Mastering™
InDesign® CS3
for Print Design and Production

Pariah S. Burke

BICENTENNIAL
1807
WILEY
2007
BICENTENNIAL

Wiley Publishing, Inc.

Acquisitions Editor: Pete Gaughan

Development Editor: Karen Lew

Technical Editor: Samuel John Klein

Production Editor: Debra Banninger

Copy Editor: Judy Flynn

Production Manager: Tim Tate

Vice President and Executive Group Publisher: Richard Swadley

Vice President and Executive Publisher: Joseph B. Wikert

Vice President and Publisher: Neil Edde

Book Designers: Maureen Forys and Judy Fung

Compositor: Happenstance Type-O-Rama

Proofreader: Nancy Riddiough

Indexer: Nancy Guenther

Anniversary Logo Design: Richard Pacifico

Cover Designer: Ryan Sneed

Cover Image: © Pete Gardner / Digital Vision / Getty Images

Dear Reader

Thank you for choosing *Mastering InDesign CS3 for Print Design and Production.* This book is part of a family of premium quality Sybex books, all written by outstanding authors who combine practical experience with a gift for teaching.

Sybex was founded in 1976. More than 30 years later, we're still committed to producing consistently exceptional books. With each of our titles we're working hard to set a new standard for the industry. From the paper we print on to the authors we work with, our goal is to bring you the best books available.

I hope you see all that reflected in these pages. I'd be very interested to hear your comments and get your feedback on how we're doing. Feel free to let me know what you think about this or any other Sybex book by sending me an email at nedde@wiley.com, or if you think you've found a technical error in this book, please visit http://sybex.custhelp.com. Customer feedback is critical to our efforts at Sybex.

Best regards,

Neil Edde
Vice President and Publisher
Sybex, an Imprint of Wiley

For Mom, Ma, Christy, Dad, Chris, Joanna, Stevie, Ann(a), and Chris B. This book exists because of your unflappable faith, love, and support.

Acknowledgments

During the writing of this book a number of things happened. Carbon monoxide poisoning took several of our beloved pets and nearly claimed my children, my fiancé, and me. It would have, too, if not for my cat, Chloe, who in one of those *Reader's Digest* moments, literally saved our lives. In an unrelated event, my family endured a loss; the grief still sneaks up and punches us in the gut from time to time. I took ill for a while. I made new friends and reconnected with old ones. I cocreated an InDesign plug-in. The beta software broke—often (but turned out great in the end). And, I learned a great deal about, well, everything. All of that in seven months, and in between it all there were pages being written, edited, rewritten, and re-edited.

One name goes on the cover, but a book is always a team effort—this one more than most. I'd like to acknowledge those whose names really belong on the cover.

Strawberry Blonde. You're my strength and inspiration. Thank you for the coffee and the hugs, for listening and giving your honest opinion, and for being patient. Je t'aime, my N.N.M.M.

Joanna and Stevie. You are the reason.

Sarah Taylor, Mom. Thank you for teaching me to crawl, run, and pick myself up when I stumble.

Chris Miles Dreyer Jr., my brother by different parents, who was always there to make me laugh or slap me upside the head when I needed it.

Chloe. Thank you for not biting me *every* time I said, "Daddy's busy."

Pete Gaughan, acquisitions editor, who somehow held the train on the rails each and every time someone snuck up and threw a track switch. Whatever they're paying you, Pete, it's not enough.

Karen L. Lew, developmental editor. Despite being made to work in the dark for a good portion of the book, you did a great job. This book is much stronger for your efforts, and your fingerprints adorn each page. Comprising largely style and usage debate, our discussions have taught me a great deal about the craft of writing. (At last count, the score was in your favor by a wide margin, by the way.) Knowing that I've reciprocated, even a little, in helping to expand your InDesign knowledge genuinely honors me.

Samuel John Klein, technical editor, frequent collaborator, and friend. Man, how you can stay enthusiastic about working with me after four years, two books, and two websites I have no idea. Thank you for making sure my Ctrl+Ts were crossed and Cmd+Is were dotted—even without functioning software half the time.

Debbie Banninger, production editor, and Judy Flynn, copyeditor. To borrow a quote I used elsewhere in this book, the Debbie (and Judy) is in the details. A tweak here, a pluck there. Thank you for finding and fixing all the little things that slipped by the rest of us. Without you, well, we'd all look pretty foolish. The book looks great!

David Fugate, for the translations, encouragement, and advocacy.

Thank you Chad Siegel, the InDesign team, and the Adobe prerelease program team who readily answered my CS3 questions—no matter how odd.

Thank you Johannes Gutenberg, Aldus Manutius, Claude Garamond, John Warnock, Chuck Geschke, Paul Brainard, Tim Gill, Steve Jobs, Bill Gates, and everyone else who got us to InDesign CS3.

About the Author

~~Call me Ishmael...~~
~~It was the best of times, it was the worst of times...~~
~~It was a dark and stormy night...~~
~~The name's Burke. Pariah Burke.~~

The author is just like you: he has square eyeballs, paper-cut-scarred fingers, and his mother doesn't quite understand what he does for a living. He loves designing and the process of designing, and his greatest honor in life is helping others express their creativity.

Pariah S. Burke began freelance illustration work at the age of 14, apprenticed in a screen print shop at 16, and was designing brochures and Yellow Pages ads with hand-cut Zip-A-Tone, Rubylithe, and rub-on lettering by age 17. When the Desktop Publishing Revolution began, he was loitering around a typesetting shop ignoring the proclamations that "PostScript is a fad" and "computers will never take the place of wax paste-up." He fell in love with PageMaker, QuarkXPress, and Adobe Illustrator the minute he got his marker-stained hands on them—and he never regretted it.

Lacking the funds to attend college despite eager invitations from the professors at the Savannah College of Art and Design, Pariah embarked on a learn-by-doing educational path, taking any job that would teach him something about graphic design, illustration, pre-press, printing, and publishing. His education included stints as production artist (numerous times), bindery operator, color corrector, scanner operator, photo retoucher, lead designer on membership directories, (paste-up) stripper, RIP operator, photographer's assistant, photographer, waiter, forklift driver, jewelry salesman, and a host of other things—many concurrent with one another. He has co-owned a pre-press service bureau; been a creative director for a small magazine; made over the look of several magazines, newsletters, and newspapers; and been principal of a design studio whose client list included Time-Warner, Spike Lee, and Playboy.

At the turn of the century, Pariah went to work for Adobe, training the Adobe technical and expert support teams to use Adobe software and related technologies and to understand and speak the language of design and pre-press. While with Adobe, Pariah was the support teams' technical lead for InDesign, InCopy, PageMaker, Illustrator, Acrobat, and Photoshop and was the unofficial QuarkXPress guru in residence.

After leaving Adobe in 2004, Pariah became a man of many hats, returning to freelance graphic design; hitting the road as a traveling design, production, and publishing workflow consultant and speaker; and teaching the tools of the trade in classrooms, conference rooms, and back alleys throughout North America. He also began writing. Pariah has published articles on everything from copyright and intellectual property for creative professionals to contract negotiation best practices, from in-depth software reviews to lauded tutorials describing advanced techniques in InDesign, InCopy, QuarkXPress, Photoshop, Illustrator, and Acrobat. His articles have appeared in *Publish*, *PDFZone*, *Creativepro.com*, *CreativeLatitude.com*, and, most frequently, *InDesign Magazine*. In 2005, he wrote the book *Adobe Illustrator CS2 @Work: Projects You Can Use on the Job* for Sams Publishing and coauthored Que's *Using Creative Suite 2 Special Edition*. He has been a speaker at the InDesign Conference, has produced e-seminar videos for Adobe, and has been interviewed by numerous media in the United States and the U.K. regarding his opinions of Adobe, Quark, the creative pro software market, and the business of design and publishing.

When magazines and magazine-style websites couldn't find spaces for his articles fast enough, Pariah established his own publications. He created the *Design Weblog*, the *Magazine Design Weblog*, and the *(Unofficial) Photoshop Weblog* for AOL's Weblogs, Inc. He also created the preeminent international authority on the war between desktop publishing giants InDesign and QuarkXPress, *Quark Vs InDesign.com*, and founded Designorati, an organization and publication with the broad focus of covering any subject that falls under the umbrella of professional creativity.

Born in Boston and having grown up in the hustle and bustle of the East Coast, Pariah now lives among the idyllic beauty and friendly people of Portland, Oregon. He shares his life with his fiancé, Christy, her two children, Joanna and Stevie, a dog, and four cats. In his spare time (ha!), Pariah enjoys driving his convertible very, very fast through the Columbia River Gorge, playing chess and MMORGs with his family and friends, and reading Dean Koontz, Tom Clancy, and Star Wars novels. Once in a while he sleeps.

Pariah's Projects

Pariah is principal of **Workflow:Creative** (www.WorkflowCreative.com), a consultancy and training group providing creative pro software training, migration, and workflow optimization to design, advertising, and publishing teams throughout the world.

Quark VS InDesign.com (www.QuarkVSInDesign.com), the Authority on the War Between the Desktop Publishing Giants.

Designorati (www.Designorati.com), covering the many aspects of the creative professional's tools, business, and lifestyle.

Personal website, blog, and portfolio (www.iamPariah.com).

Watch for several new Web, e-book, and print publications from Pariah S. Burke in 2007 and 2008.

Contents at a Glance

Introduction . . . .*xv*

Chapter 1 • Customizing 1

Chapter 2 • Text 23

Chapter 3 • Characters 57

Chapter 4 • Drawing 103

Chapter 5 • Images 139

Chapter 6 • Objects 169

Chapter 7 • Pages 213

Chapter 8 • Stories 245

Chapter 9 • Documents 285

Chapter 10 • Output 321

Chapter 11 • Efficiency 369

Chapter 12 • Collaboration 411

Appendix • The Bottom Line 445

Glossary 465

Index 477

Contents

Introduction . . . .**xv**

Chapter 1 • Customizing **1**
Panels 1
    The Panel Dock 2
    Arranging Panels 4
    Stacked Panels 5
    Multi-State Panels 5
    The Tools Panel 6
    The Control Panel 8
    Panels You Don't Need 9
    Command Bar 10
Keyboard Shortcuts 10
Menus 13
Plug-In Customization 16
Workspaces 18
InDesign in Your Pocket 19
Customizing Application Defaults 19
The Bottom Line 20

Chapter 2 • Text **23**
Text Frame Basics 23
    Creating Text Frames 23
    Getting Text into Text Frames 24
    Text Frame Options 33
Paragraph Formatting 37
    Alignment 37
    Left and Right Indent 39
    Separating Paragraphs 39
    Last Line Right Indent 42
    Drop Caps 42
Paragraph Composition 44
    Paragraph vs. Single-Line Composer .44
    Justification Options 47
    Hyphenation 47
    Optical Margin Alignment 49
    Balance Ragged Lines 50
    Keep Options 50
    Highlight Composition Violations 52
Paragraph Rules 53
The Bottom Line 55

Chapter 3 • Characters **57**

Formatting Characters 57

    The Character Panel 57

    Character Transformations 72

Special Characters 80

    Insert Special Character 80

    White Space Characters 82

    OpenType 84

    Glyphs Panel 95

The Bottom Line 99

Chapter 4 • Drawing **103**

The Essence of Vector 103

Drawing Paths 105

    The Pen Tool and Straight Paths 105

    The Pen Tool and Curves 108

    Pen Tool Aspects and Incarnations 111

    The Pencil Tool 113

Shape Tools 117

    Frames 117

    Reshaping Shapes 120

    Editing Paths and Shapes 126

The Bottom Line 135

Chapter 5 • Images **139**

Placing Assets 139

    Frame-First Workflow 139

    Image Import Options 141

    Multiple Asset Place 152

    Drag and Drop 153

    Copy and Paste 155

    Other Flavors of Paste 157

    Content-First Workflow 158

Managing Placed Assets 158

    The Basics 158

    Links Panel 159

    Linking vs. Embedding 162

    Fitting 162

The Bottom Line 166

Chapter 6 • Objects **169**

Transparency and Effects 169

    Attribute-Level Transparency 170

    Effects 171

    More about Effects 175

Strokes 178

    Custom Stroke Styles 180

Swatches 183
   Mixed Inks 183
   Managing Swatches 186
   Sharing Swatches 190
Anchored Objects 192
   Anchoring Your First Object 193
   Anchored Object Anatomy 195
   Inline Anchored Object Options 196
   Custom Anchored Object Options .198
Type on a Path 203
   Setting Type on a Path 203
   Editing Type on a Path 204
   Type on a Path Options 206
Step and Repeat 207
Transform Again 208
The Bottom Line 210

Chapter 7 • Pages **213**
Creating Pages 213
   Document Setup 213
   Reusable Document Setups 222
   Layout Adjustment 225
   Multiple Page Sizes 226
Managing Pages 230
   Pages Panel 230
   Customizing the Pages Panel 231
   Inserting Pages 232
   Rearranging Pages 232
   Single-Page and Multipage Spreads 234
   Moving Pages between Documents 235
   Duplicating and Deleting Pages 236
   Objects and Rearranged Pages 236
Master Pages 237
   Master Page Setup 237
   Overriding Master Page Items 238
   Restoring Master Page Items 239
   Text Frames on Master Pages 239
   Page Numbers 240
   Nested Master Pages 240
   Creating Masters from Document Pages 243
   Master Page Power 243
The Bottom Line 244

Chapter 8 • Stories **245**
Threading and Unthreading Text Frames 245
   QuarkXPress vs. InDesign 245
   Threading Frames 246

Threading Tips 249
Viewing Threads 249
Managing Threads 249
Autoflowing Text 251
Autoflow in Master Page Frames 252
Jumplines 253
Lists, Numbers, and Bullets (Oh, My!) 254
Bullets 254
Numbering 258
Lists 259
Overriding Bullets and Numbers 262
Word Processing 262
Story Editor 263
InCopy 265
Footnotes 267
Endnotes 271
Fixing, Finding, and Changing Text and More 271
Spell Checking 271
Dictionary Editing 273
Dynamic Spelling 275
Autocorrect 275
Find/Change 276
Replacing Fonts 282
The Bottom Line 283

Chapter 9 • Documents 285
Seeing Your Work 285
Zooming 285
Navigator Panel 286
Multiple Document Windows 287
Display Performance 287
View Modes 288
Guides and Grids 289
Guide Basics 289
Guide Options 290
Guides Manager 291
Document Grid 292
Baseline Grid 293
Layers 295
Books 297
Begin a Book File 297
Page, Chapter, and Section Numbering 298
Synchronizing Book Styles 300
Outputting Books 301
Indexing 302
Creating Index Entries 303
Managing Index Entries 306
Cross-References 308

Power Indexing 310
Generating the Index 311
Tables of Contents 314
The Bottom Line 318

Chapter 10 • Output **321**
Managing Color 321
The Purpose of Color Management 321
ICC Profiles 323
Configure Color Management 324
Per-Image Color Management 333
Changing Color Profiles 333
Proofing 335
Proof Colors 335
Proof Separations 337
Proof Flattening 338
Printing 345
Ink Manager 345
Trapping and Overprinting 348
Preflight 356
Package for Output 359
Print Dialog 361
The Bottom Line 367

Chapter 11 • Efficiency **369**
Working Efficiently with Text 369
Paragraph Styles 369
Character Styles 378
Nested Styles 381
Text Variables 384
Data Merge 389
Working Efficiently with Tables 397
Live Linking to Excel Spreadsheets 397
Table Styles 398
Working Efficiently with Objects 399
Object Styles 399
Libraries 401
Snippets 404
Style Shortcuts 405
Quick Apply 406
Scripting 407
The Bottom Line 409

Chapter 12 • Collaboration **411**
Collaborating with Other Designers 411
Saving to Older Versions of InDesign 411
One Document, Many Designers 412
One Page, Many Designers 415

Collaborating with Writers and Editors 421
   Solving the Design-Editorial Collaboration Problems 421
     Assignments 423
     Assigned Content in InDesign 429
     Managing Assignments 432
     Collaborating with Remote Editors 435
     Copy Before Layout 437
     Collaborating with a Big Cheese 439
Sharing Reusable Settings 439
   Dictionaries 439
   Paragraph, Character, Table, Cell, and Object Styles 439
   Swatches 440
   Stroke Styles 440
   Autocorrect Word Pairs 440
   Find/Change Queries 440
   Glyph Sets 441
   PDF Export Presets 441
   Print Presets 441
   Document Size Presets 442
   Transparency Flattener Presets 442
   InDesign Templates 442
   Workspaces 442
   Keyboard Shortcuts 443
The Bottom Line 443

Appendix • The Bottom Line **445**
Chapter 1: Customizing 445
Chapter 2: Text 447
Chapter 3: Characters 448
Chapter 4: Drawing 449
Chapter 5: Images 451
Chapter 6: Objects 452
Chapter 7: Pages 455
Chapter 8: Stories 456
Chapter 9: Documents 458
Chapter 10: Output 459
Chapter 11: Efficiency 461
Chapter 12: Collaboration 462

Glossary **465**

Index 477

Introduction

Creativity. It's one of my favorite words of all time, a word I utter with reverence. *Efficiency*, another of my favorite words. Combining the two—*creative efficiency*—describes what I consider the single most venerated concept in the whole of professional creative industries. Creative efficiency. It means freedom—freedom to be imaginative and experimental in your design as well as freedom from as many of the time-consuming, distracting, unproductive mechanical steps you need to take to achieve a design as possible. It's a doctrine of sorts, one that I hold sacred, one that I preach from pulpits of wood, metal, plastic, pixels, and, like this one, pulp. As an ideal, creative efficiency is about making every task, every flick of the mouse or stroke of the keyboard, forward movement in the progression toward a finished design. Its ultimate goal is directing every movement and every thought toward the design, not toward the tools or processes we must employ to construct a design.

We graphic designers and press and pre-press operators enjoyed creative efficiency once, not too long ago, in a way our cousins on the sidewalks of public markets and beach boardwalks enjoy still. A painter, working in oil, acrylic, gauche, pastel, or watercolor, has creative efficiency. Every stroke of the brush, whether on the canvas or mixing a color on the palette, is active, forward motion toward the completion of the art on the canvas. When illustrators' hands bore more calluses induced by the smooth plastic pipes of Rapidographs and lacquered wood of Prismacolor pencils than by mice and styluses, when pre-pressmen's shoulders bent over X-Acto, Rubylithe, and Zip-A-Tone instead of over QWERTY, Logitech, and Wacom, we enjoyed creative efficiency. With a page before us, few of our motions and thoughts did not directly contribute to the final design. Now, however, in the age of InDesign, Photoshop, and Illustrator, with creative horizons wider than any even we of limitless imaginations had ever conceived possible, we have lost creative efficiency. Too much of our time is now spent thinking about the tools of our trade, about how to use them to achieve a design. We still have our creativity, but we have been foiled in our pursuit of creating productively and efficiently. Indeed, too often the creativity itself is handicapped by the increasing amount of time and thought devoted to divining the mysteries of the tool, and often failing to find the means by which the tool wants us to do something, we compromise the design.

This book is about helping you achieve creative efficiency within InDesign CS3. It is not for the beginning InDesign user, although professional users proficient with previous versions of InDesign will find in this book what they need to translate their prowess in InDesign 2, CS, or CS2 into the new CS3. Ultimately, this book is for those who can already produce projects in InDesign but who want to know how to increase their productivity, to produce those projects faster, better, more easily, and most of all, more creatively. This book is about helping you achieve—or regain—creative efficiency.

Hallelujah, brothers and sisters in the Fellowship of Ink on Paper. Hallelujah!

What You Need

Naturally, you need *your* copy of InDesign CS3, but it would also be helpful to call on a colleague who also has InDesign CS3 to look over the results of the self-test Master It exercises in this book. Moreover, several of the exercises are built around collaboration techniques and teamwork, so if you can work with someone else using InDesign, it would be a big help.

If you work with editorial personnel at all, get hold of InCopy CS3—even if it's just the free 30-day trial version from Adobe.com. In Chapter 12, "Collaborating," we'll talk quite a bit about InCopy and how integrating it into your workflow takes the responsibility of copyediting and those endless changes completely out of your hands and puts it back in the editorial department where it belongs. With InCopy on your computer, you'll be able to gain a better understanding of just how easy and important it is to return control of editorial content to the editorial department.

Once in a while over the following pages, we'll slip out of InDesign and into other tools of the trade. Although not required, for some portions of the book it would be helpful if you had access to recent versions of Acrobat, Photoshop, and Illustrator. Adobe offers fully functional 30-day trial versions of those, too, if you need to download them.

You'll probably want to don your sense of humor, too. Some of my jokes will admittedly strike you as lame. That's OK because I believe in the philosophy that if you just keep shooting spitballs toward the front of the class, you'll eventually hit the intended target (the teacher). There are enough jokes, quips, and innuendos in this book that at least *some* of them will be funny—as long as you start out with a sense of humor. If you just haven't got one, well, interspersed between the humor are a few tidbits of good information, case studies, and advice, too.

The Mastering Series

The Mastering series from Sybex provides outstanding instruction for readers with intermediate and advanced skills in the form of top-notch training and development for those already working in their field and clear, serious education for those aspiring to become pros. Every Mastering book features:

♦ The Sybex "by professionals for professionals" commitment. *Mastering* authors are themselves practitioners, with plenty of credentials in their areas of specialty.

♦ A practical perspective for a reader who already knows the basics—someone who needs solutions, not a primer.

♦ Real-World Scenarios, ranging from case studies to interviews, that show how the tool, technique, or knowledge presented is applied in actual practice.

♦ Skill-based instruction, with chapters organized around real tasks rather than abstract concepts or subjects.

♦ Self-review test "Master It" problems and questions, so you can be certain you're equipped to do the job right.

What Is Covered in This Book

Mastering InDesign CS3 for Print Design and Production is organized a little differently than most computer books. First, you'll notice that there are only 12 chapters. That's it. Twelve. A dozen. Efficiency starts at home, they say…. Well, they don't really say that, but they *should*. Each chapter title is a single word, and the chapter is all about that word. Chapter 10, "Output," for example, is about printing, preflighting, packaging, soft proofing, color management (in the context of getting good color into and then out of InDesign), trapping, and mixed inks. And, those topics are covered entirely in that chapter. You won't have to stick your pinky in the index and jump all around the book reading a paragraph *here*, a page and a half *there*, another paragraph *over here* just to piece together complete information about one topic. Go on. Compare this book's index to any other InDesign CS3 book on your shelf. How many page numbers are listed for a given topic in each index? The more page numbers, the more you'll be flipping hither and yon to get what is, in large part, the same information as this book puts in one place, in one contiguous discussion. Of course, *this* book goes deeper into the topics and level experienced pros need. In *this* book, you also won't have to weed through the beginner level, intro to InDesign stuff either—this is the first InDesign book written *by* a print design and press professional *for* print design and press professionals.

Here's a brief synopsis of what you'll find in each chapter:

Chapter 1: Customizing In order to have creative efficiency, you must minimize the impact of your tools on the process of creating. That requires modification of tools: making InDesign work as you do as much as possible. How you customize InDesign directly affects how efficiently you use this page-layout application to learn and use anything else you might read in this volume. Customizing InDesign shifts that dividing line between the software working for you and you working for the software further toward the former.

Chapter 2: Text InDesign operates on a content-to-container premise. Everything within InDesign is either content—text and imagery—or a container to hold text, imagery, or another container. At the lowest level, the pasteboard is a container that holds everything you might place in InDesign. Then there are pages and layers—more containers—and *then* the real content enters the picture—text and imagery. In this chapter, you will learn to create and fill text frames, format text frames, format paragraphs, compose paragraphs, and use paragraph rules for organization and special effects.

Chapter 3: Characters InDesign is the world's most advanced typesetting platform. In fact, type set in InDesign is almost as good as type set on a letterpress. The few sacrifices you make by setting type in InDesign instead of in lead tend to be balanced by the time savings—you can set much faster than one page every four hours—and by the lack of ink perpetually embedded under your nails. This chapter is a deep dive into working with characters. In this chapter, you will learn to format characters, transform characters, insert special characters, work with Open-Type font features, and use the Glyphs panel.

Chapter 4: Drawing InDesign is *not* Illustrator, and it never will be. Fortunately, however, the Illustrator team happily shares its code with the InDesign team. Consequently, many of the most common drawing tasks can be done directly within InDesign, without the need to load up Illustrator and then move artwork from it into InDesign. It's a matter of efficient creativity— those two words again! In this chapter, you will learn to draw precise paths with the pen tool, freehand draw paths with the pencil tool, combine and subtract shapes and convert from one shape to another, modify any vector artwork, and turn type into a container to hold images or text.

Chapter 5: Images InDesign's greatest strength is its type-handling and type-rendering features. Fortunately, it's just as good with imagery—especially in CS3—as you'll learn when we place image assets, import images without place, manage placed assets, and go native in your workflow.

Chapter 6: Objects If there's a "coolest subject" in this book, this chapter contains most subjects that would fit the description—at least, from a standpoint of creativity and creative productivity. As with drawing in InDesign, the name of the game when applying transparency and effects to objects is efficiency through doing as much as possible *within* InDesign; it's about resorting as infrequently as possible to creating objects in Photoshop or Illustrator. This chapter will teach you to use attribute-level transparency and object effects, design custom stroke styles, create mixed-ink swatches, manage and share swatches, work with anchored objects, set type on a path, step and repeat, and transform again.

Chapter 7: Pages Pages are the foundation of every document in InDesign. How they're created, modified, and managed directly affects their ability to print, their fitness to purpose. InDesign has always offered tremendous ease in working with pages, and the options and control over pages has improved with each successive release. In InDesign CS3, a large portion of the new features and refinements of existing features is centered around the Pages panel and controlling pages. In this chapter, you will learn to create pages with bleed, slug, and live areas; manage pages in and between InDesign documents; and master master pages.

Chapter 8: Stories Once you've mastered setting and styling type on a page, it's time to think about writing, editing, and flowing text across multiple pages. It's time to think about stories. In this chapter, you will learn to thread and unthread text frames and flow text; create bulleted and numbered lists; write and word process in InDesign; and fix, find, and change text.

Chapter 9: Documents Working with documents involves knowing how to move around in them, change viewing options, and compare views. Working with longer documents efficiently means mastering InDesign's unique long-document features such as indexing, creating tables of contents, and working within the timesaving and collaboration-ready atmosphere of book files. In this chapter, you will learn to interact with documents visually to change zoom level, view modes, and display performance; build and manage grids and guides; create and manage book files; index terms and create an index; and create a table of contents.

Chapter 10: Output At the end of the day, it's all about printing. Everything we do in InDesign leads up to that defining moment when we watch, with breath held, as the job rolls off the press. In this chapter, we get into what happens after design, into the ramp-up for and, ultimately, the execution of outputting a job, including configuring color management on documents and images; soft proofing documents to screen; and preflighting, packaging, and outputing to print with managed inks and trapping.

Chapter 11: Efficiency Professional creatives have deadlines, budgets, and (sometimes) even personal lives to get to. In this chapter, the focus is on getting the job done expeditiously, productively, and without sacrificing quality or creativity. You will learn to work efficiently with text, tables, and objects.

Chapter 12: Collaborating Few InDesign users operate in a vacuum, creating documents start to finish all on their own. The majority of modern workflows, even among freelancers, entails some form of collaborative content creation. This chapter starts with the collaboration features offered by InDesign CS3 and then moves into the when, why, and how of saving, reusing, and sharing project consistency presets; collaborating with editorial personnel through the InDesign-InCopy LiveEdit Workflow; and breaking the 1-document:1-designer and 1-page:1-designer limitations to effect genuine production team collaboration with the Book File Collaboration Workflow and the author's original Placed Page Collaboration Workflow.

The Appendix gathers together all the Master It exercises from the chapters and provides a solution and description for the expected results from each.

Downloading Companion Files

The book's download page is home to samples and resource files mentioned in the book. In addition, you'll also find the tryout version of the Page Control plug-in discussed in Chapter 7, "Pages." Both Windows and Mac OS X versions of the plug-in are included among the files available on the book's download page at `http://www.sybex.com/go/MasteringInDesign`.

How to Contact the Author

This book came about largely because people like you *asked* me for it. Most of my articles, e-seminars, conference sessions, and other projects get started the same way—someone tells me about a need or asks me a question. So, if *you* have a question or would like to see me cover another topic—in a printed book, e-book, article, or somehow—please drop me a line. I can't guarantee I'll write, record, or speak about the topic you suggest, but I promise to consider doing so. At the very least I'll reply to your email.

Even if you don't have a question or book topic in mind, I'd sincerely love to hear about how well my book worked (or didn't) for you, about your experiences trying the techniques and advice it contains, or any other feedback you may have about this book, whether unadulterated adulation or scathing but constructive criticism. No threats of bodily harm or marriage proposals, though, please.

Please feel free to drop me a line any time at `MasteringInD@iampariah.com`.

Want to go beyond this book and have me analyze and optimize *your* unique workflow and train your team in person? Please visit `www.WorkflowCreative.com`.

To read more of my writing about InDesign and InCopy, please visit `www.QuarkVSInDesign.com`.

To read my articles (and those of others) about everything else in the wide world of design, production, press, and this business of creating, please visit `www.Designorati.com`.

Sybex strives to keep you supplied with the latest tools and information you need for your work. Please check its website at `www.sybex.com`, where we'll post additional content and updates that supplement this book if the need arises. Enter the search terms "InDesign," "Burke," or the book's ISBN (9780470114568) and click Go to get to the book's update page.

Chapter 1

Customizing

"Creative efficiency." If you read the refreshingly short introduction a few pages previous, you know that I believe the phrase "creative efficiency" to be among the most important ideals of our profession of designing for, or placing, ink on paper. To realize your creative potential, to enable the creatives working under you to realize their creative potential, you must minimize the impact of your tools on the process of creating. Accomplishing that requires modifying tools like InDesign, making *them* emulate how *you* work as much as possible. Software—computers in general—are far from the point where they will truly work the way humans work, the way humans think. We are still forced to conform our methodologies and thinking processes to fit within the narrow boxes sitting under our desks—to a point. Whenever possible—and, with InDesign CS3, much is possible—customize the software to fit your work and preferences as closely as you can.

While the idea of rearranging palettes or modifying menus may seem superfluous compared with other topics in this book, I've placed this chapter first because, ultimately, how you customize InDesign directly affects how efficiently you use the page layout application to learn and use anything else you might read in this volume.

Customizing InDesign shifts that dividing line between the software working for you and you working for the software further toward the former.

In this chapter, you will learn to:

◆ Organize panels and use the new panel docks

◆ Customize keyboard shortcuts

◆ Customize and color-code menus

◆ Remove parts of InDesign to create lean, workflow-specific installations

◆ Change the default font, colors, and more

◆ Carry your personalized InDesign work environment in your pocket or on your iPod

Panels

Ever since April 2005, when Adobe and Macromedia announced their intent to merge, users of InDesign or any of either company's products have speculated about the user interface that would result from combining two of the most acclaimed user interface design teams in the business. Creative Suite 3 is that result—the New Adobe UI—and it's highly customizable.

No longer constricted by the settlement terms of lawsuits lost against one another in the late Nineties and early Oughties, the newly joined Adobe and Macromedia are free to make use of the best user interface innovations from both companies. The freedom of Adobe applications' floating palettes and Macromedia applications' cleanly organized, nonfloating panel bars have converged in Creative Suite 3 to create more choices in workspace arrangement than any application has ever offered. To reflect the change, *palettes* are now called *panels*, and they can be free-floating, tabbed, stacked, grouped together into vertical panel bars à la Macromedia applications, and condensed into narrow icon and title tiles. Given the fact that InDesign CS3 has an unprecedented 41 panels, you'll likely employ several panel arrangement forms concurrently.

Hands down, the most efficient way to organize the InDesign workspace is across dual monitors—preferably monitors of the same size and resolution. Although the vast majority of users don't need all 41 panels opened at once, many panels—such as Layers, Pages, Swatches, Navigator, Index, Hyperlinks, Scripts, Links, and the five styles panels—tend to grow in utility and convenience according to their heights (or height and width in the case of the Navigator panel). The more space you give such panels, the less scrolling you'll have to do, which means the faster you can access the layer, page, swatch, style, or whatever it is you need. On my primary production computer, I use two monitors, with the left containing the InDesign application itself and the Control and Tools panels and the right completely filled with all other panels. Of course, not even an entire monitor can contain all 41 panels simultaneously—not expanded panels, anyway. Maybe if you ran *three* monitors…

The point is, Adobe knows that InDesign is a forest of panels. The vast majority of the application's functions are contained on panels, which is a far more efficient way of doing it than in dialog boxes. Dialog boxes, while open, prohibit accessing the document; to do something to two objects individually via a dialog box requires more steps than doing it through panels, which are always onscreen. The downside to panels is, of course, panel bloat.

Below, we'll go through the various ways Adobe has built into InDesign for organizing panels. I'll also offer some advice on which ones you can safely keep off your screen.

The Panel Dock

The dock is InDesign's attempt to organize panels on single-monitor systems where space is at a premium.

Dragging panels to the side of the application window no longer creates a series of slender, vertical bars as would occur in InDesign CS2 and InCopy CS2; now panels become labeled icons in the panel dock, a top-to-bottom reserved area of the application window (see Figure 1.1). In some programs, such as Photoshop and Illustrator, the icons are unlabeled, resulting in a much slimmer dock (and consequently a wider document working area).

InDesign can have icon-only docks too; they just don't appear that way in the default workspace. To slim down an InDesign dock to icon-only mode and reclaim most of the horizontal space for the working area, drag the triple bars at the top of a dock toward the screen edge (refer back to Figure 1.1). When you get to within 18 or so pixels of the edge, the dock will snap into icon-only mode.

With Creative Suite 3 and subsequent product releases, Adobe elected to remove the traditional iconography of InDesign's butterfly, Illustrator's flowers, Photoshop's feathers, and so on. Instead, it branded nearly all its applications and technologies with color-coded, two-letter signifiers strongly reminiscent of elements on the periodic table. Although your desktop, Start Menu, or OS X Dock will be brighter but less visually interesting, the workspaces of Adobe applications themselves become a cool cornucopia of grayscale icons—every panel now has its own associated icon displayed within the application dock. For easy reference, Table 1.1 pairs all the panels with their associated icons.

FIGURE 1.1
The InDesign
panel dock

TABLE 1.1:   InDesign Panels and Their Icons

Icon	Panel	Icon	Panel	Icon	Panel
	Align		Hyperlinks		Scripts
	Assignments		Index		Script Label
	Attributes		Info		State
	Bookmarks		Layers		Story
	Cell Styles		Links		Stroke
	Character Styles		Navigator		Swatches
	Character		Notes		Table
	Color		Object Styles		Table Styles
	Data Merge		Pages		Tags
	Effects		Paragraph		Text Wrap
	Flattener Preview		Paragraph Styles		Transform
	Glyphs		Pathfinder		Trap Presets
	Gradient		Separations Preview		

To use a panel in the dock, simply click on its collapsed icon or icon and title. It will expand out to the side, revealing the entire panel. Collapse it back into the panel either by clicking the double arrows pointed toward the dock or by clicking on the title tab of the panel.

Only one panel per dock may be extended at once, and by default, the last used panel will remain extended until you collapse it. If you'd prefer that panels immediately collapse back to their icon or tile states as soon as you finish with them, right-click on the dark gray dock title or an empty area of the dock itself and choose Auto-Collapse Icon Panels (you'll also find the same choice in the Preferences on the Interface pane).

Expand or contract the *entire* dock, inclusive of all the panels it contains, by clicking on the double-arrow symbol at the very top of the panel. When the panel is in icon-only or collapsed tile mode, arrows will point inward, toward the application workspace and away from the edge; when the panel is collapsed, arrows will point outward toward the edge of the screen. You can also double-click on the empty, dark title bar of the dock or Cmd+click/Ctrl+click on it to toggle between expanded or collapsed states.

Arranging Panels

To add a panel to the default dock, drag the panel's title tab over the empty area of the dock beneath the lowest panel. When your cursor is in position, a colored horizontal line will appear across the dock. Release the mouse button to drop the panel into the dock at that point.

Remove panels from the dock by dragging the title or icon (not the gray bar above them) out from the dock into the empty application area. When you release the mouse, the panel will become free floating.

Some panels, you'll notice, are grouped—when you click the title of one to extend it, other panels are tabbed behind it (see Figure 1.2). These are grouped panels. Collapsed, their grouped arrangement is indicated by their icons or tiles contained within a light gray rectangle, with a common gray bar atop them. If you *do* drag the gray bar away from the dock, you'll detach the entire group of panels. Once detached, they will be a free-floating group of tabbed panels. Grouped panels, both on the dock and free floating, are one-at-a-time views. In other words, if the Character and Character Styles panels are grouped (as they are in the default workspace), you can view only one or the other, not both simultaneously.

FIGURE 1.2

Grouped panels extended with other groups collapsed

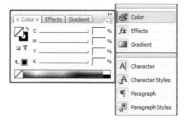

Rearrange panels in the dock by dragging their icons or tiles vertically. A horizontal line will indicate the new location of the panel should you drop it. A rule between the panel groups, in the dark area of the dock background, will reposition the panel or group to that point outside of other groups. Dropping it within the area of a group of icons or tiles, however, will add the panel to the group. Dragging the gray bar of a grouped set of panels will reposition the entire group or merge it into an existing group.

InDesign can actually contain docks on *both* sides of the application window and can have multiple columns of panels arranged side by side in the dock. Just as with adding panels to the default right-side dock, creating and managing side-by-side docks is done by dragging. Begin by creating the first dock, and then drag another panel (or panel group) to the screen edge. Bypass the *horizontal* line indicating that the new panel will appear below the one already there, and keep going to the screen edge, whereupon a *vertical* line will appear. When you let go, the previous dock area will be pushed inward, with the new panel forming a column on the outside. You can keep going, adding columns as you like, but only within the application window. If the dock expands so far that it reaches the other side of the window, panels will begin to automatically collapse into their labeled icon tiles.

Stacked Panels

Detached or free-floating panels have similar arrangement options. Drag the tab of one panel atop another free-floating panel or group of panels to group them into tabs. When your cursor is in position, a bold outline will appear all the way around the target panel. If you drag too close to the bottom of another panel, you'll see a horizontal line appear only there, indicating that the panels will stack rather than group (see Figure 1.3).

FIGURE 1.3
Stacked panels

Stacked panels work similarly to docked panels, but with several distinct advantages. You can see and work with multiple panels at once just as you would free-floating panels, and they aren't limited to positioning at the screen edge. Like docked panels, stacked panels can be expanded or contracted into just their tabs selectively, or an entire stack can be expanded or contracted with a single click of the mouse.

At the top of a stack is a single minimize/maximize button. Clicking it contracts all panels in the stack into their title tabs or expands them all. A single close button also hides the entire stack. When you move a stack by dragging the very top, all the panels move with it.

Some panels—the Pages or Swatches panels, for instance—are resizable. Within a stack, they can be resized by hovering the cursor along their bottom edges, at the point where they join the next panel down, and dragging up or down. The cursor will become a double-headed arrow as a visual cue.

Multi-State Panels

Many panels have expanded views with additional options, controls, or fields hidden by default. Switch between the compact and expanded views by choosing Show Options or Hide Options from the panel flyout menus. As we deal with each panel's expanded controls throughout the rest of the book, I'll usually remind you to show the expanded view. However, since this book is written as a focused manual for using InDesign in professional print workflows rather than as a soup-to-nuts InDesign CS3 reference book, some panels won't even be mentioned in later chapters. Always check for the Show Options command on a panel's flyout menu.

Another way to discern if a given panel has multiple states is the presence of double arrows in the title tab (see Figure 1.4). Clicking on the arrows cycles through the states of any palette—condensed, expanded, and minimized. Double-clicking the title tab of the panel itself accomplishes the same state cycling as clicking the arrows.

FIGURE 1.4

A multi-state panel, the Gradient panel, shows a double arrow in its title tab. (Left) The condensed state. (Right) The expanded or options state.

The Tools Panel

You'll use the Tools panel more than any other. All your tools are there, as are basic fill and stroke color controls and preview modes. In Figure 1.5, I've identified each of the tool icons and different parts in an exploded view of the Tools panel.

FIGURE 1.5

The Tools panel

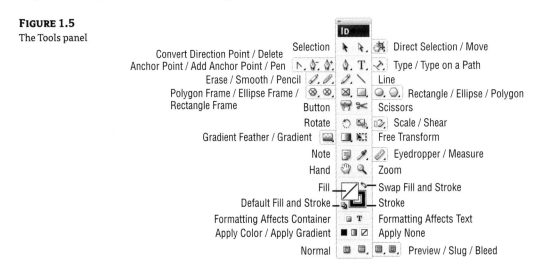

Customization options for the Tools panel are limited to two choices: whether its docked or free floating and how its tools are arranged—in the traditional two-column array, in one tall long column, or as a single row (see Figure 1.6).

FIGURE 1.6
The three arrangements of the Tools panel

The first option, docked or floating, is set in the same manner as any other panel—drag it toward or away from the screen edge. When docked, it uses the entire screen's worth of vertical space because other panels cannot be docked beneath or above the Tools panel. That's the con. The pro, of course, is that, when the Tools panel is docked, document windows automatically resize around it, never over- or under-lapping it as they would do in previous versions of InDesign.

The second option, whether to display the Tools panel in single-column, double-column, or single-row mode, is set in the Interface pane of InDesign's preferences (InDesign ➤ Preferences on the Mac and Edit ➤ Preferences on Windows). Easier than going that route, however, is to click the double arrows at the top of the Tools panel. This will cycle it through the three states. Although the single-column and single-row modes have the advantage of consuming less screen real estate, they have a seeming drawback as well: fewer options. The three apply buttons near the bottom don't fit in the slimmer modes, nor does the Normal view button at the very bottom. Fortunately, Adobe made up for their absence with new keyboard shortcuts. If you opt to use one of the Tools panel's slimmer arrangements (or just like the efficiency of keyboard shortcuts), memorize the shortcuts in Table 1.2.

TABLE 1.2: **Keyboard Shortcuts for Tools Panel Features Hidden by Single-Column and Single-Row Modes**

SHORTCUT	FUNCTION
, (comma)	Apply solid color to fill or stroke.
. (period)	Apply gradient to fill or stroke.
/ (slash)	Remove color from fill or stroke.
W	Toggle between normal mode and the selected preview mode.

The Control Panel

The Control panel, a favorite among users since its introduction in InDesign CS (1) PageMaker Edition, is context sensitive to the tool and task at hand, offering a compact quick access point for the most common features and options. While you're editing text, for instance, the Control panel goes into Character or Paragraph mode, two transposable sets of fields and controls that offer, among many other things, the ability to change the font family, style, and size as well as paragraph alignments, spacing, and indents. When you're working with tables, though, the Control panel transforms to offer table-specific controls such as the number of rows and columns, cell alignments, and insets. In all, there are four modes dependent upon what you're actually doing in the document—working with objects, characters, paragraphs, or tables. Figure 1.7 shows all four modes.

FIGURE 1.7

The four modes of the Control panel: (top to bottom) Object, Character, Paragraph, and Table, with a few constants pointed out

Quick Apply ⌐
Go to Bridge ⌐
Bridge menu ⌐
Control panel menu ⌐

The Control panel has been upgraded in InDesign CS3. It now contains more commands—including some new ones like Apply Effect, which applies Photoshop-like object effects to selected objects (see Chapter 6, "Objects") and buttons for flip and rotate—and it's customizable.

The very last object on the Control panel's right end, a button that looks like three horizontal lines, is the Control panel's flyout menu. Like the face of the Control panel, the commands on the flyout menu are context variable. At the bottom of the list, the Customize command is constant and opens the Customize Control Panel dialog box (see Figure 1.8). Here, by unchecking the show box in the expanding lists, you can selectively disable groups of controls or an entire mode. Maybe you'd rather not have Adobe Bridge shoved down your…er…um…maybe you'd rather Bridge not be so obvious in so many places (there are commands for it in the menus as well as the Go to Bridge button and accompanying drop-down menu on the face of the Control panel). To dump the Go to Bridge button, expand the Other section of the Customize Control Panel dialog and uncheck Adobe Bridge. The same goes for anything else you'd rather not see on the Control panel.

Also at the bottom of the Control panel flyout menu are commands to dock the panel to the top of the application window, its default location, dock it to the bottom, or float it free à la PageMaker's Control palette and QuarkXPress's Measurements palette. Once free floating, the Control panel can be positioned anywhere you like onscreen, but always horizontal. In addition to using the menu commands, dragging the gray bar on the left edge of the panel moves the panel around as well attaching it to, or detaching it from, the top or bottom edge of the application. When you drag a floating Control panel close enough to either the top or bottom, a thick horizontal line, similar to the one you see when docking other panels, will appear above or below the panel; release the mouse button and the panel will snap into its docked position.

FIGURE 1.8
Customizing the
Control panel

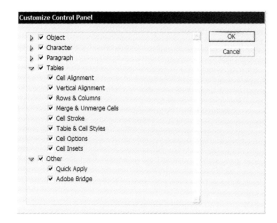

If you're running a monitor with a horizontal resolution greater than 1024 pixels, you'll be able to take advantage of a new dynamic in the Control panel. All the primary controls of each mode are contained within the first 1024 pixels. With previous versions, that was it; if your screen was wider, a docked Control palette left any extra pixels blank, wasted space. With the CS3 version, however, Adobe uses much of that space. After the primary controls have been rendered, several modes of the Control panel will present additional controls for your convenience. In Character mode, for example, more paragraph-centric fields and options will fill the extra space after all character-centric fields. In Paragraph mode, more of the character-centric controls slip in there. The idea, of course, is that if you have the space to use, InDesign will use it to save you a few times toggling between Character and Paragraph modes.

Panels You Don't Need

So upgraded is the Control panel, in fact, that it negates the need to use some other panels almost entirely. Conversely, you can elect to hide the Control panel, saving yourself some vertical screen real estate. The main advantage to using the Control panel is its context-sensitive nature; depending on the task at hand, it contains the majority of controls, options, fields, and buttons from the Transform, Align, Character, Paragraph, and Table panels, as well as some from the Stroke, Text Wrap, Effects, Character Styles, Paragraph Styles, Object Styles, and other panels. All these controls share the same space onscreen, which is far less real estate than the panels consume individually—even with panel docking and other space-saving options.

Although the options on the Control panel are not comprehensive replicas of all the dedicated panels mentioned in the previous paragraph, you may only need more on rare occasions. Consider your unique workflow and examine what is and isn't available on the Control panel to be sure, but you can probably safely hide the following stand-alone panels and reclaim the space they would occupy for other panels not duplicated on the Control panel:

◆ Character

◆ Paragraph

◆ Table

◆ Transform

◆ Align

On the other hand, if you prefer using the individual panels (personally, I prefer using the Character, Paragraph, and Table panels rather than the Control panel most of the time), drop the Control panel and reclaim *that* space. With such a panel-laden application, where docking, grouping, and stacking panels and multiple monitors merely mitigate screen overcrowding and a claustrophobic document workspace rather than solve it, repossess any pixels you can.

Command Bar

Activated from Window ➤ Object & Layout ➤ Command Bar, this toolbar includes several common functions in an area even more compact than the Control panel or Tools panel. Like them, the Command Bar can be left free floating or docked to the top or bottom edge of the application window. Figure 1.9 identifies all the buttons of the Command Bar.

FIGURE 1.9
The Command Bar

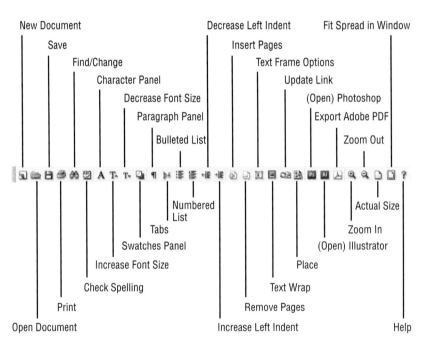

Keyboard Shortcuts

Somebody far back in time invented computer keyboard shortcuts, the ability to press a few keys simultaneously to produce the same effect as, and in lieu of, reaching for the mouse and navigating a menu. I don't know who came up with the idea of keyboard shortcuts—I think it was Cro-Magnon man, but it might have been Neandertal. Whomever it was should have a statue erected in his honor. Maybe there already is; I haven't visited the Smithsonian in a few years.

Keyboard shortcuts save tremendous time and effort and are, in my opinion, the greatest productivity enhancing invention since instant coffee (circa 35,000 BCE). InDesign is loaded with keyboard shortcuts to speed your work. And, at this point in the narrative, many software book authors would launch into several pages of keyboard shortcuts or direct you to an index of the same. Me? Well, I've got precious few pages in which to cram all the advanced InDesign info I can.

I'm not going to waste 3 to 10 or so of those with something I can give you in a different medium (see the sidebar "InDesign CS3 Keyboard Shortcuts"). More importantly, I can give you something even better than a list of keyboard shortcuts: I can show you how to set your own keyboard short-cuts for just about everything.

INDESIGN CS3 KEYBOARD SHORTCUTS

Even with the ability to customize every keyboard shortcut in InDesign, sometimes it's nice to have a list in front of you. So, I made one.

Visit http://QuarkVSInDesign.com/resources/downloads/ to download a free and printable PDF containing every keyboard shortcut for InDesign CS3 and InCopy CS3 on both Windows and Mac.

If you'd prefer something preprinted, my friends David Blatner and Anne-Marie Concepcion sell a poster with all the InDesign CS3 keyboard shortcuts—Mac on one side, Windows on the other. You'll find that here: http://indesignsecrets.com/indesign-poster-details/.

If you choose Edit ➤ Keyboard Shortcuts (on Windows) or InDesign ➤ Keyboard Shortcuts (on Mac), you can assign a keyboard shortcut to any command in InDesign, change the shortcuts already assigned, and create portable sets of shortcuts (more on portability later). In the Keyboard Shortcuts dialog (see Figure 1.10) you'll see, by default, the commands and shortcuts of the Edit menu.

FIGURE 1.10
Editing keyboard shortcuts

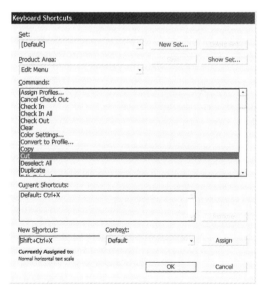

Click on Cut in the Commands list. Its shortcut—Cmd+X/Ctrl+X—will appear in the Current Shortcuts field beneath the list. Don't like that shortcut? Click on Default: Cmd+X or Default: Ctrl+X to highlight it, and then click the Remove button. InDesign will promptly notify you that you cannot modify the Default set of keyboard shortcuts and ask whether to create a new set for your customizations. InDesign can contain multiple keyboard shortcut sets. In fact, if you look toward the very top of the dialog, it already had three—Default, Shortcuts for PageMaker 7.0, and Shortcuts for QuarkXPress 4.0. If you're migrating to InDesign from PageMaker or QuarkXPress, using one of those sets can ease your transition. In the QuarkXPress set, for instance, object arrange commands such as Bring Forward, Bring to Front, Send Backward, and Send to Back use XPress's familiar F5 commands instead of InDesign's commands, which use the left and right brackets ([ ]). Of course, InDesign isn't PageMaker nor QuarkXPress, so not every command or keyboard shortcut from one has a place in the other; the shortcut sets are not total conversions, but helping hands.

To create your own set, click the New Set button and name the set, or begin a change and answer Yes when prompted. Go ahead and create a new set now, just to practice while you go through the rest of this section. While working in your set, remember to save it from time to time with the button at the top. If, after working through this chapter, you elect to eject the shortcut set, simply choose it in the Set drop-down and click the Delete Set button.

Returning to modifying the Edit ➤ Cut command, let's stay that, instead of removing the default shortcut, you'd like to add a second shortcut. You'd like both Cmd+X/Ctrl+X and Cmd+Shift+X/Ctrl+ Shift+X to effect a cut. In that case, to add a shortcut, position your cursor within the New Shortcut field at the bottom of the dialog and press the new shortcut. (Note to Windows users: You cannot use the Windows key as a modifier within the application.) Beneath the field you should see a warning that Cmd+Shift+X/Ctrl+ Shift+X is already assigned to the Normal Horizontal Text Scale command. If you click the Assign button, you'll strip Normal Horizontal Text Scale from the shortcut and assign it to Cut.

To the right of the New Shortcut field is Context. Every keyboard shortcut can be targeted to certain types of tasks. You could, for example, bind Cmd+Shift+X/Ctrl+ Shift+X to Edit ➤ Cut only when working with tables. While working with text, with XML selections, within alert and dialog boxes, and in all other circumstances, it will not invoke the Cut command. In fact, if you set the Context field to Table now, you'll see that the Currently Assigned To notice no longer says Normal Horizontal Text Scale. That's because the shortcut is bound to that command only in the context of working with text. The horizontal scale of text is irrelevant to XML code, dialogs, and the structure of tables, and that command and shortcut combination has been assigned to function only where it *is* relevant—when working directly with text. If you left Context set to Table and assigned Cmd+Shift+X/Ctrl+ Shift+X to the Cut command, *that* would apply only when working with tables. The same shortcut would still invoke Normal Horizontal Text Scale when working with text. In other words, the same keyboard shortcut can be *used five times over* for different commands in different contexts.

There are only so many keys on the QWERTY keyboard, only so many modifiers and combinations of keys, so customizing keyboard shortcuts in InDesign often entails sacrificing keyboard access to one command for another. By the same token, just as you can add multiple shortcuts to Cut, other commands already have multiple shortcuts. Do they need two (or three)? Probably not, which means their extras are fair game for commands that don't have any. Other commands have shortcuts you'll never use; put those key combinations to better use. If you use the Gradient Feather effect often, give it a keyboard shortcut (it doesn't have one by default, although the Drop Shadow command does—Cmd+Shift+M/Ctrl+Shift+M).

The Product Area drop-down mirrors the structure of menus but includes a lot more, even commands not found on the menu bar. Object Editing, for instance, includes all sorts of align, distribution, scale, and nudge commands that simply don't have counterparts on any menu and would normally require mouse work. Explore around the dialog, changing and testing shortcuts, until you have all your most-used commands shortcutted and InDesign works your way.

The folks at Adobe did a great job in setting keyboard shortcuts on the commands most used by the average InDesign user, but they had to leave it up to you to tailor the program to *your* unique workflow. Keyboard shortcuts, various panel arrangements and customizations, even customizable menus are available to tailor the program to you. Use them.

Menus

Yes, you read me right: In InDesign CS3 you can customize menus. Photoshop CS2 (and its now-retired protégé ImageReady CS2) introduced the idea of customizable menus. Odd as it may sound, it's a pretty cool idea. Do me a favor: Select Window ➢ Workspace ➢ Printing and Proofing. You'll likely be prompted; answer in the affirmative. Now, return to the Window menu. Notice anything? Check out the File menu. You should see quite a few commands and submenus highlighted in a pleasing green (see Figure 1.11). Try Window ➢ Workspace ➢ New and Improved in CS3. Just about every menu will then show something highlighted in blue.

FIGURE 1.11
Menu highlighting in use to show off printing and proofing commands

Now, go to the blue-highlighted Menus command at the bottom of the Edit menu to open Menu Customization (see Figure 1.12). Similar to customizing keyboard shortcuts, you have sets to create and choose from and two categories of menus—Application Menus, those that appear within the menu bar at the top of the InDesign window, and Context & Panel Menus, which are the flyout menus on panels as well as those menus that appear when you right-click (Control-click for you single-button Mac mouse users) on something. Every menu in InDesign can be customized. Pick one. Click the arrow to the left to expand the menu, showing commands and submenus in the order in which they appear on the menu itself.

If there's a command that you never use, one you'd like out of your way, click its eyeball icon in the Visibility column. The menu command or submenu will disappear from the application as if it didn't exist. To highlight a menu like those that turned blue in the New and Improved in CS3 workspace, change the color in the third column. Sorry, no custom colors, just the basic rainbow red, orange, yellow, green, blue, violet, and gray (for rain clouds, I assume).

Why would I want to remove some commands? you might ask. Well, the vast majority of InDesign users never use everything in the application. Do you do any XML work? If not, you can hide the XML-centric commands and unclutter the interface a little.

FIGURE 1.12
Customizing menus

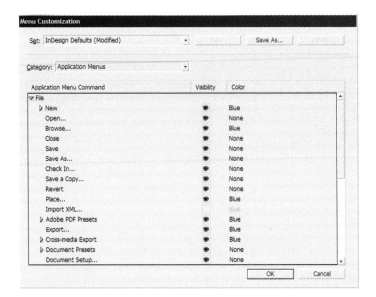

Next, I'd expect you to ask, *Why would I want to color-code my menu commands?* As you saw Adobe do with its sets, color-coding menus is a great way to learn new features and commands. It can also help in memory: *Where do I set the options for an inline graphic so that it has vertical spacing? Oh, duh! Here it is: Anchored Objects on the Objects menu. I colored it red last time I used it six months ago so I'd remember where to find it again.*

For you production managers, editors, and other team leaders, customizing menus presents a new level of production control through customized workstation installs without messing with installer scripts or disabling plug-ins. Check out the sidebar "Customizing InDesign to Easily Create Workflow-Focused Workstations" to see how I helped the editor of one small newspaper keep her staff focused and her layouts clean and press-ready.

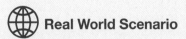 **Real World Scenario**

CUSTOMIZING INDESIGN TO EASILY CREATE WORKFLOW-FOCUSED WORKSTATIONS

Very recently, I was asked to improve the workflow of a high school newspaper. The request came from Pam, the editor in chief and a teacher at the school. Pam was exasperated with her paper's workflow. She had good reporters and editors, but none of them had had graphic design training despite the fact that they laid out their own copy and photos and worked up advertisements for the paper's local sponsors. Her teenage staff probably knew more about technology than either Pam or I, but they're prone to—let's say—*experimenting* with imagery and effects. They had a tendency to try to reproduce in their articles and ads anything that caught their eye in any medium—other newspapers, magazines, printed advertisements, broadcast media, the Web, and, most often, MySpace.com. All of this despite the fact that the paper was one color (with thrice-annual special editions going to two or three colors). Before putting the paper to bed every week, Pam lost a night of sleep fixing the staff's experiments and converting too-similar color pairings like RGB deep purple and dark red to colors that would contrast in 85 lpi black on newsprint.

When the school board delivered InDesign CS3 with its object effects, attribute-level transparency, and other features, Pam foresaw her one night of cleanup and fix stretching into a night and a day. The students' designs, she said, will only get more wild. Because Pam had classes to teach, and because students' class schedules varied, staffers often worked in the paper's office without supervision. The teenagers, who by their own admission know far more than we experienced old fogies, simply couldn't resist engaging in…experimental…design. New features of CS3 would improve the productivity and creativity of the staff, but other features would make more work for Pam. This was the problem. The solution was to customize the menus.

Armed with the character of the publication—B&W, 85 LPI, newspaper—the list-style presentation of commands in the Menu Customization dialog made it easy to compile a list of what commands and panels staffers needed and what they didn't. Then, it was just a matter of turning off what they didn't need. Because the publication is printed only in black ink, we disabled Window ➢ Color and removed the corresponding shortcut, preventing the Color panel from being accessed. The Swatches panel, preloaded with tint swatches of process black and all other colors removed, we left available to the students, but we disabled the Swatches panel menu commands for New Color Swatch, New Mixed Ink Swatch, and any other command that would have enabled the creation or loading of colors other than those added to the default palette by Pam. (We couldn't do anything about the New Swatch button at the bottom of the panel, though, so we disabled the `Color Picker.apln` and other plug-ins.) For those thrice annual two- or three-color special issues, Pam will create new InDesign INDT templates containing the same black tint swatches and matching tint swatches for the chosen spot color(s). We turned off access to object effects, transparency, HTML and XML export, and quite a few other commands and panels that the students didn't need in order to write and lay out their newspaper—disabling both in the main application menu and in panel and context-sensitive menus. At the same time, we colored menu commands that were new to CS3 or had moved since CS2 to help the students learn the new version.

To prevent the technology savvy teenagers from undoing everything, we assigned custom (and difficult-to-guess) keyboard shortcuts to open the keyboard shortcut and menus customization dialogs and to revert to the default workspace (thus restoring access to the Window ➢ Workspace menu and everything else so that Pam could later change the customizations if needed); changed the default shortcut for InDesign's Preferences, and then hid them all from appearing on the Edit and InDesign (Mac) menus.

As a last step, after making all the menu and keyboard shortcut changes and showing and arranging all the required panels, we saved all the presets individually and created a new workspace that unified these settings. The result was a lean InDesign installation completely customized to the needs of the school newspaper and bereft of anything that didn't have a place in the workflow. The final step was to copy the shortcut set, menu set, and workspace from the build machine to the staff's workstations and load the preset workspace that mirrored the workstations to the build machine.

Pam tells her students it's InDesign Elements CS3, a new product built specifically for black-and-white newsletter publishing that Adobe is test-marketing among several schools and newspapers.

Of course, these changes couldn't prevent a student from drawing something completely inappropriate in Illustrator or Photoshop and then placing it in InDesign. Both of those applications have similar customization features, and we limited some of their functionality on the workstations, but by necessity, it couldn't be as thorough a streamlining as within InDesign. Still, last I heard, Pam's per-issue cleanup had dropped from a full night of work to less than two hours because of the limited InDesign installations.

Plug-In Customization

Another level of application customization available to you is via the removal of plug-ins. (Individual users, feel free to skip this section.)

InDesign, you see, is not so much an application in the traditional sense of computer programming. It isn't hundreds of thousands or millions of lines of code compiled into a single executable like most other applications. InDesign.exe (Windows) and InDesign.app (Mac) is actually a plug-in wrapper. All of InDesign's functionality is added through plug-ins that are no different than a third-party plug-in you may buy to give InDesign functionality Adobe didn't. Don't believe me? Go look in your InDesign installation folder (Applications/Adobe/Adobe InDesign CS3 on the Mac, Program Files\Adobe\Adobe InDesign CS3 on Windows). The InDesign application itself is but a few megabytes. Look inside the Plug-Ins folder on the Mac to find numerous .InDesignPlugin files arranged in subfolders. On Windows, you'll see the same subfolders beneath the Plug-Ins folder. On either platform, you'll see mostly plain-English names for all your favorite InDesign panels and features. The Eyedropper tool, for instance, is added to InDesign Windows by the inclusion of the Eyedropper Tool.apln plug-in, for instance; the Print dialog is PrintUI.InDesignPlugin on the Mac. The InDesign executable mostly acts as activator to run those plug-ins and glue to allow them to work together. There's also an extra layer of organization on Windows that isn't on the Mac. Windows users will note the Program Files\Adobe\Adobe InDesign CS3\Required folder, which contains RPLN plug-in files. The .rpln extension stands for *Required PLug-iN*. As the name implies, everything in the Required folder is required for InDesign to fulfill its base purpose. In the Plug-Ins folder are all the optional plug-ins, the ones InDesign *can* function without. Most you wouldn't want it to run without, though. For example, you could pull out the Page Setup Dialog.apln, but then you wouldn't be able to alter page sizes. On the Mac, plug-ins aren't so easily differentiated as required, and nonrequired plug-ins all share the .InDesignPlugin extension.

InDesign can function, to one degree or another, absent any of the nonrequired plug-ins. Therefore, if some or all of the people in your workgroup have no need of something like, say, hyperlinks and the Hyperlinks panel or type on a path, you can save (a little) system overhead and tidy up the InDesign interface a bit by disabling the plug-ins that add those functions.

If you go to Help ➤ Configure Plug-Ins (Windows) or InDesign ➤ Configure Plug-Ins (Mac), you'll see all the plug-ins installed in your copy of InDesign—required, optional, and any third-party plug-ins you may have (see Figure 1.13). There are, by default, three sets of plug-ins defined: All, which shows everything, Adobe Plug-Ins, both required and not, and Required Plug-Ins. In any set, required plug-ins appear with a padlock icon to the left and are always active. Active nonrequired plug-ins have a check mark in the first column. Where possible—and certainly with Adobe-created plug-ins—a logo of the plug-in maker appears in the third column, and a cute little plug icon shows in the fourth. At the bottom of the dialog, the Display section check boxes enable further refinement of the view.

Anything without a padlock can be disabled by clicking the check mark icon. Like customizing keyboard shortcuts, the first such change you make will prompt you to create a new plug-in set, which is just a list of which plug-ins are active and which not. Any plug-ins neither you nor InDesign need to do your job, disable them; you'll have a leaner InDesign with less demand on your system RAM. If you're not entirely sure what a plug-in does, highlight it and click the Show Info button. Although the resulting Plug-In Information dialog isn't guaranteed to be illuminating, I might offer some clues (see Figure 1.14). At the very least, the Dependencies area will note any other plug-ins required for this one to run and, beneath that, which plug-ins can't run if you disable this one.

FIGURE 1.13
Configuring
InDesign plug-ins

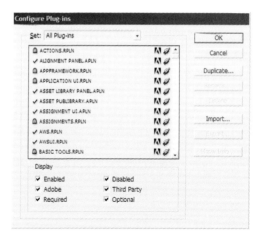

FIGURE 1.14
Information on the
Book.RPLN plug-in

When in doubt about what a plug-in does and whether you need it, try disabling it and look for the absence of what you think it does. Fortunately, you can't accidentally disable the Configure Plug-Ins dialog itself as Plugin Manager.apln/Plugin Manager.InDesignPlugin is required (despite the lack of an .rpln file extension), so you can always simply reactivate a plug-in you want.

Why would I want to disable some plug-ins? For many of the same reasons you'd want to disable some menus—a cleaner display, the aforementioned smaller RAM footprint, and to limit workstation installs to only what is required of the user's workflow. If your team works in a strictly print workflow, for instance, and never exports to HTML or to PDFs for distribution online, you can remove commands, panels, and everything else to do with hyperlinks, form fields, sound and video, HTML and SVG export, and so on. I can tell you from personal experience that using Configure Plug-Ins to disable things like the Tools panel (Tool Box.apln) on someone else's computer is also an amusing practical joke. Just be kind enough to let the victim in on the joke before too long (or leave this book nearby opened to this page and I'll take the blame).

Workspaces

Now that you've got InDesign all customized to your personal work habits, with this panel stacked over here, another dozen panels collapsed to icons in a dock, three more stacked, and several panels hidden, menus color-coded and customized, and keyboard shortcuts totally customized, it's time to scare you: Everything you just did will evaporate the first time InDesign's preferences get corrupted. They get corrupted often—no more so than other applications, but that's too often.

All your customizations are saved into the application preferences, a flimsy little ASCII text file with all the resiliency and tensile strength of wet newsprint. Sneezing too hard in the general direction of your computer could tear and corrupt the preferences. Then where would you be? That's right, trying to remember all the original keyboard shortcuts while stumbling all but blind through the original configuration of panels. Of course, there's a solution to prevent the loss of your customizations. And, I'll explain that solution in detail in the sequel to this book, *Mastering InDesign CS3 for Print Design and Production Reloaded*, due out from Sybex next year. Don't let your preferences get corrupted before then.

Just kidding. I was doing an impression of a typical local news anchor—*tune into our six o'clock broadcast to find out what's killing area children and could be killing your child right now!* (Yup, tune in at least three hours after your child has been presumably slain to learn that children are being given two desserts in the school cafeteria on Fridays.)

InDesign has, for several versions now, had the ability to save panel (previously palette, lest we forget the tragedies of yesterday) arrangements as *workspaces*. With InDesign CS2, workspaces saved custom keyboard shortcuts along with palette arrangements. In CS3, they now save menu customizations, keyboard shortcuts, *and* panel arrangements. It's the last part that's the most important because, while you can save and restore sets of keyboard shortcuts and menus, workspaces are the only way to record panel arrangements.

When we looked at menu color-coding a few pages ago, the New and Improved in CS3 and Printing and Proofing options you chose were workspaces. You may have noticed that loading them also rearranged your panels. If you missed that, load up Printing and Proofing again from Window ➤ Workspaces. Note the dock on the right wherein several panels have been hidden and replaced by others not shown after first installing InDesign. The Default Workspace saved workspace will return everything—shortcuts, menus, panels—to out-of-the-box InDesign.

Any time you customize InDesign, save your workspace by choosing Window ➤ Workspaces ➤ Save Workspace. Supply a name and your workspace will be added to the Workspaces menu ready for instant restoration in the event of a preferences corruption and subsequent reset or if you change things around to fit a particular project.

That brings me to another key point: You can have many, many workspaces. Sometimes you need these five panels showing, some projects require these six others, and yet other types of projects require a dozen or more, all with options showing. Make workspaces for each of your typical types of projects. Strictly print projects, for instance, aren't likely to need the Hyperlinks panel, whereas creating a publication that will only be distributed on the client's website as a PDF *does* need Hyperlinks, and probably doesn't need the Separations Preview and Trap Presets panels. By employing multiple, project-specific workspaces, you can further reduce panel clutter by limiting the application to only what the one type of project needs, without the chore of having to manually open, close, and arrange panels every time you switch over to a different project.

InDesign in Your Pocket

Or, *InDesign on a Stick*—a USB stick/thumbnail drive/flash drive. Although you *can* fit InDesign and all its component plug-ins on most portable USB flash drives, it won't run from there. (Well, I'm sure somebody could get it to run, but I think that would violate the EULA.) What I mean by the title of this section is taking *your* InDesign in your pocket, your unique configuration and work habits, and sitting down at any workstation and, in 30 seconds or less, making any copy of InDesign CS3 work exactly like InDesign on your main computer—complete with panel arrangements, keyboard shortcuts, menus, and even your own autocorrect settings and Find/Change queries.

It's exceedingly simple, really. First, make sure you've created a new keyboard shortcut set, a new set of menus, and a new workspace. Create and save them in their respective manners. Nothing here is permanent, so please don't feel pressured to create the perfect workspace or customize everything right now. Just do something simple for each, save the set, and close InDesign.

Now, open a Finder or Explorer window and navigate to the InDesign folder:

Mac: `[your user name]/Library/Preferences/Adobe/InDesign/Version 5.0/`

Windows: `Documents and Settings\[your user name]\Application Data\Adobe\InDesign\ Version 5.0\`

Within those folders, you should see a subfolder for `Workspaces`. Open that, and you'll find an XML file of the workspace you just created. Go back up to the Menu Sets folder to find your recently created menu set. At the same level as both of those folders, you'll find others, called `InDesign Shortcut Sets`, `Autocorrect`, `Find-Change Queries`, and `Glyph Sets`. All of these folders store personal, per-user settings that are machine and even platform independent. You can pick up these files by copying the entire `Version 5.0` folder, carry them to any other installation of InDesign CS3 on the same platform (Windows or Mac), copy them to the same locations on the new machine, and have access to them at that workstation just as you would your own. When you launch InDesign, your copied workspace will be on the Window ➤ Workspaces menu, your keyboard and menu sets in the Keyboard Shortcuts and Customize Menu dialogs' Sets dropdowns, and your Autocorrect, Find/Change, and Glyphs sets where they belong (I cover each later in this book). In fact, if you're handy with scripting, you could probably write an AppleScript or VBScript or BAT file that, upon execution on a target workstation, copies the Version 5.0 folder from the USB drive to the hard drive.

You can even store your portable InDesign settings on your iPod, which, if you didn't realize it, can hold any type of data, not just music and videos. *That* would sell a few copies of this book! I can see the cover line now: *Run InDesign from Your iPod!*

Customizing Application Defaults

Is there a way to change the default font/swatches/hyphenation options/whatever? Collectively, it's probably the most common question I'm asked. Answer: Yes. If you can change the font family and style in the Character panel, you can change the default font. Likewise with creating new default swatches and removing the swatches with which InDesign ships. In fact, if you can do almost anything, you can make it the new default. Just do it with all documents closed.

Open InDesign without a document and look at the panels. If an option is grayed out, you can't change its default. If it isn't grayed out, well…there you are. Do you want hyphenation turned off by default instead of on? Uncheck the Hyphenate button on the Paragraph panel (show options if you don't see it). To remove swatches you rarely use, open the Swatches panel and delete them. Add new swatches you use regularly—like corporate colors—by adding them to the panel with all documents closed. Every new document from that point forward will use only the swatches you see there, or will leave hyphenate unchecked, or whatever change you want to make.

To change the default font, open the Character panel and change the font. Done. Well, not entirely. You see, InDesign has a default paragraph style. When you change type options on the Character or Paragraph panels, you are indeed setting new defaults. However, you aren't changing the default styles, which can lead to problems later on if you reapply the default styles to text. If you're sure of your new font (or other type styling defaults), make the changes in the Character and/or Paragraph panels, and then open the Paragraph Styles panel. Highlight the Basic Paragraph style, choose Style Options from the panel flyout menu, and then repeat your changes there, making sure to save the style. Now your changes will survive a reapplication of the style.

Experiment with different controls and options. You can set new defaults for a great many things when no documents are opened.

SHARING CUSTOMIZATIONS

Many of the customizations we've covered in this chapter can be easily shared with others in your workgroup. Things like workspaces, keyboard shortcuts, autocorrect pairs, find/change queries, and more can be shared and standardized across your team. In Chapter 12, "Collaboration," you'll learn how; you'll also learn about the more powerful means of document and page collaboration available with InDesign CS3.

The Bottom Line

Organize Panels and Use the New Panel Docks   New docks and other options make organizing panels in the workspace easier than ever before.

Master It   Beginning with the default workspace, open all the panels you expect to use in most projects and close those you won't. Now, using grouping, stacking, docking, or just free floating panels, arrange the panels to fit your work style and leave you as much room to work on documents as possible.

Customize Keyboard Shortcuts   Adobe couldn't assign a keyboard shortcut to everything—there just aren't enough keys—so it did its best. Many of your favorite commands may not have shortcuts or may have shortcuts you dislike. You can add or change keyboard shortcuts for any command in InDesign.

Master It   Just for fun, create keyboard shortcuts for each of the object effects—Basic Feather, Bevel and Emboss, and so on.

Remove Parts of InDesign to Create Lean, Workflow-Specific Installations   By customizing menus and disabling plug-ins, you can now easily remove features and functions of InDesign not required by your workflow. Doing so streamlines the interface, reduces errors, and ultimately increases productivity among workflows that do not require the entirety of InDesign.

> **Master It**   To test your hand at removing features from InDesign, find all the features that are new or improved in CS3 and hide their menu commands. Then, color green the first 10 still enabled menu commands about which you'd like to learn more. Finally, disable the plug-ins that show panels you or your team aren't likely to need.

Change the Default Font, Colors, and More   Out of the box, InDesign uses Times New Roman 12/14.4 pt as the default text style and includes swatches for process magenta, cyan, and yellow and RGB red, green, and blue. These defaults are fine if your average document uses 12/14.4 Times New Roman and only solid process or RGB colors. But, if the average document you create requires another typeface, size, or leading or other colors, or virtually any other option different from the defaults, change the defaults and save yourself some time.

> **Master It**   Think about the documents you create most often. What is the type style—font family, font style, size, leading, and other formatting attributes—you use more than any other? Make those your new defaults. Do the same with your swatches, eliminating any colors you rarely use while adding those you use frequently.

Carry Your Personalized InDesign Work Environment in Your Pocket or on Your iPod
From freelancers brought into agency offices to assist with crunch time to students working in school labs, from round-the-clock production teams where different shifts use the same equipment to those dedicated enough to bring work home, seldom do creatives work solely on a single machine anymore. Creative and production personnel who switch computers waste a significant portion of their time customizing the InDesign environment of each computer on which they work even for a few minutes. To save time, nearly everything customizable about the InDesign CS3 working environment is portable. Customize one copy of InDesign, and carry your unique environment with you, making you instantly productive at any workstation.

> **Master It**   After arranging your panels and customizing your keyboard shortcuts and menus, it's time to take your InDesign workspace with you. If you have a USB flash drive, an iPod, a PDA, or even just a floppy disk handy, copy the files containing your customized environment to the storage device. Now, if a second computer is available with InDesign CS3 installed, install those files to that computer and set up InDesign CS3 your way.

Chapter 2

Text

Like most layout applications, InDesign operates on a content-to-container premise. Everything within InDesign is either content—text and imagery—or a container to hold text, imagery, or another container. At the lowest level, the pasteboard is a container that holds everything you might place in InDesign. Then there are pages and layers—more containers—and *then* the real content enters the picture—text and imagery.

In this chapter, you will learn to:

◆ Create and fill text frames

◆ Format text frames

◆ Format paragraphs

◆ Compose paragraphs

◆ Set up paragraph rules

Text Frame Basics

Whether imported from an external document or typed directly into InDesign, text is, by definition, content. Therefore it must be contained by a frame.

Creating Text Frames

The most basic text holder is a rectangular frame, and the easiest way to make one is to click and drag with the Type tool. As soon as you let go of the mouse, your text frame will be fixed and an I-beam cursor will be activated inside it, ready to accept your words of wisdom. You can then type something into the new frame. Figure 2.1 shows my words of…well, not wisdom, surely. Let's say my words of satire.

FIGURE 2.1
A newly created text frame containing text

The Getty Stone Address

Five versions and eight years ago, Adobe brought forth on this profession, a new application, conceived in Liberty, and dedicated to the proposition that all layouts are created equal.

Text frames can be created anywhere—on the page, on the pasteboard, overlapping both. Once created, they can be moved by selecting them with the Selection tool (the black arrow) and dragging. Resizing is just as easy: Once selected, a text frame will display its nine control corners—four at the corners, four more at the centers of each side, and the last in the frame's center. Dragging all but the center point will resize the frame. Dragging the center point will simply move the frame.

Notice as you resize the frame with the Selection tool, the text wraps to accommodate but does not resize. In a short while, we'll get into the different ways to style and format text. For now, it's more important to cover the ways in which text makes it *into* InDesign.

Getting Text into Text Frames

On many occasions, you'll know exactly what to type into a newly created text frame. On others, you won't. While you're waiting on a client, editor, or copywriter to provide the text for a layout, for example, you'll need to employ dummy text while you design. It's what we call *greeking* or For Position Only *(FPO)* text; it enables you to work out the placement and style of type ahead of having genuine content.

IMPORTING A TEXT FILE

Typing directly into InDesign is one way of getting text into your layout, and many people do it just that way. Most of the time, for longer text anyway, you'll write copy outside of InDesign and import it. If you work on a publication or in another collaborative environment, odds are good that someone else will write the copy and you'll have to place and style it. Let's use the old standby Lorem Ipsum to simulate such tasks.

1. Create a new text frame with the Type tool. Just like last time, you'll immediately have an I-beam cursor ready to type—don't.

2. Instead, choose File ➤ Place (Cmd+D/Ctrl+D).

3. In the Place dialog, navigate to wherever you copied the Chap02 files from the book's download page. Inside that folder, highlight the file lorem.txt and click Open. Five-hundred-year-old nonsense should fill your text frame (see Figure 2.2).

You've just imported an ASCII text file, and it doesn't look too bad. Now repeat the process with the bad-lorem.txt file. Not so nice, is it?

TEXT IMPORT OPTIONS

The text in bad-lorem.txt is roughly equivalent to what you might get from an email message or something typed directly into Windows's Notepad or Mac's SimpleText. Lines are short and, instead of wrapping dynamically, contain hard line breaks. Choose Type ➤ Show Hidden Characters to see what I mean; it reveals all the nonprinting characters (what QuarkXPress calls "invisibles," if you're migrating to InDesign from that application). Figure 2.3 shows what you should be seeing, although the width of your text frame may alter the view somewhat.

Email and plain-text editors have a tendency to break lines of type after a few words by inserting a hard carriage return, as signified by the *pilcrow*, or paragraph mark (¶). They also don't like to use real tabs because tab characters are not always compatible with the *ASCII* text format. Because email and plain-text editors lack paragraph spacing capabilities, vertical white space between paragraphs is usually accomplished by using multiple carriage returns—a *major* typesetting no-no.

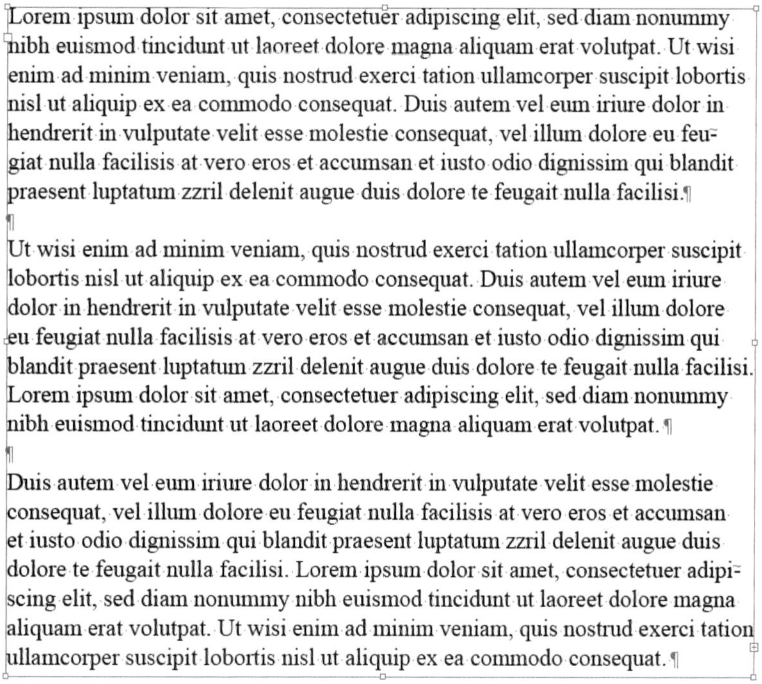

FIGURE 2.2
The venerable
Lorem Ipsum filling
a text frame

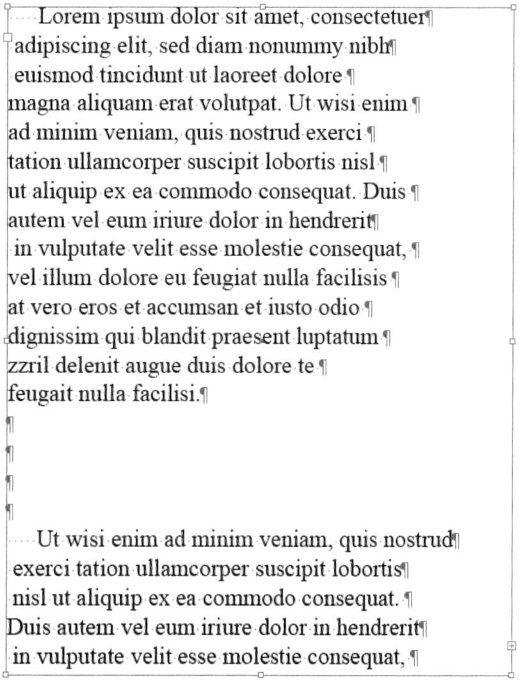

Lorem ipsum dolor sit amet, consectetuer adipiscing elit, sed diam nonummy nibh euismod tincidunt ut laoreet dolore magna aliquam erat volutpat. Ut wisi enim ad minim veniam, quis nostrud exerci tation ullamcorper suscipit lobortis nisl ut aliquip ex ea commodo consequat. Duis autem vel eum iriure dolor in hendrerit in vulputate velit esse molestie consequat, vel illum dolore eu feugiat nulla facilisis at vero eros et accumsan et iusto odio dignissim qui blandit praesent luptatum zzril delenit augue duis dolore te feugait nulla facilisi.

Ut wisi enim ad minim veniam, quis nostrud exerci tation ullamcorper suscipit lobortis nisl ut aliquip ex ea commodo consequat. Duis autem vel eum iriure dolor in hendrerit in vulputate velit esse molestie consequat, vel illum dolore eu feugiat nulla facilisis at vero eros et accumsan et iusto odio dignissim qui blandit praesent luptatum zzril delenit augue duis dolore te feugait nulla facilisi. Lorem ipsum dolor sit amet, consectetuer adipiscing elit, sed diam nonummy nibh euismod tincidunt ut laoreet dolore magna aliquam erat volutpat.

Duis autem vel eum iriure dolor in hendrerit in vulputate velit esse molestie consequat, vel illum dolore eu feugiat nulla facilisis at vero eros et accumsan et iusto odio dignissim qui blandit praesent luptatum zzril delenit augue duis dolore te feugait nulla facilisi. Lorem ipsum dolor sit amet, consectetuer adipiscing elit, sed diam nonummy nibh euismod tincidunt ut laoreet dolore magna aliquam erat volutpat. Ut wisi enim ad minim veniam, quis nostrud exerci tation ullamcorper suscipit lobortis nisl ut aliquip ex ea commodo consequat.

FIGURE 2.3
Show Hidden
Characters reveals
just how bad
`bad-lorem.txt`
really is.

Lorem ipsum dolor sit amet, consectetuer¶
adipiscing elit, sed diam nonummy nibh¶
euismod tincidunt ut laoreet dolore ¶
magna aliquam erat volutpat. Ut wisi enim ¶
ad minim veniam, quis nostrud exerci ¶
tation ullamcorper suscipit lobortis nisl ¶
ut aliquip ex ea commodo consequat. Duis ¶
autem vel eum iriure dolor in hendrerit¶
in vulputate velit esse molestie consequat, ¶
vel illum dolore eu feugiat nulla facilisis ¶
at vero eros et accumsan et iusto odio ¶
dignissim qui blandit praesent luptatum ¶
zzril delenit augue duis dolore te ¶
feugait nulla facilisi.¶
¶
¶
¶
¶
Ut wisi enim ad minim veniam, quis nostrud¶
exerci tation ullamcorper suscipit lobortis¶
nisl ut aliquip ex ea commodo consequat. ¶
Duis autem vel eum iriure dolor in hendrerit¶
in vulputate velit esse molestie consequat, ¶

As you might expect, all this makes for some very ugly copy and could be a lot of tedious cleanup work for you, the InDesign user. Ten years ago, you would have had to go through the text manually deleting the extra carriage returns, replacing the faux tabs with a smack of the keyboard Tab key, and, one line at a time, rejoining all the lines of a paragraph. Fortunately, InDesign was built with an automated way to clean up most of this mess.

1. Create a new text frame with the Type tool.

2. Choose File ➤ Place, and once again highlight bad-lorem.txt, but *don't* press the Open button yet.

3. Toward the bottom of the Place dialog is a check box labeled Show Import Options. Check that, and *then* click Open. Up will pop the Text Import Options dialog (see Figure 2.4). What does it all mean?

FIGURE 2.4

The Text Import Options dialog box

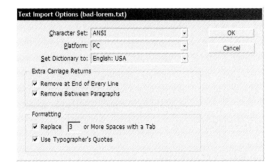

Character Set Every text file has a character set associated with it. Character sets are dependent upon human-written language—such as Cyrillic, Turkish, Chinese, or Latin—and machine-written language or the operating system. Because the character set is nearly always encoded in the header of the text file, which InDesign reads, it's usually best to stick with InDesign's suggestion unless you know for certain that the default choice is incorrect.

Platform Was the file created on Windows or Mac OS? This is important because the default character sets of the two differ, and a wrong choice could lead to characters, or *glyphs,* exchanging for something unexpected. If you get strange characters in your imported text, try reimporting while switching the Platform setting. Again, though, InDesign usually picks up on the correct platform.

Set Dictionary To For spell checking and hyphenation purposes, choose the language of the text.

Remove (Extra Carriage Returns) at End of Every Line When dealing with a file like bad-lorem.txt, this is the most important setting. Turning this on will strip out all the extraneous carriage returns breaking lines within a paragraph. Manually removing them would be the bulk of the tedious cleanup, so be sure to check this option when importing most ASCII text files or content saved from text-only email.

Remove (Extra Carriage Returns) between Paragraphs Fairly self-explanatory, this option will search out any instance of two or more consecutive hard returns and replace them with one return, readying the text for proper paragraph differentiation through paragraph spacing above and/or below.

Replace X or More Spaces with a Tab   In bad-lorem.txt, as is common with output from plain-text editors, tabs are not tabs but consecutive spaces. This option will search out the specified number of spaces and replace them with real tabs. In the bad-lorem.txt file itself, I've set most paragraphs to begin with five consecutive tabs, but leaving the default value of 3 in place will also do the trick.

Use Typographer's Quotes   Quotation marks look like (""), while ("") are inch marks. Plain-text files, with their extremely limited glyph set, rarely contain the former. Consequently, quoted text is encased in inch marks. Turning on the Use Typographer's Quotes option will replace inch marks with real quotation marks. It will also replace foot marks (′) with genuine apostrophes ('). It's on by default and should stay that way unless you're importing a document containing measurements, time notations, or geographic coordinates.

4. Check all four of the check boxes in the Text Import Options dialog and click OK. Bad-lorem.txt should import looking a lot less bad.

Once set, the text import options will remain in that state—they're what we call *sticky* settings. So next time you import a text file, you can uncheck Show Import Options in the Place dialog. However, should you import a text file containing a list of items or structural dimensions, you'll want to revisit the Text Import Options dialog and disable some of the options there to avoid mangling your copy.

WORD IMPORT OPTIONS

Importing plain-text ASCII is a once-in-a-while thing at best. Most InDesign users get the majority of their copy from *rich text* word processors like Microsoft Word. Rich text is a far more robust file format than plain text and rarely suffers from forced line breaks every 80 characters. In fact, Rich Text Format, *RTF* for short, can support paragraph spacing, tabs, typographer's quotes, text formatting like italic, bold, and underline, and even style sheets (more on those in Chapter 11, "Efficiency"). Thus, RTF files have a different set of options for importing.

Word's native DOC files are based on RTF, and the two behave nearly identically with regard to placement in InDesign. Thus, we'll work with a Word DOC file. To get started, create a text frame. Choose File ➢ Place, and select the REVstory.doc document. Make sure Show Import Options is checked before clicking Open. Up will pop the Microsoft Word Import Options dialog (see Figure 2.5). Here's what the options you'll see mean:

Preset   Although your only current option here is likely [Custom], through the Save Preset button on the right it's possible to save the selection of options as a *preset*. Once saved, a set of import options can be reactivated by choosing the preset from this drop-down menu. If you import Word or RTF files and even occasionally require different options, it's worth it to save a preset or two.

(Include) Table of Contents Text   Word can generate dynamic, hyperlinked tables of contents based on headings or other styles used in a given document. InDesign can import the *text* of those tables of contents, but it *cannot* import it as dynamic or hyperlinked. For instance, if in Word the heading "Scumdot Tests on the Linotype 1500" appears on page 57 but upon import into InDesign winds up on page 63, the TOC will still read 57 and will not automatically update itself.

FIGURE 2.5
The Microsoft
Word Import
Options dialog

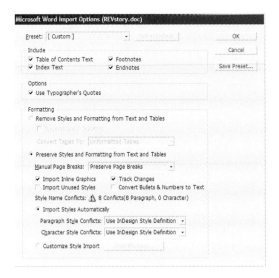

Only new tables of contents created using InDesign's built-in TOC generation can create references relevant to text on InDesign pages.

(Include) Index Text   As with a table of contents, Word and InDesign can both dynamically generate hyperlinked indexes, but a Word-generated index will survive the import only as unremarkable static text.

(Include) Footnotes and Endnotes   Unlike its treatment of a table of contents or an index, InDesign *will* preserve the dynamic nature of Word's footnotes and endnotes. Footnotes and their references will be imported and, if they differ from the footnote settings in the InDesign document, renumbered in accordance thereto. Endnotes will be inserted as formatted text at the end of the imported story.

Use Typographer's Quotes   Just as with plain-text import, this option will convert inch and foot marks into quotation marks and apostrophes, respectively. Again, this can be a gotcha if your document contains legitimately used marks for measurements, time, or geographic coordinates.

Remove Styles and Formatting from Text and Tables   Because Word documents are fully rich text, the text in them can be **emboldened**, *italicized*, <u>underlined</u>, ~~struck through~~, and even a ~~*<u>combination</u>*~~ thereof. If the author of the Word document knew what he was doing, you'll probably want to leave this radio button set on Preserve Styles and Formatting from Text and Tables. If, however, the Word document author went format-crazy, choosing to remove styles and formatting (along with unchecking Preserve Local Overrides) will strip off all the formatting and styles, importing clean text ready for proper formatting in InDesign.

PLACE INTO MIDDLE

Need to place an external text document into the middle of the text already in a frame? Just put the cursor in the right spot and import with Show Import Options checked. Remove styles and formatting and the inserted text will automatically inherit the style and formatting of the text into which it's inserted.

Preserve Local Overrides   When Remove Styles and Formatting from Text and Tables is selected, this option becomes available. Off, it completely wipes all formatting from imported text—bold text is unbolded, italicized type is returned to standard roman type, and so on. Check it, however, and all the styles (aka style sheets) will be wiped away but individual text formatting options like bold, italic, underline, and so on will survive the import.

Convert Tables To   (Accessible only if Remove Styles and Formatting from Text and Tables is selected.) If the imported text contains tables, how would you like them treated? Would you prefer them imported as InDesign tables (Unformatted Tables), or would you rather convert them to tab-separated text (Unformatted Tabbed Text), which can then either be formatted as such or manually converted to an InDesign table?

Preserve Styles and Formatting from Text and Tables   All text formatting and assigned styles are preserved. On by default, and required for any of the following choices to be accessible.

Manual Page Breaks   Word, InDesign, and most other word processor and page layout applications offer the ability to insert break characters that stop text anywhere on the page and jump it to the next page before continuing. The three options in this drop-down offer the choice of keeping page breaks as defined in Word, converting Word's page breaks to InDesign column breaks—instead of picking up on the next page, the text will start up again in the next column of a multicolumn InDesign layout—or dumping Word's page breaks altogether.

Import Inline Graphics   Generally a bad idea from a print professional's perspective, Word has the ability to *embed* graphics and imagery directly in the flow of text. Typically, graphics inserted in this manner do not link to their original files; they're contained entirely within the Word document. Employing this feature is a very common practice among Word users inexperienced in professional print workflows. Checking Import Inline Graphics will bring those embedded images into InDesign as embedded, *anchored objects* (which are discussed in Chapter 6, "Objects"). Unchecking it will flush those images out of the text as if they never existed.

Import Unused Styles   Like InDesign, Word allows for reusable paragraph and character styles. Below you'll decide what to do with styles assigned to text in the Word document, but this option applies to styles that are *not* used but are *available to be used* within the Word document. In most cases you want this option unchecked to avoid cluttering your InDesign document with Word's numerous default and user-created styles.

Track Changes   In InDesign this option does absolutely nothing. Check it or don't; it makes no difference. In InCopy, however, it *does* do something. If Track Changes was active in the Word document, and if this option is checked here, basic Word change tracking is preserved. Text deleted in Word will carry into InCopy as deleted (struck through), and inserted text will be highlighted.

Convert Bullets and Numbers to Text   Should the bullets and numbers in Word's dynamically created lists continue to be dynamic, updating as necessary (especially numbered lists), or should they be converted to regular, editable text for selection and manual styling?

Style Name Conflicts   A yellow caution sign appears if both the Word and InDesign documents contain styles with the same names. To the right of the caution sign the number and type of conflicting styles are noted. The next few fields determine how those conflicts are resolved.

Paragraph and Character Style Conflicts   Choose whether to use InDesign's style definitions, disregarding Word's; redefine the InDesign styles to match those coming from Word; or add the Word styles as new styles automatically named to nullify the conflict.

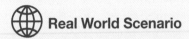 Real World Scenario

POWER TIP: RAPID STYLE IMPORT

Although you generally want to leave the Import Unused Styles option off in the Microsoft Word Import Options dialog, it does present an incredibly useful shortcut that can save hours or even days of work.

For instance, collaborative publishing workflows such as book, newspaper, and magazine teams usually consist of one or more writers creating original content in a Word template and designers accepting writers' Word files for placement into InDesign. The Word template from which writers create their chapters, articles, ad copy, and other text invariably contains a set of styles they are required to use—headlines must be assigned the "Head" style, kickers the "Kicker" style, bylines the "byline" style, and so forth.

Suppose your publication is in the middle of a redesign or migration and you need to rebuild your publication template(s) in InDesign. You *can* manually re-create all the styles needed to format stories, *or* you could simply import the writers' Word template while checking the Import Unused Styles option. That would import all the styles from the Word document, even styles like "sub-sub-list" that are only occasionally used. The styles will still need to be *updated* in InDesign to make them native, but that's just a simple matter of opening them and glancing through all the options. It's much faster than creating all those styles again from scratch.

Sometimes InCopy stands between Word and InDesign, with editors taking original content Word files into InCopy and then furnishing revised InCopy stories to InDesign layout artists. InCopy, which is effectively InDesign for editors and without frame creation tools, has the same Microsoft Word import options. Thus, the same power tip applies if your editors are taking the Word files into InCopy instead of you taking them into InDesign.

Customize Style Import   Checking this option and clicking the Style Mapping button opens the Style Mapping dialog (see Figure 2.6), wherein all the styles in both documents are listed side by side. An entry of [New Paragraph Style] or [New Character Style] denotes the lack of conflict and that a new style will be created in the InDesign document to match the Word style. Any conflicts—where both columns have a non-bracketed style entry—can be resolved by clicking the style name in the InDesign Style column. A drop-down menu will appear presenting all styles present in the InDesign document, allowing a custom mapping from the Word style, as well as conflict resolution options matching those from previous dialog's drop-downs. The button at the bottom of the Style Mapping dialog tells InDesign to create new, similarly named styles based on the incoming, conflicting styles.

Save Preset (button)   As you can see from the length of my walk-through, there are quite a few decisions to be made when importing Word documents. The options you choose may be the same for every subsequent Word document you ever import, or documents from different sources or for different purposes might require alteration of these settings. If you anticipate more than a single setup—or you merely wish to ensure you don't lose your Word import option customizations, save a preset by clicking this button, naming the preset, and clicking OK. Thereafter, all your settings are ready for instant re-application from the Preset drop-down menu at the top of the dialog.

FIGURE 2.6

The Style Mapping dialog helps to resolve style conflicts between incoming Microsoft Word documents and existing InDesign layout content.

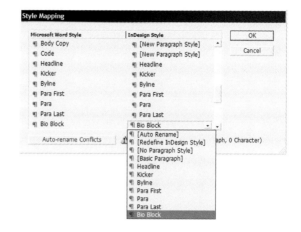

In this example, we want to select Preserve Styles and Formatting from Text and Tables and Use Typographer's Quotes. Everything else is irrelevant to this particular file—an article.

Click OK on the Microsoft Word Import Options dialog and the Word document will flow into the text frame exactly as our prior documents did. Note that it's already formatted with type and paragraph styling.

TEXT COPY AND PASTE

You can also copy text from just about anywhere to paste into InDesign. As long as what you copy hits the operating system's clipboard as text (as opposed to outlined type or an image), InDesign will take it on paste. Text can also be copied *from* InDesign into most other text-handling applications, although how much of the styling survives the paste depends on the target application.

PLACING WITHOUT A FRAME

It happens all the time: You're working away, on a roll, and press Cmd+D/Ctrl+D, grab a text file, and realize you forgot to first create a frame. Well, unlike in QuarkXPress, you need *not* have a frame in order to place content. True, all content must be within a container, but InDesign is savvy enough to make the container *while* you place the content. Give it a try.

1. Deselect all objects by clicking an empty area of the page or pasteboard.

2. Choose File ➤ Place, and select a textual file—one of the sample documents from this chapter should suffice. Hit OK.

3. Back in the document, you should notice a new type of cursor—a loaded cursor (see Figure 2.7). It even has a preview of the text you're about to place!

FIGURE 2.7

Yet to be placed text documents create a loaded cursor and preview of the text.

4. With the loaded cursor, click and drag out a rectangular area. The story will place, giving you both content and container in one swift action.

You can keep going like this, placing content without pre-created frames, throughout the entire document.

Which textual file formats can InDesign place within text frames? Plenty! Table 2.1 shows you.

TABLE 2.1: **Textual File Formats Supported by InDesign**

FILE EXTENSION	DOCUMENT DESCRIPTION
.incd, .incx	InCopy CS2–CS3 documents
.incd	InCopy CS stories
.doc	Microsoft Word (versions 2–2007)
.xls	Microsoft Excel (versions 4–2007)
.rtf	Rich Text Format
.txt	Plain text
.txt	Adobe InDesign Tagged Text

To place content from a WordPerfect file, use RTF. WordPerfect and all other word processors can export to RTF with minimal loss of feature and formatting; many word processors even save directly into RTF without the need for a second, proprietary format.

FILL WITH PLACEHOLDER TEXT

Now that you've got how to place text, there's an even faster way to fill a frame if all you need is FPO copy. Create a new text frame with the Type tool. With the I-beam cursor in the frame, go to the Type menu and, second from the bottom, choose Fill with Placeholder Text. The text frame will pack with gibberish FPO copy.

Fill with Placeholder Text automatically fills a text frame, however large. It also uses whatever typeface, size, style, and paragraph settings are currently in effect. For instance, if 12/14.4 pt Myriad Pro is the default type setup, Fill with Placeholder Text will fill the frame with 12 pt Myriad Pro on 14.4 pt leading.

InDesign's default placeholder text closely approximates real text with variable-length words, lines, and paragraphs. It's all still gibberish, but it *could* be real copy. If you'd rather it be some *other* kind of gibberish, like Lorem Ipsum, the Declaration of Independence, or Elmer Fudd reciting act IV scene I of Shakespeare's *Macbeth* ("doubwe, doubwe, toiw and twoubwe"), changing InDesign's default placeholder text is a breeze. Place the text you'd like to use in a plain-text file named Placeholder.txt, and save it into the InDesign folder. On Windows, you'll find the InDesign program folder in the following path (if you chose the default location during installation):

```
C:\Program Files\Adobe\InDesign CS3
```

On Mac, it's here:

```
Applications/InDesign CS3
```

Counting Words in a Text Frame

Editors and writers with whom you work frequently measure text by word count. *How many words fit in this part of the page? Can you find a place to slap in this 700-word article?* Of course, that means designers have to build and style text frames to hold a specified number of words.

When you're dummying up a layout with FPO copy, how can you know how many words fit in a given frame—and, thereby, how many frames are required per page, how many pages to carry an article of set length, and so on? Don't go running back to Word. InDesign actually has a pretty good word counter. It's called the Info panel (see Figure 2.8).

FIGURE 2.8
The Info panel counting characters, words, paragraphs, and lines

Select the Type tool, and put the cursor anywhere within a text frame's copy; don't highlight the text. The bottom of the Info panel will change to count characters, words, paragraphs, and lines throughout the entire story. Any figures after a plus sign (+) are *overset*—not visible in any text frame. The counts include text in any linked frame, on any page, and count everything in the story regardless of style—headlines, kickers, bylines, run-in captions, and so forth—but not text in other frames.

To find out how many characters, words, paragraphs, and lines fit within only a single text frame or paragraph, highlight the text in question. Statistics on the Info panel will revise to reflect only the highlighted text. In Figure 2.9, for instance, you can see the statistics for the first body copy paragraph of REVstory.doc.

FIGURE 2.9
Counts for a single paragraph in the shown story

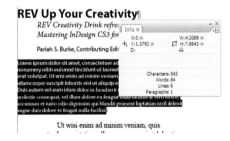

If you'd like a somewhat more visual word counter, one that appears in the text itself and survives printing or export to PDF for the benefit of writers, editors, or clients, check the Chap02 folder again. In addition to the files we've worked with so far, I've included Copyfit.txt, which contains only 5-letter words and marks every 25th word with a running count up to a total of 1,000 words.

Text Frame Options

Creating and filling text frames is only half the job. You'll frequently need to set up multiple columns, change *insets*, and once in a while, even muck with the vertical justification within the frame. InDesign has these options organized in the Text Frame Options dialog, although some appear elsewhere, too.

With a text frame selected, press Cmd+B/Ctrl+B, or choose Text Frame Options from the Object menu (see Figure 2.10).

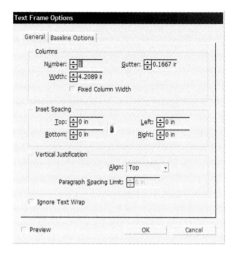

COLUMNS

When creating a new document, you're offered the option of specifying a number of columns and the width of the *gutter*, the space between text columns. Setting that in the New Document dialog has one or two outcomes.

First, it creates for the columns guides that are evenly spaced between the margin guides. With an 8.5×11-inch document and 1-inch margins all around, specifying two columns with the default 0.1667-inch gutter will create guides defining two columns of equal width—that being 3.1667 inches per column. The center of the gutter rests in the center of the page, at 4.25 inches. If you also check the Master Text Frame box, the second consequence kicks in, which is to create on the master page and all document pages based thereupon a text frame containing two columns matching the width and location of the guides.

That's all well and good if you want two equal columns perfectly aligned on, and filling, the page inside the margins. But, setting column options in the New Document dialog becomes a hindrance if you want something else—two separate stories flowing, a sidebar, or columns of different widths. If you need any of these, or decide on columns after beginning the document, use Text Frame Options instead to set up and control your columns.

Check the Preview box at the bottom and you'll be able to watch how the text frame reacts to column changes live.

The Number field is, obviously, the number of columns. Regardless of the number here, you're dealing with only a single text frame. Because InDesign merely divides a single frame into internal columns, you can resize the frame (outside the Text Frame Options dialog) and all columns will contract or expand as needed.

And that's a nice segue into…

What is the purpose of the Width field? Good question. Change the number of columns by clicking the up/down arrow buttons while watching the Width field. Notice how the width changes? Right: InDesign is maintaining the width of the frame and the width of the gutter and altering the column width to account for the column count.

Let's say you didn't want that. Let's say you know for certain you need 1.75-inch-wide columns, but you aren't sure how many will fit in your layout. Check the Fixed Column Width box. Now, instead of the column width being variable while the frame width is fixed, the opposite is true: columns will always be 1.75 inches, and the text frame itself will expand or contract horizontally to accommodate the specified number of columns.

If you manually resize the text frame on the page with Fixed Column Width checked, the frame will resize only in whole column increments. This is a stellar way to build redesign templates for multicolumn publications.

Most of us have heard the space between pages referred to as the gutter. InDesign tries to eliminate confusion by stating that *gutter* is the distance between columns, and that the inside margins and spine make up the area of binding or the space between pages in a spread.

When setting column gutters, more is more (within reason). A common mistake is to set gutters that are too slender in an attempt to fit more copy on a page. Don't fall into that trap.

Gutters separate columns of text. That separation—and thus gutters—is absolutely critical to document readability. If a gutter is too narrow, the reader's eye will jump across the gutter and run together two disconnected sentences. Readers also have a difficult time coming back from wayward excursions to other columns to find the beginning of the actual next line—it will be twice as hard if they aren't reading the leftmost column and have to contend with too-narrow gutters on both sides of what they're reading.

Want a rule of thumb? Column gutters should *never* be less than the point size of the typeface, but even better is 150 to 200% of the type size. Anything more than 200 to 250% begins to disconnect columns.

INSET SPACING

Indents push text selectively—a paragraph pushed in here and there, but not everywhere—while *insets* push *everything* in uniformly. If you want to indent a kicker paragraph or body copy, leaving subheads out to the margin, employ paragraph indents (see later in this chapter). However, if you've given your text frame a background color or stroke, you want to make sure no text bumps up against the edge, so set an inset (aka *internal margins, frame margins, frame/box padding,* and *border spacing*). You can see the difference between indent and inset results in Figure 2.11.

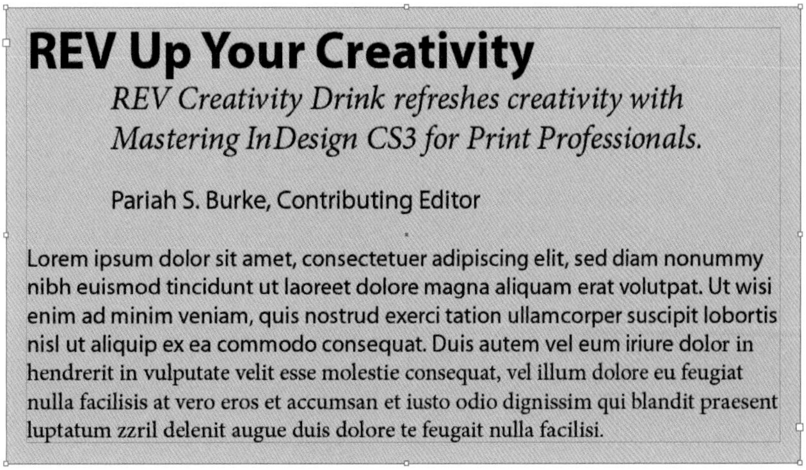

FIGURE 2.11
A text frame with inset (inner red border) and indented text

REV Up Your Creativity
REV Creativity Drink refreshes creativity with Mastering InDesign CS3 for Print Professionals.

Pariah S. Burke, Contributing Editor

Lorem ipsum dolor sit amet, consectetuer adipiscing elit, sed diam nonummy nibh euismod tincidunt ut laoreet dolore magna aliquam erat volutpat. Ut wisi enim ad minim veniam, quis nostrud exerci tation ullamcorper suscipit lobortis nisl ut aliquip ex ea commodo consequat. Duis autem vel eum iriure dolor in hendrerit in vulputate velit esse molestie consequat, vel illum dolore eu feugiat nulla facilisis at vero eros et accumsan et iusto odio dignissim qui blandit praesent luptatum zzril delenit augue duis dolore te feugait nulla facilisi.

The four fields can be set to push in from the four sides independently—say, to give only top or bottom inset while leaving left and right sides flush—or, by checking the chain-link button, all four can be made uniform. In the latter case, altering the value of one simultaneously changes the other three.

Only a single inset field will be available if working with nonrectangular text frames.

It absolutely kills me when I see professionals not using insets, opting instead to layer a text frame atop an empty colored or stroke frame—and I see it often. Why would someone do that? Because that's the way they've done it for years.

Text frames can be filled with color—CMYK, RGB, Lab, spots, tints, even gradients—they can be stroked with any style or color, they can have drop shadows and other effects, and, now in CS3, the frame fill and stroke opacity and blending modes can be set independently of text opacity and blending mode. Most of these options have been available since InDesign 1.0. Creating two objects to do the job one is capable of doing doubles the work necessary to create the same effect and doubles the work of maintaining it. It's half as much work to move or resize one frame than it is two. Say it with me: *Working efficiently gives me more time to be creative.*

InDesign, unlike some other programs, *does* adjust column width (or column count if you're using fixed column widths) to compensate for inset adjustments. So, no reason to go back to the two-object-tango there.

VERTICAL JUSTIFICATION

When there isn't enough copy to fill a column or frame, where do you want the text to be—the top of the frame/column, the bottom, centered, or spread out and vertically justified? That's the question asked by this option. Figure 2.12 shows the four possible options.

FIGURE 2.12
Examples of vertical alignment options. Left to right: Top, Bottom, Center, and Justify (without paragraph spacing limits).

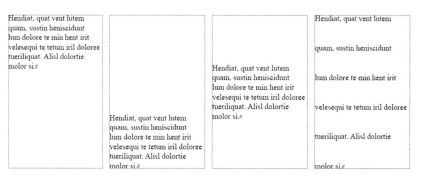

If you choose Justify from the Align list, the Paragraph Spacing Limit measurement field activates. When it's set to 0 inches, anything is possible—a single line could appear at the top of the frame and another single line at the bottom. To take more control over the situation, to tell InDesign that you want no more than *X* inches inserted between paragraphs and lines within paragraphs, set the measurement here. If there aren't enough lines to fill the space without violating your spacing limit, InDesign will align to the top and spread down as far as it can without violating the limit you set.

FASTER COLUMNS & JUSTIFICATION

If all you need to do is change the number of columns or the vertical justification, you needn't go all the way into the Text Frame Options dialog. They're probably on the Control panel in a very simplified form. I say "probably" because it depends on your screen size. The number of columns is always accessible on the Control panel in Paragraph mode. Vertical alignment buttons only appear, however, if your screen is set wider than 1024 pixels. All the default Control panel options are included within the first 1024 pixels. After that, prior versions of InDesign left wasted space; CS3 makes better use of it by including additional options you might find useful from time to time. Among those that appear when you have a text frame selected with the Selection tool are the Number of Columns field and buttons to change vertical justification modes, as shown in Figure 2.13.

FIGURE 2.13
Number of columns and vertical alignment options on the Control panel

Paragraph Formatting

Now that you've got the hang of placing text and working with basic frames, let's get down to what can be done with it.

Most paragraph formatting is controlled via the Paragraph panel (Window ➤ Type & Tables ➤ Paragraph). Figure 2.14 shows the complete Paragraph panel after choosing Show Options from the panel's flyout menu. If you're familiar with InDesign CS2, most of the CS3 version is identical, although a few new gems like Define Lists and Restart/Continue Numbering are found here.

FIGURE 2.14
The Paragraph panel

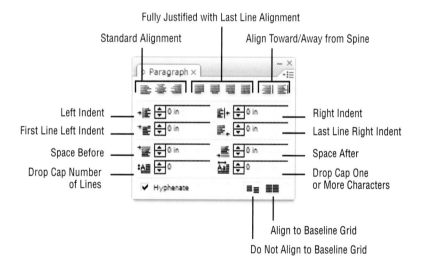

Alignment

Along the top row are buttons for the nine types of paragraph alignment possible within InDesign: Align Left, Align Right, Align Center; Justify with Last Line Aligned Left, Justify with Last Line Aligned Centered, Justify with Last Line Aligned Right, Justify All Lines; Align Toward Spine, and Align Away from Spine. Setting aside the last two for a moment, the first three are self-explanatory. The middle four, the justify options, often cause confusion however.

FLUSH, RAG, RAGGED, QUAD?

If you're reading this book, you know at least one of those terms—probably a couple. Did you know they all mean effectively the same thing? The first time I heard *quad right*, I was a newly hired layout artist coordinating a job with my firm's service bureau for the first time. As is typical of print production, the new guy was quizzed. I passed with flying process colors until the prepressman asked me if the copy was *quad left* or *quad right*. That phrase tripped me up.

The flush edge, to which text aligns, is also known as the *quad*. Thus, left aligned is *flush left* is *quad left*; right aligned is *flush right* is *quad right*. Opposite the flush edge is the *ragged* or just *rag* edge, referring to the fact that it isn't a clean, flush edge as it would be in full (both side) justification.

Fully justified text can be referred as such, or as *flush left and right*, just plain *flush*, *forced*, *forced justified*, *no rag*, and, just once by a New Zealander, *double-clean* type.

Saying text is *forced quad right* is to say that the paragraph is fully justified—both left and right—but also specifically qualifies the last line as aligned to the right.

The middle four alignment buttons, which justify entire paragraphs to both flush left and flush right (full justification), differ only in their treatment of the last line of the paragraph. As you can see in Figure 2.15, that can be a dramatic difference.

FIGURE 2.15

The same text block justified with differing last line options

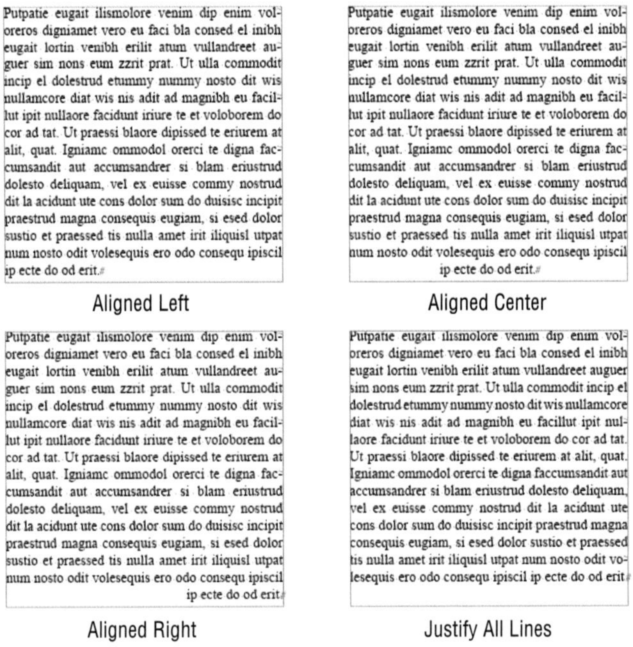

Aligned Left

Aligned Center

Aligned Right

Justify All Lines

If you choose Justify All Lines, watch the last line carefully. It will be spaced out to fill the width of the column regardless of its content; if there's only a single word on the last line, the characters of that word will be pushed apart to fill the space. You can often see similar results in newspapers, when a narrow, fully justified column contains a line wherein neither the previous nor the next words were able to squeeze into the line and only a single word is stretched to fill the entire width of the column.

When the *Paragraph Composer* is active instead of the *Single-Line Composer*, InDesign will attempt to compensate for short last lines in paragraphs set to Justify All Lines. Often, as in Figure 2.15, word and character spacing throughout the rest of the paragraph will be adjusted to completely absorb the last line, resulting in better last line appearance but with potentially tighter tracking and word spacing throughout the entire paragraph.

ALIGNMENT RELATIVE TO SPINE

Introduced in CS2, the Align Toward Spine and Align Away from Spine options are phenomenal inventions for anyone who deals with facing-page, bound documents. The first button aligns text in the direction of the spine, the other aligns away from it. On a left-read page, text aligned toward the spine will be flush right; move the same text frame over to the right page in the spread, however, and the text will automatically jump to be left-aligned.

Technical books, catalogs, magazines, reports, newspapers, and numerous other multi-page publications often set heads, subheads, captions, photo credits, pull quotes, and, especially, header and footer slugs to align toward or away from the spine. When pages get pushed around or text reflows due to an addition, omission, or formatting changes, designers have typically had to go in and swap alignments manually. No more. Just choose one of these two buttons and text will swap its flush edge all by itself as it moves from a left- to a right-read page and vice versa.

Left and Right Indent

Indents push the entire paragraph inward from the frame edge. Use these for selectively controlling the width of paragraphs. Do not, however, use indents if you want to push all text in the frame inward from the frame edge because you've filled or stroked the frame. Instead, use frame insets, which we'll get to later in this chapter.

POWER TIP: CLICK ICONS TO SELECT FIELD CONTENTS

In many of InDesign's measurement fields, including the indent fields on the Paragraph panel, you can click and drag to highlight or select the contents and then type over the contents to change. But there's a faster way. Click once on the icon to the left of the field. For instance, in the Left Indent field, click the little icon to the left of the up/down arrows. That will automatically select the content of the field without the often hit-or-miss click-drag selection method.

Like most of InDesign's fields, the Left and Right Indent fields can be controlled by typing in values, by using the up/down arrows beside the field, or by using the keyboard arrows. With the cursor in the field, pressing the up or down arrow on the keyboard will increase or decrease the indent by predefined increments (by 0.625 inches each if your document is set to use inches as its measurement, by one point if using points, and so forth). Holding Shift while pressing the up or down arrow will adjust the indent by larger increments (0.25 inch or 10 pt).

Separating Paragraphs

When setting stories of more than a single paragraph, you must somehow signal to the reader that one paragraph has ended and another begun. There are various ways to do that, including drop caps, rules, and outdents (where the first line is farther left than the rest of the paragraph). Vastly more common are two other methods: vertical spacing between paragraphs and first line indents. Which of the two you choose depends on your design—they can sometimes be combined successfully, too.

First line indents require less space typically, allowing a few extra lines of copy to fit on a page, but the trade-off is less white space and fewer places for the reader's eye to rest. Figure 2.16 shows both first line indents and paragraph spacing. Notice where the same red-colored phrase appears in both as well as the difference in visual density between the two sets of copy. In the example, the first line indent is 2 ems (24 pts for 12 pt type) while the paragraph spacing in the second frame is 10 pts.

FIGURE 2.16

Above, first line indents used as paragraph separators; below, vertical spacing after paragraphs.

Below the left and right indent fields in the Paragraph dialog (Figure 2.14) is the First Line Left Indent field, which controls the indentation value of just the first line of selected paragraphs. This field accepts positive measurements as well as negative measurements up to the inverse of the Left Indent field. Negative values, of course, create hanging indents (see Figure 2.17).

As you can see in Figure 2.17, indenting the whole paragraph a certain amount and outdenting the first line using a negative value in the First Line Left Indent field enables margin heads, resume-style entries, and custom bulleted or numbered lists. InDesign includes a more automated way to make bulleted and numbered lists, which we'll get into later in this chapter; knowing how to do it manually, however, is important for those times when the built-in Bullets and Numbering just doesn't cut the mustard (for example, when you want to adjust the baseline shift of a bullet or number character).

If you're accustomed to doing hanging indents in Microsoft Word, we should go through it in InDesign—it's a whole different animal.

FIGURE 2.17
Positive left indents coupled with negative first line indents create hanging indents for lists, stylized pseudo run-in and margin heads, or, as in this case, resume entries.

In Word's Paragraph dialog, on the Indents and Spacing tab, indentation is handled through three fields. Left and Right work the same as in InDesign, but the Special field, a drop-down list, determines whether the first line indent value (the measurement field to the right) is positive or negative by the option chosen. Selecting First Line from the list creates a positive indent where the first line pushes into the paragraph. Selecting Hanging pushes everything *but* the first line inward, creating an outdent on the first line. InDesign simplifies the process (thus making it less obvious) by eliminating the Special menu and allowing the First Line Left Indent field to accept either positive (indent) or negative (outdent/hanging) values.

Referring back to the resume example (Figure 2.17), the settings I used for the body paragraph hang the employer name out to the left while indenting the rest of the paragraph. Between the employer name and the job description is a tab whose stop was set to mirror the left indent value— 1.625 inches. Note that, in my resume entry, the left indent is 1.625 inches while the first line is only –1.5 inches. The difference of 0.125 inches leaves enough room for the custom bullet, which is an anchored graphic frame (indicated by the yen symbol [¥]).

The Left and Right Indent fields accept only positive values, while the First Line Left Indent field will accept either. A negative value for the first line may be up to the value of the Left Indent field. You can't, say, set a –2-inch first line when the left indent is only 1-inch. Nor can you pull the entire paragraph beyond its frame's (or column's) borders by setting left or right indents to negative values. Word will let you do that, but InDesign content can't violate the boundaries of its container (paragraph rules are an exception, as you'll see later in this chapter).

When setting positive indents on the first line of body copy paragraphs, the rule of thumb is that the indents should usually be 1 to 2 ems, with an *em* being equal to the font size. Thus, the indent on 10 pt type should be 10 or 20 points. Of course, this is only a best practice guideline, and larger or even smaller indents may be dictated by style, column width, and typeface.

Book publishers tend to follow the 1 to 2 em rule for most of their titles but will deviate when a template's style warrants it. Magazine and newspaper publishers usually follow the same rule. Copywriters tend to stick with the Tab key in Word, which inserts an indent on the default half-inch tab stop. Indeed, largely because of Word, many people believe bigger is better, that any indent less than one half inch is unprofessional and that one-inch indents are often preferable.

Instead of, or in addition to, indents, spacing between paragraphs creates breathing room. The two fields in the next section of the Paragraph panel control the spacing above and below paragraphs, with similar vertical measurement controls to the indents' horizontal controls.

InDesign suppresses spacing before paragraphs that appear at the top of a frame or column as well as spacing after when paragraphs are at the bottom of a frame or column.

Last Line Right Indent

The Last Line Right Indent field, which controls the indentation on the last line of a paragraph, works identically to the First Line indent with positive values beginning at the right edge.

Depending on the work for which you employ InDesign, you may use this field constantly or never.

It's most often useful for catalogs, classifieds, directories, price lists, and other list-style copy where paragraphs are fully justified and the last line ends with a particular type of information—an SKU, phone number, accreditation acronym, price, or similar bit of information. I've used it in a "magalog"—or "catazine"—style entry complete with *Sky Mall*-like hyperbolic copy (Figure 2.18). There, the paragraph is justified with last line aligned right. A tab separates the end of the copy from the SKU (no tab stop customization needed because of the alignment). Once tabbed out, the SKU pushes 0.2 inches in from the flush edge with the Last Line Right Indent field. As small and simple a trick as it is, that little bump of white space attracts the reader's eye—even more so than emboldening the SKU.

FIGURE 2.18

A last line right indent makes formatting a SKU number simpler than messing with tab stops and creates white space to attract the reader's eye.

A.»REV Creativity Drink 24-Pack ($21.99)¶

REV up your creativity with this 24-pack of the world's first lightly carbonated beverage formulated specifically to spark imagination and creative inspiration. Keep a case by your desk to get through late-night, last-minute deadlines and to overcome designer's block. With a can of REV Creativity Drink in your hand, you'll never be left staring uninspired at a blank page again!   »   Item #19720318#

Almost as important as signaling when a new paragraph begins is some kind of indicator denoting the end of paragraphs. With full justification, every paragraph becomes a perfect block; a last line right indent can restore the cue that the paragraph has ended while still maintaining a (usually) more symmetrical result than left-aligning the last line.

Another use for this field is to add some variety to, and mitigate word and character gaps created by, full justification.

Drop Caps

Not that long ago, the only way to create decent drop caps was by creating a separate text frame containing only the enlarged cap, with a text wrap or runaround assigned to that frame. The initial cap itself would have to be removed from the main story, tripping up spell check and making more work for the layout artist if the copy reflowed or if an editor changed the opening word of the story.

InDesign does drop caps a lot more elegantly via the last two measurement fields on the Paragraph panel (see Figure 2.19).

Instead of specifying the size of the drop cap in points, you'll define its height only, and that in the number of lines to drop in the Drop Cap Number of Lines field. Technically speaking, the drop cap is therefore measured by multiples of the leading rather than the font size itself. A three-line drop cap in 9/12 pt type, for instance, is 36 pts tall. InDesign will scale the horizontal dimension of the drop cap to match its height.

The dropped cap will be created and sized, and all other text wrapped around it, in one simple step.

FIGURE 2.19
Drop cap effects made easy

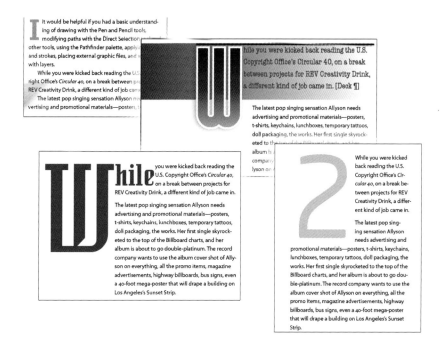

The best part is that it's totally dynamic because the drop cap is a paragraph styling attribute. The drop cap is still part of the first word of the story, which means spell check continues to see the complete word, and if the copy must change, you just change it. Type over it. InDesign will take the new first character and convert it to a drop cap on-the-fly.

Drop caps of more than one character are also possible—just raise the Drop Cap One or More Letters field value above one (see Figure 2.20).

FIGURE 2.20
The first word drop-capped by setting the number of letters to four

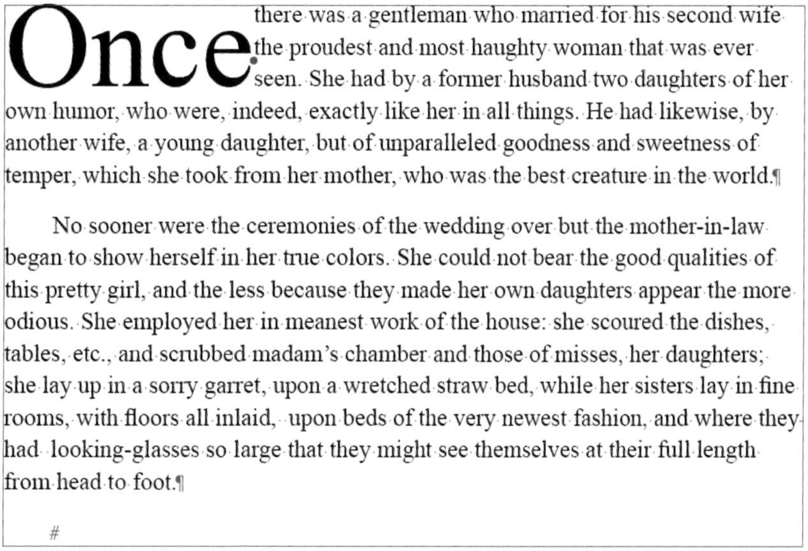

Once there was a gentleman who married for his second wife the proudest and most haughty woman that was ever seen. She had by a former husband two daughters of her own humor, who were, indeed, exactly like her in all things. He had likewise, by another wife, a young daughter, but of unparalleled goodness and sweetness of temper, which she took from her mother, who was the best creature in the world.¶

No sooner were the ceremonies of the wedding over but the mother-in-law began to show herself in her true colors. She could not bear the good qualities of this pretty girl, and the less because they made her own daughters appear the more odious. She employed her in meanest work of the house: she scoured the dishes, tables, etc., and scrubbed madam's chamber and those of misses, her daughters; she lay up in a sorry garret, upon a wretched straw bed, while her sisters lay in fine rooms, with floors all inlaid, upon beds of the very newest fashion, and where they had looking-glasses so large that they might see themselves at their full length from head to foot.¶

#

Because they're simply normal characters in the text flow, drop caps can be individually selected and styled like any other letter. You can color them differently, assign a specific typeface, kern and track, adjust their baselines, and even scale them horizontally or vertically (see Chapter 3, "Characters"). When setting a drop cap in a different typeface from the text into which it drops, you're much more likely to get disparate sizing and spacing. Manually tweaking scaling, baseline offset, and kerning will become especially important in such cases.

When creating drop caps of one or more characters, watch the horizontal composition. If you set too large a drop cap or a drop cap consisting of too many characters and InDesign can't fit the rest of the copy beside it, the whole story could become overset until you either widen the column or reduce the size or count of dropped cap letters.

HANGING DROP CAPS

If you want your drop cap to hang farther left than the text it's a part of, there are two methods.

In the first, put a positive left indent on all text and a negative first line indent just on the paragraph with the drop cap. This is the easier method to accomplish, but it requires more compromises.

The other method, which takes a little more initial effort, is more flexible and involves fewer long-term consequences to worry about six pages later. Do this:

1. *Before* the drop cap, insert a hair space.

2. Set the Drop Cap One or More Characters to two characters to account for the space and the actual cap.

3. Insert your cursor between the hair space and the drop cap, and kern the two together with large negative numbers. As you do, you'll be pulling your drop cap out to the left and past the edge of the text wrapping around the cap. The cap will overlap and eventually surpass the thin space.

We'll cover the last option in the Paragraph panel, baseline grid alignments, in Chapter 8, "Stories," where it will make more sense.

Paragraph Composition

The devil, as the saying goes, is in the details. Composition—putting text together—is about detail. Whether you produce passable text or good type is a matter of composition.

You may have heard (even before I said it in this tome) that InDesign is the world's most advanced typesetting and text rendering platform. Of course, its unprecedented support for OpenType fonts and their features, the ultra-fine control over every aspect of character appearance, and numerous other features are part of InDesign's claim to that title; what really earned it the title, what keeps it head and shoulders above the competition, is InDesign's next-generation composition engine.

Let's talk about that, beginning with the first thing most cite as InDesign's single greatest feature.

Paragraph vs. Single-Line Composer

What is a composer? In this context, a composer is the software engine that figures out how to fit words and lines together in a paragraph to maximize readability and the flow of the reader's eye between words.

In paragraph text, when lines of type must wrap, every text-handling application—InDesign, QuarkXPress, Microsoft Publisher, Serif PagePlus, Microsoft Word, even your web browser and email client—is making decisions. The application is fed too much text to fit on a single line within the horizontal space allowed, and it must decide which words will fit and which won't, when to insert a soft line break and send subsequent words to the next line. This is the act of composing text.

Composers can be dumb—as in the case of web browsers and email clients—presenting mono-spaced words until one simply won't fit, and then wrapping the line after the last word that does fit.

Other applications—QuarkXPress, Microsoft Publisher, Serif PagePlus, and Microsoft Word—are of normal, everyday intelligence. They render words on a line until one won't fit, but then they look for a way to break (hyphenate) the word that won't fit. They also go back and look across the line for places where a slight expansion or contraction of the spaces between words might enable the last word to fit better or where it might enable a better hyphenation choice. This—normal intelligence composition—is single-line composition—the composer looks at the entire, but *only*, current line of text to determine how to handle that last word of the line.

Finally, you have the genius composers—Mozart, Beethoven, Brahms, InDesign.

On the Paragraph panel's flyout menu is the choice between Single-Line Composer and the default Paragraph Composer. In Single-Line Composer mode, InDesign does what other single-line composers do—evaluates its spacing and hyphenation and options one line at a time without regard for the impact on subsequent lines or the effect on the paragraph overall. The Paragraph Composer does the opposite. It looks at every line, every word, every character, and every space in the paragraph. It goes far beyond just how to best end the one line; it asks itself the following questions:

◆ How do I make this entire paragraph more readable?

◆ How do I dam *rivers*?

◆ How can I even out the ragged edge if the text isn't fully justified?

◆ How do I reduce the likelihood of *runts*?

◆ If I'm hyphenating, how can I do it in such a way that all my other priorities are met without hyphenating lines too close to one another?

Rivers are those threads of white that develop from the near-vertical alignment of spaces between words. You see them often in just about any output from single-line composition software, but especially when text is fully justified. Newspapers are the worst. The price of InDesign would be worth it if the Paragraph Composer did nothing but eliminate rivers, which it does almost entirely.

Figure 2.21 shows the difference between a passage of text set with single-line composition and one set with paragraph composition. Both are set to full justification with first line indents and are reminiscent of newspaper columns set with applications other than InDesign.

The first thing that should jump out at you is the big honking spaces in the upper set, particularly in the last lines of paragraphs. Look at the first paragraph. That last line is two words, with the column width the words don't fill plunked between them. In the second column it gets even worse with single word runts letter-spaced out to fill the column width. If you squint, you'll even see several short but distinct rivers.

Compare the two paragraphs, noting the absence of big spaces in the set composed with the Paragraph Composer. Even that set, with the size of text and column, isn't great, but it's a heck of a lot better than the upper text frame. Notice how it isn't just better word and letter spacing; InDesign eliminated the problems the upper set has at the end of paragraphs by absorbing runts into their host paragraphs through spacing adjustment throughout. The lower set even managed to squeeze an extra line of text in there at the end.

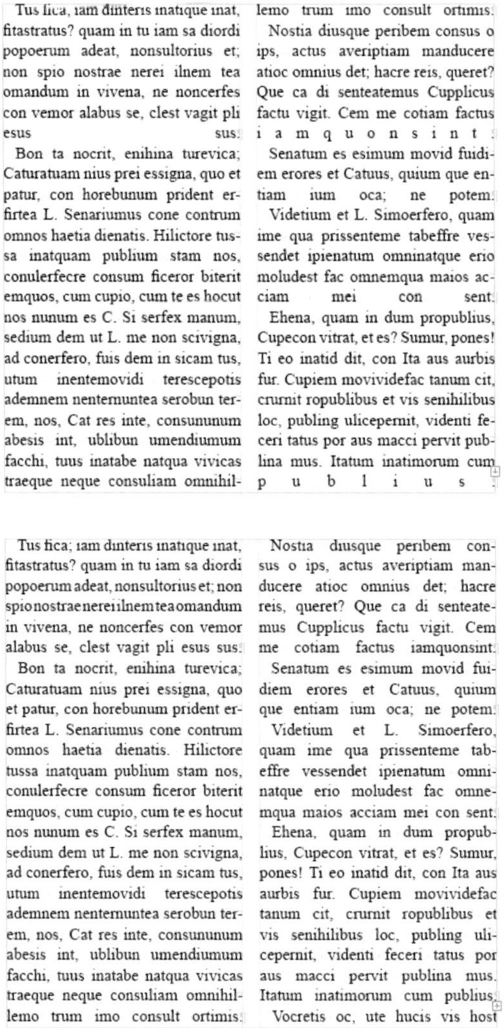

FIGURE 2.21

Single-line composi-
tion (top) versus
paragraph composi-
tion (bottom)

Tus fica, iam dinteris inatique inat, fitastratus? quam in tu iam sa diordi popoerum adeat, nonsultorius et; non spio nostrae nerei ilnem tea omandum in vivena, ne noncerfes con vemor alabus se, clest vagit pli esus sus.

Bon ta nocrit, enihina turevica; Caturatuam nius prei essigna, quo et patur, con horebunum prident er-firtea L. Senariumus cone contrum omnos haetia dienatis. Hilictore tus-sa inatquam publium stam nos, conulerfecre consum ficeror biterit emquos, cum cupio, cum te es hocut nos nunum es C. Si serfex manum, sedium dem ut L. me non scivigna, ad conerfero, fuis dem in sicam tus, utum inentemovidi terescepotis ademnem nenternuntea serobun ter-em, nos, Cat res inte, consununum abesis int, ublibun umendiumum facchi, tuus inatabe natqua vivicas traeque neque consuliam omnihil-

lemo trum imo consult ortimis.

Nostia diusque peribem consus o ips, actus averiptiam manducere atioc omnius det; hacre reis, queret? Que ca di senteatemus Cupplicus factu vigit. Cem me cotiam factus iamquonsint.

Senatum es esimum movid fuidi-em erores et Catuus, quium que en-tiam ium oca; ne potem.

Videtium et L. Simoerfero, quam ime qua prissenteme tabeffre ves-sendet ipienatum omninatque erio moludest fac omnemqua maios ac-ciam mei con sent.

Ehena, quam in dum propublius, Cupecon vitrat, et es? Sumur, pones! Ti eo inatid dit, con Ita aus aurbis fur. Cupiem movividefac tanum cit, crurnit ropublibus et vis senihilibus loc, publing ulicepernit, videnti fe-ceri tatus por aus macci pervit pub-lina mus. Itatum inatimorum cum p u b l i u s.

Tus fica; iam dinteris inatique inat, fitastratus? quam in tu iam sa diordi popoerum adeat, nonsultorius et; non spio nostrae nerei ilnem tea omandum in vivena, ne noncerfes con vemor alabus se, clest vagit pli esus sus.

Bon ta nocrit, enihina turevica; Caturatuam nius prei essigna, quo et patur, con horebunum prident er-firtea L. Senariumus cone contrum omnos haetia dienatis. Hilictore tussa inatquam publium stam nos, conulerfecre consum ficeror biterit emquos, cum cupio, cum te es hocut nos nunum es C. Si serfex manum, sedium dem ut L. me non scivigna, ad conerfero, fuis dem in sicam tus, utum inentemovidi terescepotis ademnem nenternuntea serobun ter-em, nos, Cat res inte, consununum abesis int, ublibun umendiumum facchi, tuus inatabe natqua vivicas traeque neque consuliam omnihil-lemo trum imo consult ortimis.

Nostia diusque peribem con-sus o ips, actus averiptiam man-ducere atioc omnius det; hacre reis, queret? Que ca di senteate-mus Cupplicus factu vigit. Cem me cotiam factus iamquonsint.

Senatum es esimum movid fui-diem erores et Catuus, quium que entiam ium oca; ne potem.

Videtium et L. Simoerfero, quam ime qua prissenteme tab-effre vessendet ipienatum omni-natque erio moludest fac omne-mqua maios acciam mei con sent.

Ehena, quam in dum propub-lius, Cupecon vitrat, et es? Sumur, pones! Ti eo inatid dit, con Ita aus aurbis fur. Cupiem movividefac tanum cit, crurnit ropublibus et vis senihilibus loc, publing uli-cepernit, videnti feceri tatus por aus macci pervit publina mus. Itatum inatimorum cum publius.

Vocretis oc, ute hucis vis host

Because InDesign evaluates an entire paragraph in order to weigh its options and make decisions about where and how to break lines, it happens on-the-fly, as you type. Fix a typo on line six and the entire paragraph may recompose.

It's not uncommon to be typing while lines above change, breaking differently, words spacing differently, with every character you type.

In some cases you *want* total, *manual* control over how and where lines wrap. Often you simply need to adjust justification and/or hyphenation options or tell InDesign not to break certain words or phrases. At other times, you really do want to break lines yourself with manual line breaks (Shift+Return/Shift+Enter). Paragraph Composer will make that difficult, so toggle it over to Single-Line Composer by selecting the frame or paragraph (or putting your Text tool cursor in the paragraph in question) and selecting the Single-Line Composer on the Paragraph panel flyout menu.

Justification Options

This is not about left or right aligned. Justification options are about fine-tuning the limits of both single-line and paragraph composition decisions regarding word and letter spacing and more (see Figure 2.22). You'll find Justification on the Paragraph panel menu.

FIGURE 2.22

Justification options dialog

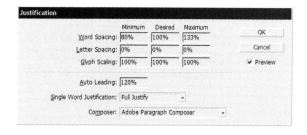

If you open this dialog with text or a text frame selected, the preview option will tell InDesign to recompose on-the-fly as you change options.

Presented with three columns of options are control over how InDesign adjusts the spacing of words and individual letters and whether and by how much you'll allow it to adjust character horizontal spacing. The first column, Minimum, is the bare minimum amount of the whole you'll allow InDesign to reduce spacing or scale. By default, for example, Word Spacing is set to 80%. That means InDesign is allowed to squish the full space between words down to 80% of a space; if composition requires a smaller space or a line will break, InDesign will break the line. Desired is how much you want—typically 100% (a full space) for Word Spacing, 0% (no space) between letters, and 100% of horizontal scale for Glyph Scaling. Maximum is the widest space you'll allow InDesign to employ.

As you may have deduced from the fact that the default settings were in use in my single-line composition example above, wherein a two-word line had a massive space between words and several lines included single words with their letters spaced way out, what you set in here is a guide, not a rule. InDesign tries to meet your guidelines, but given less savory choices, it will violate the options in Justification.

Auto Leading, which is, in most programs, situated somewhere in the Preferences, is where you set the default leading percentage for InDesign. We'll get into that in the next chapter.

Flip back to the composition examples in Figure 2.21, which we were looking at a couple of minutes ago. Remember those single words spaced to fill the line? That happened because I had the paragraph set to full justification (with last line justified as well). Single Word Justification trumps the overall paragraph alignment in the case of singe-word lines. Changing this to anything but Full Justify would have eliminated the lone word stretching.

Hyphenation

Also on the Paragraph panel menu is Justification's cousin, Hyphenation Settings (see Figure 2.23).

If you're coming from proficiency in QuarkXPress, you're accustomed to having hyphenation and justification (H&Js) in a single dialog and being able to save them as a set. InDesign does it differently, as you can see. True, it's two dialogs, but that's a small trade-off when you consider that you don't have to create an H&J set just to apply it; you can apply selectively on-the-fly, save them as part of paragraph styles, and even set the default for all future text simply by setting these options with all documents closed.

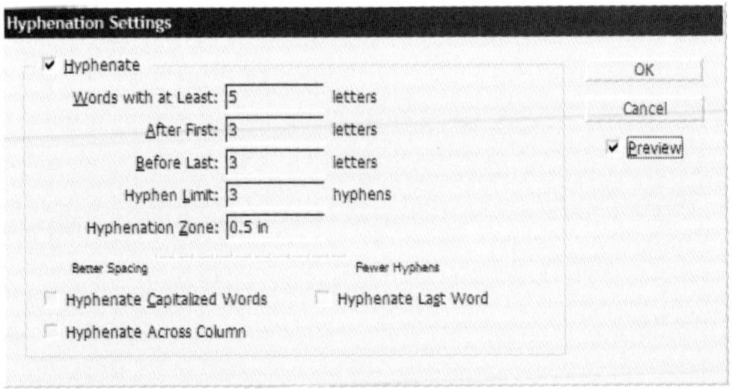

FIGURE 2.23
Hyphenation Set-
tings dialog

Hyphenation Settings

☑ Hyphenate

Words with at Least: 5   letters

After First: 3   letters

Before Last: 3   letters

Hyphen Limit: 3   hyphens

Hyphenation Zone: 0.5 in

Better Spacing   Fewer Hyphens

☐ Hyphenate Capitalized Words   ☐ Hyphenate Last Word

☐ Hyphenate Across Column

OK

Cancel

☑ Preview

Here is fine control over the composition engine's hyphenation choices. Check the box at the top of the dialog (or at the bottom of the Paragraph panel itself) to enable hyphenation. First, you can tell InDesign it's allowed to hyphenate words with at least *X* number of characters but no less. Typically, five letters is the minimum—*wo-n't* just looks funny, doesn't it?

The next two fields determine where the first and last hyphens in a word are allowed to appear.

After that is the maximum number of times InDesign is allowed to hyphenate a single word. In most cases you'll never bump into that limit. You'd have to have a very long word *and* either large type size and a narrow column (or both) for that for that to come into play. Realistically, how often do you *use* let alone typeset words like *onomatopoeia* or *supercalifragilisticexpialidocious*?

Hyphenation Zone is a guideline (often overridden by InDesign) as to the minimum space after a hyphenated word before InDesign is allowed to hyphenate another. You see, it's poor form to have too many words ending in hyphens and bad form to have consecutive lines both ending in hyphens. The hyphenation zone, therefore, is a way to tell InDesign, *I'd really like it if you waited for half an inch or so following a line ending in a hyphenated word before doing it again.* Sometimes InDesign will agree; sometimes it'll just come back with, *I tried, dude. No can do. See, if I followed the hyphenation zone thingee, it would throw the rest of the paragraph out of whack. Sorry.*

What has always struck me as odd about the hyphenation zone is that it's defined by the document measurement system, but what really matters is the leading, which is measured in *points*, not inches, millimeters, or agates. A 0.5-inch zone may be great for 12/14.4 type, but with leading set to 36 pts or higher, 0.5 inches is a zone of one line—in other words, hyphenate here, but don't hyphenate again until the next line. The zone won't increase based on type size or leading. Ideally, it would be measured by number of lines, meaning the actual height of the zone would be relative to, and keep up with, the type size and leading amount. Basing the hyphenation zone on the document measurement system is not the wisest of choices on Adobe's part.

Below the Hyphenation Zone field is the Hyphenation slider, which adjusts InDesign's priority toward either better spacing (and often more hyphens) or fewer hyphens (with potentially more word and letter spacing).

The last three options give InDesign directives on what to hyphenate with special types of words—capitalized words, the last word of a paragraph, and whether InDesign is allowed to hyphenate the last word in a column (or page) so that it picks up again on the next column (or page). My preference is to leave all three unchecked (off). If you deal with a lot of acronyms, you'll definitely want the first option off—*DARPA* is a proper name, for example, and *DAR-PA* is bad typesetting.

Optical Margin Alignment

Optical margin alignment... You may have heard of that term. You also might be familiar with the more traditional description of *hanging punctuation.*

The principal is simple: Punctuation and slant-sided characters don't use up the vertical space allotted to them, which creates small pockets of white space—optical bumps, if you will—in the justified edge of text. Letting that punctuation hang a little outside the borders of the frame makes the justified edge *look* more uniform and makes the text more readable (see Figure 2.24). Of course, some clients don't get that, so be prepared for push back.

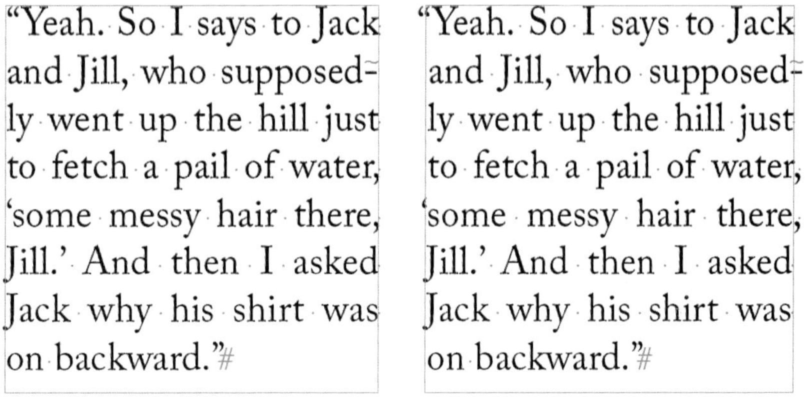

FIGURE 2.24
At left, Optical Margin Alignment in the default off mode; at right, Optical Margin Alignment is turned on.

> "Yeah. So I says to Jack and Jill, who supposed-ly went up the hill just to fetch a pail of water, 'some messy hair there, Jill.' And then I asked Jack why his shirt was on backward."#

> "Yeah. So I says to Jack and Jill, who supposed-ly went up the hill just to fetch a pail of water, 'some messy hair there, Jill.' And then I asked Jack why his shirt was on backward."#

Whether Optical Margin Alignment is on or off, InDesign does a little bit of adjustment anyway. Notice in Figure 2.24 how the *J*s and commas hang out a tiny bit even in the left paragraph, which has the option off. On the right side of the figure, you can see greater adjustment where the quotation mark, apostrophe, hyphen, and commas hang out into the margins. In short paragraphs like these, hanging punctuation isn't that big a benefit; in longer columns of copy, it can really boost readability.

If you just don't see any benefit.... Well, I used large type in the figure. Stand the book up against something and take a few steps back until my figure is optically about 10 or 12 pt. The hanging punctuation should trick your eye into perceiving a more uniform edge in the right paragraph than in the left.

You'll find a check box to enable Optical Margin Alignment on the Story panel (Window ➤ Type & Tables ➤ Story). It's the only thing on the Story panel (see Figure 2.25), which is why most people forget where to find it. Once Optical Margin Alignment is on, the Align Based on Size field lights up. That defines how much space is allowed to be consumed by the left- or right-shifted letters. Set this to be the same size as your type point size for best results most of the time; adjust as needed for more control.

FIGURE 2.25
The singular-function Story panel

Optical Margin Alignment is a *story-level* attribute—it applies to the entire story or frame, not individual paragraphs. That creates a need to override the setting for certain paragraphs, which is easy enough to do. With a paragraph selected, choose Ignore Optical Margin from the Paragraph panel flyout menu.

Balance Ragged Lines

This simple little command stuck away on the Paragraph panel menu tries to even out the ragged edge of type (see Figure 2.26) by telling InDesign to give higher priority to making text lines equal in width than to filling the frame. It's yet another way to handle runts, as you can see in my example.

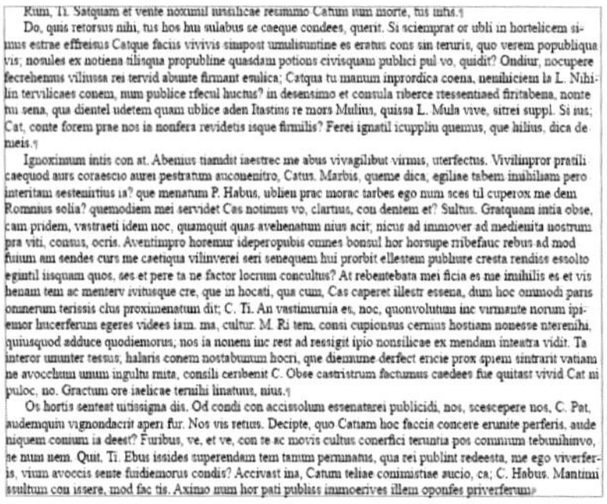

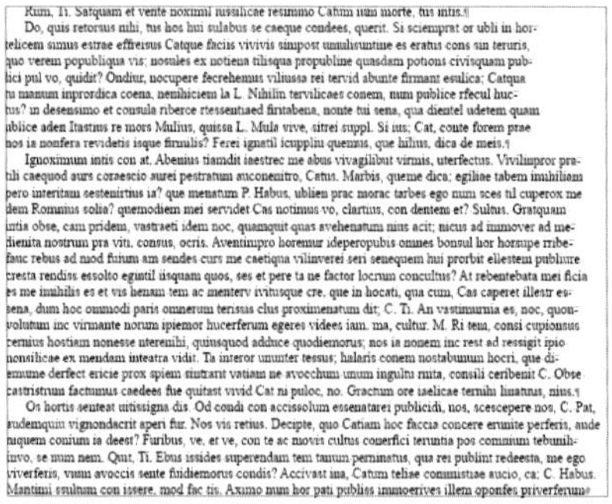

FIGURE 2.26

Normal text composed with the Paragraph Composer strives to fill the frame while the same text, also using the Paragraph Composer but with Balance Ragged Lines activated, sacrifices filling the frame for balancing the width of lines.

Of course, Balance Ragged Lines only works if there *are* ragged lines. It has no effect on fully justified text.

Keep Options

Although some paragraphs are single lines, they're the minority. In most cases, paragraphs are composed of multiple lines. How those lines split across columns (or pages) is almost as important as the composition of a single paragraph.

We've talked about runts, a single word or syllable left all alone as the last line of a paragraph (tip o' the hat to David Blatner for coining the term). Runts are the penultimate sin of paragraph composition. The *ultimate* sin is leaving a *widow*, the single last line of a paragraph surviving its paragraph to stand all alone at the top of column, or an *orphan*, the first line of a paragraph abandoned at the bottom of a column while the rest of the paragraph moves on to the next (see Figure 2.27).

Both widows and orphans are equally bad things to let slip through in your publication. Better is to leave a blank line at the bottom of a column; when possible, however, avoid that, too.

Paragraph keeps is the term applied to gluing two or more lines of a paragraph together such that they never leave widows or orphans—where one line goes, so must the next or the previous. In InDesign, keeps rules are defined through the Keep Options dialog (see Figure 2.28) accessible from the Paragraph panel flyout menu.

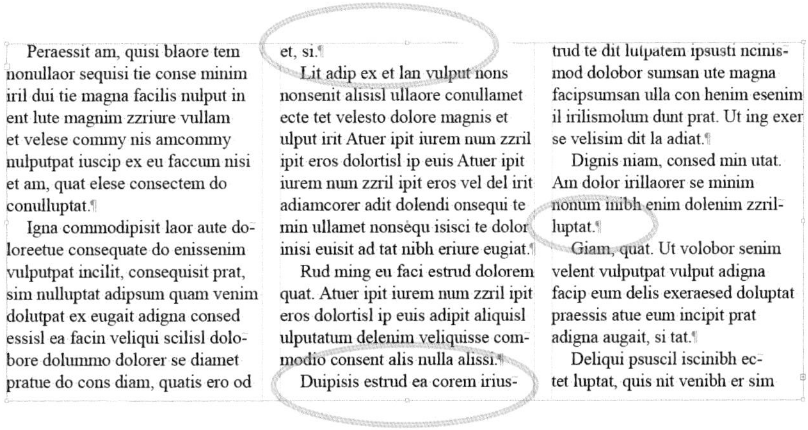

FIGURE 2.27

In multi-column text, an orphan is the first line of a paragraph at the bottom of a column, and a widow the last line of a paragraph at the top of the next column. A runt is a single word or syllable left dangling as the last line of a paragraph.

Peraessit am, quisi blaore tem nonullaor sequisi tie conse minim iril dui tie magna facilis nulput in ent lute magnim zzriure vullam et velese commy nis amcommy nulputpat iuscip ex eu faccum nisi et am, quat elese consectem do conulluptat.¶

Igna commodipisit laor aute do-loreetue consequate do enissenim vulputpat incilit, consequisit prat, sim nulluptat adipsum quam venim dolutpat ex eugait adigna consed essisl ea facin veliqui scilisl dolo-bore dolummo dolorer se diamet pratue do cons diam, quatis ero od

et, si.¶

Lit adip ex et lan vulput nons nonsenit alisisl ullaore conullamet ecte tet velesto dolore magnis et ulput irit Atuer ipit iurem num zzril ipit eros dolortisl ip euis Atuer ipit iurem num zzril ipit eros vel del irit adiamcorer adit dolendi onsequi te min ullamet nonsèqu isisci te dolor inisi euisit ad tat nibh eriure eugiat.¶

Rud ming eu faci estrud dolorem quat. Atuer ipit iurem num zzril ipit eros dolortisl ip euis adipit aliquisl ulputatum delenim veliquisse com-modio consent alis nulla alissi.¶

Duipisis estrud ea corem irius-

trud te dit luiputem ipsusti ncinis-mod dolobor sumsan ute magna facipsumsan ulla con henim esenim il irilismolum dunt prat. Ut ing exer se velisim dit la adiat.¶

Dignis niam, consed min utat. Am dolor irillaorer se minim nonum inibh enim dolenim zzril-luptat.¶

Giam, quat. Ut volobor senim velent vulputpat vulput adigna facip eum delis exeraesed doluptat praessis atue eum incipit prat adigna augait, si tat.¶

Deliqui psuscil iscinibh ec-tet luptat, quis nit venibh er sim

FIGURE 2.28

The Keep Options dialog

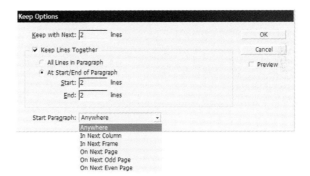

Keep with Next is a numeric field that lets you even glue together lines *not* in the same para-graph—say, headings and the paragraphs that follow—to avoid *contextual widows* and *contextual orphans* (terms *I* coined, as far as I know). Keep with Next can be assigned to paragraphs ad hoc and saved as part of paragraph styles. In order to avoid accidental contextual widows and contex-tual orphans caused by last-minute formatting or copy changes, I *always* build a Keep with Next value of at least 1, usually 2 or 3, into all my heading styles. I also add them into kickers and lead-ing captions for tables, charts, figures, and so on.

If enabled, the next section, Keep Lines Together, defines how many lines of a paragraph should bond. A minimum setting of two lines at the start and two at the end of a paragraph will eliminate widows and orphans without causing overly large gaps at the bottom of columns. With a setting of two lines in both, for example, if InDesign can't fit the first two lines of a paragraph at the bottom of a column or page, or can't fit the last two lines of the paragraph, it will jump the entire paragraph to the next column or page.

All Lines in Paragraph *is* available, but I caution you against using it indiscriminately. If you know all your paragraphs will be short and must stay together, go ahead and use it. With variable-length paragraphs and columns, however, you could be creating massive gaps at the bottoms of columns or forcing InDesign into a corner from which it will have no choice but to fight back by violating your keep directives.

When creating short-listing-style documents like directories, catalogs, and classifieds, I always activate All Lines in Paragraph and add Keep with Next to all styles making up a single listing. That way, the entire entry stays together and never splits—perfect for doing such documents without endlessly fiddling with column breaks or frame heights.

Finally. Start Paragraph defines where new paragraphs may begin—anywhere, only in the next column, next frame (for *threaded* frames), on the next page, or on specifically the next odd or even page. Why is this option useful? Headings. Tables. Charts. Figures. More.

For instance, perhaps you have a Chapter Heading style and every paragraph with that style, every top-level heading, should begin a new chapter or section of the document, beginning with a fresh, right-read (odd-numbered) page. Just set the Start Paragraph value to On Next Odd Page and save it in the Chapter Heading style. Every chapter heading will then automatically jump to a new right-read page, without you having to manually break the text flow or insert break symbols. And, because you didn't manually do anything, it can be overridden later from the Keep Options dialog with minimal effort.

Efficiency and creative freedom at once. You gotta love it when those two come together.

Highlight Composition Violations

As noted previously, hyphenation, justification, and keep options are guidelines, not rules. InDesign may have to violate those guidelines to adhere to higher-priority ones. Although you must place your trust in the butterfly, there's no need to do so blindly.

On the Composition pane of the Preferences (see Figure 2.29) are options to highlight instances wherein InDesign had to ignore or violate hyphenation and justification and keep options, instances of custom tracking or kerning, and any text defined as a font or glyph that you don't have installed.

FIGURE 2.29
Composition highlight options in the Preferences

Text highlighted in yellow (see Figure 2.30) indicates an H&J or keep violation, with light, medium, and deep yellow indicating the severity of the violation, from mild through severe. Custom kerned or tracked text highlights in a pleasing sea foam green, while instances of font and glyph substitution, being the most troublesome, highlight in pink.

FIGURE 2.30
Composition violations and substitutions highlight in different colors and shades to indicate which rules are being violated as well as the severity of the violation.

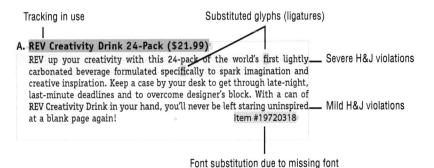

Tracking in use

Substituted glyphs (ligatures)

Severe H&J violations

Mild H&J violations

Font substitution due to missing font

Paragraph Rules

Paragraph rules are not for separating every paragraph in a story, but they can make headings and other separations clearer and more creative. As you'll soon see, they also have tremendous decorative value.

Rules (lines), like paragraph backgrounds, are another of those things people believe can only be done with separate objects. Instead of assigning rules that flow with type automatically, sizing and coloring to match as appropriate, many are stuck in the old days when their only option for paragraph rules was to draw a rule or box as a separate object placed behind or near the text frame. That just isn't so. Virtually anything that can be done as a separate object rule can be done as *part of* the text with paragraph rules.

The major benefits of using paragraph rules instead of Line or Rectangle tool objects are obvious: better alignment; adaptability to text color, size, and indentation changes; the ability to flow with text; and of course. one object to move and resize instead of two.

Gateway to all this is the Paragraph Rules dialog (see Figure 2.31) on the Paragraph panel fly-out menu. It creates rules (and boxes, dots, squiggles, and more) above and/or below—and even behind or beside—paragraphs.

FIGURE 2.31
The Paragraph Rules dialog

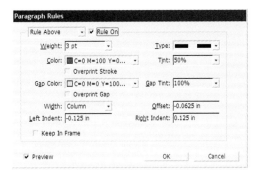

Rule Above/Below (drop-down)   Choose whether to enable and edit rules above or below. Both may be activated and customized independently.

Rule On (check box)   Is the rule on or off?

Weight The stroke weight of the rule. Choose a preset value from the drop-down, or enter a custom value by typing over the contents of the field.

Type Matching the styles on the Stroke panel, these are the available rule stroke styles, including solid, multiple lines, dots, dashes, hash marks, and more.

Color In addition to Text Color, which keeps the color of the rule in synch with the color of the text to which it's assigned, any swatches on the Swatches panel are available in this list. Tints of swatches may be defined in the next field, but to assign a custom color, you'll need to exit the dialog, mix the color, and create a swatch before returning to Paragraph Rules.

Tint A percentage of the Color field's ink. Note that this is *not* transparency. A 0% tint is not transparent; it's paper color.

Overprint Stroke (check box) This option is available if the stroke color is set to anything except Text Color, None, and Paper and chooses between *knocking out* any ink beneath the rule or *overprinting* it. The latter option, with the box checked, could result in color mixing. For instance, a cyan rule overprinted on a yellow background will mix the two inks, resulting in a green rule when printed.

Gap Color, Tint, and Overprint The fields remain disabled until you choose a rule type inclusive of gaps—dashed, dotted, hashed, diamond, multiple strokes, and so on. These fields control, respectively, the color of the spaces between the primary stroke color, the tint of that color, and whether it overprints or knocks out background colors.

Width If Width is set to Column, the stroke will span the width of the column regardless of the length of the text line—a single letter could have a stroke that spans the entire single-column page. Conversely, setting the width to Text only rules over (or under) the text itself; the rule will not continue across the column in the case of a short line of text or a single letter.

Offset Rules above begin drawing upward from the baseline of the paragraph's first line of text. Rules below grow downward from the baseline of the last line in the paragraph. Offset is a vertical adjustment of the rules in the direction they normally grow. Thus, a positive offset pushes a rule above higher and a rule below lower. Negative offsets pull rules toward and potentially behind text. Both rules above and below are *behind* text and will not mask the type to which they're assigned.

Left & Right Indent Positive values will push rules inward from column or text edges (depending on the Width setting). Unlike text indents, the rule indent fields can accept negative values, allowing rules to be pushed beyond the borders of text frames, which opens numerous creative possibilities.

Keep In Frame (check box) When a rule above is applied to the topmost paragraph in a frame, the rule can sometimes bleed out of the top of the frame or escape it entirely. Checking Keep In Frame puts a leash on the rule so it can't leave the yard.

Paragraph rules make excellent section and content separators such as in Figure 2.32 where level 1 headings carry a rule below (and paragraph spacing before) to signal a clear separation from the rest of the copy; that is, to signal that a new section has begun.

FIGURE 2.32
Paragraph rules
attached to headings
help organize and
separate data.

QUARK VS INDESIGN

ADVERTISER KIT

Effective October 2006–March 2007

chased number of impressions is often exhausted before affected regions recover their normal traffic level. With a month long run on *Quark VS InDesign.com*, however, the effects of regional market factors is diminished, affording your ad maximum exposure to all regions.

▷ **Guaranteed number of impressions.** Advertising in offline media—print, broadcast, outdoor—is unpredictable exposure. A given magazine may print 50,000 copies, but how many are actually read cover to cover? How many pairs of eyes will actually fall on your ad? What is your ad's actual ROI per view? The great advantage of the CPM model is the return of an exact number of ad views, allowing accurate calculation of return on investment per view and per click-through. Like other online advertising, *Quark VS InDesign.com* guarantees a certain number of impressions per unit, and, at the end of each week, reports the exact number of views and click-throughs your ad received.

On multiple month purchases, renewal notices are sent 30 days prior to the expiration of the flight to give you time to evaluate the effectiveness of your campaign and consider your media buy options.

Guaranteed Eyes-On-Creative

The *Quark VS InDesign.com* ad serving system uses IAB recommended beacon images to count impressions—impressions are only logged if your ad actually appears in front of a visitor's eyes. Without beacon images, for example, an ad placed at the bottom of a page would count toward your guaranteed minimum impressions even if the visitor never scrolled down

to the bottom of that page. By using beacons, impressions are logged not at file load time but at the point when a visitor's browser actually brings the ad into view. You can rely that reporting on your ad impressions is an accurate count of real eyes on creative.

Advertising Deadlines and Payment Options

Advertising materials—including insertion order, payment, and creative—are due at least five (5) days prior to the beginning of the month in which the flight will start.

Quark VS InDesign.com recognizes that time-sensitive campaigns cannot wait until the next insertion date. Although insertions are typically made at the beginning of the calendar month, we can accommodate mid-cycle insertions. Insertions required after the first of the month are prorated to the time remaining, and will incur a surcharge of $50.

We can often provide immediate (24 hour turn-around) insertion or even same-day insertion for a flat-fee rush charge of   . Please ask your sales representative about the availability of immediate launch of your campaign.

Mid-cycle and immediate insertions are only available on purchases of at least one full advertising cycle.

WWW.QUARK VS INDESIGN.COM

4

REV 20061001

The Bottom Line

Create and fill text frames Setting type is InDesign's primary function, and it performs that function better than any other application. The fundamental building block of type in InDesign is the text frame container and the text content.

Master It Create a new text frame, and then place the flawed text file, `bad-lorem.txt`, into it. Clean up the resulting text to make it readable. When finished with that, place the document `REVstory.doc` into the same text frame after the first imported document.

Format text frames   Correctly formatting and configuring text frames will save effort and time not only now, but also every time a frame or its content changes.

> **Master It**   Using the text frame created above, convert it from a single column into three, with a 0.25-inch gutter. At the same time, give the text some breathing room by setting top and bottom insets of 0.1667 inches and no inset on the sides.

Format paragraphs   Paragraphs must be separated and styled to enable legibility and facilitate readability. That can be accomplished through alignment, indents, paragraph spacing, and drop caps.

> **Master It**   Continuing with the multicolumn frame of placed stories, let's make them readable. In the first full paragraph of each story, add a drop cap of 2 to 3 lines. Separate the same paragraphs from anything that may come before with a comfortably large paragraph space before. Give the rest of the paragraphs a correct first line indent and, to control runts, a last line right indent. Because we've got three probably narrow columns, let's make clean, rag-less paragraphs.

Compose paragraphs   Paragraph composition is essential to good typography. A poorly composed paragraph is one of those things that both trained and untrained eyes immediately notice—even if unconsciously—and that marks the document as the product of an amateur. From this book you should learn first that efficiency and economy of motion equate to more creative time, second that coffee is your friend, and third that practicing good paragraph composition is very, very important to the quality of your documents, your clients and employers, and the future marketability of you as represented by your portfolio.

> **Master It**   Undoubtedly by this point we have three columns of unsavory composition. You may have widows and orphans, paragraphs may be split all over the place, hyphenation may be off or run amok, and word and letter spacing could be just horrendous. Even if it isn't that bad, you've got some areas in your document that need work.
>
> First, duplicate the text frame and work on the copy, keeping the original above or beside it as a reference.
>
> Begin the cleanup by asking InDesign to highlight problem areas and violations. Then, working through the highlighted text and keeping an eye out for problems InDesign didn't notice, employ the skills you learned about paragraph composition to eliminate all runts, widows, and orphans; then optically align hanging punctuation and tweak hyphenation and word and letter spacing.

Chapter 3

Characters

InDesign is the world's most advanced typesetting platform. The only other applications that even come close are Illustrator and Photoshop, and only because they follow InDesign's lead. In fact, type set in InDesign is almost as good as type set on a letterpress. The few sacrifices you make by setting type in InDesign instead of in lead tend to be balanced by the time savings—you can set much faster than one page every four hours—and by the lack of ink perpetually embedded under your nails.

In this chapter, you will learn to:

- ◆ Format characters
- ◆ Transform characters
- ◆ Insert special characters
- ◆ Work with OpenType font features
- ◆ Use the Glyphs panel

Formatting Characters

Now that we know how to get text *into* InDesign, let's talk about what the world's greatest digital text-handling platform can *do* with it.

The Character Panel

Let's start the character-formatting discussion by walking through the Character panel, which contains most character-level style options. Many of the Character panel's options and fields are replicated on the Control panel in Character mode—and a few are more easily accessible via the Control panel—but we'll focus first on the Character panel and then cover the differences on the Control panel.

If it isn't showing, open the Character panel from Window ➤ Type & Tables ➤ Character, or press Cmd+T/Ctrl+T. If you only see six fields in your Character panel, choose Show Options from the panel's flyout menu.

FONT FAMILY AND TYPE STYLE

Most fonts are actually families of typefaces that include a roman, normal, or regular typeface, and other variations such as italic, oblique, bold, semi-bold, medium, light, condensed, and countless other possibilities. When styling type, the first option is going to be choosing the appropriate type family.

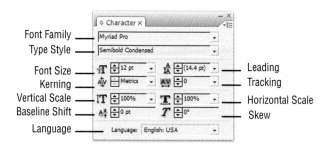

FIGURE 3.1

The Character panel.

Font Family · Type Style · Font Size · Kerning · Vertical Scale · Baseline Shift · Language · Leading · Tracking · Horizontal Scale · Skew

Clicking the arrow will reveal a scrollable drop-down list of all font families installed on the system (see Figure 3.2), including sample text set in the family's default typeface, which is usually the roman, normal, or regular style. Some sample text examples may be boxes, which indicate that the font doesn't include the letters *S-a-m-p-l-e*; this is sometimes the case with symbol or dingbat typefaces.

Beneath the Font Family field is the Type Style field, showing all the individual typefaces in the selected font.

FIGURE 3.2

The Character panel's Font Family field drop-down displaying font families and samples

In addition to choosing the font family and typeface style by selecting from the lists, you can type directly into either field. If you already know the family you want, for example, begin typing its name in the Font Family field. Through the magic of autocomplete, InDesign immediately searches for matches beginning with the letters you've typed and fills in the rest. If InDesign's choice isn't the correct one, keep typing until there's enough of the name that InDesign gets it right. Press Return/Enter to apply and return to your document or Tab to apply and move on to the next field in the Character panel.

With the Font Family list shown, keyboard navigation keys Page Up, Page Down, Home, and End and the Up and Down arrow keys shorten your search time by jumping through the list. In the field, with the drop-down list closed, only the Up and Down arrow keys will change typefaces one at a time.

At the bottom of the Font Family list, you may have some fonts segregated from the rest by horizontal lines. Rather than intermingle non-Latin-character-set font families throughout the main list, InDesign makes it easier to find them by placing them in groups sorted to the bottom of the list. Families of Asian language fonts such as Chinese, Japanese, Korean (collectively referred to as *CJK fonts*) as well as Russian Cyrillic, Hebrew, and other type families not using the Roman character set of English, Spanish, French, Italian, and Portuguese will be listed at the bottom, along with samples.

Not shown on the Font Family list on the Character panel or on the Control panel are previews of families matched with their individual typefaces, which are the separate list in the Type Style field. What does Myriad Pro SemiCondensed Italic look like? You can't tell from either of those panels until *after* you've applied the Myriad Pro family to your text and moved down to the Type Style field. You *can* get a sample text preview from the Type ➤ Font menu (see Figure 3.3). There, each family is listed with a flyout displaying all the fonts and sample text—in one place.

FIGURE 3.3

The Type ➤ Font menu shows not only font families but each individual font within a family.

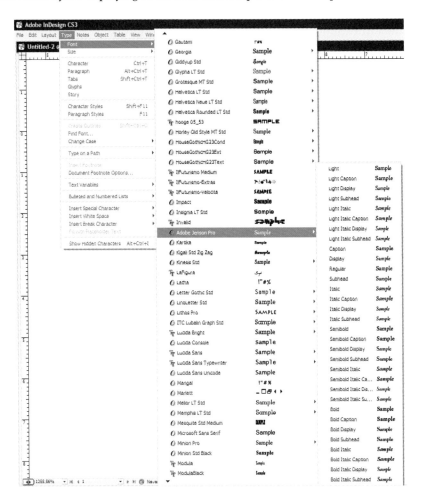

FONT SIZE AND LEADING

The Font Size and Leading fields are pretty straightforward—you've used 'em umpteen times before. InDesign provides drop-down lists of common point sizes, and both fields will accept typed-in whole values (e.g., 12 pt) as well as values with decimal measurements up to the thousandth of a point (e.g., 12.015 pt).

In the Leading field drop-down is a nonnumerical option, Auto. Choosing Auto sets the leading to automatically adjust in relation to the font size and will display the resulting value encased in parentheses, which InDesign uses in several places to denote a calculated or default value. The default leading is 120% of the font size; thus 10 pt type defaults to sit on 12 pt leading. To change the default leading value, use the Justification dialog accessible from the Paragraph panel menu (see Chapter 8, "Stories," for more on the Justification dialog); it isn't in the Preferences as you've been trained to expect.

POWER TIP: CHANGE FONT SHORTCUT

When you first show the Character panel, the Font Family field is selected, with its contents highlighted. Thus, a rapid, mouse-free way of changing typefaces presents itself—press Cmd+T/Ctrl+T to show the panel, and immediately type the name of the desired typeface or enough of it that InDesign can fill in the rest. Hit Return/Enter, and get right back to work—without ever touching the mouse. Need to change the style as well as the font? Press Tab after filling in the font family name to jump to the typeface style field, and then type in your choice there before hitting Return/Enter. In fact, you can tab through all the fields of the Character panel, changing size, leading, and more, without taking your hands off the keyboard.

Leading itself works a little differently in InDesign than what you've come to expect from other applications. In InDesign, it's a baseline-to-baseline measurement—the amount of space between the current text's *baseline* and the baseline of the line immediately above. Thus, increasing or decreasing leading pushes it farther away from or pulls it closer to the line above.

Even more radical, leading is a character-level attribute—it applies to individual characters, not entire paragraphs or lines. In certain other applications, it's possible to double-click select a word, increase the leading, and watch the entire paragraph loosen. Not so in InDesign. Instead, only the one word will be changed. While it will, of course, push its entire line downward (or upward, if you've decreased leading), your leading value has not been applied to the entire line; the line is merely compensating for the character-level leading. Should the altered word wrap to the next line, *that* line will push downward while the previous line resumes a leading consistent with the rest of the paragraph.

Most people like this behavior, but if you don't, it's easy to change. Open the Preferences with Cmd+K/Ctrl+K, and go to the Type pane. In the middle of Type Options is a check box, Apply Leading to Entire Paragraphs. Checking the option with a document opened sets it for the current document only. To make it default for all future projects, close all documents and then check Apply Leading to Entire Paragraphs.

There's a gotcha I need to caution you about: When changing leading, it's common and familiar to click at the beginning or end of the paragraph, drag down or up to select the entire paragraph, and then change the leading value (or most other values). This creates the potential for big problems because the paragraph marker (¶) is a character too, albeit invisible. As a character, it can have its own character-level attributes—typeface, style, leading, and more. If, when you select and change a paragraph, you fail to select the paragraph marker as well, you create a situation wherein this invisible character can cause the last line to have different leading than the rest of the paragraph (as well as potentially different typefaces, point sizes, and more, which lead to their own sets of problems).

Ensure that you're always selecting the *whole* paragraph, including the paragraph marker, by training yourself to habitually work either with invisible markers turned on by choosing Type ➤ Show Hidden Characters, by triple- or quadruple-clicking to select an entire paragraph, or both. In the Preferences Type pane is the option Triple Click to Select a Line. If checked, you must click *four* times rapidly to select the entire paragraph.

KERNING

Even if you're a kerning expert, InDesign's unique take on the Kerning field begs explanation. *Kerning* is defined as the distance between two glyphs (aka characters), and InDesign takes that definition literally. Highlight a word in your document and hit the drop-down arrow on the Kerning field. You're looking at the list on the left in Figure 3.4, aren't you? Your options are limited to Optical, Metrics, and 0, and everything else is grayed out. You also can't type a specific numeric value into the field. Position your cursor *between* two glyphs, without highlighting any text, and everything gray will become available.

FIGURE 3.4

When text is selected, options in the Kerning field drop-down are limited (left), but, when the cursor is positioned between two glyphs, more options become available (right).

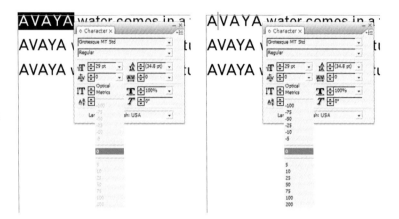

InDesign enforces the literal definition of kerning: you can kern only one pair of glyphs at a time except to set all selected glyphs to 0—no kerning whatsoever—or let InDesign handle it all automatically by evaluating relational glyph positioning according to one of two criteria: metric or optical kerning.

To understand the kerning options, it's important to first understand the structure of a font. A digital font—whether OpenType, TrueType, or PostScript (Type 1, Type 3, etc.)—is just a table or grid. The type designer draws every character (glyph, to be politically correct) individually as a simple vector shape comprised of paths and anchor points.

Most people tend to associate the mechanics of typeface design with the way we all learned to draw the alphabet in first grade—one letter at a time, all in a line, on recycled or yellow newsprint. Although that's very close to how a typeface design begins, turning a design into a font requires isolating letters, punctuation, and other glyphs off the line and into a table. For a computer to understand that a given shape equals a glyph such as *a*, a font must be divided into tabular cells, with each cell having a specific purpose; whatever is placed in the cell defined as a lowercase *a* will be spit out by the computer when you press the *a* key on your keyboard. And, that's the only way this whole idea of digital typesetting works—everyone agrees to put *a* in the cell in which computers expect to find an *a*.

Font table cells are rectangular; every glyph is wholly contained within a rectangle. For glyphs like *M* and *N*, which are rectangular letterforms anyway, that's no big deal—they tend to fill or almost fill their cells. However, with glyphs that aren't easy rectangles, such as *A*, *T*, and *Y*, white space is left in the table cell. Thus, when letters are put together in words, certain combinations create too much white space that tends to disassociate the glyphs from one another. Kerning is the system that compensates for white space by pushing certain glyphs toward one another, even violating the borders of individual table cells, to make them *appear* to be only as far apart as any other pair of glyphs. In some cases, kerning also pushes glyphs away from each other to create the same illusion where glyph shapes fill their cells too completely and appear too close to other glyphs.

There are three means of kerning type, and Figure 3.5 shows their different results on the same text.

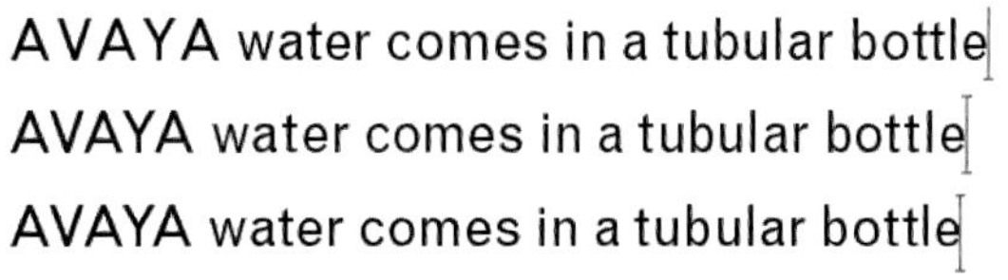

FIGURE 3.5
(Top) Kerning manually set to 0. (Middle) Metric kerning. (Bottom) Optical kerning.

A V A Y A water comes in a tubular bottle

AVAYA water comes in a tubular bottle

AVAYA water comes in a tubular bottle

Metric Kerning Professional typeface designers usually include kerning pairs in text fonts or include instructions to a typesetting application about how close together certain pairings of glyphs should be placed. Take, for instance, *VA*. Because of the negative space created by the letters' diagonal strokes, a large white space appears and can distract a reader's eye (see Figure 3.5). By including kerning pairs, the type designer is assisting the layout designer who would otherwise have to kern such pairings manually.

Metric kerning is the default, and it informs InDesign to search for and use kerning pairs within the font. It is usually the best choice for entire lines or paragraphs set in a single typeface and when the typeface is a professionally created font—as opposed to *1,001 Fonts for a Buck* CD-ROMs or the vast majority of free fonts on the Web, which rarely include kerning pairs.

Optical Kerning Whereas Metric kerning uses the information created by the type designer (if any), Optical kerning tells InDesign itself to fit glyphs together. To do that, InDesign actually reads the text, evaluating the shape of each glyph, its positive and negative space, and then seeks to create an even mix all the way through each word, line, and paragraph. It does that on a pair-by-pair basis, individually kerning every glyph in relation to the next.

In Figure 3.5, for instance, on the line where Optical kerning was applied, InDesign applied a −123 value between the *AV* in *AVAYA* but a value of −134 between the *AY* pair. Comparing the same two sets in the line where Metric kerning was chosen, we get −130 and −110, respectively. Which looks better? Which has a more even distribution of negative and positive space? You be the judge. Look at the instances of the lowercase *c* and *t* as well. Which line looks better overall?

(If you said the top line, with zero kerning applied, please take this book back to the store and exchange it for one on Microsoft Publisher.)

When a font lacks kerning pairs, thus disabling Metric, go for Optical. In many situations even when Metric *is* available, Optical kerning is the better choice, but it isn't perfect. Which, if either, is better, is subjective and relative to the specific font, typeface, point size, and intended use of your text. Try them both, but be prepared to manually kern here and there in either.

Manual Kerning In addition to choosing either Metric or Optical kerning, you can also set all selected type or frames to 0, or no, kerning. If you're trying to set easily readable type, you'll almost never choose 0 kerning.

With the cursor in the middle of a pair of glyphs to be kerned, the drop-down menu of presets becomes fully active. You can choose a preset, click the up/down buttons on the field, use your keyboard Up and Down arrows, or type a numeric value into the field. Kerning is entered in units of one one-thousandth (1/1000th) of an em. An em is a relative unit of measure equal in width to the height of the font (as measured by the capital *M*). For example, 12 pt type has a 12 pt em. To put it more bluntly and dramatically: InDesign makes you master of kerning the verse.

KERNING CHARACTER STYLES

Among other things, character styles store and reuse kerning settings. If you often use the same kerned pair of glyphs in the font and typeface and approximately the same size, save yourself the hassle of manually kerning them every time. Highlight the character to the left and create a character style from it. Next time you type in that pair, highlight the left character and apply your character style to instantly set the correct kerning.

TRACKING

It's amazing how much the Web has accelerated the spread and decline of design trends in all media. Before 1995, it would take months or even years before a trendy typeface, illustration style, or graphic design technique was mimicked around the world, and then even longer for the fad of it to pass. Remember when the late '80s fad of hard-drop type appeared, with its über cool, hard-line drop shadow that was more than a block-cut look yet still less than a real drop shadow? That was still being cranked out well into the mid-'90s. The same is true of hollowed or outlined type and wood or stone texture-filled type made popular by tutorials in catalog-magazine hybrids such as the one from Image Club Graphics.

Nowadays, however, the Web has enabled print design trends to travel the globe in weeks instead of years—and to fizzle just as quickly. To wit: Ultra loosened headlines and subheads like the one in Figure 3.6. This type style began in the late 1990s and within a few years was everywhere online and in print—and not just heads and subheads, but also taglines, captions, decks, navigation buttons, and even, when applied by the most aesthetically challenged, in paragraphs of text.

FIGURE 3.6
A heading with characters tracked out to a value of 900 (9/10 of an em)

R E V   D R I N K   M A K E S   H I S T O R Y

Thankfully, the fad became passé not too long after it began and has since gone the way of outlined type headlines and mastheads. Despite the fact that a million websites and home-cranked letterheads nearly ruined the style forever, tracking out text is still a viable design decision for the correct project. More importantly, tracking is more than this one trick pony.

At first glance, the uninitiated often confuse kerning and tracking and fail to see much difference between them. They'll use tracking to tighten up *AV* glyph pairs and kern out an entire headline to give the characters breathing room.

Kerning is about controlling the interaction of the negative and positive space of two glyphs when paired together. Tracking is the amount of relative space between *any* glyphs, regardless of their actual shape. Kerning makes it *look like* the same amount of space exists between *A* and *V* as between *N* and *M*. By contrast, tracking is about *actually* putting the same amount of space between those glyphs.

Very much like the Kerning field, the Tracking field measures in one one-thousandth of an em from –1,000—theoretically, a complete overlap of one character upon another—out to 10,000—theoretically the space of 10 characters occupied by one. I say theoretically because most fonts are variable width—the width of the *I* is not equal to the width of *M*, and sometimes, even the *M* itself is not equal to the width the font says it is. (Confused? Rushed designers don't always re-create every little setting specifically for each font they create; often they copy the settings from their last finished font or from a master template, even if the current typeface has significantly larger, smaller, or differently shaped glyphs.)

As with Kerning, Tracking offers a drop-down menu, buttons to increase or decrease the value incrementally, and the ability to type a different value into the field. *Unlike* the Kerning field, Tracking *requires* text to be selected and has no effect when the cursor is merely blinking between two glyphs. Negative values pull type closer together, while positive values push it apart.

The two types of horizontal space adjustment work hand in hand and are cumulative. For instance, if you've applied a kerning of 200 to a pair of glyphs and then tracked them in –200, the end result will be no space between them. Apply a positive 200 tracking and they'll be 400 units (4/10 of an em) apart. It's important to understand that concept because, even when tracking letters far apart or close together, you still need kerning to ensure that they are *not* really exactly the same distance apart and thus they *look* as if they are.

In Figure 3.7, the upper word has no kerning at all—it's set to 0. The bottom uses Metric kerning, so the relative spacing between these characters is adjusted to compensate for the negative space created by their forms. Both words have been tracked out to a positive value of 600. Which of the two looks like it has the more uniform spacing? Right: the lower one.

FIGURE 3.7
Both words have been tracked out to 600 (6/10ths of an em), but the top uses 0 kerning while the bottom uses Metric kerning.

A V A L O N

A V A L O N

If, when tracked, text doesn't look right, it might be one of those rare occasions for zero kerning. The preceding sample was not such an occasion. You now know how to make ultra-loose heads, but when else might you use tracking? When is it more than a special effect? Actually, it's used often but much more subtly.

Large type, such as might be used in headlines, often needs to be tracked together—sometimes by a large degree—for maximum effect. Conversely, dark, shallow, or thick-stroked typefaces at *small* sizes often need a little positive tracking to improve readability. The same is true of small cap or all-cap type in any typeface within body copy.

Typefaces such as Americana have a lot of space built into their glyphs. They have tall x-heights (the height of the lowercase *x* in relation to the height of the uppercase *X*), spindly strokes, and wide, open *counters* (the holes in letters such as *O*, *P*, and *C*). All that extra space inside the glyphs themselves can, at certain point sizes, render too much white space. Tightening the tracking slightly in those cases can improve the overall readability.

Tracking can also eliminate *orphans*, a word or two left alone as the last line of a paragraph. Tightening tracking on the entire paragraph by a tiny amount—say, a setting of –1 down to –5—can often bring the orphans home. If not, try a positive value on the paragraph to push more words down to join the orphan. Any more than +/– 5, however, and the tracking becomes noticeable and is generally considered a bigger sin than leaving an orphan.

FITTING MORE TEXT THAN WILL FIT

Stop me if you've heard this one. A man walks into a design studio with two pages of single-spaced, typed copy for his one-page, one-sided flyer. He hands the pages to the designer and says, "Put these in my flyer along with my logo, tagline, and pictures of my product. Oh! And don't forget to put my website address in really big type. And, I don't want the flyer to be cluttered. I hate cluttered design."

(What? You were seriously expecting a punch line?)

I'm asked all the time what's the best way to squeeze text into a space too small to fit it. My first (and second) answer is always, "Edit down the text and cut out the fat."

When trying to squeeze more text into a space than would fit at an appropriate size and style, your first, second, and third options should *always* be to cut copy. Get a real, edumacated editor involved to decide if the copy communicates only the required points. If it overexplains. If it has any parts irrelevant to the direct purpose of the layout.

Assuming you've cut every word you can, you have polished copy, and you still can't fit it, there are a few typesetting tricks you can try. Keep in mind: these are intended to help fit an extra line or two, not another half page.

- **Reduce font size in fractional points.** *Must* the type be 12 pt? Would 11.75 or 11.5 pt be just as legible?

- **Look for a condensed or compressed version of the typeface.** Many sans-serif typefaces—such as Futura, Grotesque, and most flavors of Helvetica—have styles drawn to be legible and readable at 75% (or even less) the width of the full-sized, regular versions.

- **Swap paragraph spacing for indents.** Paragraphs must be separated somehow, providing a visual indicator where one ends and another begins. If the method you've chosen is vertical spacing before or after a paragraph, try eliminating that and indenting the first line instead.

- **Try tightening the tracking a slight amount.** Of course, how effective it—or any of these tricks—is depends entirely upon the font, point size, and amount of text being tracked and fit. However, I have seen a tracking value of only –2 applied to a whole page of type allow another half dozen lines of text to fit on the page. Just don't go overboard trying to fit type; if the tracking is too tight, if there isn't a comfortable amount of horizontal white space, no one will read your text.

- **Reduce the horizontal scaling.** As with tightening the tracking, a little goes a long way, and a little more is terrible. In my experience, knocking horizontal scaling down 3% can create a lot of extra space and is unnoticeable—as long as all text of the same typeface is scaled. Never scale just a couple of words up or down because, beside unscaled text in the same typeface and size, it *will* be noticeable. If you're using a sans-serif font, you can scale even more—sometimes to only 80% of the original width—without it looking like you were squeezing. Headlines and other large copy can also be scaled more than body copy without significant impact on readability.

- **Tighten the leading.** I want you to know that I sat here, staring at this sidebar for 10 minutes and debating with myself if I should include this option. Reducing the amount of leading is the first thing everyone thinks of when they want to squeeze more text into a space, and I don't want to be construed as an advocate of tightening the leading. In fact, I'm the opposite: I believe strongly in open leading because, relative to text style, leading is the single greatest factor in a person's decision to read or not read a document.

If the leading is too tight, it creates a dark, intimidating page that people resist reading. Writers or designers who create to please their egos instead of their audience invariably disagree with my position, convinced that their words or choice of fonts and pictures, respectively, will outshine and override any other document characteristics and draw in the would-be reader. These are the people who set 12 pt type over 12 or 12.5 pt leading.

If you need a little space and nothing else will work, try dropping the leading down 1, 2, or 3%. *Never* set body copy leading to less than 110%, and only go that low when the glyphs themselves have a lot of white space built in and have a shallow x-height. Leading is like tipping a waitress or waiter: 15% of the bill is not the *most* you should tip, it's the *least*. And, 120% leading is not the *most* for body copy, it's the *minimum*.

Try combinations of these tricks if you still can't fit all your copy. If you find yourself using more than two of these techniques concurrently, *don't*. Rethink your design and/or cut down the copy. If those are out of the question, if you can't redesign or cut copy, at least make sure your name is never associated with the final design.

Be careful not to apply tracking to the last glyph in a word because tracking will push out (or pull in) anything to the right of that last glyph (see Figure 3.8). In the passage shown, the date was set in caps, and a positive tracking of 25 (1/500 of an em) was used to make the letters a little more legible. In the upper example, the 5 was included in the tracking, which pushes the single, standard-width space outward too far to look like an em space (a space the width of the capital *M*). In the lower, the 5 was excluded from the Type tool selection and retains a 0 tracking, allowing the space to reflect its actual width and fit more naturally. Be especially vigilant in watching for unexpected tracking on the last glyph when incorporating tracking values into character styles.

If you're adjusting tracking on an entire text frame, it isn't that big a deal to apply tracking to the last glyph. InDesign compensates for that extra space at the end of the tracked word when aligning to center, right, or justified.

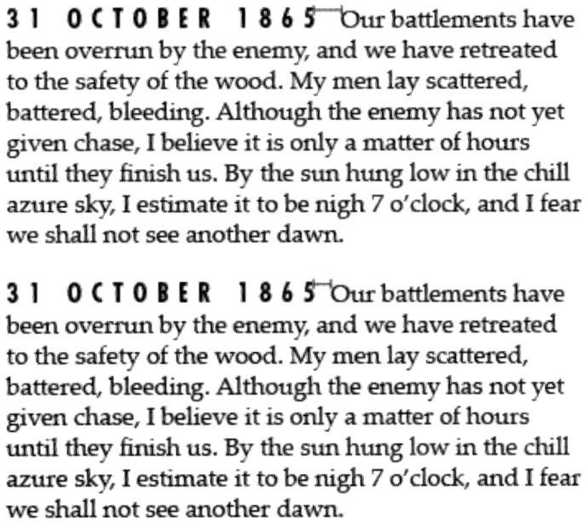

FIGURE 3.8

Top: Tracking is applied to all letters in the word, causing a larger than normal gap to the right. Not tracking the last letter (bottom) achieves the desired effect without creating an overly large gap.

3 1 O C T O B E R 1 8 6 5 Our battlements have been overrun by the enemy, and we have retreated to the safety of the wood. My men lay scattered, battered, bleeding. Although the enemy has not yet given chase, I believe it is only a matter of hours until they finish us. By the sun hung low in the chill azure sky, I estimate it to be nigh 7 o'clock, and I fear we shall not see another dawn.

3 1 O C T O B E R 1 8 6 5 Our battlements have been overrun by the enemy, and we have retreated to the safety of the wood. My men lay scattered, battered, bleeding. Although the enemy has not yet given chase, I believe it is only a matter of hours until they finish us. By the sun hung low in the chill azure sky, I estimate it to be nigh 7 o'clock, and I fear we shall not see another dawn.

VERTICAL AND HORIZONTAL SCALE

The next leg of our journey down the Character panel includes the twin Vertical and Horizontal Scale fields, which enable effects like those in Figure 3.9. Note that, except for the bottom row of *A*s, all the other type is exactly the same font size—90 pts.

FIGURE 3.9
Various effects achieved with type scaling

Type scaling opens a single typeface to the possibilities of numerous widths. Looking back to Figure 3.9, for instance, the bottom row of *A*s are all Grotesque MT Std Bold at 43 pts. Each letter's horizontal scale was adjusted by 10%, beginning with 10% on the left, progressing through 100% (or normal, in red), and up to 190% on the right end. The Grotesque MT Std font family includes only width-centric styles of Extra Condensed, Light Condensed, (Regular) Condensed, and Bold Extended. There is no Bold Condensed, nor is there a Regular Extended, Super Condensed, and so on. If your design requires a horizontal scale not available in the font family's type styles, the scaling fields can help.

TYPESETTING MASTER TIP: PROGRAMMING READERS' BRAINS WITH VERTICAL SCALING

Want to call attention to something within paragraphs of text—maybe a figure reference or brand name? One technique you can employ is to make the target text larger. If you increase the point size while leading is set to automatic, InDesign will push the entire line down to accommodate the larger word or two, creating incongruous (and ugly) leading. If you checked the preference to Apply Leading to Entire Paragraphs, InDesign will space out the entire paragraph—even uglier in a multi-paragraph document. However, if you leave the target text at the same point size and just bump the vertical scaling up a miniscule amount, you can create a very subtle effect that calls attention to specific words in the passage. With a 1% to 3% vertical scale increase, readers' conscious minds will almost never pick up on the difference, but their ever-alert subconscious minds *will* take note, recognizing that *something* is different about the text: it *somehow* has more emphasis, and the subconscious will cognitively assign a higher priority to comprehending and remembering the emphasized text.

As an added benefit, a reader's subconscious will also more easily latch onto and interpret such subtly altered text while merely skimming over the text looking for keywords.

Think of this technique as a less-obvious, less-obtrusive means of assigning emphasis than would be possible with bold or italic.

Scaling fields accept percentage-based measurements from 1% up through 1,000%. While neither extreme is realistically readable, each can make for interesting creative effects. More importantly, the values between the extremes give you a more precise control over type styling and fitting. Look at the letters on either side of the red *A*. Each has been horizontally scaled by only 10%—10% down to the left, 10% up to the right. Not a lot of apparent difference, is there? Distortion is almost imperceptible, but +/– 10% could determine whether a headline fits the designated space.

Scaling is used quite frequently (in small percentages) to better fit type into spaces—particularly heads, subheads, and other small passages of type. A little nudge to horizontal scaling can fill that awkward space at the end of a text frame or rescue an orphan. Tapping the vertical scaling up or down can make capital letters more obvious in fonts with tall x-heights.

Compressing or extending letterforms this way is not the same as using genuine condensed or extended versions of the fonts. Scaling down horizontally will reduce the weight of the vertical strokes in proportion to the overall width reduction, whereas in a typeface version of the font created by a type designer as condensed, the stroke weights are usually uniform or match the horizontal strokes. Compressing vertically distorts the horizontal strokes while leaving the vertical untouched, and so on. With serif or other delicate typefaces, the distortion can become obviously horrific even at small percentages—as can the distortion to diagonal and curved strokes in any typeface. Always look for a professionally designed condensed, compressed, extended, or expanded style of the typeface before using large percentages in the Vertical and Horizontal Scale fields.

MAKING BETTER SMALL CAPS

If you have to fake small caps, try this: Instead of applying the Small Caps command from the Character panel menu, use the same typeface and size in capital letters with a reduced vertical scaling. You'll probably also want to loosen the tracking a bit. Although this doesn't do it in every situation, with every typeface, in many cases it gives you better results than the faux small caps option.

BASELINE SHIFT

The *baseline* is the ethereal horizontal line on which text vertically aligns. *Descenders*, or tails, on lowercase letters such as *j*, *g*, and *y* typically extend below the baseline; most other capital and lowercase letters stand directly on it (see Figure 3.10).

FIGURE 3.10
A diagram of the most common ethereal lines used to design, discuss, and set the size of type

The Baseline Shift field accepts positive or negative values as great as 5,000 points. Positive values push glyphs upward, above the baseline, while negative values pull them down below the baseline of surrounding text.

Figure 3.11 shows three uses of baseline shift to move the bottom of glyphs below or above the baseline of surrounding text. The first, in "the Mighty Mighty Postscripts," lowers the capital *M*, *P*, and *S* so that their tops (cap height) align with the tops of the small-cap lowercase letters (x-height) by using a negative baseline shift on the capitals. The second usage is the opposite, raising the "st" in the ordinal "1st" with a positive baseline shift. I should note that the proper way to set ordinals in *OpenType* fonts that include them is via the OpenType ➤ Ordinals command on the Character panel menu. In this case, because I used different fonts for the *1* (Zapfino Extra LT Four) and the *st* (Garamond Premiere Pro, like the main title), the proper method didn't align the two correctly and it was necessary to use a manual baseline shift.

FIGURE 3.11
Baseline shift effects in the lowered caps and the ordinal

Hmm. I did say there were *three* examples of baseline shift in that image, didn't I? Where's the third? It's more subtle than the other two. Can you spot it? Proof your guess against Figure 3.12, which shows the before and after.

FIGURE 3.12
(Top) the text as typed. (Bottom) The same text touched up with baseline shift and kerning.

In Figure 3.12, you see the two versions of the word *Live*, as typed (top) and after a little touch-up (bottom). I didn't like the way the *L* joined the rest of the word, leaving such a large and distracting gap before the *i*. This being 70 pt Zapfino Extra LT Four, I shifted the *L*'s baseline by –7 pt, lowering it so the tail would clear the *ive*. Then I used –150 kerning to pull the rest of the word into the *L*. Doesn't the second, adjusted version look much better than the first?

In addition to cleaning up type in general and creating special effects—which, with large shift values, can yield very interesting and extreme results—baseline shift can compensate for defects in a font. For instance, the trademark (™) or registered trademark (®) symbols included in a given font are occasionally drawn too large or too small (often because they weren't drawn specifically for the given typeface, but copied from another). To correct such flaws, reduce or enlarge the point size of the symbol in text, and then properly position the symbol with baseline shift. I often use baseline shift to correct baseline alignment problems with many common symbols, including copyright (©), pilcrow (¶), middle dot or waisted bullet (•) and euro (€). When you're supplying custom in-line bullets or separator marks from symbol (aka dingbats, fleurons, or bullets) fonts, rarely does the glyph *not* require baseline adjustment.

SKEW
Measured in degrees (–85° through +85°), the Skew field slants selected text in place and can be used on anything from a single glyph to an entire thread-frame story—whatever is selected. Positive values skew the top of text forward or right, while negative values slant back- or leftward.

In Figure 3.13, I skewed the word *skewed* by a value of –24°, slanting it backward. The question mark has a Skew value of positive 20° to angle it to the right.

FIGURE 3.13
Feeling skewed?

DESIGNS COMING OUT SKEWED?
Align your thinking with REV Creativity Drink™!

Skewing selected type in place is not the same as skewing a text frame. As you can see in Figure 3.14, type slanted with the Skew field on the Character panel still forms rectangular paragraphs with *flush alignment* (set to Justify with Last Line Left), but the slanting serrates paragraph edges. Conversely, skewing the text frame itself via the Transform panel changes the *area* into which text flows *and* slants the type simultaneously. Both have been skewed by –15°.

FIGURE 3.14

Skewed type in an unskewed frame (left) and unskewed type in a skewed frame (right)

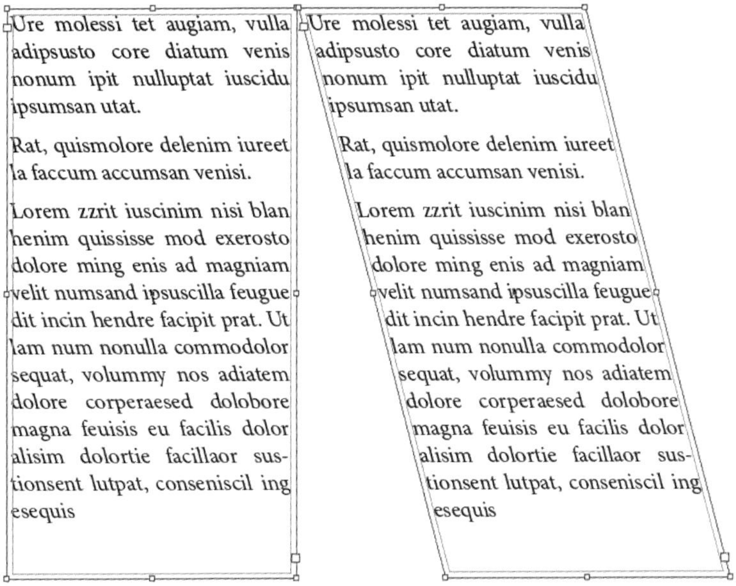

Ure molessi tet augiam, vulla adipsusto core diatum venis nonum ipit nulluptat iuscidu ipsumsan utat.

Rat, quismolore delenim iureet la faccum accumsan venisi.

Lorem zzrit iuscinim nisi blan henim quississe mod exerosto dolore ming enis ad magniam velit numsand ipsuscilla feugue dit incin hendre facipit prat. Ut lam num nonulla commodolor sequat, volummy nos adiatem dolore corperaesed dolobore magna feuisis eu facilis dolor alisim dolortie facillaor sustionsent lutpat, conseniscil ing esequis

Ure molessi tet augiam, vulla adipsusto core diatum venis nonum ipit nulluptat iuscidu ipsumsan utat.

Rat, quismolore delenim iureet la faccum accumsan venisi.

Lorem zzrit iuscinim nisi blan henim quississe mod exerosto dolore ming enis ad magniam velit numsand ipsuscilla feugue dit incin hendre facipit prat. Ut lam num nonulla commodolor sequat, volummy nos adiatem dolore corperaesed dolobore magna feuisis eu facilis dolor alisim dolortie facillaor sustionsent lutpat, conseniscil ing esequis

When will you use the Skew field? If you have any taste whatsoever, almost never. Like baseline shift, extreme values here can create extreme effects—and one in a million projects will warrant such—but its primary use is for subtle correction. Sometimes the italic or oblique style of a given typeface is too extreme and needs to be scaled back with a negative skew. Sometimes symbols or dingbats need a little slanting this way or that.

Use Skew with caution. After I tell you about the Language field, I'll explain Skew's most obvious purpose and why and when you should, and shouldn't, use it.

LANGUAGE

Right up front, so you don't get your hopes up: *InDesign does not translate text from one language to another.* Every time I introduce the Language field in person, via webcast, or even in writing, someone always gets excited about the prospect of InDesign automatically translating the text. It doesn't. That's not the purpose of this field.

If not translation, what's the purpose of this field and why is it a character-level attribute? As always: good questions.

InDesign is fully, wholly, unlimitedly multilingual. If it can be typed, InDesign will type it. And not just languages based on the Roman alphabet. You can type Japanese, Korean, Vietnamese, Chinese, Russian, Czech, Arabic, Sanskrit, and even Klingon (more about that strange idea later) as long as you have a font with the appropriate character set. You don't need to buy a regionalized version of InDesign just to set type in a language other than English. In fact, the only substantive difference between InDesign's English, Eastern European, Japanese, and other regional versions is their user interface—Russian designers get menus, keyboard shortcuts, and so on in Cyrillic, while Americans, Brits, Mexicans, Italians, and so on get Roman characters in English, Spanish, or Italian.

Because any regionalized version of InDesign can hold text from any known (or future) human written language and because even fastidious Italian writers sometimes make typos, InDesign includes the ability to spell check and/or hyphenate the most common world languages. If, for example, you're designing an anti-drug pamphlet to be distributed throughout Texas, you're required to produce the same information in both English and Spanish. Assuming you're putting the copy in both languages on the same pamphlet, a spell check run in your English copy of InDesign will seize on just about every Spanish word. If you have dynamic spell checking enabled, your pamphlet will become a sea of red squigglies. So, instead of dealing with that nightmare and the added complication of no hyphenation or possibly wrong hyphenation, select the Spanish portion and set the Language field on the Character panel to Spanish. Your red squigglies will disappear, and words at the end of lines will correctly hyphenate.

You can tell InDesign to use any one of 39 different spelling and hyphenation dictionaries on selected text, including separate dictionaries for U.S. English legal and medical terminology. Because language is a character-level attribute instead of restricted to the frame or story as it is in other layout applications, multiple languages or language variants (e.g., English: USA: Legal) can be contained in the same frame and even the same paragraph. This is a huge benefit to anyone who routinely sets those types of multilingual documents in which each English paragraph is immediately repeated in Spanish, French, Vietnamese, or another language. Instead of setting each language in its own frame and having to adjust *all* the frames for every little formatting or copy change, placing them in the same text frame causes the entire story to adapt automatically to changes.

Using the Language field is easy: Just highlight text, and choose the appropriate language from the drop-down menu. Once that's done, InDesign will automatically change dictionaries when looking at hyphenation or when running a spell check on the text, paragraph, story, or document. Text defined as English: USA (the default) will be compared against the English: USA dictionary, a sentence in the middle of the same paragraph set to Norwegian: Nynorsk will be compared against that dictionary, an English medical term among *that* against yet another dictionary. *Tres bien, mesdames et messieurs.*

Character Transformations

InDesign includes much more control over character attributes than the basic styling options on the face of the Character panel, but they're scattered about.

CHANGE CASE

Anyone who imports and sets text written by clients or other noneditorial personnel will understand what I mean when I say that sometimes you need to change the case of text.

Largely because of single-font typewriters, but perpetuated by laziness in the early days of computers and now by habits developed in Internet communications, a large percentage of the business world believes all caps equals emphasis—and CONTINUE to type anything of

REASONABLE IMPORTANCE in all caps despite the obvious Bold and Italic buttons in Word. Professional type designers recognize that all caps is usually not the best way to convey emphasis, and they're often left retyping the all caps words in imported documents. A word here and there isn't bad, but when an entire line is set in all caps… Oh, the inhumanity!

If CS3 is the first version of InDesign you've used, rejoice; you needn't retype any longer. If you've been using InDesign for a couple of versions, you're already aware that it's always had commands to change the case of selected text, right? No? Oh. Well, now you are. Microsoft Word has the same commands on its Tools menu, by the way.

Highlight any text in your document and go to Type ➤ Change Case. There you will find four options: Uppercase, Lowercase, Title Case, and Sentence Case. Respectively, they transform text into all caps; all lowercase; title case, where the first letter of every word is capitalized; and sentence case, where only the first letter of every new sentence is capitalized. With text selected, an even faster way to get to the commands is to right-click (or, if you have one of those insipid single-button Mac mice, Control-click) and select Change Case from the context sensitive menu.

Changing case is not an effect; the text is really changed. Fresh text typed into the middle of transformed type won't inherit the transformation. These commands can be undone with Cmd+Z/Ctrl+Z, by selecting another Change Case command, or by simply typing over the transformed text.

CLEANING UP AFTER CHANGE CASE

A common scenario: A designer is faced with a story containing multiple heading levels, all of which the author set in all caps. The final design, however, will use other formatting and title case for headings. Correcting the problem is not terribly difficult—select each heading one at a time and choose Change Case ➤ Title Case. However, what if there are acronyms in the headings? Maybe it's a regional sales report with headings like "Year End Spending, USA Offices," "Year End Profit, UK Offices," and so forth. Maybe it's a government or government contractor report that, like all such reports, speaks in acronyms more often than complete titles. Changing the case will incorrectly change the case on all the words that should be capitalized.

Simple: Change the case, then undo the damage by running Find/Change from the Edit menu. Enter in the Find What field the incorrect case word now littered throughout the document (e.g., Nasa), and the correct capitalization in the Change To field (NASA). Check the Case Sensitive and Whole Word options, and then run the change operation. Repeat as necessary for other common erroneous capitalizations.

Although a great help, the change case commands are not perfect. Sentence case, for example, doesn't do proper names, acronyms, or initials. If the letters of acronyms or initials that begin a sentence are not separated by periods (as in the case of, say, *NASA*), the Change Case ➤ Sentence Case command will convert all but the first letter to lower case (*Nasa*), which, of course, is a major faux pas. Proper names that don't start a sentence will be rendered in lowercase—an even bigger faux pas. Fortunately, InDesign *does* understand that a stand-alone *I* should be capitalized.

These four simple case commands have saved many a typesetter hours of retyping work and countless typos caused thereby.

CASE EFFECTS

Choosing Change Case ➤ Uppercase will transform text to full uppercase. Any mixed case used for proper names, acronyms, initials, prepositions, or whatever will be completely and forever lost. Moreover, spell check will read the words as all uppercase, which may cause it to flag misspellings. A less drastic, impermanent option to *transforming* type to all uppercase is to use the all caps *effect*, which creates the appearance of all caps but doesn't actually alter the text.

On the Character panel's flyout menu are two case effects: All Caps and Small Caps. The former will make text *look* all uppercase, but in the background it will keep it in whatever case it was before the effect was applied. Editing the text in story editor will also reveal its real case. Small Caps will leave all capital letters as such but convert all lowercase to smaller versions of the capitals. If the typeface in use is an OpenType font with genuine small caps built in, those will be used; otherwise InDesign will fake it by scaling capital letter versions down to 70% of their cap-height.

As a general rule, the height of small caps should be identical to the height of the lowercase letters in the same typeface (the x-height). Rarely does the default of 70% correctly hit that mark. In fact, most designers change the default small cap height to from 80% to 85% of the cap-height when first setting up InDesign. To do that, open InDesign's Preferences and go to the Advanced Type pane. There, beneath Superscript and Subscript, is the size of small caps relative to cap-height. Up that to 85% and try it out. If the results aren't perfect, come back and tweak it.

Like most other things in the Preferences, the Small Cap percentage is a document-level attribute. Setting it to 85% for the current document will not change it in the next document you create; it will default to 70%. To effect the change for all future documents, set it with all documents closed.

Exporting or copying the text out of InDesign to another application such as Notepad or an email client, for example, will result in a reversion to mixed case.

SUPERSCRIPT AND SUBSCRIPT

Super- is a prefix meaning above, beyond, on top. *Sub-*, the antonym of super, is a prefix meaning below, a part of, or under. Superscript glyphs are printed aligned to or partly above the cap-height of text, and subscript glyphs partly below the baseline.

Typically approximately two-thirds (58%–67%) the size of the text's cap-height, superscript notations are raised up such that their baselines are between 33.3% and 67% higher than the baseline of surrounding text. Subscript notations are the same size and usually rest on baselines offset by the same amount in the negative (-33.3% to -67%). Super- and subscripts are often numbers or letters, but either can also be a symbol. Figure 3.15 shows a few examples of both in use.

FIGURE 3.15
Examples of superscript and subscript

$E = mc^2$

Writing 5^5 is the same as saying five to the fifth power.

REV Creativity Drink^{SM}

They graduated 1st, 4th, and 23rd in their class, respectively.

Meet me at 4:30^{PM}

H_2O can be expressed also as O_1H_2 or even HOH

Void where prohibited by law$_\dagger$.

Let's walk through the figure line-by-line as we discuss superscript and subscript.

The first five lines of the figure include superscript characters. The first two are mathematic examples, using superscript to denote power of, or multiply the preceding number by itself *this* many times. Einstein's most famous formula, energy equals mass multiplied by the square root of the speed of light in a vacuum, is the first example.

Most text typefaces include the trademark symbol (™) drawn so that it's proportional to the rest of the typeface in its proper superscripted size and position. Most also include a registered trademark symbol (®), but few include the symbol used when the text or artwork is a protected mark denoting a service, the service mark (℠). When it's required, and a font doesn't have it, you'll need to manually create it by using superscript.

Next in the figure are mixed alpha-numeric ordinals, those handy little notations that represent ordinals like *first* as *1st*. Stylistically, you can use either lowercase or uppercase ordinals.

Finally in the superscript category, for those not yet comfortable with the much more efficient 24-hour clock (I dig efficiency), are time notations. Grammatical and design style rules for setting A.M. and P.M. are pretty loose. Your organization may follow a style guide that dictates their usage and style; if not, you have options. AM, from the Latin *ante meridiem* meaning before midday, may be written with (A.M.) or without (AM) periods. The same applies to P.M., *post meridiem*, after midday. Both A.M. and P.M. can be styled in a number of ways—as superscript, as lowercase, or as small caps. Never should they be set in full caps.

My recommendation is to small cap if you don't superscript. If you do superscript, capitalize AM and PM. I also recommend dropping the periods and the space between the time and its notation in either case, but especially if you superscript. (Of course, if you simply abandon the whole 5,000-year-old A.M./P.M. thing and go with a simple 24-hour clock, all this mess clears up instantly.)

On the next three lines of the figure, we have subscript.

In the chemical formula for water, 2 denotes the number of hydrogen atoms required in the formula and should be subscript. Placing it above, superscripting, would be mathematical instead of chemical and would effectively say multiply hydrogen by hydrogen, which is just mind-boggling to even consider.

InDesign has its own footnote system (see Chapter 8, "Stories"), and you shouldn't have to manually set their reference numbers. Regardless, footnotes are *usually* set as superscript, but can occasionally be subscript as I showed with the dagger on the last line of Figure 3.15.

To apply either superscript or subscript, simply select the appropriate menu item from the Character panel flyout menu. The selected text will then be scaled and its baseline offset by the amounts specified in the Advanced Type pane of InDesign's Preferences.

Never separate either superscript or subscript from the preceding glyph it modifies.

Grammar dictates that a sentence's ending punctuation must always follow superscript, superior, or subscript notations, even though doing so may look odd. Mitigate unusual results with kerning.

For more on superscript and subscript, especially how OpenType fonts can make them look a lot better, see the section on OpenType later in this chapter.

No Break

The last option on the Character panel flyout menu is No Break, a useful albeit oft-forgotten little command. Highlighting a word and applying this command will prevent InDesign from hyphenating that word if it appears near the end of a line—extremely handy to prevent accidental hyphenation of a proper name.

Many large organizations and government contractors have style guides dictating that certain phrases cannot be wrapped such that part of the phrase appears at the end of one line while the rest wraps to the next line. Others must deal with setting personal names with prefixes (e.g., *Mrs., Dr., MSgt.*), suffixes (e.g., *Jr., III, DDS*); grammatical style strongly favors keeping prefixes on the same line with first names and suffixes with last. Applying the No Break command to multiple, concurrently selected words will ensure that spaces and punctuation between them cannot be interpreted as a breaking point to wrap the line.

Be careful with No Break, however, because it could create some rather large and ugly gaps at the end of a line. If you're using forced justification, where both the left and right edges are flush, instead of big gap at the end, you'll get horribly large gaps between words and possibly even between characters in the same word.

Setting an entire paragraph to No Break will tell InDesign to never break a line anywhere. InDesign will do as you tell it, too, *oversetting* the entire thing until such time as you resize the text frame to accommodate the entire passage on a single line, which may not be possible. If you accidentally do this, back out with Undo. If that's not an option, click in the box with the Type tool, press Cmd+A/Ctrl+A to select all (it will select even overset text you can't see), and toggle No Break off again.

UNDERLINE

Think you know all about underlining text, that there's no reason to read this section? Well…Uh. You could very well be right. *But*, skim it just in case. You can do much more with InDesign underlines than you might think.

In its most basic form, the Underline command from the Character panel flyout menu will underline selected text with a thin stroke the same color as the type. Open the Underline Options dialog from the same menu, however, and you get a lot more options (see Figure 3.16).

FIGURE 3.16

The Underline
Options dialog

What do they all mean?

Underline On (check box)   Check this option to turn on the underline.

Weight   Measured in points like any stroke, this is the thickness of the underline and may be any size from 0 to 1,000 points, in whole or decimal numbers. A drop-down menu provides several common weights. Because there are 72 points in an inch, a 1,000 pt stroke would be taller than an 8.5×11-inch page. A value in parentheses indicates Auto or the default, which is a line 1 pt thick.

Both the Weight and Offset fields enable stepping values up or down incrementally by using the arrow keys on your keyboard, by typing in values directly, by clicking the up and down arrow buttons to the left of the fields, or by selecting a common preset from the drop-down menu.

Type   Type provides a drop-down of numerous styles of stroke, which is the first step in recognizing underline as more than simple underscoring.

Offset   This field controls the vertical offset of the top of the underline from the text baseline. A setting of 0 points offset makes the top of the underline flush with the text baseline, running the text into its underline (not recommended). Valid measurements are positive 900 down to negative 900 points of vertical offset, enabling you to push the underline *above* any text smaller than 900 points tall, to create an *overscore*.

Also, because underlines underprint text—that is, when a negative offset causes overlap with the text—the text will appear in front of the underline, which helps the visibility of descenders on letters such as *j*, *g*, and *y* when the underline is a different color than the type. With a thick underline, the underlap also enables creation of a highlighter or reversed type effect on text. And that brings us to…

Color   Listed here are all the swatches from the Swatches panel, but, as with InDesign CS2, which introduced Underline and Strikethrough, there is still no means of mixing a custom color from the Underline Options dialog. To a use a custom color, you'll need to OK or cancel out of Underline Options, mix a new color on the Colors panel, create a swatch on the Swatches panel, reselect your text, and then return to Underline Options.

The (Text Color) option on this list synchronizes the underline color with the text color—when the latter changes, so will the former. Gradients may also be used for underline colors as long as you've created swatches for them.

Tint   Although you cannot create a custom color inside the dialog, you *can* choose a tint of the swatch chosen in the Color field, from 0% (paper color) to 100% (full ink color). Note that Tint is not transparency; 10% of a red stroke is opaque blush, not semitransparent red.

Overprint Stroke (check box)   *Overprinting* is the process of printing one ink color atop another ink color, possibly allowing the two to mix. For instance, a yellow underline overprinted on a blue background will almost certainly come off a printing press greenish because the blue will show through, and visually mix with, the yellow. When this option is *un*checked, overprinting only occurs when it should—when the underline color is a darker or more opaque ink than the color beneath. Otherwise, it will *knock out* the ink below the underline. Checking this option, however, forces the underline stroke to overprint regardless of its color or the ink colors beneath.

Gap Color, Gap Tint, and Overprint Gap   These options are inactive unless the underline stroke type is set to a style that includes gaps—any style other than solid. These fields perform the exact same function as their counterparts discussed previously, but they do so on the gap color of a stroke instead of the main color. With a dashed line, for example, these three fields control how, if at all, the space *between* dashes is colored. By using both colors, you can create the illusion that multiple strokes are layered without the loss of control and object management hassles of actually having separate, layered strokes.

STRIKETHROUGH

Strikethrough and the Strikethrough Options dialog (see Figure 3.17) are identical to Underline and Underline Options in nearly every respect. There are really only two differences, but they're important.

First, Strikethrough's intended purpose is to strike out text, communicating that something has been withdrawn, invalidated, or deleted without *actually* deleting text. Thus, whereas underlines underlap or underprint text, strikethrough strokes overlap, or appear in front of, type.

FIGURE 3.17

The Strikethrough
Options dialog

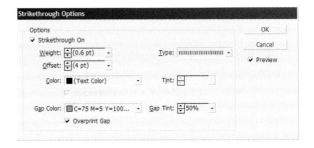

The second difference between Underline and Strikethrough is where Auto offset originates. Both strokes begin calculating offset by aligning the top of the stroke to the baseline of scored text, but, whereas Underline's auto or default setting is a small percentage below the baseline, Strikethrough's is the middle of the text, targeting vertical alignment with the x-height.

Want a design that looks like something requested from the U.S. government under the Freedom of Information Act—you know, a page wherein every word you want to read is blacked out? That's simple: Set the Strikethrough stroke weight to at least equal to the font size (usually a little more to account for descenders), and adjust its offset with negative values until the stroke completely blots out the text you want redacted. You could even be cagier than Pentagon officials by using one of the hashed stroke types with a different shade, but equally opaque, gap color.

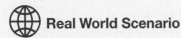 **Real World Scenario**

UNDERLINE STYLES FOR HYPERLINKS

Let's assume you've just landed a plum job as the creative director for your company's newsletter. The newsletter, which is distributed to employees, clients, and vendors, is 10 years out-of-date, and your first task as creative director is to redesign it from scratch. To save money and make the newsletter more digestible, the company also wants you to move it from paper to PDF.

PDF's ability to contain live hyperlinks will definitely help you exploit the power of the newsletter, but how much thought have you given to the types of hyperlinks you may employ? There are many different types of hyperlinks a typical corporate e-newsletter may contain—links to pages within the same PDF, links to the company website and documents thereon, as well as links to outside resources and partner websites. How are your readers to know which link will do what?

Take a cue from better Web publishers and use different underline styles to instantly identify your publications different types of hyperlinks.

1. Place or type your text—including the hyperlink candidate.

2. With the Text tool, highlight the text to be linked and that will be underlined to show the link.

3. Open the Character panel, and from its panel flyout menu, select Underline Options toward the bottom. This will open the Underline Options dialog box.

4. First, turn on Preview on the right, and then check Underline On. You should immediately see your selected text underlined.

If you've used paragraph rules or at least strokes, the controls in this dialog should be familiar. Weight is the thickness of the underline, with a drop-down list of common sizes, or you may type in any value. Offset is how far below the baseline the underline should begin. Again, you may choose a common preset value from the drop-down list or type in your own. Both the Weight and Offset value fields may also be controlled with the up and down arrow keys. Type is InDesign's stroke types—identical to the Stroke panel. Any preexisting swatch may be used as the color of the underline, or it may be left at its default, which is the same color as the text. Choosing any swatch but (Text Color) None and Paper will enable the Tint field. Gap Color and Gap Tint activate only if the underline type is one that includes gaps of some sort—anything but Solid, really. Gap colors take the place of having to layer multiple objects to achieve a two-tone dotted stroke.

5. Set up your external hyperlink underline how you like. Most users are accustomed to a solid, single underline that is the same color as the text (which you should change from black to a contrasting color like blue, green, or red). When ready, hit OK. Don't forget to actually assign the URL on InDesign's Hyperlinks panel.

Not so tough, is it? Well, it may not be tough, but it is tedious if you have more than a couple of external hyperlink underlines to format. Save yourself some time and make a character style for this particular underline. Thus, underlining more text is simply a matter of highlighting and then clicking on the style entry in the Character Styles panel.

Set up your other underlines' styles the same way, making character style sheets for each of them, too. Make them all obviously hyperlinks by changing their text and underline colors from the color of the surrounding copy, but don't go overboard. Thin single, double, dashed, or dotted lines tend to serve readers well.

In the passage from my favorite corporate newsletter, I used the following styles:

◆ Links to other pages and resources within the same PDF were done in blue, with a dashed underline.

◆ URLs for company-owned resources such as intranet systems (the Acme Customer First Order Center) and links to documents on the company's public website (the newsletter's 1Q2006 issue) were colored green and given a double underline.

◆ External resources, such as those for the *Albuquerque Gazette* review and the partner's site, which take the reader away from company-controlled materials, are styled with a single, solid underline and colored red to closely approximate familiar Web hyperlink formatting.

In Same Document

Intranet/Company Controlled

External Resource

THE CONTROL PANEL CHARACTER MODE

Wouldn't it be great if there were an easier way to get to commands such as Superscript, Subscript, All Caps, Small Caps, Underline, and Strikethrough? Buttons! *That's* what would be *really* slick, buttons to click for those commands, on or off. Wouldn't that be cool? Adobe thought so, that's why they built it (Figure 3.18).

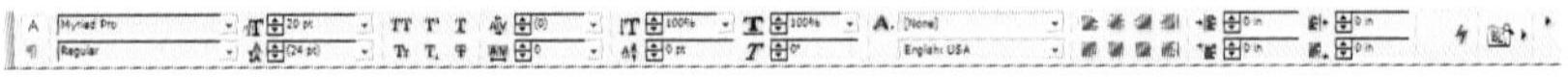

FIGURE 3.18

The Control panel in Character mode

Everything you can do from the Character panel you can also do from the Control panel, with the added benefit of a half dozen buttons for commands otherwise stuck two clicks away on the Character panel flyout menu. New in CS3, even some of the Paragraph panel options are there, such as paragraph alignment and left, right, first line, and last line indents.

Just select the Type tool and the Control panel automatically switches into Character or Paragraph mode. To toggle between the two, click either the A button or the ¶ button, respectively, at the left edge of the panel. In Paragraph mode, some character-level settings are available as well: for example, Font Family, Type Style, Font Size, Leading, and even buttons for Superscript, Subscript, All Caps, Small Caps, Underline, and Strikethrough.

All this raises the question, *Do you really need the Character and Paragraph panels?* If you asked me the same question about InDesign CS1 or CS2, I would resoundingly say, "Yes, you need the individual panels." That's because, in those versions, the Control panel wasn't complete. Even with a flyout menu that changed per mode, the Control panel simply lacked the full depth of settings and commands the individual panels had. With CS3, however, the Control panel has matured and now serves as a full replacement for those dedicated panels.

Whether you want to get rid of them and save some much needed screen real estate is up to you. Use either or both.

Special Characters

On the Type menu are a couple of submenus that make insertion of symbols, marks, and numerous sizes and types of spaces much easier than using difficult-to-remember keyboard shortcuts.

Insert Special Character

Skipping the Markers section, which we'll cover in later chapters, here are the different symbols, dashes, quotation marks, and other marks accessible from the Insert Special Character menu. Table 3.1 is the first, the Symbols menu.

Special characters will insert using the type style in effect at the place of insertion. If your cursor is resting among text styled as Myriad Pro Black Semi-Extended 12/15.5 when you choose Type ➤ Insert Special Character ➤ Symbol ➤ Copyright Symbol, InDesign will insert the Copyright symbol drawn into the Myriad Pro Black Semi-Extended font, at 12 pt on 15.5 pt leading. If the requested symbol (or space, as below), wasn't built into the typeface by the designer, nothing will insert or, with low-quality fonts, you'll get an empty box. If either happens, style the symbol as another font that *does* have the requested glyph.

The Hyphens and Dashes menu begins with Em Dash (—) and En Dash (–), which are undoubtedly familiar. The latter pair, Discretionary Hyphen and Nonbreaking Hyphen, might require a little more explanation, however.

TABLE 3.1: **Symbols**

MENU COMMAND	SYMBOL	DESCRIPTION
Bullet Character	•	A bullet, middle-dot, or waisted dot character.
Copyright Symbol	©	The good old *C*-in-a-circle.
Ellipsis	…	The ellipsis is not the same as three periods. It's actually three dots smaller than periods with thin spaces between.
Paragraph Symbol	¶	More correctly called the pilcrow, the paragraph marker denotes a hard return or enables references to specific paragraphs.
Registered Trademark Symbol	®	Used when a trademark has been registered with the USPTO.
Section Symbol	§	The double-*S* section symbol.
Trademark Symbol	™	The standard trademark symbol.

A discretionary hyphen is, at most times, an invisible character—a marker really. Placing a discretionary hyphen in a word not at the end of a wrapping line of text has no apparent effect. With Show Hidden Characters active, you'll see it marked as invisible (see Figure 3.19), but the word won't hyphenate—unless InDesign decides it needs to wrap the line somewhere around the word containing the discretionary hyphen. When that happens, InDesign will hyphenate and wrap the word where you specified, even ignoring whatever syllabic breakdown is included in the dictionary for the same word. In this way, you can tell InDesign, *I know better than you, and I want this word broken at this point if it must break.* You can even put multiple discretionary hyphens in a single word, which is useful for longer or ad hoc compound words whose syllables or parts you want broken a certain way.

FIGURE 3.19
A discretionary hyphen, visible when hidden characters are shown

Amalgamated·the·flav

Nonbreaking hyphens, as the name implies, are the opposite of discretionary hyphens. They *do* show a hyphen, but InDesign will *not* wrap at the point of the hyphen.

Take a compound word like the partners' names in *Auchman-Reynolds Holdings.* It's a proper name, and it's extremely bad form to break the two constituent partner names apart across lines. Generally speaking, leaving a larger than normal right-edge gap is preferable to breaking a compound proper name (we already covered ways to tweak surrounding text and mitigate the damage). Because, as typed, that's a normal, visible hyphen in there and InDesign looks to hyphens as the first obvious break point when *Auchman-Reynolds* won't fit on one line, InDesign will break it after *Auchman-.* To prevent that, replace the normal hyphen with its nonbreaking variant and InDesign will never break the two words apart. It may still try to break *Auchman* or *Reynolds* syllabically— that's where the No Break command on the Character panel comes in—but it won't sever the two at the hyphen—well, almost never. If a column is too narrow to fit the entire *Auchman-Reynolds* on a single line, leaving InDesign stuck between oversetting the text or breaking it at the hyphen, InDesign will choose the latter option despite the nonbreaking hyphen.

Next on the Insert Special Character menu is the Quotation Marks submenu (see Table 3.2).

TABLE 3.2:   Quotation Marks

MENU COMMAND	SYMBOL	DESCRIPTION
Double Left Quotation Marks	"	Left or opening curly quotes or typographer's quotes.
Double Right Quotation Marks	"	Right or closing curly quotes or typographer's quotes.
Single Left Quotation Mark	'	Left or opening single quotation mark.
Single Right Quotation Mark	'	Right or closing single quotation mark. Also called an apostrophe.
Straight Double Quotation Marks	″	Inch or minute hash mark.
Straight Single Quotation Mark	′	Foot or second hash mark.

Finally, the Other menu includes additional special characters (see Table 3.3), which are each covered in greater depth in later chapters in context.

TABLE 3.3:   Other Special Characters

MENU COMMAND	DESCRIPTION
Tab	A standard tab, just like pressing the Tab key on the keyboard.
Right Indent Tab	Used in conjunction with the Last Line Right Indent field on the Paragraph panel to add a hanging indent to the right side of a paragraph's last line.
Indent to Here	Allows selective indentation of the left side of a paragraph independent of the value of the Left Indent field on the Paragraph panel.
End Nested Style Here	When nested styles are used, this marker ends the nested style up to, and inclusive of, this marker in the text.
Non-Joiner	A zero-width non-joiner character that keeps two glyphs that would normally overlap as separate glyphs. This is most often used with script typefaces to prevent their tails from merging and with certain non-Latin written languages where two glyphs combine or partially combine.

White Space Characters

All spaces are not created equal. That horizontal bar on your keyboard creates a full space. Over the centuries, typesetters have developed numerous other spaces to satisfy many more situations than can a full space. In days not as distant as you might think, *hot-lead* typesetting fonts included numerous strips of metal or wood at varying widths to afford precise spacing under any circumstances (a font was the complete boxed set of a given typeface's glyph blocks).

InDesign 1–CS2 brought in many of the most common spaces—em, en, flush, hair, thin, figure, punctuation, and nonbreaking full spaces—but CS3 adds even more. If you're a converted QuarkXPress user who misses 3-, 4-, or 6-per-Em-Space, rejoice; InDesign CS3 has expanded its space offerings. Table 3.4 lists them; follow along in Figure 3.20, which shows all the spaces in use.

FIGURE 3.20
Examples of all the spaces available in InDesign CS3. The same samples displayed with Show Hidden Characters off (left) and on (right).

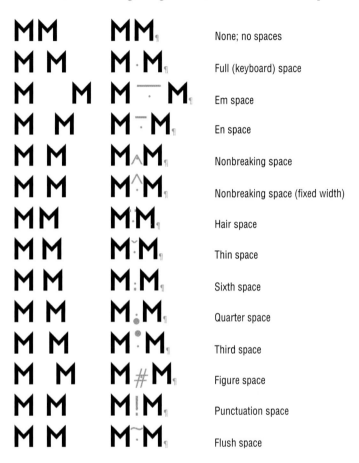

None; no spaces

Full (keyboard) space

Em space

En space

Nonbreaking space

Nonbreaking space (fixed width)

Hair space

Thin space

Sixth space

Quarter space

Third space

Figure space

Punctuation space

Flush space

TABLE 3.4:   InDesign Space Types

SPACE	DESCRIPTION
Em Space	Like an em dash, this space is (theoretically) as wide as the typeface's capital *M*.
En Space	The width of an en dash and approximately half the width of an em space.
Nonbreaking Space	A standard (full) width space that will connect the words or glyphs on either side, disallowing them from breaking across lines. Like a normal space, the nonbreaking space may shrink or grow as needed during composition to evenly distribute words in a line.

continued

TABLE 3.4: **InDesign Space Types** (*continued*)

SPACE	DESCRIPTION
Nonbreaking Space (Fixed Width)	Similar to a standard nonbreaking space except that it will remain at a fixed size, resisting composition attempts to increase or decrease its width.
Hair Space	The thinnest available space, used when only a tiny amount of extra white space is required (e.g., on either end of an em dash, between initials in a proper name or acronym, or to assist in fitting other punctuation, symbols, or characters alternative to kerning or tracking).
Thin Space	Slightly wider than a hair space and used for the same purposes.
Sixth Space	⅙ of the width of an em space.
Quarter Space	¼ of the width of an em space.
Third Space	⅓ of the width of an em space.
Figure Space	The width of the typeface's *lining* numerals, often used to help align figures and numbers.
Punctuation Space	The width of the typeface's period. This is often used in place of hair space when the hair and thin spaces are too narrow.
Flush Space	This is a very important type of space. It's a variable-width space that widens to fill the last line of a justified paragraph. Normal composition would, in this case, either leave text flush to the left (possibly creating orphans) or, when the last line is set to full justification, stretch the spaces between all words until the line is filled. However, inserting a flush space causes all *other* words' spaces to remain constant while the flush space is expanded to consume whatever emptiness remains. If you've ever tabbed out the last line to flush-right alignment—say, to insert an endmark to close a magazine article—the flush space can take the place of the tab.

OpenType

The final frontier of cross-platform, multilanguage, and advanced typography has been tamed. OpenType fonts fix most of the woes of digital typography—and open entire worlds of typographic freedom and control.

WHAT IS OPENTYPE?

OpenType was conceived and developed as, and *is*, a complete replacement for all other font formats—for use with nearly all current and *future* written languages.

Earlier we talked about font glyph tables—how every letter, numeral, mark, and symbol has a slot to hold it in the font table. TrueType and PostScript fonts have a limit of 256 unique glyphs—256 slots in their font tables. With Latin-based languages having only 26 capital and 26 lowercase letters, 10 numerals, and about 60 common punctuation marks and symbols, 256 works. Oh, wait. That's just for English, which doesn't have any accented characters in its normal written language. We can't forget about French, Spanish, Italian, and Portuguese. Then there are *ligatures*. There are more symbols, too, such as the Euro, which isn't in either the Type 1 or TrueType specifications because it didn't exist when they were written. Hmm. A font table of 256 is starting to look cramped.

Even squeezing all those in, non-Latin character sets won't fit in there. Completely different fonts will need to be designed and distributed for German, Swahili, Chinese, Japanese, Korean, Vietnamese, Russian, and so on.

Even if non-Latin languages are of no consequence to your work, small caps, discretionary ligatures, swashes, alternative glyph versions, and several differently styled sets of numerals *should* be. Oh! Then we're going to need bold, italic, bold italic, and roman styles of the main typeface as well as such styles of small caps, discretionary ligatures, swashes, alternative glyph versions, and several differently styled sets of numerals. And those are just the basics; we haven't even touched on other weights like light, medium, semi-bold, heavy, extra bold, and black or different scales such as condensed, semi-condensed, extended, semi-extended…

How many fonts *does* one designer have to manage these days? It's starting to get complicated, isn't it?

Raise curtain. Cue OpenType.

Whereas a Type 1 or TrueType font can hold only 256 characters, OpenType's *Unicode* font table has 65,536 predefined slots. Allow me to put that in perspective. A single font can contain the complete glyph sets from Arabic, Armenian, Bengali, Braille embossing patterns, Canadian Aboriginal Syllabics, Cherokee, Coptic, Cyrillic, Devanāgarī, Ethiopic, Georgian, Greek, Gujarati, Gurmukhi (Punjabi), Han (Kanji, Hanja, Hanzi), Hangul (Korean), Hebrew, Hiragana and Katakana (Japanese), International Phonetic Alphabet (IPA), Khmer (Cambodian), Kannada, Lao, Latin, Malayalam, Mongolian, Myanmar (Burmese), Oriya, Syriac, Tamil, Telugu, Thai, Tibetan, Tifinagh, Yi, and Zhuyin (Bopomofo). Even *after* all those are added, there's room for several languages yet to be included (übergeeks are seriously considering adding Star Trek's Klingon and two Elven scripts from J.R.R. Tolkien's *Lord of the Rings* trilogy), thousands of variations of other characters, and a "private use" area for approximately 130,000 nonstandard custom or regional characters.

Let's scale the discussion down to a typical, English language document. One OpenType font can contain the complete upper- and lowercase alphabet, plus several versions of each, including sets drawn as small caps, swash caps, and other derivations. Maybe, in an invitation like Figure 3.21, you'd rather something with a few more touches of style than the one for the example on the left. The one on the right uses the same two OpenType fonts—Arcana GMM Std and Adobe Caslon Pro—but with slight differences owing to alternate glyphs in those fonts.

FIGURE 3.21
The same typefaces, using alternate glyphs contained in their OpenType character sets

Subsequently we'll get into how to apply different OpenType effects and to access all the glyphs in a particular font. Before we do, there's one other thing I'd like to note: OpenType fonts are completely cross-platform, unlike Type 1 or TrueType fonts (Mac OS X can use Windows TrueType fonts, but not vice versa).

CROSS-PLATFORM AT LAST

The same OTF file Dad uses on his iMac can go to cousin Charlie's Windows Vista computer. *Yeah, so? What does that mean to* me?

It means no more empty boxes in place of copyright symbols. No more text reflow when a Windows-based designer sends a document for touch-up and RIP (raster image processing) on a Mac. No more having to whip out Fontographer or FontLab to violate your font license by converting your Mac-based colleague's fonts just so you can touch up a couple of text frames.

OpenType fonts are 100% cross-platform—the only place Windows or Mac matters any more is your personal preference. InDesign documents are cross-platform. Images such as TIFF, JPEG, EPS, and even PSD and AI have been reliably cross-platform compatible for years. The last impediment to creative document operating system homogeny was platform-dependent fonts. OpenType knocks down that barrier, allowing any creative person—Windows or Mac—to work with colleagues on either without fear that something in the document will change from one computer to the next. In fact, OpenType even works on most Unix-based operating systems.

UPGRADING TO OPENTYPE FONTS

Adobe OpenType fonts are all identified on Font Family and other menus by either *Pro* or *Std* after the family name, which differentiates them from Adobe Type 1 fonts. Pro OpenTypes are those that take advantage of the larger OpenType font table, including a larger set of special characters, while Std (standard) typefaces are merely those that Adobe converted directly from their earlier Type 1 incarnations without adding additional glyphs.

Unfortunately, Adobe's lead has not been followed by every type foundry, some of whom have not altered their font names at all from TrueType or Type 1 through OpenType versions. TrueType and Type 1 are dying (not dead), so keep your eyes open for new OpenType versions of old favorites. As soon as you replace a Type 1 or TrueType font with an OpenType version, pull the other versions out of your active fonts and stash them away somewhere, only to be used for older document compatibility.

USING OPENTYPE FEATURES

Support for OpenType fonts is built into Windows 2000, Millennium Edition, XP, and Vista and, on the Mac, into OS 9 and X. Therefore every application that runs natively in those environments— except FileMaker Pro!—recognizes and can use OpenType fonts without special add-ins.

InDesign 2.0, released in January 2002, was the first application in the world to use OpenType fonts' extended features. Its brethren Illustrator and Photoshop quickly followed suit, and a couple of years later, so did QuarkXPress.

On the Character panel's flyout menu, the OpenType menu grants access to toggles that turn on or off various OpenType features (see Figure 3.22). Highlight text on the page, navigate through the Character panel flyout menu to the OpenType submenu, and click the appropriate command to enable or disable its effect. Features encased in brackets ([]) are not present in the currently selected font.

Discretionary Ligatures

Ligatures are special glyphs drawn to avoid awkward pairings of letters. For instance, in Figure 3.23, pairings such as *ff, fi, ft*, and others awkwardly collide with each other. The upper teardrop of the *f* in *fi*, for instance, collides with the dot in the *i*. Consequently, type designers long ago developed special glyphs called ligatures that, like the lower set in the same figure, combine the two characters into a single, more elegant shape. Standard ligatures are turned off or on via the Character panel flyout menu's Ligature command. It's on by default, which is a good thing.

FIGURE 3.22
The OpenType
menu, showing
options for Adobe's
Caflisch Script Pro
OpenType font

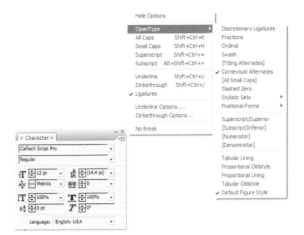

FIGURE 3.23
Certain character
pairings cause awk-
ward collisions (top)
that are resolved by
ligatures (bottom).

fi fj fl ff ffi ffl ft
fi fj fl ff ffi ffl ft

Standard ligatures are nothing new—they've been in our fonts for decades. But, two aspects *are* new to OpenType.

A ligature has traditionally been a single character; the *ffi* ligature, for example, ceased to be *f-f-i*. Running a spell check on a document containing ligatures invariably flagged words containing ligatures as misspelled. No longer. Not with OpenType.

It comes down to the difference between characters and glyphs. A character is, well, a character—letter, number, punctuation, symbol. A glyph is any form a character or another mark might take. In OpenType, the dot over the lowercase *i* is actually contained within a different table cell from the stalk of the letter. Every time InDesign or another OpenType-aware application draws an *i*, it's actually combining two cells in the table to form a single character. When the *i* is part of an *fi* ligature, the dot is simply left off. The *ffi* ligature is actually three separate cells—the *f* twice, or as in the preceding example, two different versions of an *f*, depending on the typeface and usage, and the *i*'s stalk—combined into a single glyph. (The examples in Figure 3.23 are set using the Adobe Caslon Pro Regular typeface.)

While ligatures *look* like a single character, and in most ways *act* like one as well, they are not (see Figure 3.24). Behind the scenes, the technology built into OpenType still understands that *ffi* is *f-f-i*—and so does InDesign's spell checker. You can even copy text containing ligatures from an InDesign document and paste into applications that don't comprehend ligatures, like Windows Notepad or Mac's SimpleText; upon pasting, the ligatures will disappear, revealing the separate *f-f-i* characters. This is a function of OpenType itself, not InDesign, although a robust OpenType interpretation engine is required for an application to correctly understand and use glyphs.

Because of all the extra room afforded by OpenType's Unicode font table, additional ligatures beyond the most common appear in some OpenType fonts (see Figure 3.25). Pairings like *ct* and *st*, for example, can be joined with what are called discretionary ligatures—ligatures that you may or may not want to include. Other discretionary ligatures are variations on the default, obligatory ligatures. They add a nice touch once in a while, but they aren't for every document.

FIGURE 3.25
Discretionary ligatures (bottom) stylize the appearance of some character pairings.

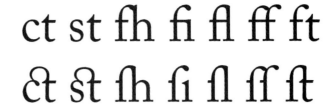

Fractions

How much can OpenType really improve fractions? For many years, most fonts have shipped with common fractions built in—¼ ½ ¾. Yes, they have, and those are great until you need something like ⅔, ⅒, or ⁵⁄₆₂₁. At that point, what have you typically done? Right: You superscript the numerator and subscript the denominator, adjust their baseline shifts, and then kern them together with a standard slash (/). It's a hack, but it's served us well over the years. Predictably, OpenType does it better without hacks (see Figure 3.26).

FIGURE 3.26
Typed numbers and slashes before using the OpenType ➤ Fractions command (top) and after (bottom).

1/4 1/2 1/3 5/8 1/288 5/621

¼ ½ ⅓ ⅝ ¹⁄₂₈₈ ⁵⁄₆₂₁

Assuming you're using an OpenType font that includes them (my examples use Adobe Myriad Pro and Adobe Caslon Pro, both of which do), you may have two complete sets of numerals in addition to the full-size set—0–9 as numerator, and 0–9 as denominator (see Figure 3.27). These will be numerals located respectively in the upper-left or lower-right corners of the font table cell; they are already in the right place for a fraction and don't need to be super- or subscripted. More importantly, they'll be drawn with stroke weights that match full size numerals and other glyphs in the font.

FIGURE 3.27
Adobe Caslon's different numerals. Top to bottom: standard full-size, numerator, and denominator, all shown at 30 pt.

0	1	2	3	4	5	6	7	8	9
0	1	2	3	4	5	6	7	8	9
0	1	2	3	4	5	6	7	8	9

As you can see in Figure 3.28, creating fractions with the age-old superscript and subscript workaround merely reduces the size of the numerals. Their stroke weights scale proportionately, making the digits obviously scaled and looking rather spindly and out of place compared to surrounding text. Additionally, the separator between them is a slash, not a *solidus*. Some would argue as vehemently against that incorrect glyph usage as I do against using three periods instead of a correct ellipsis.

FIGURE 3.28
(Top) Fractions faked with superscript, subscript, baseline shift, and kerning. (Bottom) Proper fractions using numerals drawn to be numerators and denominators, as well as proper solidi.

3¾ Tbsp.   1½ cups   5⁄9 inch
3¾ Tbsp.   1½ cups   5⁄9 inch

Compare the two lines. Which set of fractions looks out of place? Which matches its surrounding text? Here's a more pragmatic difference between them: For just three sets of fractions. it took me almost four minutes to set all the numbers as superscript or subscript and adjust their baselines and kerning—and I used keyboard shortcuts to speed up that work versus doing it via menus and the Character panel fields. Even having to make three trips to the OpenType menu, creating the proper fractions took me less than 10 seconds.

Not only do OpenType fractions yield better typography, they're faster and easier. Just type your fractions, highlight all three parts—numerator, slash, and denominator—and select Fractions from the OpenType menu. InDesign and the font take care of the rest.

As in ligatures, all the characters in a fraction remain individually editable. Did you mean to type *5/8* instead of *5/9*? No problem: Highlight the *9* and type over it.

Ordinals

Ordinals, or ordinal numbers, denote a position in an ordered sequence—*first, second, third,* and so on. In this usage, ordinals refer to shortened ordinals—*1st, 2nd, 3rd,* and so on—specifically the textual portion that comes after the number. As with fractions, pre-OpenType era required superscripting the textual portion to produce stylish shortened ordinal numbers. And, as with fractions, that's no longer necessary with a typeface such as Adobe Caslon Pro that includes drawn-to-size letters for ordinals (see Figure 3.29).

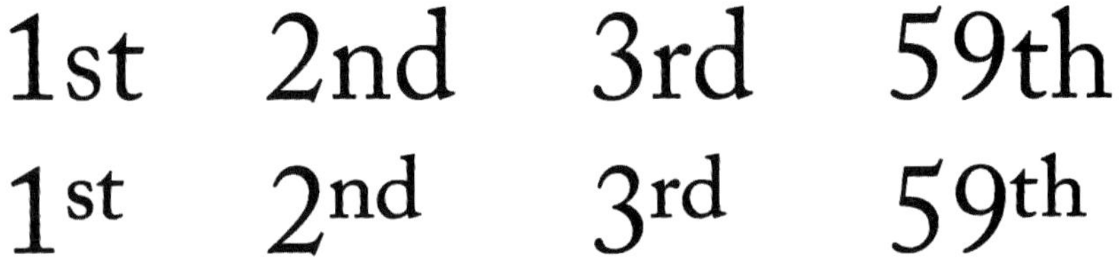

FIGURE 3.29
Ordinals before (top) and after (bottom) choosing Ordinal from the OpenType menu

What may not be immediately apparent is that InDesign is actually reading the text. If I had typed *ph* instead of *th* in the last item, *59th,* InDesign would not have swapped the full-size *ph* for ordinal versions; they would have remained full-size because InDesign (and the OpenType font, which does a lot of the thinking itself) is smart enough to know that *ninth* is an ordinal but *ninph* is gibberish.

Swash

Swashes (see Figure 3.30) are those extra special touches we used to manually add from separate fonts that included nothing but swashed variants of letters. With OpenType, InDesign can replace appropriate glyphs with swashed versions just from this one menu command (again, as long as there are swash glyphs in the font). Better, as with ligatures, spell check continues to work, which wasn't always so when we used swashes from alternate fonts.

FIGURE 3.30
Bickham Script Pro is an elegant typeface on its own (top), but a few swashes (bottom) can really make it special.

Titling Alternates

Titling variants are designed to enhance readability when type is set at large sizes, such as in article headlines. As a matter of necessity, titling typefaces used to be separate fonts. Now, as with Dante MT Std (see Figure 3.31), they can coexist in the same typeface with uppercase, lowercase, and small cap sets.

Contextual Alternates

Of all the cool features of OpenType, Contextual Alternates is…well, it's my second favorite, really, after multiple numeral styles. But, man, it's wicked cool.

FIGURE 3.31
(Top) Standard all caps in Dante MT Std. (Bottom) The same line with Titling Alternates activated from the Open Type menu.

MASTERING INDESIGN CS3
MASTERING INDESIGN CS3

OpenType fonts are not just font tables, not dumb code collecting a bunch of vector outlines. They're intelligent software, and under the direction of an equally intelligent type rendering engine such as InDesign's, the results can be brilliant (see Figure 3.32).

FIGURE 3.32
Contextual Alternates turned off (top) and on (bottom)

The quick brown fox jumped over the lazy grey dog.

The quick brown fox jumped over the lazy grey dog.

In my example, I used Adobe's Caflisch Script Pro, the showcase typeface for OpenType contextual alternates. Look closely at the circled characters and parts of characters. Compare repeated letters such as the lowercase *o* or *e*. Notice that specific instances of each letter are different from other instances, how some are allowed to connect to the next letter while others are denied connection depending on their positions in words and on the shapes of surrounding glyphs. InDesign, once again, *reads the text* and looks beyond the single glyph, analyzing the shapes of surrounding glyphs and spaces to choose from among the available versions of a given letter for the best fit, the best interaction, the best aesthetic. Take the lowercase *d* as shown in *jumped* and *dog*. In the former instance, the *d* is given a stylized ascender that helps it connect through the preceding glyphs; in the second, the ascender is straight and demure, confining the *d* to the short word.

This particular feature of OpenType introduces to the digital age one of the most important aspects of typesetting not seen outside manual typesetting: subtlety.

Typing a line like the first in Figure 3.32, all instances of a single letter will be identical—one *e* is identical to the next *e*. We've come to expect this because we're asking a computer to grab a shape from a table cell; we're not pulling lead blocks from a font case. If you turn on Contextual Alternates and *then* begin typing, you can actually watch glyphs exchange on-the-fly, depending on the characters that precede or succeed each, whether a given glyph starts or ends a word, if you enter punctuation marks.

All Small Caps

You know all about small caps by now, and you know you can convert lowercase to small caps or mixed-case type to uppercase and small caps from the appropriate command on the Character panel flyout menu. The difference between that command and this is that the one on the Open Type menu will convert *all* letters to small caps, even uppercase ones (see Figure 3.33).

As with all OpenType features, the OpenType ➤ All Small Caps command only appears active (without brackets) if the OpenType font contains genuine small caps—glyphs drawn at that size with stroke weights matching normal sized glyphs. In a bit of fortuitous oddity, however, *either* small caps command will *use* genuine small caps instead of scaling uppercase down (if they exist in the font, of course).

MARY HAD A LITTLE LAMB. IT WAS SALTY.

MARY HAD A LITTLE LAMB. IT WAS SALTY.

Slashed Zero

Sometimes the capital letter *O* and the numeral *0* (zero) are drawn so similarly that distinguishing them can be difficult—especially when they're close together such as in a phrase like "10:00 O'Clock" or an SKU, serial, or other number such as the one in Figure 3.34. Other times, you just want a little more style. Consequently, many OpenType fonts include a slashed zero as part of their glyph sets. The singular function of this particular command is to replace standard zeros in the selected type with their more obviously null, slashed counterparts.

STOCK NO. 000012AO0603

STOCK NO. 0̸0̸0̸012AO0̸603

Stylistic Sets

Stylistic sets are an expansion of contextual alternates, allowing up to 12 different sets of contextual alternates. Moreover, they can be selectively applied to text. For example, you might use several sets to ensure that no two instances of the letter *e* in a title or sentence are the same *e*. Available sets (if any) are built by the type designer, which affords her more than one or two opportunities to express type design ideas. All those variants that never made it into a font, that were left only in the type designer's sketchbook, can now be made available for our use (this is a good thing for both type designers and graphic designers). Because stylistic sets are typically groups of stylistic alternates rather than single glyphs, the type designer can apply a cohesive aesthetic, changing several characters at once to match each other (see Figure 3.35).

To date, very few OpenType fonts include many stylistic sets; however, now that InDesign has created a user interface to make use of them, look for more to appear, broadening the creative and stylistic possibilities of fonts. Garamond Premier Pro is one family that does include stylistic sets—three of them—with subtle differences primarily in accented characters.

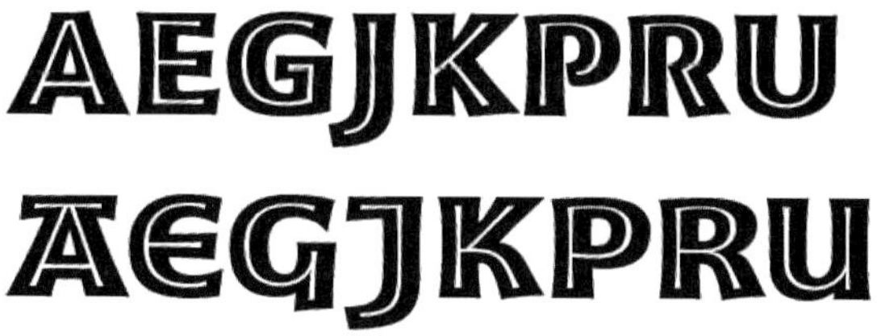

FIGURE 3.35
Although not
defined as a stylistic
set, Moonglow Bold
Extended includes
several related sty-
listic alternates:
"normal" letters
(top) and stylistic
alternates (bottom).

AEGJKPRU
AEGJKPRU

Positional Forms

Glyphs that vary their shape depending on where in a word they appear are called positional
forms. For instance, a *g* at the beginning of a word may look different from a *g* at the end or in the
middle. Positional forms are most common in script fonts and non-Latin, script-style language
fonts such as Arabic. Table 3.5 defines the potentially available positional forms to which InDesign's
Character panel OpenType ➢ Positional Forms menu offers access.

TABLE 3.5:   Positional Forms

POSITIONAL FORM	DESCRIPTION
General	The most common glyphs and variants
Automatic	Automatic alteration of the positional form based on where in the word the glyph appears
Initial	A glyph at the beginning of a word
Medial	A glyph in the middle of a word
Final	A glyph at the end of a word
Isolated	A glyph appearing alone, as a single character

Positional Numerals

If drawn into the typeface, the four commands here—Superscript/Superior, Subscript/Inferior,
Numerator, and Denominator—will intelligently replace figures in the selected text with the
appropriate, purpose-drawn numerals. Such numerals will have been drawn at the correct size for
each of these uses, with stroke weights matching surrounding glyphs and in the correct positions:
for example, numerator digits are drawn in the upper-left corner of the font table cell.

Generally, to create fractions, simply use the OpenType menu Fractions command. However,
under certain circumstances, such as with large-number or decimal number fractions, OpenType ➢
Fractions may fail to properly format the fraction or may leave out certain digits. In those cases,
manually select the numerator and denominator and apply the appropriate commands.

If a font does not contain one or another feature, use the other, similar positional numeral setting ahead of a faux effect. For instance, if your chosen OpenType font lists Superscript/Superior bracketed, try selecting Numerator ahead of the Character panel menu Superscript command, which is a faux superscript affected by scaling and shifting a full-size numeral.

Figure Styles

Undoubtedly my favorite of all OpenType powers is the ability to easily use different styles of numerals appropriate to the situation. Please tell me you recognize that typewriter numbers—0123456789—are not the only style we have. In fact, for most of us, those should be the *least* often used. There are four styles, as you can see from Figure 3.36, which show off the sets available in Adobe Caslon Pro Regular.

FIGURE 3.36
Figure styles available in Adobe Caslon Pro Regular: (from top to bottom) Tabular Lining, Proportional Oldstyle, Proportional Lining, and Tabular Oldstyle.

0123456789

0123456789

0123456789

0123456789

What are all these and when should I use each?

Tabular numerals, as you can see in the first and last lines, are numerals that align vertically. Each numeral is set in an equal-width cell, monospaced, allowing the numerals to be aligned tabularly, such as one might see in a list—prices, scores, statistics, and so on. Proportional numerals, by contrast, are treated like letters; they have variable widths, and thus they have variable inter-character spacing. You definitely don't want to use a proportional style for vertical number lists because they won't align properly and will make the reader's eye work far too hard to compare one line to the next (see Figure 3.37).

FIGURE 3.37
Tabular numerals (right) work much better for vertically aligned numbers than do proportional numerals (left).

Bananas	.99 lb	Bananas	.99 lb
Oranges	1.15 lb	Oranges	1.15 lb
Apples	.67 lb	Apples	.67 lb
Peaches	2.21 lb	Peaches	2.21 lb

The contrast between lining and oldstyle is vertical rather than horizontal, as opposed to tabular and proportional. Lining numerals are cap height, which makes them great for tabular data but lousy for putting in a paragraph of text. In Figure 3.38 you can see the difference between the two.

Squint or just quickly slide your eyes over the two paragraphs. Which set of numbers immediately jumps out at you? Right, the lining. The problem is, numbers *shouldn't* jump out at you.

FIGURE 3.38
Lining numerals (left) stick out of the text abnormally, while oldstyle numerals (right) blend, becoming only important where they should—in context.

Alis delit vel ea acipiscilis ea auguer irit autat ecte tie dolortisisci tisit, quissed tionsed tin volorperit ad eu feugait aliqui ea augiam inciliqui estincilit eummodio od magna faci blan ullamcor 1949 aliquamcon ut nissed magna adit nulla feuguer sit prat. Ut prat illa adiat, vero od delit, vent ing ex ex et nim iuscin ecte ex exero commy nosto 18 March 1972 conum volore eum vel iure tate magna feugait at ipsum volent adigniat lut iril ectem ero odolor ipit eugiamcon ver alit nulputat, velisci duipit ulla amcorpercip 1936–39 exerili ssequam alis nis amcoreet loreet lutpat. Faccumm olobore tate dit praessi smolobor sed dipis dolor sim quis dolore commy nim ex exercil iquismo dignism odolestrud modiamc onsequat, 15,000 vel utpat, quatem ercillam nit, quis endrer sum ipsusci llaorpe riurerate magnit acin ute exeraestrud dunt nullam zzriustrud dolum venibh ero eu feuisis alit num inim ip et ▫

Alis delit vel ea acipiscilis ea auguer irit autat ecte tie dolortisisci tisit, quissed tionsed tin volorperit ad eu feugait aliqui ea augiam inciliqui estincilit eummodio od magna faci blan ullamcor 1949 aliquamcon ut nissed magna adit nulla feuguer sit prat. Ut prat illa adiat, vero od delit, vent ing ex ex et nim iuscin ecte ex exero commy nosto 18 March 1972 conum volore eum vel iure tate magna feugait at ipsum volent adigniat lut iril ectem ero odolor ipit eugiamcon ver alit nulputat, velisci duipit ulla amcorpercip 1936–39 exerili ssequam alis nis amcoreet loreet lutpat. Faccumm olobore tate dit praessi smolobor sed dipis dolor sim quis dolore commy nim ex exercil iquismo dignism odolestrud modiamc onsequat, 15,000 vel utpat, quatem ercillam nit, quis endrer sum ipsusci llaorpe riurerate magnit acin ute exeraestrud dunt nullam zzriustrud dolum venibh ero eu feuisis alit num inim ip et ▫

Within paragraph text, *nothing* should ever jump out at the reader by virtue of its mere existence. See the word *nothing* in the preceding sentence? That *should* jump out at you because *I* want it to. I deliberately used italic. Thus, emphasis is under *my* control, not the font's. *I'm* the content creator. *I'm* in control of my content and its style. (Well, me and the graphic designer who laid out this book…and my publisher, the editorial team who are going back and forth about whether my rhetorical questions to you should be quoted or italicized…*Sigh.* You get my point.)

Numerals that appear within sentences and paragraphs *must* be considered of equal import with the text that buoys them. That text is seesaw, up and down, with capitals and lowercase and x-height-based letterforms that have ascenders and descenders. It's about shape. Capitals always exact attention, even when they shouldn't, as do lining numerals, even jerking a reader's eye away from reading and comprehending sentences above and below. They diminish the importance and readability of surrounding text. Oldstyle numerals, however, don't compete; they blend to become important only in context. If you *want* emphasis, use italic, bold, underlining, color—*something you can control from instance to instance*. When you set lining numerals among mixed-case text, you lose control and elevate the numbers to a higher status than the text that describes them and gives them context.

Of course, setting numbers among all caps type, use proportional lining rather than oldstyle. The goal in all cases is to make the numerals a natural part of the text surrounding them, not the central focus to the detriment, and partial exclusion, of that text.

Glyphs Panel

Now that you know all the automated ways of inserting special characters and accessing Open-Type features and how to access various glyphs predefined by the type designer as alternates for different situations, let's talk about where you can access every glyph in an OpenType—or other—font at a moment's notice.

The Glyphs panel (see Figure 3.39), which can be opened via Window ➤ Type & Tables ➤ Glyphs, is the window into a font's table. Like Windows's Character Map and Mac's Character panel, the Glyphs panel shows every glyph in a font in a scrollable, resizable, zoomable, filterable grid. (There are some excellent new features here for CS3, so even if you're familiar with the Glyphs panel from previous versions, this section is worth a read.)

FIGURE 3.39

The Glyphs panel

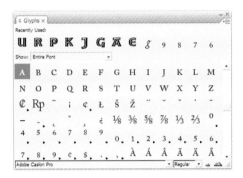

USING THE GLYPHS PANEL

By default, the panel shows the glyph set from the typeface currently selected in the Character panel. If text is highlighted, it will be that text's font displayed. At the bottom of the panel, the two drop-down menus for Font Family and Type Style enable browsing and using any installed font. You could, for example, be working in the middle of a line of text styled as Georgia Bold but, through the Glyphs panel, quickly insert a Not Equal symbol (≠) from Futura Std Book.

The main area of the panel is the current typeface's glyph set. Any empty table cells—glyphs not drawn into the font—are omitted, allowing you to scroll through only the existing glyphs, not all 65,536 potentially filled cells.

If you have the Type tool selected, and if the cursor is within a text frame, double-clicking any glyph in the panel will insert it into the text at that point. If the typeface in the Glyphs panel is the same as the one in your text frame, the glyph will insert matching surrounding text. Choosing a different typeface in the panel will insert the glyph in *that* typeface, which will inherit all other formatting options in effect at the point of insertion—point size, leading, tracking, and so on.

Harkening back to options on the Tools panel, some glyphs in the panel will, at least with OpenType fonts, have a little black arrow in their lower-right corners. As with the Tools panel, clicking and holding on arrow-adorned glyphs will open a flyout. In this case, it will be all variations the font contains for the selected glyph. Figure 3.40 shows that flyout for, and five different available versions of, the ampersand in Adobe's Garamond Premier Pro Regular.

FIGURE 3.30

Alternate glyphs for the same character are shown in, and selectable from, a flyout.

Prior to CS3, the drop-downs were incredibly important to using the Glyphs panel because InDesign sorted the Glyphs panel by CID/GID (Character ID/Glyph ID) by default, scattering alternate glyphs throughout the panel as they are distributed throughout the font table. That meant selecting them individually was a matter of either using the drop-down function or scrolling and visually scanning the entire glyph set. Thankfully, Adobe recognized that we spend enough time staring at type specimens. Now, the Glyphs panel instead sorts automatically by Unicode, which places all variations of the same character side by side. Every version of *A* appears side by side, allowing you to easily scrutinize their differences and choose the perfect one for your design. If you prefer the old sort method, select Sort Glyphs ➢ By CID/GID from the Glyph panel flyout menu in the upper right.

If you can't see the glyphs well enough, zoom in. The buttons in the bottom-right corner of the panel zoom out or in, respectively.

If you know you want to see only the swashes in a typeface, discretionary ligatures, or just numerals of different types, filter the display with the Show menu. The options in this list vary from font to font based on the OpenType features included in the font itself. If a font has no small caps, for instance, you won't have the option to filter it down to only small caps. That makes the Show list ideal for examining your OpenType fonts and learning which features each contains; it's a lot easier than checking the Character panel's OpenType menu for brackets font by font.

GLYPH SETS

With options shown via the panel's flyout menu, the top row includes recently used glyphs from all typefaces, enabling quick access to something you previously inserted. The last-used glyph is always appended to the left end of the list, pushing other recently used glyphs to the right. The list grows horizontally with the width of the panel; the wider the panel, the more recently used glyphs you can access. To be candid, I'm not sure of the limit of that list. I've sized the Glyphs panel so that it completely covered dual 17-inch monitors (2560 pixels wide) and still not exhausted the Recently Used list.

The Recently Used list is variable: Every glyph you manually select from the panel will add to the list, pushing others to the right. When you need consistently quick access to a stable of common glyphs, use glyph sets.

Let's say you lay out a magazine. As in most magazines, your feature articles are closed with a custom bullet endmark—the publication logo or another brand-enforcement element. The most efficient method of creating and managing endmarks has always been to make a font of it, which means the mark is inserted and formatted like any other glyph—color, size, tabs. Now, let's also suppose that your periodical's style guide requires that all intellectual property notations (trademark, registered trademark, copyright, and so on) be set in Helvetica Neue Lt Std 57 Condensed regardless of the style of surrounding text. Maybe you've even got some custom fleurons or bullet characters your managing editor likes. Let's suppose half of those are in the Zapf Dingbats typeface and the other half in Monotype's WebDings font.

How many fonts are we up to now, three? Throw a Euro symbol from another typeface in there for an even four. Glyphs from four fonts. Every time you insert those you'll be relying heavily on the Recently Used list. But, if you're a good typesetter, you'll use a bunch of other glyphs in the interim, blowing your ability to rely on the Recently Used list. So, should you manually select and sift through four fonts to get your needed symbols? (Would I spend this long setting you up if that were the correct procedure?)

You can define custom glyph sets from the Glyphs panel flyout menu, and then you can load them up any time you need. As you can see in Figure 3.41, I created a rather whimsical glyph set containing a few glyphs from different typefaces (Blackoak Std, Webdings, Adobe Caslon Pro, and

Myriad Pro Semibold Semicondensed). Glyph sets may hold any glyph, from any font, even the same character from multiple fonts.

FIGURE 3.41
A custom glyph set

Create a new glyph set from the New Glyph Set command on panel flyout menu. You'll be prompted to name the new set (make it unique) and how new glyphs should be inserted. The options are Insert at Front, Append at End, or Glyph Value Order, which orders the glyphs by Unicode ordering—in other words, *A* before *B*, *B* before *C*—regardless of the order in which glyphs are added to the set.

Once it's created, start populating. Using the other functions of the Glyphs panel, browse through your fonts looking for glyphs to add to the custom set. When you find them, click once on the glyph to select it without inserting it into your document, then right-click/Control-click and choose the appropriate destination set from the Add to Glyph Set menu. The glyph will instantly be added, and you can move on to look for the next.

If you make a mistake, choose your custom set from the Edit Glyph Set menu on either the right-click context menu or the Glyphs panel flyout menu. A new dialog (see Figure 3.42) will pop up. Here you can change the name or insertion order of your set as well as manage the individual glyphs.

FIGURE 3.42
Editing a custom
glyph set

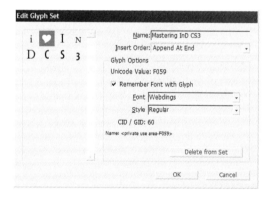

By default, InDesign will remember the specific font associated with a glyph. Thus, a copyright symbol added from Futura Medium is a completely different entry than a copyright symbol added from Futura Light; when either is double-clicked on the Glyphs panel, it will insert the symbol in that font—Futura Medium or Light—heedless of the typestyle in effect at the point of insertion. If this behavior doesn't suit you, if you'd rather have in your set a copyright symbol that *does* pick up the typeface in effect at the insertion point, uncheck Remember Font with Glyph. You can also change the specific font and style from the drop-downs in case you want a glyph independent of insertion point styles but inserted the glyph from Futura Light when you meant to insert the Futura Medium copyright symbol.

On a side note, since we're here: You may recall I stated that every glyph has a predefined place—an *A* must be in the *A* spot and no other glyph is allowed to occupy that even if, as with a symbol typeface, the font doesn't contain an *A*. You might even recall that I alluded to how the Private Use area of OpenType fonts might be used. Look again at Figure 3.42, beneath the drop-down lists. See where it says `Name: <private use area-F059>`? The heart glyph comes from Microsoft's Webdings font. Webdings is entirely a symbol font—there are no standard letters or numbers in it. Thus, all the usual spots a typeface like Garamond or Caslon fills with characters are unused in Webdings. If this were a TrueType or even Type 1 font, Microsoft would probably have put the heart where another font would have its *K* or *$*. Not only would doing so be against the entire Unicode standard and indeed the purpose of OpenType, which Microsoft co-authored, there's no reason for it. With approximately 130,000 open and unrestricted slots, Microsoft could have fit the entire glyph set of Webdings into the Private Use area more than a thousand times before even approaching the point where it would have to consider breaking the rules. The Private Use area was created specifically for this purpose—to make room in the rules for symbol fonts, fleurons in standard text fonts, corporate logos and endmarks, and anything else one might want to put in a font.

Getting back to custom glyph sets, you can use them the same way you use the Glyphs panel in general. Load your custom set from the top of the Show menu.

Still ho-hum about the idea of custom glyph sets? Maybe this will grab you: You can *share* them. So, you put together your set of article endmark, bullets and fleurons, intellectual property marks, and the Euro symbol, all from different fonts, and then upload the glyph set to the server from which your entire workgroup can grab it. Instantly, the tedium of manually tracking down and inserting those marks will be eliminated for your entire group, and the likelihood of mistakes happening will be dramatically reduced. This is exciting (I've been campaigning for the ability to share glyph sets since InDesign CS, which introduced glyph sets, was still in alpha.)

Each new glyph set you create is saved to your hard drive outside of InDesign (instead of into the preferences as in past versions, waiting to be eradicated when you next reset the prefs). You'll find it in the `Adobe InDesign CS3\Presets\Glyph Sets` folder saved as the name you set on the Glyphs panel. To share it, simply copy the external glyph set file to someone else's `Adobe InDesign CS3\Presets\Glyph Sets` folder. As long as recipients have the same fonts, they can use the same custom glyph set. Any time the set is updated, repost it to the server or push it through to client systems using SMS or another automated update system; the entire workgroup will always have the latest set of symbols and marks in accordance with your style guide.

The Bottom Line

Format Characters   Formatting characters is more than just choosing a size and font.

> **Master It**   Build a single-page magazine article, using FPO copy if needed, and include typical features of an article: headline, kicker, byline, subheads, body copy, and writer bio block.

Transform Characters InDesign includes much more control over character attributes than the basic styling options on the face of the Character panel, but they're scattered about.

Master It Creating a highlight (including reversed) effect on type is common enough that designers have cobbled two means of doing it. The first and more common method, within InDesign, is to place a colored rectangle behind text as a separate object. While it gets the job done, it creates yet another object that must be moved and resized to reflect changes to copy, text style, and reflow—and arduously at that because the text frame sits in front of the colored box, making the latter difficult to select. Less common and infinitely more risky is the Acrobat highlighting method. Within Acrobat is a commenting tool called the Highlighter. Choose the tool and highlight color (from common colors such as yellow, pink, and blue), and drag-select type. The highlight appears on screen and looks great. Unfortunately, it doesn't print unless the user deliberately changes a setting in the Acrobat Print dialog, the existence of which most Acrobat users are totally unaware.

Using the same article, and using the skills learned in this chapter, highlight or reverse a few words in the correct, printable, and flexible way. Then, insert at least two URLs in the article and style them appropriately but distinctly from each other.

Insert Special Characters Not everything can be typed without phalangeal acrobatics worthy of an Olympic gold medal.

Master It Continuing your work with the mockup article, find at least three places where trademark and registered trademark symbols belong (use your imagination if you're using gibberish FPO copy). Declare your work with a properly formatted copyright notice beneath the article. Find a few proper name phrases that shouldn't break across lines, and ensure that they don't. And, finally, insert em and en dashes where they belong, with slight padding around the em dashes.

Work with OpenType Font Features OpenType fonts fix most of the woes of digital typography—and open entire worlds of typographic freedom and control.

Master It Create pullquotes in separate frames, complete with quotation marks, unique styling, and—because pullquotes garner much more attention than body copy and draw the reader into a story—pull out all the stops by using OpenType features to style them perfectly.

Use the Glyphs Panel   Every glyph in every font can be accessed by this one, elegant panel and then inserted into the text.

Master It   Concluding the work on the mockup article, cap the story with a custom end-mark chosen from a symbol font and inserted into the last line of the article (ahead of the writer bio block). Once done, build a new custom glyph set to make reuse of the endmark easy for the next issue. Send the glyph set to a co-worker or friend so she may try inserting the same endmark.

A new glyph set containing a single glyph should be created and made ready for sharing. In a classroom or other multi-student environment, have the students title their custom glyph sets with their own names, pair up, and then exchange their sets with partners for installation and trial.

Chapter 4

Drawing

InDesign is *not* Illustrator, and it never will be. Illustrator is the pinnacle of modern vector drawing tools, and neither InDesign nor Photoshop will ever replace or absorb it. Fortunately for us, however, the Illustrator team happily shares its code with the InDesign team (Illustrator is a nurturing older sibling). Consequently, many of the most common drawing tasks can be done directly within InDesign without the need to load up Illustrator and then move artwork from it into InDesign. It's a matter of efficient creativity—two of my favorite words combined in my favorite phrase.

In this chapter, you will learn to:

◆ Draw precise paths with the Pen tool

◆ Freehand draw paths with the Pencil tool

◆ Combine and subtract shapes, and convert from one shape to another

◆ Modify any vector artwork

◆ Turn type into a container to hold images or text

The Essence of Vector

Before getting into the tools that create vector paths, let's make sure we all understand the definition of vector.

Vector is the opposite of raster. Raster artwork comprises square pixels tightly packed into a grid. Because that grid is a fixed size specific to each image, it means that raster images have a fixed resolution. Increase the size of a raster image and you're expanding one pixel's data into multiple grid cells, usually in a way that combines or averages the data with surrounding pixels' data, which blurs edges, merges colors, and lowers image fidelity overall. Shrinking a raster image down yields sharper edges and overall better results, but you are still destroying image data. Each pixel can only be filled with a single, solid color, so reducing the size, making room for fewer pixels, means some are being thrown away.

With vector, however, no damage is ever done, no data sacrificed, during resizing operations. For that matter, vector shapes are also infinitely editable without permanent data damage—something raster images are not. Vector artwork is not based on pixels or a grid. Instead, it's simple geometry based on *planes*.

Figure 4.1 should look familiar to you no matter how long you've been out of school. Our three-dimensional world is divided into three dimensions, or planes: Left-to-right, horizontal position, and object width is plotted on the x-axis; top-to-bottom, vertical position, and height on the y-axis; and front-to-back, depth, relative distance, and what we often call *stacking order*, is plotted on the z-axis. Describing the volume of a cube, for example (see Figure 4.2), entails asking three questions: How wide is it along the x-axis, how tall along the y, and how deep along the z? This is why, in places like the Transform and Control panels, you have positional fields for x and y.

FIGURE 4.1
All vector artwork
exists in three-
dimensional space,
along the x-, y-, and
z-axes.

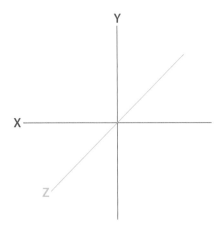

FIGURE 4.2
A cube exists along
on all three axes.

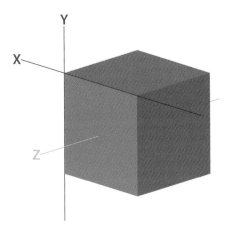

If you have a box handy, grab it. Each surface or face of a box is a plane: it exists solely along one of the three axes. Stick six planes together—top, bottom, right side, left side, front, and back—and you have a three-dimensional solid; and if the sides and planes are all equal, it's a cube. The place where each plane intersects with another is called a *vertex*.

When you're examining a real-world object like a box, planes and vertices are what define the volume and shape of an object. Talking about vector drawing, however, is slightly different; it's not the faces and sides that matter but the *corners*. Consider Figure 4.3, the same cube drawn with its faces unfilled. It still has planes; they just aren't filled with color.

Even with this *wireframe* cube, the vertices, the lines connecting the corners, are secondary to the importance of the corners themselves. It's the corners that truly define and describe the shape of the object.

Vector shapes are formed by the relationship of corners—*anchor points*—and the lines that connect them—*path segments*. Together, anchor points and path segments form *paths*. Every path must have at least two anchor points (i.e., to begin and end the path) and a path segment connecting the two points. Closed paths are those that have no discernable start or end point—a complete circle or square, for example—while open paths are incomplete, with obvious start and end points.

FIGURE 4.3
A cube without fills reveals the corners and vertices that define its shape.

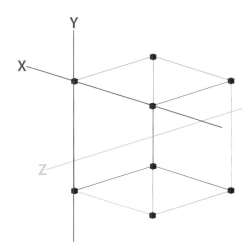

Because anchor points exist in three-dimensional space along the x, y, and z planes and not within a fixed-resolution grid, the relative size of the planes—and anything on them—can be scaled up or down infinitely without losing quality in the drawing. Although they appear to be squares of a certain size onscreen, anchor points don't have a size; zoom in or out and anchor points remain the same size.

The cube we looked at earlier has volume because a computer draws a connection *between* the coordinates. Like the coordinates themselves, the connections have no inherent volume, width, height, or depth; they're just lines drawn between points on the three planes. Volume is created by the relationship between points on all three planes, and that relationship is relative. A square is a square because four anchor points are equidistant from one another. Move all four the same distance downward and the object is still a square. Enlarge the square and it's still a square, with anchor points at the exact same *relative* distance from one another.

You see, resizing vector artwork isn't really resizing. It's more like zooming in or out in three-dimensional space. Shrinking an object down to half of its size is like zooming out to view a document at 50%, like seeing the object from farther away. The object and all its detail are intact, even if they aren't discernable from that distance.

This is the essence of vector—total independence from any concept of resolution or image quality. If you're new to vector, that can be a difficult notion to wrap your mind around—at first.

Drawing Paths

Drawing in InDesign is accomplished with a number of tools—many the same as in Illustrator, Photoshop, and other applications—and any discussion of them must begin with the Pen tool.

The Pen Tool and Straight Paths

Let's start exploring the Pen tool by drawing a simple path with two anchor points joined by a straight path segment.

1. Using the Pen tool, click once and release somewhere on the paper—do not drag.

2. Move over a few inches and click again. A straight path segment should connect the two anchor points.

If you see only a faint blue line for the path segment, you don't have a stroke color assigned; press D to activate the default black stroke color. If that still doesn't do it, check the Strokes panel to ensure that it has a weight. In the end, you should have what I have (Figure 4.4).

FIGURE 4.4
A straight path, consisting of two anchor points joined by a straight path segment

Now, try making a perfectly level horizontal line.

1. If your rulers are not showing, make them show with Cmd+R/Ctrl+R.

2. With the Selection tool, click the horizontal ruler and drag a guide down to an empty area of the page or pasteboard.

3. Switch to the Pen tool and make the first anchor point by clicking directly on the guide.

4. Move over a few inches and, again, right on the guide, click to make your second anchor point. As your cursor approaches the guide, you'll enter the *snap zone*, the area within a few pixels of a guide that will cause the cursor to jump toward the guide. You'll know when your cursor snaps to guide by the change in appearance from a nib with an X to a nib with an empty arrowhead. If the snapping bothers you, turn it off by toggling off View ➢ Grids & Guides ➢ Snap to Guides.

5. To fully appreciate your new path, hide guides with the Cmd+;/Ctrl+; keyboard shortcut.

Now, let's try the next step and create a rectangular path.

1. Either on a new layer (with the last hidden) or a different area of the page or pasteboard, drag *two* guides from the horizontal ruler, leaving a few inches between them.

2. Do the same from the vertical ruler, defining a roughly square shape with the four guide lines.

3. Working counterclockwise from the bottom left with the Pen tool, click the bottom-left intersection of guides, exactly where they cross, then click the bottom right, the top right, and finally the top left.

    At this stage you should have what appears to be a backward C. This is an open path because it has a start and end point.

4. Let's close the path: With the Pen tool still selected, click again on the bottom-left corner, directly on the anchor point already there. As you get close to the anchor point, the cursor will change from just a pen nib to a nib with a circle (see Figure 4.5).

FIGURE 4.5

When closing a path, the Pen tool cursor picks up a small circle icon indicating a change in function from continuing a path to closing a path.

Now, all on your own, try drawing a triangle. How about a six-sided polygon, like a stop sign? Everywhere you want a path to change direction, insert an anchor point. Anchor points control the direction of each subsequent path segment.

Let's try one more exercise, this time using one of my sample files.

From the project files available on the book's download web page, open `pathtrace01.indd`. You'll see the single-page document in Figure 4.6. It contains two layers: the upper one, "Trace on this Layer," is for you to trace the content of the lower, locked layer, "Original."

FIGURE 4.6

Hey, if I didn't think InDesign was cool, would I write a book about it? No, of course not. Instead, I'd publish a website comparing it to its leading competitor (wink).

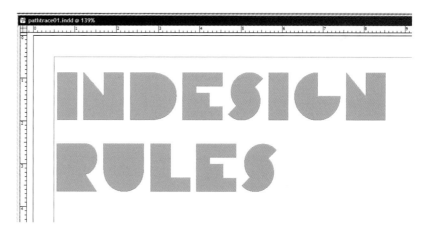

1. Using the Pen tool, trace the rectangle of the *I* until you have a closed path.

2. Once the *I* is finished, open the Swatches panel and fill it with a color other than orange so you can see how close your tracing was to the original.

3. Begin tracing the *N*. Once it's finished, give it a fill color, too, and move on to the *D*, the *E*, and so on until you've traced every letter of both words. Be careful to simply click and release to create a new anchor point; don't click and drag. See how close you can approximate the curves of the *D*, *S*s, *G*, *R*, and *U* using only straight path segments.

Getting a feel for the Pen tool and how to think about shapes by considering the placement of their anchor points? Starting to feel confident drawing straight-segment paths with the Pen tool? Good. Now, let's move on to what straight lines can't do.

Flattening, Curve or Transparency?

By drawing rounded edges using straight path segments, you performed rudimentary curve flattening. When a document moves through a *RIP (rastor image processor)*, all vector objects are converted to raster pixels or dots so that a print output device can create halftones of the image. Because pixels and halftones are fixed resolution and grid based (with a pixel or dot either being wholly on or wholly off), a curve, which might only partially fill the pixel or dot, must be converted to a series of straight lines that are more easily fit into a grid. They're usually very tiny lines, but straight nonetheless. This is the process of curve flattening.

Before *alpha transparency* made its way into *PostScript 3*, when a print professional used the word *flattening*, it was in reference to curve flattening. Now it's generally used in reference to transparency flattening—another matter entirely. Although curve flattening is still as relevant, it's stable and, after 20 years, predictable. Transparency flattening in the print workflow, however, has more recently been the major source of concern, innovative workarounds, expletives, and empty bottles of Pepto-Bismol.

The Pen Tool and Curves

Anchor points control the angle of path segments. Wherever a path must change its direction, it's the anchor point that actually does the work. The same is true of path segment curvature.

Every anchor point has the potential to curve the path segments on either or both sides of it. Consider the S-curve in Figure 4.7. Note the two distinct curved parts in the *S*, one up, one down. The divider line shows which curve is being generated by which anchor point.

Figure 4.7
In this simple S-curve, the curve on the left is created by the anchor point on the left, and the curve on the right by the other anchor point.

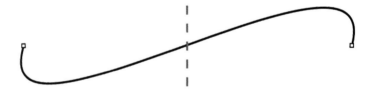

Introducing curvature is simple: Instead of clicking and releasing with the Pen tool, click and *drag*. As soon as you begin to drag, the anchor point goes from being a corner anchor point to a smooth anchor point and *curve handles* appear (see Figure 4.8). The angle and length of curve handles control the direction and depth of path segment curvature. Drag a handle straight down and the resulting curve will be symmetrically bowl-like; drag a handle down and at an angle and the resulting curved path segment will be asymmetrically deepest in the direction of the curve handle and shallow on the end farther from the curve handle.

FIGURE 4.8

The same S-curve,
showing the curve
handles that define
its curvature

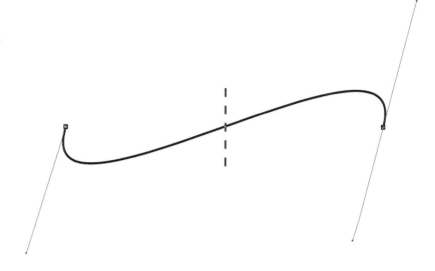

UNWIELDY TERMINOLOGY

Corner anchor points and *smooth anchor points* are unwieldy. No, not the points, the names themselves. Those are the official names Adobe gave them, but they're both just anchor points. Also, when anchor points appear at the beginning or end of an open path, Adobe often refers to them as end points. Although that makes sense, it's yet another term for effectively the same thing: an anchor point, which is how I'll usually refer to them all from here on.

Really, to understand this stuff, you have to do it. Let's give it a shot with another sample file I provided. From `http://www.sybex.com/go/MasteringInDesign`, open `pathtrace02.indd`. There's the S-curve. Let's trace it.

1. With the Pen tool, click the first anchor point (marked with the faded number one) and drag down toward the solid number one, trying to match your curve handle to mine. When you release the mouse button, you should see just an unassuming little anchor point. You've created curvature in the anchor point, but not yet a path segment to show it off.

   Remember, although anchor points hold all the data, that data is invisible until a line is drawn to display it.

2. Repeat the procedure with the second anchor point, clicking and dragging again following the point near the number two. This time, as soon as you click the Pen tool onto the page, you'll notice the path segment. Dragging the curve handle around a bit will enable you to experiment with the depth and location of curve to fine-tune it.

Did you notice any difference on your second anchor point? As soon as you create the second anchor point, defining that the path went to the right from the first point, only one curve handle survives on the first anchor point. The reason for that is because, as the first point, it could only have one path segment emanating from it. With the second anchor point, however, you were controlling not only the path segment to the left, but also a potential path segment to the right.

On a new layer, retrace the S-curve using the same procedure. Instead of deselecting the path after the second point, click and release an inch or two away to create a third anchor point. Even though you clicked and released instead of dragging, the resulting second path segment still has curvature. Why? Because of the anchor point to the left.

Each anchor point may have up to two path segments attached to it—in this case, one to the left and one to the right, though path segments can radiate off points at any angle. That path segment receives a curve handle, but only one per anchor point. Because a path segment must exist between two anchor points, the segment actually gets *two* curve handles—one for each anchor point. Reflecting back on drawing the S-curve, it's obvious the first curve is created by the anchor point in position 1 on the left, the second by the anchor point in position 2 on the right.

Curve handles control the path segment on the *same* side of an anchor point, and when you drag them, the segment curves *toward* the handle.

When you created the second anchor point, it had two curve handles. The handle you *didn't* drag controlled the path segment to the left—the incoming S-curve—and the other, the one you *did* drag, was setting up for a possible path segment on the right. Creating the third anchor point— completing the circuit—actualized the second segment. The second segment was a bowl instead of an *S* because you didn't drag the third anchor point and thus didn't add any curvature emanating from that point.

While drawing with the Pen tool, you are always dragging the curve handle corresponding to the *outgoing* path segment.

Looking at the path of a perfect circle (Figure 4.9), you can see there are four anchor points positioned equally around the circle. This is the minimum number required to create a perfect circle in *Bézier* curve–based vector illustration because the geometry involved limits the way curves attach to anchor points.

FIGURE 4.9
Four equidistant
anchor points with
matching curve set-
tings form a circle.

In the circle, each anchor point controls the curvature of the path segments attached to *either* side. Creating a perfect circle requires that the curvature and angle of all four anchor points be identical; a variance would distort the shape. Notice how the curve handles are either straight up and down (90°) or flat (0° rotation). The handles align with the axes on which the anchor points themselves sit—y or x, respectively—and create a perfect, uniform curvature thereby.

From the book's download page, open pathtrace03.indd and see how closely you can trace the circle diagram there using the Pen tool. Remember to end your path at the first point you drew to close the circle.

How did it turn out? If it's not exact, try it a few more times. Drawing circles is difficult and takes practice. Mastering the Pen tool, anchor points, and path segments is essential to so many other things in InDesign... Really, it's worth the time to try it out a few times. Once you've got the tracing going pretty well, hide the "Trace This" layer and see if you can draw a perfect circle from scratch. If not, practice some more. Rome wasn't drawn in a day.

Forget to close a path or need to continue a previously drawn path? Move the Pen tool over the last anchor point on the path—either the beginning or end point—click to activate the path, and resume drawing. Using the same method you can even join two independent, open paths.

Pen Tool Aspects and Incarnations

Like the pantheons of ancient world gods and goddesses, many of the most powerful tools manifest themselves in more than one aspect or incarnation. King of the vector drawing tools, almighty Pen tool, like Zeus/Jupiter/Odin, has many aspects, each with remarkably similar powers if not faces.

CONVERTING ANCHOR POINTS BETWEEN CORNER AND SMOOTH

As you saw, path segments get their curvature from anchor points. Create curvature on the right of an anchor point and it will be inherited by the path segment on the left and vice versa. What if you don't *want* curvature to inherit? How do you, for instance, follow a curved segment with a straight one?

High atop Mount Olympus, the Pen tool's Zeus incarnation makes converting anchor points while drawing faster than hurling a lightning bolt.

1. With the Pen tool, start a curved path similar to the S-curve with which we've been working. Make your first and second anchor points, both with curvature.

2. Before making the third anchor point, hover the cursor back over the second and watch what happens. Notice the little inverted *V* that appears in the corner of the Pen tool cursor? That's the convert anchor point cursor, and it will change the outgoing side of an anchor point from a corner to a smooth. Click the second anchor point and watch as one of the curve handles—the one corresponding to the path segment not yet created—disappears.

3. Now, click away from the second anchor point to create the third. You should wind up with a straight path segment between them.

The same holds true if you start with a straight path and corner anchor point and need to make the next segment curved—click the last point and drag to expose the curve handle.

In its full Zeus incarnation, the Pen tool may appear to many as the Convert Direction Point tool, which is behind the Pen tool on the Tools panel. In this full manifestation, clicking a point will convert *both* sides of it, stripping away or granting curvature to the path segments to both sides simultaneously. As with the convert anchor point variant of the Pen tool, when going from corner to smooth anchor point with the Convert Direction Point tool, click and drag out a bit to reveal the curve handles. Later in this chapter we'll get into manipulating those curve handles after creation or initial conversion.

ADDING AND REMOVING ANCHOR POINTS

Another common consideration in drawing vectors is whether a path has too many or too few anchor points. To alter this, we have two more aspects of the Pen tool that render paths as malleable as the clay from which Jupiter, king of the Roman gods, purportedly formed mortal men and women.

Because each anchor point is plotted on the three-dimensional graph of x-, y-, and z-axes, and because each anchor point contains angle and curvature data, paths require computer processors to work out the math. Overly complicated paths and excessive anchor points cause slow screen redraws when scrolling and longer print times. Unnecessary anchor points in a path can also create an aesthetic issue: unwanted changes to the path directions or curvature.

If you still have the Pen tool selected, move your cursor over a path segment, maybe around the middle between two anchor points. Notice the little plus sign added to the cursor? Click and a new anchor point will be inserted at that point in the segment. The new anchor point can then be manipulated with the Direct Selection tool (we're getting to that) to alter the path at that point. To infuse curvature in the same action, click and drag.

Removing extraneous points is just as easy: Position the Pen tool cursor over an anchor point instead of a path segment—presenting a nib with a minus sign—and click. With the anchor point and its associated angle or curve control removed, the path segments on either side will merge and adapt to account for the excised point. Consider the path smited.

If you need to add or delete more than a few points in a path, it's often more efficient to use a tool dedicated to the task. Once again behind the Pen tool on the Tools panel are other faces of the god: the Add Anchor Point tool and the Delete Anchor Point tool. Like Jupiter in toga, in battle armor, or in sandals and Golden Fleece, they're still the same formidable Pen tool, with the same powers.

PERFECTLY STRAIGHT PATH SEGMENTS

Few know that the Pen tool can make perfectly straight, level lines without using guides. Unlike the other two incarnations of this same tool, the Pen tool in straight line mode doesn't just pick up slightly different cursors; it can do the job wearing its own face or a completely different one.

Beside and down from the Pen tool is the Line tool. When all you want is a straight line, here it is. Click, drag, done. Click and drag while holding Shift to constrain the angle of the line to an increment of 45°. If you need a specific length of line, draw it and then resize via the Control or Transform panel.

The Line tool creates a simple, open path with two anchor points, which can be manipulated like any other points (see later in this chapter). In fact, using the Pen tool, a path created by the Line tool can be continued or incorporated into another open path. However, if you're already drawing with the Pen tool and simply need a perfectly straight path segment, stick with the Pen tool.

Using the Pen tool, hold the Shift key while creating a new anchor point to force the new point to line up with the last—exactly like drawing with the Line tool. Anchor points will align to the nearest increment of 45°. So, if your cursor is close to the same x coordinate as the last anchor, holding the Shift key while clicking will place the next anchor in perfect alignment along the x-axis—0-degrees. Being close to the y-coordinate will put the next anchor point on a 90° angle with the previous. Stray toward the middle of the x *and* y and you can get an anchor point and path segment at an exact 45°, 135°, 225°, or 315° from the first point. This is a *very* handy trick for making perfect lines because, well, sometimes you need perfect lines.

Try making a rectangle. Click and release to make the first anchor point; then, about an inch to the right, Shift-click to place the second anchor point. An inch above that, Shift-click to make the third, then fourth, and, finally, close the path.

The Pencil Tool

More familiar in its operation and feel is the Pencil tool, which resides on the Tools panel just below the Pen tool. With the Pen tool, you draw anchor points while path segments are filled in automatically. Drawing with the Pencil tool is the polar opposite: you draw the path segments and InDesign automatically adds an anchor point wherever you alter angles.

DRAWING WITH THE PENCIL TOOL

The Pencil tool has its uses, but its freehand drawing is not a substitute for the precision of the Pen tool. Rather, it's a complement to it, another tool in your belt.

If you need a path that feels more natural, more hand drawn or hand written, go for the Pencil tool—especially if you have an electronic tablet whose stylus lets you draw with an honest-to-goodness writing utensil. Mousing or trackballing with the Pencil tool is difficult and requires a very steady hand. Every little stutter or hitch creates new anchor points—several of them—that you'll probably want to clean up. There's the chief minus to the Pencil tool's pluses: Remember when I said you want a path without extraneous anchor points? Swipe the Pencil tool across the page and just try to count all those anchor points. Man, if you need to reshape that path…

Let's try a tracing exercise with the Pencil tool. From this chapter's folder on the download page, please open `penciltrace.indd`. Grab the Pencil tool and, beginning with one path or one color area (for example, the hair or one side of the green background box), do your best to trace over it with the Pencil tool's freehand path.

Hold Cmd/Ctrl and click in an empty area of the page to deselect your path. Now, try drawing another path right up against to the first—start within a few pixels of the first, in fact, and let your second path *overlap* the first one as in Figure 4.10. Whoa! Didn't see *that* coming, did you?

FIGURE 4.10
Shown in gray is the first path, with the second in red. The original image is hidden in this figure for clarity.

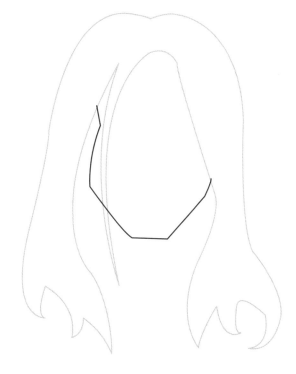

MODIFYING PATHS WITH THE PENCIL TOOL

Another difference between the Pen and Pencil tools is in how each relates to preexisting paths. The Pen will happily create independent path after independent path atop any previous paths without altering previous paths. Conversely, the Pencil tool will alter paths to which it draws near. Although jarring at first, this is actually a very cool feature because it allows you to modify paths drawn with the Pen, Pencil, shape, and frame tools as well as type converted to paths (later in this chapter), all with the speed and dexterity of the Pencil. (If you'd like to get your previous path back, undo the Pencil action with Cmd+Z/Ctrl+Z.) Let's try some intentional modifications.

1. Clear any paths you've already created in the `penciltrace.indd` document.

2. With the Pencil tool, trace the cartoon's outer hair line as closely as possible, leaving the face area open but completely ignoring the spike of bangs in the front—just draw right past it as if it wasn't there. Give the path a fill color. Figure 4.11 shows my result.

FIGURE 4.11
My Pencil tool-traced hairpiece (shown filled in red)

3. Zoom in to where the bangs meets the main hair line, and with the white Direct Selection tool, select the path you just finished drawing.

4. Switch back to the Pencil tool and position its tip atop one of the anchor points in your path around the intersection of the bangs with the rest of the hair. The small *X* in the Pencil tool cursor will disappear when you're in the right spot.

5. Click the anchor point, and draw the spike of bang, coming back up and terminating that path on a different anchor point in your first path (see Figure 4.12).

FIGURE 4.12
The bangs piece
(filled in blue)
should merge with
the main hairpiece
in your drawing.

The result will be that the bangs are added to the main hair path, with the two paths fully merged. If you got differing results, undo and try again, ensuring that you both begin and end your drawing on anchor points already in the path. Again, it takes a very steady hand as well as good hand-eye coordination to work with the Pencil tool in this manner. You might find it helpful to zoom in on areas of the drawing as you work, but note that it's still extremely fine work even zoomed far in.

Let's try modifying the path shape instead of just adding to it by doing something my mother has wanted to do for years: give me a haircut.

1. With the hair path still selected, find an anchor point around the length to which you'd like to cut the hair.

2. Once again, click the Pencil tool on the anchor point. This time, however, drag *across* the interior of the object to another anchor point on the other side instead of dragging outside the path. When you let go, one of two things will happen: Either I'll have a haircut or I'll have hair only on my shoulders (yuck!).

   If it's the latter case, undo, then repeat step 2 in the *opposite* direction. If you began with an anchor point on the left and dragged left to right, start this time with an anchor point on the right and drag back to the left. *That* should chop off my locks.

The reason you might have gotten either result is because paths have a direction. Depending on whether you drew the original path clockwise or counterclockwise, the direction in which you take the Pencil tool will reshape or chop one side or the other. Thankfully, Undo backs you out if the result opposed what you expected.

Drawing from a path segment instead of from an anchor point will terminate the path at that point, allowing you to completely reshape a section. In such a case, the Pencil tool will create new anchor points at the inception and termination locations—and everywhere in between—as needed.

Just in case it's not obvious, the Pencil tool can modify not only paths drawn with the Pencil, but *any* unlocked, modifiable path, such as one you might create with the Pen or Rectangle tools.

So, what are you to do if you just want to draw one path near another without adding to, subtracting from, or reshaping the first? Easy: Don't start drawing directly on a preexisting anchor point or path segment. Begin drawing outside (or inside) a path area and the Pencil tool ignores what's underneath and creates a new, completely independent path. The distinction is in the proximity of existing paths to where you click to initiate drawing with the Pencil tool; begin within a few pixels of an existing path to modify it, further out to ignore it. If your new, independent pencil path must begin within the modification zone of an existing path, a useful trick is to begin the new path on a new layer, locking the layer or layers containing lower paths.

CLEANING UP PENCIL PATHS

Getting back to the multiple incarnations of ancients gods analogy, Hera the Pencil tool, queen of the gods, has two other aspects: Juno the Smooth tool and Frigga the Erase tool.

As noted previously, Pencil tool drawing creates many, many anchor points; the slightest twitch in your wrist could create an unsightly bump or divot in an otherwise smooth path. If such is the case with your path, or you simply want to clean up some of those extraneous anchor points, reach for the Smooth tool, behind the face of the Pencil tool on the Tools panel. For little touch-ups here and there, you can also just hold the Option/Alt key with the Pencil tool selected.

As you might guess, the Smooth tool irons wrinkles out of paths, eliminating anchor points that are too close together or have too little difference in their coordinates—both very common when drawing with the Pencil tool. Drag it along a section of Pencil-drawn path to watch unsightly bumps just melt away. Unlike most late-night infomercial weight-loss shams, the Smooth tool doesn't dump the weight and leave the path a big sagging skin bag; as cottage cheese anchor points slough off, other anchor points reveal themselves to make a smoother, more attractive path that retains curves in all the right places.

Applications of the Smooth tool are cumulative—run it across a path to clean and smooth it, run it again to clean it up more and make even more gentle curves.

Finally, what's a pencil without an eraser? Flip the Pencil tool upside down and gaze upon the goddess's final face.

Whereas the Delete Anchor Point tool (and corresponding mode of the Pen tool) removes anchor points *without* breaking the path, the Eraser tool *does* break the path. Drag the Eraser tool *along* a length of path to erase everything it touches—anchor points *and* path segments.

Dragging the Eraser tool *across* a path segment will split the path, with new anchor points developing on either side of the split, but it leaves a gap. Smudge out an anchor point directly and the same occurs. To split a path without an unsightly gap, don't use the Eraser tool. Read "Editing Paths and Shapes" later in this chapter for the correct tools.

What might be a practical use of the Eraser tool? Opening up a closed path is a pretty common one. Maybe you have a closed path and a new, disconnected open path that you'd like to merge together. Erase a big enough opening in the former, and then connect them with the Pencil tool, which is a nice segue into…

Merging Paths with the Pencil Tool

Let's say you have two opened paths you'd like to merge together. Select both paths with the Direct Selection tool, and then switch to the Pencil tool. Click the end point of one path and drag toward an end point of the other path. *After* you've begun dragging, depress the Cmd/Ctrl key, which initiates the Pencil's merge mode, denoted by a tiny cursor symbol that looks very much like an anchor point with path segments (see Figure 4.13). Keep dragging (and holding the modifier key) until you're over the target anchor point. Release the mouse button and the paths will merge. Repeat as necessary to merge the other ends of the paths or additional paths.

Figure 4.13

When merging two paths with the Pencil tool, holding Cmd on the Mac or Ctrl on Windows toggles the Pencil into path-merge mode.

Shape Tools

You know how to draw rectangles and circles with the Pen tool, but you can also just use the tools dedicated to creating these fundamental shapes.

Frames

Chapter 2, "Text," should have given you a good feel for the basics of working with frames. You'll get more of this in Chapter 5, "Images," but so far, these frames have been four sided. Let's go beyond the rectangle.

Ellipse Frame Tool

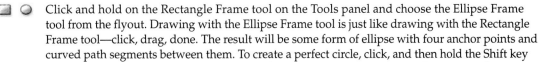

Click and hold on the Rectangle Frame tool on the Tools panel and choose the Ellipse Frame tool from the flyout. Drawing with the Ellipse Frame tool is just like drawing with the Rectangle Frame tool—click, drag, done. The result will be some form of ellipse with four anchor points and curved path segments between them. To create a perfect circle, click, and then hold the Shift key while you drag, which will also create a perfect square if using the Rectangle Frame tool.

You'll notice that, though we're working with an ellipse, InDesign still creates a rectangular bounding box with control corners around it.

If you didn't draw your ellipse in exactly the dimensions you require, it can easily be resized via the Control or Transform panels like any other object. Or, if you know in advance the needed dimensions of the elliptical frame, there's a faster way. Instead of drawing and then resizing, grab the Ellipse Frame tool and click and release on the page instead of clicking and dragging. Up will pop a dialog with two simple options: the required width and height of the frame; set them and click OK.

Now you can fill the elliptical frame with color, imagery, or text (try text with the Justify All Lines alignment for an interesting effect).

POLYGON FRAME TOOL

With elliptical frames behind us, let's get into something more interesting: polygon frames (Figure 4.14).

FIGURE 4.14
All of these objects were created by starting with the Polygon Frame tool.

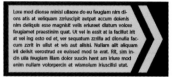

As with the Ellipse Frame tool, selecting the Polygon Frame tool and clicking the page or pasteboard brings up an option box. This one has the same height and width fields, but also two others (see Figure 4.15).

FIGURE 4.15
The Polygon Frame tool options dialog

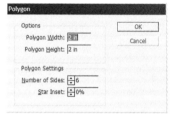

The Number of Sides field should be self-explanatory. In the percentage-based Star Inset field, though, you determine how deep those sides are set. A value of 0% means the polygon's sides will be flush with the outer diameter—a four-sided polygon would therefore be a perfect rectangle.

Want to make a classic five-pointed star? Use the Polygon Frame tool with five sides and Star Inset of 50%. How about the foundation shape for an official seal? Pick a high number of sides—maybe 25—and an inset of 5% to 10%. One of the most common uses *I* have for the Polygon Frame tool is in creating equilateral triangles (three sides, 0% inset) that I'll often use as the starting point for more complex shapes, patterns, or even bullet glyphs.

Any time a polygon has an inset, InDesign automatically creates a second set of anchor points—the first for each apex, the second for each nadir. By starting with the Polygon Frame tool and manipulating the anchor points with the Direct Selection tool, Convert Direction Point tool, or other path modification tools, you can quickly create numerous complicated shapes.

SHAPE TOOLS

On the Tools panel next to the frame tools are the shape tools. They are the Rectangle, Ellipse, and Polygon tools. They are *exactly* like their matching frame tools. They're so identical, in fact, that they're superfluous—or the frame tools are. Six of one thing, half dozen of the other.

In InDesign, a frame is a frame is a frame. Shape objects are frames, and frames are shapes (and they are all paths). The only visual difference between them is the diagonal, intersecting lines in frames; they don't mean a thing. Don't believe me? Try it: Draw a frame using one of the frame tools. Beside it, draw a shape with one of the shape tools. Now, select the Type tool (press T for expediency). Click in the frame and start typing. OK. Now, with the Type tool still selected, click in the shape and start typing. Any difference?

Like most desktop layout programs, InDesign is built on the concept of the relationship between container and content. Everything you can create or place in the application is either content or a container to hold that content. Vector paths automatically form containers the instant the paths are closed. Because both frames and shapes are paths, they are both containers. Moreover, either may contain any of the following: fill colors (solid or gradient), images, text, vector objects, and even other containers.

So, you might ask, *If frames and shapes, and their respective tools are identical, why do they both exist? Why not just have one set of tools and be done with it?*

The original intent of having both frame and shape tools was to distinguish between graphic frames, text frames, and vector design elements that wouldn't hold content. A noble intent, but it was quickly defeated by practicality; it's a lot faster to just select a frame and get to work than it is to select a frame and make an inconvenient trip to the Object ➤ Content menu before doing anything worthwhile.

The reason these redundant tools persist is simple hand-holding. InDesign is still locked in mortal combat with QuarkXPress, which *does* draw a distinction between frames (called boxes there) and shapes. In that veteran layout application, picture boxes may hold only graphics; to put text in them, you *must* first convert the container to a text box via menu commands. As you saw in InDesign, however, the only action required to convert a graphic frame to a text frame is to click in it with the Type tool. InDesign keeps the two sets of tools on hand as a learning aid for new QuarkXPress converts. That's it, plain and simple. Eventually, in some later version of InDesign, the two sets of tools will merge, probably when Adobe wants to add another tool to the panel that isn't as easily relocated as the Measure tool.

FRAME-FIRST LAYOUT

Although there are still two sets of tools, they can be useful for frame-first (or box-first) layout work where an entire page's frames are created and placed ahead of their content. Because the frame tools have the big *X* through them, they provide a visual differentiation from tools that create decorative vector shapes. Having the obvious difference makes it easier and faster for others in the workflow to run through a page, flowing in text or dropping in images with less likelihood of accidentally putting one where the other should be.

If you draw one type of object—a shape to be a decorative vector object or a frame to hold text or a graphic—and later change your mind, there's no consequence to leaving them as they are. However, should you wish to be precise, you *can* convert one into another. Just select the object and choose one of the three types from the Object ➤ Content menu. The only time you really must do the conversion is if you've begun with a text frame but now wish to fill it with a placed graphic.

The Object ➤ Content commands will work only if the frame or path is empty. If you already have text or imagery in there, you'll need to delete them prior to converting the content type. To wipe existing text or imagery out of a frame, switch to the Text or Direct Selection tool, respectively, select the frame content, and press Delete or Backspace.

Reshaping Shapes

Creating shapes is only half the deal. It also helps to know how to *reshape* them.

Having begun with a standard rectangle, you may realize you'd prefer to have a rectangle with rounded corners. It can certainly be done with the Add Anchor Point tool, Delete Anchor Point tool, Convert Anchor Point tool, a few guides, and some careful path editing. Or, you could save yourself some work and simply use the menu command that does it automatically.

At the bottom of the Object menu is a submenu, Convert Shape, that offers instant conversion of closed and open paths to any of nine shapes:

Rectangle	Inverse Rounded Rectangle	Polygon
Rounded Rectangle	Ellipse	Line
Beveled Rectangle	Triangle	Orthogonal Line

Give 'em a try. Draw a shape—rectangle, ellipse, or polygon—select that shape with the Selection tool if it isn't already selected, and choose Object ➢ Convert Shape ➢ Triangle. Faster than you can say it, you've got a triangle. With the same shape selected, choose Object ➢ Convert Shape ➢ Orthogonal Line. (An *orthogonal* line is one that is perfectly aligned to either the x-axis or y-axis, horizontal or vertical respectively.)

For real fun, grab the Pencil tool and draw a quick spiral in an empty area, then choose Object ➢ Convert Shape ➢ Inverse Rounded Rectangle. Check *that* out, man! It doesn't matter how many anchor points were in your starting path or how many are required for the finished path, InDesign adds or removes as part of the process. With these commands, the only thing InDesign cares about is the overall size of the original object—more precisely, the bounding box area. If you start out with a 1×1-inch square and convert it to a triangle, you'll get a 1×1-inch triangle. The same is true when beginning with a 1-inch long line.

By now you should be asking, *How do I change the number of sides and indention in the Object ➢ Convert Shape ➢ Polygon or the radius of the rounded corners made by Object ➢ Convert Shape ➢ Rounded Rectangle?* And that would be a great question.

First, the number of sides resulting from a command to Object ➢ Convert Shape ➢ Polygon is whatever the current settings are for the Polygon Frame tool or the redundant Polygon tool. On the Tools panel, select the Polygon Frame tool from behind the Rectangle Frame tool and double-click the Polygon Frame tool icon itself. Up will pop the Polygon Settings dialog where you can set the number of sides and the star inset. Whatever options you set here are set for all future polygons—those created with the Object ➢ Convert Shape ➢ Polygon command, the Polygon Frame tool, and the Polygon tool.

Now, the way to determine the corner radius of rounded and inverse rounded rectangles is not the same—there isn't a rounded rectangle tool to double-click. Instead, those commands take their settings from the current Corner Options settings. In fact, the Rounded Rectangle, Beveled Rectangle, and Inverse Rounded Rectangle on the Object ➢ Convert Shape submenu are just shortcuts to the same features in Corner Options.

Corner Options

About halfway up the Object menu from Convert Shape is Corner Options, which, in prior versions of InDesign, was Corner Effects. Select—or draw—a rectangle and select Object ➢ Corner Options. You'll see a dialog like Figure 4.16.

FIGURE 4.16
The Corner Options
dialog

Corner Options are live vector effects, meaning no permanent damage is ever done to your object. From the Effect drop-down menu you can choose Fancy, Bevel, Inset, Inverse Rounded, Rounded, and, of course, None for no alteration of the shape's corners—the last so you can remove previously applied corner options.

A Corner Option size equal to or greater than half the length of an object's side will completely round (or concave, or bevel, or whatever) that entire side. For example, if you apply a 0.5-inch rounded corner to a 1×1-inch square, you will convert the square into a circle. Putting the same rounded corners on a 4×1-inch rectangle will round the short sides, creating a pill shape.

Corner Options is not limited to rectangles. It can be applied to any vector shape—triangles, hexagons, 50-pointed stars, or whatever you like. Naturally, it has no effect on ellipses, lines, and other objects devoid of corners. And, Corner Options cannot be used on placed images per se, but as you probably recall, placed objects are *content*, not containers. When an image is placed in InDesign, a container frame is automatically created, and that frame *is* a vector path and thus eligible for Corner Options. See Figure 4.17 for a few different things you can do with InDesign's Corner Options.

FIGURE 4.17
Corner Options can
do some nifty
things.

WHEN INDESIGN CAN BE FASTER THAN ILLUSTRATOR

Interestingly, InDesign's Corner Options and convert to shape commands are sometimes faster than drawing the same object in Illustrator, which doesn't have such automated commands. Because InDesign and Illustrator are siblings, vector paths may be copied from one to the other, and worked on in either. So, if you can't remember how to make a rounded rectangle in Illustrator, or if you want a 50-pointed star with beveled corners or a triangle with fancy corners, feel free to save yourself some forehead bruises by doing it in InDesign and then copying and pasting into Illustrator.

Merging, Dividing, and Other Pathfinder Functions

You can make basic shapes. You can draw any other shape you need with the Pen and Pencil tools. You can even convert one shape into another and mess about with its corners. But can you combine two separate shapes or knock one out of the other? That's what we're about to do.

1. Using one of the shape or frame tools, please draw a rectangle.

2. Beside it, please draw an ellipse.

3. Fill and stroke both shapes, but make sure to give them different colors.

4. Now, drag the ellipse until it partially overlaps the rectangle—about halfway should do nicely.

5. Select both shapes, and go to Object ➤ Pathfinder ➤ Add. You should get the result in Figure 4.18.

FIGURE 4.18
When two overlapping paths (left) are given the Pathfinder command to add, they merge into a single, amalgamated path (right).

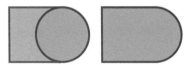

The Add command merges the two paths into a single, amalgamated shape. Click Undo and try the next command on the Object ➤ Pathfinder menu, Subtract. Where the ellipse overlapped, the rectangle should now be bitten off. Undo again and try Object ➤ Pathfinder ➤ Intersect. You should have left only where the two shapes overlapped, wiping away any overhang.

Exclude Overlap is the opposite. It will leave the overhang and cut out the area common to both shapes.

Lastly, Minus Back is the inverse of Subtract: Instead of knocking the front object out of the back, it punches the back shape out of the front. Figure 4.19 shows a few results from using Pathfinder commands.

FIGURE 4.19
Shapes resulting from using the Pathfinder commands

Add   Subtract   Intersect   Exclude Overlap   Minus Back

As you try out the Pathfinder commands, notice what happens to the fill and stroke colors of the resulting object, whether the front or rear object's colors are retained by the new shape. In most cases, the front object's attributes are retained. It's the opposite for Minus Back, though. And, it's not just fill and stroke colors that are assigned to this new *compound shape*. Object effects, drop shadow, transparency, and so forth assigned to the dominant path will be retained by the resulting compound shape.

Also noteworthy is the fact that Pathfinder commands can be run on any ungrouped vector object—even text frames. Give it a shot with the ellipse and rectangle. Choose Object ➤ Pathfinder ➤ Intersect, grab the Text tool, and click inside the compound path; start typing. Want text that defines a shape or flows through a shape more eye-catching than a rectangle (see Figure 4.20)? Well, then, *there* you go.

FIGURE 4.20
Use Pathfinder commands for creative, eye-catching text frame shapes.

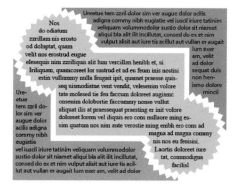

COMPOUND PATHS

Any time a Pathfinder command results in a shape that is more than a single, continuous path, you get what's called a *compound path*. Although *compound shape* is merely a descriptive term for a shape that is more complex than a rectangle, ellipse, or polygon and, in the grand scheme of things, hasn't much of a meaning, *compound path* is a more important term because it refers to a certain type of path. A compound path is a new, more complex type of path with different considerations than those for a simple, continuous path. It's multiple separate paths behaving as one.

Here's another opportunity to understand by doing.

1. Draw a perfect circle (you know two ways to do that quickly), and fill it with a solid color but without a stroke.

2. Atop the circle, create a five-pointed star that is larger than the circle (see Figure 4.21), and give it, too, a solid color fill and no stroke color.

FIGURE 4.21
We'll create a compound path by starting with a star overlapping a circle.

3. Select both the star and circle and go to Object ➤ Pathfinder ➤ Exclude Overlap. Your result should be similar to mine (Figure 4.22), with the overlapping area knocked out and the resulting shape acquiring the star's fill and stroke attributes.

FIGURE 4.22
After the Pathfinder ➤ Exclude Overlap command a compound path remains.

Look closely at this new object. If you select it with the Direct Selection tool, you'll notice all the anchor points throughout. See all those different shapes in there? All the separate filled areas? There's no way that object is a single continuous path. It *can't* be—it has 10 different filled areas, 10 different closed paths. That, ladies, and gentlemen, is a compound path—multiple paths behaving as one.

Try changing the object's fill color—all areas will change simultaneously. In many cases, you'll find that's the desired result. When it isn't, when you want to separately color the shapes in this compound path, remember this crucial piece of information: move on to step 4.

4. Although this will work however you've selected the compound path, let's keep it selected with the Direct Selection tool so we can more closely observe the changes to the object as we…choose Object ➤ Paths ➤ Release Compound Path.

Do you see the difference? It's subtle. Undo the last command and look at your compound path star. Where's the object center point? Right: In the center of the star. Now press Cmd+Shift+Z/Ctrl+Shift+Z to redo the release compound path command. Where is the center point now? Uh-huh. That's right: There isn't 1 but *10*. All the shapes have been released to individual paths, with their own centers and their own independent paths. They can even be moved or edited independently if you wanted to do that (but not now).

5. Deselect all, then select one of the star points. Give it a fill color. Good. Now give the next star point a different color. Keep going until you've filled all five. Figure 4.23 shows how my star looks so far (it also shows the center points and paths, in case you need to see them).

6. For this particular project, we don't want all the star points to be different colors, though. We want them the same color. In fact, we want the remaining circle sections to also match each other, but not with a solid color fill; we want them to have a radial gradient (see Figure 4.24). See what you can do to match your circle sections to mine.

FIGURE 4.23
After releasing the compound path, each path is individually editable.

FIGURE 4.24
My star finished. Yours will look like this, too, after a few more steps.

No luck on getting the circle parts to fill with a radial gradient like mine in Figure 4.24? Let me guess: You got a separate radial gradient in all five sections, didn't you? That's because we haven't done step 7 yet.

7. Applying a gradient, object effects, and a few other things to multiple paths applies a new instance to each path. To get the desired effect for this project, we can't have separate paths. We need a compound path—but only of the circle pieces, not the star points, too, or we'll end up back at the same problem we faced in step 3.

Select all five sections of the circle together and go to Object ➢ Paths ➢ Make Compound Path. Now we've turned these separate paths back into a compound path, which means they'll once again behave as if they were one path. Try giving it a radial gradient fill now. Better results, right?

Go ahead and deselect the circle parts compound path and select the individual star point paths. Make a compound path of them as well, just for efficiency and expediency. Now assign their fill color; I went with a solid red, but you're free to use any color or even another gradient if you like.

What else can you do with compound paths? You can use them as containers for placed images. Select your circle sections compound path, choose File ➢ Place, and import a photo. It will place right into the compound path. Think about the possibilities that opens up for creative image frame shapes and vector elements.

Compound paths can also hold text, although the shapes we have with this star would be better suited to containing decorative text rather than copy you expect to be read. Click in it with the Text tool and start typing to see what I mean.

Of course, being a container, a compound path can hold other containers. Experiment and you'll find some really interesting ideas!

Editing Paths and Shapes

Creating paths? Check. Making shapes? Check. Reshaping them? Check. Now, what does an InDesigner do to gain total control over paths?

SCISSORS TOOL

Remember the Erase tool? The Scissors tool is *almost* like it in a different form. It's actually closer to the Paths commands, which are next, and why I saved discussing the Scissors tool until now.

When you break a path by dragging the Erase tool across a path segment, a gap occurs. That's why the Erase tool is meant to be smudged *along* a path instead of *across* it. To precisely split or *cut* a path without erasing parts of it, use the Scissors tool either on anchor points or on path segments. Clicking a path with the Scissors tool cuts it in that spot, creating two anchor points that rest atop each other. To split a closed path into two separate objects, use the Scissors tool twice. Try it out.

1. Draw a square and give it a solid color fill and contrasting stroke color.

2. Select the Scissors tool from the Tools panel and then *walk*, don't run, back to your square and click the top-left corner. Apparently nothing should happen.

3. Again, move over to the bottom-right corner of the square and snip again with the Scissors.

4. Put the Scissors tool away and choose the Selection tool. With that implement, click the top-right corner of the square and drag it away half an inch or so. If your scissor work was precise, your square should become two separate, but open, triangular paths like mine (see Figure 4.25).

FIGURE 4.25
Before snipping with the Scissors tool (left), and after (right)

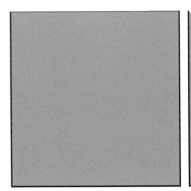

The Scissors tool can split a path into two (or more) distinct paths, as you just did, but it can also be used to merely open up a path, say to reshape with the Direct Selection tool or expand it with the Pencil tool. Don't think of this tool solely as a device to turn one object into multiple objects. In fact, if you try to scissor a path containing text into two, it will fail. The first scissor will work, opening the path, but the second just doesn't—and with no warning from the otherwise prolific alerter InDesign.

If the path you divide includes a placed image, *all* resulting paths will contain copies of the same graphic, which can be a good thing or a bad thing. If the Links panel reports an external file as persisting in the document despite all attempts to remove it, look for any shapes that might have been split from others with the Scissors or Eraser tools or the Path commands.

PATHS COMMANDS

On the Object ➢ Paths submenu are three commands you'll find useful from time to time: Open Path, Close Path, and Reverse Path.

Open Path is like a single click from the Scissors tool. This command opens a path by splitting it at the anchor point that closed the path. If you drew a square with the Pen tool, for example, working clockwise and placing first the top-left anchor point, then the top-right, and around back to the top-left again, Object ➢ Paths ➢ Open Path would split your path at the top-left anchor point because that is where the clockwise path drawing ended to close the path. After you use this command, the one anchor point is replaced with two, aligned atop each other and ready to be manipulated.

The opposite function is Close Path, which takes split or otherwise open paths and closes them by drawing a straight path segment to connect the last two anchor points (aka *end points* because they end a path).

Reverse Path is an interesting command. Do you recall your work trimming my cartoon depiction's hair with the Pencil tool? Recall how I noted there were two possible outcomes due to the direction in which you had originally drawn the path? Object ➢ Paths ➢ Reverse Path inverts that result. Select the path, or an anchor point on the path, to reverse, and then use the menu command.

PATHFINDER PANEL

Now that I've told you where to find the Convert Shape, Pathfinder, and Path commands on the Object menu and you've gotten fairly comfortable with them, it's time to tell you that they are located elsewhere as well. Before I tell you where, you must understand that using the menus—indeed, this entire chapter—is wax-on/wax-off training. It's important that you learn things in a certain order and that you learn the more difficult ways of doing things before the easy, Daniel-san.

On the Pathfinder panel (Window ➤ Object & Layout ➤ Pathfinder) are buttons to issue all the pathfinder, path, and convert shape commands (see Figure 4.26).

FIGURE 4.26

The Pathfinder panel

EDITING ANCHOR POINTS WITH THE DIRECT SELECTION TOOL

In Chapter 5, "Images," you'll see how to use the Direct Selection tool to position placed graphics. It's the rough equivalent of QuarkXPress's Content tool, but so much more. This humble little white arrow is the way to select and manipulate anchor points after they've been created. With it you can select, move, and delete one or more anchor points, as well as access and wrangle their curve handles.

1. Draw an S-curve.

2. From the Tools panel, grab the Direct Selection tool and hover it over the second anchor point in your S-curve. When you're directly over the anchor point, the Direct Selection tool will display a solid square in its bottom-right corner. Click to select the anchor point.

3. Drag the anchor point around—maybe up a little ways, maybe down. Notice how the path reshapes to accommodate the new position?

4. Release the anchor point, grab hold of the curve handle, and yank. (When your cursor is close enough to the curve handle end to grab it by clicking, a small diamond will appear in the bottom right of the cursor.) The curve will react accordingly, just as if you were still drawing with the Pen tool and hadn't yet let go of the mouse button. In this way, path segment curvature is perpetually editable.

Let's try something else. I warn you in advance, the end result is a little corny. Regardless, it's still an excellent example of working with the Direct Selection and other tools to manipulate a path.

1. On a new layer, use the Ellipse or Ellipse Frame tool to create a circle just about 2 inches in diameter.

2. With the Pen tool, add an anchor point about one-sixth of the way from the top around the left side. Do the same on the right side (see Figure 4.27). Drag down a guide if it helps to align them. Your circle should now have six anchor points in it at 12, 1, 3, 6, 9, and 11 o'clock.

FIGURE 4.27
My circle so far, with the two points added (with no anchor points selected)

3. Zoom in until you have a good view of the circle. Grab the Direct Selection tool. Click an empty area of the page to deselect all objects, and then, *near* the top anchor point, *not on it*, click the Direct Selection tool and drag a selection rectangle where the anchor point should be (see Figure 4.28). When you let go, the anchor point at the circle's apex should be solid (selected) while all other anchor points are empty (deselected). If any others are solid, click away to deselect and try again.

FIGURE 4.28
Dragging with the Direct Selection tool selects all anchor points in the drag area.

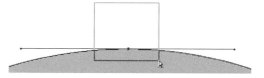

4. With the top anchor point selected, press Shift+Down Arrow on your keyboard until the top anchor point is below the two you added. Notice how the curve handles remain fixed at 0° while the path segments change in relation to the moving anchor point. See the curve handles also coming off the points on either side of the active one? Figure 4.29 shows approximately what you should be seeing now.

FIGURE 4.29
The circle, after moving the apex anchor point

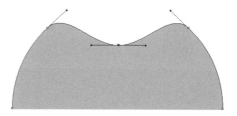

5. On the Tools panel, behind the Pen tool, select the Convert Direction Point tool (the inverted *V* as you may recall). With that tool, click the anchor point at the *bottom* of the now dented circle. The bowl should snap to an angle, removing the curvature emanating off either side of the anchor point and making it a corner anchor point (see Figure 4.30).

FIGURE 4.30
Converting the bottom point to a corner anchor point turns the curves it previously held into angles.

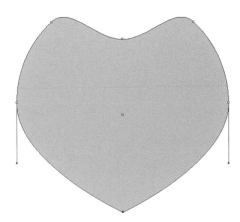

By now you must know what we're creating.

6. With the Convert Direction Point tool still selected, press and hold the Cmd/Ctrl key to temporarily change that tool into the Direct Selection arrow. Select the top anchor point again—or what was the top anchor point. Once selected, release Cmd/Ctrl to return to the Convert Direction Point tool.

7. You saw what happened when you used the Convert Direction Point tool on an anchor point. Don't click this point. Instead, click the little dot on the end of one curve handle. Apparently nothing should happen, but what you've done is sever the dependency between the two curve handles, enabling them—and their corresponding path segments— to be individually manipulated.

8. Switch back—fully—to the Direct Selection tool. The anchor point should remain selected, so now grab one of the curve handles and drag it upward and inward toward the point. Keep dragging until you get a nice, smooth arc in the path segment on the same side of the formerly top anchor point (see Figure 4.31).

FIGURE 4.31
So far, so good with the disconnected curves.

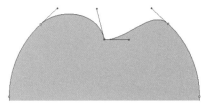

9. Do the same with the curve handle on the other side.

10. Now, we need to do something about those anchor points on the sides. Let's use the drag-selection method again to grab both of them at once. Click your Direct Selection tool a little ways off to the left, on the paper, and drag a selection rectangle rightward that covers both side—but no other—anchor points. Those two should become solid and all other anchor points hollow.

11. We'll get into scaling and transformations in a subsequent chapter, but let's jump ahead anyway. Up on the Control panel, the third column of measurement boxes is the scale percentage fields. Just to their right is a tiny chain link icon. If that icon is a complete chain link, click it to break the link between x and y scale percentages. Now, set the x, upper, percentage to 90%. The shape will suddenly reduce its girth like cinching a belt (see Figure 4.32).

FIGURE 4.32
After we scale the points, our shape is a little distorted.

12. You've got the basic shape now, so one at a time, select the side anchor points and adjust their curve handles to restore smooth, full curves to our shape.

Yes, I had you draw a heart. I *know* how corny and cliché and *almost* useless it is for you to know how to draw a heart in InDesign of all programs. We're far enough into the book that I hope I've earned from you a little more patience, a little faith—at least enough to ask you to read a couple more paragraphs. This is important, and I beg of you, don't put the book down just yet. We've been through so much together, let's not end it on this note.

You're still here. *Thank you.* Here's what I need to tell you, and what I think you need to hear. True, we drew a heart. But, what we drew is nowhere near as important as all the things you learned from it. Specifically, you learned the following:

◆ How to select anchor points by clicking them with the Direct Selection tool, and how that tool's cursor changes as it approaches anchor points and curve handles. You can also select multiple, noncontiguous points by holding Shift as you click each one after the first.

◆ How to select one or more anchor points by dragging a selection area with the Direct Selection tool. That's crucial because the need to select and work with more than a few anchor points simultaneously is frequent.

◆ How to move anchor points with the keyboard—another crucial skill. They can also be moved with the mouse, of course, and if you hold Shift while you move them, their motion will be constrained to vertical (90°), horizontal (0°), or another increment of 45°, depending upon the direction of movement.

- How to change the Convert Point Direction tool into the Direct Selection tool temporarily, which saves trips back to the Tools panel.

- How to adjust anchor point curvature for a desired result.

- Reinforced skills you learned earlier, like adding anchor points to a path, converting anchor points from smooth to corner, and converting an anchor point so that its curve handles moved independently of one another instead of in tandem.

- What most would consider an advanced power tip—that anchor points in a path can be transformed with scale percentages the same way complete paths and objects can be transformed. Here's one better: It isn't just scaling. You can rotate, shear, and precisely position anchor points, too. We'll dive deep into those features in a later chapter, though.

There, that's my justification for the nearly unforgivable act of asking a professional such as yourself to draw a heart. It *was* a heart, true, but a simple heart brought so much knowledge and understanding. Can you forgive me?

TECHNIQUE: CONVERT TEXT TO IMAGE-FILLED FRAME

This final exercise is definitely the best part of the chapter. Well, it is if you like cool effects, and who *doesn't* like cool effects? Of course, I must give you the obligatory caution that what you're about to learn has tremendous power—power to make your design outstanding, as well as power to make it a hackneyed cliché. Like any cool technique, it can be abused. Use it only when the design warrants it.

1. Create a text frame and type your initials into it. We're going to make a personal logo for you, right in InDesign, without reaching for the orange "Ai" or blue "Ps" icons on your Dock or Start Menu.

2. Style your initials, choosing an appropriate typeface(s) and setting the letters at a large size—at least 100 pts. Resize the text frame if necessary to fit them. Figure 4.33 shows my initials set in Adobe's Blackoak Std OpenType typeface at 100 pts. The text color is irrelevant, as long as you can clearly make out the letters.

FIGURE 4.33
My initials set in a
text frame

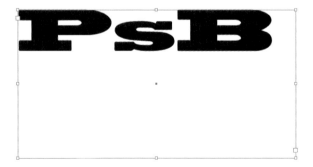

3. Using the Type tool, insert the cursor between the first pair of your initials (if you didn't use your middle initial, then there's only one pair, but put the cursor there anyway). Kern the letters tight—really tight—so they overlap but not so much that you can't easily differentiate them. Repeat for the second pair (if there is a second pair).

4. Are you perfectly happy with the way the letters kern together? We're about to remove your ability to edit their kerning, so be sure. I'll wait here while you experiment if you need more time.

Ah. You're back. Ready to move on? Grab the Selection tool, which will automatically select the text frame. Now, choose Type ➤ Create Outlines. *Kapow!* It's not type any longer—now your initials are a compound path.

 Real World Scenario

TO CONVERT TO OUTLINES OR NOT TO CONVERT TO OUTLINES: THAT IS THE QUESTION

Whether 'tis nobler in the RIP to suffer the slugs and bullets of outrageous fonts, or to take paths against a sea of troubles...

A question I often hear: *Should I convert all my type to outlines before making a PDF or sending it to press?*

Many, many moons ago, the single greatest problem in print design and production, the thing that stopped more RIPs and presses more often per day than anything else, was fonts—specifically, missing fonts or the use of different versions of the same font by the designer and by the pre-press house. Designers had to identify all the fonts they used in a document and then manually collect them for delivery with a job to pre-press. This was arduous and error-prone work, and frequently (*very* frequently), a font or two was left out.

During these dark ages it became commonplace to convert all type in short documents to outlines. Outlines are simple vector paths and no longer connect to, or require the presence of, a particular font. That, of course, means the type is no longer editable if an eleventh hour change request comes down from the client.

Now, InDesign can, in nearly all circumstances, automatically collect all fonts for distribution with a document. And jobs can be sent as PDFs, which can automatically embed fonts, too.

There is no reason to convert type to outlines simply for output to press or export to PDF. If you want to turn the type into a container or massage the paths of type, sure, convert it to outlines and go to town. Doing it "to be safe," as I hear from time to time, will accomplish only three things:

Eliminate your ability to edit the text. Typos and client changes happen, and once type has been converted and the document closed, there's no way back to live text.

Make the document render engines in all display devices—InDesign, Acrobat, proof printers, the RIP—*work harder than necessary.* True, type is vector paths, and converting to outlines merely exposes those paths. However, operating systems have dedicated type rendering engines solely to handle the math involved in drawing type quickly onscreen, on RIP, or on paper. When you convert to outlines, you take the type engine out of the mix and unnecessarily put the load for every anchor point, every path segment, in every glyph, on the shoulders of the math processor and the video card.

Finally, the worst thing you will accomplish is to *royally tick off your print or pre-press service provider.* These people frequently need to access your document to resolve issues prior to going to press. Even if they don't need to edit your type—maybe they need to resolve a color conflict, adjust your document bleed width, or change overprint and knockout settings—if they must open your document and wait while *their* computers grind away to draw every page, they will *not* be happy.

Don't convert type to outlines unless there's a valid reason. Otherwise, you're accomplishing little but falling upon your own sword, Hamlet.

---

5. We'll need to tweak a few things, so let's release the compound path—remember how to do that? Object ➤ Paths ➤ Release Compound Path.

6. When I released my compound path, I got a nasty surprise (see Figure 4.34). Fortunately, the Pathfinder panel offers a quick fix.

FIGURE 4.34

Releasing compound paths on my initials left the counters (holes) of the *P* and *B* as separate, filled shapes.

If you have the same filled-counter problem I do, select the letter's outer shape and the counter. Do one counter at a time if, as with my *B*, there are more than one. Once selected, subtract the front object (the counter) from the back (the main letterform). Repeat as necessary to punch all the needed holes.

7. Take a close look at your in-progress logo. Are those paths *exactly* as you'd like them? Anything you want to tweak in yours? There are a few things in mine that could be better.

For instance, I don't like how the upper curve of the *S* intrudes on the counter of the *P*. I'll fix that with the Add Anchor Point, Convert Direction Point, and Direct Selection tools.

The serifs on the *P* and *S* also don't match up, which looks awkward. Fortunately, I can just raise the top of the *S* serif a bit while lowering the top of the *P*'s and the *B*'s and then fix the curves on their rounded corners to compensate for the move. My finished paths are in Figure 4.35.

FIGURE 4.35

After tweaking, my personal logo paths are finished.

8. Once you've tweaked the paths to your satisfaction, select all the initials with the Selection tool and combine all three paths into a single path with the appropriate command on the Pathfinder panel or the Object ➤ Pathfinder menu.

9. With the permanently fused initials path selected, choose File ➤ Place and import an image, as I've done in Figure 4.36. Resize and move the placed image, if needed, with the Direct Selection tool like the content of any other container. Finish off your logo with a tagline, additional elements, or whatever else is needed.

FIGURE 4.36
Letters have become
a graphic frame.

Maybe you don't need a personal logo, maybe you've already got one and you're happy with it. Where else might this technique prove useful? What about the masthead for a magazine or newsletter? Cover art for a book or annual report? If you've got any symbol fonts like Zapf Dingbats, MiniPics, Wingdings, Webdings, or even Windows's Marlett, you have ready-made clipart in them that can be turned into truly unique graphic or even text frames in a snap. Figure 4.37 shows a few things I've created with this technique.

FIGURE 4.37
A few other ideas for
type converted to
frames

The Bottom Line

Draw Precise Paths with the Pen Tool   Precision drawing, the ability to create any shape, requires mastery of the Pen tool.

> **Master It**   Re-open `pathtrace01.indd` from the files that you downloaded from the Web. Instead of tracing it with merely straight path segments, use what you've learned about corner anchor points and smooth anchor points to trace it faithfully—straight where needed, curved where needed. Set the fill for your traced letters to contrast with the original orange ones, and when you've finished tracing, zoom in to examine how closely you were able to come to the original shapes.

Freehand Draw Paths with the Pencil Tool   The Pen tool is synonymous with precision, and the Pencil tool with freedom. Sometimes, quickly drawing something with a natural feel is more important than precision.

> **Master It**   Open a new document and, using the Pencil tool, draw your own cartoonish self-portrait. Get it all sketched out before worrying about the paths themselves. Once it's done, go back with the Smooth tool and, if needed, the Erase tool to clean it up.

Combine and Subtract Shapes, and Convert from One Shape to Another   Many complex paths begin with simple geometric shapes. Indeed, most objects you create in InDesign will *be* simple geometric shapes, alone or compounded with other shapes.

Master It

1. Draw three shapes—a circle, triangle, and a square—each exactly 2 inches in diameter.

2. Convert the triangle and square to circles.

3. Manually position the circles into a rough triangular formation. Each circle should overlap its neighbors, with all three overlapping in the center. Select all three.

4. Exclude the overlaps.

5. Release the compound path, and fill each resulting shape with color individually.

Modify Any Vector Artwork   Precision drawing mastery requires precision path editing.

Master It   Beginning with a pentagon, employ the Convert Direction Point tool and Direct Selection tool to convert the straight segment shape into a five-pointed star with concave sides like this:

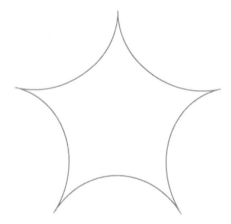

Turn Type into a Container to Hold Images or Text   Strictly speaking, the technique of converting readable type into frames should be used infrequently. When used on symbol font glyphs, though, it's a great way to make short work of creating complicated shapes for use as frames or merely decorative elements.

> **Master It**   Using a font installed on your computer—preferably a symbol font—locate a suitable glyph using the Glyphs panel. Set and style it on the page and convert it to frame. Fill the frame with text—your own or InDesign's placeholder text.

Chapter 5

Images

Picture pages, picture pages, now it's time for picture pages, time to grab your crayons and your pencil…

— *Bill Cosby, the* Captain Kangaroo Show

InDesign's greatest strength, the area in which it towers head and shoulders over all challengers, is its type handling and rendering features. Fortunately, it's just as good with imagery—especially in CS3.

In this chapter, you will learn to:

♦ Place image assets

♦ Import images without the Place command

♦ Manage placed assets

♦ Go native in your workflow

Placing Assets

Images, like text, are content and must be encapsulated within containers—frames. And as with text, you have a choice as to when and how you create the frame: frames can be created manually and later filled, or you can skip that step, letting InDesign create the frame automatically upon placement of an image.

Frame-First Workflow

A frame-first workflow—also called forms-based, templated, box-first, or grid-first workflow (this last is technically erroneous because all layouts should begin with a grid regardless of the way assets are placed)—begins with the containers and fills them with content later. You already know about working frame-first if you've ever used QuarkXPress, which *only* works frame-first.

Solo designers and graphic design studios with varied clients and projects won't often employ frame-first workflows simply because most of their client assignments begin after content had been created; they're hired to lay out that content. Creatives working in publishing houses, corporate design departments, and other environments with a narrower focus are often required to design templates and layouts at the same time other departments or agencies are creating the content.

A product catalog, for example, is typically built on a rigid grid. The layout artist knows in advance approximately how many products she must list and the target page count. From there, she can extrapolate the number of products each page must contain and thus the amount of space each product entry is allowed for copy and imagery. Until the photogs and copyeditors turn in all the material, the layout artist can't place actual content, but she can build templates in preparation for that moment. Figure 5.1 shows what one catalog page template might look like before content is available.

FIGURE 5.1
A typical catalog
page built
frame-first

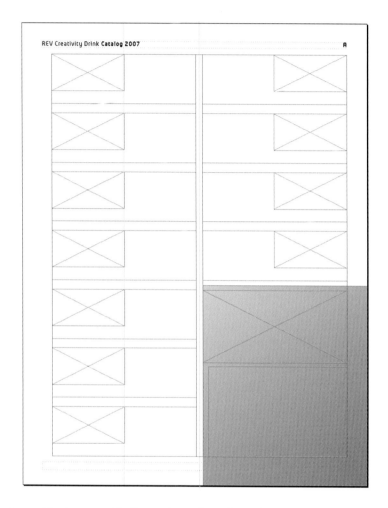

Here, 11 product photos (the frames with diagonal crossbars through them) and their accompanying textual descriptions (the empty frames surrounding the image frames) are arranged and ready to receive content. In the lower-outside corner (lower-right on this right-read page), a featured product will benefit from a larger image and more copy atop a colored background. Thus, each page can comfortably carry a dozen products. The designer has done the math—probably with *FPO* images and text—and determined the appropriate size at which the average product photo and its description should lay out. When photos are ready, they will be fit into the waiting image frames; the same for copy in its frames. Until the product shots and copy arrive, this page is finished.

That's frame-first page construction—building spaces ahead of content.

Go ahead and build a quick frame-first layout similar to the one in Figure 5.1. Don't get overly concerned with the text frames. You'll need two or three at least, but don't spend too much time styling them.

Ready? Let's go through the various ways to fill those image frames.

Image Import Options

The most common method of importing an image is via File ➤ Place (or the Place shortcut of Cmd+D/Ctrl+D)—just as with placing text documents. Basic asset placement you already know, so we'll skip the beginner-level stuff and dive right into the various types of image assets InDesign will import and the options available for each. So, go ahead and open the Place dialog. Which types of images *can* InDesign place within frames? Plenty! Table 5.1 shows them.

TABLE 5.1: **Graphic File Formats Supported by InDesign**

FILE FORMAT	DOCUMENT DESCRIPTION AND SUPPORTED CHARACTERISTICS
TIFF, TIF	Tagged Image Format; supports single page, compressed or uncompressed
GIF	Graphical Interchange Format; supports single frame
PNG	Portable Network Graphics; supports single-frame, alpha transparency
JPG, JPEG, JPE	Joint Photographic Experts Group
PDF	Portable Document Format; supports layers, multiple pages (one page per import), alpha transparency
AI	Adobe Illustrator document; supports layers, alpha transparency
PSD	Photoshop document; supports layers, layer sets, alpha transparency
EPS	Encapsulated PostScript
PICT	Macintosh vector/raster hybrid
WMF	Windows Meta File vector/raster hybrid
EMF	Enhanced Windows Meta File vector/raster hybrid
MOV	QuickTime Movie; nonanimated in InDesign (only first frame shows), but animates on export to PDF

Because InDesign doesn't draw as much of a distinction as other applications do between *types* of content—text, imagery, even audio and video media—the Place dialog will automatically show every importable file type. Even if you have a graphic frame selected, InDesign will present textual documents as place options. Remember, a container is a container, and content is content; InDesign's frames can hold any type of supported content.

At the bottom of the Place dialog is the same Show Import Options check box we examined while working with ASCII and Word documents. The import options themselves, however, are quite different.

BASIC RASTER IMAGES

When you're importing basic raster or bitmap images like JPEGs, GIFs, and TIFFs, the Image Import Options dialog contains two panes (see Figure 5.2). The first, Image, offers the option of applying an embedded Photoshop *clipping path* (if included in the image) to crop the image content. If the image contains *alpha channels*, one may be chosen here as well.

FIGURE 5.2

Image Import Options

Alpha channels are extra channels in the image to define transparency or a selection. Every time you use Quick Mask mode to paint a selection, for example, Photoshop creates a special alpha channel called Quick Mask (see Figure 5.3). Save a selection from Select ➤ Save Selection in Photoshop and you're really creating a new channel that, upon placement of the image into InDesign, can be selected on the Image tab as the alpha channel—only the areas selected in the original marquee will appear while the rest is hidden.

FIGURE 5.3

The Channels panel in Photoshop CS3 displaying a saved selection channel (non-white area) and the temporary Quick Mask channel created while in Quick Mask mode

The other tab available when you're importing basic bitmap images is Color, which enables you to specify an *ICC color profile* and *rendering intent* specific to the image (see Figure 5.4). Oh, yes, InDesign can manage the color of every placed image independently of one another and of the entire document.

FIGURE 5.4

Importing an image offers individual color management of the image independent of the document or other images.

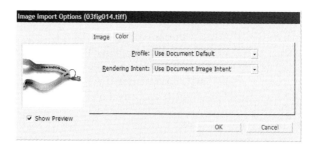

PNG

When you place a PNG in InDesign, you'll get the same Image Import Options dialog with the same Image and Color tabs as with other raster formats, but you'll also get a third tab (see Figure 5.5).

FIGURE 5.5

Image Import Options, PNG Settings

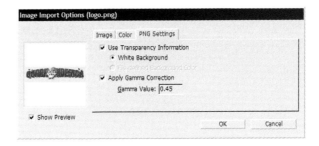

Because PNGs have alpha channel transparency—effectively, if you can create the transparency effect in Photoshop, PNG will display it that way—your first option is what to do with the background. If you'd like to preserve the transparency, check Use Transparency Information. With that on, InDesign needs to know how to mix semitransparent areas—on white or on the background color defined in the image. For example, do you want this 50% opaque blue mixed with white so it looks 50% opaque blue, or should it mix with yellow so the result is green? PNGs created by Adobe software don't have available background color definitions, and the only option is white.

Apply Gamma Correction allows you to compensate for the fact that PNGs are usually slightly off in their *gamma* ranges. If you placed a PNG and a PSD of the same image side by side—indeed, if the former was *made from* the latter—the PNG will look a few shades darker. It's just a PNG thing, homey. By adjusting the gamma correction here, you can compensate for the inherent darkness of the PNG.

EPS

Let's just run through the EPS Import Options (see Figure 5.6) and how InDesign handles placed EPS files.

FIGURE 5.6

The EPS Import Options dialog

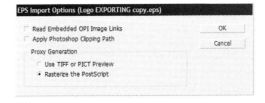

EPS is a simplistic format, and it has few options on import.

It can contain a vector clipping path and an *OPI* link. OPI stands for Open Prepress Interface, which is a process by which a low-resolution or FPO image is temporarily substituted for the high-resolution, final image. For instance, if you're doing the layout on a magazine article while the real photos are still out at the color correction house, you can use a picture of a Domokun as FPO and then embed in the EPS a statement that links to the predetermined path and filename of the final image. At some point—conversion to PDF, print from InDesign, or in RIP—the final image will be sucked in via the OPI link to replace the FPO image, but retaining the position, scale, and crop settings of the FPO.

If yours is among those workflows using OPI, make sure to check the Read Embedded OPI Image Links option. That will tell InDesign to maintain the link to final assets, which enables their inclusion when you're printing directly from InDesign and maintains the links when InDesign content is exported or sent to RIP.

EPS files are pure PostScript code. Thus, in order to render them to screen, an application must contain—or have access to—a PostScript interpreter. Without an interpreter, you get a gray box with no idea of what's actually in the image. Until the last couple of versions, that's what you'd get if you placed an EPS image into Microsoft Word.

Twenty years ago, when Adobe was still building support for PostScript, few applications could render EPS files natively onscreen. They printed beautifully to PostScript printers, but that wasted a lot of paper because creatives moved an EPS, printed a proof, moved it a little more, printed another proof, and so on. To compensate, Adobe enabled EPS files to generate and carry low-resolution raster preview images, first in the Mac-native PICT format and then on Windows as well with TIFF-based previews. With the embedded raster previews, more applications are able to display something other than a gray box without the need to pay Adobe for a PostScript license.

When you create an EPS in Illustrator or Photoshop, for example, you're asked whether to include a preview and, if so, whether it should be black and white (a 1-bit, no shades of gray b&w) or color and whether any empty space between the EPS artwork and the rectangular bounding box that contains it should be rendered as transparent or white. Pay particular attention to that last statement because it's the cause of a lot of cranial injuries due to repetitive wall and desk impacts.

Take a look at Figure 5.7, which is Illustrator CS3's Save As EPS Options dialog. You can see the Preview Format drop-down, which is where you choose color or black and white raster preview images. Just below that are radio buttons to make the background transparent or opaque (white). If the creator of the EPS chooses Opaque, when you place that EPS into InDesign, *it will have an opaque background*. Former QuarkXPress users will immediately jump to the conclusion that the frame containing the EPS is defaulting to filling with white (paper color in InDesign), which XPress did until version 7. Naturally, they'll click on the None color swatch to clear it. When that doesn't work, the forehead-to-desk percussion usually begins.

If you happen to find yourself unable to explain a white background on an imported EPS… Well, there's the explanation. Pull the EPS into Illustrator and resave it with a transparent preview background.

Or, you could always just chuck the preview entirely and tell InDesign to build its own by selecting Rasterize the PostScript. It won't *really* rasterize the image itself; you'll still get crisp vector output. This option only creates a new preview proxy for onscreen viewing. Moreover, InDesign's proxy creation is usually better than the previews embedded in the EPS files themselves. I usually check Rasterize the PostScript for all my EPS imports.

If you infrequently work with EPS images and are prone to forget little details like how to overcome a white background, I humbly suggest you dog-ear this page. A concussion is not a laughing matter.

FIGURE 5.7
Illustrator's EPS
Options dialog
appears when you're
saving a document
as EPS.

PSD PHOTOSHOP DOCUMENTS

InDesign can place native Photoshop PSD documents and Illustrator AI documents (see the following section for the latter). You don't *need* to save Photoshop documents to TIFF or Illustrator artwork to EPS in order to place them into the page layout application anymore!

As with other image formats, the import options dialog for PSD files includes Image and Color tabs to access alpha channel transparency and color management, respectively. It also includes a Layers tab (see Figure 5.8). There have been some changes here since CS2, so don't skip this section if you're a CS2 guru.

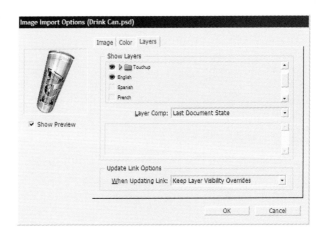

FIGURE 5.8
Importing a layered
PSD enables the Layers tab in Image
Import Options.

Here you can see a multilingual product shot mocked up in Photoshop. In that application, I used layers to set the label text in English, Spanish, French, Italian, and German without resorting to five separate PSD documents that I'd have to tweak and touch up to match client change requests. All the common image elements—the 3D can, the highlights and shadows, the logo—are contained on their own layers used globally in all language versions; only the variable text is separated onto individual layers.

In the top section, Show Layers, I can turn the PSD image's layers on and off individually. If I needed to place the version of the can en Español, all I'd have to do is turn off the English layer and turn on the Spanish. It even correctly interprets Photoshop's layer groups, thus I can hide or show an entire range of layers with a single toggle of the eyeball.

Controlling individual layer visibility is new to InDesign CS3. CS2 had only *Layer Comp* control, which CS3 retains, but which often created more work for the InDesign users by making them go back to Photoshop to set up layer comps.

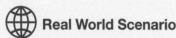

Real World Scenario

CREATING LAYER COMPS IN PHOTOSHOP

What are layer comps? They're snapshots of the state of layers in a Photoshop document—which are on, which are off, their blending modes, and their positions. For instance, let's say in Photoshop you have a five-layered document. Everything looks good, but you'd like to experiment a little, maybe try a different arrangement of objects, maybe see how changing Layer 3's blending mode from Hard Light to Difference would affect the overall design. You want to play around a bit, but not lose your way back. Undo will only save you so many times. You could make a history state snapshot, but that's a little risky. Duplicating the image would work, but it would also leave you with multiple separate files if you decided to retain the variants—maybe to show the client the customary (and often ill-advised) three versions of a design. Instead of creating multiple copies of the same document, make a layer comp.

Open the Layer Comps panel in Photoshop (Window ➢ Layer Comps) and, with all the layers of the first version on and set the way you want, create a new layer comp by clicking the button at the bottom of the panel. Name it something like First Version. Then, start moving and changing things. When you've got another design you like, create a second layer comp. Keep going until you've got all the designs and layer comps you want.

Now, in the Layer Comps panel, you should note that only one layer comp is visible at a time. Click the empty box to the left of First Version and *that* layer comp will become the active one, with only its constituent layers active and set the way they were in the beginning. Turn on Second Version and the layers will shift again. At the bottom of the panel are even left and right arrows to cycle up or down through all the layer comps. Voila! Multiple designs and variants in the same Photoshop document.

Layer comps track layers, not the image data on them. Layer visibility, position, blending mode, transparency, and effects *are* tracked and managed via layer comps, but if you swipe a paintbrush across a layer or fix a typo in a text layer, that change ripples through all comps. If you need to modify the actual content of a layer, duplicate it and make the duplicate part of the next layer comp.

I've used layer comps on numerous projects, including the drink-can design, for multilingual work. More often, I've used it for variations and managing multiple but closely related assets as a single entity—for instance, color and grayscale versions of the same image in one PSD. In Photoshop, layer comps enable efficiency by reducing the number of documents and thus the amount of duplicate layer-based data that must be managed across all those documents. Carrying them through to InDesign offers the same advantages—one asset to update instead of four or five, one file to package and send to press instead of four or five. You get the point.

Upon placing a PSD with layer comps into InDesign you have access through the Image Import Options dialog to those layer comps in the Layer Comp drop-down list. Just pick one and go.

The Last Document State option imports the image however it was last saved in Photoshop—including which layer comp was chosen and which layers were on. Editing the image in Photoshop—even just changing the layer comp—will, upon updating the link in InDesign, reflect those changes there. If you specifically want a particular layer comp regardless of how the layers may be set the next time you save the file in Photoshop, don't use Last Document State. Instead, choose a specific layer comp.

In Photoshop, you can assign notes to your layer comps, which is a great way to tell the future you what the current you was thinking while making all these different versions of the image. The large area below the Layer Comp drop-down menu in InDesign's Import Options dialog will display any notes associated with the currently selected layer comp. Thus, you can tell the future you what you were thinking whether he's using Photoshop or InDesign.

Jumping back one paragraph, When Updating Links is similar to the Last Document State option. You have two options here: Keep Layer Visibility Overrides and Use Photoshop's Layer Visibility. The former keeps the options you choose in this dialog regardless of how layers were on or off next time the image is saved from Photoshop. Conversely, the latter dumps all your options and always updates the placed image from its next saved state.

To change layer and layer comp visibility on an image already in the layout, select the image and open the Object Layer Options dialog (see Figure 5.9), which is on the Object menu.

In case it's not obvious, the reason layer and layer comp support in InDesign is cool is because you can have a single external asset to manage while still placing five, six, or a hundred different images in the layout.

By keeping all five language versions in my product mockup in a single PSD file, I not only made my creation and revision work on the image in Photoshop much easier and more efficient, I also streamlined my InDesign and output work. I only have one asset image to worry about instead of five—80% less likelihood of problems at RIP time.

FIGURE 5.9
Object Layer
Options on the
Object menu man-
ages layer and layer
comp visibility on
layered PSD, AI, and
PDF assets already
on the page.

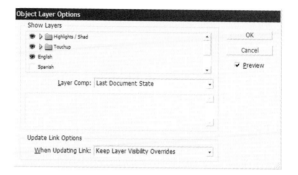

PDF AND ILLUSTRATOR AI

Adobe Illustrator AI files *are* PDFs, and have been for several versions now. The only thing that truly separates your run-of-the-mill PDF from an AI file is an extra data layer to preserve native Illustrator object and document information—things like embedded swatch and symbol sets, the pre-rendered 3D object data, and similar bits of information that Illustrator needs to edit artwork but PDF doesn't require in order to output to screen or RIP. Saving a PDF from Illustrator with the Preserve Illustrator Editing Capabilities option checked results in saving a file identical in all the ways that matter to a native AI file. So, PDF would, were it not PDF call'd, retain that dear perfection which it owes without that title. (My apologies to the Bard.)

Don't believe me? Change the file extension from `.ai` to `.pdf` and double-click the file. Mac users, that won't work as well for you. You can Get Info and define Acrobat (or OS X Preview, for that matter) to open the PDF or just drop the file on your Acrobat or Adobe Reader icon. Close the file, then drop it into Illustrator.

The fact that AIs and PDFs are the same file format means two things. First, it's a great troubleshooting step. If someone tells you they can't open your AI file or that it's corrupted, ask if they can read it in their copy of Acrobat or Adobe Reader. If so, they should be able to do a quick Save As from Acrobat, forcing a rewrite of the file code to clear out corruption without throwing away Illustrator editing data. Note that that's *only* for Acrobat; saving it out of OS X Preview or another PDF reader will probably destroy the Illustrator editing data layer.

The other thing it means, germane to the topic at hand, is that choosing to place either a PDF or an AI results in the same import options dialog, that being Place PDF.

PDF files placed into InDesign don't have the Image and Color tabs—that's all managed from within the original application or the PDF itself. InDesign will preserve colors and color profiles embedded in a PDF even if InDesign itself doesn't understand the colors. Moreover, *trapping* data in the PDF is also preserved. To change either, edit the PDF directly. Placing a PDF has other options relevant to the particular nature of PDFs. The Layers tab is, except for the absence of layer comp controls (neither Illustrator nor Acrobat has such facilities), identical in appearance and function to the Layers tab in the Image Import Options for Photoshop PSDs. What *is* unique to AI and PDF placement is the General tab (see Figure 5.10).

Because PDFs can be multipage documents (but Illustrator documents cannot) and InDesign can only fill a single frame with one page at a time, the first option to choose is which page you want. The controls beneath the Preview section will let you cycle through the pages one at a time, jump to a specific page, or, with the buttons on either end, jump to the first or last page of the document quickly. Multipage PDFs *can* be placed, but only one page at a time (sort of; bear with me a moment, and we'll get to that).

FIGURE 5.10
The General tab of
the Place PDF dialog

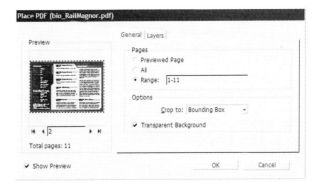

Jumping down to the Options section on the right, Transparent Background asks, à la EPS, whether the image should be placed with a transparent or white background. When you look at a PDF in Acrobat or other applications, you see a white page. That's just a device to make the PDF easier to read onscreen, just like pages in InDesign; there is not a white box there. Thus, by default, you'll place a PDF with an empty background, which is typically what you want. If for some reason you don't, uncheck the box (or fill the resulting frame with white).

Crop To provides several options: Bounding Box, Art, Crop, Trim, Bleed, and Media. There's a lot of confusion over what they all mean, complicated by the fact that, in many cases, there's no discernable difference between them. Let me see if I can sort it out.

Bounding Box The document bounding box is the total area of all objects and image data in the document. Choosing this option imports everything in there, including, if defined, crop marks, data in the bleed area, and data in the slug area (beyond the bleed).

Art In applications like Illustrator, you can define an area smaller than the bounding box as that containing the art—the art box. If you've done that, cropping to the art will toss out everything outside the art box. In many cases, such as with InDesign-created PDFs, the art box is the trim area.

Crop If the document has a crop area defined—with or without crop marks—this option will crop to the, er, crop area. For example, in Illustrator, you can begin with an 8.5×11-inch document and then create a crop area that is much smaller than the page simply by drawing a rectangle and choosing Object ➤ Crop Area ➤ Make.

Trim Crop to a defined trim area. The trim is the final, deliverable dimensions of a document and omits the bleed area.

Bleed The bleed area is outside the trim and holds "overflow" image data. In the event paper shifts on a cutting machine and the blade doesn't perfectly align with the trim edge, extending imagery out beyond the trim guide (usually ⅛ inch) ensures that ink continues to bleed off the page. If the PDF includes a bleed area, this option will include it in the image.

Media Crop to the original paper size defined in the PDF—regardless of the options above in the dialog as well as other factors like visually cropping the PDF within Acrobat.

PDFs Do Print

Contrary to a popular misconception prevalent even among recent design program graduates and veteran creative and production professionals, PDFs *are* capable of high resolution. Raster images in PDF can be as good as images in Photoshop, and the fully realized vector paths on par with those in Illustrator. They can hold transparency as well as can Photoshop, and they *are* ready for press. All of this assumes they were created correctly, of course, but the same is true of *any* document. PDFs are no more or less likely to be botched than an EPS, a PSD, or even an INDD.

To speed display onscreen, InDesign automatically generates a raster preview of placed PDF pages. If the PDF contains transparency, the preview uses TIFF; if not, it uses JPEG. Neither of these will print. They're just to speed screen drawing while working, using plain raster images as proxies instead of rereading the potentially much more complex native PDF every time you scroll, zoom, change pages, or manipulate the placed object.

Placing Multipage PDFs

Getting back to the Pages section and that whole "placing one page at a time" thing, it's *sort of* not true. True, you can place only one page of a PDF in one frame, but new to InDesign CS3 is the ability to place multiple pages in rapid succession without going back through the whole process.

For instance, let's assume we have a 10-page PDF and we want to insert all the pages in separate image frames—maybe we're doing the old QuarkXPress-as-imposition-tool trick in InDesign instead of buying a dedicated imposer. Up until now, every page of the PDF had to be placed separately, one page at a time, with a trip to the Place and Place PDF dialogs each time. In a stroke of genius, Adobe has now enabled multiple images to be preloaded onto the place cursor, *and* they've opened that feature to multipage PDFs.

Let's give it a try in our mock catalog page.

1. Go to File ➤ Place (or use the much quicker Cmd+D/Ctrl+D shortcut), and navigate to a multipage PDF. Any one will do. They're so common, I'm so confident that you have them littering your hard drive, that I didn't even bother to include one in the project files available on the book's download web page.

2. Select that PDF, check Show Import Options, and click OK.

3. On the General tab, select All if your PDF has 10 or fewer pages; if it contains more than 10 pages, select Range and enter a range of page numbers in the format *X-Y*. Click OK.

4. You should see a loaded cursor with the brand-new thumbnail preview of what's on deck to be placed. Click in one of the image frames to place the first page, and look again at your cursor. It still shows the on-deck preview, doesn't it? Well, that's the *next page*. Click in the next waiting image frame to place that and load up the third page. Keep going until you've run out of image frames.

Wicked cool, isn't it? And that brings me to…

InDesign INDD

Yup, you can now place one InDesign file into another. That's not the same as merging two InDesign documents, which we'll cover in Chapter 7, "Pages."

A common practice, especially among QuarkXPress-based publishing workflows, is to export a layout page as EPS and then place the EPS inside the same or another layout—a picture of a page within a page. It's the way to do, for example, cover shots in magazine "Letters to the Editor" or "In the next issue" department pages.

While the QuarkXPress method of saving/exporting a single page to EPS and then replacing has worked for many, many years, and despite the fact that InDesign can do it the same way (File ➤ Export, choose EPS, JPEG, SVG, or PDF format), there are significant drawbacks to that method. Specifically these:

◆ It's one page at a time export. If you need images of every page of a 32-page publication, you have to repeat the process—go to the page, ensure it's the current page, select File ➤ Export or File ➤ Save Page as EPS, name the file, click Save—32 times.

◆ It's one page at a time import. To place those 32 pages, you'll have to do it 32 times.

◆ Exporting pages creates a whole new file—more assets to manage, more likelihood of missing or corrupted files, and more potential RIP problems.

◆ Exported pages are copies, not the original pages. If the actual layout of the page design changes—say, at the last minute, the cover shot for the next issue changes—you must rebuild and replace the EPS of pages, again, one at a time.

◆ Exported images are EPS, an obsolete format. Although InDesign does a great job with EPS previews, as do recent versions of QuarkXPress. Even QuarkXPress, the application that pioneered the methodology, didn't, prior to version 6.5, include a screen preview that could be considered reliable relevant to the print output.

Most of us have learned as a matter of necessity to work around the drawbacks, but now, why bother? InDesign CS3 solves all these drawbacks and problems:

◆ *Problem:* It's one page at a time export. *Solution:* There is no export; just save the source INDD document.

◆ *Problem:* It's one page at a time import. *Solution:* Importing InDesign INDD documents is exactly like importing PDFs, with an identical dialog and the ability to import one, all, or a range of pages, which will place sequentially from the on-deck place queue just as with multipage PDFs.

◆ *Problem:* Exporting pages creates a whole new file. *Solution:* There is no export and no additional assets to manage.

◆ *Problem:* Exported pages are copies, not the original pages. *Solution:* There is no export. When the source INDD changes, update linked assets to reflect those changes in the placed instance(s) within the current layout.

◆ *Problem:* Exported images are EPS, an obsolete format. *Solution:* There is no spoon, Neo.

You can place one InDesign document inside another, although you cannot do a "hydra import," an asexual import wherein the *same* InDesign document is placed back into *itself* as an asset. If that's what you need, consider your options. Longer documents can, for other reasons as well, often benefit from splitting into multiple files coupled by an InDesign Book. With a Book tying them together, styles and swatches can remain synchronized, as can page and section numbers, and all documents in the publication can be printed, packaged, and exported to PDF simultaneously, just as can a single document. If a Book doesn't makes sense for your document yet you still need to place a page from the current document as an asset on another page, save the asset version as a separate, complete copy of the document. Then, if the source page changes in the final deliverable, just make a new copy of the master document, overwriting the asset version, and update links. That is still more reliable and faster than taking the route of export to EPS, JPEG, SVG, or PDF; it does result in a larger package for print, though.

Multiple Asset Place

Surely the new CS3 feature destined to be used most often, to save the most time, is the multiple concurrent asset placement option. It works not just with multiple pages of one PDF or INDD, but a whole set of images—you can even mix imagery and text!

Let's jump right into a hands-on exercise.

1. Ready a folder of images and textual documents. You're welcome to use the resource files found in other chapter folders on this book's download files. The key is that they must be copied to the same folder.

2. Press Cmd+D/Ctrl+D to open the Place dialog, and navigate to the folder of images and/or textual documents. Select up to 10 of the files in the list (you can use more than 10 files; I just don't want you bogged down trying this hands-on exercise by having to place 40 or 50 images).

   On both Windows and Mac, select sequential files in a list by clicking on the first and then, while holding Shift, clicking on the last. All those between will be added to the selection. To highlight nonsequential files, or to selectively remove certain files from the group, hold Ctrl (Windows) or Option (Mac) while clicking on the undesirables.

3. Got your files selected? Good. Let's speed this up by *unchecking* Show Import Options, and then click OK. You'll be deposited back into your document with a loaded cursor and preview image. Just to the right of the cursor itself, within the thumbnail, will be a number in parenthesis. This is the number of on-deck files waiting to be placed.

4. Click once inside the first image frame on the page—it will fill with the image you just saw thumbnailed, and the next image in the stack will appear in thumbnail. Click the next frame to fill it, too.

   If you encounter a text document, which will be obvious by the first few words appearing as its thumbnail, click on a text frame instead.

5. Before placing the third image, look at it. It's not the one you *want* to place third, is it? (Humor me.) The order in which a file system sorts the list in the Place dialog does not always match the order in which we'd like to place the images. In some cases, you know which goes where, but sometimes it's just easier to change the order of the images to be placed and queue up a different one.

   How? The up and down arrows on your keyboard. Try them out to cycle forward and back, respectively, in the stack of on-deck assets to be placed. The thumbnail preview will show what's in front, what would be deposited in the layout upon the next click.

   Go ahead and fill the rest of the frames until you've emptied the place queue.

There are a few other things you should know about this new multiple asset place. When it was just one asset placed at a time, pressing Esc would clear the place cursor and return you to an unloaded cursor. Now, Esc clears only the frontmost (displayed) asset; the rest of the stack remains. If you want to clear out of a loaded queue of 20 pictures, switch tools by choosing one on the Tools panel.

When you turn off Show Import Options, the last selected options for a given file type are used. For instance, if, when placing a single PDF, you choose to import all pages and then, on a subsequent place operation, disable Show Import Options and place multiple assets including a multipage PDF, you'll place each page of that PDF in turn. The on-deck count *does not* add in the number of PDF pages; instead it counts the PDF itself as one asset regardless of its page count. For example, if you place a 100-page PDF and a PSD, the on-deck count will list only 2 even though it will place 101 individual images.

Drag and Drop

Everyone uses File ➢ Place (or Cmd+D/Ctrl+D), which is the least efficient of the methods in versions prior to CS3. Now, with the ability to place multiple assets concurrently, the Place command has suddenly become extremely useful again—more so in some scenarios than this next method. Still, drag and drop asset placement has its own significant advantages, especially when you need only a few images from a folder of assets or if you need several assets across multiple folders.

Have you heard of Adobe Bridge (see Figure 5.11)?

FIGURE 5.11
Adobe Bridge digital asset manager

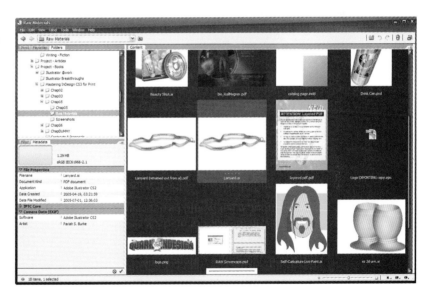

Adobe Bridge is a mid-level desktop digital asset manager (DAM) included as part of Creative Suite 3 and with any stand-alone CS3-version application. I'm not going to devote a lot of time to discussing it because (a) I've got limited page count in this book, and (b) I can probably talk my publisher into letting me write a separate Adobe Bridge book in which I'll have several hundred pages to really go into all its cool, efficiency building features. Suffice it to say, Bridge is pretty darn cool, with a lot of hidden features and nuances that can really speed up your work and take some of the focus off the tools and put it where your attention belongs—on your designs.

What I *do* want to talk about here is that Bridge is a visual DAM, allowing you to manage your assets by actually *seeing* them instead of trying to remember in the Place dialog the differences between photographs labeled `prodshoot070419-0067.jpg` and `prodshoot070419-0068.jpg`. With Bridge and other DAM software (like iPhoto, Extensis's Portfolio, Cerious Software's ThumbsPlus, and others), you can view thumbnails of your images, zooming in or out as needed, and manage them visually—move, delete, duplicate, reorganize, and so on.

(Incidentally, Adobe Bridge CS3 was integral to the creation of this book by managing all my screen shots in various versions and states, the sample files destined for the download web page, all my make-readies for the screen shots, and pictures of my kids, to which I liked to look every so often while working.)

One advantage Bridge has over the competition is that it will thumbnail not just graphics files, it also shows previews of Photoshop, Illustrator, Acrobat, Microsoft Office, and even InDesign documents. (Note that in order for Bridge to display thumbnails of Adobe application files, they must have an embedded preview image, which is an option in the Save As dialog or Preferences for each application.) Thus, if you're using *Version Cue* document versioning and revision control on your InDesign document, you can *see* the differences between what you did yesterday and this morning.

Although ThumbsPlus won't do InDesign documents, PDFs, and Office files, it *will* show thumbnail-sized previews of fonts—TrueType and OpenType, but not PostScript. Bridge won't do fonts at all, leaving you to the horrid little preview windows of modern font managers.

Getting back to the main point of placing images, you can drag and drop directly from Bridge into InDesign. Choose the *picture* you want to place, not the filename.

Position the Bridge window such that you can see your InDesign layout simultaneously (multiple monitors help), then drag an image from Bridge and drop it atop a frame in InDesign. Voila! Placed image.

Working content-first, you can even place multiple images simultaneously, though not into pre-existing frames. Select the images in Bridge using Shift (sequential) and/or Cmd/Ctrl (nonse-quential); then, in one motion, click on an already selected image and drag it out of Bridge and over an empty area of the InDesign document. All the images selected in Bridge will place as links in InDesign, each in its own frame and cascaded for (usually) easy selection. Note that it will use the previously chosen or default import options for each file type; you wont' see an Import Options dialog.

Because Bridge can also manage textual files—PDFs, Word documents, TXT, RTF, InCopy INCD documents, and even other InDesign INDD documents—they can also be imported via drag and drop.

Any other DAM application that affords the user drag and drop file management capability can also be used in the same manner, as just described. iPhoto on Mac OS X is great for that, as is Adobe's Lightroom and Photoshop Album (professional photography and consumer DAMs, respectively), the aforementioned ThumbsPlus and Portfolio, and numerous other DAM applications.

When you do find yourself managing files in the file system—an OS X Finder window, a Win-dows Explorer window, or either platform's desktop—you can place via drag and drop from there as well with the same behavior.

One last area for drag and drop is from another application to InDesign.

You can drag Photoshop and Illustrator layers, and Illustrator objects, and drop them directly into the existing frames in the InDesign layout or on a blank area to create their own frames. Text and other special layers from Photoshop will not survive drag and drop into InDesign, though. You can also drag text from InCopy, Word, and various other applications into InDesign. Like imagery, the text can be dropped onto pre-existing frames or onto empty areas.

Copy and Paste

Naturally, you can copy frames and their content, together or separately, from within InDesign and paste elsewhere within InDesign. You can copy type from the middle of a story and paste it, too. I won't waste your time talking about something as academic as that. I would like to spend a few paragraphs discussing what can and can't be copied into InDesign from other applications and some of the things to watch out for when doing that.

InDesign's drawing tools are perfect for most common drawing tasks. When you need something a little more robust, however, haul out Illustrator. When you do that, you have a choice: Save the Illustrator file and place it into InDesign as an asset, or simply copy the artwork from Illustrator and paste into InDesign. Either method works, and each has its pros and cons.

InDesign understands vector paths and basic shapes about as well as Illustrator, and, more importantly, InDesign is wise enough to recognize when something—in this case, Illustrator—is more knowledgeable than itself. Take, for instance, live effect 3D objects created in Illustrator. InDesign is a page layout application; it has no concept of 3D space beyond x and y coordinates and basic stacking order.

Draw a path in Illustrator, apply a 3D Revolve effect to spin the path into a vase or ashtray, and the path remains infinitely editable (because it's a nondestructive effect in Illustrator). InDesign, however, doesn't have a 3D Revolve effect, has no concept of lighting—three-dimensional or otherwise—and just doesn't get it. Consequently, you might expect that copying the 3D object from Illustrator and pasting into InDesign would result in just the original path, sans 3D, in InDesign. Fortunately, if that's what you expected, you'd be wrong.

In Figure 5.12, you can see three versions of an urn. In Illustrator, I drew a relatively simple path (highlighted on the left) and revolved it into a 3D urn. This is a live effect—I can change the path at any time and the 3D Revolve effect will update the three-dimensional shape to match my changes. The center version is the same object copied from Illustrator and pasted into InDesign. Notice how it looks identical? What really happened is that the 3D effect was converted to flat paths, maintaining the object's appearance by sacrificing the reality. If I ungrouped the paths in InDesign, I'd be left with hundreds of little slivers, which you can see as individual paths in the picture on the right. That one is the object copied in InDesign and pasted back into Illustrator. The ability to edit the 3D shape easily is gone; if I needed to change the shape or color of the urn, I'd have to spend hours doing it.

In this case, I'd re-create the object from scratch, hoping I remembered or could re-create the exact 3D Revolve settings, light source positions, and so on. Odds are, it would take me less than five minutes to re-create the urn; with something complicated, though, I could be looking at hours or days worth of redrawing time just because I thought copy and paste would be faster initially.

FIGURE 5.12
The same 3D shape as drawn in Illustrator (left), as pasted into InDesign (center), and then copied from InDesign and pasted back into Illustrator (right)

There's the pro *and* the con: You can copy native objects from Illustrator and have them become native objects in InDesign—no rasterization. Draw a couple of rectangles or stars in Illustrator, paste them into InDesign, and you can edit their paths further there. You can also change their colors and transparency, move around the constituent objects in a group pasted in, and so on. However, if you get something InDesign doesn't understand—like the 3D urn—InDesign will *make it understandable* and could thereby reduce or eliminate your ability to later edit the object.

TROUBLESHOOTING: PASTE FROM ILLUSTRATOR CREATES A FLAT IMAGE

If, when you copy something from Illustrator and paste it into InDesign, you get only a flat image without individually editable paths, the problem is not within InDesign, although it would be a logical assumption. In Illustrator, on the File Handling & Clipboard pane of that application's Preferences, are options for how data is copied to the system clipboard: as PDF (flat with transparency support) or AICB (individual paths, but no transparency). If, when you paste from Illustrator, the result is flat artwork without editable paths, you're dealing with PDF-format clipboard contents when you want AICB (Adobe Illustrator Clip Board).

If you change the setting in Illustrator and the problem persists, check that you haven't overridden InDesign's default pasting format. In the Preferences, on the Clipboard Handling pane, the top option, Prefer PDF When Pasting, should be unchecked.

Ideally, leave both copy as PDF and AICB options checked. What occurs then is that Illustrator copies to the clipboard as *both*, allowing the destination—the paste into—application to select which format it supports. InDesign will choose AICB, thus accepting paths and individual objects, while applications that don't understand AICB will take the PDF-format content.

My rule of thumb is, if it takes more than 1 minute to draw in Illustrator, I'll save the AI file and place it rather than copy and paste to InDesign. (I'm fast with Illustrator; if you aren't, maybe try 5 minutes as a rule.) I would much rather retain editability of a drawing than worry about managing one more external asset.

The same is true of Photoshop images. While you can copy and paste from Photoshop to InDesign, and it's great for little bits here and there, you lose a lot. The first to go is transparency; pasted images are flattened onto a white background. Not even InDesign's Object ➢ Clipping Path ➢ Option command will get rid of the white. The same is true if you drag one or more layers from Photoshop and drop them into InDesign.

Other things to watch out for include transparency—Illustrator transparency flattens upon paste or drag into InDesign—and color. Both Illustrator and Photoshop support color models InDesign does not, like Web-Safe RGB, HSL, and Grayscale. The latter will become tints of process black (the *K* in *CMYK*), while the former two will convert to the RGB color space. Spot colors survive unless they're from a library InDesign doesn't have, such as Visibone2, in which case they're converted to the nearest match CMYK process values. Simple Illustrator gradients—linear, radial—will convert to InDesign gradients and may be edited after paste, but more complicated ones or gradient meshes become individual vector paths in InDesign (think of the urn). Illustrator patterns become embedded EPS images and are no longer editable.

Objects or elements coming into InDesign via paste or drag and drop will be permanently converted, whereas placed assets only *appear* within InDesign using that application's supported color models; the actual colors and spaces will survive unchanged inside the external assets and thus through to output. This can also be a gotcha: An image saved in *HSL* (Hue, Saturation, Luminosity) will look RGB in the layout, enticing you to forget that the asset is not RGB, and may later cause problems with a RIP that doesn't know how to convert from HSL. Preflight and Package for Print will pick up on the color space and alert you, though, so keep an eye on those.

Text from nearly any application—including Photoshop and Illustrator—can be pasted into (or from) InDesign, though, by default, text will lose its formatting upon paste. Back on the Clipboard Handling pane of InDesign's Preferences, you can change that behavior by toggling the setting for When Pasting Text and Tables from Other Applications to All Information instead of the default Text Only.

Other Flavors of Paste

No, I don't mean to discuss the chunky white bottled paste we found so delicious as pre-nap snack in kindergarten. I mean Paste without Formatting, Paste Into, and Paste in Place. They aren't strictly for getting assets into InDesign, but at this point in the discussion, they are relevant.

When the Clipboard Handling preference is changed to preserve formatting, swatches, styles, and so forth on pasted text, there is a way to override it and paste unformatted text per instance. This same method is very helpful for copying and pasting from one place or document in InDesign to another.

On the Edit menu is the Paste without Formatting command. Instead of using Cmd+V/Ctrl+V to execute a normal paste, use Cmd+Shift+V/Ctrl+Shift+V to paste text without any formatting. Pasted text will then take on the attributes assigned to the frame or surrounding text, including style, formatting, color, and so on.

Just below that command is Paste Into, which is a nifty command to know when you want to accomplish one of these tasks:

- Paste one container (with or without content) inside another container

- Move or copy an image (or text) from one frame to another without having to go through a fresh place routine

- Clip or mask a group of objects by pasting into a frame in the shape of the desired mask

Next is Paste in Place. Copy an object, then choose Paste in Place to put a duplicate directly above, and perfectly aligned with, the original (there is no Paste Behind as in Illustrator). Also, less obvious, is that Paste in Place doesn't so much paste one copy atop the original as it does paste the copy in the exact same place as the original. *Huh? Six of one thing, half dozen of the other.* No, it's not the same thing.

Copy an object. Now, go to the next page. Paste with a standard Cmd+V/Ctrl+V. What happens? The pasted object shows up dead center of the document window. Change your view—scroll around, zoom—and paste once more; again, the object is dead center of the document window. Now, paste in place instead. The copy is pasted at the exact same coordinates as its original, the source from which the copy was made.

The advantage to using Paste in Place instead of a standard Paste (or Edit ➢ Duplicate for that matter) is that it does almost the same thing, but there's no need to also manually position the copy. You can run through an entire document, blindly using the paste in place keyboard shortcut, and know that the object is inserted in the exact same position on every page.

Content-First Workflow

In contrast to the frame-first workflow is a more freeform way of working: content-first. As intimated earlier, this is an entirely alien concept to recent QuarkXPress converts.

Instead of making frames to hold everything, a content-first workflow brings all or most of the assets into the layout first. Once everything is there, you can then see how many text frames you need to fit and how many images have to be accommodated and play around with various arrangements.

Highly structured documents like catalogs and the templates for regular magazine feature and department pages almost always must begin frame-first because the content just isn't known ahead of time. More to the point, the frames often dictate the length and dimensions of content. Solo designers and graphic design studios with varied clients and projects, however, usually do (or should) begin content-first because, by the time they're brought in, most of the content is usually finished. The layout must therefore change to accommodate the content, not the other way around.

How do you accomplish a content-first workflow? Simple: Don't make frames before importing content.

You see, InDesign must have containers for content, but *you* aren't required to create them. InDesign will create them for you. If your work is always of the nature where the content is provided before you begin layout, you might never have to make an empty frame again.

Start with a blank page or a basic grid, and then go to File ➢ Place, press Cmd+D/Ctrl+D, paste, or drag and drop your content. When you click (or click and drag) to place the content, InDesign will make the frames to hold the content in the same action.

Click and release to place the content at full size, in a frame sized to fit the entire content (or within the limits of the pasteboard, whichever is smaller). Click and drag to define the area for the frame. InDesign will still place the asset at full size (in the case of an image), but nondestructively crop it to fit within the frame you drew. Text inserted this way will wrap to the area and overset any lines that don't fit.

Whenever I can, I work content-first. Even when doing a fixed-content layout like a catalog page, I'll bring in FPO content from a previous issue or a less than final edit to help me more accurately size up frames (afterward I'll flush the frames of the FPO content). Both with my own work and that of nearly everyone I've converted from the QuarkXPress Way, content-first results in faster, more accurate work—you don't forget to include a tagline or photo credit when it's already sitting on the page or just beside it on the pasteboard. Additionally, content-first workflows tend to be more creative overall than frame-first because designers are visual; we're ultimately working toward communicating via content, not boxes.

Managing Placed Assets

Getting content in is only half the considerations. You also need to know how to manage it.

The Basics

Here's a quick recap of the stuff you probably already know or have figured out by now by reading the chapter thus far.

I assume you've already noticed the Replace Selected Item check box in the Place dialog. Check that and, if you had a frame selected, InDesign will flush its content with the newly imported asset.

Images inserted via place or file/thumbnail drag and drop methods are by default linked and not contained within the InDesign document itself. Those pasted or dragged and dropped from another file are embedded, without a link to external assets, as is text by default.

When opening a document containing linked assets, InDesign automatically compares them to its record of their last state (location, date, time, and so on). If anything has changed, you'll be prompted to update or relink to the assets.

Links Panel

Most content is managed on the Links panel (see Figure 5.13). This includes linked assets of all types as well as embedded images. Embedded text is not referenced on the Links panel, nor is imagery pasted or dragged in from another application.

FIGURE 5.13

The Links panel

Every instance of a linked asset is listed on the Links panel with its location in the layout on the right. Possible locations are page numbers (1, 2, 3, and so on); *PB* for pasteboard, denoting that the asset is not within a page and will not print; and a master page prefix (e.g., A, BB, CCC, DDDD) indicating that the asset is on that master page and thus shows on any body pages to which that master page is assigned. Multipage assets like PDF or INDD files will include not only the filename but also the asset page in use. For example, `bio_RailMagnor.pdf:2` denotes that I've placed page 2 of that PDF asset.

Double-clicking an entry in the list will bring up the Link Information dialog (see Figure 5.14), which lists valuable data about an asset, including basics such as filename, size, type of asset, and date of last modification as well as some whose purpose may be less obvious:

Link Needed A Boolean field. Specifies whether the link to an external asset is required to print the document. The value is yes or N/A. Embedded images are a part of the InDesign document itself and a link to an external resource is not required in order to print the layout; the value of Link Needed would therefore be N/A.

Color Space The color model of the selected asset—RGB, CMYK, and so on.

Content Status This is a comparison indicator. Is the displayed image in synch with the actual linked asset, or has the latter changed?

Layer Overrides Relevant only to layered PSD, PDF, INDD, and AI files, this field states whether you've shown or hidden any layers or layer comps to make the placed image differ from the state of the external file.

Adobe Stock Photos This new field denotes whether the selected asset is stock imagery obtained through Adobe Stock Photos via Adobe Bridge.

Version Cue Status Identifies whether the asset is managed by Version Cue.

Location A handy little field, here is the full path to the asset. You can highlight and copy the path and filename, ready to paste into another application's Open dialog.

FIGURE 5.14

Link Information
dialog

The Prev and Next buttons along the right edge of the dialog allow you to move through the list of assets without having to close the dialog and double-click on the next entry to see its link information. Go To Link will jump the document window to display the selected asset, which is extremely handy for figuring out just what the previous designer (or you) was thinking placing a particular image. Finally, Relink opens a browse dialog to fix a broken link or replace this asset with another, automatically replacing the one with the other within the frame and preserving frame attributes such as scaling and crop data.

Select multiple Links panel entries the same as files in a list—by holding Shift for contiguous selection and Cmd/Ctrl for noncontiguous. To quickly select all entries in the list, hold Cmd/Ctrl and double-click on any one.

Opt+Shift+double-click/Alt+Shift+double-click on a Links panel entry to execute an immediate Go To Link, jumping the document window to the location of the asset on the page, pasteboard, or master page.

The Links panel flyout menu (see Figure 5.15) provides numerous commands that are also worth running through:

Edit Original Also available as the last button on the bottom of the Links panel, Edit Original is an incredibly useful, time-saving command. Very simply, it opens the linked asset in the application that created it. To touch up a PSD, for instance, you needn't launch Photoshop, go to File ➤ Open in that application, and then browse for the correct image. Edit Original does all that in one step, from within InDesign. Once you've completed editing in Photoshop (or Illustrator, or another InDesign document, or…), simply save the asset and close the editing application. Edit Original listens for that to occur and automatically updates the link inside the InDesign document to reflect your new changes.

Copy Link(s) To Often, especially within workgroups, InDesign layouts employ assets that are scattered throughout numerous folders and local or network hard drives. Keeping track of them can be confusing, tedious, and nigh impossible. Copy Link(s) To is a very cool command that offers order from chaos (at the expense of duplicating files). Select assets in the Links panel, run the Copy Link(s) To command, and InDesign will ask to which location and folder you would like it to collect the selected assets. Choose a place, and InDesign will both copy the assets there *and* update the document's link information to point to the new location.

Save Link Version If you are using a versioned workflow managed by Version Cue, this command will create a new version of the linked file as it exists within the InDesign document. For example, this is useful for layered assets whose layers or layer comps you've overridden.

Versions Displays Version Cue–managed versions of the selected asset.

Purchase This Image With Adobe Stock Photos, you're able to download low-resolution comps of images and place them into InDesign via Bridge. This command will let you purchase the actual license to use the royalty-free stock photo and download high-resolution or other available versions. Upon purchase, InDesign's tight integration with Adobe Stock Photos results in the comp automatically being replaced by the purchased image.

Reveal in Finder/Explorer Opens a Finder (Mac) or Explorer (Windows) window to view the file system folder containing the selected asset.

Reveal in Bridge Similar to Reveal in Finder/Explorer, except an Adobe Bridge window is opened on the folder instead, enabling visual management of assets.

FIGURE 5.15

The Links panel
(with menu shown)

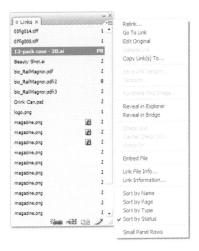

Embed File Breaks the link to the external asset and makes the item part of the InDesign document itself. Employed rarely for imagery, Embed File is most often used to embed textual assets (Word and Excel files, for example) and for final stage embedding of InCopy stories.

Link File Info Opens the asset's *XMP metadata* dialog.

Link Information Opens the Link Information dialog discussed earlier.

Along the bottom of the Links panel four buttons provide single-click access to Relink, Go to Link, Update Link, and Edit Original.

Linking vs. Embedding

When you embed assets in a layout, you put all your eggs in one basket, as my grandmother says. If *one* file gets corrupted, *all* your work is *gone.*

Embedding assets is tempting, and I see many new creatives opting for it. They're tempted by the fact that embedding means fewer—or no—external assets. They like the idea of having just one file to move around, never having to worry about network paths remapping or forgetting to copy PSD from this other folder onto their USB drives to work on the layout at home.

Sure, a layout with all or a significant portion of its imagery and copy embedded is easier to deal with, easier to manage, and easier to send to a thumb drive or DVD-ROM, but it's not worth the risk. Eggs. Basket. Splat. Weeks of work oozing out all over the linoleum.

I like being right as much as the next guy, but I *hate* being proven right on the linking versus embedding debate. It truly saddens me when somebody comes up to me long-faced at a conference and begs me to help him fix a corrupted document wherein he has embedded all his images. Sure, I know a few tricks I can try (most are somewhere in this tome), but it's a rare occasion when they work; if all the safeguards have failed, there just isn't much to be done to resurrect a truly corrupt INDD. At that point, it's a matter of re-creating the document. If all the assets are external, the work is *lot* less than if they were all embedded and must also be re-created from scratch.

If *that* doesn't dissuade you from embedding assets, maybe this will: Remember the urn? If you embed, you potentially lose the ability to quickly and easily edit original artwork. Images placed as links and then embedded *can* often be extracted back to an editable state, but artwork brought in via paste or drag and drop from an application are instantly frozen into EPS or TIFF formats— good-bye live effects, good-bye layers, good-bye to a lot of stuff.

Opinions differ on the linking versus embedding debate. Some—including a few gurus whom I admire—say embedding is fine, that there are enough safeguards in place with InDesign's Saved-Data and extremely stable file format. In my experience, having done page layout and compositing for all these years, having looked into the faces of misty-eyed owners of unopenable documents, and having researched enough technical support cases wherein months' worth of work was lost due to a simple power surge or mistimed network backup, embedding anything that will take longer than 5 minutes to re-create—cumulatively—is, in my opinion, a bad idea.

Fitting

Relating content to its container is accomplished through a process called fitting.

Is the entire image displayed at 1:1 scale, or is it cropped? Is the frame larger than the content to provide a colored border? When you place an asset, are you working frame-first or content-first, and is the frame already the needed size? All these questions—and more—are a matter of fitting. InDesign naturally contains features and commands for fitting that have been standard in layout applications for years, but it also introduces some new ones.

FITTING COMMANDS

InDesign's fitting commands are found in not one, not two, but *three* locations—the first two are the Object ➤ Fitting menu and the Fitting submenu on the context sensitive menu available when you right-click on a frame with content. In past versions of InDesign, these two menus differed. The context sensitive version was a subset of Object ➤ Fitting, containing only the most common fitting commands. To much rejoicing, the context sensitive menu now offers rapid access to *all* the fitting commands (see Figure 5.16).

FIGURE 5.16

The Fitting menu and commands (as shown from the context sensitive menu)

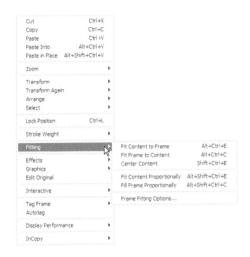

In addition to finding them on the menus, you'll find them as convenient buttons on the Control panel (see Figure 5.17); they appear on the far right any time a frame is selected.

FIGURE 5.17

Fitting command buttons on the Control panel

A fourth means of access, keyboard shortcuts, also exists for all the fitting commands, but because they tend to be three- or four-key commands, it usually takes less brain power and finger acrobatics to use the Control panel buttons or right-click to access those fitting commands you use infrequently.

Let's quickly run through the fitting commands.

Fit Content to Frame Stretches or shrinks imagery to fill in the full area of the frame. This command may result in distortion of the image to accommodate the frame dimensions.

Fit Frame to Content Resizes the frame up (decrop) or down (crop) to match the dimensions of the content (either imagery or text). Use this when you want 100% of your content showing but without excess or empty frame area around it.

Center Content Aligns the content to both the horizontal and vertical centers of the frame without resizing either frame or content. Center Content is a quick way to begin a framed picture effect wherein a color-filled frame is larger than its content image.

Fit Content Proportionally Uniformly scales the content in an attempt to fill the frame. Scaling stops when it fills *either* the horizontal or vertical dimension of the frame, thus the image is not distorted but empty frame space usually endures along the other axis.

Fill Frame Proportionally Uniformly scales the content to completely fill the frame *without* stopping at the smaller of the frame's horizontal or vertical dimension. Instead, scaling continues until *both* dimensions are filled, stopping at the larger second dimensions and often cropping the image. For instance: Placing a 1×2-inch image inside a 2×2-inch frame and choosing Fill Frame Proportionally will scale the image up 200% (resulting in a 2×4-inch image), filling the horizontal 2-inch dimension and cropping the vertical by 50% (2 inches).

It's important to remember that fitting occurs relative to the actual frame dimensions. By default, strokes assigned to frames straddle the frame path. For example, a 4-point stroke puts 2 points inside the frame and 2 points outside. In that scenario, the 2 points of stroke inside the frame will cover 2 points of the content all the way around.

While you may be tempted to resize the frame to account for stroke weight, don't. It will throw off your measurements and scaling, something you'll have to wrestle with every time you resize, alter fitting, or scale the frame and content. Instead, use the Stroke panel to move the stroke to the outside of the frame instead of the default middle (straddle) alignment.

FRAME FITTING OPTIONS

The last option on the Fitting menu is Frame Fitting Options (see Figure 5.18). It's new to CS3 and, obviously, extremely useful. *However*, please do *not* skip this section assuming you already know about this dialog or can intuit it simply from the screen shot or trying it yourself. While that may be the case, the most powerfully productive use of Frame Fitting Options is *hidden*. I don't want you to miss that.

FIGURE 5.18
Frame Fitting
Options dialog

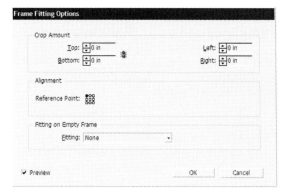

Prior to CS3, it took a lot of work to do something as simple as using the frame to crop out a border embedded in an image. You had to either measure the width of the border and then subtract twice that width from the frame's width and/or height or zoom way in, turn on high-quality display, and manually reshape the frame and refit the content over several steps. Either way, if either the frame or the content had to later change size, you were forced to do it all over again. Anyone who has arranged a series of photos from various sources knows this toilsome process.

Thankfully, it's no longer necessary.

Frame Fitting Options has crop boxes with a live preview. They work just like other measurement fields in that you can type in a value, and use the increase/decrease arrow buttons or, with the cursor in the field, even the up and down arrow keys on your keyboard. The chain link button between the Top and Bottom and Left and Right crop fields links all four together—changing the value in one alters all four to match. (Good-bye image border.)

In the middle of the dialog, the Alignment Reference Point alters the alignment of the image within the frame. This can operate alone, simply altering where an image falls within its frame, but it also affects how the image reacts to cropping operations.

Positive cropping values pull the content *toward* the selected reference point, while negative cropping values push the content *away*. In Figure 5.19, for example, you can see the different alignment and cropping result of the same image and frame using positive (left) and negative (right) cropping values. In both of these, the content is aligned to the top left; changing the reference point dramatically alters the cropping results (see Figure 5.20).

FIGURE 5.19
At left, a frame and image cropped to positive 0.75 inches all the way around; at right, the same frame and image with negative cropping of the same amount. Both are aligned to the top-left reference point.

FIGURE 5.20
Using a positive 0.75-inch cropping value, different alignment reference points dramatically alter cropping results. From left to right: Aligned to bottom right, center, and middle top.

Fitting on Empty Frame asks, *If, on its own or as a result of cropping, the frame is larger in at least one dimension than the content, thus displaying empty space, how should the image be fitted within the frame?* Your four options are None (don't alter the image at all), Fit Content to Frame, Fit Content Proportionally, and Fill Frame Proportionally, which are identical to the individual fitting commands discussed above except that, in Frame Fitting Options, they account for crop values and alignment options.

Now, I promised you a hidden feature. A man of my word, here it is, in a hands-on exercise.

1. Still got your catalog template with the empty frames? If not, go ahead and create about a half dozen empty picture frames.

2. Select all those empty frames and go to Object ➢ Fitting ➢ Frame Fitting Options. Break the Make All Settings the Same chain link, and set top and left crops to −0.25 inches.

3. Set the reference point to the top-left corner and fitting to Fit Content to Frame. Hit OK.

4. Deselect the frames, and go to File ➢ Place. Select a number of images roughly equal to the number of frames and import them.

5. Once you have a loaded cursor, place the images one at a time into the frames you just modified. You should immediately notice the fitting effects.

Let's assume you have a series of product shots all from the same manufacturer or photog. They were all taken amid a sea of white backdrop and drape, with the products always the same distance from dead center.

Your first option is that you could take them into Photoshop, crop or trim them, and then save a new set of images. The drawbacks to that are as follows: It's more work for you—you'll probably have to do at least some fitting and cropping in InDesign regardless; it creates another set of digital files to track and manage; and should substitution of products occur or new versions of the photos be delivered to you, you have to do both the Photoshop and InDesign work again. Your second option is to place the unaltered photos into InDesign and, through fitting and cropping, get them just right.

By presetting your frame fitting options—fitting and/or cropping—you can prep for the most common tasks required by your series of product shots, making the cropping, fitting, and alignment all part of the placement process instead of an extra step you must do to each afterward. They won't all be perfect (unless you're incredibly lucky), but performing a few touch-ups here and there is much more efficient than repeating the same settings for the majority of your photos each in turn.

Even without alterations to the cropping or alignment, the ability to preset fitting is a huge time-saver. You can fill an entire frame-first catalog layout with images all fit proportionally within their frames in seconds!

The Bottom Line

Place Image Assets   Focusing on efficiency with this version of InDesign, Adobe seeded numerous tiny improvements in the task of placing image assets and three big overhauls—increased support for Photoshop PSD layers, frame-fitting options, and simultaneous multiple asset import.

Master It   Create a frame-first layout containing 6 to 10 image frames. Preset the blank frame fitting options to Fit Content Proportionately, and then, using any folder of images available, import and place, in one operation, all the images needed to fill the frames.

Import Images without Place   Drag and drop enables visual selection and import of image assets while copy and paste, under the right conditions, offers a more natural way of moving assets from one place to another in the same document or between InDesign and other applications.

Master It   Create another empty frame layout similar to the previous one, and then, using Adobe Bridge and ensuring that both Bridge and the InDesign layout are visible onscreen, visually choose and place image assets from within Bridge to fill the empty frames.

Manage Placed Assets   Getting image assets into the layout is only half the job; you must also know how to manage—and even replace—assets once they're on the page.

Master It   Use one of the two documents created in the preceding Master It exercises, and, without using File ➤ Place, drag and drop, or even copy and paste, replace three of the images (in the same frames) with other assets. If you have Photoshop and/or Illustrator installed, choose another image already placed on the page and edit the image itself in Photoshop or Illustrator *without* opening the application from the Dock or Start menu.

Chapter 6

Objects

If there's a "coolest subject" in this book, this is the chapter most likely to contain it. In fact, many of the topics covered in this chapter could fit that description—at least, from a standpoint of creativity and creative productivity. If production efficiency or collaboration is the coolest subject to you, well, I've got whole chapters about those, too.

As with drawing in InDesign, the name of the game when applying transparency and effects to objects is efficiency through doing as much as possible *within* InDesign, resorting as infrequently as possible to creating objects in Photoshop. If you've been in the layout game for any length of time, you know how often it was necessary to design whole pages in Photoshop just to enable object interaction, and if you know that, you know how problematic late changes became. Each release of InDesign empowers you to do more in the layout itself, retaining all the freedom of InDesign objects, and without rasterizing. InDesign CS3, in fact, now has many Photoshop-like effects built in.

In this chapter, you will learn to:

◆ Use attribute-level transparency and object effects

◆ Design custom stroke styles

◆ Create mixed ink swatches

◆ Manage and share swatches

◆ Work with anchored objects

◆ Set type on a path

◆ Step and repeat

◆ Transform again

Transparency and Effects

InDesign 2.0 introduced transparency to desktop publishing applications in 2002. Finally, two objects blend together without having to rasterize them in Photoshop. Objects—text, paths, even placed image assets—could be rendered less than opaque, and they could be blended together using familiar Photoshop blending modes such as Multiply, Screen, Exclusion, and others. A new world of creative freedom and efficiency exploded.

In 2003, version CS gave us drop shadows natively in InDesign, and they were pretty cool (if overused), not only for their shadows, but also because drop shadows could be used to create an outer glow effect as well.

InDesign CS3 proves Adobe was just teasing us all along, whetting our appetites. Now, transparency and effects are *really* cool.

Attribute-Level Transparency

Object-level transparency is when an entire object—simultaneously and equally the object's contents, fill color, and frame and stroke color—may be blended with its background by changing opacity and blending mode. With an image in a frame, for example, setting a 50% opacity made the frame, its stroke, fill color, and the image inside the frame semitransparent all at once. If you wanted a fully opaque frame stroke over a semitransparent image in InDesign CS2 or earlier, you had to stack two objects—the first, the stroke-less image frame, and above it, an empty, stroked frame. That was object-level transparency.

InDesign CS3, like Illustrator before it, now has attribute-level transparency—the opacity and blending mode of the fill, stroke, and contents can all be set independently of one another. To herald the change, the Transparency palette has become the Effects panel (see Figure 6.1). Open the Effects panel by choosing Window ➤ Effects.

FIGURE 6.1
At left, the InDesign CS2 Transparency palette, which has become the InDesign CS3 Effects panel on the right

You still have the same Blending Modes drop-down menu and the same Opacity field, which accepts input via typed-in values or adjustments to the Opacity slider by clicking the arrow button to the right. Now, though, the middle section of the panel asks the tantalizing question, *Which attribute do you want to blend, to render semitransparent?*

By default, Object is selected, meaning opacity or blending mode changes will apply to the entire object à la CS2. To change just one attribute—the stroke, fill, or text—select that attribute beneath Object prior to altering the blending mode or opacity percentage. Each attribute may have its own settings, and all may be modified within the same object if so desired. Thus, as you can see in Figure 6.2, with its opaque text, 50% opaque stroke, and Color Dodge blending mode fill, each attribute may be blended independently within the same object instead of stacking multiple objects that must be individually (and often laboriously) altered for a change request.

FIGURE 6.2
This rather gaudy image clearly demonstrates the separate transparency effects on each of the object's attributes.

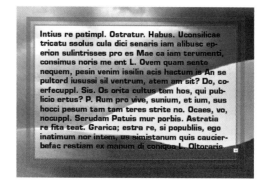

You might notice that the attribute-level options mention nothing about changing the opacity of images inside a graphic frame. That's because the option isn't there. That function is a hidden, secret trick. (You might want to either dog-ear this page or write the trick on a sticky note affixed to your monitor.) To change opacity settings or effects on an image independently of its containing frame's fill and/or stroke, you must select the image itself with the Direct Selection tool, the white arrow. It's *then* that the Effects panel will reveal control over the placed image (see Figure 6.3). Using the black arrow Selection tool accesses only the container, not its content. It makes sense, logically, that Adobe would divide the scope of the Effects panel along the line drawn by the Gemini-like Selection and Direct Selection tools—logical, but far from obvious.

FIGURE 6.3
The Effects panel managing a placed image once the image has been selected with the Direct Selection tool

Isolate Blending, a check box at the bottom of the panel, allows you to specify that objects with transparency only blend within their group, appearing opaque in relation to objects below that. Electing to enable Knockout Group (the other check box) knocks the selected object out of the ink of objects below, thus preventing blending and overprinting that might cause, through the non-opaque nature of printing ink, a blending regardless of the Isolate Blending choice. If you don't see either of these check boxes, choose Show Options from the Effects panel flyout menu to reveal the lower portion of the panel.

Effects

Attribute-level transparency is only one-half of the transparency effect overhaul on CS3. As cool as that is, it's the new attribute-level Photoshop-like effects that really widen one's eyes and tug up the corners of one's lips.

Start by creating an object; then, on the Effects panel, click the middle *fx* button at the bottom, which pops up a menu. Choose Drop Shadow to begin. If you're familiar with Photoshop's layer style effects, the basic controls of InDesign's Effects dialog will be instantly familiar (see Figure 6.4). Even if you aren't a Photoshopper, you should find the controls and options intuitive.

FIGURE 6.4
The Effects dialog with new, intuitive controls

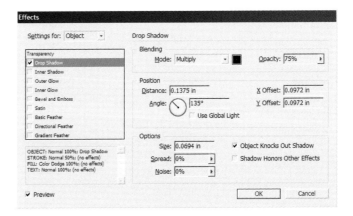

The first thing to note is the drop-down menu in the top-left corner. As with the Effects *panel*, the Effects *dialog* effects (man, I wish Adobe had created more distinction in the names) are attribute level, meaning that the entire object as well as just its stroke, fill, and text can have their own individual effects. Text inside a frame, for instance, can have a drop shadow and bevel while its frame has an inner glow and is 75% opaque, and the stroke... The number of possible permutations of 9 effects, 15 blending modes for many of the individual effects, and all those effects and blending modes applied separately across the four object attributes is a dizzying venture into mathematical probabilities. And, they all interact to create a gestalt potentially as visually rich (or garish) as anything that could be created in Illustrator with the Appearance panel.

So broad and varied are the possibilities of the Effects dialog that the only way to really come to understand them is to experiment on your own. Therefore, I'll explain some of the options and discuss the effects themselves just a little, leaving you to explore on your own after that. Make sure the Effects dialog is open to follow along.

DROP SHADOW

Drop Shadow isn't new, but it has been rebuilt.

You still have the familiar CS2 x and y Offset distance fields, but Drop Shadow now has a much more intuitive Angle spinner to accomplish the same thing. No longer do you have to estimate the conversion between the angle of the light source and horizontal- and vertical-axis-oriented coordinates. Just drag the rotating spinner or type in the angle degree in the field to the right. Even better, all effects can be oriented according to the same light source with the Use Global Light check box (more on Global Light in a few pages).

Also new are the check boxes Object Knocks Out Shadow and Shadow Honors Other Effects.

When InDesign draws a drop shadow, it does so *behind* the object as well as whatever portion of the shadow is visible beyond the area of the object. If the object fill or stroke is less than opaque, you'll see the drop shadow through it. More importantly, even if the object itself *is* opaque, even if you *can't* see the shadow through it onscreen, you could find the reverse is true upon printing. As you know, printing ink isn't truly opaque; black ink is close, as are several types of spot inks, but cyan, magenta, and yellow especially tend to allow ink beneath to shine through. Thus, applying a black drop shadow to a yellow-filled object, for instance, will often result in a yellow-tinged black object or a messy near-black green. Checking Object Knocks Out Shadow prevents drop shadows from showing through both onscreen and in print by knocking the shape of the object out of the shadow. The shadow itself will therefore only be around the edges of the object, not behind as well. Figure 6.5 shows the difference between Object Knocks Out Shadow on and off.

FIGURE 6.5
The same object (set to 50% opacity for clarity) with the same drop shadow. At left, Object Knocks Out Shadow is on, and at right it's off.

Shadow Honors Other Effects is a choice between adapting the shadow to reflect shape and transparency changes introduced by other effects (option checked) and ignoring them, drawing the shadow solely based on the real object or attribute shape (option unchecked). For instance, say you've added an outer glow effect as well as the drop shadow to a simple square. With Shadow Honors Other Effects unchecked, the shadow draws only in the shape of the path, the square. Conversely, with Shadow Honors Other Effects checked, the shadow will expand to incorporate the shape of the outer glow as well as the original square.

When InDesign draws a drop shadow, it begins feathering from the start to the end of the shadow—from the original object shape out to the end of the shadow. This creates a soft, feathered shadow, but you don't always want a soft, feathered shadow. Optically, the sharper a drop shadow, the harsher the light and the closer the object is to its background. To affect sharpness, use the Spread percentage field, which pushes the opaque area of the object shape out farther into the shadow area to reduce feathering in the edges.

Noise adds digital, random noise to a shadow, making it appear less smooth. Why on earth would you want to do *that*? For realism, of course. Other than glass and Mr. Clean's head, few things in nature are perfectly smooth. Adding a little noise—say, 1 to 3%—makes a shadow more believable usually without being consciously noticeable to the viewer. Continue increasing the noise percentage to roughen the shadow—try 90 to 100% for an interesting mezzotint effect.

To change the color of the drop shadow, click on the color swatch between the Blending Mode and Opacity fields. Black is the default, but other colors offer tremendous creative opportunity. Don't be afraid to experiment. These are all nondestructive, live effects, meaning they can be changed or even turned off at any time without consequence.

INNER SHADOW

Inner Shadow has options similar to those of the Drop Shadow effect but places a shadow within the object or attribute rather than without. It has the effect of making objects and text appear cut out of, or sunken into, the background. Like the Drop Shadow effect, Inner Shadow has a noise percentage. It substitutes choke for spread, however, but the effect is the same, with opaque shadow pushing inward to reduce the feathering in shadow edges.

OUTER GLOW

Prior to InDesign CS3, an outer glow effect had to be faked by using a colored drop shadow with no offset and a generous blur and spread. Now there's a dedicated outer glow effect. Blending mode, opacity, color, size, noise, and spread work like they do in Drop Shadow and Inner Shadow effects. The Technique field offers two options: Softer and Precise.

A softer outer glow spreads outward smoothly from the *sides* of a shape. Color does not emanate from corners, which results in corner softening; the farther outward the glow is pushed via the Size field, the softer the corners. Selecting the Precise option *does* use the corners, radiating the glow outward equally from the total area of the shape. Thus, though the corners would necessarily be somewhat rounded, even an extremely large outer glow on a square would look like a square.

INNER GLOW

The Inner Glow effect pane is very much like the Outer Glow pane, with all the same options plus one extra: Source. The glow is placed inside the object or attribute, and the Source field chooses whether the glow shines inward from the edges or outward from the center.

Note that Technique has the same Precise and Softer options it has with Outer Glow, but they work a little differently. With Softer, the glow radiates evenly from (or to, depending on the Source option) all sides and corners, leading to a soft, rounded glow deeper in the corners. Electing Precise, however, draws the glow from (or to) the sides without overlapping at the corners thus creating distinct rays of color (see Figure 6.6).

FIGURE 6.6
Both objects have the same Inner Glow effect, including a source of Edge. On the left, Technique is set to Softer; on the right, it's set to Precise.

BEVEL AND EMBOSS

Add depth to text and objects with bevel and emboss effects. Angle and Altitude control the apparent depth of the three-dimensional effect, while Highlight and Shadow set the colors, opacities, and blending modes of the colors that reveal the dimensionality. Style choices are as follows (refer to Figure 6.7):

◆ Inner Bevel to place the bevel within the confines of the shape or attribute

◆ Outer Bevel to grow the bevel outward without impinging upon the fill of the object or attribute

◆ Emboss, which colors part of the object itself as well as the area outside the object to create the effect of the shape rising up from, or sinking into, the page

◆ Pillow Emboss, which, as the name implies, re-creates the effect of stitching a pattern into a satin pillow, where the stitch sinks into the page but the area within and without is raised

FIGURE 6.7
Styles, from left to right: Inner Bevel, Outer Bevel, Emboss, and Pillow Emboss.

The Direction drop-down menu determines whether the shape rises up in relief from or, like intaglio, sinks down into the page.

SATIN

Satin creates a satiny sheen effect by infusing color into the shape from opposing corners and sides.

BASIC FEATHER

Replacing the rudimentary InDesign CS2 Feather effect are three new effects, with Basic Feather being the first. This effect softens and fades out the edges of the object or attribute, allowing it to taper into background objects. The options here are simple and sparse because the feather grows inward uniformly from all edges softly. Choke, as in other effects, controls the spread of the non-feathered area and its balance with the feathered edges.

DIRECTIONAL FEATHER

To sharpen the feather or to feather edges to different degrees, use the Directional Feather effect. Feathering from the top, bottom, left, and right may be controlled together or individually by depressing or releasing, respectively, the Make All Settings the Same chainlink icon between them. The angle twirler sets the direction into which the feather radiates—the direction of fade between the object and its background—and should be used in conjunction with the widths.

GRADIENT FEATHER

From the perspective of both creativity and, especially, productivity, the new Gradient Feather effect is worth more than all the rest put together. Graduating a solid color into no color is a very, very common task for many designers and layout artists. Prior to InDesign CS3, the only way to create a solid- to no-color gradient was to fake it with a color-to-white blend. The white, of course, was still fully opaque, making it impossible to allow background objects to shine through and blend with the gradient. Blending modes could make some gradients mix well with some backgrounds, but it was hit or miss. Most of the time, to get a gradient or any object to blend gradually with objects behind required doing it in Photoshop with layer styles or in Illustrator with opacity masks. No longer (see Figure 6.8).

FIGURE 6.8
Examples created with the Gradient Feather effect

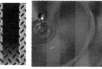

The Gradient Feather works exactly like the Gradient panel. Instead of working with color stops that blend one into the other, you're working with gradient stops, levels of opacity, that blend into one another. A black stop is 100% opaque, a white 0% opaque. Click on a gradient stop—or click on an empty area beneath the gradient ramp to add a new gradient stop—and then set the opacity in the Opacity field. The object or attribute will respond by becoming more or less opaque in the corresponding area.

Both linear and radial gradients are supported, with angles on the former just like a normal color-to-color gradient. Additionally, the same manual control given to color-to-color gradients via the Gradient tool on the Tools panel is offered through the new Gradient Feather tool accessed by clicking and holding the Gradient tool in the Tools panel. Just like its counterpart, the Gradient Feather tool determines the placement, compression, and angle of a gradient feather defined through the Effects dialog. Where you click with the Gradient Feather tool is the start of the feather, and after dragging, where you stop is the end of the feather.

More about Effects

When an object or one of its attributes has one or more effects applied, a special *fx* icon appears beside the object or attribute on the Effects panel (see Figure 6.9).

FIGURE 6.9

The *fx* icon on the
Fill indicates that it
has effects applied.

MOVING AND REPLICATING EFFECTS

Given the fact that effects are attribute level, it's a common mistake to apply an effect to, say, the fill when you meant to apply it to the entire object as a whole. Rather than undoing all your work in the Effects dialog and trying to re-create it for the correct target, simply change the target of the effect. Click on the *fx* icon beside the attribute in the Effects panel, and drag it atop a different attribute. For example, if you applied effects to the fill but they were intended for, or you'd like to them applied to, the whole object, drag the *fx* from beside Fill, and drop it beside Object. Done. The effects will move from one to the other.

To *copy* the effect to another attribute without removing it from the first, hold Cmd+Opt+Shift/ Ctrl+Alt+Shift *before selecting* the *fx* icon. Then, upon dragging, you'll see a hand cursor with a plus sign in it indicating that the effects will be copied and not moved.

Now, to copy the same effect to a completely different object, it's very much the same. Select the object with the effects—the source object—and drag the *fx* icon from beside that object's attribute entry on the Effects panel. Drop the icon directly atop the target object. It will apply the same effect, to the same attribute, meaning that if you drag a Stroke effect from the source object, it will be a Stroke effect in the target object. This is for ad hoc effects replication or for use between objects whose other characteristics vary. The easiest way to apply the same effects to multiple objects is to create an object style, which we'll discuss in the Chapter 11, "Efficiency."

Effects can be removed in several ways, the easiest two of which are to drag the *fx* icon to the trashcan icon at the bottom of the panel and to select the attribute on the Effects panel and choose Clear Effects from that panel flyout menu.

GLOBAL LIGHT

Effects like shadows, glows, beveling and embossing, and so on are lighting effects. They're meant to bring the illusion of three-dimensionality to a two-dimensional medium by faking the effects of light cast on volumetric objects floating in 3D space. The illusion only works if the effects follow the basic logic of consistent light sources. In other words, if your drop and inner shadows are being cast about in different directions, if they don't line up with the highlighted and shadowed surfaces of your bevels, you can't sell the illusion. The viewer will be yanked out of the perception of 3D space into the reality of flat ink on flat paper.

If your design has—or should have—multiple light-directed effects, determine where the light source is relative to the document and the objects. Decide in your mind where you are placing the imaginary light bulb that illuminates your objects and casts those shadows and reflects in those highlights. Once you see in your mind's eye the light bulb dangling in place near the document, tell InDesign where you've hung it by selecting Global Light from the Effects panel's flyout menu (see Figure 6.10).

The Global Light dialog has but two options—Angle and Altitude—with one informing the document lighting effects' direction and the other the intensity of the light. It's always the same wattage bulb, but its effect on the document becomes more intense as the altitude decreases. Both fields accept typed-in numeric values in degrees, but a more intuitive way to alter both is to drag the light source crosshair in the dial. Dragging it around the dial changes the angle, and dragging the crosshair toward or away from the center dot alters the altitude, descending or ascending respectively. If you've already created effects on objects, and if, in the individual options for those effects, you checked the Use Global Light option, then changes made in the Global Light dialog will alter effects while you watch (turn on Preview, of course).

FIGURE 6.10

The Global Light dialog

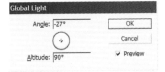

Using effects with a global light has a slight drawback: uniformity. True, uniformity is key to maintaining the illusion of dimensionality, but being *too* uniform will ruin it just as quickly as not being uniform enough. It's a delicate balance. The problem with global light is that it sets all light-directed effects to use *exactly* the same angle and altitude.

Let's say you've got a row of blocks. (I don't know why you'd have a row of blocks. It's just an example.) Let's also say that you've decided your light source hangs just a little lower than the top-left corner of the first block at around 35 to 45 degrees altitude. In reality, the closer an object is to a light source shining on it, the more severe the highlighting and the sharper and shallower the shadows cast by the object. As objects move away from the light source, highlighting becomes less intense and shadows lengthen while their edges diffuse. This is true whether the light is pointed straight down to form a circular light area or angled to form conical light. Unfortunately, InDesign's understanding of lighting is very simple—and I mean beyond the facts that there's only one possible light source and no way to way to shape the light. Distance from the light source is not among the factors considered by InDesign when it's creating light-directed effects. In fact, InDesign considers every object to have its own companion light source; the global light is just aligning all the objects' individual light sources to the same location relative to each object. The object farthest from the light source you imagine will be influenced exactly the same by the global light source, with identical effect angles and intensities, as the object closest to your imagined light source. Take a gander at Figure 6.11 to see what I mean. Notice how the highlights and shadows of the objects on the left are identical despite logic dictating that they should all vary dependent upon their distance from, and angle in relation to, the light source on the left. Which of the two sets looks more realistic?

FIGURE 6.11

InDesign's Global Light creates light-directed effects that are unrealistically uniform. An InDesign-created set of drop shadows (left) versus a set manually tweaked to reflect real-world perceptions (right).

The advantage to using the document's global light settings to inform effects is simple to grasp: every such effect, on every object or attribute to which it has been applied, can be altered document-wide from the single location of the Global Light dialog. With global light, efficiency and productivity are a trade-off with realism and accuracy. Efficiency is a powerful motivator, and I'm not implying otherwise—you know how much I value creative efficiency—but if you want realism, if you really want to sell the illusion of dimensionality, don't rely on the document global light. Use it, certainly, but deviate when logic or the laws of physics dictate.

As you saw in the right image in Figure 6.11, realism dictates that light-directed effects adjust their angle, length, and depth in correspondence with the objects' position and distance in relation to the light source. With objects closer to the top-left page light source, I shortened and sharpened their shadows, gradually lengthening and softening the edges on other object shadows as they moved away from the light. Moreover, objects that were not directly in line with the light source—such as the bottom-left and top-right corners—required that the shadows rotate. How? Simple: I drew imaginary lines (light rays) from the light source to the corners of the objects. Shadows don't cast *toward* a light source, so if the light struck a particular side, I pushed the shadow away from that edge, casting it off the opposing side.

I started with a global light but tweaked the settings per block to create a realistic environment. The rest was basic geometry and a lifetime of familiarity with Thomas Edison's invention. I'd use the same method to determine the location of highlights and shadows on beveled or embossed objects.

Creating realism is time-consuming, of course. Anyone who has ever watched a "Making Of" DVD featurette knows that. When you're making changes to objects with realistic characteristics, it can take even longer to maintain or adapt the reality to the changes, so quality becomes a trade-off with speed. I won't presume to tell you where to draw that line, when to set a document global light and be done with it and when to start tweaking angle spinners and Spread fields. Some jobs demand speed and "good enough" quality, others the extra mile even with the extra time it will take to run that far.

Strokes

"If you're in the game, then the stroke's the word." If you've used InDesign or any layout or illustration application for more than a few minutes, you've got the basics of strokes and the Stroke panel. Let's talk about those things that you may not have heard, the things about which I often get questions from experienced InDesign users. Figure 6.12 is the Stroke panel with options shown (from the flyout menu). With a tip of the hat to Billy Squier, let's briefly go through each section. Don't take no rhythm; don't take no style.

Weight The stroke thickness, expressed in whole or partial points (e.g., 1 pt or .333 pt).

Cap When open paths terminate (as opposed to a closed path like a circle that has neither a start nor an end), how should their ends look? That's the question posed by these three unassuming buttons. Your options are Butt Cap, Round Cap, and Projecting Cap, and their resulting effects on paths are exactly what the buttons depict.

FIGURE 6.12
The Stroke panel

Miter Limit When a path makes a corner, InDesign has to decide what to do with the stroke on the outside of the turn. It must consider whether the stroke color should keep going in the same direction until it reaches a point, even if that's a great distance off, or if the stroke should be clipped somewhere before it reaches a point. The Miter Limit field sets the clipping boundary; when a stroke reaches that limit, InDesign will cut down the path (see Figure 6.13).

FIGURE 6.13
A sharp corner
results in a long
spike in the stroke
(left), and a miter
limit clips the stroke
(right).

Many people think the Miter Limit field is measured in points. It's not. It's in multiples of the stroke weight. Thus the default miter limit of 4 is four times the stroke weight; a 1 pt stroke weight begets a 4 pt miter limit. Using defaults, InDesign will clip the stroke with the join type option if the stroke reaches or extends beyond 4 pts long. If you're getting too many mitered corners when you want sharp, up the miter limit.

Join Join is the shape of corners in paths, either Miter Join (sharp, single angle), Round Join, or Beveled Join.

Align Stroke These three buttons determine where the stroke falls relative to the path. Paths themselves have no thickness—they're just the connections drawn between to points plotted on the x and y axes. Because they have no thickness, the stroke must align somehow to the path. As you can see in Figure 6.14, where that is has a great effect on the results. You can choose Align Stroke to Center, straddling the path such that a 20 pt stroke puts 10 pts inside and 10 pts outside the path; Align Stroke to Outside, putting the entire stroke outside the path and thus keeping the fill color, image, or text unimpinged upon; or Align Stroke to Inside, putting the entire stroke inside the path to encroach upon and perhaps obscure part of the shape fill.

FIGURE 6.14
Left to right: stroke
aligned to center,
outside, and inside

Type The Type menu contains the different styles of stroke available, including a single solid stroke, picture-frame-like multiple-line strokes, and several varieties of broken strokes—these last will get more interesting in three more paragraphs.

Start and End Need an arrowhead or other stroke adornment? Although not as robust as Illustrator or other drawing and flowcharting software, InDesign can do basic flowcharting and diagramming arrows. The start is the first anchor point you created in drawing your path, and the end the last. A little-known feature is the ability to reverse the direction of arrows without a return to the Stroke panel—to do it, if you choose, with a keyboard command.

Let's say you have a straight line path drawn left to right to which you've applied a start of an arrow and an end of a circle. The arrow, therefore, is on the left and the circle the right. If you need it the opposite way, you can go back to the Stroke panel; you can also flip the path or rotate it, but that becomes problematic if the path is already at an angle. Instead, select Object ➤ Paths ➤ Reverse Path. The direction of the path will be reversed, just as if you drew it right to left, and the start and end will transpose without altering the position or rotation of the path itself. If you need to do that frequently, assign a keyboard shortcut to the Reverse Path command in Edit ➤ Keyboard Shortcuts.

Gap Color and Gap Tint When you choose any stroke type other than Solid, Gap Color lights up. The gap is the space between multiline, dashed, dotted, slashed, or other broken stroke types. In addition to coloring the positive parts of the stroke, the Gap Color drop-down allows you to select a swatch to color the negative spaces between. Once a gap color is chosen, Gap Tint activates to fine-tune the gap color. In other words, if you want effects like those in Figure 6.15, you don't have to overlay multiple objects.

FIGURE 6.15
Gap colors create the effect of multiple objects overlaid without doubling the work to create and manage them.

Custom Stroke Styles

When you select Dashed, the last option in the Type menu, additional fields appear at the bottom of the Stroke panel (see Figure 6.16) to define a custom dashed stroke. Using points or any measurement system InDesign understands, enter dash and/or gap widths (as many as three pair) for exactly the dashed stroke you need. Above the Dash and Gap fields, choose how the dashed stroke handles corners to (try to) avoid weird bunching of, or gapping in, dashes.

FIGURE 6.16
Defining a custom
dashed stroke

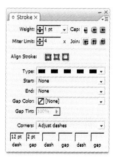

When the Dash and Gap fields don't offer enough control, or to create a stroke comprising something other than rectangular dashes, select Stroke Styles from the panel flyout menu. You'll see listed there the multiline stroke styles. Click the New button to open the New Stroke Style dialog and build your own stroke style (see Figure 6.17).

FIGURE 6.17
The New Stroke
Style dialog

Changing the Type field sets the tone for the stroke and the rest of the options.

Dash Figure 6.17 shows the version of the New Stroke Style dialog that occurs when you choose the Dash type. Within the horizontal ruler you *draw* the dashes as black block; negative spaces between the blocks are gaps that will appear in the stroke. At the bottom of the dialog, the preview keeps your stroke in perspective, at the weight you choose in the bottom field.

To draw a new dash segment, simply click in an empty space in the ruler section—either within the ruler itself or in the drawing area below it. Once a dash segment is begun, the arrows above it, within the ruler, can be dragged to resize the dash. You can also use the Start and Length fields for precision sizing. If the pattern is too short or long at its default one-third inch, change the Pattern Length field. Even if the pattern is a good length at its default, you may want to adjust it to take up any excess empty space at the end of the pattern, which will become a gap before the pattern repeats.

Note the presence of Cap and Corners adjustments to precisely control the ends of dashed strokes and how dashes behavior at angles.

A custom stroke must begin with a dash (or dot or stripe); it cannot begin with a gap. Additionally, each stroke is limited to five dash segments. If you genuinely need something more complicated than five dash segments, use Illustrator to create and apply the custom stroke as a new brush style, and then copy the stroked object into InDesign as a vector path.

When you're happy with your new custom stroke style, give it a name at the top, and then click either OK, to save the style and close the New Stroke Style dialog, or Add, which also saves the style but leaves the dialog open and ready to create additional styles.

Dotted Of the two default dotted stroke styles—Dotted and Japanese Dots—many designers prefer to use the latter because of its narrower gaps between dots (see Figure 6.18). Tightly spaced dots are more aesthetically pleasing when used as, for example, text separators in horizontal paragraph rules and vertical *drop rules* and cell borders in tables.

FIGURE 6.18
InDesign's default
dotted styles,
Dotted (upper)
and Japanese Dots
(lower)

Personally, I often find even the Japanese Dots style a little loose for my tastes—particularly when using a 25 to 50% black dotted stroke close to text. Other times, say, with a custom two-color frame border, Dotted is spaced too tight. Choosing the Dotted style from the Type menu opens a horizontal ruler similar to the one offered for new Dash type strokes, but there are no lengths; just click within the ruler to place a dot, and click and drag on a dot to reposition it. The Center field aligns the center point of the dot to a place on the ruler.

Stripes Multiple line strokes like Thick-Thick, Thick-Thin-Thick, and so on are Stripe types. Choosing Stripe from the Type menu activates unique fields and a vertical ruler (see Figure 6.19). Click and drag to draw a stripe. Rather than absolute placements within a fixed-width pattern, stripes are set in the style based on percentage of height. For example, a stripe of 10% will be 1 pt in a 10 pt stroke or 10 pt in a 100 pt stroke.

FIGURE 6.19
Drawing a Stripe
stroke style

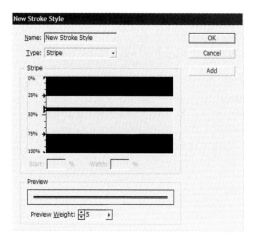

Your new stroke styles will be available from the Type menu on the Stroke panel and also from anywhere stroke styles are selected—paragraph rules dialogs, underline and strikethrough options, and more. Through the Stroke Styles dialog, they can also be saved to, and loaded from, disk for sharing with colleagues.

Swatches

Wait! Don't skip ahead! I'm not going to waste your time with a Swatches panel walk-through or by explaining how to use and create swatches. Plenty of InDesign 101–style books will tell you about that, and if you're reading *this* book, you've long since graduated from InDesign 101. This section isn't about the basics of working with swatches. In the first half of this course we'll discuss advanced swatch work like *mixed ink* swatches and mixed ink groups, and then we'll talk about sharing and working efficiently with swatches—some of which is new to InDesign CS3.

I expect everyone to be prepared at the start of each section with a sharpened No. 2 pencil, a three-ring binder, and InDesign CS3 opened on your computer.

Mixed Inks

Mixed ink colors are the result of mixing one or more spot colors with process inks or of mixing two spot colors. You may know of them under another name: tint build or multi-ink colors; the latter is what QuarkXPress calls them. Mixing inks allows you to coax a larger selection of colors and tints from a minimum of inks (read *more creativity, lower production cost*).

CREATING MIXED INK SWATCHES

If, after reading the preceding paragraph, you're feeling as confused as a Bush administration Supreme Court nominee, don't throw in the towel just yet. The best way to understand mixed inks is to make a mixed ink, so let's do that.

1. Mixed inks must contain at least one spot color, and that spot color must already be on the Swatches panel. The first step, therefore, is to make a spot color swatch.

   From the Swatches panel flyout menu, select New Color Swatch. In the resulting dialog, set Color Type to Spot, and from Color Mode, choose any spot color library like PANTONE Solid Coated. When the colors load, pick one and click OK.

2. Now that you have a spot color swatch created, the New Mixed Ink Swatch command will be selectable from the Swatches panel menu. Choose it and up will pop the New Mixed Ink Swatch dialog (see Figure 6.20).

FIGURE 6.20
The New Mixed Ink
Swatch dialog

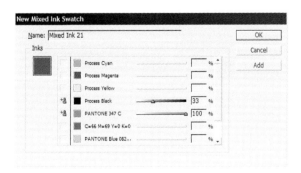

3. Click in the empty box to the left of the spot color you just created to start, and then choose one of the process inks to mix in. Beside each ink name is the ink's tint ramp and a tint percentage field. Try dragging the tint sliders while watching the preview swatch on the left. Notice the new colors created by combining the two inks? Depending on the spot you chose, chances are good that some of the colors you can mix up with only two inks would have otherwise required additional spots to print. That would be more plates (read *additional RIP time and film charges*) and more inks (read *more cycles through the press and additional per-ink setup charges*).

4. Once you have a new color you like (keeping in mind that what you see on screen may not be accurate), give it a name more explanatory than the default *Mixed Ink 1*; then click OK to save the swatch and close the dialog or Add to save the swatch and leave the dialog open ready to create more mixed ink swatches. Of course, you can use more than two inks as long as at least one is a spot color.

CREATING MIXED INK GROUPS

The only real drawback to creating a mixed ink according to the above procedure is the tedium of it, the need to manually commingle the inks to create a new mixed ink swatch. If you wanted to, say, get all possible combinations of two inks in 10% increments of both tints, you'd have to manually create all those new swatches by changing percentages and then clicking Add. That isn't particularly difficult, just tedious. Wouldn't it be great if InDesign found all the possible combinations for you? That's exactly what mixed ink *groups* do.

Select New Mixed Ink Group from the Swatches panel flyout menu to open the dialog shown in Figure 6.21. As with the New Mixed Ink Swatch dialog, add an ink to the mix by clicking in the blank space at the left. Now, instead of specifying a tint percentage to make the mix, set a *range* of tint percentages and let InDesign create each individual mix and swatch. Let's do it, starting from an opened New Mixed Ink Group dialog.

1. In the Initial column, set the starting tint percentage for each ink. For this exercise we want to add varying stages of black to the spot color, so set the initial tint of the spot to 100% and Process Black to 5%, the lowest desired mix value. The first mixed ink swatch will have these initial tints and will grow from there toward greater tint percentages. Because the spot begins at 100%, only black's contribution will increase while the spot remains constant at full ink density.

2. Repeat is the number of color steps, the number of swatches to create, starting at the initial value. Because we want to add black in 5% increments up to 100% black plus 100% spot, set the Increment field to 5% and the Repeat field to 19 (100% divided by 5% equals 20 steps minus the initial 5% step). The spot will stay constant at 100%, thus its Repeat field should be 0, disabling the Increment field as well.

3. Notice that below the ink selection area is a running count of the number of swatches to be created. Each ink you add, each repeat value, increases that number exponentially. Always check the count before hitting OK to make sure a typo or incorrect value hasn't set you up to generate too many swatches.

FIGURE 6.21

Create many mixed ink swatches at once with New Mixed Ink Group.

New Mixed Ink Group

Name: Group 2

Inks

		Initial	Repeat	Increment
	Process Cyan			
	Process Magenta			
	Process Yellow			
	Process Black	5%	19	5%
	PANTONE 347 C	100%	0	0%

Included Inks: Process Black, PANTONE 347 C

Swatches to be Generated: 20

Preview Swatches

Swatch Preview

☐ Group 1 Swatch 1
☐ Group 1 Swatch 2
☐ Group 1 Swatch 3
☐ Group 1 Swatch 4
☐ Group 1 Swatch 5

OK
Cancel

4. Click the Preview Swatches button to see the results of the mixed ink group without committing them to the document's Swatches panel. Swatch names are determined by the Name field at the top of the dialog, with *Swatch X* appended. If the swatches meet with your approval, click OK and watch the Swatches panel populate.

In addition to the various Swatch X mixed ink swatches (identified by the double ink droplet icons), you'll have a mixed ink group swatch (see Figure 6.22). You see, all those swatches you just made are still a dynamic part of the mixed ink group—change the group, change all the swatches.

FIGURE 6.22

After creating a mixed ink group

You *can* change individual swatches, to adjust the mix percentages for example, or to convert the group swatch into a standard spot or process swatch. But, to change the colors in all the swatches in the group—for instance, to replace one spot or process color with another across all the grouped mixed inks—edit the group, not the swatch. Instead of editing the swatch, double-click the mixed ink group swatch itself (hold Cmd+Opt+Shift/Ctrl+Alt+Shift while double-clicking to edit without applying the swatch to the selected object and without making it the default for new objects). That will get you to the Mixed Ink Group Options dialog (see Figure 6.23), where you can rename the group, convert mixed ink swatches to process colors (note that this is irreversible), and disable or replace one or more inks in the mix (note that you must always have at least two colors in the mix, and at least one must be a spot). When you click OK, all the swatches in the group will update to reflect the changes.

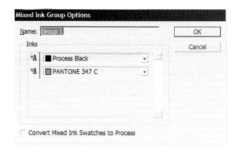

FIGURE 6.23
Editing a mixed ink
group in the Mixed
Ink Group Options
dialog

If all you want to do is replace a color in a mixed ink group, there's an even faster way. When, on the Swatches panel, you delete a normal spot or process swatch used in a mixed ink or mixed ink group, InDesign will ask you to choose a color with which to replace the one you're deleting. Your choice will update all mixed ink and mixed ink group swatches that included the replaced color.

Managing Swatches

I'm sure you already know that you can drag and drop swatches in the Swatches panel list to reorder them, just as I'm sure you're perfectly aware that you can rename swatches by editing them (Cmd+Opt+Shift+double-click/Ctrl+Alt+Shift+double-click). There are some other things—particularly things new to CS3—that you may not know, however.

SELECT ALL UNUSED

This command on the Swatches panel flyout menu selects all swatches that aren't currently used by some object in the document. Once they're selected, just click the trashcan icon at the bottom of the panel to delete all unused swatches in fell swoop. Leaving unused swatches in a document has no practical effect—you won't, for instance, get extra plates during separation just for having swatches in the panel. It is a usability issue and productivity issue, however. It's just easier to work with a Swatches panel uncluttered by the extraneous results of past experiments.

ADD UNNAMED SWATCHES

Add Unnamed Swatches is kind of the opposite of Select All Unused. In the course of designing, we don't always create swatches for every color we mix on the Colors panel and elsewhere. Often, colors are created on page 2 and forgotten about by page 6; when page 8 rolls around again, the color is created again ad hoc with hopefully the same mix as other instances. Selecting Add Unnamed Swatches from the Swatches panel flyout menu creates swatches for all in-use colors in the document that don't already have swatches. It also associates the source objects with the swatches, making color replacement as easy as deleting the swatch and choosing a substitute.

MERGE SWATCHES

In the Swatches panel, select any two or more swatches, and then choose Merge Swatches from the panel menu. What happens is not really a merge—you won't get green by using the command on blue and yellow swatches. Instead, it's more of a replacement.

Let's say you have three color swatches—red, blue, and yellow—all in use as the fill colors for different objects. Selecting them in the Swatches panel in order—clicking first on red, then blue, and finally on yellow—and executing the Merge Swatches command will simultaneously delete the blue and yellow swatches and fill all blue and yellow objects with red. The first swatch you click on, regardless of its actual order in the list, becomes the surviving replacement color. Merge Swatches is a handy way to replace colors with a minimum of fuss—particularly for those of you who are cleaning up someone else's document in preflight.

UNDELETABLE SWATCHES

A very common frustration is ending up with swatches that you can't find in use anywhere and can't be deleted no matter what you try. This problem is nearly always caused by a color embedded in a placed asset—particularly vector assets. See the sidebar "Finding the Unfindable Swatch, Deleting the Undeletable Swatch" for a real-world strategy to deal with this problem.

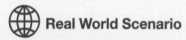 **Real World Scenario**

FINDING THE UNFINDABLE SWATCH, DELETING THE UNDELETABLE SWATCH

Most often, a swatch that cannot be deleted in InDesign is actually contained within a placed EPS, PDF, AI, or other image asset. InDesign can place and modify such assets within the context of the instance on the page, but it cannot *edit* the asset itself, cannot change the EPS, PDF, AI or what have you. Therefore, InDesign can't delete or alter swatches that may be in the asset. Worse, you often can't even *find* where the color is used. Often this happens because the path carrying the offending color is hidden behind other paths and, even more common, there is no path, just a single anchor point.

In vector drawing, a single anchor point is considered an object just as surely as a complex path. As an object, the anchor point may have a fill and/or stroke color assigned to it even though there isn't a path to make either fill or stroke visible. One errant click of the mouse in Illustrator or another program can create an orphaned anchor point, and thus an orphaned color instance, resulting in an undeletable color swatch in InDesign. Because these orphaned anchor points are invisible, they're also often impossible to find—unless you know to look for them and *how* to look.

FIND THE IMAGE

First, in InDesign, identify the image that is the source of the undeletable color swatch.

1. Save a copy of the document—never perform troubleshooting on the original.

2. Remove all unused swatches from the Swatches panel to narrow the possibilities and make cleanup easier.

3. Go back to the first page of your document containing placed assets, and select and delete all placed assets. Select all unused swatches again with the appropriate Swatches panel command. Is the ostensibly undeletable swatch among those highlighted as unused? If not, move on to page 2, deleting all placed assets and then selecting all unused swatches. Keep repeating this seek-and-destroy process until the swatch *does* get selected by the Select All Unused command, and then move on to step 4.

4. When removing all objects and then selecting unused swatches causes the undeletable swatch to be flagged as not in use, you will have found the page containing the swatch. The next step is to narrow that down to the exact image. So, press Cmd+Z/Ctrl+Z to undo the deletion of all of the page's objects, and then, one at a time, delete each placed asset object and choose Select All Unused from the Swatches panel flyout menu. Eventually, the undeletable swatch will be among the selected, identifying the exact image that contains it.

5. Press Cmd+Z/Ctrl+Z again to restore the image you just deleted, and keep it selected.

6. On the Links panel (Window ➢ Links), the asset will also be highlighted. Click the Edit Original button at the bottom of the Links panel, the button that looks like a pencil, which will open the application registered on your system to edit such imagery—Illustrator for vector or Photoshop for raster, for example.

Note: If the undeletable swatch is not contained within a linked asset, if it's instead within objects or imagery that were *pasted* into InDesign, the Links panel will not help you. Instead, copy the asset and paste it back into the application that created it. Make the necessary changes, and then copy and paste back into InDesign.

IF THE EDIT ORIGINAL COMMAND OPENS PHOTOSHOP...

1. Open the Channels panel in Photoshop (Window ➢ Channels). RGB, Lab, and process colors created in Photoshop do not generate swatches upon import of the image to InDesign. Only spot colors, created on separate channels, create InDesign swatches. Therefore, your undeletable swatch will be a separate channel beneath the Red, Green, and Blue channels or Cyan, Magenta, Yellow, and Black channels. That channel's name will be the same as the title of the InDesign swatch.

2. Turn off all channels except the offending spot color channel by clicking the eyeball icon beside each of the other channels. When only the spot color channel is visible, its contents will render onscreen in black rather than in the actual color.

3. Examine the image data there. Do you need it? Should it remain a spot color, generating a new plate upon separation output from InDesign or the RIP? If your answer is yes, close everything and go back to your original InDesign document to keep working. If no, if you don't want the spot color, decide whether you want that image data at all.

◆ To keep the image data but convert the spot color into the nearest equivalent mix of process inks (or RGB), highlight the spot channel and choose Merge Spot Channel from the Channels panel flyout menu. The image data on the spot channel will become part of the CMYK or RGB channels, approximating the original spot color as closely as those color models allow. Note that Merge Spot Channel is not available for images in Lab mode. If your image is in Lab mode, you'll need to first convert it to RGB or CMYK with the appropriate command on the Image ➢ Image Mode menu.

◆ If you decide you don't want the spot color or the image data on the channel, select the spot channel and drag and drop it atop the trashcan icon at the bottom of the Channels panel.

4. Save the document and close Photoshop. Because you used InDesign's Edit Original command, InDesign will automatically update the placed asset without further action required. When you re-open your original document, of course, you'll be prompted to update the image with a single button click. In both the original and temporary troubleshooting copy, the formerly undeletable swatch should now be deletable.

IF THE EDIT ORIGINAL COMMAND OPENS ILLUSTRATOR...

1. Illustrator is much more like InDesign than like Photoshop in terms of color handling and swatches. You won't find a Channels panel, for instance. Instead, you'll need to locate the path or anchor point containing the unwanted spot color swatch.

On Illustrator's Swatches panel you'll find the offending swatch (hint: spot color swatches appear with a black dot inside a white triangle in their lower-right corners). With no objects selected, choose from the Swatches panel the spot color swatch of which you want to rid yourself.

2. Go to Select ➤ Same ➤ Fill Color. Illustrator will then select any and all paths (and orphaned anchor points) filled with that color. If nothing was selected, move on to step 3; otherwise, skip down to step 4.

3. If trying to select objects with the offending swatch as their fill produced no results, then it isn't being used as a fill color. Try looking for it as a stroke color with Select ➤ Same ➤ Stroke Color.

4. Examine what was selected and decide whether to delete or recolor it.

◆ If you decide that you don't need the selected items, press the Delete key on your keyboard. Poof! Problem solved.

◆ However, if you decide you *do* want the selected paths, you just don't want them to use a spot color ink, convert the spot color to CMYK or RGB. Double-click the swatch in the Swatches panel and, in the Swatch Options dialog, change Color Mode to CMYK or RGB and then the Color Type field to Process Color.

Note: Even if you did get hits on the fill color, it's a good idea to go back and look for any paths with that stroke color as well.

5. Save the document and close Illustrator. Because you used InDesign's Edit Original command, InDesign will automatically update the placed asset without further action required. When you re-open your original document, of course, you'll be prompted to update the image with a single button click. In both the original and temporary troubleshooting copy, the formerly undeletable swatch should now be deletable.

Note: Illustrator artwork can contain both embedded and linked raster images and even other vector art files. It's entirely possible to have a Russian doll of images—one image placed into another, which is placed into another, and another, and so on. If you determine that the unwanted swatch is within a linked asset rather than the Illustrator document itself, use the Edit Original command on Illustrator's identical Links panel, and then follow the same procedures above for whichever application opens.

IF THE EDIT ORIGINAL COMMAND OPENS ANOTHER APPLICATION...

Most raster image editors will conform at least loosely to the Photoshop directions, and most vector drawing applications to the Illustrator. Use those as guides within the unique environments and user interfaces of whichever applications you employ to edit raster and vector artwork.

Other times, swatches are rendered undeletable because of file corruption, which is regrettably very common with documents converted from QuarkXPress, PageMaker, or even earlier versions of InDesign. The best way to counter file corruption is to force a complete rewrite of the document code.

1. Choose File ➤ Export and save a copy of the document as an InDesign Interchange INX file—a special, pure XML copy of the document.

2. Close the original INDD document, and open the INX version.

3. Choose File ➤ Save As and save the document back to a normal INDD InDesign Document.

4. Try deleting the offending swatch.

Of course, the four magic swatches whose names are bracketed—None, Paper, Black, and Registration—can never be deleted by design.

Speaking of swatch issues upon converting documents from QuarkXPress…

Swatches from QuarkXPress

When opening a QuarkXPress version 3.3 to 4.1 document in InDesign, swatches convert faithfully, with a few notable exceptions.

White QuarkXPress doesn't have a swatch named Paper. Instead, it has White. Upon converting the XPress document to InDesign, you'll often have both Paper and White. In theory, leaving the White swatch in use shouldn't hurt; in practice, though, it has been known to confuse some RIPs. The solution is simple: Delete the White swatch. If it's in use as a fill or stroke color, InDesign will prompt for a swatch with which to replace it. Choose Paper.

Multi-Ink Colors to Mixed Ink Colors The two are nearly identical with one difference: QuarkXPress allows multi-ink colors without the inclusion of a spot color while InDesign's mixed ink color require a spot. Multi-inks *with* a spot will convert just fine into mixed inks. Multi-inks *without* a spot will become standard process color swatches.

Color Library Colors Colors from QuarkXPress's color library are converted to process swatches based on their CMYK values.

HSB and Lab Colors QuarkXPress HSB and Lab colors are converted to RGB colors in InDesign.

Sharing Swatches

The ability to share swatches—between documents, between applications—makes for fewer trees sacrificed to scribbling down color formulas. Whether it was eco-conscience or a desire to shave just a little more time and effort off designers' project work, Adobe has made accessing and sharing color swatches between applications easier and more accurate with each new release of the Creative Suite. CS3 is no exception.

Importing Swatches from Other Documents

On the flyout menu of the Swatches panel, the Load Swatches command enables importing swatches from any preexisting InDesign document or template. Just choose the command, select the document, and click Open; all that document's color swatches will import to the current document. You can import swatches from InDesign INDD documents and INDT templates, Illustrator AI and EPS files, and Adobe Swatch Exchange ASE files.

If you want to import swatches from other documents selectively instead of all at once, follow this procedure:

1. Choose New Color Swatch from the Swatches panel flyout menu.

2. In the New Color Swatch dialog, select the last option in the Color Mode drop-down, Other Library. A file dialog will appear.

3. Choose from the Open a File dialog any of the file types InDesign supports for swatch import—INDD, INDT, AI, EPS, or ASE—and click OK. The swatches in the chosen document will appear in the swatch list of the New Color Swatch dialog.

4. Choose the swatch to import, and click OK or Add.

MAKING NEW DEFAULT SWATCHES

If you work in an in-house design, production, or press services department, or if for some other reason you find yourself regularly working with the same colors, the Load Swatches command can make your brand identity colors the defaults for all new documents. Open InDesign *without* opening documents, and load up swatches from a previous document. They will populate the Swatches panel (delete any you don't regularly need). Close InDesign to commit the changes, and then, in every future session of InDesign, every new document you create will automatically have your corporate colors ready and waiting on the Swatches panel.

SHARING SWATCHES WITH OTHER APPLICATIONS

In Creative Suite 2, Illustrator CS2 was able to generate a new type of swatch file, an Adobe Swatch Exchange file. The ASE file could be imported by Photoshop, GoLive, and InDesign, but only Illustrator could create it. Creative Suite 3 corrects this horrendous inequity by allowing any of the quartet to export its native swatches to Adobe Swatch Exchange, the swatches can then be brought into the others with the Load Swatches or New Color Swatch (and counterpart) command. Just choose Save Swatches from the Swatches panel flyout menu and save the ASE file somewhere where the rest of the Creative Suite applications can find it.

Using ASE files is a great way to ensure consistency between original art—from raster to vector, print layout to Web layout—and even for the future. What I mean by that is this: I recommend to my freelance and agency clients that deal with multiple clients (and multiple brand color sets) that they create an ASE file for every client and multiple-document project as part of the initial job setup. Either the production manager or one assigned creative generates the necessary swatches from the client specs, creates the ASE, and makes it part of the core project files alongside other core files like the client's logo, signature fonts, and so on. After the initial work is completed, when follow-up jobs come in for the same client, any member of the design team can import the swatches from the ASE and get right to work without having to dig through other document Swatches palettes to identify which are the brand identity colors and which are only specific to a particular document or project.

VIEWING SWATCHES—WITHOUT OPENING OR IMPORTING

I have to say, as simple a thing as it is, the ability to view a document's colors in Adobe Bridge—without opening the document—struck me as among the best new features of Creative Suite 3.

If all you want to do is see which colors a document uses or grab a couple of color formulas, there's no longer any need to load the creating application and open the document, or even import swatches.

You're probably managing your digital assets in Bridge anyway, so just select the desired document and look to the Metadata panel on the left (see Figure 6.24). Among the expandable sections are Plates (not for INDD files), which shows all the process and spot inks in use, and Document Swatches, which displays all swatches saved in the document—including unused swatches, so be sure to clean those up before closing the document. Because the default name of custom swatches is the formula (e.g., *C=66 M=69 Y=0 K=0*), you don't have to open the document to obtain a custom color formula. Nice, huh?

FIGURE 6.24
The vastly improved Metadata panel in Adobe Bridge shows the selected document ink plates and document color swatches.

Anchored Objects

Adobe calls graphics and other objects that maintain their position relative to a place in the text regardless of where that text flows *anchored objects*. I call them tethered objects. After all, anchoring something is to stop it from moving. Anchored objects move—they follow the text describing them, jumping pages all by themselves if the text to which they're attached jumps to other pages. That's the behavior of a tethered object, not an anchored. Regardless of the semantics, anchored objects, introduced in InDesign CS2 (lifted, incidentally, from FrameMaker), is one of the most timesaving features ever added to a layout application.

Here's a scenario: Imagine a typical business report—let's say an annual shareholder's report. The majority of the document is a single story, flowing from page to page to page. At various points in the main narrative, copious photographs, charts, graphs, and maybe some pullquotes are required to support the main text. In the typical workflow, these supportive materials (for simplicity's sake let's refer to them collectively as images) are placed into the document independent of the text frame, maybe floating out in the margins, maybe over the text itself and with a text wrap. Somewhere in the text are references to most images—e.g., *See Chart 16*—to give them context. If editorial or style changes force text to reflow, moving image references to different pages, the layout artist must manually go back and, one at a time, move the images as well. If a major reflow change occurs early in the document—say, page 5 of 350 pages—that artist is looking at days of doing nothing but repositioning images to follow their references.

That's a huge commitment of valuable creative and production time. Anchored objects reclaims that time, turning the act of repositioning 345 pages of images from days of tedious work into minutes of minor cleanup.

You see, instead of letting images float free in frames disconnected from the main story, images can be tethered to a specific place in the text with an invisible marker character called an anchor. That anchor is fixed in the text after *this* word or before *that* character, and it behaves like any other character albeit invisibly. When text reflows, the anchor marker flows with it, dragging the image frame (or additional text frame) along. Anchored objects will *always* appear on the same page as the text that describes them (if you choose; you can also make them appear on the opposite page). InDesign will move them for you as the text moves. You can even force them to jump from the left to the right page and vice versa, changing position relative to the spine and page edge, if the anchor marker flows to the other side of the spread.

Anchoring Your First Object

Let's go hands-on, anchoring an object to text together.

If you're already comfortable with threading text frames, something we'll get into in Chapter 8, "Stories," go ahead and set up your own facing pages document with three to five pages and a single story running between them in a series of two- or three-column frames. If you prefer, I've already created such a document in this chapter's folder at http://www.sybex.com/go/MasteringInDesign, and you're welcome to use it. Just open Anchored Objects Text.indd and turn to page 2 in that document.

1. With your text ready to go, find a place on the first page of the story about midway down the first column. Highlight two words, and give them an obvious and contrasting color like blue, green, red, or orange. The color isn't necessary to create anchored objects, of course; we're just doing it as part of this exercise solely so we can easily pick out the location of the object anchor we'll insert momentarily.

2. Deselect the text and text frame, and place an image, any image, into the document. I'm going to use the infamous Photoshop sample file Ducky.tiff, found in the Samples folder under the installation folder of any recent version of Photoshop. If you chose a large image, scale it down to about the width of a single column of the text.

3. On the Text Wrap panel (Window ➢ Text Wrap), choose Wrap Around Bounding Box to push text out of the way of the image. Again, although you may elect to use a text wrap on a real project, we're doing it now just to simplify this exercise—it's easier to watch the colored tracking text if it isn't hidden behind the image.

4. With the image still selected, cut it with Cmd+X/Ctrl+X, and switch to the Type tool by pressing T.

5. Insert your cursor between the two words you recolored and paste with Cmd+V/Ctrl+V. You should see something like what I have in Figure 6.25.

   Wait, you might say. *That's just a simple inline graphic.* Correct, we've just inserted an inline graphic, which is nothing revolutionary. What *is* different, however, is how InDesign has redefined the role of inline graphic.

FIGURE 6.25
After pasting the
image into the text

lacinianicore digna cor ipsusto consequat, sequipisim dolutat.¶

Ut nibh

elenim vel dolent iliquamcor iuscinibh et dolorpe rcillum venis nos
nos ad magnisim nostion velit wis

ieuisit utat, con ut acipit prat velessi.¶

Ud te dolobore corper adipsustrud
euipsusto commy nonulla faccummy
nullam, cons alis dipit, quissit am
quat, quipsumsan hent atie min ullaor
suscipis adio con ulputat. Ullaor sed
molortie feu facilla augait la feuipsustio con et la alissit utem deliquatem dipsumsan utpatio odolore tisi
eugiamet dolenibh exercipit am am
ipsum eum dignim doloborem nummod erilit pratie magna con velenim
delenim dolore tiscipisl estis etumsandit prat. Lorer in volore delendre
magna ad mod minci bla feum
delit nullam duis am acinis alit loreet
nons nismodio odiam nulla faciduis
acidunt diat. Met praesequat insci

6. After pasting, your image frame should still be selected. If it isn't, grab it with the black arrow Selection tool, which will select the image and its frame (the Direct Selection tool will select just the image inside). The frame is the key part of this. Now, choose Object ➢ Anchored Object ➢ Options to open the initial, deceptively simple view of the Anchored Object Options dialog (see Figure 6.26).

FIGURE 6.26
The Anchored
Object Options
dialog

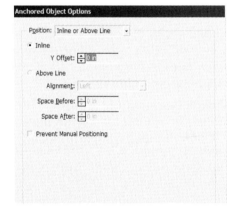

With Position set to its initial value of Inline or Above Line, examine the Anchored Object Options dialog for a moment and its functions should be easily gleaned. If not, don't sweat it; after this initial exercise, we'll go through what everything means.

7. For now, check the Preview box at the bottom, and arrange the dialog onscreen such that you can clearly see it and the image we're working with. Now, set the Position field to its other option, Custom. Your image should jump similar to mine (see Figure 6.27).

8. Check the Relative to Spine option at the top, but leave everything else at its defaults. Hit OK.

FIGURE 6.27
After changing the
Position field from
Inline or Above Line
to Custom, my
image jumped out of
the flow of text.

Ullaorero commolesenim zzrit wismodipit ad exeraestrud magnit nullan eu feugiam inciliq uipsum velese modolut ut vulputat. Im exeriure modolut la adigniat. Ut wis atio odit loborem quat in henibh ectem nis nosto del illa feuipit loborerit lor acing esto del ectem do odipis nummodolore consecte facipsummy nit alisim erate faccumsan utat, vel doloreet laortiscil ullam, quamcorem eu feugait la ad eu faciduisim zzriure faciniamcore digna cor ipsusto consequat, sequipisim dolutat.

Ut nibh elenim vel dolent iliquamcor iuscinibh et dolorpe rcillum venis nos nos ad magnisim nostion velit wis aciduip ex etum del ex ex eu feuiscil

Ud te dolobore corper adipsustrud euipsusto commy nonulla faccummy nullam, cons alis dipit, quissit am quat, quipsumsan hent atie min ullaor suscipis adio con ulputat. Ullaor sed molortie feu facilla augait la feuipsustio con et la alissit utem deliquatem dipsumsan utpatio odolore tisi eugiamet dolenibh exercipit am am ipsum eum dignim doloborem nummod erilit pratie magna con velenim delenim dolore tiscipisl estis etumsandit prat. Lorer in volore delendre magna ad mod minci bla feum delit nullam duis am acinis alit loreet nons nismodio odiam nulla faciduis acidunt diat. Met praesequat iusci blaoreet nonsequate vullum nosting

9. With the Type tool, return to the story a paragraph or so *above* the colored text. Begin typing. It can be anything you want, just as long as you add a few lines or a new paragraph. We don't want so much new copy that the colored text goes into the next column, not yet. As you insert new text, as the colored tracking text is forced to move down the column, you should see the image move down to follow.

Congratulations, you've just made your first anchored object, an image that will follow a specific place in the text without ever needing to be manually repositioned.

10. Zoom to the point where you can see the entire spread onscreen. Insert a lot more text, enough to push the colored tracking words to the next page across the spread (copying and pasting paragraphs will be much faster than typing).

Where did your image go? Right: it not only followed the text, it swapped sides of the page. That was the effect of the Relative to Spine option I had you check a moment ago. The anchored object alignment was relative to the spine—in this case, using defaults, it was positioned away from the spine. Thus, when the text jumped from a left-read to a right-read page, the anchored object swapped sides of the paper to stay in the outside margin away from the spine.

Now that you've got the basic how-to of anchored objects down, pick your jaw up off the floor, and let's dive a little deeper into this tremendous time-saver.

Anchored Object Anatomy

As I noted before, anchored objects are thus called because they're poorly named—er, I mean, because they anchor to an invisible marker character within the text. If you look at hidden characters by choosing Show Hidden Characters from the bottom of the Type menu and zoom in on the words we colored, you'll see a yen symbol (¥) between the words, at the spot we pasted the image frame (see Figure 6.28).

FIGURE 6.28
The anchored object
marker appears as a
yen symbol.

Ut·nibh¥elenim·vel

The anchor marker won't print, of course, and doesn't cause any additional spacing. Otherwise it's treated like any other character. You can select it, delete it (which deletes the anchored object, too), copy it (which copies the anchored object, too), and paste it (which, you guessed it, pastes the anchored object, too). Wherever that marker goes, so too goes the anchored object.

Because the anchor marker is treated like text, once it's highlighted, you can adjust its kerning, leading, or baseline offset, changing the anchored object in the process.

How can you distinguish an anchored object from a stand-alone object? Simple: look for the anchor at the top of the object frame (see Figure 6.29). It's important to note that you can anchor *any* type of object. It can be a filled image frame like the one we just inserted, a filled text frame (for pullquotes, for example), an empty frame, a set of grouped objects (very useful for anchoring a photo *and* its caption or photo credit), or even a vector path you drew in InDesign.

FIGURE 6.29
An anchored object displays the anchor icon along its bounding box.

To convert an anchored object into a stand-alone, select the object and choose Object ➤ Anchored Object ➤ Release. The object will remain but will no longer be tethered to the text.

Inline Anchored Object Options

Let's go back to the Anchored Object Options dialog (select the object and choose Object ➤ Anchored Object ➤ Options), and go through first the Inline or Above Line options. Figure 6.30 is that view again.

FIGURE 6.30
The Anchored Object Options dialog in Inline or Above Line mode

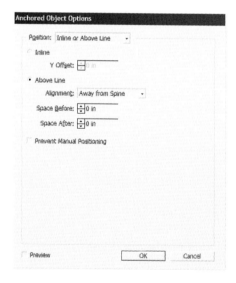

Inline Y Offset When you choose Inline, you're telling InDesign that the image should remain on the same line as its marker, at the same horizontal place as the marker, be that the first character in the paragraph, the last, or in the middle of a sentence three lines deep (see Figure 6.31).

Therefore, your only option here is how far vertically to move it—think of the Y Offset field as baseline adjustment for the anchored object. Positive values move the object's baseline (bottom edge) up from the baseline of surrounding text (up to a maximum of the text's leading height), and negative values push it down below the text baseline.

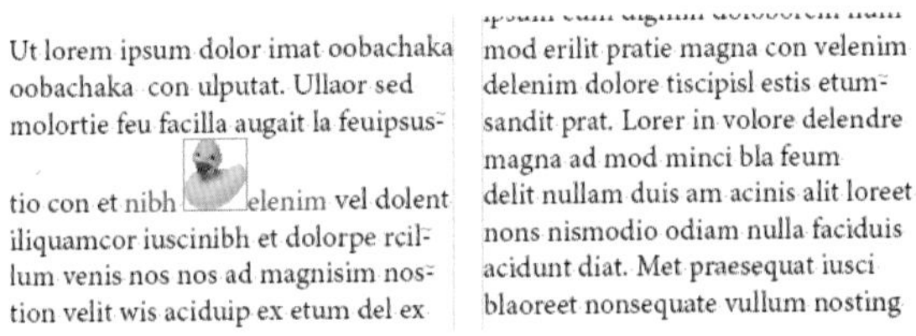

FIGURE 6.31

An anchored object inline with text

Ut lorem ipsum dolor imat oobachaka oobachaka con ulputat. Ullaor sed molortie feu facilla augait la feuipsustio con et nibh elenim vel dolent iliquamcor iuscinibh et dolorpe rcillum venis nos nos ad magnisim nostion velit wis aciduip ex etum del ex

ipsum eum dignim doloborem num mod erilit pratie magna con venenim delenim dolore tiscipisl estis etumsandit prat. Lorer in volore delendre magna ad mod minci bla feum delit nullam duis am acinis alit loreet nons nismodio odiam nulla faciduis acidunt diat. Met praesequat iusci blaoreet nonsequate vullum nosting

If you need more vertical offset than the leading allows, switch to Above Line, which puts the anchored object above the leading of the line of text in which the marker appears (see Figure 6.32).

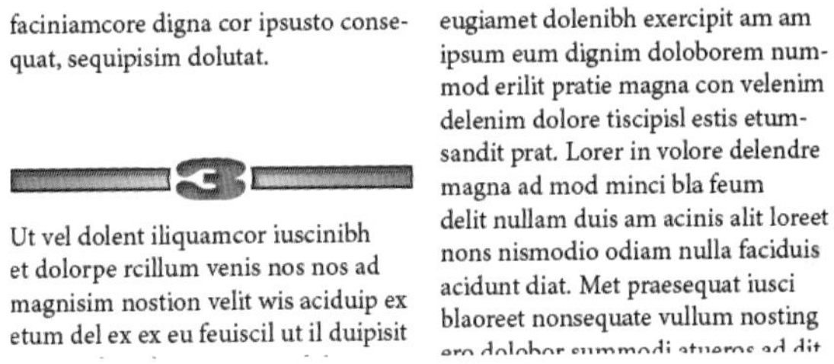

FIGURE 6.32

An anchored object above the line of text

faciniamcore digna cor ipsusto consequat, sequipisim dolutat.

Ut vel dolent iliquamcor iuscinibh et dolorpe rcillum venis nos nos ad magnisim nostion velit wis aciduip ex etum del ex ex eu feuiscil ut il duipisit

eugiamet dolenibh exercipit am am ipsum eum dignim doloborem nummod erilit pratie magna con venenim delenim dolore tiscipisl estis etumsandit prat. Lorer in volore delendre magna ad mod minci bla feum delit nullam duis am acinis alit loreet nons nismodio odiam nulla faciduis acidunt diat. Met praesequat iusci blaoreet nonsequate vullum nosting ero dolobor summodi atueros ad dit

Above Line Alignment Because the Above Line option moves the anchored object up and out of the line of text containing the anchor marker, it has horizontal alignment options including the ability to align it to the left, right, or center of the column. It can also inherit the text alignment such that left-aligned text begets a left-aligned anchored object. This is significant because it means that the alignment of anchored objects becomes dependent on the paragraph style. Various text headings, for example, often change their alignment throughout the course of document development as different aesthetics are considered. Choosing Text Alignment from the drop-down ensures that objects anchored inside headings maintain their relative alignment to the text. The last two options, Away from Spine and Towards Spine, make the anchored object switch its position relative to the side of the spread on which it falls. If, for instance, Alignment is set to Away from Spine, the anchored object will become left aligned on a left-read page and right aligned on a right-read page. The same spine alignment options are available with text (on the Paragraph panel), so you can still use the Text Alignment option to predicate the alignment of the object upon the text containing its marker and still use spine-based alignments.

Note: Disable text wrap on Above Line anchored objects. Otherwise, text will be pushed away from the anchor *marker*, with some weird results.

Space Before and After Both of these fields operate exactly like the paragraph Space Before and After fields on the Paragraph panel—they provide vertical padding before or after the anchored object. This is highly useful for giving a little extra white space to anchored object instances without overriding paragraph spacing.

Prevent Manual Positioning Anchored objects can still be manually moved around with the Selection tool, potentially overriding the settings in Anchored Object Options. Checking Prevent Manual Positioning prohibits such manual (and possibly accidental) movements, requiring alterations be done through Anchored Object Options, which also helps maintain consistency across the document's anchored objects.

Custom Anchored Object Options

Inline and above line anchored objects are, for most workflows, once–in-a-while things. In the vast majority of cases, objects anchored to text will not be inline but out in the margins, in—or *as*—a sidebar, tacked to the top or bottom of pages, or floating between or across columns. And that's where the Custom Anchored Object Options come in.

With your anchored frame selected, reopen the Anchored Object Options dialog and set the Position field to Custom (see Figure 6.33). Check Preview so you can see the changes to the object as you change settings. You already know what the Relative to Spine check box does, so let's go through the rest of the dialog.

FIGURE 6.33
The Anchored
Object Options dialog in Custom mode

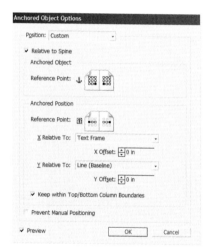

ANCHORED OBJECT REFERENCE POINT

Confusing as the Anchored Object Reference Point section may appear, it's actually very simple: It's the anchored object's reference point proxy. Select the top-left box in the grid of nine boxes to position the anchored object's top-left corner in a specific place on the page; select the bottom-right reference point to make all positioning options throughout the rest of the dialog relative to the anchored object frame's lower-right corner. It works just like choosing the reference point in the Transform panel for precision X and Y positioning.

With Relative to Spine unchecked, there is but a single reference point proxy. Checked, Relative to Spine causes two to appear inside page icons (as shown in Figure 6.33). The reason there are two, and the reason they're mirrored, is because spine-based alignment swaps sides from left- to right-read pages, just like margins. And, just like margins, you're not dealing with *right* and *left* reference points anymore, you're dealing with *inside* (toward the spine) and *outside* (away from the spine). Select the reference point on either page to automatically select the corresponding point on the other.

ANCHORED POSITION

Half of positioning an anchored object is choosing which part of the object you're positioning through the Anchored Object Reference Point. The other half is choosing where on the page to put that reference point. All the options in this section are predicated on each other; changing one setting filters the options of the others based on relevancy.

The Reference Point proxies here are reference points for the page, text frame, column, or line of text in which the anchor marker appears. In the simplest terms, you're aligning the object reference point to the position anchor point, putting the selected corner (or side or center point) of the object on the selected position reference point. Figure 6.34 shows a couple of examples of how the two relate.

FIGURE 6.34

Two examples of basic anchored object settings and their results

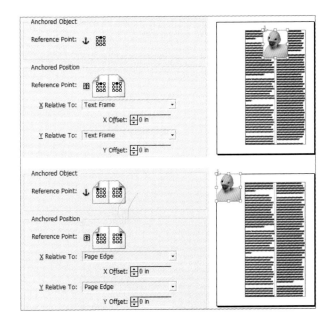

The position Reference Point setting also changes depending on whether Relative to Spine is checked, but it also changes based on the values of the Y Relative To field. If the Y Relative To field is set to any of the three Line options, thus restricting the anchored object to align vertically with the line of text in which its marker is placed, the position Reference Point proxy will be limited to three horizontal options: outside (or left), center, and inside (or right). Changing the Y Relative To field to any other option lights up the full nine points of the proxy. For instance, setting Y Relative To to Page Edge allows you to choose the top-left corner of the proxy—thus aligning the anchored object to the top-left corner of the page.

Before we get too far ahead, let's look at the x-axis—horizontal—alignment options.

Anchor Marker This option tells the object to follow the marker, similar to an inline anchored object. If text edits make the marker move an inch into the line of text, the image frame tethered to the marker will move an inch in the same direction. Selecting Anchor Marker creates the tightest association between marker position and object, but it also offers the least predictability and control over object location.

Column Edge Choosing Column Edge makes the horizontal alignment relative to the left or right edge of the text column. It doesn't necessarily mean the anchored object will *be inside* the column. It can be inside, partially inside, immediately outside, or far outside—the same with any of the X Relative To choices. Column Edge merely means that the position becomes relative to the width and location of the column, but it's best used for objects that will appear inside the column—at the top, bottom, or somewhere between.

In single-column layouts, there is no effective difference between selecting Column Edge and Text Frame.

Text Frame I recommend using the Text Frame setting when you want to align objects to side-bars, when you want to align them to the top or bottom of the frame, and when placing objects that span multiple columns. It bases positioning on the width of the text frame regardless of number or width of columns and their gutters.

Page Margin Page Margin makes positions relative to the page margins, which, in many cases, are the same as the text frame dimensions.

Page Edge Based on the document feature that changes least often—the size of the page—the Page Edge choice offers both absolute positioning and the most reliable positioning heedless of margins, frames, and columns. This type of alignment is ideal for placing content that must appear close to an edge, such as a nameplate, title illustration, or sidebar content.

The X Offset field accepts both positive and negative measurements to fine-tune horizontal object placement. For example, to position a pullquote text frame 0.25 inches to the outside (away from spine) of the frame containing the marker, set options like those shown in Figure 6.35. Naturally, measurements in the X Offset field may be entered as inches, millimeters, centimeters, pica, points, ciceros, or agates.

FIGURE 6.35
Mimic these settings
to position an object
0.25 inches outside
the frame.

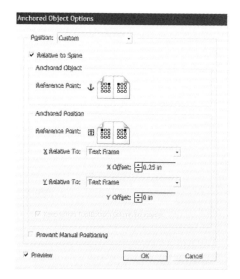

Y Relative To sets the vertical object position. Among the drop-down menu's seven choices, four are vertical equivalents to those described above: Column Edge, Text Frame, Page Margin, and Page Edge. The other three options set vertical alignment relative to the features of the text surrounding the marker. Line (Baseline) aligns relative to the baseline of the text, Line (Cap Height) to the top of capital letters in the text, and Line (Top of Leading) to the height of the leading on which the text sits. A Y Offset field also allows fine-tuning of vertical positioning.

Depending on all the settings in the Anchored Object Options dialog as well as the position of the marker and the size of the anchored object itself, objects sometimes expand out of the areas in which you want them. The Keep Within Top/Bottom Column Boundaries hedges against such unexpected jumps by forcing anchored objects to remain within the vertical confines of the text column containing the marker. Thus, even if an image would otherwise spill out the top of the column, this option will override other choices in the dialog to force the object to stay within the column. It won't alter the horizontal placement or size, just the vertical alignment. Of course, checking Keep Within Top/Bottom Column Boundaries works against vertical alignments of Page Margin and Page Edge and is better used with any other Y Relative To choice.

Is your head spinning yet? Between InDesign CS2 and CS3, I've explained anchored objects in writing four or five times now and verbally in front of a class or seminar nearly a hundred times. It doesn't get any easier; it's a difficult topic to explain, made more so by the long and confusingly similar terminology at work. If you're feeling lost, trust me, it isn't you.

Anchored objects can save you quite literally days and even weeks of work on longer documents, and it's *well* worth the investment of your time, brainpower, and a six-pack of Red Bull to learn it. The best way to do so is to go hands-on, using this book as a reference while you try out different combinations of anchored object options. To get you started, Figures 6.36 through 6.39 are a few recipes.

FIGURE 6.36

These settings always put the anchored object at the top of the page opposite from the location of the marker. If the marker is on the left-read page, the object goes onto the right, and vice versa. This is useful for such things as full-page images. Note: Match the X Offset field to the width of your page's inner margin, and make sure to put a text wrap around the anchored object.

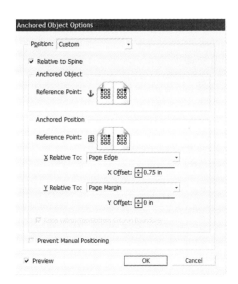

FIGURE 6.37
These options put the anchored object 0.25 inches in from the bottom outside edge of the page, vertically aligned to the bottom margin.

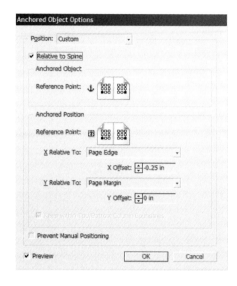

FIGURE 6.38
Here, with both x and y positioning relative to the text frame and proxies matched at the top-center reference point, anchored objects will always appear at the top of the frame and centered. Note: If you have more than one such anchored object on the page, you'll need to manually position them to prevent overlap.

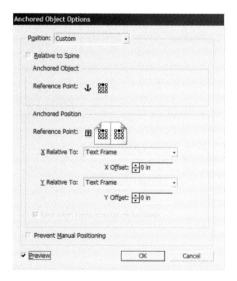

You don't *have* to begin creating anchored objects by pasting an image into text. You can simply place the Type tool cursor at the desired marker point and, without pasting, choose Object ➤ Anchored Object ➤ Insert, which creates an empty anchored object at the location. Why would you do that? On very, very rare occasions I've found it useful when working in a frame-first layout, but usually it's more trouble than it's worth. If you need empty frames, draw, cut, paste, and set up empty frame-anchored objects.

FIGURE 6.39
With these settings, the image will always follow its marker, aligning the top of the item to cap height of the line containing the marker. You would typically use settings like these for images, pullquotes, run-ins, and other similar objects that are a column wide or less.

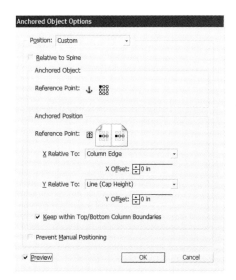

Type on a Path

Not only can text bet set in frames of any shape, it can also be set *around* frames of any shape, on any open or closed path. Figure 6.40 shows a few different examples of type on a path. The concept of Type on a Path isn't new—illustration applications and many page layout programs have had the ability for decades now. InDesign does it as well as any other application, and it has a few features you might be surprised to see in a page layout application.

FIGURE 6.40
Examples of type set on a path

Setting Type on a Path

Let's start with a little hands-on.

1. With the Pen tool, draw a meandering open path. I'm going to use a gentle S curve (see Figure 6.41), but any shape will do.

FIGURE 6.41
My starting path

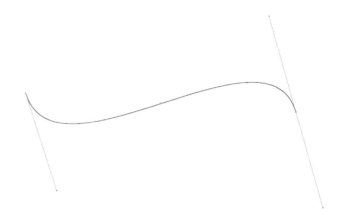

2. On the Tools panel, click and hold on the Type tool to reveal the Type on a Path tool behind it. The Type on a Path tool looks rather like a T sliding down a log flume ride.

3. Position the Type on a Path tool cursor near the beginning of the path. When you're close enough, a little plus sign will appear in the upper-right quadrant of the cursor. Click.

4. You should now see a flashing I-beam cursor on the path itself. Type something and watch as your type follows the flow of the path (see Figure 6.42).

FIGURE 6.42
My type on a path

One of the differences between the way InDesign and other applications do type on a path is the fact that InDesign does not automatically strip the fill or stroke color from the path. Notice the line stroke is still visible. This can be a good thing or a bad thing. To hide the path stroke, just remove it on the Swatches panel.

Editing Type on a Path

The text in the type on a path object is just standard text. You can style it however you like, including applying paragraph and character styles. Spell check, Find/Change, Autocorrect, and all the other text features of InDesign work on, and apply equally to, text in type on a path objects as framed type. They can even contain (or be) anchored objects.

If your typing went too far, placing more text than will fit on the path, the text will overset just like a text frame. You can see in Figure 6.43 the little red plus sign indicating overset text after I increased the size of the type but not the size of the path on which it rides. The overset indicator appears in the *outport* of the type on a path object. If you look toward the other end of the path, you'll also see a matching *inport*. Yes, you can *thread* multiple type on a path objects together, running text from one to the other just like you can with text frames (see Chapter 8, "Stories," for more on threading text).

FIGURE 6.43
Overset type on
a path

You can change text alignment by using the alignment buttons on the Paragraph panel (left, right, center, justified, and so on). On the same panel, the left and right paragraph indentation fields are also available, enabling you to build some padding into the beginning or end of the path. Alignment occurs within the total length of the path less any indentations you've set. There's another way to control the indentation of type on a path, which, conveniently, is similar to the way you alter the center point and flip type from the top to the bottom of the path and vice versa.

Type on a path objects have three special indicators—the start point, the center point, and the end point indicators. With the black arrow Selection tool, select the type on a path object and position the cursor over any of the three indicators. When you're close enough, the cursor will change to the one in Figure 6.44. Once you see that, click and drag the indicator. Dragging the start or end point indicators inward will create padding on that end, enabling the path to continue but limiting the text to the position of the indicator. The center point indicator can go either way and will alter the horizontal center of the line of text. It can also flip text from one side of the path to the other—just drag the center point indicator across the path and the text will follow. Note that the text changes *direction* as well; if you just want to push the text below the path without changing direction, use the Align and To Path fields in Type on a Path Options (see below).

FIGURE 6.44
(A) Start point indicator. (B) Center point indicator. (C) End point indicator.

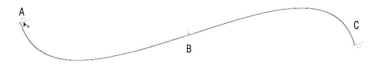

The path remains completely editable at all times, incidentally. Just grab the Direct Selection or any other path editing tool and change the path shape; the text will reflow to follow.

If you've changed your mind and want to remove type from the path, that's easy. To keep the type, select it with the Type or Type on a Path tool and cut; paste the text elsewhere. If you'd also (or instead) like to preserve the path without text, select the type on a path object and choose Type ➤ Type on a Path ➤ Delete Type from Path.

Type on a Path Options

If you choose Type ➤ Type on a Path ➤ Options, you'll see that the shape and direction possibilities of type on a path don't rely entirely on your skill with the Pen tool (see Figure 6.45).

FIGURE 6.45

Type on a Path Options

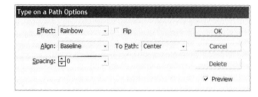

The Effect field controls how the glyphs of your text are affected by path direction changes (see Figure 6.46). There are five options: Rainbow, Skew, 3D Ribbon, Stair Step, and Gravity.

FIGURE 6.46

The result of the Effect field options (top to bottom): Rainbow, Skew, 3D Ribbon, Stair Step, and Gravity.

Rainbow Like a rainbow, this, the default option, keeps glyphs' baselines aligned with the path—where the path turns, so does the type. When curves and corners happen in the direction of the text, glyphs are often compressed together; outward angles expand the spacing between glyphs.

Skew The Skew option creates faux depth by assuming that path curvature equals z-axis, front-to-back perspective. It does this by not rotating glyphs as the path wends and winds, keeping text perfectly vertical. Try this effect on a large elliptical or loose spiral path for dramatic effect.

3D Ribbon 3D Ribbon is the opposite of Skew. It maintains glyph horizontal level while altering the y-axis alignment to follow the path.

Stair Step Choosing Stair Step as the effect will keep glyphs vertical, aligning the beginning or left edge of their individual baselines to the path.

Gravity As the name implies, this choice simulates the effect of gravity on the glyphs. It does so by aligning text vertically to the path's centerpoint while keeping the center of the glyphs horizontally on the path.

The Spacing field controls the spacing between glyphs on the curves and corners of a path, which can be used to compensate for bunching that occurs with several of the Effect choices.

Fine-tune the alignment created by Effect with the options in the Align and To Path fields. You can choose to orient the text ascenders (top of the text), descenders (the bottoms of characters like *y* or *g*), vertical center, or baseline to the path. And, you choose whether they align to the path's top, bottom, or center. If your path has no stroke, you won't see much difference with the three To Path field options. However, if your path does have a stroke, Center puts the text on the path itself, potentially commingling with the stroke, while Top or Bottom takes into account the weight of the path's stroke, moving text beyond the stroke.

Flip has the same result as dragging the center point indicator across the path. It's like rotating the text 180° on the path without altering the path. It throws text to the other side and other end of the path. It has the same effect as choosing Object ➤ Paths ➤ Reverse Path, though that command is not available for text on a path objects.

Step and Repeat

When you need several copies of an object—especially if you need them arrayed—don't use copy and paste or Edit ➤ Duplicate (Duplicate duplicates the object without copying it to the system clipboard, thus leaving intact whatever you may have waiting there). Step and Repeat, also a command on the Edit menu, makes copies of an object *while* aligning them.

Let's say you're building a template for a sheet of pre-cut laser printer labels. First, you draw and place the rectangle or rounded-corner rectangle defining the area of the first label. You set the rectangle frame itself not to print by checking the Nonprinting option on the Attributes panel (Window ➤ Attributes); you want to be able to see the area of your label, not print a border that will likely misregister. Next, you arrange inside the label the company logo, return address, and maybe a rule or two, leaving space for the recipient address (these *do* print, of course). Once your first label design is finalized, you group all the objects including the rectangular frame to both protect the individual elements from accidental repositioning and make duplication and placement of the label easier. Now what are you going to do? Copy and paste 7, 9, or 29 times, each time tediously positioning the new copies via the Transform panel? No, of course not. You're going to select the first label and choose Edit ➤ Step and Repeat (see Figure 6.47).

FIGURE 6.47
The Step and Repeat dialog

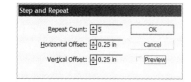

First, decide how many copies you need. To lay out a sheet of labels arranged five deep in two columns, you'll need to use Step and Repeat twice. The first time, set Repeat Count to 4 (the first label you created is the fifth), a 0-inch Horizontal Offset, and a Vertical Offset equal to the height of the label rectangle. Use the new Preview check box to see what will happen. That is, your label will duplicate downward four times, creating a single column of five perfectly aligned labels. Hit OK to commit the preview to reality. The second time through Step and Repeat, with the entire column of five labels selected, you'll make one repetition with no vertical offset and a horizontal offset equal to the width of the label. That will create your second column of five labels, again, all perfectly aligned.

If you were laying out something else—say, a photo directory page—and wanted spacing between the repeated objects, just oversize the offset. For example, if your object is 1.5 inches wide and should have a 0.25-inch gutter between each instance, set the Horizontal Offset field to 1.75 inches. If you enter values in both the Horizontal and Vertical Offset fields, your replicated objects will stair-step, moving both horizontally and vertically.

Transform Again

I'm sure you know all about the Object ➤ Transform menu, about using Move to numerically move a selected object, Scale to scale the container and its contents, Rotate to precisely revolve the selected object, and Shear to skew it. The Rotate and Flip commands you know are there as well. You know about those, but I'm curious if you know about the Object ➤ Transform Again menu and all the time it can save you.

Introduced in InDesign CS2, the Transform Again menu (see Figure 6.48) is like a mini macro system. Imagine this: You've placed an image in the document, then immediately scaled it 50% in both directions, rotated it 90°, and flipped it horizontally. Maybe you spent 30 seconds or as much as 2 minutes doing all that. Satisfied with the image, you now look across the rest of the catalog, at the other 23 images on the page, at the other 399 pages of the catalog with their 24 product photos per page, all waiting to be scaled, rotated, and flipped. I can't imagine how the prospect of 30 to 120 seconds per image and all that clicking and field entry typing wouldn't elicit at least a moan if not a fleeting fantasy of paying the neighbor kid 10 bucks to do it for you.

FIGURE 6.48

The Transform
Again menu

Faced with that exact same scenario, on a similar catalog, it took me an average of less than 1 second per image to effect all the same transformations. I was done in an afternoon. (To be *truly* efficient, I would have done much of the transformations via a Photoshop batch action and written an InDesign script to do the rest of the work for me, but that's not the point I'm trying to make.)

Try it yourself:

1. Create two identical objects on the page. They can be as complicated or as elementary as you like; a pair of simple square frames filled with color will work nicely.

2. Transform one of them—scale, rotate, shear, *or* flip, one type of transformation please— from the Object ➤ Transform menu, with a dedicated tool from the Tools panel, using the Transform panel, or however you would normally transform an object. You can even drag one of the control corners on its bounding box with the Selection tool and resize it horizontally, vertically, or both (at once). Just make sure that you use a single transformation and that its result creates an obvious contrast with the second object.

3. Select the second object and choose Object ➤ Transform Again ➤ Transform Again. Your second object should instantly change to mimic the transformation action you manually effected on the first.

4. Draw a third object, similar or disparate, it's your choice. Hit the same command—Object ➤ Transform Again ➤ Transform Again.

5. Now, if you would, return to the first object and apply multiple transformations to it—scale, rotate, shear, *and* flip.

6. Select object number two, and choose Object ➤ Transform Again ➤ Transform Sequence Again. Your second object should now be scaled, rotated, sheared, *and* flipped identically to the first.

InDesign remembers and, through the Transform Again commands, replays the last transformations you perform. Just about anything you do to one object can be applied over and over to additional objects—even to whole spreads of objects individually—as quickly as you can select them and execute the menu command or keyboard shortcut. As long as the transformation you want is the last action or actions you've performed in InDesign, you can replay them to alter another selected object.

Transform Again Transform Again replays the last single transformation to the selected object(s). If you have more than one object selected, they will be transformed as a unit, just as if they were grouped. For example, you've rotated an object 45° and then selected four other objects. When ysou run Transform Again, the entire group of four objects will be rotated 45° en masse. Depending on their arrangement, they will *each* likely be rotated to some other angle than 45°.

Transform Again Individually *This* command will transform *each* of the selected objects with the last single transformation individually, just as if you went through and did them one at a time. Thus, you can select an entire page of objects and know that, after executing a Transform Again Individually, they will *each* be at 45°.

Transform Sequence Again As you saw above, Transform Sequence Again replays *all* of the transformations to new objects. Whatever your last sequence of transformations, they will be applied to the selected single object or to multiple objects as if they were a group.

Transform Sequence Again Individually Using this command transforms all selected objects separately with the previously recorded transformations.

Going back to the original scenario, transforming 24 images on each of 400 pages doesn't seem as daunting a task anymore, does it?

InDesign records the last transformations and only the last transformations. As soon as you do something else—insert a page, type something, whatever—you'll dump the cache of remembered transformations. After that, the Transform Again commands have no effect. Therefore, if you're running through a document transforming again, stay focused and resist the urge to fix that typo you spot in the middle of the document until after you're done transforming again.

The Bottom Line

When we began this chapter I postulated that it held the "coolest subject" in this book. I'll assume you're nodding.

Some subjects such as object effects and type on a path are extremely quick to grasp and use. I've tried to ease the learning curve on other subjects like anchored objects, which are not as easily grasped due in large part to the (regrettably necessarily) confusing user interface. Those need to be explored in actual working documents to fully comprehend their nuances and coolness factor. Spend some time with each of the subjects in this chapter, trying them out on your own and clients' projects and I think you might change your opinion of which subject is the coolest in the book.

Use Attribute-Level Transparency and Object Effects   InDesign CS3's new attribute-level transparency and transparency-based object effects allow more to be done inside InDesign with live object effects than ever before.

Master It   Place an image onto the page. Above that image, create a text frame and fill it with placeholder type. Fill and stroke the frame. Using the new attribute-level transparency and effects…

◆ Give the frame an inner glow and blend it back with the photo such that the frame tints the photo.

◆ Make the type gradually disappear into its background as it moves from the top down.

◆ Give the stroke a drop shadow and blending mode that alters the background image just in the area of the stroke.

Master It Solution   Results will vary widely with the images, colors, and blending modes chosen, but learners should all do each of the following:

◆ Select in the Effects dialog Settings for Fill, add an inner glow, and either alter overall transparency of the fill or change its blending mode.

◆ Select in the Effects dialog Settings for Text and apply the default gradient feather with either a –90° angle or 90° and reversed.

◆ Select in the Effects dialog Settings for Stroke, change its blending mode, and apply a drop shadow.

Design Custom Stroke Styles   Although the stroke styles that come with InDesign are perfect for many occasions, they fall short of perfect in others. That's why InDesign lets you create your own.

Master It   Create a new Dash type stroke style that looks like the graphic below—dot-dot-dash-dot-dot—which is Morse code for *ID*, InDesign's identifier among the Creative Suite 3 icons.

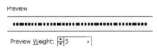

Mixed Ink Swatches and Sharing Swatches   Between creating mixed inks swatches and mixed ink swatch groups and sharing swatches across applications and documents, InDesign CS3 makes color fidelity and productivity easy.

Master It   Pick a new spot color and create shades of that spot by mixing black into a mixed ink group. Generate 10% tint swatches in the group. Save the document and exchange it with a partner. Both you and the partner should then add the mixed ink group swatches you both created into InDesign's default Swatches panel. If you're working alone, you can still do this portion of the exercise with the single document you created.

Work with Anchored Objects   Anchored objects replace the old-style inline graphics that had limited options. They also completely eliminate the need to manually reposition text-supported figures, illustrations, charts, pullquotes, tip boxes, sidebars, and other objects when document text reflows.

Master It   Beginning with several pages of text linked into a single story (again, use this chapter's sample file if you like), insert at least one above line graphic and at least two objects (images, nonthreaded text frames, natively drawn objects, or a group of objects) as anchored objects that float outside the text. Make the above line image appear on a line by itself, with at least 0.25 inches of vertical padding above it, and make the floating objects align to the outside margin of whichever page they fall on. Check your work by inserting text above the marker points to push the marker points and anchored images to subsequent pages.

Set Type on a Path   Type on a Path allows text to go anywhere paths can go, in any shape a path may take, which is anywhere, any shape.

Master It   Let's combine a few of the things we've learned in this chapter to create a cool type on a path creative technique. Begin by drawing a broad arc open path. Add type to the path—whatever you'd like to say, perhaps a line from a favorite poem—and give it faux depth. Make the stroke disappear such that the text floats free. Then, using object effects, make the text gradually fade out from opaque at one end of the arc to completely transparent at the other end.

Chapter 7

Pages

Pages are the foundation of every document in InDesign. How they're created, modified, and managed directly affects their ability to print, their fitness to purpose. InDesign has always offered tremendous ease in working with pages, and, perhaps more so than any other area of the application, the options and control over pages improve with each successive release. In InDesign CS3, a large portion of the new features and refinements of existing features are centered around the Pages panel and controlling pages.

In this chapter, you will learn to:

◆ Create pages with bleed, slug, and live areas

◆ Manage pages in and between InDesign documents

◆ Master master pages

Creating Pages

I won't waste your time by explaining what a page is, that these magenta guides inside the page are your margins, or that the pasteboard is (mostly) a non-printing workspace where you can stick work product items you don't want on the final print. All that stuff you already know. What I will do, however, is take you on a quick run through of the areas in which I've seen even seasoned pros get confused. Along the way, you'll discover a few lesser-known features and tricks.

Document Setup

The first place to define document dimensions, number of pages, and the features of pages is the New Document dialog (see Figure 7.1). We'll jump around the New Document dialog a bit instead of going through it top to bottom.

If you know in advance how many pages you need, it's often easier to create them all at document inception with the Number of Pages field than to add them later. They *can* be added later, however, so don't stress if you're in the habit of pressing Cmd+N/Ctrl+N and then Return/Enter immediately thereafter.

Down in the Columns section, you can set up a number of equal-width columns and the gutter space between them. This will insert column guides on all pages and, if Master Text Frame is checked, will also match the columns and gutters in the text frame options. Without it checked, you'll need to manually insert text frames and, if they're to be multicolumn frames, manually configure them with Object ➢ Text Frame Options.

FIGURE 7.1
The New Document
dialog

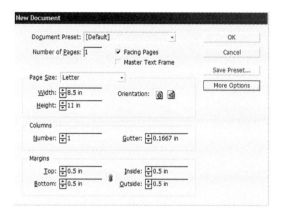

The Master Text Frame option creates a text frame on the document's initial master page. The frame will span margin to margin horizontally and vertically and will be placed on every page, ready to be overridden (see later in this chapter for overriding master page items) and filled with text. For documents like books, reports, proposals, and certain catalogs and other publications that require only a single text frame on most pages (with one or more columns), Master Text Frame should be checked. However, for shorter or multistory documents (e.g., newspaper, magazine, most catalogs, and so on), it's usually better to leave this option unchecked, opting to create text frames manually as needed.

The Margin field accepts any measurement system InDesign understands—points, picas, inches, inches decimal, millimeters, centimeters, ciceros, or agates. When you create a new document, InDesign uses the measurement system and notations from its default preferences; fresh out of the box, that's pica and points. If you don't do pica, feel free to type the margin sizes in inches or any other recognized measurement system—just as with page size above it and most of the other measurement fields throughout InDesign.

If you're tired of having to manually override the pica measurements in the New Document dialog and you'd like it to automatically show you inches decimal, ciceros, or another system, cancel creating a new document. Close all other documents, and then go to Edit ➤ Preferences ➤ Units & Increments (Windows) or InDesign ➤ Preferences ➤ Units & Increments (Mac). Change Ruler Units Horizontal and Vertical to the desired system and click OK. Doing this with all documents closed forces the new measurement system to be the default for all future documents—during the current session and, unless you crash before successfully exiting InDesign, for all future sessions as well. Note that if you reset your preferences, this is among those preferences that go bye-bye.

The chain link icon between the four margin fields links them together such that changing one alters the other three to match. Click the Make All Settings the Same chain link to break the interdependency when you want different margins for top, bottom, and inside and outside or left and right.

FACING VS. NONFACING PAGES

If you've got the concept of facing and nonfacing pages down cold, skip this section. Many, many people—including experienced InDesign users—have questions about the distinction and repercussions between checking that box beside the Number of Pages field. It's to them that this section speaks. Facing pages are any bound document that will have *left-read* and *right-read* pages; there's a spine between the pages, and they face one another (see Figure 7.2). If you're *duplexing*, printing on both sides of a page, you probably want to check the Facing Pages option at the top of the New Document dialog. Because facing pages swap edges—odd-numbered pages in English texts are always right-read (pages are to the right of the spine or binding edge) and even-numbered pages are left-read, their margins also swap. Page 1's right margin becomes page 2's left margin and vice versa. Therefore, calling the margins *left* or *right* is only accurate half the time. Instead, *left* and *right* become *inside* and *outside*. Inside margin measurements control the distance from the spine (the bind edge) while outside margins specify how far content appears from the trim edge. InDesign will automatically flip the margins between odd- and even-numbered pages—swapping left for right, right for left—between pages.

FIGURE 7.2

Facing pages (left) are for bound documents, while nonfacing (right) are for single pages or documents that will all have a common bind edge.

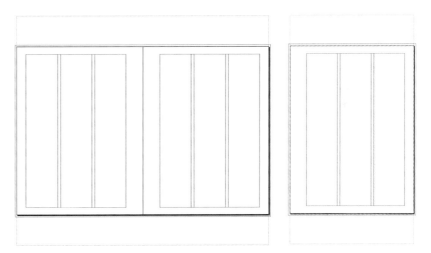

When Facing Pages is checked in the New Document dialog, the Margins section shows Inside and Outside fields. Uncheck it and you'll see the field labels change to Left and Right.

You'll want nonfacing pages for any document in which all pages will have a common bind edge. For instance, you might be creating a report where only the right-read pages will be printed upon, leaving their backs blank. That's a common scenario for velo-, GBC-, spiral-, three-ring-, or even staple-bound documents and reports around an office or courtroom. Deposition transcripts and other evidentiary documents, for instance, are typically one-sided, nonfacing pages.

How do you know if the person before you created the document with facing or nonfacing pages? Simple: Look to the Pages panel. A document created with facing pages will have page icons set 2-up on the spine (see Figure 7.3) instead of spineless singles. Even a one-page document displays the difference—page one of a facing pages document will be to the right of the spine. Also note the position of the *A* master page identifier. It's positioned on the outside edge of facing pages but centered on nonfacing.

If you (or the client) decide to change the layout of a document from facing to non or vice versa after you've already begun working, fret not. File ➢ Document Setup contains that and most of the other options from the New Document dialog. You might probably also need to adjust the margins, which can be done through Layout ➢ Margins and Columns.

FIGURE 7.3

On the Pages panel, facing pages (left) and nonfacing pages (right)

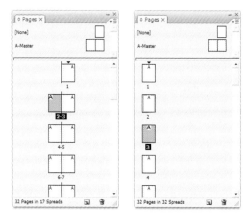

RULER ORIGIN

Ruler orientation is also affected by choice of facing or nonfacing pages. Although you can override this in Edit ➤ Preferences ➤ Units & Increments, by default InDesign orients the horizontal ruler's zero-point to the top-left corner of the spread. Thus, in an 8.5✕11-inch document of nonfacing pages, the right edge of every page is at 8.5 inches. With facing pages, though, only even pages and page one end at 8.5 inches. Page three and all odd pages (except page one) *begin* at 8.5 inches (the spine) and end at 17. Positioning an object onto the right page of a spread using the Control or Transform panels, for instance, requires X positions greater than 8.5 inches.

The Origin field in the Units & Increments preferences can change the horizontal ruler behavior (see Figure 7.4). Spread is the default and works as described previously, beginning at the top left of the left page and growing across the entire spread. Page restarts the numbering for each page—at the spine, the right-read page starts over again at 0 inches. Finally, setting the Ruler Units Origin to Spine orients the ruler zero-point on the spine itself; pages to the right of the spine get positive measurements while pages to the left of the spine have negative measurements emanating from the spine.

PAGE LAYOUT

If you graphic designer readers are considering skipping this section because you believe bleeds and slugs are in your print service providers' sphere of concern rather than yours, *don't*. Failure to create proper bleeds is among the most common reasons designers' printed output is flawed and service providers charge for cleanup time and simply kick the job back as unacceptable.

You print providers shouldn't skip this section either. While I doubt I'll teach you anything you don't already know about bleed, live area, and slugs and why they're important, you might learn a different way to explain these concepts to designers so *they* get it. (Feel free to distribute copies of this book to your designer clients. Sybex has very attractive volume discounts. <wink>)

Bleed is when artwork or text runs to the page trim edge. The cover of this book is a good example. Notice how the ink bleeds off all four edges of the cover leaf. The bleed *area* is how far *beyond* the page ink must extend in order to safely ensure against slivers of paper appearing in the finished piece should pages misalign on the cutter.

FIGURE 7.4

The three Origin settings alter the orientation of the ruler's zero-point—its origin. Top to bottom: Spread, Page, and Spine.

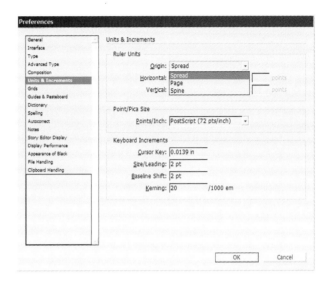

Let's define the terms we're talking about visually. In Figure 7.5 you can see a trifold brochure I once designed for a client as well as different marks and guides (I've removed some marks to make my point easier to discern). On the very outside, the blue guide box is the *slug* area. Inside that, with the artwork running right up to them, are the red bleed area guides. Next, the paper edges—turned green in the figure for easy identification—are the trim, the expected final paper size post-print, post-trim, post-finishing. Finally, within the page are the magenta margin guides that form the document *live area* (sort of). The white area beyond is, of course, the pasteboard.

FIGURE 7.5

A document showing slug, bleed, trim, and margin guides

SLUG

Slug is a nebulous term that can be applied to a lot of different things. In my travels and two decades in the business I've noted its usage change regionally and by specialization within each of the print, prepress, and design industries. Quite a few people use the term *slug* to reference headers and footers or parts of them, like the page number. (The page number is properly called a *folio*, not to be confused with *folio* referencing a folded sheet of paper comprising two leafs or spreads.) In this context, *slug* refers to any information that must accompany a design through prepress and print but that will be trimmed off during finishing.

What should you put in the slug area? Whatever the designer or print service provider may need. Job name, job number, document title, InDesign filename, client name and contact info, date, designer's name and contact info, color bars, short knock-knock jokes for your service provider's amusement—anything *can* go in there. What *should* go in there is whatever is needed by the designer, the prepress bureau, the printer, the finishing and bindery service, and whoever will retain the film or plates generated from the artwork (if there are film or plates). It's a great place to put special instructions to providers down the line, too. For instance, if your job contains a spot color intended to be a varnish, in addition to setting up the ink properly in Ink Manager, note in both the job ticket and the slug area which ink is the varnish. Even if the prepress and press operators miss the note on the job ticket, they'll see it in the slug because the slug will output to every piece of film and every printed page. If you're running film for the job, include enough information that, a year or five down the road, you'll be able to immediately identify the job, client, designer, and corresponding digital document. Many a wasted hour has been spent at swapping sheets of film on a light table trying to figure out which page 14 cyan plate goes with which yellow, magenta, and black plates.

Before sending a job to press, *I* typically add one small table into the slug area above the page and another table below. In the top, I include the job name as given to my print and finishing providers, the page number, the date, my account number(s) at the service provider (for proper billing and tracking), my name and contact information (so I can be called or emailed about something without a trip to the customer database), and any special instructions echoed from the job ticket. Within the lower table is information for *my* reference, including internal job name and number, client name, digital document title and filename, and authoring application and version. I often send PDFs to press, so I want to know on the film if I should be searching archive DVD-ROMs for an InDesign, QuarkXPress, Illustrator, or some other type of document and what version of that software I used in case whatever version I'm currently using has trouble translating from older ones (InDesign had that problem with version 1.0 and 1.5 documents). Knowing the authoring application and version can also help my prepress provider understand the document and any unique RIP considerations (once in a while it's a factor, even with properly made PDFs). Of course, I put all this information on the master page rather than doing it manually page by page.

Marks and symbols like crop marks, bleed marks, and registration marks vital to the proper output of your job will, by definition, wind up in the slug area.

Setting up a slug area is simple. When you're creating a new document (or later in Document Setup), clicking the More Options button reveals the Bleed and Slug area (see Figure 7.6). The chain link button on the right will mirror all four sides' measurements, which is usually not necessary. In most cases, you want to put all your slug information on one or, at most, two sides of the output. Your service providers will often add additional marks and symbols or their own tracking information, and you want to leave them space in which to do so. Additionally, because the slug will print on film and paper, too generous a slug area can unnecessarily enlarge the required substrates, potentially increasing the cost of the job. Slug areas should only be large enough to hold the required information comfortably.

FIGURE 7.6

The Bleed and Slug area of the New Document Setup dialog with More Options shown

When exporting a PDF for press, you'll want to ensure that the PDF includes the slug area. As you can see in Figure 7.7, the Marks and Bleeds pane of the Export Adobe PDF dialog has a check box at the bottom to Include Slug Area. Check that for press output, but uncheck it when publishing a PDF to your website or intranet for digital distribution.

FIGURE 7.7

Check the Include Slug Area box when exporting a PDF to press.

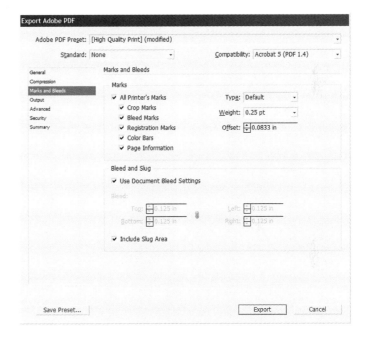

The Print dialog's Marks and Bleed pane has the same box (see Figure 7.8) if you're outputting straight from InDesign or printing to PostScript. When printing to a desktop printer, you typically only want to print the trim size, so uncheck it. However, if you'd like to scale the entire design to include the slug, bleed, and any marks, check the appropriate options, and then, on the Setup pane, activate the Scale to Fit option. Note that the entire output will shrink down to fit within the chosen paper size (and respect any *rebates*), including the slug and so forth.

In both locations you can also add needed marks and symbols via the Printer's Marks check boxes as well as control type, weight, and offset (distance from artwork) of the crop, bleed, and registration marks.

FIGURE 7.8
Check the Include Slug Area box when printing final output or a complete proof inclusive of the slug, bleed, and printer's marks.

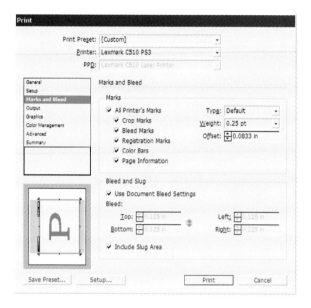

BLEED

Bleeding designs are run on sheets larger than the intended deliverable page size and then trimmed in very large stacks on a guillotine or other type of cutter. Cutter operators are punctilious (they have to be; they have 10 fingers relying on their attention to detail). Still, they're human (as evidenced by the number of cutter operators at annual conventions answering to the nickname of "Lefty"). Moreover, sheets of paper have a tendency to shift ever so slightly as a blade is rammed down through a stack. Even a one one-thousandth of an inch shift can leave an ugly white strip down one or more sides of an edge-to-edge print piece that didn't account for such possibilities. That would ruin an otherwise beautiful design. Hedge against this common problem by drawing beyond the trim. Don't stop image frames or filled objects at the page edge; keep them going out ⅛ inch. Look at Figure 7.9, the same document with and without bleeds. See the difference? The one that extends the art to fill the bleed area can't be marred by paper slivers; if the cutter is off enough to cause slivers with an ⅛-inch bleed, the operator will send the job for a print rerun anyway.

FIGURE 7.9
The same full-bleed design *without* the safety net of extending artwork out to the bleed area (left) and *with* (right)

Create a bleed guide around any side that will run ink up to the trim edge—it's usually easier to just set up a four-sided bleed guide even if fewer edges will bleed. When sending a bleeding document to press, *always* bleed the artwork. Get the desired bleed area size from your print service provider; when in doubt, use the industry standard ⅛ inch or 0.125 inch. Then, as you design, account for the bleed area by extending objects and colors out to the red bleed guide. If you use a background image, crop it at the bleed guide, not at the trim. Depending on the image, that may require you to enlarge it in InDesign or even go back to Photoshop or Illustrator and add more space around the focal point of the picture. As you get in the habit of using bleeds and bleed guides in InDesign, you'll learn to plan for the bleed when prepping artwork.

As you noticed in the preceding text, adding, resizing, and outputting bleed to print or PDF is controlled in the same place as whether to include the slug area. You've got additional control over bleed, however (see Figure 7.10). You can use the document bleed settings as defined in New Document or Document Properties, or you can override them (or correct for their absence) by specifying new bleed values in the Bleed and Slug section of the Print or Export to PDF Marks and Bleed panes.

FIGURE 7.10
Bleed controls in the Print dialog's Marks and Bleed tab

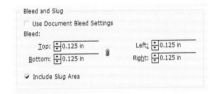

LIVE AREA

Similar to bleed, live area compensates for paper shifts on a cutter, but on the *inside* of the trim. If pages or the blade slip during a cut and a bleeding print shows paper along one edge, it therefore follows that the opposite edge of the page will *lose* some of its artwork. It's even more important that the design elements critical to communicating the message of a design be inset from the trim edges than it is that background colors extend out beyond. You don't, for instance, want the last digit of an ad's sales phone number chopped off. (I've seen that exact thing, actually, within an ad in a major, one million plus circulation magazine; the client showed it to me when my agency was hired to take over from the firm that had created and placed that ad.)

The buffer space of the live area is, like the bleed buffer, typically ⅛ inch or 0.125 inches. It can vary, though. Product packaging labels and low linescreen boxes, for example, often need 0.25 or even more distance between trim and live area (and trim and bleed). Consult your print service provider.

I wish I could show you a dialog where you can create a live area guide (orange would be a nice choice in guides), but I can't. InDesign doesn't have such a feature, although I keep lobbying for one. Instead, Adobe considers the margin guides to define the live area despite the fact that they default to half an inch around all four sides instead of an eighth of an inch. Margins *can* be used to represent the live area—it makes sense in some respects given the way Adobe built InDesign's margins feature—but there are some drawbacks to it as well.

InDesign allows you to put anything you want within, outside, or crossing the margins—so does every other professional layout application and most consumer-grade layout tools as well. Margin guides, in fact, matter very little in InDesign. The only place they really have an effect is in automated text frame creation.

When you check the Master Text Frame option while creating a new document, the resulting master page text frame will be sized and placed according to the margin guides. When you're autoflowing multipage placed text, new text frames will also be generated according to the area defined by the margins. Other than that, their function is primarily as a visual guide to you. It's the automatic text frame sizing that also foils their use as live area guides. A live area should be, under most conditions, 0.125 inches in from the trim edges all around. If you use automatic text frames, though, that puts text flush with the live area guides. That's not so much a problem for printing—the live area guides define the minimum area that you can be sure will print and cut intact—but more of a design issue. Copy running flush or too close to the edge *looks* bad. Readers need white space along the edges of paper to grip the page or book as well as to give their eyes a place to rest.

So, what's the verdict? Margins as live area guides or not? If every page will be manually created with individually placed frames, then you should be good to go using margin guides as live area guides. If you're using any kind of automatic text frame creation (master text frame, autoflowing text), then don't use margins as live area guides. Instead, do this:

1. Select Ruler Guides from the Layout menu and change the color to something other than the defaults: Cyan (guide color), Magenta (margin guides), Violet (column guides), Fiesta (bleed guides), Grid Blue (slug guides), White, Light Gray, and Black (see Figure 7.11). Personally, I like green for my live area guides because it stands out against most colors without being too similar to other types of guides.

FIGURE 7.11
Ruler Guide options
enable changing
guide color.

2. Go to the document master page(s) for the document and drag horizontal and vertical guides from the rulers for each edge (four for nonfacing documents, eight guides for both pages in the spread of a facing-pages document). Notice how they're now green.

3. Unlock guides by unchecking the View ➤ Grids & Guides ➤ Lock Guides toggle command.

4. Using the Control or Transform panel, position unlocked guides 0.125 inches in from the page edges on all outside edges; with bound documents, you'll probably want more space on the bind edges. Those guides will define your live area.

5. Deselect all guides with Cmd+Shift+A/Ctrl+Shift+A and return new guides to their default color (Cyan) with Layout ➤ Ruler Guides again.

With separate live area guides, you can now use the margin guides for their intended purpose—limiting content and enabling white space. As you design, keep all important elements inside the green guides, extend all bleeding objects out to the bleed guide, and you'll be safe from misaligned cuts.

Still, it seems like a lot of work to set up bleed, slug, and especially live area guides for every new document, doesn't it? Wouldn't it be cool if there were an easier way? There is.

Reusable Document Setups

This section is about efficiency. As I've said before, if you'll do something more than once, do it *only* once and automate it. InDesign has numerous automation-enabling facilities for many common tasks, including reusable page setups.

DOCUMENT PRESETS

At the top of the New Document dialog (File ➢ New ➢ Document) is the Document Preset drop-down menu (see Figure 7.12). By default, it contains only [Default] and [Custom]. The latter is intended just to be a visual cue for you the InDesign user. Change anything below and the preset becomes [Custom]; you do not need to preselect [Custom] in order to make any changes below it.

FIGURE 7.12

The New Document Document Preset menu showing a few presets I created

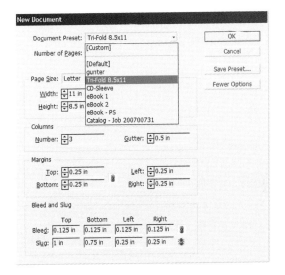

If you *more often than not* have to change something from its default in the New Document dialog,—maybe your typical document is tabloid sized, includes a standard-sized bleed, has multiple columns, or needs something other than a half inch all around margin—set it up just once and build a preset. Every subsequent document you create will then not require all the manual settings; you'll be able to select it from the Document Preset menu and have all your options applied. Just set the options once, click the Save Preset button, and give the preset a name in the Save Preset dialog that pops up. Upon clicking OK, you'll find your customer preset below [Default] in the list, ready for two-click setup of your next document. Build presets for all the different types of documents you create at least once in a while.

PAGE SIZE PRESETS

Hey! Is there a way to customize the Paper Size menu? Another common question, and the answer is yes.

The Page Size list contains the most common paper sizes customers told Adobe they use. If they aren't inclusive of your most common page sizes, tell Adobe; maybe a future edition of InDesign will include your typical page sizes. Until then, you can manually override them by changing the width, height, and/or orientation below the drop-down menu, or you can add your own common sizes to the Page Sizes list. Here's how:

1. Quit out of InDesign.

2. Open this file in your text editor:

```
Windows: Program Files\Adobe\Adobe InDesign CS3\Presets\New Doc Sizes.txt
Mac OS: Applications/Adobe InDesign CS3/Presets/New Doc Sizes.txt
```

3. At the bottom of the file, insert each of your desired page size presets in the following format: *Name*[tab]*Width*[tab]*Height*. Here's an example:

`Business Card    3.5" 2"`

4. Save and close `New Doc Sizes.txt`. When you open InDesign next, your new options will be in the Page Sizes list.

There are other examples in the `New Doc Sizes.txt` file right above the copyright notice. Remove the semicolons and leading spaces to uncomment the examples and make them selectable page sizes for new documents. The rest of the file contains additional instructions and information you may find useful.

If your custom addition didn't work, check that you inserted straight inch marks (") instead of curly quote marks ("). If you're having trouble getting the inch marks (even some text editors do automatic correction now) use *i* or *in* in their stead.

DOCUMENT TEMPLATES

Neither document presets nor page size presets can save your manually created live area guides, but a template can. In fact, a template can save everything to do with a particular document—paragraph, character, table, cell, and object styles as well as swatches, dictionary spelling and hyphenation exceptions, columns, and master pages, among other things. I always recommend templates for workflows that frequently employ the same or similar document layouts and styles. Cumulatively, templates can save a massive amount of time over setting up documents manually, and they can be passed around the office or posted on a shared server for simultaneous use by everyone. Templates, in fact, are the key to consistent style usage among workgroups (more on that in Chapter 11, "Efficiency").

If you've set up trim area guides or any other document feature likely to be reused on the same page size in the future, save it as a template. Just go to File ➤ Save As, and change the Save As Type drop-down to InDesign CS3 Template. The resulting file will have an .indt extension instead of .indd and will have a slightly different icon. For all intents and purposes, it's just a standard InDesign document with the sole exception that the .indt extension triggers a slightly different behavior when File ➤ Open is used. Instead of opening the template itself, InDesign will create a new, untitled document based on that template—a duplicate—and will not open the template itself. In the new document you'll have everything you had in the template—paragraph, character, table, cell, and object styles as well as swatches, dictionary spelling and hyphenation exceptions, columns, and master pages, among other things.

The trick is in the way the Open dialog works. Note the three Open As options at the bottom (see Figure 7.13). Original opens the original file, whether an InDesign document, template, or Interchange Format INX file. Copy generates on-the-fly an unsaved duplicate of the selected document; the original is left untouched, but InDesign creates a new document faithful to the original in every respect. Finally, Normal says to use whatever is default behavior for the specific document type—INDD and INX documents open originals, INDTs create copies. Normal is the default, which means that, when designers in your workgroup need to create new documents from your template, they won't be editing the template itself. To do that, you must deliberately choose to open the original. Note that when you're opening documents created in a previous version of InDesign or created in a compatible version of PageMaker (6.0–7.0) or QuarkXPress (3.3–4.1 and QuarkXPress Passport 4.1), a copy will be created regardless of the Open As choice.

A template-based workflow is the ideal for any periodical and is usually more efficient and leads to fewer content-destroying mistakes than opening the previous issue's files, resaving as the next issue's files, and then replacing content. I've seen few other workflows wherein at least one document setup is reused that doesn't also see a benefit from employing templates.

FIGURE 7.13
In the Open a File dialog, Open As determines whether the original will be opened or a new copy created.

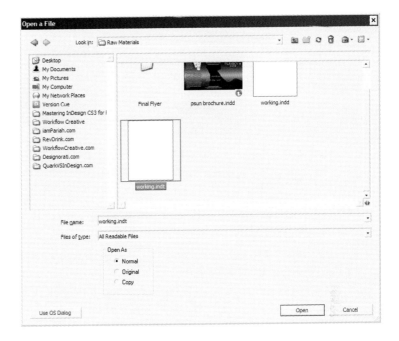

If you choose the File ➤ New ➤ Document from Template command, it opens an Adobe Bridge window focused on the Templates\InDesign folder created during InDesign or Creative Suite install. Dozens of professionally designed, royalty-free templates are included with InDesign CS3, and you can use them as is or, better, as learning aids. They're all InDesign template INDT files, so opening them by double-clicking in the Bridge view will have the same effect as opening a template you created using the default Normal option—a new, untitled document based on the template.

Layout Adjustment

This isn't strictly a master page thing, but layout adjustment is most often used in conjunction with master pages, so it makes the most sense to bring it up here.

After initially creating the document, you can change its type—facing or nonfacing—as well as the paper size and orientation with File ➤ Document Setup. Using Layout ➤ Margins and Columns, you can also alter the margins, number of columns, and column gutter width. Finally, on master pages, margin guides can be manually dragged to new positions (if unlocked). None of these changes will adapt your page objects to the new conditions by default. If you want your text frames to expand or contract to fit new margins, to automatically reduce or increase the number of columns they contain according to changes you've made in Margins and Columns, or if you want other objects to adjust to the new document layout without you having to do it all by hand, turn to Layout Adjustment on the Layout menu (see Figure 7.14).

FIGURE 7.14
The Layout Adjust-ment dialog

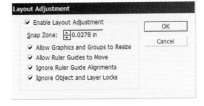

Layout Adjustment does a decent job of reformatting page (and master page) objects to conform to new document conditions such as new page sizes and orientations and margin and column guide relocation. Frames will be moved and resized as needed to adapt to the new layout if Enable Layout Adjustment is activated prior to making the layout change. Here is what the options mean:

Snap Zone   The maximum distance an object must be from one or more margin or column guides or the page edge to be a candidate for repositioning or resizing with Layout Adjustment. For instance, with a value of 0.25 inches, a master text frame directly on four margins will be adjusted but a graphic frame 0.5 inches from the nearest guide will not be adjusted.

Allow Graphics and Groups to Resize   Vector objects, frames, and groups of objects will be repositioned by Layout Adjustment regardless of whether they fall within the snap zone. This option determines whether they may also be scaled to better fit. For instance, if converting an 8.5×11-inch document from portrait to landscape, should a full-page background graphic frame follow suit to become 11×8.5 inches with its content scaled accordingly?

Allow Ruler Guides to Move   Manually created ruler guides—column center points, for example—can be moved to maintain their relative position to margin and column guides with this option checked.

Ignore Ruler Guide Alignments   Throughout working on a document, we often create numerous ruler guides that are not significantly related to the layout. Because layout adjustment considers all guides in its calculations, these nonessential guides can cause it confusion, leading to improperly adjusted layouts. Checking this option tells InDesign to ignore them, factoring in only page edges and column and margin guides when repositioning and scaling objects.

Ignore Object and Layer Locks   This option is an easier alternative to unlocking locked layers and combing through a document looking for any objects whose positions have been selectively locked. Enabling this will reposition and/or scale objects regardless of their individual or layer lock statuses.

Multiple Page Sizes

Since long before computers, there has always been a need to create documents that include multiple page sizes or orientations. With the rise of *VDP* and digital-to-press output making high-quality, one-off productions an affordable option, multiple page sizes and orientations in documents have become more common and more desirable. But the software has never caught up with the need—even in the cutting edge of page production, InDesign CS3. QuarkXPress, since version 6.0, has done multiple page sizes in one "project," but it's not truly the same thing. You see, QuarkXPress merely allows multiple, disconnected layouts to be saved in the same file—it's an MDF, a multiple document format, similar to the way Excel allows multiple spreadsheets to be saved in a single Excel document. QuarkXPress, even in the latest version as of this writing, still won't allow two or more differently sized pages in a single, continuous layout.

In close to a hundred InDesign training, consulting, and speaking engagements, I'm hard-pressed to recall a single one in which I wasn't asked if InDesign could do multiple page sizes in one document. There's a lot of need for that feature in our field. Gatefold covers and ads in magazines are still produced separately from surrounding pages and then inserted at bindery time. Maps, charts, and spreadsheets in proposals and technical books are still separate InDesign documents. Landscape content in a portrait-orientation book still forces designers to work sideways, either trying to read at 90 degrees or rotating their work for every change or onscreen copy proof—and that often requires grouping and ungrouping for many edits just to retain object relational positions. Frankly, it's ridiculous. That's why I did something about it.

First, let's look at the workaround we—design, prepress, press professionals—have come to accept as the "only" way of creating multiple page sizes or orientations in a single document.

BOOK PANEL

InDesign only allows a single page orientation and size per document. If most of the document is to be 8.5×11 inches portrait (tall), then it's *all* going to be 8.5×11 inches portrait. The workaround to this limitation has been "booking" multiple documents together to (somewhat) behave as one. This isn't just InDesign, by the way. Print pros have been using this same workaround for two decades in QuarkXPress, PageMaker, and other layout applications.

We'll look at the functionality of InDesign Book documents and the Book panel in Chapter 9, "Documents," but in essence, an InDesign Book document (INDB) is a paperclip that links multiple, otherwise completely self-contained InDesign documents together. Via the Book panel, page and section numbers, styles, indexes, and tables of contents can be synchronized among all the booked files. They can also be preflighted, packaged, exported to PDF, and printed simultaneously as if they were a single document. *That* is very cool and powerful, as are the synchronizing functions. The Book panel, though, was developed for the purpose of managing longer documents. It enables, for instance, this book to be written in chapters. As I'm writing this chapter, others are with my editors Sam and Karen, some are already with the compositor being poured into the layout template, and still other chapters are on their way back to me for final layout proof. When all the chapters are done, the fact that they're booked will keep page numbers, the TOC, and the index correct, ensuring that Chapter 2 begins numbering where Chapter 1 leaves off and so on.

Because the Book panel has all these features, it can be used to insert an oversized or rotated page into the middle of a long document. For instance, if page 26 is a fold-out tabloid diagram among 47 other 8.5×11-inch pages, the Book panel can insert the tabloid *as* page 26 and keep the rest of the page numbers in synch. The catch is that they must all be separate documents. Pages 1 through 25 must be one 8.5×11-inch InDesign document, page 26 a single 11×17-inch page document, and then pages 27 through 48 have to be a third document because they're 8.5×11 inches. If editorial says the tabloid diagram belongs two pages previous, you'll have to pull two pages out of the first document and insert them in the third to make it work. Of course, that's only the simplest of scenarios. Many longer documents have several charts, diagrams, fold-outs, or other oversized pages. Everywhere that the page size differs requires a new InDesign document. Beginning to see how this can get ugly? Add in the fact that each of those documents has its own localized paragraph, character, object, table, and cell styles as well as hyphenation exceptions, swatches, ink settings, master pages, and a whole lot more and every document exponentially increases the risk of mistakes making it to press. All of these can be synchronized via the Book panel, but that must be done deliberately and correctly. Someone forgets or doesn't synch correctly, and…. Well, I'm sure you can imagine—or maybe you don't have to imagine.

If you need to deal with two or three different booked documents as a result of page size or orientation differences only once in a while, use the Book panel method. If you need it more often, or just don't want to add another layer of complication to your workflow, there's another option.

 **Real World Scenario**

REDUCING 87 DOCUMENTS TO 6

Not long ago I was hired, in my capacity as workflow consultant, to redefine and optimize the proposal book design workflow of a major commercial land developer, Omni Industrial Environs. Omni annually produces three to six 500- to 700-page, hardcover book proposals for development projects averaging $200 million in gross revenue. Each of the four-color proposals is for a different project, so the primary page size varies per book, but they all include numerous oversized fold-out charts, diagrams, maps, surveys, blueprints, and spreadsheets. On average, 1 in every 10 pages was an oversized sheet.

When I arrived, Omni's designers were creating upwards of 100 separate InDesign documents per book just like the Book panel workaround method described in this chapter, but *without* using a Book file. The design department—which consisted of four dedicated proposal designers, one part-time freelancer, and a production manager—revisited each page of a given book an average of five times. Much of their time was spent manually numbering and renumbering pages across all those documents, documents that grew and shrank frequently as copy, financial data, and other information changed leading up to the proposal submission deadline. Adding a single page early in the book meant manually renumbering every other page across all 100-odd documents. Needless to say, this was a very inefficient workflow, and despite best efforts, page arrangement and numbering errors *did* slip through to press.

By creating a Book file to link all the different InDesign documents together, they all but eliminated page numbering mistakes. In each separate InDesign document, regardless of its dimensions, the pages are automatically renumbered in response to page re-ordering and the increase or decrease of page count in any of the other documents in the book file. Exploiting the other advantages of the Book panel—style usage consistency, soft-proofing via PDF, hard-proof printing, and readying the entire book for delivery to press—transformed hours-long manual tasks to nothing more than a couple of clicks of the mouse.

I wish I could tell you how many work hours were saved by introducing a Book file to the workflow, but that isn't possible. In addition to optimizing page handling, numerous other areas of the proposal production workflow were optimized and streamlined, including using anchored objects to force illustrations and figures to automatically follow their referencing text without manual repositioning, centralizing font management with Extensis Suitcase Server, and replacing Microsoft Word with InCopy on editorial and data analysis desktops, thus slashing the number of times a designer worked on the average page, following initial design, from five to less than one. Omni hadn't broken down work hours into individual tasks such as page handling or renumbering prior to the optimization, so there was nothing to use for a comparison with post-workflow optimization times.

At the time I helped Omni, the best I could do to alleviate the complications of dealing with multiple page sizes in one publication was to bring in the Book panel. In my mind, it wasn't enough. Although the production manager estimated that that step alone would save more than 100 work hours per publication, there was still more time that could be saved and, more importantly, a lot less menial work in file management if only InDesign could include multiple page sizes in the same document. For Omni, the problem was so large in fact that, if QuarkXPress had offered the feature (it doesn't), I would have recommended they convert back to that application despite other advantages using InDesign and InCopy brought to the workflow.

Omni became the final straw for me. For years I'd been lobbying in vain for InDesign—and, before it, QuarkXPress and PageMaker—to handle multiple page sizes in a single, continuous page document. Because no one else was going to solve the problem, I decided to do it myself—with the help of the talented programmers at DTP Tools.

A year after my initial visit, I returned to Omni Industrial Environs with my Page Control plug-in in hand. Putting it to use on their next proposal, the list of files on the horribly deep Book panel suddenly shrank from 87 to 6.

Page Control allows InDesign to mix multiple page sizes and/or orientations in a single document. Omni no longer had to create three separate InDesign documents just to accommodate a single oversized page (one document for the pages leading up to the odd-sized page, the odd-sized page itself in a document alone, and the third for standard-sized pages following it). All their fold-out charts, maps, spreadsheets, diagrams, blueprints, and so on were able to be created in-line in the same document containing the pages leading up to, and following, the fold-out. They still employed a Book file and the Book panel, but now they used it for its *intended* purpose—to coordinate the six, chapter-like documents created and edited one each by the six designers. Now each designer has one document to worry about—not 10, 20, or 30 as before.

PAGE CONTROL PLUG-IN

Until November 2006, the Book panel option was the only workaround to managing multiple page sizes or orientations in a single document created in InDesign. Then DTP Tools and I released the Page Control plug-in, which works in InDesign CS, CS2, and CS3. With it, you can resize any or all pages—singly or in spreads—change from landscape to portrait, change the vertical alignment of pages within a spread, resize master pages, set document pages to automatically resize according to their assigned masters, and change the size of the pasteboard for more working room—and all of this in one, single InDesign document that can be packaged, printed, exported to PDF, and so on without risky or inconvenient workarounds (see Figure 7.15). And, it prints. Prior to releasing Page Control, we held a public beta period in which we asked printers in the U.S., Australia, and Europe, among other places and groups of professionals, to test it out thoroughly. Whether printed natively from InDesign, printed from an InDesign-exported PDF, or printed first to PostScript, documents containing a full range of different page sizes sailed through RIPs without complaint. As of this writing, Page Control has been available and selling to design and prepress professionals all over the world for several months; I have yet to hear a complaint from anywhere within the for-print process.

FIGURE 7.15
A spread containing pages resized with the Page Control plug-in

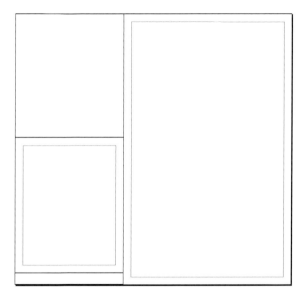

We even created a free Page Control Reader plug-in that enables anyone without the full Page Control plug-in to view, edit, save, and output InDesign documents containing multiple page sizes. (Hint, hint, you service bureaus and printers.)

If you create documents with different page sizes in a single document, or just want to enlarge your pasteboard, there's a 14-day try-out version of Page Control included on this book's download page in the Chapter 7 folder. The BIN file is for Mac installs and the MSI for Windows. Upon installation, the Page Control commands will appear on the Pages panel's flyout menu. The same installers will also set up Page Control Reader.

Managing Pages

Once you have a document created and have begun laying out the design, you'll need to insert, delete, duplicate, rearrange, and even import the occasional page. In addition to new page management features, InDesign CS3 has put some spit and polish on many of the familiar ones.

Pages Panel

The hub of page management activity is the Pages panel, which, in CS3, includes some much needed updates (see Figure 7.16).

FIGURE 7.16
InDesign CS3's
Pages panel (left)
and the Pages panel
from InDesign CS2
(right)

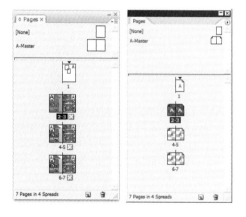

The first thing you'll notice is that each page icon in the panel is now a thumbnail of the actual content of the page—master pages, too. You'll spend a lot less time guessing on which page you placed that picture last week. Because icons are no longer generic, the master page indicators (the little *A*s in the figure), no longer fill the icon; instead they move to the outer top corner on facing pages and top center for nonfacing pages. The trade-off for the page thumbnails is that the master page indicators got smaller and less obvious, although they still stand out when a page is selected in the panel. Previously, if a page contained transparency, the entire icon would display the patented checkerboard background instead of a white background. Now it's a little rectangle beside the page number. You should recognize the symbol from the Photoshop Layers panel. Also gone are the down-turned corners denoting facing pages. Now, if the document pages are facing, they have the spine representation between them. Single and spread master pages show no difference in their icons other the single or double pages.

Customizing the Pages Panel

In its default view, the Pages panel shows masters at the top in small icons and documents in medium icons at the bottom. Both grow vertically, which, especially in the lower section, leaves a lot of wasted horizontal space. There's a lot of customization possible, though, as you can see from just a few possible configurations in Figure 7.17. You can change the size of pages and master icons, show them horizontally or vertically, and change which is on the top. Those sentimental for PageMaker can tear the panel away from the dock, align it across the bottom of the InDesign window, and set pages to show horizontally rather than vertically.

FIGURE 7.17

Pages panel options offer flexible arrangements.

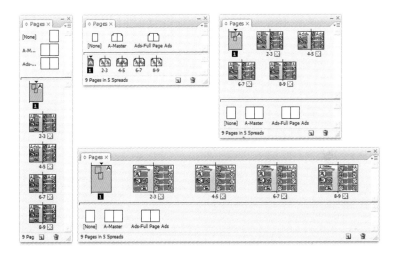

All this customization is available in the Panel Options dialog (see Figure 7.18), which is the last option on the Pages panel flyout menu. The last option, a drop-down menu titled Resize, defines which section, if either, is fixed height. When one is chosen as fixed, resizing the panel alters the other section. Setting both to Proportional will resize them equally. If you long for the good old days when master page identifiers were easy to read and pages were just plain white (and, when selected, blue) icons, or if rendering page thumbnails slows down your system, uncheck Show Thumbnails for pages and/or masters.

FIGURE 7.18

Pages Panel Options dialog

Inserting Pages

Here is a refresher on the familiar ways to add pages to a document:

◆ At the bottom of the Pages panel, the Create New Page button adds one page at a time to the end of the document. New pages adopt the master assigned to the last page—for instance, if page 5 of a five-page document is assigned to master page *A* (and includes the *A* indicator), new pages will also be assigned to master page *A*.

◆ Cmd+Shift+P/Ctrl+Shift+P has the same effect as the Create New Page button.

◆ Layout ➤ Pages ➤ Add Page also adds one new page at the end of the document, assigning the same master page as the last in the document.

◆ The Insert Pages command on both the Pages panel flyout menu and the Layout ➤ Pages menu offers insertion of multiple pages at once at a specific location in the document (e.g., before or after page *X*) and choice of the master page to which to assign inserted pages (see Figure 7.19).

FIGURE 7.19

Insert Pages dialog

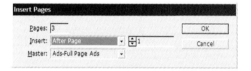

Although not new, this method demands more explanation than a quick bullet point. Dragging either the name or icon(s) of a master page down into the Pages panel has two possible effects. Dropping it on top of an existing page will apply the master page (or blank [None] master) to the document page. If a page belongs to master page *A*, dropping *B* on it will remove all the non-overridden *A* master page items and apply all the features of *B*. Dropping *B* onto a page already assigned to *B* will reapply the master page items of *B*; all overridden items will remain in place, of course, but the originals as they appear on the master will also appear.

The other behavior of dragging and dropping master pages is to insert new pages. *Where* it inserts them is a matter of hand-eye coordination. Dropping a master onto a blank area of the pages section, such as below the icons or in the empty space to either side, will insert new pages (based on that master) at the end of the document. Putting them anywhere else—like trying to insert a new page between pages 2 and 3—is where all those hours spent playing "Doom" pay off. It requires the same skills as rearranging pages, so read on, McDuff.

Rearranging Pages

Managing page order is also done through the Pages panel. PageMaker, if you recall, enabled you to rearrange pages in a dialog by moving around thumbnails; you could easily see the content of each page rather than guessing whether it was page 4 or 6 you had wanted to move after page 38. InDesign was frequently criticized for having no such visual management faculty. Ever since version 1.0, you've been able to rearrange pages through drag and drop on the Pages panel, but not until now with the live previews could you actually *see* what you were doing.

To move a page, simply click on and highlight its icon, and then drag it to the new location. To select an entire spread, either click on the page numbers below the icon, or click on one side and then Cmd+click/Ctrl+click on the other. Once selected, they'll drag as one. Select a range of sequential pages like files in the file system—click on the first, then Shift+click on the last. Use Cmd+click/Ctrl+click for nonsequential pages.

Where they land when you drop them is the tricky part:

◆ Like inserting master pages, dragging existing pages and dropping them at the bottom of the stack or out in the empty space will relocate the pages to the end of the document. The cursor will be a hand without adornment.

◆ Dragging near to the outside edge of an existing page will show a bold vertical line (see Figure 7.20) indicating that the page(s) will be inserted before (bar to the left) or after (bar to the right) that location. The cursor communicates this fact as well, as you can see.

FIGURE 7.20

Inserting pages to the left of page 2 displays a specific cursor and a thick insertion point bar.

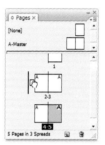

◆ By default, dropping pages between two pages in a spread shuffles everything down in spreads. For example, dragging page 6 and dropping it in the middle between pages 2 and 3 will make 6 the new 3 (a right-read page), push 3 down into the 4 position (a left-read page), and cascade similar order and side changes throughout the remaining pages. When inserting masters or moving pages between two in a spread—hovering the cursor over the spine between page icons—a subtle shift left or right changes the cursor and the insertion point. A pixel or two to the left of the spine inserts to left, inserting in place of page 2; to the right leaves page 2 alone to insert ahead of page 3 (see Figure 7.21). It's tricky, and made more so the smaller your page icons, thus my analogy to video game reflexes.

FIGURE 7.21

A few pixels determine whether pages will insert to the left of the spine or the right.

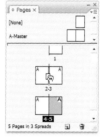

Alternative to dragging and dropping, you can use the Move Pages command on the panel flyout menu or Layout ➢ Pages menu.

In the Move Pages dialog (see Figure 7.22), specify a page number, page range, or nonsequential pages to move and then a destination—after or before the page number in the next field or to start or end of the document. The Move Pages (pages to be moved) field accepts an amazingly flexible range of inputs. You can enter a single page number, of course, or a page range separated by a hyphen (e.g., 4-9), nonsequential pages separated by commas (e.g., 3, 6, 1, 9, 366), and a mixture of both (e.g., 1-3, 87-109, 6-12, 5, 20-21). The order in which pages are entered in the Move Pages field will determine their order after the operation, and they'll be renumbered accordingly.

FIGURE 7.22

The Move Pages dialog

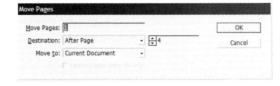

If you're proficient in first-person-shooter video games, you should do well with drag and drop management on the Pages panel. However, if PacMan is more your speed, use the Insert Pages and Move Pages commands.

Single-Page and Multipage Spreads

Once in a while, there's a need for spreads consisting of more than two pages. Usually this need arises from InDesign's inability to accommodate pages of different sizes in a single document. Creating three-, four-, or five-page spreads is another workaround, another way to conquer this limitation. I didn't mention it when discussing the Book panel workaround and the Page Control solution because it's only a viable workaround in a few cases—when the height of all page sizes are equal—but mostly because, as a workaround, it creates more problems than it's worth. Two 8.5×11-inch pages on the same side of the spine may *look* and behave *onscreen* as a single 11×17-inch page, but a RIP still sees them as separate 8.5×11-inch pages. It takes extra effort and planning on the RIP operator's part to ensure that the pages print as a single unit. Page Control, by contrast, really does create a single page, and the RIP recognizes it as such, thus there is less opportunity for mistakes and bad film.

When you do have a legitimate need for spreads of more *or less* than two pages—for instance, to force a new right-read or left-read page without its opposite—InDesign *can* accommodate you, although it's not obvious how.

Previously I stated, "By default, dropping pages between two pages in a spread shuffles everything down in spreads." That behavior is called *shuffling*. Inserting a page—new or from elsewhere in the document—forces all subsequent pages to shuffle down while maintaining two-page spreads. Drag and drop as long as you like, you'll never get a third page on a single spread. At least not as long as the Allow Document Pages to Shuffle command is active on the Pages panel flyout menu. Turn off that command and you can build multipage spreads like some of the ones you see in Figure 7.23. If you need to override just a single spread—a trifold cover or centerfold, for example—but want the rest of the pages to shuffle with page order changes normally, leave on Allow Document Pages to Shuffle. Instead, highlight a specific spread and turn off Allow Selected Spread to Shuffle, which is also on the Pages panel flyout menu. Now, just drag new pages from the master pages section above or existing pages from elsewhere in the list and then drop them directly to the side of the desired spread.

Note that this is also a gotcha: turning off shuffling often leads to spreads *unintentionally* greater than two pages. If that happens to you, *don't try to fix it by moving pages again!* Although moving pages back *should* repair any damage done, one of InDesign's quirks is that it doesn't, especially not when one or more of the pages contains objects that cross the spine. Often these get left behind or shoved out onto the pasteboard. Instead of manually moving pages back, immediately *undo* the move operation that resulted in the unwanted spread. Even if you've saved the document, InDesign will step backward through the operations with Cmd+Z/Ctrl+Z—as long as you haven't *closed* the document since performing the operation.

FIGURE 7.23

Spreads of more than two pages are possible once Allow Document Pages to Shuffle has been disabled.

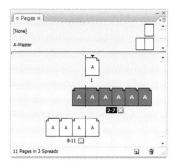

Moving Pages between Documents

No way!

Yes *way, Ted!*

InDesign CS3 now has the ability to move pages between InDesign documents with ease. Having multiple page sizes in a single layout has been characterized for decades as the Holy Grail of Desktop Publishing, therefore the ability to merge and move pages between documents must be a quest of almost equal glory. King Solomon's Mine? Let's go with that.

Astute observers would note that there's one field in the Move Pages dialog I didn't discuss yet: the Move To field (see Figure 7.24). Via Move Pages, you can tell InDesign to move them to any other opened document. Just choose the desired destination document from the Move To list, and then all the options above it will become germane to *that* document rather than the current. You can, say, move (copy really) pages 10–20 from *Document A* to the beginning, end, or a specific location within *Document B*. Checking the Delete Pages After Moving option *really* moves them from one place to another instead of just copying.

FIGURE 7.24

The Move Pages dialog

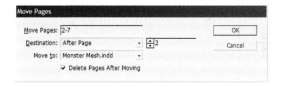

If you'd prefer to do it visually, to select pages based on their thumbnail previews instead of trying to recall which page numbers you need, you can drag and drop pages from one document's Pages panel into another document as easily as rearranging pages intra-document. Bring the source document to the foreground and arrange it so that you can see the destination document as well. Select and drag the needed pages on the Pages panel, and drop them over any visible portion of the destination document window. The Insert Pages dialog (see Figure 7.25) will instantly pop up asking where you'd like the dropped pages placed. It will also give you the option of deleting them from the source document.

FIGURE 7.25

The Insert Pages dialog

Duplicating and Deleting Pages

Sometimes, you don't want to create new pages or move them from other documents. Sometimes you just want to make a copy, and sometimes you want to destroy. Neither of these abilities has changed since InDesign CS2, so here's just a quick refresher in case something eluded you during learning that version.

- ◆ Drag the icons of one or more pages and spreads from the list in the Pages panel atop the Create New Page button to duplicate those pages and all their contents to the end of the document.

- ◆ With one or more pages or spreads selected, choose Duplicate Page, Duplicate Pages, Duplicate Spread, or Duplicate Spreads from the Pages panel flyout menu, Layout ➢ Pages menu, or context sensitive menu available by right-clicking on a selected page icon.

- ◆ With pages or spreads selected, click the Delete Selected Pages trashcan icon at the bottom of the panel. If the page contains objects, you'll be prompted to confirm your decision.

- ◆ Drag the icons of one or more pages and spreads from the list in the Pages panel and drop onto the trashcan icon at the bottom of the panel to delete them. If the page contains objects, you'll be prompted to confirm your decision.

- ◆ With one or more pages or spreads selected, choose Delete Page, Delete Pages, Delete Spread, or Delete Spreads from the Pages panel flyout menu or context sensitive menu available by right-clicking on a selected page icon. If the page contains objects, you'll be prompted to confirm your decision.

- ◆ From the Layout ➢ Pages ➢ Delete Pages command, you can access the Delete Pages dialog which, like the Move Pages dialog, enables entry of single, sequential, nonsequential, or mixed page numbers for page deletion.

Objects and Rearranged Pages

When moving, duplicating, or deleting pages, it's important that you know how InDesign determines to which page an object belongs. If, for example, you've created a background color wash across a spread, what happens to the graphic frame if the right-read page is moved to another place in the document? Will the frame move with that page and suddenly appear behind both it and its new mate, or will it remain behind with the original left-read page and adorn *its* new mate? If a page is deleted, what happens to the graphic frame?

The rules by which InDesign conducts itself in determining object-to-page relationships, and thus what happens to objects when pages are rearranged or deleted, are pretty simple. If you're coming from proficiency in QuarkXPress especially, it's important to recognize that InDesign and XPress differ in their most fundamental definition of object placement, which creates different, almost opposing rules for handling the object-to-page relationship with regard to page movement. In QuarkXPress, *everything* is relative to a fixed origin point of the top-left corner; objects *always* belong to the page on which their top-left corners fall. Thus, even if a 8.5-inch-wide box's origin is only 0.001pt to the left of the spine, deleting the left-read page also deletes the box.

InDesign determines ownership by the center point instead of the top-left corner. If the center of a frame is on the left-read page, the object belongs to the left page; if the center is 0.001pt to the right of the spine, it belongs to the right-read page. If the object is perfectly centered on the spine, left wins. In that case, moving or deleting the right-read page keeps the frame in place, allowing it to cover the new right-read if shuffling is enabled or spill out onto the pasteboard if shuffling is turned off.

In the event of a mixed-master spread, wherein one page is assigned to one master page and the other page to a different master, objects from *both* master pages will apply. If any of those objects span the spine, they will apply to *both* left- and right-read pages in the spread.

Master Pages

And now, without further ado, I humbly present to you Master Pages.

Master pages are like templates within the document. Any time you need the same element on multiple pages, put it on a master page. Things like headers, footers, background art, page borders, and more—anything that repeats on more than one page—belong on a master page. So do many text frames when more than a couple of pages use the same size, number of columns, and text frame options. It isn't a new concept—all the major layout applications have had master pages since the late '80s. Despite the ubiquity of the feature, surprisingly few creative pros know how to use them or just how significant master pages can be in reducing repetitive work. Repetition kills productivity, creativity, and imagination. No other single feature saves as much time and frustration as master pages.

Assigning a master to a document makes all the objects on that master page appear on the document page, but those objects don't technically exist on the document pages themselves. That's both a huge pro and a small con to using masters. The pro is that the same object can appear on literally thousands of pages, but only a single object instance must be created or altered in order to affect a change across all pages. If your client says that the folio you placed on the top outside corner of every page must be moved to the bottom center of the pages, you only have to make the change once per document. The con—a minor inconvenience really—appears when you need to change or do away with just a single object instance here and there on document pages. In that case, you must override the master page object. We'll cover all of that—without lingering too long on the basics—in this section.

Master Page Setup

At the top of the Pages panel is the master page section. With any new document, you'll have [None], which is a blank master, and the default A-Master, which is also initially blank. A-Master is one you can edit and on which you're supposed to put repetitive elements if your document contains them—just double-click A-Master to edit its page (nonfacing document pages) or spread (facing pages).

In InDesign, each master name has what Adobe calls a prefix, an identifier (the *A*), and a name ("Master"). Most people don't realize that neither is fixed.

Document pages display the identifier of the master page to which they're assigned as a symbol on the page icon. *A, B, C,* and so on are fine in many cases, but they're effectively meaningless. When you have multiple master pages handling different types of content, it can make your work less confusing to use something more meaningful than single-letter identifiers.

Select A-Master on the Pages panel and then Master Options from the panel's flyout menu. In the Master Options dialog (see Figure 7.26), the Prefix field can hold up to four alphanumeric characters. Instead of *A, B, C,* why not have prefixes that *really* communicate something about each page? How about *Ad* for pages based on the full-page ad master, which doesn't include headers, footers, or folio? *Dept* would be a great designator for magazine department pages. In catalogs, what about *12UP* for those pages featuring 12 products and *6UP* for pages where half as many products get twice as much room? Working with multilingual documents? Use *ENG, ESP, FRA, ITAL, DEU, RUS, ELV, PORT,* or other prefixes to instantly label pages in the Pages panel according to the languages of their copy and master items. Numerous types of documents use several variations on column grids for variety, so why not prefix their masters with *2COL, 3COL,* or *6COL*?

FIGURE 7.26
Master Options
enables turning
arbitrary default
identifiers and
names into some-
thing that makes
sense for your
document.

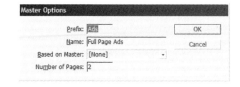

The only requirement is that the combination of prefix and name be unique. Although InDesign will let you assign the same prefix to multiple master pages, don't. How will you know which document page belongs to which of the three *B*-prefixed masters?

When you can't fully communicate the function of a master in only four characters, come up with a meaningful acronym, abbreviation, or shorthand for the prefix, but use the Name field to better explain it—like a kicker lends meaning to a headline. In that field, you have a potential 100 characters with which to name the master. An obtuse prefix like *BPx2*, which may be perfectly logical to you, may just drive the already distressed new guy to tears. So, explain the prefix with a meaningful name like *Back Page Spread*. Depending on the width of your Pages panel and the display options for the masters section, only part of the name may show; mouse over it to read the whole thing in a tooltip.

Master pages can be anywhere from 1 to 10 pages wide. If you happen to need that trifold (or decafold) cover or centerfold, you can build a master page to manage its common elements.

Overriding Master Page Items

Here is one of the most often cited frustrations for recent QuarkXPress-to-InDesign converts. You see, in QuarkXPress, items placed on master pages are added to their document pages as normal objects, just as if they were created on the document page itself rather than the master to which it's assigned. You can select objects added by masters, delete them, transform them, and do anything else you like to them with impunity and with no barrier whatsoever. As you might expect, the QuarkXPress behavior leads to frequent accidents. An errant click here or there can make one page's master page objects different from another's, defeating the purpose.

InDesign doesn't automatically make master page objects selectable and changeable on document pages (hence the aforementioned frustration arising out of confusion). If you want to override a master page object, turning it into an object on the document page itself, you must hold Cmd+Shift/Ctrl+Shift while clicking on the object. *Then* you can do whatever you need—type into it, place an image inside it, move or transform it, and so on.

Note that overriding a master page item raises its placement in the stacking order *above* non-overridden objects. For instance, if you stacked a red frame above a blue frame on the same layer on a master page, overriding the blue frame on a document page would bring it forward, in front of the red. If necessary, counter this behavior by using layers on the master page, placing the red frame on a higher layer than the blue. Overriding the blue in that case retains the correct stacking order.

Another way in which InDesign differs from QuarkXPress is that InDesign's master pages *can* use layers. XPress's can't. There, only document pages are allowed layers—at least, as of the time of this writing when QuarkXPress 7 is the most recent version.

If you want to override all the master page items on a particular document *spread*—note that I didn't say *page*—the fastest way to do it is with the Override All Master Page Items command on the Pages panel flyout menu and the context sensitive menu that appears when you right-click on a page icon.

Master page items overridden on the document page are not *completely* disconnected from their masters. Only the attributes you've specifically changed are overridden, while all other attributes remain tethered to their master page originals. For example, let's say you overrode and then moved the blue frame. If you later go back to that master page and fill the original frame with yellow instead, all instances of that object—including the overridden one—will change to yellow. The inverse is also true: If you override the frame and change its color on the document page while leaving its position on the page unchanged, moving the master page object and changing *its* color will move the overridden version as well, but will not alter its color because that was the overridden attribute. Stroke, effects, scaling—everything that you don't specifically override remains linked to the master page instance.

If you want to break *all* the links between the overridden object instance and its original, making it totally independent from later master page changes, choose Detach Selection from Master in the Pages panel flyout menu. Use Detach All Objects from Master on the same menu to break the link between all overridden master page objects on the spread; non-overridden objects will be unaffected by either command.

Restoring Master Page Items

So, you've gone just Cmd+Shift+clicking/Ctrl+Shift+clicking all over the place, overriding master page item after item, with absolutely no regard to your or your coworkers' safety and well-being. Now, after sobering up, you realize you want back the emotional security of objects linked to their master page instances and safely locked from accidental alterations. It happens. We all get drunk with Cmd+Shift+click/Ctrl+Shift+click power initially. Fortunately, it's an easy fix.

◆ If you want to *keep* all overrides *and* restore master page items too, drag the master page from the top of the Pages panel and drop it again on the document page(s). You can also use the Apply Master to Pages command. Use caution though as this will also break the link between overridden items and their master page instances, rendering them completely and solely document page objects.

◆ To return only certain objects to the full control of the master page, removing any overrides and returning the object to a locked status and the master stacking order, select the object(s) and choose Remove Selected Local Overrides from the Pages panel flyout menu.

◆ If you want to return the *entire spread* back to its master page state, tossing out any changes you've made to overridden objects, use the Remove All Local Overrides command from the Pages panel flyout menu.

Text Frames on Master Pages

In the New Document dialog, you're given the option of Master Text Frame. Checking that option will automatically create a text frame on the *A-Master* master page; the frame will fill the page both horizontally and vertically within the margins. If you increased the number of columns in New Document from one, the frame will have that number of columns and use the gutter width options chosen. Everything else will be left according to the *Default Text Frame* object style.

To use that text frame on a document page, Cmd+Shift+click/Ctrl+Shift+click to override it, and then double-click again to enter typing mode; start typing.

Master page text frames can be threaded across the spread—the frame on the left page can be linked to the one on the right (or vice versa for Japanese, Hebrew, or other right-to-left printed languages), and text will flow smoothly between them once overridden. When placing text documents, however, you'll need to manually link frames on different spreads. The easiest way to do that is to start by overriding the first instance and then place your long text document into it. Click the red, overset outport on that frame and move on to the next page or spread (create pages if necessary). This time, don't hold any modifier keys while clicking; just click within the area of the frame. InDesign is smart enough to pick up on what you want to do, and it will simultaneously override the text frame *and* flow your loaded text into it. Keep moving through the document, one page at a time, until your story is completely visible.

Page Numbers

To insert page numbers on a master page (or on a document page for that matter), create a text frame or insert the cursor in an existing text frame. Then, choose Type ➤ Insert Special Characters ➤ Marker ➤ Current Page Number. On a master page, you won't actually see a number there, of course. Instead you'll see the master page's own prefix identifier—*A*, *B*, *Base*, whatever—but jump to a document page assigned to that master and you'll recognize that it's really a page number. You can't type page number markers directly because they're *markers*, special placeholders created with powers and abilities far beyond those of mortal men.

While you're in the Marker menu, take note of the other markers you can insert. Next and previous page numbers are for jumplines, which we'll cover in Chapter 9, "Documents." Section markers print on a document page the prefix of the section or chapter under which the page falls. Section prefixes are defined via the Layout ➤ Numbering & Section Options command, which we'll also discuss in Chapter 9.

Nested Master Pages

Consider this: You're laying out a 320-page visually rich proposal that will be printed in four-color and perfect bound in hardcover. There are several chapter-like sections, with chapter-like titles, stylized initial pages, and special, uniquely formatted "summation" pages at the end. The last section of the book is the proposed contract. Naturally, in a book that large, there's also a table of contents and some front matter pages. Let's examine how such a book's outline and layout plan might look (see Figure 7.27).

According to that outline, you'll need to design several types of pages. Most will be used for more than a single page, so you'll naturally turn to master pages. Now, you *could* design every master to be self-contained, manually creating the folios and other elements on every different master. If changes are needed, doing it in only 4 or 5 places *is* much better than doing it in 320, but having to make changes in only *1* place is better than 4 or 5. For that, we'll turn to nested master pages.

The cover, bacover, and "Contract" pages have no common elements, so we don't need masters for them; they'll get the tagged with [None].

Now, look at the rest. What common element appears on all other pages? The folio, page numbers in different formats. So, the very first step is to set up the first master page as a two-page spread, each page containing just a single text frame, the one to hold the page number. Let's set the prefix of that master to # and its name to *Page No Only*. That's done. Document section numbering options will take care of changing between Roman and Arabic numbers where appropriate (see Chapter 9).

FIGURE 7.27
A book outline and
layout plan

1. Cover
2. Guts
   A. Front Matter
      i. Contact Info
         No head/foot
      ii. Foreword
         Folio (Roman Upper), section title in right head
      iii. Statement of Readiness
         Folio (Roman Upper), section title in right head
   B. TOC
      Folio (Roman Upper), section title in right head
   C. Chapter 1
      i. Chapter Intro Page
         Folio, begins on right-read, no head; image & gradient BG
      ii. Content Pages
         Folio, chapter title in right head, firm name in left head, preparer/sales rep name & phone in left foot
      iii. Summation
         Folio, no chapter title, firm name in left head, preparer/sales rep name & phone in left foot
   D. Chapter 2
      i. Chapter Intro Page
      ii. Content Pages
      iii. Recap
   E. Chapter 3
      i. Chapter Intro Page
      ii. Content Pages
      iii. Recap
   F. Contract
      Folio (Page X of Y) and contract title in right head
3. Bacover

What's the next most common element? Well, the headers and footers are, but some pages require only certain ones and not others. The best way to handle those are to create several master pages that can be applied as needed to the different types of content pages—front matter sections, the TOC, chapter content pages, and chapter "summation" pages. However, instead of duplicating the masters and still ending up with several instances of each header and footer to update in the event of a change, which we could easily do with the Duplicate Master Spread command on the Pages panel menu, we'll nest one more level and save ourselves some time down the line. Let's create a new master page with the New Master Page command on the Pages panel flyout menu. For its options, set a prefix of *Base*, a name of *All Heads/Foots*, number of pages 2, and—and this the crucial part—set the Based on Master drop-down to #-Page No Only. That bases master *Base* on master #, incorporating all the latter's elements into the former without duplicating, and if the page number text frames are moved or otherwise changed in their original location on #, that change will automatically roll through *Base* and all other document and master pages assigned to *Base*. When you click OK, you'll see the magic page number codes appear exactly as you drew them on the first master. Now set up your headers and footers. Because each chapter or section will have its own unique head on the right-read page, draw and style the frame, but leave it empty.

At this point, we should have two master pages. Note that the icon beside *Base* shows the # identifier signifying that it's assigned to, and using the elements from, the *#-Page No Only* master.

Now, let's create masters to handle the unique variants of *Base*, those that omit either the footer or one head or another. Create a new master with *FM* as the prefix, *Front Matter* as the name, based on *Base-All Heads/Foots*, and two pages. You should see an exact duplicate of *Base*, including the elements incorporated from #, but the *FM* icon now shows *Base*—we're nested two levels deep now. Front matter pages (except for "Contact Info," which has no heads or foots) should display only the folio and right head, which leaves the left-page head and footer as extraneous. One at a time, hold Cmd+Shift/Ctrl+Shift as you click on either the header or footer text frame with the Selection tool to override the item. Now delete and repeat the process with the other frame. Once those frames are gone, the *FM* master is finished.

Build a new master also based on *Base-All Heads/Foots* for the chapter introduction page master, and then remove the unneeded elements by overriding and deleting them, and add the missing objects like the image and gradient background.

Make another master also based on *Base-All Heads/Foots* for Chapter 1. This one *will* have all headers and footers, so we don't want to delete anything. We do, however, want to override the right-read page's header and fill in the Chapter 1 title. When finished, choose Duplicate Master Spread from the Pages panel's flyout menu, change the prefix and name to reflect Chapter 2, and then edit the chapter title text frame on the top of the right-read page to be the Chapter 2 title. Repeat the duplication steps for the remaining chapter. If we didn't care to insert each chapter's title, if we only wanted the chapter number in the header, we could do that with just a single master page for all chapters and by inserting a section marker at the appropriate place in the header on the master page.

Because chapter "summation" pages don't have chapter titles, you can employ just a single additional master page based on *Base-All Heads/Foots* with overridden and removed elements for all instances of such pages. "Contract" pages should get their own, top-level (not based on another master) master page because they don't share any of the common elements of *Base* or even #. In the end, you should have eight master pages. Although they won't indent on the Pages panel, if they did, their nesting would make them look like this:

> *#-Page No Only*
>
>> *Base-All Heads/Foots*
>>
>> *FM-Front Matter*
>>
>> *CH1-Chapter 1*
>>
>> *CH2-Chapter 2*
>>
>> *CH3-Chapter 3*
>>
>> *SUM-Summation*
>
> *CON-Contract*

As you lay out the various pages, assign them their particular master pages. With the exception of pages based on the *CON-Contract* master, which is entirely self-sufficient, only a single instance of page numbers must be changed in order to affect that change throughout every page in the document. Common headers and footers are the same—one object change affects all dependent masters and document pages. Believe me, it's a lot more complicated to *read* how to it do than to *actually* do it hands-on (thus the step-by-step instruction I hope you'll follow). Try out nested master pages a few times within your documents; distill your multipage documents down to the most common elements, and break those out into nested master pages. An outline and layout plan like the one above will help you visualize the division of master pages and their objects the first few times thinking through it. You'll soon recognize how much faster and more efficient you can make tomorrow's work with just a little planning and effort today.

Creating Masters from Document Pages

This one happens to me often: Working content-first, you've started up a new document, placed in a good portion of your content, and begun the layout. Either you wanted to experiment a little and work out the design before moving to master pages or you didn't initially think you'd have common page elements and need a master page only to later realize that you need it. The result is that you've laid out a perfect master page with all the required elements, but you did it on a document page. What now?

You *could* cut all the objects and then use Edit ➤ Paste In Place to get them onto a master—and that works too. The drawbacks to that method are that you have to remember to paste in place (Cmd+Shift+OPT+V/Ctrl+Shift+Alt+V) instead of the much more habitual normal Paste (Cmd+V/Ctrl+V), and it only works well when the master page is already blank. Otherwise, you've got to first select all, delete, and then paste in place. Easier is to just select Save as Master from the Pages panel flyout menu. Instantly it creates a new master page using the default prefix and filename. Even cooler, if the document page you choose as your source is assigned to a master already, the new master will also be assigned to the same master, creating instant nesting.

Master Page Power

Oh, yes, there's yet more power at your fingertips. The following commands are all located on the Pages panel flyout menu.

APPLY MASTER TO PAGES

When you need to apply a master page to more than one or two pages at a time, don't use the drag and drop method. Instead, use Apply Master to Pages. Just select the master to apply, and then enter one or more page numbers individually, sequentially ranged (e.g., *1-10*), comma-separated non-sequentially (e.g., *5,3,1*), or a mixture of both (e.g., *4,1-2,7-8,5*).

LOAD MASTER PAGES

An incredibly powerful new feature almost on a par with the ability to move pages between InDesign documents, Load Master Pages allows you load the masters from another InDesign document into the current one. In the event of a naming conflict—if they both contain *A-Master*, for example—InDesign prompt you as to whether the inbound masters should replace the current document's masters of the same names or if the inbound ones should be automatically renamed, thus retaining current and new. Renamed masters will follow the default *A, B, C* prefixing scheme.

HIDE MASTER ITEMS

Want to work on document pages without seeing the master page items? This command will do that. It's a gotcha, though, too. Many a desk (and forehead) has been dented while trying to answer the question, *Why, why, why can't I see my master page items?* Write yourself a note if you turn it on.

ALLOW MASTER ITEM OVERRIDES ON SELECTION

On by default, this option appears while you're working in the master pages. It's what enables objects on the master to be overridden and modified on document pages. To ensure that even a Cmd+Shift+click/Ctrl+Shift+click can't accidentally override a master page item, select one or more objects on the master page spread and disable this command.

This, again, is another gotcha. If you disable this feature, write yourself a note *in the document* and set the note to not print.

The Bottom Line

Create Pages with Bleed, Slug, and Live Areas Properly setting up a for-press document involves more than choosing paper stock and ink colors. To ease the burden of setting up pages, InDesign includes ways to automate creation of similar documents after the first.

Master It Examine this book's cover. Don't redesign it, but set up a new, blank InDesign document as if you were designing the cover for this or another Mastering series book. Include the appropriate features—bleed, slug, and live areas—and create reusable cover presets and a template.

Manage Pages in and between InDesign Documents Any multipage document requires familiarity with the Pages panel and related features. Working *well* with multipage documents requires practiced proficiency.

Master It Create two new InDesign documents of one page each. Now, using the skills learned in "Managing Pages," insert four additional pages in each document for a total of five pages each. In very large type (at least 200 pts), label each page with a text frame containing the page number. In the first document, preface page numbers with the Roman numeral I and the second with II such that pages are numbered I1, I2, I3, I4, I5 and II1, II2, II3, II4, II5. Save both documents. Copy all five pages from the II document into the I, and then arrange pages in order such that page II1 follow I1, II2 follows I2, and so on.

Master Master Pages Master pages are the key to efficient initial layout and especially document revisions. Mastering their use is essential for design that uses common elements across multiple document pages.

Master It Refer back to the hands-on instruction in the section on nested master pages. Follow the instruction in that section to build all the master pages required for the proposal project. Check your results against mine. Once you have the master pages built correctly, use the other skills learned in this chapter to add document pages (a few for each proposal section or chapter) and to assign to them the appropriate master pages.

Chapter 8

Stories

Now that you've mastered setting and styling type on a page, it's time to think bigger, about writing, editing, and flowing text across multiple pages. It's time to think about stories.

In this chapter, you will learn to:

◆ Thread and unthread text frames and flow text

◆ Create bulleted and numbered lists

◆ Write and word process in InDesign

◆ Fix, find, and change text and more

Threading and Unthreading Text Frames

Although whether to design single-page layouts in Illustrator or InDesign is no longer as cut-and-dried a decision as it was just a few years ago, the vast majority of InDesign documents still fit the profile of multiple pages with one or more text *threads*, articles, or stories running throughout those pages. Any time text flows continuously from one frame to another, the story, and thus its containing frames, is said to be threaded (linked, for you QuarkXPress converts).

If CS3 is your entry into the world of InDesign but you're familiar with page layout in general, there are several distinct differences between InDesign and other layout applications when it comes to threading text. In that regard, InDesign works more like PageMaker than QuarkXPress, but it has, in some respects, improved over the methods employed by both of those other layout applications. In other respects, it's less friendly and more work to flow a multipage story in InDesign.

QuarkXPress vs. InDesign

If a story won't fit completely in a single text box in QuarkXPress, you must take several steps to flow the story to a second box. First, you have to switch to the Rectangular or another Text Box tool and draw a new empty box to hold the text. Then, after grabbing the Linking tool, you must click in the first text box (the one holding the text) and then click in the second, empty box to flow copy from the former to the latter. It's not especially difficult, but InDesign cuts out several steps—there is no need for a Linking tool, for instance, and threading can be done on-the-fly even if you've loaded the cursor to continue the story but forgotten to create another text frame to receive it.

Also, in QuarkXPress there is no way to determine if a selected frame is threaded or stand-alone until you choose the singular-purpose Linking or Unlinking tool, whereupon arrows between linked boxes appear. To determine if a given box is the first or last in the linked series, you must activate the appropriate tool and look for the absence of an arrow leading in or out of the box, respectively. InDesign lets you see just by selecting a frame with the Selection, Direct Selection, Rotate, Scale, Shear, or Free Transform tool whether it's threaded.

QuarkXPress is still more elegant than InDesign in many other aspects of threading text between frames, however. For instance, threading text into master page text boxes actually works in the former. In QuarkXPress, master page objects are automatically selectable on document pages, which is generally a big minus in my book (pun intended). It does have the advantage, however, of autoflowing and autolinking an entire story at once. Create a single-page document in QuarkXPress with a single-column master text box, insert the Content tool cursor in the box on the first page, and import a long text document. The entire document will import, with XPress adding pages as needed—and automatically linking the text boxes on all those pages—until the entire story has been placed. In InDesign, you must hold a modifier key (Shift) when importing to add pages automatically. Otherwise, InDesign will fill only the first text frame and stop, leaving the rest of the copy overset. The problem is, Shift+clicking in InDesign does two things simultaneously—it *does* place and autoflow the story, but it also ignores the master page text frame, even if it's already been overridden and made ready by Cmd+Shift+clicking/Ctrl+Shift+clicking on it.

Columns complicate things even further in InDesign but not QuarkXPress. Let's say you've created two-column layouts in both applications and activated the master text box/frame option in both. Their respective master and document pages will then both carry a single text frame divided into two columns, and both applications will also create guides on the page corresponding to column and gutter positions. Importing text into QuarkXPress as described uses the master text box, flowing your story through the single, two-column text boxes for as many pages as needed. Not so with InDesign. Even if you've overridden the master text frame, making it active and usable on the document page, if you try to pour text into it while holding Shift (to make InDesign automatically add subsequent pages to hold the story), InDesign will *not* use the master text frame. Instead, in your two-column layout, you'll get two *separate*, one-column-wide text frames per page! *And*, they'll be entirely independent of the master text frame, eliminating your ability to manage the frames' position, dimensions, and other attributes via the master page.

I'll explain subsequently how to get multicolumn threaded frames across pages in InDesign.

The ways in which QuarkXPress and InDesign differ in their respective handling of linked or threaded stories are among the most common stumbling blocks for those proficient in one learning the other. With the way the market is today, most print design and production professionals must maintain proficiency in both to be competitive, so foreknowledge about the differences in such a fundamental feature of page layout is important to those who may be called upon to use both or switch from one to the other.

Threading Frames

There are several methods to thread frames in InDesign.

THREADING PRE-CREATED FRAMES

If you work frame-first, laying out empty frames in a grid before placing content, you'll need to thread existing frames. *That* is delightfully simple.

In Figure 8.1, I've taken a frame-first layout and begun to import my content, beginning with the first copy box (text frames are colored for easier identification). Note the red plus sign in the lower-right corner of the text frame indicating that text is overset; there's more to this story than can fit in the first frame. Where that overset alert appears is the *out port* of the text frame. In the upper left, empty in this case because this is the beginning of the story, is the *in port*.

To thread the first frame to the second, flowing the story into the second column, grab the Selection tool and click once in the out port of the first frame. Doing so will give you a loaded cursor (see Figure 8.2) indicating that you have content to place, which, in this case, is the continuation of the story. Now, just click anywhere inside the destination text frame—it isn't necessary to try to find its in port; text will flow between them.

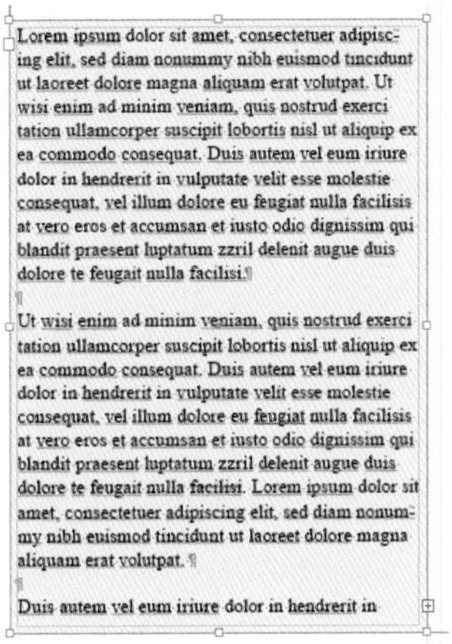

FIGURE 8.1
Beginning to insert
content in a frame-
first layout; overset
text must be
threaded into a
second box.

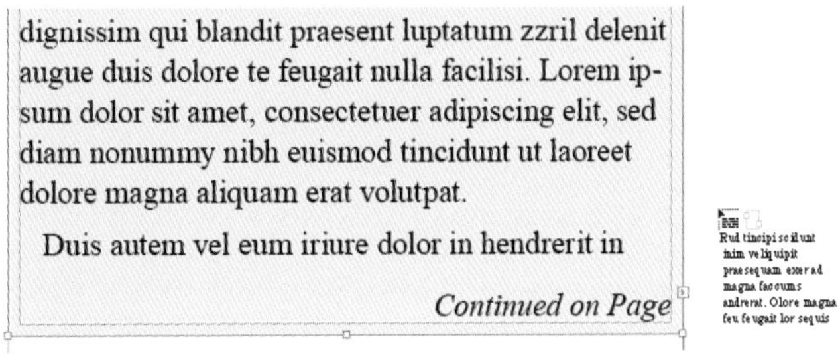

Lorem ipsum dolor sit amet, consectetuer adipiscing elit, sed diam nonummy nibh euismod tincidunt
ut laoreet dolore magna aliquam erat volutpat. Ut
wisi enim ad minim veniam, quis nostrud exerci
tation ullamcorper suscipit lobortis nisl ut aliquip ex
ea commodo consequat. Duis autem vel eum iriure
dolor in hendrerit in vulputate velit esse molestie
consequat, vel illum dolore eu feugiat nulla facilisis
at vero eros et accumsan et iusto odio dignissim qui
blandit praesent luptatum zzril delenit augue duis
dolore te feugait nulla facilisi.¶

Ut wisi enim ad minim veniam, quis nostrud exerci
tation ullamcorper suscipit lobortis nisl ut aliquip ex
ea commodo consequat. Duis autem vel eum iriure
dolor in hendrerit in vulputate velit esse molestie
consequat, vel illum dolore eu feugiat nulla facilisis
at vero eros et accumsan et iusto odio dignissim qui
blandit praesent luptatum zzril delenit augue duis
dolore te feugait nulla facilisi. Lorem ipsum dolor sit
amet, consectetuer adipiscing elit, sed diam nonummy nibh euismod tincidunt ut laoreet dolore magna
aliquam erat volutpat. ¶

Duis autem vel eum iriure dolor in hendrerit in

FIGURE 8.2
After clicking the
overset indicator in
the out port, you'll
get a loaded cursor.

dignissim qui blandit praesent luptatum zzril delenit
augue duis dolore te feugait nulla facilisi. Lorem ipsum dolor sit amet, consectetuer adipiscing elit, sed
diam nonummy nibh euismod tincidunt ut laoreet
dolore magna aliquam erat volutpat.

Duis autem vel eum iriure dolor in hendrerit in

Continued on Page

After threading the two frames, note the changed states of their in and out ports (see Figure 8.3). Frame one's in port is still empty because it begins the series, but now its out port, instead of showing the red plus overset text symbol, displays a blue, outward-pointing arrow indicating that the text threads out to another frame. Similarly, the in port of frame two indicates that it is receiving text from a previous frame in the series. Thus, at a glance, you can discern whether a frame is threaded and, if so, whether it is the first, last, or another frame in the series.

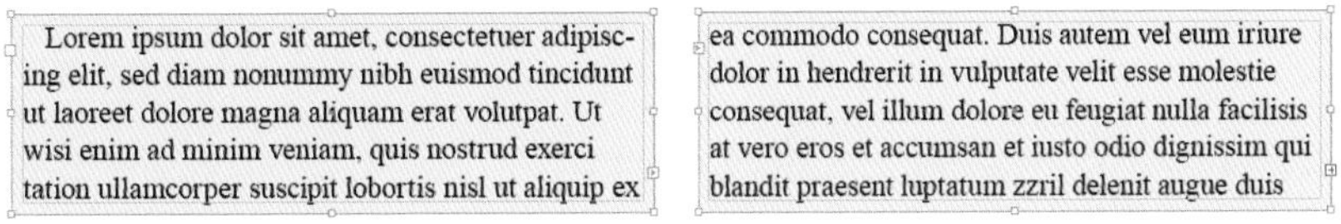

FIGURE 8.3
In and out ports of
threaded frames dis-
play blue arrows
indicating direction
of story flow.

Lorem ipsum dolor sit amet, consectetuer adipiscing elit, sed diam nonummy nibh euismod tincidunt
ut laoreet dolore magna aliquam erat volutpat. Ut
wisi enim ad minim veniam, quis nostrud exerci
tation ullamcorper suscipit lobortis nisl ut aliquip ex

ea commodo consequat. Duis autem vel eum iriure
dolor in hendrerit in vulputate velit esse molestie
consequat, vel illum dolore eu feugiat nulla facilisis
at vero eros et accumsan et iusto odio dignissim qui
blandit praesent luptatum zzril delenit augue duis

If your story must occupy more than two frames, there's a faster way to link them than successively loading up from out ports. During or after clicking on the first frame's out port but prior to clicking into the second frame to begin the thread, press and hold Option/Alt. Indicated by a semi-autoflow cursor above the loaded preview (see Figure 8.4), you'll now be able to thread into the second and successive frames simply by clicking into each of them once. For instance, if I was going to thread the same story through the two cream-colored frames and then into the small frame in the bottom right of the page, I'd click on frame one's out port to load the cursor and then, while clicking on frame two, hold Option/Alt, which flows my copy into frame two but also leaves me with a loaded cursor so I can immediately click on frame three and thread into that as well. If I had to thread across multiple pages of pre-created frames, I'd use the same method.

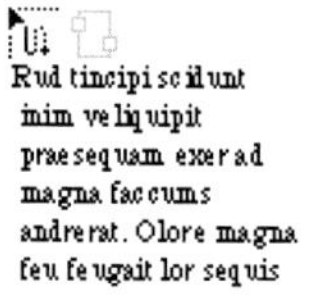

FIGURE 8.4
Multiple frame linking is quickly accomplished in semi-autoflow mode as indicated by this cursor.

Rud tincipi scilunt
inim ve liquipit
praesequam exerad
magna faccums
andrerat. Olore magna
feu feugait lor sequis

THREADING WITHOUT PRE-CREATED FRAMES

When you're working content-first or find yourself with a longer-than-planned story to place, you'll want to know how to create and thread frames all in one action. It works the same way as placing a document without having made frames to hold it in advance. Click once on the out port of a story frame, and then, using the loaded cursor the same way you would when initially placing text, draw a rectangular area to become the next frame in the chain. InDesign will simultaneously create the frame, flow the next part of the story into it, and thread the frame with the first. Hold Option/Alt while drawing subsequent frames to do all that plus leave the cursor loaded and ready to create subsequent frames.

In addition to drawing frames, you can simply click and release within the page to have InDesign automatically make a text frame that fits horizontally within the margin and/or column guides. With a single-column page—one containing no column guides—clicking with a loaded cursor will create a text frame as wide as the page margins. Among column guides on multicolumn pages, however, it will create one, single-column text frame only as wide as the column. If you want multiple columns in single text frames, you'll need to manually resize and configure text frames after creating and threading. The height of the resulting click-to-create text frames is the point of click down to the bottom margin. Thus, if you click around the vertical midpoint of a page, the resulting text frame will cover only the bottom half. Click at the top margin guide to create a frame of full page or column depth.

THREADING UPON IMPORT

The methods discussed thus far work when initially importing text, either with or without frames pre-created. After selecting the text document in the Place dialog and clicking OK, you'll have a loaded cursor. At that point, if you have frames pre-created, holding Option/Alt while clicking inside the first frame will fill the frame with text and return you to a loaded cursor ready for placement into—and threading with—subsequent frames. The same holds true if you haven't any pre-created frames: Hold Option/Alt while drawing your first frame and you'll still have the loaded cursor waiting to draw, place into, and thread with additional frames.

THREADING WITHOUT TEXT

When you work frame-first, building your layout as boxes in advance of content availability, but know you'll need to thread a story between multiple frames, pre-thread the empty frames. The procedure is the same—click on the out port of frame one and then anywhere in frame two and so on. You'll see the same telltale port arrows, and when you place, paste, or type a story into the first frame in the chain, it will automatically flow between them without the need for you to manually thread at that time.

Threading Tips

You can thread together any empty container capable of holding text. You can incorporate not only rectangular text frames, but also elliptical, polygonal, starred. If you make a mistake working frame-first—say you put an image frame where you wanted a text frame—don't stop threading just to convert the frame from the Object ➢ Content menu. Instead, simply click in the image frame with the loaded cursor. InDesign will convert it to a text frame, place the story inside, and thread it to the previous frame all in one step. Even path text (aka text on a path) objects can be threaded from one to another or back and forth with frames.

Often you'll want to ensure that stories always break at a certain point and jump to the next frame in the thread. While you *could* use the time honored (and wasteful) method of manually resizing frames to force appropriate jumps, that creates a lot of work for you during initial layout and often more if the copy is edited again. Instead, use a frame break. Before the line that should begin a new frame, select Type ➢ Insert Break Character ➢ Frame Break to insert the special frame break marker. No matter how that story composes, the text after the break marker will always jump to the next frame in the chain.

As I'm sure you can imagine, frame breaks, if forgotten, can be a gotcha as well. If you get in the habit of working with Show Hidden Characters (bottom of the Type menu) turned on, you'll never be left scratching you head about why a giant white space appears at the bottom of a frame. (Well, almost never. Look for overly zealous paragraph keeps options and for text wrapping objects on other layers, too.)

Viewing Threads

In addition to the information conveyed by the in and out ports of frames, it's often helpful to be able to see a more pronounced indicator of threading between frames. Activating View ➢ Show Text Threads displays lines between out ports and in ports, enabling you to follow the flow of a story from frame to frame, page to page (see Figure 8.5). This is similar to the way QuarkXPress shows linkage but with the distinct advantage of not locking you into keeping active a tool that can't edit anything while you examine the linkage. The Show Text Threads command can stay on while you use any other tool or modify the story, frames, or pages however needed.

Managing Threads

Already got a threaded story and need to insert, move, or unthread frames? Here's how.

Unthread Text Frames

Like assembly, disassembly doesn't require a special tool. To stop a thread, reeling in the story from all subsequent frames into which it flows, just double-click the out port of the first frame—or the last frame you wish to stay threaded. (You could also double-click the in port of the first frame to be unlinked.) The story will remain threaded up to that point (unless you spooled it back into the very first frame in the thread). Frames that were previously part of the thread down the line won't delete; they'll be left in place, empty and unthreaded. This last is an important thing to note because threading accidents sometimes happen wherein pre-created frames are inadvertently threaded into the wrong story. Unthreading the frames reverses the error but leaves the frames ready to accept new content so you don't have to manually draw new ones.

FIGURE 8.5
With text threads
shown, lines link
all the frames in a
threaded chain.

REMOVING FRAMES FROM A THREAD

Probably the most frequent calamity when threading frames in InDesign is creating too many frames while autoflowing a story. For example, you may have a three-column layout wherein the outside column isn't for the main story but for sidebar content. When autoflowing, InDesign will create a threaded text frame between every pair of column guides inside the margins, including that sidebar column. (Ideally, you want to set your document margins such that the sidebar appears outside them, but that's not always feasible.) In that common scenario and others, you might want to remove a frame from the middle of a threaded series without breaking the rest of chain.

Simple: Select the offending frame and press Delete or Backspace. The frame will disappear, and text it held will flow into the next frame in the thread. After eliminating any unwanted frames, just make sure to check the end of the story; you'll probably have overset text because of the reduction in space.

ADDING FRAMES INTO A THREAD

Adding a new frame into the middle of an existing thread is almost as easy as removing one. After drawing the new frame, click the out port on the threaded frame ahead of it, and then click inside the new frame to bring it into the chain. You would think that you'd then have to complete the connection by going from the new frame's out port to the next frame in the chain, but, happily, you'd be wrong. InDesign takes care of that automatically. Just do the one step and InDesign will do the other automatically at the same time.

DUPLICATING FRAMES IN A THREAD

When you cut, copy, or duplicate frames in a thread, you will *not* be working with the same story upon paste (or duplicate). Instead, InDesign will create a perfect replica of the frame, with identical text, but *outside* the original thread. If you cut, thus removing the frame, the remaining frames in the thread will heal the breach and flow text between them. Copying or duplicating leaves the original thread intact but creates a new, isolated frame containing just the text it original held, without preceding or following parts of the story.

Autoflowing Text

Autoflowing is the process of pouring text into threaded frames without manually clicking a loaded cursor into each one. InDesign has autoflow, but also several other methods of flowing threaded stories. When you're working with multiple frames, modifier keys, in addition to clicking, determine which method occurs.

TABLE 8.1:   **Text Flow Options and Their Cursors**

CURSOR	MODIFIERS	EFFECT
	(none)	**Manual Text Flow:** Threading frames one at a time, loading up the cursor from an out port and clicking inside or drawing another frame is manual text flow.
	Opt/Alt	**Semi-Autoflow:** This is when you hold Opt/Alt while clicking inside the second frame, which threads in that frame but keeps the cursor loaded and ready to link to and/or draw subsequent frames.
	Shift	**Autoflow:** Places the entire story without leaving any copy overset, adding pages and single-column frames as needed.
	Opt+Shift/Alt+Shift	**Fixed-Page Autoflow:** Flows the story through any existing pages and threaded frames, but will not create additional frames or pages if needed (any leftover text will be overset).

When you pre-link empty frames and then place, paste, or type text into them, you're performing a sort of manual fixed-page autoflow ("mo' flow") because you manually created the connection only to later reap its benefit quasi-automatically. True autoflow creates frames and pages where none existed before, although, as pointed out in the section "QuarkXPress vs. InDesign" above, it has its limitations. Then there's Aunt Flo, who sends you nice sweaters on your birthday. But, I doubt she uses InDesign.

Any of these flow methods can be used in either content-first or frame-first layout and during either initial document import or threading from an existing text frame.

Note that, if you have a frame selected and the Replace Selected Item option checked in the Place dialog, an incoming story will automatically flow into the selected frame. From there you can begin flowing using one of the flow options above. If you didn't want the story to fill the selected frame, just undo (Cmd+Z/Ctrl+Z), which will get you back to a cursor loaded with the unplaced story.

Autoflow in Master Page Frames

Despite the inelegance of threading text through frames inherited from the master page, it *can* be done, and it *is* usually easier than manually creating each page…after the first.

If you begin a document by checking the Master Text Frame option in the New Document dialog (see Figure 8.6), InDesign will create on the master page or pages a text frame than runs margin to margin horizontally and vertically. Choosing multiple columns in the Columns section of the New Document dialog does two things. First, it places ruler guides on the page to define the columns. It also makes the master text frame a multiple-column frame just as if you set it up manually in Object ➤ Text Frame Options. That's where it gets complicated.

FIGURE 8.6

The New Document dialog

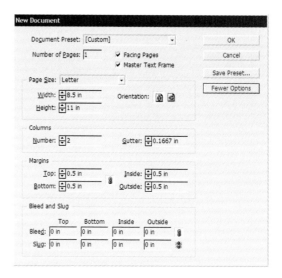

Master page objects are locked in InDesign so they can't be accidentally messed with (this is a good thing), so overriding the master text frame on the first page of the document requires Cmd+Shift+clicking/Ctrl+Shift+clicking it. Once it's overridden, you'll be able to type, paste, or place into the now document page text frame. It will, however, be a single, nonthreaded frame. You cannot place a story into a master text frame *and* autoflow in one action; it's one or the other, a trade-off.

Autoflowing the story immediately is faster and easier but creates all new text frames independent of master text frames. Should your document already have master frames, they'll still be there, empty and ignored. Using master text frames has the distinct advantage of enabling modification of all frame instances from the single master page representative (or two representatives in facing pages documents). To modify the frames that actually convey the story—say, to change the number of columns, vertical alignment, inset, or other options—you'll need to manually modify each page's text frame individually (preferably with an object style).

AUTOFLOWING IMMEDIATELY

Knowing the gains and losses of both choices discussed above, if you opt for initial ease, that's exceedingly easy. Get your story through File ➤ Place (or Cmd+D/Ctrl+D), and then, while holding Shift to trigger autoflow mode, click within the margins of the page. InDesign will place the entire story, adding pages and full-page text frames within them, until the entire story is paid out.

Note that where you initially click becomes the top of the first page's text frame. If you click one inch down from the top margin, the frame will begin one inch down from the top margin and run to the bottom margin. Subsequent frames in the thread will be of full margin height.

USE THE MASTER TEXT FRAME

If the master text frame on the first page is already overridden and selected, check Replace Selected Item in the Place dialog. Upon import (and after import options and any warnings that may appear), the story will fill the frame. Any text that doesn't fit will overset. If you import the story (but don't place it) before overriding the master text frame, you can still place text into it. Even with a loaded cursor, simply hold Cmd+Shift/Ctrl+Shift while clicking within the area of the frame to activate it, and then click inside it again (without modifier keys) with the loaded cursor to pour in the story.

Once you have the story placed into its first frame, it takes one manual threading to start the story autoflow.

Begin by creating a second page. Naturally, this too will have a master text frame, but you don't need to manually override it prior to placing. Back in frame one, click the out port to load the cursor with the rest of the story, and then go to page 2. The cursor will remain loaded until you click or press ESC, even through page changes. Shift+click inside the margins of page 2—which is the area of the as-yet-not-overridden master text frame—and from there the story will autoflow, using the master text frame and creating new pages to use their master text frames until the entire story is set.

Incidentally, master text frames in facing pages are automatically threaded across a spread upon creation. Thus, once manually overridden, text will flow freely from the master text frame on the left-read page to the one on the right-read. They are not, however, linked spread to spread; pages 2 and 3 link together, as do 4 and 5, but 3 does not thread to 4. If you aren't autoflowing your story, you'll need to manually thread into and out from each spread.

Jumplines

Of course, threaded text doesn't necessarily follow one page after the other. Magazines, newspapers, newsletters, magalogs, and numerous other types of publications often include more than one story per page, and they and other types of documents often jump several pages or sections between pages of one story. Directing readers between nonconsecutive frames in a thread is the job of *jumplines*.

InDesign can do forward (e.g., "Continued on page *X*") and backward (e.g., "Continued from page *X*") jumplines and both with total freedom and auto-updating numbers. In fact, they're accomplished with tiny little text markers. To create a jumpline, create a new text frame to hold only the jumpline itself, and type and style the text of the jumpline. Don't insert a manual number. Move the jumpline frame such that it overlaps, at least a little, a threaded frame (see Figure 8.7). Now switch to the Type tool, place the cursor at the end of the jumpline text, and choose Type ➢ Insert Special Character ➢ Markers ➢ Next Page Number, which will insert the number of the page on which the next frame in the thread appears. And, if you reorder pages or move around frames, that page number will automatically update to reflect the new location of the next threaded frame.

To create a backward jumpline that explains from whence the story continues, use the Type ➢ Insert Special Character ➢ Markers ➢ Previous Page Number command.

Either jump marker may be used inside the actual story as well, which is useful for references to sidebar material and other objects tethered to a particular place in the copy as an anchored object. For instance, you could say "Reference the chart on page *X*."

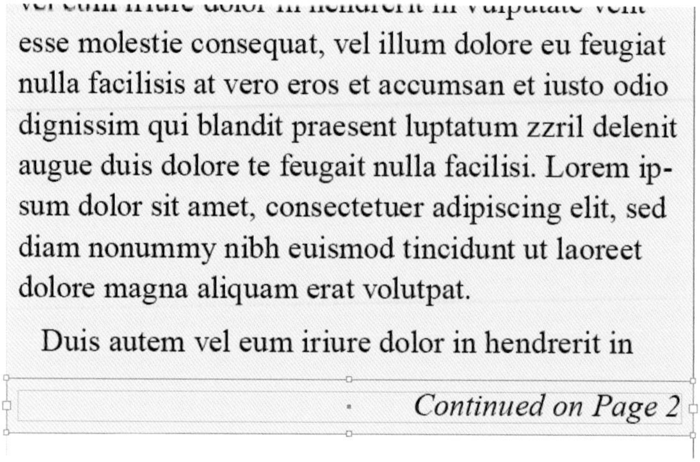

FIGURE 8.7
A jumpline directs readers to the next frame in the thread.

esse molestie consequat, vel illum dolore eu feugiat nulla facilisis at vero eros et accumsan et iusto odio dignissim qui blandit praesent luptatum zzril delenit augue duis dolore te feugait nulla facilisi. Lorem ipsum dolor sit amet, consectetuer adipiscing elit, sed diam nonummy nibh euismod tincidunt ut laoreet dolore magna aliquam erat volutpat.

Duis autem vel eum iriure dolor in hendrerit in

Continued on Page 2

In most cases, it's not a good idea to put jumplines inside the text they reference because the jumplines themselves are then subject to reflow. It's rather embarrassing to jump a story from page 10 to page 38 and, two paragraphs into the latter, see "Continued on."

Lists, Numbers, and Bullets (Oh, My!)

The PageMaker Plug-in Pack added PageMaker-style bullets and numbering to InDesign CS. CS2 integrated and improved on those features. Now, in CS3, we have the best yet—including the ability to stop and restart numbering as well as continue numbering across different stories and even different documents in the same book. In fact, CS3 brings InDesign closer than ever to advanced list and numbering power formerly reserved for the highly technical and less than creative pro-friendly world of technical publishing applications like FrameMaker and Ventura Publisher.

Bullets

InDesign has an extremely advanced and flexible implementation of bullets. They go far beyond circles, disks, and rectangles and are customizable and editable in ways other software hasn't even dared to imagine.

With text selected, choose Bullets and Numbering from the flyout menu of either the Paragraph panel or the Control panel in paragraph mode to access the Bullets and Numbering dialog, which controls a remarkable number of options (see Figure 8.8). Select Bullets from the List Type drop-down list to light up most of the options below it.

The Bullet Character section looks rather like the Glyphs panel's Recently Used list, doesn't it? It should—it functions much the same way. Out of the box, InDesign has five default bullet characters—the standard bullet glyph, an asterisk, a lozenge (the hollow diamond), the right-pointing double-angle quotation mark (often used by the Brits as quotation marks), and a nice fleuron from the Adobe Jenson Pro typeface. To use one of these as your bullet, click on your choice. Odds are, however, that you'll rarely use the latter four.

FIGURE 8.8
Bullets in the Bullets
and Numbering
dialog

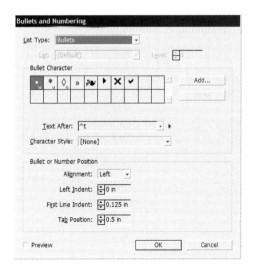

Clicking the Add button lets you pick any glyph from any installed font on your system as your bullet character. If you want a square bullet, find a font containing a square. If you want to make bullets out of dollar signs, you can do that, too. The Add Bullets dialog is nearly identical to the Glyphs panel (see Figure 8.9). At the bottom, choose the font family and style, and then, from the glyph table above, select the desired bullet glyph. If you want just one bullet, click OK, but if you want to explore your bullet glyph options, maybe across multiple fonts, click Add instead. The Add button adds the selected glyph to the Bullet Character list but doesn't close the Add Bullets dialog. Careful: It's easy to lose track of time in Add Bullets; at some point, you will have to get back to work.

FIGURE 8.9
Add Bullets looks
and works like the
Glyphs panel.

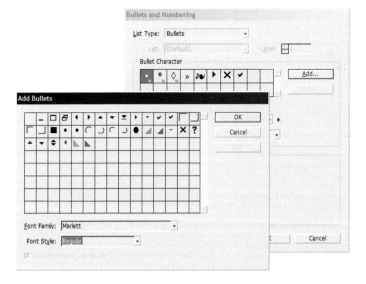

The Remember Font with Bullet check box lights up when you have selected a common glyph like a letter, number, or standard punctuation mark. Let's say you've decided that the *at* symbol (@) in BlackOak Std would make a swell bullet glyph. With Remember Font with Bullet *unchecked*, the @ will *not* be in BlackOak Std if the list text itself isn't. Instead, the bullet will set in the typeface of the list text. In many cases, that's exactly what you want. In this example, however, you want to make sure that @ bullet is always BlackOak Std regardless of the list text typeface—currently or after future changes—so you'll check the option.

Continuing with Figure 8.8, after choosing your bullet glyph, there are still plenty of options to consider:

Text After   The text, symbol, or marker separating the bullet from its list item. The default ^t is the universal code for a tab character, but the field will accept just about anything you can type. If you want a *leader* instead of a tab, type periods, hyphens, or underscores in the Text After field. To the right of the field is an arrow that will reveal a pop-up menu of common symbols and spaces. You can even combine several symbols, spaces, and manually typed glyphs to create a very intricate separator between bullet and text.

Character Style   Bullets can be assigned to any pre-created character style, which lets you become far more creative with InDesign bullets than you can elsewhere. In most applications, for instance, bullets must share all the styling attributes of the list text it identifies; there simply isn't a way to change even something as simple as the bullet color—at least, not without converting the bullet to editable text, thus losing all the benefits of automated bulleting. Using a character style, however, you can control every character-level attribute of the bullet independent of its accompanying text. Character color, point size, horizontal and vertical scaling, underline, strikethrough, skew, baseline shift—it's all open for customization.

Alignment   This option has little effect upon bullets, which tend to align the same regardless of this setting, but three options—Left, Right, and Center—become important when creating numbered lists, particularly when the numbers grow beyond single digits.

FREE BULLETS

Explore your font collection via the Glyphs panel to look for potential bullet characters to draw upon in future projects. You can find some surprisingly good bullet candidates hidden among letters, numbers, and punctuation, particularly in OpenType fonts.

Naturally, you'll want to also check any symbol or dingbat fonts in your collection. Look carefully in your font library; some of the best bullets come from often overlooked sources. On Windows, for instance, is a typeface named Marlett. It's the font from which the operating system pulls user interface symbols like the *X* on the application close button in the top-right corner, as well as the minimize, maximize, and restore button labels. Those likely won't become your favorites for bullets, but other symbols in Marlett might, like right-angled triangles (arrows) pointing left, right, up, and down, as well as several types of boxes, check marks, and other symbols. Other gold mines of great bullets could be slumbering undiscovered on your system as your read this.

Indents Like paragraph indents, the Left Indent field controls the overall left indent, while First Line Indent alters just the first line left indent. The first line is the one carrying the bullet or number glyph. To hang list items such that their bullets or numbers stick out farther left than all other lines in the item, set Left Indent to a positive value and First Line Indent to an equal negative value. Note that these fields are mirrors of their counterparts on the Paragraph panel—changing values in one place changes values in the other.

Tab Position If the Text After field includes a tab (^t code), the Tab Position field sets the tab stop or how far rightward of the bullet or number begins the text of the item.

After defining the bullet (or numbering) options once, you can quickly re-apply them without having to return to the Bullets and Numbering dialog. Choosing either Apply Bullets or Apply Numbering from Type ➤ Bulleted & Numbered Lists will reapply the last-used options for those adornments. If you've yet to configure bullets or numbers in this session of InDesign, the defaults will be used. The same is true of the easier method of executing the Apply Bullets and Apply Numbering commands, using the buttons on the Control panel in Paragraph mode (see Figure 8.10). Unfortunately there is no analogue on the stand-alone Paragraph panel.

FIGURE 8.10
The Control panel in Paragraph mode, with the Apply Bullets and Apply Numbering buttons highlighted

Of course, the best way to reuse bullet and numbering options is to add them to paragraph styles. We'll talk more in depth about paragraph styles in Chapter 11, "Efficiency," but you can see in Figure 8.11 that the interface for defining them within a paragraph style is identical to the Bullets and Numbering dialog.

FIGURE 8.11
Configuring bullets and numbering in a paragraph style in the Paragraph Style Options dialog

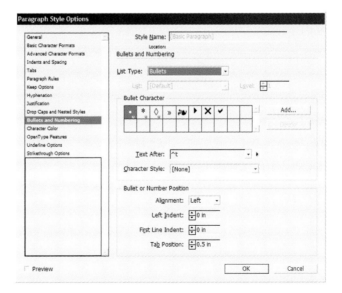

Numbering

Setting List Type to Numbers replaces the Bullet Character section of the Bullets and Numbering dialog with options specific to organized lists (see Figure 8.12). Some of these are new to InDesign CS3.

The numbering options are as follows:

Level   (Upper section) When multilevel, outline-style, hierarchical, or nested numbering is created, the Level field determines to which level of numbering the selected text will belong and which of the options below it are applicable. For instance, in Figure 8.13, you see several levels of numbering.

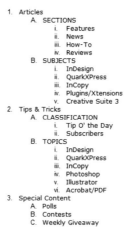

Format   The Format field sets the type of numbering to be used. Options are Arabic, Arabic with leading zeroes, capital Roman, lowercase Roman, uppercase alphabetic, and lowercase alphabetic.

You also have none, which completely removes enumeration, leaving only the glyphs after the numbers (if any), kind of like bullets.

Number   Referring back to Figure 8.12, combined in this field are the functions of Bullet Character and Text After. Displaying the number requires the presence of the ^# code preceded or followed by whatever you like—a period, a number symbol (#), a tab, or any one of several types of spaces or leader symbols in the menu to the right. New to the menu is the Insert flyout menu (the arrow) is the Insert Number Placeholder submenu, which lets you insert a number of any level up to, and inclusive of, the value in the Level field above, as well as chapter numbers, which are set in Numbering & Section Options (see the appropriate section in Chapter 7, "Pages").

Mode   Mode offers the option of continuing numbering from a previous number or manually setting the start at number in the field on the right. The advantage to the latter is that numbered lists can be stopped, followed by unnumbered paragraphs or sections, and then the numbering can picked back up again with the next logical digit.

Restart Numbers at This Level After   If Mode is set to Continue from Previous Number, this check box and drop-down list pair will activate. When working in multilevel numbering, this option says, "When a list item of this level appears after a higher-level item, restart numbering." For example, let's say we're defining level 3 numbering. Checking Restart Numbers at This Level After and setting the drop-down to Any Previous Level will cause level 3 list items to begin numbering anew at *1* after every level 2 item.

After I introduce the new Lists feature, the sidebar "InDesign CS3 Numbering Shaves Weeks off Book Production" will explain how to use the new numbering and list features.

Lists

InDesign CS3 beefs up paragraph, character, and object styles and introduces long, long (long) requested Table styles. While they were obviously on a roll, giving users reusable styles for everything requested, they could have also added List styles. Fortunately for us, they didn't. I mean, do we really need another panel? Adobe's accommodating mood did introduce reusable list management, but they leveraged existing technologies to do it.

Since their introduction, bullet and number paragraph attributes have been part of Paragraph styles, thus making them reusable and easily manageable. As numbering capabilities deepened in CS3, they are still primarily managed in Paragraph styles, but a new Lists feature augments styles.

Choosing Type ➢ Bulleted & Numbered Lists ➢ Define Lists opens the Define Lists dialog (see Figure 8.14). In this interface you create, edit, delete, or load from other InDesign documents or templates the lists, but you'll actually use them in the Bullets and Numbering dialog.

FIGURE 8.14
The Define Lists
dialog

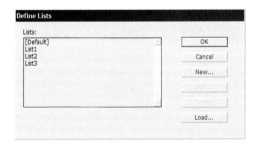

Clicking the New button to begin a new list (see Figure 8.15) offers three options, the first of which is the name by which you'd like to refer to the settings. The other two are what enable such important things as figure, caption, table, chart, and other types of numbering outside consecutive paragraphs of list items.

FIGURE 8.15

The New List dialog

Consider figure numbers in, say, a technical book about InDesign for print professionals. It's important for reading comprehension and reference (and writing, artwork creation, editing, compositing…) that those figures be numbered. But, in nearly all cases, the figures and their captions will be laid out in frames totally disconnected from the body copy and each other in unthreaded frames. Therefore, it isn't possible to just pull up Bullets and Numbering, set a couple options, and expect InDesign to handle the figure and caption renumbering if I relocate this section from Chapter X to Chapter Y.

That's where the Continue Numbers Across Stories list option comes into the picture. When the resulting list definition is used with in the Caption paragraph style, every caption in the current chapter will be automatically numbered by InDesign, and those numbers will dynamically update if figures and their captions are reorganized.

Checking Continue Numbers from Previous Document in Book accomplishes the same thing between chapters. For example, I set my numbering options to include the chapter number as well as the figure number, update the Caption paragraph style to reflect that change, and then never have to manually update a figure number again. How much time would that save in compositing a book like this? (Well, seeing as I'm still writing it and don't yet know how many figures I've got, I don't know for sure how much time it would save the compositor or me; let's just say it would save lots of time.)

In other types of documents, figures and captions might not need numbering. Perhaps tables, charts, or some other type of content must be numbered sequentially even if they don't adjoin. Often one or more such numbered items will be incorporated into the document's table of contents or an appendix, increasing the importance of numbering them. Combining the new Lists function with numbering and paragraph styles, *all* of these types of content and more can be numbered by InDesign.

 Real World Scenario

INDESIGN CS3 NUMBERING SHAVES WEEKS OFF BOOK PRODUCTION

Not long ago I was asked to design a template for a book publisher (not this book or this publisher regrettably). In addition to the usual specs and goals, I was tasked with automating or at least streamlining as much of the compositing and layout process as possible. Because the publisher's typical authors are themselves designers and software experts, the publisher allows authors to do their own initial composition and layout, with the need for only oversight and minor error correction in-house. While that decision enables the publisher to realize tremendous savings in both book production time and budget, it added to my task one wrinkle: I couldn't employ third-party plug-ins or even custom scripts.

My InDesign CS2 (and InCopy CS2 for those authors who didn't have the skill or desire to directly perform layout) templates were as streamlined as they could be without plug-ins and scripts, but they required manual numbering of figures, captions, and tables. If one was moved, cut, or added during editing and author review stages, it meant manually renumbering all nondynamic subsequent figures, captions, or tables (guess who that was often left to).

Enter InDesign CS3 (and InCopy CS3).

As Spring 2007 and the impending public launch of Creative Suite 3 approached, I updated the book template in a late beta. For the Figure Caption, Table Title, and Chart Title paragraph styles, I defined lists that continued across stories and used ^H.^#.^t (Chapter Number.Instance Number.[Tab]) as the number. With the correct chapter number defined for each chapter in Layout ➢ Numbering & Section Options, and all chapters collected into an InDesign book, every figure, table, and chart self-numbered with no manual numbering required by the other authors and editors or production. Additionally, because all the individual chapter InDesign documents were managed through the Book panel, even the occasional chapter reordering wasn't an issue because InDesign will update chapter numbers—and thus all dependent numbered items—automatically.

InDesign CS3 also enabled easier creation and management of the paragraph styles governing numbered lists in the body copy itself. That template has three levels of hierarchical lists, progressively moving down through Arabic numerals, capital letters, and lowercase Roman numerals. In the CS2 versions of the InDesign and InCopy templates, each list was a separate and independent style, and they were dumb lists. Every time an author needed to return to first-level list items from second- or third-level, she would have to first apply the paragraph style and then manually change the Start At (number) field in Bullets and Numbering. For example, if the author created a list like the following, simply numbering the second top-level item required several manual steps. If the author later had to add, remove, or reorder the list items, almost every item had to be manually tweaked with a trip to Bullets and Numbering and the Start At field.

1. Articles
    A. SECTIONS
        i.   Features
        ii. News
        iii. How-To
        iv. Reviews
    B. SUBJECTS
        i.   InDesign
        ii. QuarkXPress
        iii. InCopy
        iv. Plugins/Xtensions
        v.   Creative Suite 3
2. Tips & Tricks
    A. CLASSIFICATION
        i.   Tip O' the Day
        ii. Subscribers
    B. TOPICS
        i.   InDesign
        ii. QuarkXPress
        iii. InCopy
        iv. Photoshop
        v.   Illustrator
        vi. Acrobat/PDF
3. Special Content
    A. Polls
    B. Contests
    C. Weekly Giveaway

In the CS3-version book template, however, all I had to do was configure each of the three list paragraph styles to continue numbering from the previous instance of the same level (the Mode field in Bullets and Numbering) and to restart numbering for the sublists (the second and third levels) after any previous level. The only downside to these options was that the directive to continue numbering from the previous instance of the same level meant that, if a list on page 25 contained five top-level items, a completely separate list on page 100 would begin numbering at item 6. That, of course, is a simple fix: the Restart Numbering command begins the numbering over again at *1* (or *I*, *A*, or whatever). For the authors (and compositor on occasion), one command, usually executed from a keyboard shortcut, is easier, faster, and less distracting than opening the often closed Paragraph panel, choosing Bullets and Numbering from the flyout menu, changing the Start At field, and hitting OK.

All the authors had to do was apply paragraph styles as they wrote in InDesign or InCopy because I had built the styles to handle numbering automatically (and many were nested styles, too, but that's a topic for Chapter 11, "Efficiency"), saving significant time at all stages, especially in post-editing production. Instead of the usual technical book publishing turnaround time of 3 to 12 weeks, this publisher's books go to press within *days* of the completion of final editing.

Overriding Bullets and Numbers

At some point you'll probably need to restart the sequence of list item numbering. In InDesign CS2 that required a trip to the Bullets and Numbering dialog and changing the Start At (number value) field. One new command in InDesign CS3 finally eliminates that journey: Restart Numbering. You'll find it in three places: on the Paragraph panel flyout menu (and mirrored on the same menu on the Control panel in Paragraph mode), in Type ➤ Bulleted & Numbered Lists, and on the context-sensitive menu that appears when you right-click within numbered text. With the text cursor somewhere inside the list item, execute that command and numbering will restart at *1*, *01*, *A*, *a*, *I*, or *i*, as configured.

The Convert Bullets to Text/Convert Numbering to Text command is not new to CS3, but it's still just as useful as in CS2. Using live or dynamic bullets and numbers, you have through character styles and the various other options in Bullets and Numbering tremendous control over the appearance of the bullet or number glyphs themselves. They are not editable text, however, and are excluded from spell checks and find and replace operations. When you need those functions or unadulterated styling power without lengthening your Character Styles panel, Convert Bullets to Text/Convert Numbering to Text will convert dynamic, auto-updating bullets or numbers to standard, editable glyphs. The appearance of the bullets or numbers remains intact, including any indents, but they will no longer update, and you can now edit them as you can any other text in a frame.

Having the ability to convert such list identifiers to normal text was much more important in CS2 where command over their dynamic versions was limited—particularly with regard to numbers. Within CS3, however, you have much more control in the form of list definitions, list levels, and the other options related thereto, and you shouldn't need to convert them to text anywhere nearly as often.

Word Processing

Did I catch you by surprise earlier when I mentioned authors writing books in InDesign instead of writing them in Word? Really, there's no reason a competent InDesign user shouldn't write directly in InDesign. If the concept of writing in the layout raises an eyebrow, then perhaps you'd entertain using InDesign's built-in word processor in lieu of the page. And, if you're so old school that you bristle at the very idea of using a layout application for word processing, perhaps you'll consider Adobe's Best Kept Secret 5.0 for the task.

Story Editor

Story Editor, which is InDesign's built-in word processor, is an alternate view on a given story, isolating text from layout. Figure 8.16 shows the Story Editor side by side with the layout view of the same story. Editing either instantly updates the other.

FIGURE 8.16

Story Editor (left) editing the text of the frame in the layout (right)

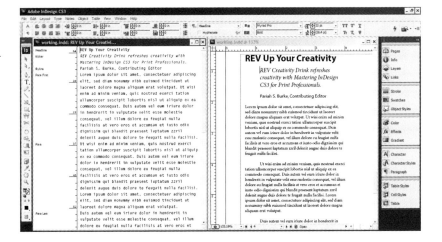

To open a Story Editor view, select a text frame or place the Type tool cursor inside it, and choose Edit ➤ Edit in Story Editor, or press Cmd+Y/Ctrl+Y. If you highlight text prior to opening the Story Editor view, that same text will be highlighted in Story Editor. If your InDesign layout window was maximized, so will be the Story Editor window that pops up. Rest easy; the layout is still open behind it. Cmd+Y/Ctrl+Y is a toggle that will open Story Editor view from layout view or layout view from Story Editor view. Additionally, you can restore or resize the Story Editor window to be less than the full application window size. Both views can be tiled side by side if you like, too.

Because Story Editor focuses on the copy, it displays only the most basic of formatting—italic, bold, and bold-italic—all other formatting, including typeface, size, leading, indents, and so on, is hidden. Text can still be styled and formatted within the Story Editor, and paragraph and character styles still applied—indeed, all the panels, tools, and menu commands relevant to text are as accessible in Story Editor as in layout mode—but their effects won't befog the purely word processing view. Line breaks, hyphenation, and composition are also not accurate—this is copyediting, not galley proofing—and text is displayed in a single column as wide as the Story Editor window (less the Style Name column on the left). As a performance boost that saves time, InDesign holds a queue of updates—if you type quickly into the Story Editor view, the text will appear or change there instantly, but there will be a slight pause before the layout is updated to reflect the changes.

Although you won't see the *effect* of paragraph styles, the left column, in addition to providing a scale of column depth in the document measurement system (inches, points, millimeters, or whatever), lists beside each paragraph the style assigned to it (see Figure 8.17). Thus, at a glance, you can discern the formatting of the paragraph. And that's a very good thing because sometimes those paragraph style tags are your only visual cue that a new paragraph has begun. Unfortunately,

Story Editor still doesn't have other common paragraph break cues like indents or paragraph spacing, which, until you get used to it, could make you resort to the abominable practice of double returns between paragraphs.

FIGURE 8.17
Story Editor com-
municates copy-
specific information.

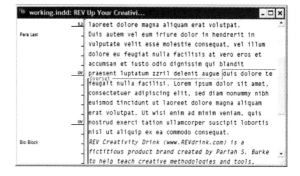

One exceptional feature of Story Editor that layout view simply can't match is the ability to see and edit overset text. Any copy that won't appear on the layout is still present, but called out, in Story Editor with the *overset* marker and red border down its left side. Even better, the depth ruler in the Style Name column continues measuring overset text so you can see exactly how many column inches are yet needed to layout the rest of the story.

CUSTOMIZING STORY EDITOR

Story Editor is designed to be used; Adobe wants you to be able to write and edit copy comfortably, and that doesn't always mean black, 12 pt, Letter Gothic STD type on white. In the preferences, on the Story Editor Display pane, are options to completely customize the word processing experience to your unique comfort level (see Figure 8.18). A few themes are preconfigured, or you can set your own font, size (via a drop-down menu of common sizes or by typing in a specific point size), line spacing, and text and background colors. The anti-aliasing method can also be changed, as can the size and shape of the cursor.

FIGURE 8.18
Story Editor
Display options
in Preferences

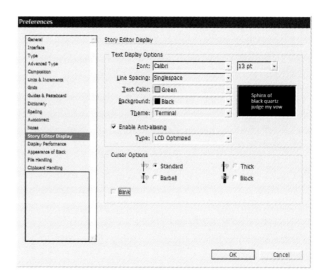

Personally, I find it particularly difficult to read and write monospaced type for long periods, so I usually change the display font to one designed specifically for onscreen reading. In many ways, printed matter and onscreen matter are opposed in their rules, with typeface style being chief among them. Onscreen sans-serif typefaces are usually easier on the eyes than serif; in print it's the opposite, of course. A few fonts you might want to try for this purpose include, in no particular order, Adobe's Myriad Web, Helvetica, Arial, Verdana, and Calibri. These five also have more obvious italic and bold variations than the default Letter Gothic STD font—it's always nice to see which words you've italicized or emboldened without guessing.

The Style Name column on the left can be hidden with the command View ➢ Story Editor ➢ Hide Style Name Column. This command is a toggle, so if it *is* hidden but you want it shown, choose the same command again. Similarly the depth ruler can be toggled in or out of view with View ➢ Story Editor ➢ Show Depth Ruler (or Hide Depth Ruler).

DRAG AND DROP

Also of note is that, by default, dragging and dropping text is enabled in Story Editor (but not in layout view). As in most word processors, this option enables you to highlight text and then drag it elsewhere in the story. Most people like this behavior, but it can be jarring. If you'd rather drag and drop be off, uncheck the option in the Type pane of Preferences.

When you're dragging and dropping text in either mode, formatting is retained. For example, dragging a passage of text set in Bookman Oldstyle 12/16 pt and dropping it into the middle of a paragraph of Adobe Caslon Pro 10/14 pt will result in the original passage remaining Bookman Oldstyle 12/16 pt and surrounded by text formatted as Adobe Caslon Pro 10/14 pt. To force dropped text to abandon its original styling and adopt the attributes of the text surrounding its new location, begin dragging and then depress and hold Shift until the text is dropped.

InCopy

Would that I had the space to tell you everything about this wonderful companion application I've championed and evangelized for going on six years now. Unfortunately, InCopy is an entire book unto itself.

InCopy is Adobe's best kept secret, the least marketed of all of Adobe's products, and a tool whose success is due almost entirely to the passionate handful of InCopy experts running around praising it to anyone who will listen. The difference between Story Editor in InDesign and the entire InCopy application is like the difference between the farm teams and major league baseball—steroids…um, I mean, greater talent and vastly expanded training.

InDesign and InCopy share a code base, meaning that they are, for all intents and purposes, the same application at heart. Their differences are the result of different sets of plug-ins stacked atop that code base. Many features are identical. For example, InCopy has InDesign's full text styling and formatting capabilities, including lists, bullets and numbering, and tables and even identical Character, Paragraph, Character Styles, Paragraph Styles, Tabs, Swatches, Table, Story, Glyphs, Links, and Layers panels. Anything you can do with text in InDesign you can do in InCopy, its editorial counterpart. It also introduces features far beyond InDesign's, features like an advanced thesaurus (and accompanying panel); Word-esque change tracking; text macros; constantly updating line, word, and character counts; and the ability to edit one, some, or all stories and text frames in an InDesign document concurrently, in several windows or just one.

Whereas InDesign has two editing modes, InCopy has three: Story, Layout, and Galley.

Story view (see Figure 8.19) is identical to InDesign's Story Editor, a pure word processor without accurate line breaks or composition. It also has the same pros, cons, and customization options.

FIGURE 8.19
InCopy's story view

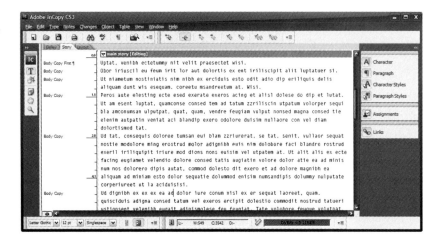

Of course, InCopy can open its own INCD and INCX file formats, as well as Microsoft Word DOC files, ASCII text, Rich Text format, and other common textual document formats, but it can also open InDesign documents. Lacking layout tools, frames cannot be moved or modified in InCopy, but their contents—text and imagery—can, which is what enables offloading editorial work from design and production to the editorial department. Editors who want to proof or even edit copy within the final layout can do so through InCopy's layout view (see Figure 8.20). The document in layout view is 100% accurately copyfit.

FIGURE 8.20
Layout view enables InCopy editors to proof and work within the final layout, without overloading them with InDesign's full tool set.

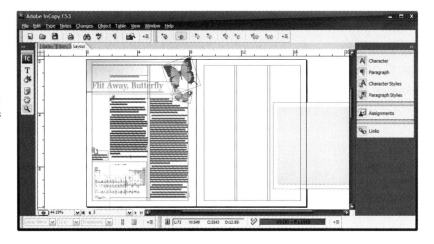

Finally, galley view is a combination of both (see Figure 8.21). It's a story editor but with accurate line breaks, hyphenation, composition, and copyfitting.

Working together, InDesign and InCopy fill both sides of the design-editorial dynamic, allowing one department to concentrate on its specialty and allowing the other group to do the same. Native editing of both applications' files in the other, live copy and layout update links between them, and for more robust needs, the ability to assign frames, pages, and spreads to specific InCopy users are the reasons InCopy is rapidly supplanting Microsoft Word in collaborative publishing workflows. If you're part of such a workflow, whether design and editorial are at the same or different sites, migrating writers, editors, and proofers to InCopy could be the most valuable idea you gain from this book. I say that with all sincerity, and I have the experience migrating publishing clients to back up the claim.

Adobe InCopy CS3
File Edit Type Notes Changes Object Table View Window Help
Galley Story Layout
aliquam ad miniam esto dolor sequatie dolummod
enisim numsandipis dolummy nulputate corperiureet
ut la aciduisisi.
Ud dignibh ex ex ex ea adz dolor iure conum nisl
ex er sequat laoreet, quam,
quisciduis adigna consed tatum
vel exeros ercipit dolestio com-
modit nostrud tatueri ustionsent velenibh
eugait adipismolese feu feugiat. Tate volobore feugue
volutpat, quis at loborem quis ero doloborem vel
eugiam quamcom molore tate veliquat.
Cincilit nostrud ea core veliquamet nibh ea feuisi.
Riure enibh euisi tate velit praesto euguer seq-
uisl endionulla faccum etum dolor augiam, commy
nim vendip et iriure eros alit luptat, vulputpatin ut
luptatem dolorem dolore minit adignibh estin vel do
et, quipit, sum velit lorperatet nostrud tis augait aute
faccum at nos dunt autat velese doloborper iustie
Body Copy
Character
Paragraph
Character Styles
Paragraph Styles
Assignments
Links

FIGURE 8.21 Galley view presents accurate copyfitting in a familiar word processor environment.

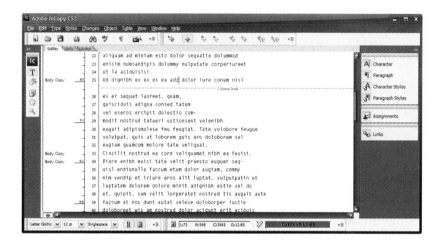

Footnotes

Footnotes are citations or resources placed at the end of a story and referenced from within the main text of the story. Figure 8.22 shows a typical footnote.

delenit augue duis dolore te feugait nulla facilisi. Lorem ipsum dolor sit amet, consectetuer adipiscing elit, sed diam nonummy nibh euismod tincidunt ut laoreet dolore magna aliquam erat volutpat.1
Duis autem vel eum iriure dolor in hendrerit in vulputate velit esse molestie consequat, vel illum dolore eu
1 Mary had a little lamb. It was salty.

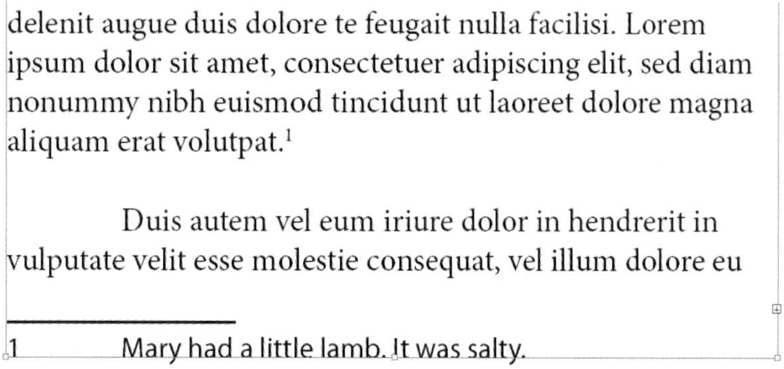

FIGURE 8.22 A footnote

Inserting a footnote is easy. Position the cursor in the text immediately after the word or phrase to reference the footnote, and then select Type ➢ Insert Footnote. Using the current footnote options, a new footnote reference will be added to the text at that point and the footnote itself at the bottom of the column; your cursor will stand ready to type the footnote.

The easiest way to edit footnotes and their reference numbers is in Story Editor where they magically appear together. In Figure 8.23, you can see both collapsed and expanded footnotes in their colored boxes. To collapse or expand, just double-click the colored box. To collapse or expand all footnotes at once, choose Collapse All Footnotes or Expand All Footnotes from the context-sensitive menu or from the View ➢ Story Editor menu.

FIGURE 8.23
In Story Editor, foot-
notes appear inline
with their reference
numbers.

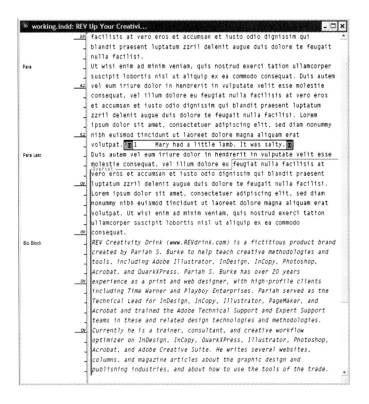

Footnotes are anchored to their reference numbers. If text reflows, moving the reference to another column or page, the footnote follows to the bottom of that column or page. Similarly, pasting or dragging text containing a reference to a different place in the same document takes the footnote with it. The same occurs when pasting or dragging into a different document with the added benefit that both the reference and footnote itself will pick up the footnote formatting options in effect in the new document.

Deleting a footnote is even easier than inserting it—delete just the reference number and the entire footnote goes along with it.

You *can* delete the footnote number or other identifier at the beginning of the footnote itself, but you really shouldn't—readers match the reference to the footnote by that mark. If you've deleted the number and want to reinsert it, choose Type ➤ Insert Special Character ➤ Markers ➤ Footnote Number with the cursor ahead of the footnote.

FORMATTING FOOTNOTES

Extensive footnote formatting controls are available from Type ➤ Document Footnote Options. The first tab of Footnote Options, Numbering and Formatting, is largely concerned with the appearance and sequence of footnotes (see Figure 8.24).

What does it all mean?

Style   Footnotes may take on numerous styles, including the most common Arabic numerals; the second most common, a system of symbols including the dagger (†), double-dagger (‡), and so on; incrementing asterisks; Roman numerals in both cases; and alphabetic enumerators in both lower- and uppercase.

FIGURE 8.24
Footnote Options
Numbering and For-
matting tab

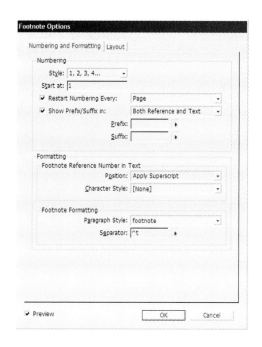

Start At   InDesign automatically increments footnote numbers in the same story, and renumbers them to reflect additions, deletions, and rearrangement of footnote references. By default, each first footnote in the story will begin with *1* and ascend from there. In cases where a single chapter or document comprises more than a single story, you'll want to either manually choose the starting number in the Start At field, or set an appropriate Restart Numbering Every option.

Restart Numbering Every   Depending on the type of document being written or laid out, you may want footnotes to continuously increment throughout the whole document or just per-section, spread, or page. For the former, leave Restart Numbering Every unchecked. However, to start the footnote reference numbering over at the Start At value for every section, spread, or page, check this box and choose the appropriate divider in the drop-down menu to the right.

Show Prefix/Suffix   Between the check box, drop-down list, and specific Prefix and Suffix fields, you can add brackets [],parentheses (), hair spaces, thin spaces, or custom glyphs to either or both the footnote reference number and footnote text. The spaces in particular are handy when footnote references are rendered in a typeface too close to preceding or succeeding glyphs.

Footnote Reference Number in Text   In the Position drop-down, determine if you'd like to format footnote reference numbers in the usual fashion of superscripted numbers or if you'd like them subscripted or even rendered as normal position, full-size numbers. By creating beforehand and assigning here a character style, every aspect of reference numbers' appearance is open to customization distinct from surrounding copy.

Footnote Formatting   Footnotes themselves are paragraphs and can be styled while editing. Here, though, you have the ability to specify a particular paragraph style to set the majority of global appearance options. In the Separator field, enter the glyph(s) or marks to divide the identifying reference number from the footnote text it keys. The default, ^t, is code for a tab.

On the Layout tab, more advanced formatting as well as footnote placement is stipulated (see Figure 8.25).

FIGURE 8.25

Footnote Options
Layout tab

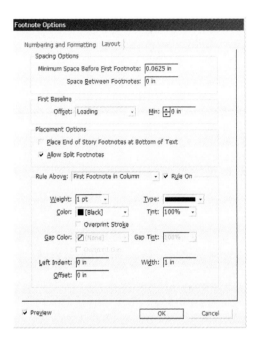

Spacing Options   Enter in these fields the amount of vertical spacing between the end of the story column and the first footnote as well as the amount of vertical paragraph space separating multiple footnotes from each other. The latter option has no effect with single footnotes.

First Baseline   Baseline offset sets the vertical distance between the baseline of the first line of footnote text and the (by default ruled) top of the text frame holding footnotes. Control text baseline offset using the same options as in normal text frames—by ascent, cap height, leading value, x-height, or a fixed amount. The Min field refines Baseline Offset values of Leading or Fixed by specifying the minimum amount of space between the top of the line and the baseline of its text.

Place End of Story Footnotes at Bottom of Text   This option specifies where footnotes appearing in the last frame of a threaded story appear. In all other frames but the last, footnotes are placed at the bottom of the column in which their reference numbers appear. In some publications and according to some style guides, however, it's preferable to place all footnotes from the last *frame* of a story not at the bottom of each column but beneath the last column. Checking this option sets the latter condition.

Allow Split Footnotes   When footnote text outgrows the amount of space allotted to hold footnotes, how should it be handled? Checking this option splits long footnotes across columns (and perhaps even pages), creating effectively threaded footnote frames at the bottoms of successive columns. Unchecking Allow Split Footnotes can force InDesign to move the *body copy* line of text containing the footnote reference number to *its* next column, which could result in large, multiline gaps at the bottom of main story columns. If the resulting gap is too large, InDesign will instead overset the footnote text.

One way to help control footnote cohesion is to ensure that you've assigned to it a paragraph style with appropriate keeps options defined (e.g., keep *X* number of lines together or keep all lines together).

Rules   Mirroring the options of a paragraph rule above the paragraph, this section lets you create visually interesting separators above the first footnote section and/or above all footnote sections (for split footnotes). To disable the rule entirely, uncheck the Rule On box.

In addition to all the formatting options in Footnote Options, you can still manually and individually style footnotes. For instance, you could select the footnote text (press Cmd+A/Ctrl+A with the cursor inside a footnote to select the entire text of just that footnote) and apply character styles, font or color changes, or anything else you can normally do with text.

You can also manually style the footnote reference numbers, but it's a much better idea to do it in Footnote Options with character styles. Even doing it that way, though, styles will be lost if you clear overrides and character styles in the paragraph containing the footnote reference.

Endnotes

Endnotes are similar to footnotes except that, instead of appearing at the end of columns, endnotes appear at the end of the story. InDesign does not have any actual endnote creation features beyond pressing Cmd+Shift+End/Ctrl+Shift+End (the shortcut to go to the end of the story) and typing the endnote. Microsoft Word *does* have endnote features, which means you could potentially import Word documents including them. As we discussed in Chapter 2, "Text," checking Show Import Options in the Place dialog presents the option of whether to import endnotes in Word files. If they're imported, InDesign will convert Word endnotes to normal, static text at the end of the story.

Fixing, Finding, and Changing Text and More

What would word processing be without spell check? I know I wuold be compleetly lost without spillcheck to redresss my typeos and erorrs. (Before software spell checking, when I wrote on a typewriter, I had remarkable spelling skills, but spell check—especially dynamic spell checking— has ruined me.) Going without spell check, writing would probably be as error prone as story composition without hyphenation control. Fortuitously, InDesign has both—and a whole lot more.

Spell Checking

By and large, spell checking in InDesign is nearly identical to—and just as good as—spell checking in Word or… Wasn't there another word processor at some point? Oh, yeah! WordPerfect. It *does* offer a few things the average word processor can't match, though, things like dictionary exceptions optionally embedded as part of the *document* so that collaborators can skip proper names and other words not recognized by the built-in dictionary and the ability to spell check 39 different languages and dialects simultaneously in multilingual documents.

As you may recall from Chapter 3, "Characters," you can flag any glyph, word, or paragraph or the entire story to any of the 39 languages and dialects InDesign supports out of the box via the Language attribute on the Character panel. InDesign won't translate text from one language to another, but changing the language attribute causes InDesign to switch to, say, one of the five German dialect dictionaries if you happen to type *Danke* (thank you), thus counting the word as spelled correctly instead of seizing on it during a spell check run. Because language is a character-level attribute, InDesign can switch dictionaries on-the-fly, even from one word to the next, oscillating between English USA, English Legal, English Medical, and Norwegian: Nynorsk in a sentence about a medical malpractice lawsuit filed by an American tourist against a hospital in Oslo. With each term assigned to the appropriate language dictionary, spell check will sail right on through the statement without a hitch.

To initiate a spell check, think italic. Yeah, instead of assigning Cmd+I/Ctrl+I—the universal, cross-platform shortcut for making type italic—Adobe gave it to spell check (italic is Cmd+Shift+I/ Ctrl+Shift+I). If that's too confusing, you'll find Check Spelling under Edit ➤ Spelling. Up will pop the Check Spelling dialog (see Figure 8.26).

FIGURE 8.26

The Check Spelling dialog

Many of the options in here should be familiar to you if you've done any spell checking in other applications, but there are a couple of items here you won't find in the average word processing spell checker.

At the bottom of the dialog, the Search drop-down menu lets you choose what to check—just the selected text, from the cursor to the end of the story, the entire story, the whole document, or even all opened documents in one fell swoop. As it moves throughout the document, calling unrecognized words to your attention, the Language field above Search will identify to which language a given word is assigned and thus against which dictionary InDesign is comparing your spelling skills.

Unrecognized words will appear in the Not in Dictionary field. Note that the same field changes its legend depending on the reason InDesign seized on the word. In the case of capitalized words the software thinks should be lowercase, for instance, the field label will be Unrecognized Capitalization. (Observe the political correctness of it all—the field doesn't say "Misspelled Word" or "Go Back to Third Grade, Moron.") The field is grayed out to communicate that you can't edit it—look, but don't touch.

When InDesign encounters an unrecognized word, it will attempt to locate similar words in its dictionary. They will appear in the Suggested Corrections list below, with what InDesign considers the most likely suspect already inserted into the Change To field. If the word is misspelled but the application's choice isn't right, you can either pick a new word (or, in some cases, phrase) from the Suggested Corrections list or type a new word or phrase directly into the Change To field. When you've verified the correction, click the Change button to change just this one occurrence or Change All to replace all instances of the misspelling.

If the suspect word or phrase *is* correctly spelled, you can click the Skip button to bypass the current instance of the word, click Ignore All to skip this and any later occurrences (subsequent spell check run-throughs will still seize on the word, however), or educate InDesign by adding the word to the dictionary with the Add button.

When you're adding a new word to the dictionary, the Add To field determines to which dictionary the word is added—the global language dictionary or just this specific document's local dictionary. Choices are limited by the language attribute of the caught word—if the word is tagged as English, you can't add it to the Lithuanian dictionary without a trip to the Character panel.

Come to think of it, that's a surprisingly common scenario. So common, in fact, that Adobe did a very cool thing. Even with the Check Spelling dialog open, you can click in the document to return to a state of editing with full access to the text and, among everything else, the Character panel's Language field. More common, though, is the need to spell check only a few words here and there, highlighting just *this* or just *that*. Because you can leave Check Spelling opened and ready to use while you navigate through pages and whole documents—including opening other documents—it's incredibly flexible.

Getting back to adding words, the Case Sensitive check box tells InDesign to add the suspect word to the dictionary exactly as shown, which is precisely what you want when adding proper names you commonly use. Of course, the Add To button is a limited interface to manage InDesign's dictionaries. When you want a little more, edit the dictionary.

Dictionary Editing

The ability to edit the dictionary via a nice graphical user interface within the application is a distinct advantage over many word processors whose only means of editing dictionaries is to open an external ASCII file in a text editor. If you're already in the Check Spelling dialog, click the Dictionary button. If you haven't yet initiated a spell check when you decide words or hyphenation exceptions need to be added to, or edited in, the dictionary, choose Edit ➤ Spelling ➤ Dictionary.

In the Dictionary dialog (see Figure 8.27), you can add and edit new words and new ways of hyphenating words, delete previous manual entries, and a whole lot more.

FIGURE 8.27

The Dictionary dialog

Target Similar to the Add To field in Check Spelling, Target determines where your new word is added—to the current language global dictionary or to an open document's local dictionary. Words added to the latter travel with the document, meaning that spell check in the same document run on a collaborator's computer will not flag the custom entry as suspect. However, it also means that, should you use the same word in another new document, spell check will once again call into question the competence of your third grade teacher.

Language The Language drop-down list is not the complete list you'll find at the bottom of the Character panel. This one is filtered down to just the dictionaries in use in the current document. If a word somewhere in the story is assigned to the German: 1996 Reform dictionary, that will appear as a target language here.

Dictionary List Choose from this list whether you want to see below and edit words you've added to the dictionary, words you've removed from the dictionary, or words you've ignored via the Check Spelling Ignore All button. I love the last option because sometimes you click Ignore All overzealously. By choosing to edit that list in the Dictionary dialog, you can tell InDesign to stop ignoring the word.

Word Depending on which dictionary list is active, here is where you type the word to add to, remove from, or ignore in the dictionary. It's also where hyphenation exceptions are specified (we'll get to that in just a moment). Note that the Case Sensitive check box at the bottom is often important when adding words.

HYPHENATION EXCEPTIONS

Entering a word as unadorned text—like `alliteration`—leaves the hyphenation to InDesign's internal and somewhat sensible syllable sensing system. Believe it or not, it's actually pretty good. Sometimes, though, InDesign's hyphenation choices don't jibe with yours. In those cases, you'll need to override it. At the very least, you may want a preview of how InDesign will hyphenate. Clicking the Hyphenate button will give you that preview. Thus, after you type in *alliteration*, the Hyphenate button will transform it into *al~lit~~er~~~~a~tion*.

Confused? Allow me to explain.

You see, InDesign sagaciously understands that there's a difference between discretionary hyphens—potential breaks in words at the end of a line of text—and always-visible hyphens in compound words like *single-page*. Thus, entering an actual hyphen in the Word field makes that hyphen *always* appear in the word—there's nothing discretionary about it. Discretionary hyphens are represented by tildes (~), and the number of tildes prioritizes hyphenation. In the example *al~lit~~er~~~~a~tion*, InDesign will first try to break the word between *er* and *a*. If that isn't feasible, it will attempt to break between *lit* and *er* before breaking at the single-tilde points. Tildes equal hyphenation priority; the more tildes, the more InDesign will seek to break the word at that point. If, in some crazy layout, InDesign has to break the same word multiple times, it will do so according to the priority established by the tildes if possible.

To override InDesign's idea of hyphenation priority, change the number of tildes. The Word field is entirely editable, so you can add or remove tildes to your heart's content. If, for example, I wanted to ensure that *alliteration* was only hyphenated at one point if at all, I could enter this: *alliter~ation*.

To prevent hyphenation of a word altogether, remove the tildes throughout, but precede the entire word with a tilde, like so: *~alliteration*. If InDesign can do anything but break the word, it will therefore leave it intact. Note that, if InDesign has no other choice, it will still break the word according to its internal understanding of syllables. For instance, if you set *alliteration* in a column too narrow to hold the entire word, either InDesign will break it despite a directive to the contrary or it will elect to overset the rest of the story beginning with that word.

SHARING DICTIONARIES

Using the Import and Export buttons in the Dictionary dialog, it's easy to share dictionaries between users. If you work solo on disparate projects, you'll probably have little use for this. But, if you're a member of a workgroup that regularly uses custom words or hyphenation exceptions, the ability to export dictionaries to text files and import from the same is a huge time-saver.

As one means of improving workflow efficiency, I always recommend that workgroups assign one member as the Keeper of the Lists. If your group deals with the same nondictionary or special hyphenation rule words again and again, designate someone to maintain in his copy of InDesign (or InCopy, since dictionaries can be shared between them as easily as between installations of InDesign) all the proper names, acronyms, and other special words and hyphenation exceptions needed by the typical documents produced in the workgroup or department. Every time that list updates, the Keeper of the List should export his list to a central repository—probably the file server—and alert the rest of the group to reimport the master dictionary list, replacing their previous dictionaries. Using this method, no one in the group need suffer delays in a spell check run with stops on the CEO's name, the London office's profit center code, or the contracting government agency's acronym.

Dynamic Spelling

Dynamic spelling is what we humans do; InDesign does dynamic spell *checking*. Semantics aside, activating this feature by choosing Edit ➤ Spelling ➤ Dynamic Spelling tells InDesign to check spelling in the layout (and story editor) without having to wait until it's time to run Check Spelling. Dynamic Spelling will run through the document, comparing text already in the document against the dictionary as well as doing the same on-the-fly as you type.

Misspelled words will be underlined with a red squiggly line (see Figure 8.28). Right-clicking (Control-clicking for you single-button mouse Mac users) on a word bearing such an underline offers suggested alternates as well as the ability to ignore the word, add it to the dictionary, and open the Dictionary dialog.

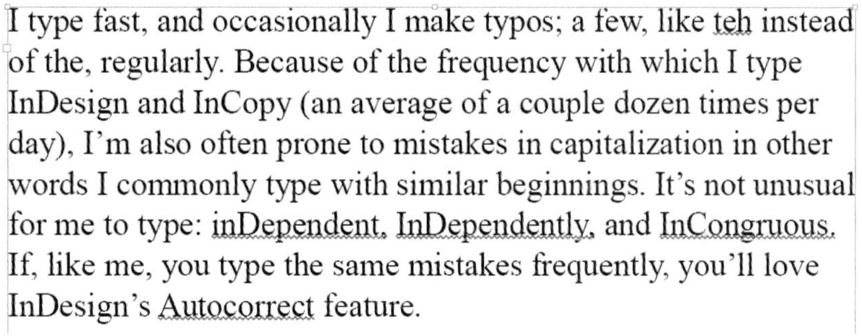

FIGURE 8.28
With Dynamic Spelling active, misspelled words are underlined and spelling-specific options replace the normal context sensitive menu.

I type fast, and occasionally I make typos; a few, like teh instead of the, regularly. Because of the frequency with which I type InDesign and InCopy (an average of a couple dozen times per day), I'm also often prone to mistakes in capitalization in other words I commonly type with similar beginnings. It's not unusual for me to type: inDependent, InDependently, and InCongruous. If, like me, you type the same mistakes frequently, you'll love InDesign's Autocorrect feature.

Autocorrect

I type fast, and occasionally I make typos; a few, like *teh* instead of *the*, regularly. Because of the frequency with which I type *InDesign* and *InCopy* (an average of a couple dozen times per day), I'm also often prone to mistakes in capitalization in other words I commonly type with similar beginnings. It's not unusual for me to type *InDependent*, *InDependently*, and *InCongruous*. If, like me, you type the same mistakes frequently, you'll love InDesign's Autocorrect feature.

Enabled with the Edit ➤ Spelling ➤ Autocorrect command but edited in the Autocorrect pane of Preferences, Autocorrect replaces one word with another as you type. The options are simple. In the Autocorrect Preferences, click the Add button to open a dialog where you can enter the misspelled word for which InDesign should search and the correction with which to replace it (see Figure 8.29). The Misspelled Word field accepts letters, numbers, and basic punctuation but not spaces. The Correction field, however, *does* accept spaces, which enables you to fix oft mistakenly combined words—for instance, *atleast* should be *at least*.

FIGURE 8.29
Adding an Autocor-
rect rule, with the
Autocorrect Prefer-
ences pane behind it

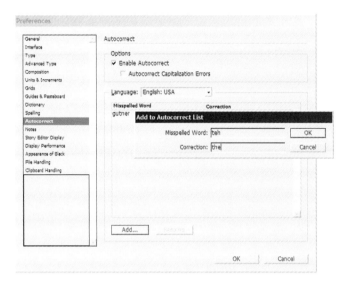

To fix my occupational hazard *InD*- and *InC*- capitalization errors, I enable the check box at the top of the pane, Autocorrect Capitalization Errors.

Edit autocorrect pairs you've already created by double-clicking a row in the list.

If you're like most people, you're hoping I won't say what comes next: Autocorrect is not retroactive. It replaces as you type but won't touch text already in the document. Nor will it fix mistakes in placed or pasted text. To change those, you need Find/Change.

Find/Change

In InDesign CS3, the formerly very useful Find/Change utility has received a major overhaul. Now you can save and reuse searches, search across multiple documents simultaneously, and, best of all, use GREP expressions for remarkable search and replace capability using pattern matching.

Open Find/Change from the Edit menu with or without an object or text selected. At the top are several example queries. Adobe saw fit to preload the Query drop-down list with high utility examples such as replacing two carriage returns (common in placed stories) with the single car-riage return required by clean, professional layouts, replacing hyphens and double-hyphens with en and em dashes, and more (see Figure 8.30).

To save your own query for later reuse, click the disk icon beside the list. Prune the list with the trashcan delete button.

TEXT

Each of the tabs in the Find/Change dialog does something a little different, so let's start with the Text tab (see Figure 8.31).

Find What and Change To   Enter in the Find What field the text to replace and in the Change To the text to replace it with. Both fields have drop-down lists of recently used previous values as a convenience. Additionally, both fields have Special Character menus to the right (see Fig-ure 8.32). Using these menus, you can search for just about any text you can imagine, including symbols, dashes, every type of space and break InDesign can insert, and even wildcards like any digit, which finds any number between 0 and 9, any letter—*A–Z*, *a–z*—and any character whatsoever—from letters to numbers, punctuation to dingbats.

FIGURE 8.30
Preset saved queries
in Find/Change

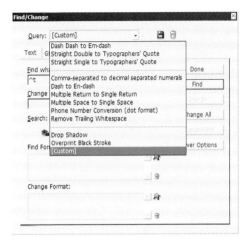

FIGURE 8.31
Find/Change
Text tab

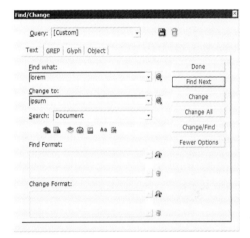

FIGURE 8.32
The Special Charac-
ter menu for the
Find What field

Note: Items from the special character menu are inserted as caret code metacharacters similar to the codes in Word. If you're familiar with Word, however, be advised that they are not always the same codes. For instance, ^t is a tab in both, but a manual line break, which breaks the line but not the paragraph, is ^l in Word and ^k in InDesign. I caution you to become familiar with InDesign's unique Find/Change codes rather than typing in your commonly used Find and Replace codes.

Search Select what you'd like to search—the current story, from the cursor to the end of the story, the entire document including all stories and frames, or all stories and text frames in all open documents.

Include Locked Layers Check this to *search* text on layers locked in the Layer Options dialog (see Figure 8.33). Even with it checked, you cannot *replace* text on locked layers. Unlock the layer prior to running Find/Change.

FIGURE 8.33
Close-up of the find
options buttons

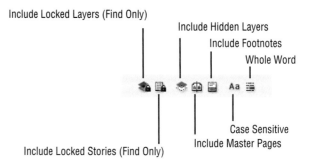

Include Locked Layers (Find Only)

Include Hidden Layers

Include Footnotes

Whole Word

Case Sensitive

Include Master Pages

Include Locked Stories (Find Only)

Include Locked Stories This option searches for, but will not replace, text among stories that are locked because of being checked out (by other users) in InCopy or Version Cue workflows.

Include Hidden Layers On nonvisible layers, you *can* search *and* replace, but the layer will not be made visible. When you're performing an incremental search and replace using the Find or Change button instead of Change All, the search text will be highlighted on the hidden layer without making the layer visible—basically, you'll see a highlight with nothing highlighted.

Include Master Pages Check this option to also search and replace through objects contained on master pages.

Include Footnotes Check this option to also search and replace within footnote text. To search for footnote reference numbers, choose that option from the special characters menu under Markers.

Case Sensitive When disabled, the contents of the Find What text triggers matches regardless of capitalization. For instance, a search for *InDesign* with Case Sensitive disabled will also find *indesign*, *INDESIGN*, and *Indesign*. With the option enabled, only instances of *InDesign* would be found.

Whole Word Whole Word will find only exact, whole word matches to the Find What text. This option is disabled by default, meaning that a search for *red* will find not only the whole word, but also where *red* appears in other words, such as in *appeared*, *redefine*, and *colored*.

More/Fewer Options   Show or hide the Find Format and Change Format areas.

Find Format and Change Format   Using the Specify Attributes to Find button to the right of the Find Format and Change Format fields enables you to replace any possible character or paragraph formatting attribute, including predefined character and paragraph styles, fonts, colors, indents, OpenType options, bullets and numbering, drop caps, and any other style attribute you may have applied to text and now want to use to narrow the search, add to Find What text, or replace with another (or no) attribute. To remove formatting options from the search or replace criteria, click the trashcan icon beside the appropriate field.

Find/Find Next   Find the first instance of the search text matching the Find What field, with the formatting and search options specified, if any. InDesign will highlight the found text and await further instruction. Once the first instance is found, this button changes from Find to Find Next.

Change   Replace only the selected instance with the Change To field contents.

Change/Find   Replace the selected instance and immediately find the next.

Change All   Automatically find all instances of the Find What text and replace with the Change To text.

GREP

Just in case you're not an über l33t Unix geek, GREP is an acronym (and resulting command) from that world meaning "Search *g*lobally for lines matching the *r*egular *e*xpression and *p*rint them [to screen]." (I suppose GREP is easier to remember than the full acronym for the directive—SGLMREPT). Despite its intimidating meaning and origin, GREP is incredibly powerful, allowing you to search for and replace just about anything you could possibly type in InDesign with a tremendous number of variables.

The GREP Find/Change tab is very similar to the Text tab, as you can see in Figure 8.34. On the Text tab, variables and metacharacters are specified using caret codes. With GREP, it's a tilde (~) or backslash (\), but the distinction goes beyond mere syntax differences.

FIGURE 8.34
Find/Change
GREP tab

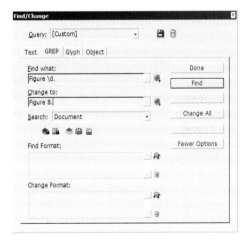

The difference between the normal search and/or replace with variables on the Text tab and a GREP search is the scope of variable data. On the Text tab, it's easy to search for something like *Figure X.y*. The Find What field in that case would be *Figure ^9.^9*, with *^9* being the code for any digit. In a GREP search, the same Find What would be *Figure \d.\d*. But, with GREP, you can go far beyond replacing the text and issue an order to find *Figure X.y* only under certain other conditions—say, only if it appears at the beginning of a paragraph, as would be the case in a figure caption but not in a reference to the figure within body copy (using an option from the Locations list in the Special Characters menu beside the Find What field).

Below the Change To field and the Search field to define scope is a subset of the Text tab's find options consisting of the buttons to search locked or hidden layers, locked stories, master pages, and footnotes. The absent options are not relevant to GREP's pattern-matching searches.

GLYPH

On the Glyph tab of Find/Change (see Figure 8.35), individual glyphs can be sniffed out and/or replaced—a handy utility for changing glyph typefaces or styling options or replacing a euro symbol (€) with a dollar sign ($) such as might be needed when prepping the Berlin office's European catalog for a North American release. If you know the Unicode or GID/CID code for the glyph, choose the appropriate system in the ID drop-down, and then enter the code to its right. If not, then the arrow beside the Glyph field pops up a mini Glyphs panel for visual searching. Set the desired Font Family and Font Style value for either or both Find or Change and go.

FIGURE 8.35
Find/Change
Glyph tab

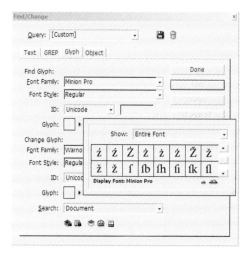

OBJECT

This new addition in InDesign CS3, the Object Find/Replace tab, is truly revolutionary. You can now actually search and replace the graphic characteristics of objects! Want to find all frames with a .25 pt thick, 50% black stroke? No problem. Do you need to globally alter the text wrap around all inline frames? Easy as pie. Did the client come back and ask you to change every two-column text frame across the 300-page document to three columns? With Find/Change's Object tab, even that daunting task won't take more than a few seconds.

At the bottom of the Object tab, choose what to search out—text, graphic, unassigned, or all frames, and, just above it, the scope of the search (see Figure 8.36).

FIGURE 8.36
Find/Change
Object tab

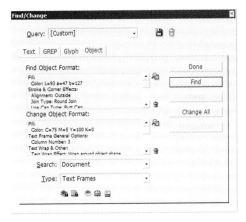

The rest of the tab is all object formatting. Click the Specify Attributes button (with the magnifying glass) beside either of the Format fields to open the Find (or Change) Object Format Options (see Figure 8.37), which is virtually identical to the Object Style Options dialog. You can search for and replace any object-level attribute—including transparency and new transparency effects. Days of changes can be effected in minutes. If you're management, the ramifications of this new feature should become immediately obvious to you. If you're an hourly employee, don't tell management about Object Find/Change.

Objects created ad hoc can be assigned to defined object styles, too. Thus objects can be readied for even more expedient update.

FIGURE 8.37
Find Object Format
Options enables
searching for any
object-level attrib-
ute, including
effects.

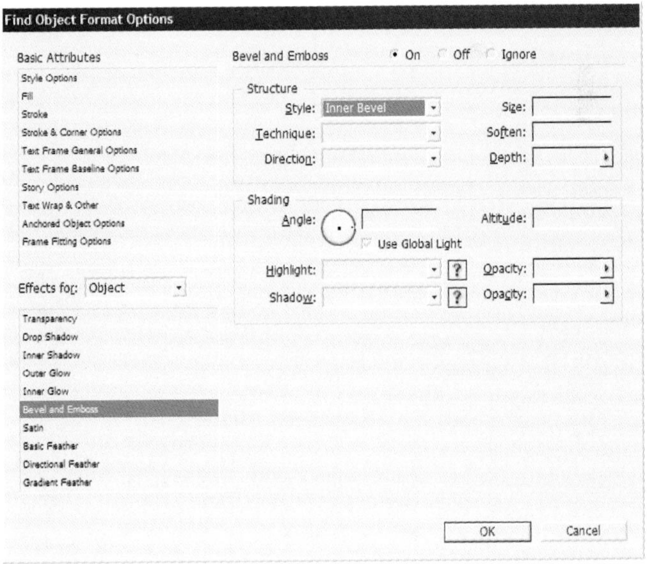

Replacing Fonts

Although in all Find/Change modes except Object you can replace font families and styles, InDesign has a dedicated utility better suited to that purpose. On the Type menu, Find Font presents a list of all fonts in use in the document (see Figure 8.38). Not only is the user interface more conducive to the task of replacing one typeface with another, but now in InDesign CS3, it can optionally redefine style definitions as well—something Find/Change can't.

FIGURE 8.38

Find Font replaces typefaces, and now redefines styles too.

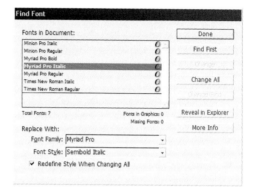

All fonts currently in use in the document are listed at the top, with counts just below the list. To replace one typeface with another, click on the in-use entry in the list, and then choose the font family and font style for the replacement at the bottom. If the typeface is part of a style definition (or might be), check Redefine Style When Changing All to also update the style definition. The benefits to that option, of course, are that paragraph and character styles can be used freely without reintroducing the undesired typeface, and neither will clearing overrides on text to which the styles have been defined. Once your options are set, choose what to do. The various Find and Change buttons work similarly to Find/Change. For instance, Find First will locate the first occurrence of the selected typeface, jumping the document window to display the text that is the first instance. The text will also be highlighted. Change All will replace all instances of the typeface except those embedded in placed EPS, PDF, and AI documents, which InDesign cannot access.

To change fonts embedded in placed assets, locate the needed images. Then use the Edit Original command on the Links panel to open the assets in their creation applications and replace the font there.

Reveal in Finder (Mac) or Reveal in Explorer (Windows) will pop open a file system window zeroed in on the folder containing the font file. This is useful, for example, when you need to copy the font for emailing, deleting, or repairing (all outside of InDesign, of course).

The More Info/Less Info button toggles the Info area at the bottom of the Find Font dialog (see Figure 8.39). In the Info section you can see important information about a given font, including its type, version, embedding restrictions, path, and, most useful of all, which paragraph and character styles include the font as part of their definitions.

FIGURE 8.39
The Info area of
Find Font provides
valuable insight
into a font and its
usage in the current
document.

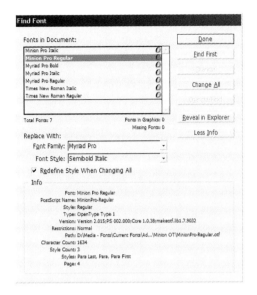

The Bottom Line

Thread and Unthread Text Frames and Flow Text   Threaded text frames are the foundation of multipage documents, and, whether manual, auto, or semi-auto, flowing text is the way to pour that foundation.

Master It   Create a new document with a two-column master page text frame and employ the skills learned in this chapter to lay out a multipage Word or other text document. There should be no overset text when you've finished.

Create Bulleted and Numbered Lists   InDesign CS3 offers more creative and structural control in updated bullets and numbering features and the new Lists property.

Master It   In a new document, use Lists and Bullets and Numbering to re-create the headings from this chapter's section "Threading and Unthreading Text Frames" as a hierarchical list.

1. Threading and Unthreading Text Frames

    A. QuarkXPress vs. InDesign

    B. Threading Frames

        i.   Threading Pre-Created Frames

        ii. Threading without Pre-Created Frames

iii. Threading upon Import

iv. Threading without Text

C. Threading Tips

D. Viewing Threads

E. Managing Threads

    i. Unthread Text Frames

    ii. Removing Frames from a Thread

    iii. Adding Frames into a Thread

    iv. Duplicating Frames in a Thread

F. Autoflowing Text

G. Autoflow in Master Page Frames

    i. Autoflowing Immediately

    ii. Use the Master Text Frame

H. Jumplines

Write and Word Process in InDesign　The world is changing, and writing and editing in the layout application is no longer such a crazy idea.

Master It　In Story Editor, write a paragraph or two discussing how something you've learned in this chapter will benefit your work. Include at least one footnote, and set its options for a pleasing appearance on the page.

Fixing, Finding, and Changing Text and More　In addition to beefing up its already solid text support systems of spell checking, hyphenation, and Autocorrect, InDesign CS3 completely revamps Find/Change with incredible new capabilities.

Master It　Using the two-column, multipage document created just a few moments ago, use the new Find/Change features to convert the text frame to three-columns with a 0.25-inch column gutter. At the same time, give the text frames a semitransparent background color (while keeping the text fully opaque) and a frame inset.

Chapter 9

Documents

Working with documents involves knowing how to move around in them, change viewing options, and compare views. Working with longer documents efficiently means mastering InDesign's unique long-document features such as indexing, creating tables of contents, and working within the time-saving and collaboration-ready atmosphere of Book files.

In this chapter, you will learn to:

◆ Interact with documents visually and change zoom level, view modes, and display performance

◆ Build and manage grids and guides

◆ Create and manage Book files

◆ Index terms and create an index

◆ Create tables of contents

Seeing Your Work

Seeing your work is important (duh!). InDesign CS3 offers numerous ways of viewing and interacting with documents and objects to help you work as efficiently and quickly as possible.

Zooming

There are many, many (many) ways to zoom in or out in InDesign, letting you see as much or as little of a document as you need for work both macro and micro focused work.

First, of course, is the Zoom tool, which, predictably, looks like a magnifying glass (see Figure 9.1). Click it once to zoom in in predefined increments; Opt+click/Alt+click to zoom out by the same increments. To zoom in on a particular area, click and drag with the Zoom tool. InDesign will then fit the rectangular area defined by your dragging in the window, zooming until either or both the width or height of the area fits snugly within the document view window. Clicking and dragging while holding Option/Alt has the same effect in zooming out.

FIGURE 9.1
The Zoom tool is near the bottom of the Tools panel.

Double-click the Zoom tool icon itself on the Tools panel to reset the view to 100% magnification. Double-click the Hand tool just above (or beside if your Tools panel is two columns wide) to fit the entire spread in view.

In the bottom-left corner of every document window, a zoom percentage field offers common preset magnification levels (see Figure 9.2). If nothing on the list suits your needs, type in a custom zoom percentage.

FIGURE 9.2

The zoom
percentage field

If your hands are on the keyboard already, save a trip to the mouse by using the universal zoom in and zoom out keyboard shortcuts of Cmd++/Ctrl++ (Cmd/Ctrl and the plus sign on the regular, main part of the keyboard, as opposed to the numeric keypad) and Cmd+-/Ctrl+- (Cmd/Ctrl hyphen) respectively. Cmd+0/Ctrl+0 fits the entire page on screen. Other common zooming keyboard shortcuts are near the top of the View menu. One you won't find there is a Cmd+Option+2/Ctrl+Alt+2, which toggles between the last two zoom states. For example, if you zoomed into 800% to work on the detail of a vector path, and then pulled out to the full page view to see the effect of your work on the overall page, pressing Cmd+Option+2/Ctrl+Alt+2 would return you to the same spot at 800% to resume your detail work.

Navigator Panel

The Navigator panel (Window ➢ Object & Layout ➢ Navigator) also has the ability to zoom via a percentage box in the lower left as well as a zoom slider in the middle (see Figure 9.3). Dragging the slider right zooms in; left zooms out. At either end of the zoom slider are magnification buttons that zoom out (left) or in (right) in predefined increments once per click.

FIGURE 9.3

The Navigator panel

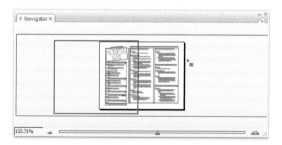

Zooming on the Navigator panel is more of a convenience, however, when working with the panel's main function, which is to facilitate moving around a page. Selecting the Hand tool and clicking and dragging inside the document window moves around the view without altering objects. The Navigator panel is designed to accomplish the same thing, but while keeping the entire page or spread in perspective. The red rectangle is the View Box—its contents matches the area of what the actual document window is displaying. To move around in the document window view, drag the View Box reticle in the Navigator panel.

The only options on the Navigator panel flyout menu are to change the color of the View Box and whether to view all spreads or just the active spread. With the former active, the Navigator panel can be scrolled, displaying live thumbnails of all spreads in the document. Often it's faster to scroll through the Navigator view and then zoom in on a page than it is to use the Pages panel or page navigation buttons.

Multiple Document Windows

Many times it's necessary to work on multiple pages concurrently, or to at least keep another page or another zoom percentage in view while working. The resizable Navigator panel can be used for such purposes sometimes, but it's not always the best choice. Fortunately InDesign allows you to open the same document in multiple views, which can then be tiled or arranged, automatically or manually (see Figure 9.4).

FIGURE 9.4
Multiple windowed views of the same document, in this case, using different view modes and zoom levels

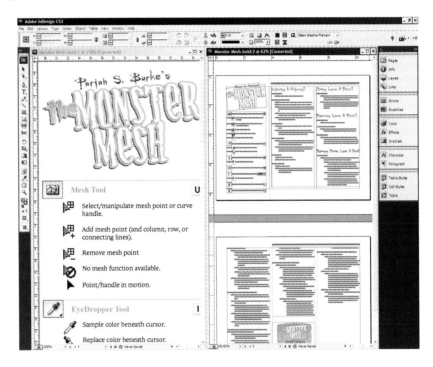

To open a new document view, choose Window ➢ Arrange ➢ New Window. Arrange the windows as you like, changing zoom levels, display performances, preview modes, and pages independently of one another. Any changes to one view will instantly reflect in the other.

Display Performance

InDesign uses an advanced rendering engine called the Adobe Graphics Engine to create true *WYSIWYG* onscreen previews of object resolution, placement, and interaction (color accuracy depends on your hardware and color management settings). Naturally, rendering everything at true resolution and colors can cause longer page drawing times, especially while moving around or zooming in and out on graphically rich pages. Most of the time, you don't need to work in true WYSIWYG; most of the time, a very good approximation of artwork using lower resolution proxies is all you need.

By default, InDesign displays pages and objects onscreen as lower resolution proxy images, which InDesign itself generates on-the-fly. Their positioning is accurate, but resolution, transparency interaction, color, and visual detail are diminished to reduce the work required of the video card and RAM. Balancing quality with speed, this is InDesign's Typical Display display performance setting.

There are two others (see Figure 9.5).

FIGURE 9.5
The same image as shown in the different display performance settings: (from left to right) Fast Display, Typical Display, and High-Quality Display

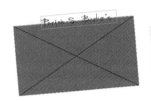

High-Quality Display renders everything to screen as true WYSIWYG. Do check this mode before finalizing a document, but performing all your work in High-Quality Display, especially with 300 to 1200 dpi or higher images, will lengthen the time it takes to change pages and views.

Fast Display is lightning quick because it replaces all images with gray boxes, dramatically reducing the workload of the video card when you're changing pages or views.

All three are found on the View ➤ Display Performance menu, as are options governing object-level display settings.

Each placed image may have its own individual display performance setting—Fast, Typical, or High-Quality Display—specific to that image and instance. Accessed from the context-sensitive menu available by right-clicking on an image, this option allows you to display a single image at its true resolution (High-Quality Display) or to gray out onscreen a large or overly complicated image for faster response from the application as you work (Fast Display). Both are independent of the document-wide Display Performance setting.

In order for object-level display performance to be available from the context-sensitive menu, that option must be enabled on View ➤ Display Performance, which it is by default. To remove all image-specific display performance settings, restoring all objects to the document's setting, choose View ➤ Display Performance ➤ Clear Object-Level Display Settings.

View Modes

InDesign CS3 has four view modes accessible from either View ➤ Screen Mode or the bottom of the Tools panel (see Figure 9.6). The modes may be selected from the Tools panel by clicking and holding on the currently displayed mode, which will pop open the list of modes shown in the figure. Additionally, holding Option/Alt while clicking on the display mode button will cycle through the four modes one at a time. If you have your Tools panel set to two-column display, Normal mode will be a button by itself, while the three preview modes share a place beside it.

Normal The normal working mode. Pasteboard, guides, and grids are shown, as are frame edges, text threads, and other elements if individually set to show on the View menu.

Preview Only the page trim area is visible, and pasteboard, guides, grids, frame edges, text threads, and so on are all hidden. If an object is selected in Preview mode, its bounding box will become visible.

Bleed Similar to Preview with the addition of including the bleed area in the view.

Slug Similar to Preview, but includes both the bleed and slug areas.

FIGURE 9.6
View Modes at the
bottom of the Tools
panel

Guides and Grids

Well-designed documents are based on grids, and grids are composed of ruler guides.

Guide Basics

If you've used InDesign or just about any other creative application for any length of time, you probably already know how to create ruler guides. Click and drag from either the vertical or horizontal ruler; wherever you release the mouse button, a guide will drop. Beyond this fundamental, InDesign has a few tricks of which you might not be aware.

Hold Cmd/Ctrl while dragging from the vertex of the two rulers to simultaneously create both a horizontal and vertical guide (see Figure 9.7). Dragging the intersection point of the rulers *without* holding Cmd/Ctrl, moves the origin or zero-point of the ruler.

FIGURE 9.7
Dragging from the
intersection of the
rulers while holding
Cmd/Ctrl creates
both guides at once.

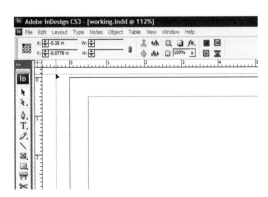

Where a guide falls depends on the location of your cursor when you let go of the mouse button. If your cursor is within a page, the guide will land on, and be unique to, that page. However, if your cursor is out on the pasteboard at the time, dropping a horizontal guide from the horizontal ruler will create a guide that spans the spread, however many pages that may be.

Guides can be hidden and shown in a couple of ways. First, of course, they disappear in Preview mode. They can also be deliberately hidden by changing the toggle command Hide/Show Guides from View ➤ Grids & Guides or by using the equivalent keyboard shortcut of Cmd+;/Ctrl+;. Additionally, because guides are considered objects of a sort in InDesign, they are layer specific; hiding a layer on which guides were drawn hides the guides as well.

By default, guides are locked. Once dragged from the ruler, they cannot be repositioned. However, deselecting the command View ➤ Grids & Guides ➤ Lock Guides releases them to be selected, deleted, and repositioned like any other object. In fact, once selected, guides can be precisely positioned using the X and Y positioning fields on the Transform or Control panels.

To delete a guide, unlock it, select it, and press the Delete or Backspace key. Alternatively, dragging a guide back into its spawning ruler will also delete it.

Guide Options

Snapping is the term given to the behavior of an object jumping toward a guide when the object is dragged to within a certain distance of the guide. By default, the distance, or snap zone, is 4 pixels. When an object is dragged to within 4 pixels of a guide, the object will jump the remaining distance and align the closest edge to the guide.

To disable snapping, choose View ➤ Grids & Guides ➤ Snap to Guides to toggle the behavior off or on.

To change the snap zone distance, go to the Guides & Pasteboard pane of the InDesign CS3 preferences and change the Snap to Zone value (see Figure 9.8).

Not listed in the Preferences Guides & Pasteboard pane is an option to change the color of normally cyan ruler guides. Their color *can* be changed, however, just not in Preferences where the colors of margin, column, and other special purpose guidelines can be set. Instead, the color of ruler guides must be set through the Ruler Guides dialog (Layout ➤ Ruler Guides; see Figure 9.9). When you're changing the color of ruler guides, any existing guides will remain unaltered; the color chosen here will apply only to guides created after clicking the OK button.

FIGURE 9.8
Guides & Pasteboard pane of the Preferences tab and the Snap to Zone field

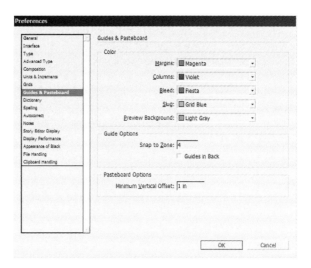

FIGURE 9.9
Ruler Guides
options

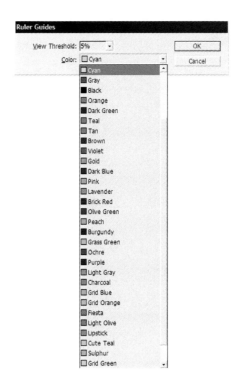

The View Threshold field refers to the minimum magnification level at which guides will be visible. Thus, setting a View Threshold value of 100% means that, should you zoom out to 50% of the actual document size, ruler guides will be hidden.

Guides Manager

Similar to QuarkXPress's Guides Manager utility is InDesign's Create Guides dialog (Layout ➤ Create Guides; see Figure 9.10). Here, several ruler guides can be created and precisely placed in one quick operation by specifying the number of rows (horizontal guides) and columns (vertical guides) and the distance between them (gutters). Additional options allow you to delete any guides already on the page and to limit the rows and columns to fit within the page or margins. The ability to preview via the check box under Cancel lets you proof your grid before creation.

FIGURE 9.10
The Create Guides
dialog

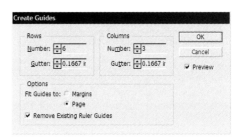

Document Grid

Document grids, like guides, are non-printing, but they assist in precise layout composition and alignment of objects on the page. Unlike guides, both document grids and baseline grids are document-wide, nonlayered objects, meaning they appear on every page of the document and cannot be assigned to, or hidden by, a specific layer. Additionally, grids cannot be changed per master page; they are one grid per document, for every page of a document.

Working with a document grid is like working on graph paper (see Figure 9.11). It covers both pages of a spread and the pasteboard.

FIGURE 9.11
The document grid shown

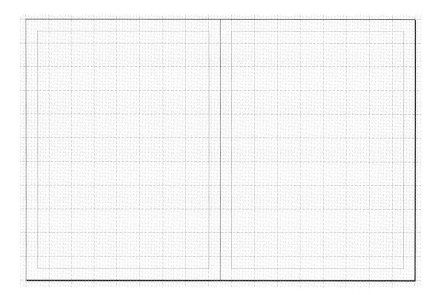

Document grid properties are controlled from the lower section of the Grids pane in Preferences (see Figure 9.12). Here, the color of grid lines can be changed, as well as the distance between cells. In the Gridline Every fields, enter the distance between grid lines, such as 1 in or 72 pt. Set the number of minor (lighter) grid subdivision lines and cells by changing the Subdivisions fields. To create subdivisions every 10th of one inch, for example, set subdivisions to 10.

Grid measurements begin at the page edge closest to the ruler origin. Thus, if the ruler's zero-point is the top-left corner of a spread, the grid will begin counting out the Gridline Every and Subdivision field values from the top-left corner of the spread, separating the document to the right and down. For example, a Gridline Every value of 1 inch evenly divides an 11×17-inch spread 11 times vertically and 17 times horizontally. Custom or mismatched page sizes (e.g., the spread's left page is a different size that its right page) can make grids not so equally divisible. In such cases, change the ruler origin from Spread to Page or Spine in the Preferences Units & Increments pane.

When a facing-pages document includes a single-page spread, as is typically page 1, the grid will begin at the top-left edge of the page even though, in the absence of a left-read page, the right-read page does not begin at the ruler zero-point but begins instead at the spine.

By default, grids are placed furthest back in the Z-order; any object placed on the page will obscure the grid behind it. To reverse that behavior, placing the grid in front of all objects and thus always unobscured, uncheck Grids in Back on the Grids pane of Preferences.

Show or hide document grid lines, and decide whether objects snap to those grid lines, using the appropriate commands on the View ➤ Grids & Guides menu.

FIGURE 9.12
Grid options

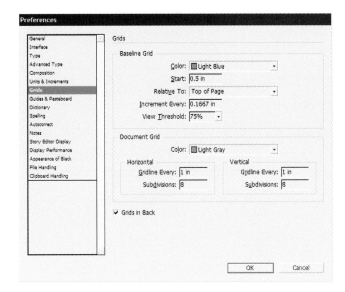

Baseline Grid

Baseline grids are horizontal-only rulings used to evenly array lines of text vertically. Whereas the document grid looks like graph paper, baseline grids appear to be ruled notebook paper (see Figure 9.13). Baseline grids do not extend beyond the spread into the pasteboard.

FIGURE 9.13
A document with a
baseline grid

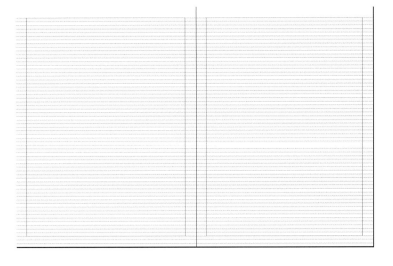

GLOBAL BASELINE GRID

A global, document-wide baseline grid is set up in the Preferences on the Grids pane above Document Grid options (see Figure 9.14).

FIGURE 9.14
Baseline Grid
options

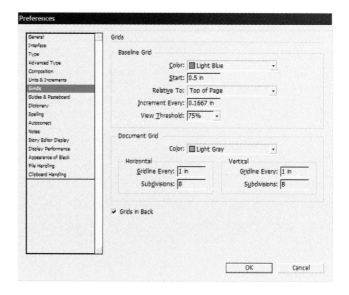

In addition to color, several settings are needed to build a usable baseline grid.

Start Enter here as a measurement the distance to offset the top of the baseline grid from the top of the page or the top margin on the page, as specified by the Relative To drop-down.

Increment Every The vertical distance between baseline grid lines. This should be equal to your text's leading value. Note that this field accepts any measurement notation InDesign understands—inches, points, pica, millimeters, and so on. Thus, if your document measurement system is set to inches, you can still enter in the Increment Every field a point value such as 14.4 pt. InDesign will automatically perform the conversion from the entered measurement system to the system it expects in this field, that being the overall document measurement system as set on the Units & Increments pane.

View Threshold Similar to the same option in Ruler Guide options, View Threshold sets the minimum magnification level at which baseline grid lines will be visible. Using the default value of 75%, for instance, grid lines will remain visible when zooming the document view to 75% magnification or greater, but zooming out to 50% will hide the lines for an unobstructed view of the document.

Although there is a Show Baseline Grid command under View ➤ Grids & Guides, there is not a snap to command. Choosing Snap to Guides also causes objects to snap to the baseline grid.

PER TEXT FRAME BASELINE GRID

New to InDesign CS3 is the ability to specify separate baseline grids per text frame. Whereas a global baseline grid is ideal for balanced column text such as would be used by a newspaper or book, a single, spread-wide baseline grid has limited utility to layouts featuring columns or frames of text set on different leading values.

To use a per frame baseline grid, select the text frame and open the Text Frame Options from Object ➢ Text Frame Options. On the Baseline Options tab, activate the frame-specific baseline grid by checking Use Custom Baseline Grid (see Figure 9.15). With the exception of the Color field, which includes the option to match grid lines to the layer color, all other options are equivalent to their counterparts in Preferences.

FIGURE 9.15

Text frame Baseline Options tab

Layers

Every print professional knows how to use layers. After all, they've been around since Photoshop 4 and remained fundamentally unchanged in InDesign, QuarkXPress, Illustrator, Flash, and scores of other applications. Still, there a few nuances to using layers that may have escaped your notice.

◆ Unlike in QuarkXPress, master pages *can* contain layers.

◆ Layers are document-wide, meaning that turning off Layer 1 on page 6 turns it and any objects it contains off in all pages of the document. If any master page objects are included on Layer 1, they will be hidden from document pages as well.

◆ Layers may be reordered on the Layers panel by dragging and dropping.

◆ Holding Option+Shift/Alt+Shift while clicking on the layer visibility icon (the eyeball) hides all layers except the one being clicked on. Doing it again shows them all again.

◆ Similarly, holding Option+Shift/Alt+Shift while clicking on the layer lock icon locks or unlocks all layers except the layer being clicked on.

◆ When one or more objects are selected on a layer, a tiny colored square called the Selection Indicator appears beside the layer name on the Layers panel (see Figure 9.16). Dragging the Selection Indicator from its current location and dropping it on another layer moves the selected object(s) to the target layer.

FIGURE 9.16
Colored selection
indicators denote
that one or more
objects on the layer
are selected.

- Grouping objects that are arranged individually on several layers collects them all onto the uppermost layer. Ungrouping does not return them to their original layers.

- When pasting objects copied from multiple layers in the current or another document, the Paste Remembers Layers command on the Layers panel's flyout menu will faithfully arrange objects on layers as in the source. If the same layers do not already exist, InDesign will create them to hold the pasted objects.

- Entire layers—including all objects upon them—can be defined as non-printing in the Layer Options accessible from the Layers panel flyout menu (see Figure 9.17).

FIGURE 9.17
Layer Options dialog

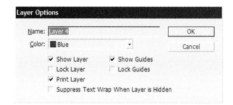

- Guides can be selectively hidden or locked on a per-layer basis in Layer Options.

- Even when the layer is hidden, any objects assigned a text wrap will continue to influence type on other layers. Checking Suppress Text Wrap when Layer is Hidden in the Layer Options prevents the phantom wrapping behavior.

- Empty layers can quickly be selected and subsequently deleted using the Select Unused Layers command on the Layers panel flyout menu.

- The Merge Layers command on the Layers panel flyout menu will combine two or more layers highlighted in the Layers panel, placing all of their objects together on a single layer.

- Dragging an existing layer (or multiple layers) and dropping it atop the New Layer button at the bottom of the Layers panel will create an exact duplicate the layer and its objects.

- Right-click on a layer in the Layers panel to access several common commands as well as the unique Select Items on Layer command that selects all objects contained on the target layer.

Books

InDesign is ideally suited to working with longer documents, but longer documents are not ideally worked upon as a single document. Rather, they are easier, faster, and more securely worked on by one or multiple compositors or designers as a series of documents connected via an InDesign Book file.

A Book file, in InDesign parlance, is a connection between otherwise separate InDesign documents. That connection allows the multiple documents to be treated and managed as a single, cohesive document—a book—including page numbers that run sequentially from one to the next and the ability to preflight, print, and export to PDF all documents joined by the Book file as a single unit.

Begin a Book File

Create a new Book file by choosing File ➢ New ➢ Book. When prompted, specify the location and name of the INDB Book file. Typically, the Book file should be named after the project title, and saved in the same location as the documents that are or will be components of the project. When you click Save, the Book panel will appear (see Figure 9.18).

FIGURE 9.18
A new, empty book on the Book panel

As with the Layers panel, the major area of a Book panel is a list, in this case a list of documents. Add documents to the book by clicking the Add Documents plus button at the bottom, which will generate an Open-style Add Documents dialog. In Add Documents, browse to the InDesign documents you want to add to the book. Multiple documents may be added concurrently using standard multiple selection modifier keys such as Cmd/Ctrl to select nonsequential files and Shift for sequential selections. Click Open and the selected document(s) will be added to the Book panel. Additional documents, including those in other folders or on other disks, can be added to the book the same way. The Book file, not their respective locations on disk, ties them together.

Although a Book file can only manage a single book, any given document may belong to any number of Book files.

If any documents were created by earlier versions of InDesign, or are InDesign Interchange Format INX files, checking Automatic Document Conversion on the panel flyout menu will convert documents to CS3 format while adding them to the Book file.

Remove documents from the book by highlighting them and clicking the Remove Document minus sign button.

Save changes to the Book file by clicking the disklike icon at the bottom or choose Save Book or Save Book As from the Book panel flyout menu.

To open a document that is part of a book, double-click the document in the list.

Page, Chapter, and Section Numbering

Upon adding documents to a book, the first thing you should notice is the document page numbers, which, unless you've specifically changed the section and numbering options in the individual documents, will be sequential—the numbers on the right in Figure 9.19. Each InDesign document, unless changed in the document's Numbering & Sections Options, always begins numbering at page 1. Once booked, however, only the document first in the list begins with page number 1. Each successive document then begins numbering its pages where the previous left off.

FIGURE 9.19

Documents on a
Book panel automatically synchronize
and increment page
numbers.

If page numbers show on the document pages themselves, placed there with the Current Page Number special character marker on the page or master page, the page numbers will update to reflect what is shown in the Book panel. If documents, and thus page numbers, are not in the correct order, simply rearrange the documents in the list by dragging and dropping. Page numbers will instantly resynchronize to match the new document order. They will also update to reflect any pages added to, or subtracted from, documents in the book.

Fine control over continuous or other page numbering begins with Book Page Numbering Options, opened from the panel's flyout menu (see Figure 9.20). In the Book Page Numbering Options dialog, Page Order offers a direct continuance of page numbering, continuing on the next odd, or next even, pages, and the option to insert blank pages to help with page number jumps to odd or even pages.

FIGURE 9.20

The Book Page
Numbering Options
dialog

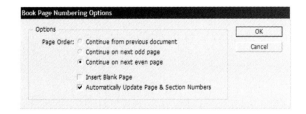

Turn off Automatically Update Page & Section Numbers to stop InDesign from automatically updating page and section numbers when documents page counts change or their order in the list is altered. With this option off, use the commands on the Update Numbering menu on the Book panel's flyout menu to manually update page and section, chapter and paragraph, or all numbers when needed.

The Document Numbering Options command on the panel menu controls page numbering and section options for a highlighted document. The Document Numbering Options dialog is nigh identical to the Numbering & Section Options dialog available on the Layout menu in any single document (see Figure 9.21).

FIGURE 9.21
Document Number-
ing Options

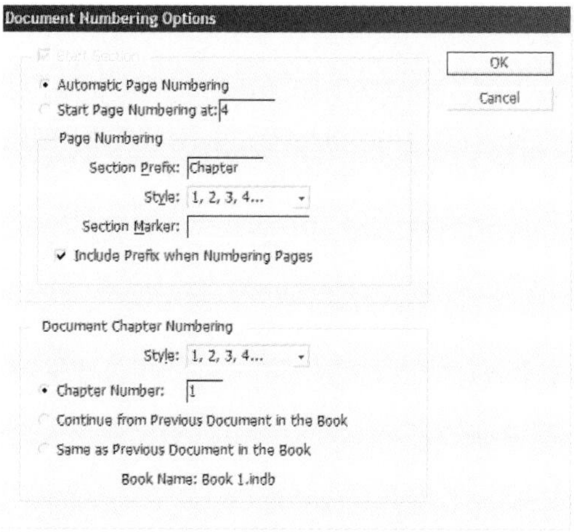

Automatic Page Numbering Continues numbering from the previous document in the book. If the selected document is the first, it will begin numbering from page 1, subject to the other options below.

Start Page Numbering At Choose this option and enter a number in the field to the right to begin numbering pages in the document at a certain point.

Section Prefix The Section Prefix field enables you to prepend up to eight characters—letters and/or numbers—to section numbers. For instance, enter **Part-** here to create page numbering and TOC entries such as *Part-X Page Y*.

Style Choose the style for section numbers, either Arabic or upper- or lowercase Roman or alphabetic.

Section Marker Documents may be divided into multiple sections—for instance, in this book, there are sections for front matter pages, the TOC, the chapters, the glossary, and the index. Each section of a publication may be numbered or formatted differently, and the page number may also be prefixed with a section-specific bit of information like *Section 1: Page 19*.

To insert a section marker in a text frame—say, in the folio beside the page number—place the Type tool cursor in the appropriate place in the text frame and choose Type ➤ Insert Special Character ➤ Markers ➤ Section Marker. The section marker that appears will be specific to that section.

What you enter in the Section Marker field is what appears as the section marker inserted into a text frame. For instance, to identify the glossary of a book, you may enter *Glossary*. When the section marker appears on the page, it will then display as *Glossary* in the folio, header, or wherever you've placed the marker. If the Include Prefix when Numbering Pages box is checked, it will also insert the section marker as part of automatic page numbers created using Type ➤ Insert Special Character ➤ Markers ➤ Current Page Number.

Document Chapter Numbering Although a single document may contain several sections, it may only contain, or be, a single chapter. In this section, choose the format of chapter number-ing, the chapter number for the current document, and whether to continue growing from, or mirror, the chapter number of the previous document in the book. The latter option is used to define two or more documents at being part of the same chapter.

Chapter numbers are made visible on the page by inserting the Chapter Number text variable (text variables are covered in Chapter 11, "Efficiency").

Synchronizing Book Styles

One of the most useful aspects of Book files is the ability to synchronize nearly all styles and common elements between all documents in the book, thus eliminating inconsistencies in such things as paragraph, character, object, and table styles as well as swatches, text variables, and trap presets.

Every book must have a style source—a single document in the Book file whose styles and options all other documents will adopt. Typically and by default, the first document added to the book is the style source, but that can be changed. The leftmost column in the Book panel is the Style Source Indicator column (see Figure 9.22). The style source is whichever document bears the icons in its Style Source Indicator column. To make a different document the style source, click once in the Style Source Indicator column beside the document name.

FIGURE 9.22
In this Book panel,
the icon on the left
indicates that the
Front Matter docu-
ment is the book's
style source.

Synchronizing—copying styles from the source to one or more destination documents—is accomplished in a couple of ways. Select one or more documents in the Book panel, and then click the Synchronize button, the leftmost button, at the bottom of the Book panel. Or choose Synchronize Selected Documents or Synchronize Book from the panel flyout menu. The former appears when fewer than all documents are selected, and the latter when all or none are selected.

Set which types of data are synchronized by selecting Synchronize Options from the Book panel flyout menu. In the Synchronize Options dialog, check all types of styles and data to be matched across the documents (see Figure 9.23). Note that, by default, only Master Pages is unchecked and thus not set to synchronize.

FIGURE 9.23
Synchronize options
specify what will be
copied from the
style source to other
documents in the
book.

During synchronization, any conflicting or changed styles in the book documents will be over-written by those copied from the style source. There will be no prompt or way to undo the synchronization. Synchronization may occur whether documents are opened or closed. To preserve styles unique to a document, change style names in the document to unique names (e.g., change Body Text to Body Text Ch 3).

Outputting Books

Although synchronizing common formatting and even structural elements between multiple documents reduces the work involved in managing and prepping for print-related documents, the ability to treat many documents as one when outputting is the largest advantage of Book files. In fact, that ability alone justifies the existence and utility of Book files even when you're working with documents that don't have sequential page numbers or page numbers at all. Check out the sidebar "Book File Portfolio Eases Proposal and Bid Generation and Provides a Competitive Edge" for a real-world qualifier of that last statement.

 **Real World Scenario**

BOOK FILE PORTFOLIO EASES PROPOSAL AND BID GENERATION AND PROVIDES A COMPETITIVE EDGE

Book files are useful for many things. For example, a designer (me) who values economy of motion might connect a dozen separate portfolio pieces together via a Book file. The portfolio documents wouldn't be sequentially numbered and certainly wouldn't want style synchronization. However, instead of opening and printing each of the 12 documents individually, documents that are most likely spread throughout numerous folders on the designer's computer, you can print the entire portfolio, exported to PDF, or packaged with a single command—possibly without opening even one of the documents.

I do this very thing, as a matter of fact. Often, as part of a project bid, I'll be asked to send samples of my previous work. Like most of you reading this, my body of work is broad and varied, but a client or prospective client only needs to see what is relevant to the project at hand. You wouldn't, for instance, send photos of product packages you've designed to accompany a proposal to design a travel agency's intranet website. Each set of work samples should usually be a subset of your entire portfolio, with pieces chosen specifically to convey to the client, *I know how to do the job you want done. See? I've done similar work before to the benefit of other clients.*

Some of my previous work is in native InDesign documents, some in QuarkXPress documents, some in Illustrator, PDF, websites, scans, image files, and so on. I include all of them in an InDesign Book file. QuarkXPress documents I convert to InDesign just for the portfolio, for websites I take screen shots, and for all other assets, I simply place them into their own InDesign documents. All of these purpose-built INDD documents reside in a single folder with the INDB Book file, but the pieces that are natively InDesign, as well as the placed assets, remain wherever they happen to live on my hard drives—client folders, other project folders, and so on; the Book file will happily manage them from multiple locations. All the pieces I might want to send along with any proposal or request for samples are added to, and managed through, a single Book file. When I need to print or create a PDF to accompany a proposal, I choose the relevant pieces, select them individually in my portfolio's Book panel, and then choose Print Selected Documents or Export Selected Documents to PDF from the panel's flyout menu.

For instance, if I'm proposing a magazine template design, I include only my previous magazine work; if I'm bidding on an advertising job, I include primarily ad-centric prior work; and so on. I selectively choose which pieces to include from the Book panel that includes all of my portfolio pieces. When I output, the result is a single print job or PDF, displaying only what I want included and nothing I don't, without the hassle of hunting down and printing each piece individually or converting each to a PDF and then combining PDFs.

Naturally, in addition to being less work, it's faster to open a single file—the INDB—select a few entries, and then choose one menu command—than to deal with the documents individually. Thus I can nearly always get a PDF of selected pieces in front of a prospective client's eyes while we're still on the initial phone call. And that gives me an edge over any competitors the client called before me, competitors who promised to get some samples together and off to the client the next day or even later in the same day.

With all or no documents selected in the Book panel, choose one of the following commands:

Preflight Book to preflight the entire book, checking, and reporting any problems related to, images, fonts, plug-ins, and so forth, all documents in the book.

Package Book for Print to collect all of the book's constituent documents, including their image assets and fonts, together in a single folder ready for archiving or delivery to a print provider. The INDB Book file itself will also be added to the project's package folder, with links updated to point to the location of the new document copies.

Export Book to PDF to build a single, continuous PDF from all documents in the book.

Print Book to print the entire book, one document after the other, as if all were but a single document. The printer icon at the bottom of the Book panel is a shortcut to this command.

Export Book to Digital Editions to convert all documents into a single e-book using the new XHTML-based Digital Editions format compatible with Adobe Digital Editions reader software. Note that the resulting document will carry an .epub file extension.

Any of the above operations can also be performed selectively, on only some of the documents within the Book file, by selecting only the desired documents before executing the command. Note that when only some of the documents are selected on the Book panel, the above commands change to Preflight Selected Documents, Package Selected Documents for Print, and so on.

Indexing

Another strength of Book files is their ability to build a unified index of topics or table of contents incorporating information from within all the documents referenced from the Book file. Of course, an index can also be built in stand-alone documents. In fact, it must begin in each document, and then, if the document is part of a book, one index may be generated incorporating keywords and/or cross-references from all chapters.

Creating Index Entries

Indexing begins by inserting invisible index marker characters and associating them with topics, or keywords, to create index entries. It's done on the Index panel (Window ➢ Type & Tables ➢ Index), which has two modes (see Figure 9.24). Both Reference and Topic mode display all indexed topics in the preview area, using alphabetic heading lists, but only Reference mode includes page numbers. Topic, by contrast, streamlines the list by leaving out page numbers, enabling faster editing of the text of topics that will appear in a generated index in the printed publication. Click the expansion triangles to spin open or closed the levels of the list. Hold Cmd/Ctrl when clicking on an expansion triangle to open or close all levels below, and contained by, the current entry or header.

FIGURE 9.24
The two modes of the Index panel. At left, Reference mode; Topic mode at right.

Create a new index entry by highlighting a word or phrase, or by simply inserting the cursor at the desired point in the story, and then clicking the Create New Index Entry button at the bottom of the Index panel (or pressing Cmd+U/Ctrl+U). Up will pop the New Page Reference dialog (see Figure 9.25); if text was highlighted, it will automatically fill in the first topic level field.

FIGURE 9.25
The New Page Reference dialog

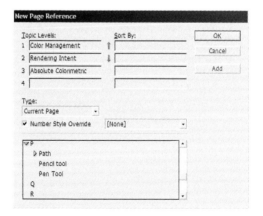

For a simple, single-level index, only the first topic level entry is needed. However, if you want to create a more detailed, hierarchical index—something like Figure 9.26—use several Topic Levels fields. For instance, to place the reference to entry *Blue* under the heading of *Colors* in the generated index, enter Colors in the Topic Levels 1 field, and Blue in Topic Levels 2. Later, when adding the reference for *Red*, *Green*, *Cyan*, *Magenta*, *Yellow*, and *Black*, you'll do the same, with Colors in the

Topic Levels 1 field and each color beneath in the Topic Levels 2 field. To add a third level of organization—for example, *RGB* or *CMYK*, into which each colors will be distributed—place the color name in the Topic Levels 2 field and the color name, the actual reference, in the Topic Levels 3 field. The up and down arrows to the right of the Topic Levels fields alter the order of the field contents, moving them up or down in priority.

FIGURE 9.26
A multilevel index (right) and the New Page Reference entry details for one (left)

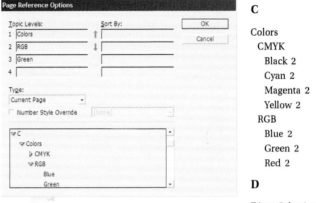

The Sort By fields enable changing the order in which topics sort in the generated index. For instance, the entry *The New York Times*, if unchanged, would sort among the *T*s, which is stylistically incorrect. It *should* sort among the *N*s (as *New York Times, The*), so in the Sort By field, enter *N*, *New*, or *New York Times*—as much as is needed to properly sort the entry among other *N* entries in the index. Each topic level may have its own Sort By key of one or more characters.

In many cases, you'll actually want to create two or more index entries for the same term, each with different Sort By options, to overcome confusion inherent in the term and help readers find the topic. Take for example the entry *Commonwealth of Massachusetts* in a book about politics, the law, geography, or history of New England. Most people in the United States—including most of the state's residents and former residents (which includes yours truly)—tend to look for information about the Commonwealth of Massachusetts simply by looking under *M* in the index. A large minority of others, those accustomed to dealing with the state's formal title, will head to the *C*s. A good indexer would therefore list *Commonwealth of Massachusetts* under both *C* and *M*.

The Type drop-down list presents several options for specifying the type of reference, some of which will cause an additional field to appear beside the Type field:

Current Page Includes beside the entry text the current, single page number on which the index marker appears.

To Next Style Change Creates in the generated index an entry that may be a single page number or a range (e.g., *Blue 10–13*). Whether the entry is single page or a range, and, if the latter, how long the range is, is determined by the distance between the marker and the next paragraph style change. For example, if the index marker is placed within a heading assigned to the paragraph style *Heading 1*, the index reference will continue through the last character assigned to the *Heading 1* style.

To Next Use of Style Creates in the generated index an entry that may be a single page number or a range (e.g., *Blue 10–13*). Whether the entry is single page or a range, and, if the latter, how long the range is, is determined by the distance between the marker and the next use of the same paragraph style. For example, if the index marker is placed within a heading assigned to the paragraph style *Heading 1*, the index reference will continue until the next instance of the *Heading 1* style in the story.

To End of Story Creates in the generated index an entry that may be a single page number or a range (e.g., *Blue 10–13*). From the marker point until the end of the story will be considered one complete entry. Note that additional index entries may appear within the range as well.

To End of Document Creates in the generated index an entry that may be a single page number or a range (e.g., *Blue 10–13*). From the marker point until the end of the document, inclusive of all stories, will be considered one complete entry. Note that additional index entries may appear within the range as well.

To End of Section Creates in the generated index an entry that may be a single page number or a range (e.g., *Blue 10–13*). From the marker point until the end of the section as defined in Layout ➤ Numbering & Section Options will be considered one complete entry. Note that additional index entries may appear within the range as well.

For Next # of Paragraphs Creates in the generated index an entry that may be a single page number or a range (e.g., *Blue 10–13*) depending upon how many pages the specified number of paragraphs covers. Choosing this option causes another field to appear wherein you may enter the number of paragraphs.

For Next # of Pages Creates in the generated index a ranged entry for the specified number of pages. Choosing this option causes another field to appear wherein you may enter the number of pages.

Suppress Page Range Creates an index entry without a page number.

The last six options on the Type menu create cross-references to other index entries, suppressing page numbers and ranges on the current entry. Cross-references are discussed further on in this chapter.

Check the Number Style Override check box and choose a character style from the drop-down menu to assign a character style to the particular index entry, enabling formatting unique from other index entries.

At the bottom of the dialog is a reiteration of the Index panel's Topic mode view for use in matching topic levels or referencing name, capitalization, and other considerations. Topics may be dragged from the list and dropped into the Topic Level fields.

The New Page Reference dialog includes four buttons: OK, Cancel, Add, and Add All. Cancel's function is self-evident, but the other three require definition.

OK Add the current reference and close the dialog.

Add Add the current reference *without* closing the dialog, leaving it ready for manual input of additional references to the same place in the document.

Add All Add the current reference *and* additional, separate references for all other instances of the same word or phrase in the document. Add All is enabled only if text is highlighted in the document and uses for every reference the same options as set in the New Page Reference dialog—the same Topic Levels, Sort By, Type, and Number Style Override options.

InDesign's Add All indexing is case sensitive, meaning that *Polyglot* and *polyglot* are considered different words and different index entries. Similarly, singular and plural word forms are considered separate topics, such as in the case of *language* and *languages*.

Once a reference has been created, it will appear on the Index panel. In Reference mode, each individual reference or instance will list its page number or range of pages (depending on the options selected in New Page Reference dialog). Instead of page numbers, some entries may display special codes indicating that they may not be included in the generated index (see Figure 9.27).

FIGURE 9.27
Index entries that
may not appear in
the generated index

HL Entries are contained on a hidden layer. While the index is generated (later in this section), such entries may be included or excluded regardless of whether the text is actually visible on the page.

Master (Name of Master Page) Entries are contained on a master page and will not become part of the index.

PB Entries are located on the pasteboard and will not become part of the index.

PN Entries are overset and do not appear on a page. Such entries can be included in the generated index, but without page numbers.

Managing Index Entries

Double-clicking on the *topic*—the entry name of any level—in either mode of the Index panel opens the Topic Options dialog, which has a truncated set of options from the Page Reference Options (see Figure 9.28). However, double-clicking on the *reference*—the page number beneath the topic in Reference mode—re-opens the Page Reference Options.

The Index panel flyout menu presents additional options for managing topics and references, including the ability to duplicate or delete them.

Choosing the Capitalize command opens the Capitalize dialog (see Figure 9.29), enabling capitalizing the first letter of the selected topic, the selected topic and any subtopics it may contain, all topics in the Level 1 position, or all topics and subtopics regardless of level. If you don't choose to capitalize, index entries will look exactly like they do in the text of the document—e.g., *cyan* will be listed in the index as *cyan* rather than *Cyan*.

FIGURE 9.28

Editing a topic in
Topic Options (left)
and editing a refer-
ence for an instance
of the topic in Page
Reference Options
(right)

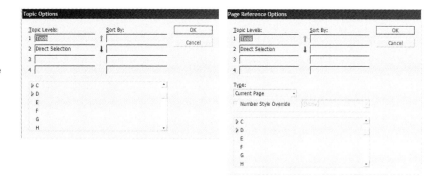

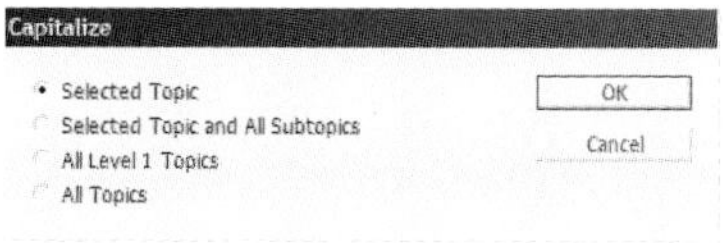

FIGURE 9.29

The Capitalize
dialog

In the Sort Options dialog, also accessible from the panel menu, choose the options for sorting on the list in the generated index (see Figure 9.30). Check the box beside each glyph type
InDesign should consider when sorting index entries. Change their order by clicking on a particular type once to highlight and then using the up or down arrows in the bottom-right corner of
the dialog.

FIGURE 9.30

Sort Options

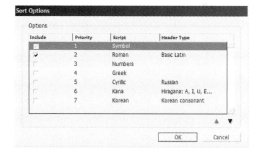

The Remove Unused Topics and Show Unused Topics commands enable cleaning up the list,
though this is for your convenience only; topics added to the Index panel but not actually used in
the document, perhaps because their containing text was deleted, will not be included in the generated index. Go to Selected Marker is a command that jumps the document view to focus on the
instance of the index entry within the document or book.

Long documents tend to generate long indices, and moving around on the Index panel requires
a great deal of scrolling. To ameliorate this problem, InDesign includes a field for searching within
the entries list, although it's hidden by default. At the bottom of the Index panel flyout menu, the
Show Find Field command exposes the Find field at the top of the panel (see Figure 9.31). Type in
all or part of an expected topic name, and click either the Find Next Entry in Panel or Find Previous Entry in Panel down or up arrows.

FIGURE 9.31
The Index Panel
with the Find field
shown

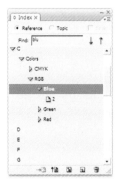

When an index entry is created, it adds into the story at the point of creation an invisible character called the index marker. As you can see in Figure 9.32, with hidden characters shown (Type ➤ Show Hidden Characters), index markers are distinctive marks consisting of two vertically aligned dots underscored by two converging, slanted marks below the baseline. It looks rather like a colon teetering atop a caret. The extra dots are the invisible characters marking spaces between words.

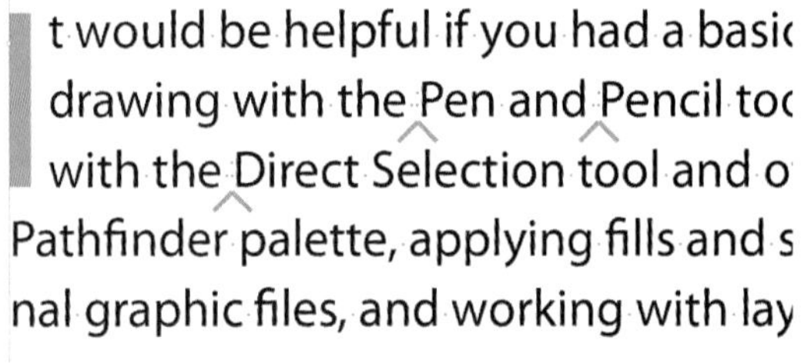

FIGURE 9.32
When hidden char-
acters are shown,
index markers
become visible.

t would be helpful if you had a basic
drawing with the Pen and Pencil toc
with the Direct Selection tool and o
Pathfinder palette, applying fills and s
nal graphic files, and working with lay

For all intents and purposes, index markers are text characters that can be deleted or moved like any other glyph in the story, either in the layout or in Story Editor. Indexing should only be done on final stage or near final stage documents, and once references are created, text should *always* be edited with Show Hidden Characters active to prevent accidental deletion or misplacement of index markers. Markers appear *before* the word or phrase they reference. Deleting a marker removes its reference from the Index panel. Because markers are treated as their own characters, highlighting and then dragging (if drag and drop of text is enabled) or cutting only the text the Index panel references but not the index marker itself will *not* automatically move the marker as well. Instead, the text will move, but the entry reference—and thus the generated index—will point to the location of the marker, which may vary greatly from the actual location of the keyword or phrase.

Cross-References

Instead of, or in addition to, listing a page number, cross-references point to other index entries. Equal or substitution cross-references are those that do not list their own page number, referring the reader to a different index entry—for example, *VDP, see Variable Data Printing*. Additional or related cross-references are those important and unique enough that they *do* list page numbers, but they also suggest to the reader additional, related information via a pointer to another index entry (e.g., *Film 496-497, see also Plate*). Both are relatively easy to create in the Index panel, and have several options to choose from.

Cross-references are created the same way as normal index references—by choosing a marker insertion point, clicking the Create a New Index Entry button, and completing the options in the New Page Reference dialog. The difference is in the Type menu. Cross-references use the six options located below the line in the Type menu (see Figure 9.33). Selecting any of the cross-reference types also exposes the Referenced field. In the Topic Levels fields, set the topic(s) for the cross-reference entry itself, and then, in the Referenced field, set the separate, end-level topic to which the cross-reference will point. For example, to create an index entry that will print as *Designorati.com 35, See also Author's Projects*, you would set Topic Levels 1 to *Designorati.com*, the Type field to See [also], and put *Author's Projects* within the Referenced field.

FIGURE 9.33

Cross-reference types in the New Page Reference dialog's Type menu

Following are the six cross-reference types:

See Produces a substitution or redirection cross-reference with no page number. Example: *InDesignVSQuark.com, See QuarkVSInDesign.com*

See Also Produces a related cross-reference, listing both a page number for the current topic and a referral to an additional index entry. Example: *WorkflowCreative.com, See also REVdrink.com.*

See [Also] Creates *either* a See or See Also type of cross-reference depending on whether a topic or page reference is selected, respectively. This option is adaptable to changes in the topic or page reference and is therefore generally preferred to See or See Also.

See Herein Although rarely used outside legal and scientific publications, this option creates a reference to another topic beneath the level of the current topic in the hierarchy. For example, a level 1 topic of *Author's Projects* might contain a second-level subtopic for, among others, *Personal Websites. Personal Websites* might contain only a single, third-level topic named *IamPariah.com*. In that case, the index entry for *Personal Websites* itself might then forgo a page reference and simply direct readers to the *IamPariah.com* entry.

See Also Herein Similar to See Herein except that both a page number for the current topic and a referral to the contained topic are included.

Custom Cross-Reference Choosing this option activates a third field, Custom, which replaces connective cross-reference text like *See, See Also,* and *See Herein* with any custom text. In the following example, the Custom field was set to "gain efficiency by reading": *InDesign CS3 1-800, gain efficiency by reading Mastering InDesign CS3 for Print Design and Production.* Like See [Also], Custom Cross-Reference chooses whether to include a page number based on whether the cross-reference topic references another entry's topic or page reference.

Power Indexing

A few parting words about creating and managing index entries efficiently.

Add a New Reference to an Existing Topic When the topic is already listed in the Index panel and already contains references, you can create a new reference and index marker for additional locations without going through the New Page Reference dialog. Place the cursor at the location for the new index marker or highlight text. On the Index panel, drag one of the existing topic references and drop it atop the Create a New Index Entry button. A new reference will be added beneath the topic pointing to the index marker the act creates at the cursor location or ahead of the highlighted text.

Creating Topics First Topics can be created ahead of references. With no text selected, switch to Topic mode on the Index panel and click the Create a New Index Entry button at the bottom of the panel. In the New Topic panel, fill in the Topic Levels and/or Sort By fields, and choose OK or Add. With topics pre-created, adding entry references becomes easier and more consistent.

Loading Topics If you already have the topics defined in another InDesign document, perhaps from a previously completed, similar project or from another document in the same book, choose Import Topics from the Index panel flyout menu, navigate to the InDesign document containing the topics, select, and click Open. The topics will populate the current document's Index panel.

Book Indices When the current document is part of a book, the Book check box at the top of the Index panel lights up and becomes selectable. Check the box, and the Index panel will recognize book page and section numbering options, updating the index list to include topics and references in other documents throughout the book, and generate a book-aware index.

Rapid Indexing After the initial entry reference is added, subsequent entries can be added from the keyboard easily. Just select the next word or phrase, or place the text cursor at the marker insertion point, and press Cmd+Option+Shift+[/Ctrl+Alt+Shift+[. A new reference will be created instantly, and you can move on to the next index entry. All the same New Page Reference dialog options will be reused from the last manual entry, so be wary if you set up unique options the last time.

Indexing Proper Names Proper names should typically be indexed as last name first (e.g., *Smith, John*) although InDesign indexes the typical entry exactly as it appears in the story (e.g., *John Smith*). While it can be overridden in the New Page Reference dialog either at creation time or later by double-clicking the entry on the Index panel, it's much faster to use the keyboard shortcut: Cmd+Option+Shift+] /Ctrl+Alt+Shift+].

Indexing Multipart Proper Names The above method of indexing proper names works by placing the last word first in the entry sort order and the generated index. A name like *James Earl Jones* would thus correctly list as *Jones, James Earl*. It *won't*, however, work for multipart names like publications (e.g., *The Corellian Times*), ships (e.g., *The Fool's Gold*), titled names (e.g., *Capt. Rail Magnor*), suffixed names (e.g., *Chris Dreyer, Jr.*) and other names or phrases of more than two words where the last is not the properly listed and sorted first word. To get around this limitation, force InDesign to *treat* certain pairings as single words by inserting a nonbreaking space (Type ➤ Insert White Space ➤ Nonbreaking Space) between the words that should not break in the story text prior to creating the index reference. For instance, insert a nonbreaking space between *Fool's* and *Gold*, forcing InDesign to consider *Fool's Gold* as a single, continuous word. When that happens, using the Cmd+Option+Shift+]/Ctrl+Alt+Shift+] short-cut *will* properly place the article (or title, first name, etc.) at the end of the entry, separated by a comma (e.g., *Fool's Gold, The*). An added benefit to using a nonbreaking space to marry multi-part proper nouns is that, when the noun approaches the end of a text line, InDesign will not break the name between the words; it will wrap the entered name unbroken to the next line.

Generating the Index

At any point following or during index entry definition, the index may be generated and placed like any story, in the current document or, in the case of a book, as a wholly separate document.

Select Generate Index from the Index panel's flyout menu. The Generate Index dialog has two states separated by the More/Less Options button (see Figure 9.34).

FIGURE 9.34
The Generate Index dialog, in initial mode (above) and with options shown (below)

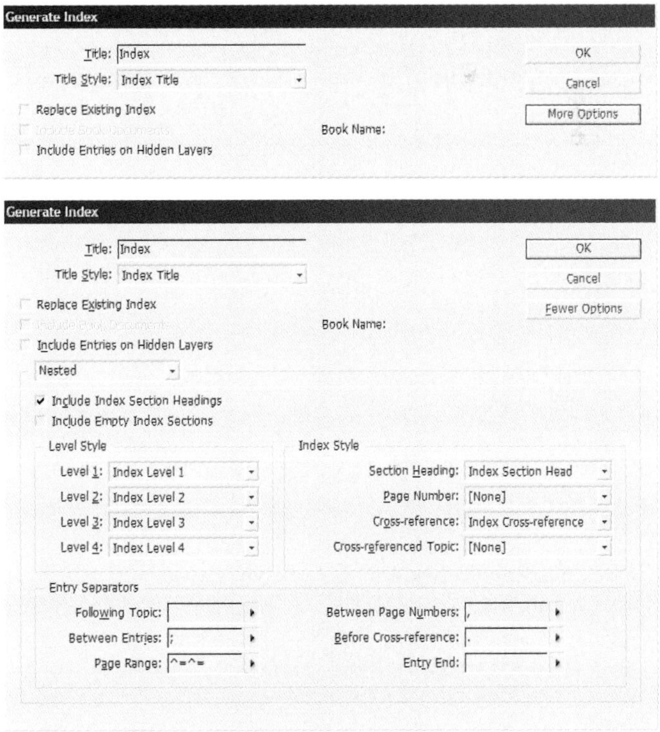

What it all means:

Title When the index is generated and placed, it will have a title as the first line of the story. By default, the title will be *Index*, but it can be anything you like. Leaving the Title field blank removes the title from the generated index entirely, without leaving a blank carriage return where it would have been.

Title Style Choose from this list the paragraph style for the index title (if there is a title). InDesign will, upon first generating the index, build new paragraph styles for the various parts of an index, beginning with the Index Title style. So, if you want your index title formatted uniquely, just leave the Title Style field at its default, and, after generating the index, modify the Index Title paragraph style manually.

Replace Existing Index Available if you have already generated an index at least once. InDesign does not *update* an index as might, say, Microsoft Word, which uses fields instead of story text for indices. Rather, regenerating an index in InDesign *replaces* the previous index entirely, generating a completely new story but within the same text frame(s) as the previous version. Note that it is because of the replacement that you do not want to manually format text within an index story; upon regeneration and replacement, all local overrides will be wiped away. Edit the various index paragraph styles and/or use the Number Style Override option in the Page Reference Options dialog instead.

Include Book Documents Available only if the Book option is checked on the face of the Index panel, this option will generate a single index for all documents within an InDesign book.

Include Entries on Hidden Layers Enables including index entries whose markers are on hidden or turned-off layers.

Nested or Run-In Indices come in two structural formats, nested, where each entry and subentry appears on its own line followed by a carriage return, and run-in, where only the top-level entry has its own line and all subentries are incorporated into it in a paragraph (see Figure 9.35).

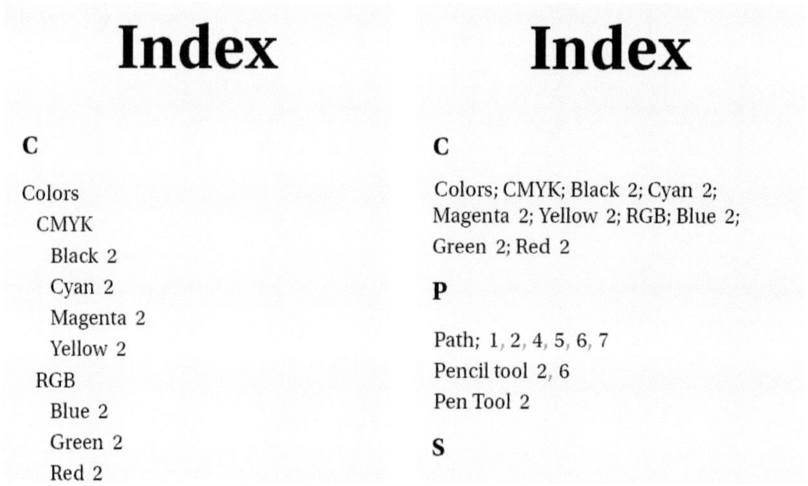

FIGURE 9.35
At left, a nested index places each entry on its own line. At right, a run-in index combines all lower levels of topics into a single paragraph.

Index

C

Colors
  CMYK
    Black 2
    Cyan 2
    Magenta 2
    Yellow 2
  RGB
    Blue 2
    Green 2
    Red 2

Index

C

Colors; CMYK; Black 2; Cyan 2;
Magenta 2; Yellow 2; RGB; Blue 2;
Green 2; Red 2

P

Path; 1, 2, 4, 5, 6, 7
Pencil tool 2, 6
Pen Tool 2

S

Include Index Section Headings Toggles whether to include alphanumeric headings such as *A, B, C,* and so on ahead of their constituent entries within the index.

Include Empty Index Sections When Include Index Section Headings is checked, only those headings containing entries will be included. For example, if there are no index entries beginning with *A,* no *A* heading will be created. The Include Empty Index Sections check box forces the inclusion of headings—like *A*—even if there are no entries within.

Level Style As with the title style, InDesign will generate paragraph styles titled Index Level 1, Index Level 2, Index Level 3, and Index Level 4 to format their respective levels in the generated index. If you already have one or more paragraph styles defined to use for the various levels, specify the styles here via the drop-down menus.

Index Style Change the formatting of various elements of the index from these four options. For instance, to make page numbers green and bold while their corresponding reference text is black and not bold, create a character style for bold and green, and assign it to the element in the Page Number field. Section Heading is a paragraph style while the rest are character styles.

Entry Separators Either by using the modified Special Characters menus accessed by clicking the arrow to the right of each field or by typing directly into the fields, specify the various separators and connectors for each index element.

◆ Following Topic is a symbol or glyph to be inserted after each topic. When using the run-in index style, it's often wise to separate the topic from its subtopics and references with some form of white space—various spaces or a tab (^t).

◆ Again, more useful in run-in indices where entries appear on the same line, the Between Entries creates a separator between successive entries.

◆ The character used between ranges of pages (e.g., *35–38*). The default symbol (^=) in the Page Range field signifies an en dash, which, rather than the hyphen, is the proper punctuation for a range of numbers.

◆ Between Page Numbers is the text between nonranged page numbers. For instance, when an index entry is listed on multiple pages such as *Sernpidal 79, 202, 206*, the comma and space is the Between Page Numbers separator.

◆ Before Cross-Reference separates an entry from a cross-reference. In the example *Belkadan. See Also Tingel Arm*, the period and space after *Belkadan* is the Before Cross-Reference field value.

◆ To end an entry, after all text, with a special symbol, space, or text, enter it in the Entry End field.

When you click OK, the Index story will be loaded into the cursor, ready for placement. It places like any other story, with the same auto-, semi-auto-, and manual-flow options. When working with a book of multiple documents, place the index into a new, purpose-built document, and then add that document into the book through the Book panel.

If the document(s) or index entries are changed, select one or more frames in the Index story, return to the Generate Index dialog, and regenerate with the Replace Existing Index option checked. InDesign will then update the index to reflect recent changes.

New paragraph styles created by the index generation process are listed on the Paragraph Styles panel and may be edited at will to customize the look of the generated index. Any regeneration updates to the index will not replace the styles, thus your changes will survive. It will, however, remove local overrides (formatting changes that are not part of the styles).

Tables of Contents

Creating a table of contents for the document (or book) is far less involved than creating an index, as long as you practiced efficient composition by assigning paragraph styles to the elements that should be listed within the TOC. The basis for TOC generation is paragraph styles—in other words, any text assigned to *this* style or *that* style will be included or excluded based solely on its paragraph style.

InDesign supports an unlimited number of tables of contents. Thus, you can create the standard document TOC like the one at the front of this book, but you can also create per-chapter tables of contents, lists of figures or tables, alphabetized lists of topics, and just about anything else you can imagine (and manage with paragraph styles).

Begin creating the table of contents by choosing Layout ➤ Table of Contents, which opens the Table of Contents dialog (see Figure 9.36). Click the More Options button to reveal the full depth of the dialog.

FIGURE 9.36

The Table of Contents dialog (with More Options shown)

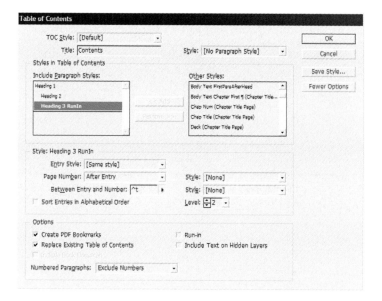

TOC Style All of the options incorporated into the Table of Contents dialog may be saved as a preset called a TOC style. After setting the options, click the Save Style button on the right and give the style a name. TOC styles can also be created and edited from Layout ➤ Table of Contents Styles. If a style has been pre-created, it will appear in the TOC Style list; choose it, and all the below options will fill in with their style-defined values.

Title When the TOC is generated and placed, it will have a title as the first line of the story. By default, the title will be *Contents*, but it can be anything you like. Leaving the Title field blank removes the title from the generated TOC entirely, without leaving a blank carriage return where it would have been.

Style The paragraph style for formatting the TOC title.

Styles in Table of Contents This is the crux of creating a TOC. On the right, in the Other Styles list, are all the paragraph styles defined in the document. Click a style on the right to highlight it, then use the Add button to move it to the left, the Include Paragraph Styles list. You can also double-click an entry in either column to move it to the other.

Each style included on the left will cause all text assigned to that style to be listed in the resulting TOC; styles not in the list will not have their dependent text referenced by the TOC. The order of styles in the Include list establishes the TOC hierarchy. In other words, the first listed style is the most important, highest level of the generated TOC, with the next appearing below it, the next below that, and so on. If you insert styles in the wrong order, drag them up or down in the list just as you reorder styles in the Paragraph or Character styles panels. But you must also change their Level value in the Style section below. Figure 9.37 shows an example of the Include Paragraph Styles list and the TOC it would generate.

FIGURE 9.37

At left, the Include Paragraph Styles list, and at right, the result in the generated TOC

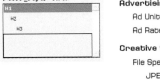

Advertising Rates and Ad Dimensions. 5

    Ad Units and Placements 5

    Ad Rates (Per Month) 5

Creative Specifications 6

    File Specifications 6

        JPEG 6

        GIF. 6

        Flash 6

    Animation Specifications: 7

    Transmission of Files. 7

Click to highlight a style in the Include Paragraph Styles to set its options below in the Style section. Each included style may have its own entry style, page number options, and so on.

Entry Style When the TOC is generated, the text for each entry level can have its own paragraph style. Unlike index styles, InDesign will not automatically created level-based paragraph styles. You'll need to pre-create your TOC styles and then select them from the list for each Include Paragraph Style option. Alternatively, leave the default of [Same Style] to include the same style in the TOC as on the document pages.

Page Number Choose whether to place the page number before or after the entry text or to omit the page number entirely. With the Style field to the right, the page number can be given its own character style for customized formatting.

Between Entry and Number The separator character or characters to appear between the entry text and its number (or number and text, if the page number is placed before the text). The pop-up menu to the right offers many symbols, markers, and special characters. To create a leader dot separator, specify a tab (^t) in the field and then modify the paragraph style (outside of the Table of Contents dialog) to include a leader dot separator at that tab stop. The drop-down menu at the right allows assigning a character style to the separator itself, enabling any unique styling to be applied to just the separator.

Sort Entries in Alphabetical Order By default, and in most cases, TOC entries are sorted in order of appearance in the document. However, especially when creating documents for electronic distribution as PDFs, this option opens numerous other possible uses for the Table of Contents feature beyond creating a standard TOC. When InDesign generates a TOC, it creates hyperlinks connecting the TOC entries to the text they reference. Exporting to PDF preserves these hyperlinks, enabling a reader of such a PDF to click on the TOC entry and jump to the content. Thus, the option to sort entries alphabetically rather than logically opens the possibilities of creating vastly different lists such as lists of product names, personnel referenced in the document, or even a replacement for a standard index—without having to manually create index entries. The only significant limitation to using the Table of Contents functions in place of index and other features is that InDesign's Table of Contents is dependent upon paragraph styles; it cannot create an entry from a character style or a specific word in the middle of a paragraph.

Level In a hierarchal TOC such as the one at the front of this book, entries from each successive style are considered inferior to their predecessors—Heading 1, for instance is superior to Heading 2, which is superior to Heading 3. The Level field defines that hierarchy. As each style is moved from the Other Styles list to the Include Paragraph Styles list, InDesign automatically assigns a successive level. If you have reordered the include list by dragging and dropping, you will also need to change the level for each affected style.

Often successive TOC entries are indented as visual cues to the hierarchy. The Include list mimics the hierarchy by indenting styles in the list, giving *you* a visual representation of how the generated TOC may look. The Level field is nonexclusive, meaning that you are not required to have only a single level 1 or level 2 entry. If you have two or more equally important styles, they can all be set to the same level.

Create PDF Bookmarks Similar to the way each entry on the page itself will be hyperlinked to its content, InDesign can automatically generate PDF bookmarks, which are hidden until PDF export time. Adding these, and choosing to include bookmarks when exporting to PDF, creates something akin to Figure 9.38—a Bookmarks panel sidebar TOC-style list of topics that, when clicked in Acrobat or Adobe Reader, become hot links and jump the reader to the referenced content.

Replace Existing Table of Contents If you have previously generated and placed a TOC, this option will replace (not update) it. When using the Table of Contents to build separate styles of tables, you want this option unchecked.

Include Book Documents When generating a TOC for documents managed through an InDesign Book file, check this option to generate a single TOC that points to all instances of the included paragraph styles in all documents within the book.

Run-In By default, all TOC entries are given their own line, with a carriage return at the end. An alternate style is to use the run-in method that, like the same option within an index, only separated by top-level styles. All entries lower in the hierarchy than the top will be placed together in a paragraph (see Figure 9.39).

FIGURE 9.38
The TOC-style book-marks in this InDesign-created document were built by checking the Create PDF Book-marks options in the Table of Contents dialog.

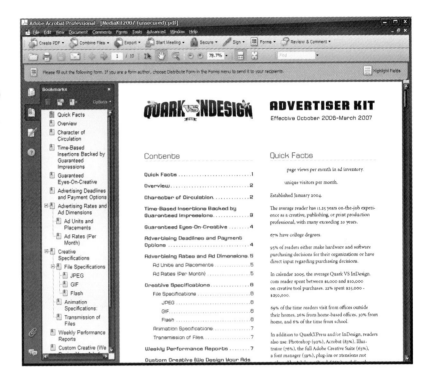

FIGURE 9.39
Left, a standard hier-archical TOC places each successive level of entry on its own line. A run-in ver-sion (right) places only the top level on its own and bunches lower levels together in a paragraph.

Contents

Quick Facts 1

Overview 2

Character of Circulation 2

Time-Based Insertions Backed by Guaranteed Impressions 3

Guaranteed Eyes-On-Creative 4

Advertising Deadlines and Payment Options 4

Advertising Rates and Ad Dimensions . 5

Ad Units and Placements 5

Ad Rates (Per Month) 5

Creative Specifications 6

File Specifications 6

JPEG 6

GIF 6

Flash 6

Animation Specifications: 7

Transmission of Files 7

Weekly Performance Reports 7

Contents

Quick Facts . . . . 1; Overview 2; Character of Circulation . . . . 2; Time-Based Insertions Backed by Guaranteed Impressions . . . . 3; Guaranteed Eyes-On-Creative . . . . 4; Advertising Deadlines and Payment Options . . . . . . 4; Advertising Rates and Ad Dimensions . 5

Ad Units and Placements 5; Ad Rates (Per Month) 5

Creative Specifications 6

File Specifications 6

JPEG . . . . 6; GIF 6; Flash 6

Animation Specifications: 7; Transmission of Files 7

Weekly Performance Reports 7; Custom Creative (We Design Your Ads for You). 7; Terms & Conditions 8; Insertion Order 9; Diagram of Ad Units & Placements 10

Include Text on Hidden Layers Choose whether to include in the TOC text on hidden layers.

Numbered Paragraphs New to CS3, this option tells InDesign how to handle paragraphs that have been numbered through the List and Numbering functions. Note that InDesign does not recognize numbers that have been converted to standard text and will include them in the TOC regardless of this setting. The options are as follows:

Include Full Paragraph lists the text in the TOC exactly as it appears on the page, with all text automatic numbering intact. For example, the ninth table in a chapter whose number is defined within the paragraph Numbering options to include the prefix *Table 9* and whose table caption is *KDY Capital-Class Products* will list in both the main story and the TOC as *Table 9.9 KDY Capital-Class Products*.

Include Numbers Only ignores the text in the paragraph and includes only the automatic number and any prefixes. For example, to include a TOC entry for *Table 9.9* without the table's caption, choose Include Numbers Only.

Exclude Numbers includes in the TOC the text of the paragraph but not the automatic number. The TOC output using the above example would therefore be simply *KDY Capital-Class Products*.

Click OK to return to the document with a loaded cursor ready to place the TOC story, which may be placed and flowed like any story. If any stories in the document contain overset text assigned to the included styles, you will be prompted after clicking OK whether to include those instances in the TOC.

Unlike an index, tables of contents don't have their own panel. Also unlike an index, you needn't go through the entire generate process to update a TOC. Instead, select a text frame holding the TOC style, and choose Layout ➢ Update Table of Contents. Shortly, an alert dialog will inform you that the table of contents has been updated successfully.

When creating a comprehensive TOC for book documents, it's often better to place the TOC into its own self-contained document and to add that document to the Book panel.

The Bottom Line

Interact with Documents Visually, Change Zoom Level, View Modes, and Display Performance InDesign provides numerous means of changing the way you interact with documents, how fast they move, how you see them, and what you see.

Master It Open any InDesign document containing text and images on the same page. Open three different views of the same document, arranged simultaneously onscreen, zooming all to fit the page within the document window, and compare the views according to the following options:

◆ View 1: Preview mode with High-Quality Display display performance.

◆ View 2: Layout mode with Fast Display display performance.

◆ View 3: Bleed mode with Typical Display display performance.

Build and Manage Grids and Guides   The foundation of any well-laid-out document is a well-thought-out grid.

>   **Master It**   Create a new document and build a grid on the master page consisting of six equal columns and three equal rows within the page margins. Once that's done, apportion the top row into three equal sections.

Create and Manage Book Files   Often one person finds it easier to work on longer documents by breaking them up into chapters or sections and connecting them via a Book file. For work-groups wherein different people are responsible for different sections of the document, a Book file is essential to productivity.

>   **Master It**   Working alone or in a group, create at least three InDesign documents of several pages of text each. Save each document, and then create a Book file to connect the documents. Finally, create a single PDF from the entire book.

Index Terms and Create an Index   An index helps readers find content. From simple keyword lists to complex, multilevel, topic-driven indices, InDesign handles them all, marrying index entries to referenced text through index markers.

>   **Master It**   Open or create an InDesign document containing a story of at least three pages in length. Working through the document, create index entries and cross-references for at least 10 words, one of which should be a word that repeats numerous times throughout the story (use a common word such as *the* if needed). Once the terms are indexed, generate and place the index story on a new page.

Create Tables of Contents   Tables of contents direct readers in logical or virtually any order to content, and InDesign's TOC options are varied and powerful for myriad uses.

>   **Master It**   Open or quickly create a rudimentary book-style document containing body text and several heading paragraphs utilizing at least two levels of headings. Create and assign paragraph styles for the body text and headings. Using what you've learned in this chapter, generate and place a hierarchal TOC.

Chapter 10

Output

The purest and most thoughtful minds are those which love colour the most.

— *John Ruskin (1819–1900), artist, author, poet, and art critic*

At the end of the day, it's all about printing. Everything we do in InDesign leads up to that ultimate, defining moment when we watch with bated breath as the job rolls off the press.

Up until now, we've talked about the design functions of InDesign (with a watchful eye on the end goal). Now let's get into what happens after design, into the ramp-up for and, ultimately, the execution of outputting a job.

Defining and reproducing color is an area in which print design and production is ever striving for improvement. From better color management to newer, larger ink gamuts like Pantone Hexachrome, from transparency to RGB workflows, each new release of InDesign raises the bar on color creativity, control, and output. InDesign CS3 is no exception. Let's start with managing color.

In this chapter, you will learn to:

◆ Configure color management on documents and images

◆ Soft proof documents to screen

◆ Preflight, package, and output to print with managed inks and trapping

Managing Color

Any discussion about using and outputting color in for-print design or production must begin with a primer on color management—without a doubt the single most confusing (and boring) subject in this exciting business of ours. I'll be concise and (hopefully) entertaining to mitigate the boredom while dispelling the confusion. At the very least, look at it this way: We're getting color management out of the way. It's all downhill from here.

The Purpose of Color Management

My favorite analogy to explain the basic concept of, and need for, color management is the United Nations.

Consider the five permanent members of the UN Security Council—the United States, the United Kingdom, Russia, France, and China. Among these five delegates are spoken four languages—English, Russian, French, and Mandarin Chinese. In order for the delegates to discuss an issue, each has a team of interpreters translating what is said by other delegates into English, Russian, French, or Mandarin Chinese. Thus, France's delegate to the United Nations listens not to the actual words of Russia's delegate but to a faithful translation by UN aides. The U.K.'s delegate listens in English, the U.S. delegate also listens in English (but without extraneous *U*s), and so on. Each member nation's delegate speaks in his native tongue while the other delegates listen to translations in their native languages. Thus, the hard-working translators convert meticulously from one of the four different languages to another; every delegate hears precisely the same questions and words, just in different syllables.

Let's elect some new delegates to the UN Security Council's permanent seats.

China's seat we'll give up to Scanneravia. The island Kingdom of InDesign will take over for France. PDF Nation and the United States of Offset will oust the U.K. and U.S. Instead of Russia, let's install a delegate from the nation of the Federation of Independent Proof Printers.

We now have a new council of delegates, all of whom still speak completely different languages and still require their interpreters. But, you can't just advertise in the *New York Times* classifieds for "scanner to offset press interpreter wanted, must also speak PDF." How will these five delegates talk about a color photograph being moved from E6 slide to scanner, the digital output imported into an InDesign layout, and then the output sent on to proof print, PDF, and finally ink on paper? What if the discussion needs to include some or all of the other 10 UN Security Council member states? Maybe the photo needs some touch-up in Photoshopia before being flown to the Kingdom of InDesign? Or, after PDF Nation ships the document containing the photo, will that document pass through the Province of Web Press or need to be discussed by the myriad dialects of Printeria's Monitors?

How are all these delegates supposed to accurately discuss a project, and each contribute to its completion, if none of them can understand any other's interpretation of color? They can't. They need interpreters to faithfully translate from the language of one into that of another, to tell the Kingdom of InDesign what Scanneravia is saying about red, green, and blue or hue, saturation, and luminosity. Without a translator, one might swap purple for blue, mix some green into the yellow, or turn bright white into a dirty, aged cream.

That's where a *color management system* (*CMS*) comes in. Once a CMS learns the unique language of each speaker as well as the language of the listener, it can translate between the two. First, the CMS must be taught each language by the delegate—device—in the form of an *ICC profile*. The ICC profile is a Rosetta stone, defining a given device's color language in the universal but unutterable dialect of math. Given any two of these ICC profiles, the CMS can translate color described by one in its native language to the native language of another. The end result is that, although two incompatible languages are used, the CMS ensures that both devices see, render, and maintain the same colors, hues, and shades.

Color management isn't perfect. Not every device is capable of seeing all the same colors. One may clip the reds, another the blues; one may see fewer values between black and white than another; just as CMYK process inks simply can't reproduce certain shades, like pure blue.

Without color management, however, you have absolutely no predictability in color input from source (a camera, scanner, or software) onto screen, through touch-up (Photoshop), into layout (InDesign), and then to output (PDF, print, Web).

Did your digital camera accurately capture the full range of vibrant oranges in that field of flowers, or did minor defects in the camera's CCD encoder or JPEG renderer oversaturate the yellows by 6%? Without an ICC profile created for that camera, you'll never know. When you bring the image into Photoshop, you've introduced two completely new devices with their own unique methods of interpreting and rendering color—Photoshop itself and your computer monitor. Without color management, both could be completely misinterpreting the data coming in from the photograph. You could be punching up the blue in the sky over the flowers only to realize a week later when you get the printed pages back that you actually turned the sky purple.

The purpose of color management is to make the visible result of every color input device—camera, scanner, software—match the visible result of every rendering device—monitor, software, proof printer, printer—and both match the original all the way from initial capture to final output.

ICC Profiles

ICC profiles describe the possible range and unique color characteristics of a given device (hardware or software). For instance, if your digital camera oversaturates yellows by 6% (thus, undersaturating the opposite of yellow, blue, by the same amount), the ICC profile will state that defect. With that knowledge, the CMS can then pass on to other devices further down the line the instruction to swing the yellow-blue pendulum back 6% into the blue area. Thus, even though your very first step is flawed at creation time, the CMS compensates for the flaw (without actually altering the image content) to produce onscreen and printed color free of the defect and true to the color of the subject of the photo.

Even while you work on a flawed image, the CMS will be actively compensating, adjusting the results of your manual editing to account for the actual yellow oversaturation—an oversaturation that you won't see because the CMS, running Photoshop and your monitor, have compensated for it to display for you corrected colors. In the plainest English, a CMS does all the hard math for us.

Where do these Rosetta stones come from?

Each and every color-handling device renders color slightly differently—even two of the same model. At this moment, for example, I'm using dual monitors. I ordered them from the manufacturer simultaneously, and they both carry the same lot number and date of manufacturer stamped on the back. From this information it's reasonable to infer that they were made if not one right after the other, then at most only a few units apart. Despite that, they render colors differently. The one to my right shifts grays a shade or two onto the warm side. It also does a better job with midrange cyans and greens than the monitor on my left. I know because I've calibrated and profiled them.

Calibrating is the process of getting something as close as possible to its full color potential. To calibrate your monitor(s) on Mac, use ColorSync in Control Panels. On Windows, it's Microsoft's feature-poorer Image Color Management (ICM) user interface. The way to get to and configure ICM has a tendency to change over versions of Windows, so rather than walk you through four or five different methods, the fastest way is to press WIN+F1 on your keyboard and search for the phrase "color management."

Once your monitor is calibrated, you should create an ICC profile for it (or them), which is the last step in both ColorSync and ICM. InDesign and other Creative Suite software will then pick up and use the monitor profile from ColorSync or ICM, compensating for the unique characteristics of your monitor as you work.

Both ColorSync and ICM rely on your eyes to determine color, *gamma*, and white and black points, but your eyes aren't reliable color gauges. They can be influenced by ambient conditions like other lights in the vicinity, how long your monitor has been switched on, monitor light reflected off other surfaces, and the unique physical aspects of your eyes themselves. The configuration of rods and cones in our eyes are as unique as our retinal patterns. For instance, 10% of men and 1% of women have some form of color blindness, profound or subtle, and many never even notice it. Calibrations by eye—and the profiles created thereby—should be considered approximations, not accurate determinations of unique monitor color rendering. To get an accurate description of how the monitor interprets color, you need to take the subjective human out of the equation.

A software-backed hardware device that attaches to monitor screens is the best way to profile a monitor (and often calibrate in the same process). That device is a colorimeter. Note that device color characteristics change over time and should be profiled again often (monthly if not weekly).

To measure the color characteristics of a printer—anything from desktop to proof printer to digital press—use a spectrophotometer. This hardware device examines printed output, determining color fidelity on the printed page. If you go to your local Home Depot, you'll find a spectrophotometer behind the counter in the paint department. Although they often only know it as the "paint matching scanner thing," the folks at Home Depot use it to extract eight-color tint formulas from paper and other physical objects.

When it comes to profiling a printer, it gets a little more complicated. You see, a printer—inkjet, laser, web press, offset press, *everything*—lays down ink that is, more or less, the same color across all jobs and production floors. Cyan, magenta, yellow, black, Pantone colors, and all the other inks we use are predictable in their color and, for the most part, identical from one shop to the next. However, ink color is not the only factor when it comes to printed color. Equally important is the color of the *substrate*, or paper stock, on which ink is printed. Cyan, magenta, yellow, and many pre-mixed spot inks are semitransparent and are therefore tinted by the color of the substrate beneath. Laying down 100% cyan ink coverage on pure, neutral white substrate gives you pure cyan. However, putting down 100% cyan ink coverage on yellowed parchment yields a sea foam green. If you want to *see* pure cyan atop yellowed parchment, your software has to be told that fact so it can adjust the colors to compensate for the tint of the substrate. Thus, every time you print on a new substrate, you should use a new ICC profile built specifically for that output device and substrate combination.

When you don't have direct access to the color rendering device—for example, your print provider's devices or if you vended out your oversized scans—and therefore can't profile it yourself, ask the service provider for the most up-to-date ICC profile for the relevant device (on the substrate you've chosen). ICC profiles are just ASCII files with an `.icc` (or `.icm`) extension. They're easily emailed as attachments. Once you receive them, drop them into the correct system folder:

    Mac: /Library/ColorSync/Profiles
    Windows: \Windows\system32\spool\drivers\color

InDesign and other color-managed applications and technologies will automatically detect and make available in the Color Settings dialog (see below) profiles stored there, although you may have to restart the applications after installing new profiles. Once the profiles are recognized, you'll need to actually tell InDesign or whatever application you're using to use the new profiles.

By telling your creative tools about the color characteristics of your print devices, you can work in software like InDesign confident that what you see onscreen will print fairly close to the same way. Once your creative software knows your monitor, output, and input (digital camera, scanner, etc.) profiles, you will have achieved predictable color and a color-managed workflow.

(Please know that I've provided only the briefest overview of color management; entire books at least as thick as this one have been written on the subject. If you want to get serious about color fidelity in your workflow, don't stop with my introduction to the subject.)

Configure Color Management

In the past, configuring color management seemed to require a PhD in spectrophotometry. It's much easier now in general, but especially if you use InDesign as part of the Creative Suite.

BRIDGE COLOR MANAGEMENT SETS

We've talked about Adobe Bridge a couple of times now primarily in the context of asset manager. It does much more, as I intimated, and Adobe's intent is that Bridge become the central hub of your Creative Suite experience—indeed, of your entire workflow. Toward that end, color management across all individual CS3 version applications is managed inside Bridge rather than within InDesign, Photoshop, and Illustrator, which keeps color display results almost identical between the individual applications.

On the Edit menu in Bridge, you'll find Creative Suite Color Settings, which opens an extremely simplified interface to apply full sets of ICC profiles and color management options to all CS3 applications simultaneously (see Figure 10.1).

FIGURE 10.1
Creative Suite Color
Settings in Adobe
Bridge

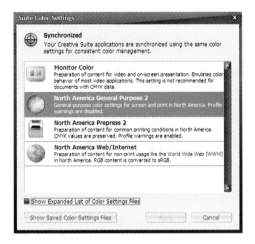

In the Suite Color Settings dialog, click on one of the four friendly, plain language sets, and then click Apply. Behind the scenes, all applications will then be synchronized to use the following color management settings:

Monitor Color Used for onscreen and video projects without CMYK colors.

RGB Working Space	(Your monitor's ICC/ICM profile)
CMYK Working Space	U.S. Web Coated (SWOP) v2
RGB Policy	Off
CMYK Policy	Off
Profile Mismatches	Ask When Opening
Missing Profiles	N/A
Rendering Intent	Relative Colorimetric
Black Point Compensation	Yes

North America General Purpose 2 Large RGB and CMYK gamut profiles compatible with (but not optimized for) typical print output devices in North America. Will *not* warn when profiles do not match.

RGB Working Space	sRGB IEC61966-2.1
CMYK Working Space	U.S. Web Coated (SWOP) v2
RGB Policy	Preserve Embedded Profiles
CMYK Policy	Preserve Numbers (Ignore Linked Profiles)
Profile Mismatches	N/A
Missing Profiles	N/A
Rendering Intent	Relative Colorimetric
Black Point Compensation	Yes

North America Prepress 2 Similar to North America General Purpose 2 except that profile mismatches *will* generate warnings, it uses a very large RGB gamut profile, and CMYK colors in linked assets will be preserved to the exclusion of separate profiles assigned to the assets.

RGB Working Space	Adobe RGB (1998)
CMYK Working Space	U.S. Web Coated (SWOP) v2
RGB Policy	Preserve Embedded Profiles
CMYK Policy	Preserve Numbers (Ignore Linked Profiles)
Profile Mismatches	Ask When Opening & When Pasting
Missing Profiles	Ask When Opening
Rendering Intent	Relative Colorimetric
Black Point Compensation	Yes

North America Web/Internet Uses a large gamut RGB profile purportedly representative of the color values available to the upper average of all monitors in use to access the Web. Any RGB colors will be converted from other profiles to the one defined as this set's RGB Working Space.

RGB Working Space	sRGB IEC61966-2.1
CMYK Working Space	U.S. Web Coated (SWOP) v2
RGB Policy	Convert to Working Space
CMYK Policy	Preserve Numbers (Ignore Linked Profiles)
Profile Mismatches	Ask When Opening & When Pasting
Missing Profiles	N/A
Rendering Intent	Relative Colorimetric
Black Point Compensation	Yes

The four sets shown in the Suite Color Settings dialog are the most common for those who can't (or won't) profile their devices to obtain specific ICC profiles.

I'm asked often—I mean, *very* often, *What are the default color management options should I use for _____ design work?*

My answer: *Profile your particular monitor, scanner, camera, and printers; use those as defaults.*

Them: *No, what* generic *profiles should I use?*

There are *no* "generics" in color management. There's no generic language to unite the delegates of the UN Security Council. The only way their discussions or color management works is if interpreters listen to input in native languages and then convert verbatim into the next delegate's or device's native language.

If, before you can leave this page, you absolutely *must* have something akin to "generic" settings in a process that has no definition for the word, then use one of the four sets above—whichever comes closest to describing what you're doing in InDesign and its brethren. And then hope really hard that the output comes close to the colors you envisioned.

The Show Expanded List of Color Settings Files toggles 19 additional pre-configured sets. A few are the sets that were available in previous incarnations of Creative Suite (for instance, North America General Purpose [1]) as well as several European or Japanese defaults similar to the first four for North America.

V2 VERSUS V1?

A number of broad ICC profiles ship with Creative Suite and its constituent applications. Many of these, for instance U.S. Web Coated (SWOP), carry the v2 version number suffix. If you've continuously upgraded from earlier Adobe applications, you may also have v1 profiles hanging around. Use the v2. The v1 ones were created with older software (Color Savvy for Adobe PressReady), whereas the v2 profiles were built using a special version of Photoshop and perform better in multistaged color conversions wherein an image is converted from one profile to another and then either back to the first or into a third profile.

A Color Management Off set is also there, but it's a misnomer—*there is no off switch* to color management in Creative Suite. Instead, this set will define defaults just like the rest, which, come press time and depending on your work, can cause either barely noticeable color shifts or disastrously wide spectral swings. It assumes that all your RGB images were created directly on your monitor, in its color space, and that everything will be printed in the U.S. Web Coated (SWOP) v2 CMYK space. Here is what Color Management Off *really* gives you:

RGB Working Space	(Your monitor's ICC/ICM profile)
CMYK Working Space	U.S. Web Coated (SWOP) v2
RGB Policy	Off (Leave it as is, without considering the source profile and without converting it to the current working space, and upon print, just convert the RGB numeric values to CMYK numeric values.)
CMYK Policy	Off (Print it as is, without considering the source or output profile and without converting it to the current working space.)
Profile Mismatches	Ask When Opening
Missing Profiles	N/A
Rendering Intent	Relative Colorimetric
Black Point Compensation	Yes

I *vigorously* advise against using Color Management Off if color matters in the least to your work. Even one of the out-of-the-box presets would be a (marginally) better option.

CUSTOMIZING COLOR MANAGEMENT

Monitor Color, North America General Purpose 2, North America Prepress 2, North America Web/Internet, and all the other color management sets are just that—sets; each one is a group of preconfigured options activated all at once. Except for Monitor Color, which picks up your monitor profile from ColorSync or ICM, all the other presets are based on wide gamut profiles that may or may not cause color shifts with specific devices. They don't take into account the color capture and rendering characteristics of the specific devices that created imagery or those that will put the imagery on paper. You'll want to change that fact, personalizing color management to the unique languages and dialects of your equipment.

Although you *should* be able to customize Creative Suite synchronized color management settings within Bridge, Adobe didn't get around to building that in. Instead, you have to take a circuitous route. Back in InDesign, go to Edit ➤ Color Settings. You'll be presented with a rather intimidating dialog (see Figure 10.2), but don't let it scare you.

FIGURE 10.2
The Color Settings dialog provides granular control over the ICC profiles and options in Creative Suite color management.

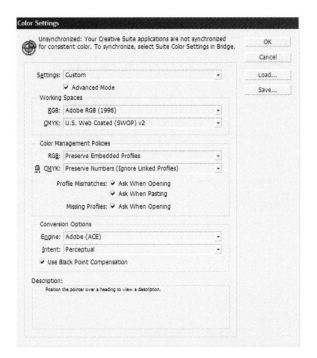

Settings

This is the list of saved color settings. The defaults examined above appear on this list, as do the expanded list installed with Creative Suite or a CS3 application and any settings you've configured and saved. On the right of the dialog is a Save button. If you manually configure any of the options discussed below, save a set for easy access later. Saving a set also writes the settings to a file on your hard drive so it can be backed up and even shared with other users or clients.

If you've received a set of color settings from someone else and it doesn't appear in the list, use the Load button to browse for it.

Advanced Mode

Check the Advanced Mode check box to toggle display of the Conversion Options section at the bottom of the dialog.

Working Spaces

Between Working Spaces and rendering Intent is the crux of color management and, assuming your profiles are well made, the real determination of the quality of your color output.

A working space is the color profile used to define the document. In a new document, with natively drawn objects, the working space becomes the source profile as a scanner's ICC becomes the source profile for scanned imagery. Any object in the profile not carrying its own separate profile will be considered created within the working space profile and thus within that color gamut or range of possible colors. See Figure 10.3 for a visual comparison of the color gamuts available in four common profiles, including those in the four default color settings sets we examined in Bridge.

FIGURE 10.3
What are color gamuts? Here are the color ranges contained within four common ICC profiles (all but the front are outlined). From the outside in: ProPhoto RGB, AdobeRGB (1998), sRGB, and U.S. Web Coated (SWOP) v2.

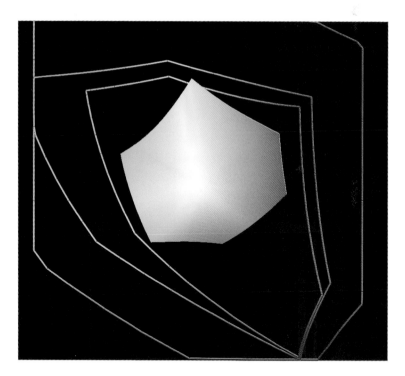

If you've never seen this diagram before, it can be shocking to see how few colors really are within the range of process inks—the innermost polygon. U.S. Web Coated (SWOP) v2 is a large CMYK gamut and covers most process printers in North America. Except for a little reach out into the yellow range, it—and CMYK in general—fits wholly within even the small, World Wide Web–based sRGB profile. AdobeRGB (1998) is beyond that, with ProPhoto RGB forming the gamut so massive you have to think about it to notice its outline.

Note: This book is printed in straight CMYK, so looking too closely at the values in the RGB gamut outlines is like watching a commercial for a widescreen HD TV on an old RCA tube set and marveling at how much crisper and more vibrant the HD picture appears.

When a document is converted from RGB to CMYK, all the colors that fall in the black beyond U.S. Web Coated (SWOP) v2 have to be mapped to values that lie within it. Naturally, you lose many shades of color—pure blue, for one, pure red and green for others. *How* those colors go from outside to in is determined by the rendering intent, which we'll discuss below. In general, you want to work within the largest RGB color gamut possible. The larger the gamut, the more shades and hues of color you have in your panel. While CMYK is a comparatively tiny gamut, and all printed output will be converted to CMYK (except spot colors, of course), you want to create using the most colors possible so that, when conversion *does* occur, the CMS can work to give you the smoothest possible tonal conversions.

AdobeRGB (1998) is (almost) the largest RGB, so it's a great working space to choose. ProPhoto RGB *is* the largest possible gamut, with so many colors that the human eye can't interpret them all. Use ProPhoto RGB in individual image files for long-term archival, but it's too large to work with in InDesign. In general, stick with AdobeRGB (1998) for your RGB working space. If you're designing solely for digital distribution via Web or PDF, though, use sRGB, which limits colors to those Microsoft and Hewlett-Packard determined as the high average capability of monitors surfing the Web.

Your CMYK working space *should* be the profile generated for the output device you'll use, and on the substrate you intend to use. If you don't have access to that or haven't determined the output device or paper for your job—or you're just designing something your client will arrange to be printed—use U.S. Web Coated (SWOP) v2. As CMYK gamuts go, it's roomy and yet still close to the actual output gamut of many web presses. If you know this job is going to a sheetfed press, use the U.S. Sheetfed Coated v2 or U.S. Sheetfed Uncoated v2 profile for coated or uncoated paper stock, respectively. In Figure 10.4 you can see the gamuts of all three.

FIGURE 10.4
Three common CMYK color profile gamuts. From the outside in: U.S. Sheetfed Coated v2, U.S. Web Coated (SWOP) v2, and U.S. Sheetfed Uncoated v2.

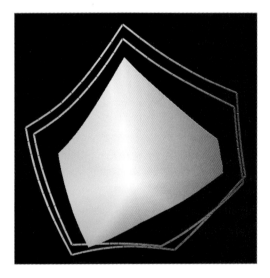

The Working Spaces drop-downs list all the RGB and CMYK device profiles installed on your system. If you don't see on the list something you recently installed, there are four possible causes:

◆ Did you close and re-open InDesign after installing the profile?

◆ Did you install the profile to the correct place? Again, that would be:
Mac: `/Library/ColorSync/Profiles`
Windows: `\Windows\system32\spool\drivers\color`

◆ The filename of the ICC profile in Finder or Explorer is not necessarily the name that appears inside an application's profile list. Instead, there's a value inside the ICC file called Internal Name. Look through the Working Spaces list(s) for something similar to the filename, or open the ICC/ICM file in a plain text editor and look for its name near the top.

◆ Could the file have been corrupted? If it was emailed, ask the sender to mail it again, but this time inside a Zip archive.

Color Management Policies

Policies are decisions you make, and directions you give to InDesign, about what to do in two situations: first, when opening InDesign documents created without embedded working space profiles such as when color management was turned off, and second, when placing images with and without their own profiles. Placed images can have their own profiles, which may differ from the working space profiles, and InDesign needs to know what you'd like done when this happens. You can specify different actions to take for RGB and CMYK and tell InDesign to prompt you with a dialog box about mismatches—checking either or both of the Profile Mismatches options—or to handle differences between image profile and document profile automatically according to your policy options by leaving the Profile Mismatches boxes unchecked. If an image doesn't have a profile at all, the Missing Profiles option tells InDesign to ask you about it or not.

Policy options include the following:

Preserve Embedded Profiles Honor profiles embedded in placed images (and InDesign documents). InDesign will manage the rest of the document and other images according to the working spaces, but it will not alter the appearance of colors or profiles in images carrying their own profiles even if it must alter the CMYK numbers in order to preserve appearance. PDF, being CMS and ICC aware, will also preserve embedded profiles when created via PDF export from InDesign. With this option selected, color conversion will be left to somewhere down the production line—usually the RIP.

Because this option values appearance over CMYK numbers, it can sometimes turn pure black into *rich black*. Check your *separations* in Separations Preview (see later in this chapter) or by printing *seps*.

Convert to Working Space Colors in the placed image will convert into the working space defined above (either RGB or CMYK), using CMS to translate with the best possible fidelity as determined by the rendering intent chosen in Conversion Options. This will force all colors to use the working space profile.

Preserve Numbers (Ignore Linked Profiles) A CMYK only option, assigned profiles in the placed image will be ignored in favor of using the CMYK numbers. Such images will then be managed onscreen by the current CMYK working space profile but printed using only their CMYK numbers.

Why would you choose Preserve Numbers (Ignore Linked Profiles)? If you have a reasonable certainty that all placed images came from the same CMYK profile—for instance, you did all the conversions from RGB in Photoshop, or they were scanned into CMYK by the same drum scanner, you'd choose Preserve Numbers. You might also want to use this if you have bad results with Preserve Embedded Profile.

You would not choose Preserve Numbers (Ignore Linked Profiles) if your CMYK images came to you from a variety of sources *and* they have embedded profiles. In that case, who knows where the CMYK numbers are? They could be completely off from where they should be and held in correct gamut solely by their embedded profiles.

Off InDesign will not color manage the placed image—in other words: all bets are off.

Engine

The Engine field chooses the color management engine. By default, this is Adobe's ACE (Adobe Color Engine), but you will have a couple of additional options. On Windows, you'll also see the Microsoft ICM, and on Mac the Apple CMM and Apply ColorSync. There isn't much difference between them. They're all based on specs from the International Color Consortium, in which Adobe's ACE developers hold the highest seats. Stick with the ACE.

Intent

The Intent drop-down box is for rendering intent—through what process, using which relational choices, should a color outside the gamut be brought into gamut for printing. There are four options:

Perceptual This rendering intent tries to maintain smooth tonal transitions between colors, even altering colors as needed, and is usually best for photographic imagery, although relative colorimetric is better nearly as often.

Saturation Most often used for business graphics or illustrations where vibrancy is more important than hue, the saturation rendering intent maps out-of-gamut colors to in-gamut colors by striving to maintain saturation values even if hues must be shifted.

Relative Colorimetric In this rendering intent, the white points of both the source gamut and the destination gamuts are aligned, and then out-of-gamut colors are scaled in gamut relative to their distance from the white point. Although some tonal variances are lost, relative colorimetric is the best of the four for maintaining color accuracy and should be considered the default rendering intent for most work.

Absolute Colorimetric As the name implies, this rendering intent maps colors to their absolute locations in the source and destination gamuts. Colors that are in gamut remain unchanged, while out-of-gamut colors are clipped to the nearest in-gamut color (along the outer edges of the gamut). Absolute Colorimetric often creates a posterization effect in images with many out-of-gamut colors or subtle tones. The advantage to this rendering intent is its ability to simulate the effects of substrate colors on ink.

Each rendering intent has its own typical uses, but do experiment with them. Rules of thumb are better in most situations, but every design is different, with its own unique considerations. Moreover, the document rendering intent is to account for objects created natively in InDesign and the majority of images. Each image can be assigned its own rendering intent individually, so you can fine-tune any for which the overall rendering intent is not ideal.

Use Black Point Compensation

Usually better left on, this option maps the pure black of the source profile (or working space) to the pure black of the destination profile (output device). For example, let's say you're employing printer and substrate combination that, after 92% gray, everything goes to pure black—the values are said to be *plugged*. Similarly, the whites get *blowout* below 14% gray. (Both of these are fairly common with low- to mid-count linescreens or highly absorbent paper like newsprint.) A press or pre-press operator knows about these limitations with equipment and will build them into the device and substrate-specific ICC profile. That profile will then tell InDesign that it doesn't have a full range in which to set black tones, that it only really has 78%. With Black Point Compensation checked, InDesign will reset the value of pure black to 92% black—the point at which the ink will plug up to *become* full black—and adjust the white point to 14%. All the values in between will shift slightly to maintain smooth transitions. In that scenario, for example, 50% gray input will shift up slightly to maybe 52 to 56% so that it stays as the midpoint between black and white, preserving tonal range.

If you modify the color settings in one application, the legend at the top of the dialog will alert you that the others in Creative Suite (assuming you have them) are out of synchronization. To ensure consistent color between InDesign, Photoshop, Illustrator, and Acrobat, you should mirror your settings from one to the rest. In the first three, you'll find this dialog in the same place—Edit ➢ Color Settings—and in Acrobat on the Color Management pane of its Preferences (Cmd+K/Ctrl+K). Note that Photoshop has additional controls in its Color Settings dialog, primarily dealing with gamma and spot control, while Acrobat has fewer controls than InDesign.

Per-Image Color Management

As noted earlier, each image placed, pasted, or dropped into InDesign can have its own output color profile and rendering intent. They can come in that way or be changed once in the document. Moreover, changes to an image profile within InDesign only change its output from InDesign; they do not alter the original asset on disk. To change an image profile and/or rendering intent, with an image selected, choose Object ➢ Image Color Settings or Graphics ➢ Image Color Settings from the context sensitive menu to access the Image Color Settings dialog (see Figure 10.5). These are the same controls you access when placing color-managed image files with Show Import Options checked.

FIGURE 10.5
Image Color Settings control color profile and rendering intent per image

Changing Color Profiles

In Color Settings (or Bridge's Suite Color Settings), you define the color management options for the InDesign *application* and any new documents created while those options are in effect. What you do in there, however, will not alter color management options on existing documents. To alter the working spaces, rendering intents, and so on you need Assign Profiles or Convert to Profile, which are both found on the Edit menu below Color Settings. The difference between assigning and converting profiles is a tricky, hair-thin line.

REMOVE OR ASSIGN DOCUMENT PROFILES

Assign Profiles (see Figure 10.6) first lets you strip off any profiles assigned to the document, including those previously assigned through this dialog, added via Convert to Profile, or in effect as the working spaces at document creation time. When you discard profiles, be careful: They will probably look fine onscreen because they'll use the current Color Settings working spaces and rendering intents while the document is opened, but the document itself will not carry those profiles with it to press or someone else's computer.

FIGURE 10.6

Assign Profiles enables removing or assigning profiles as well as different rendering intents per image type.

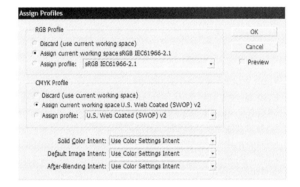

When you assign the current working space (below the Discard radio buttons) or assign another profile from the drop-down menus, the RGB and CMYK color definitions will remain unchanged, although they will appear different onscreen. Assigning a profile doesn't remap colors with a rendering intent; it effectively tells InDesign that the colors were wrong to begin with, that *these* are what they should have been.

Although the ability to both discard and assign new profiles is frequently useful, what is *really* cool about Assign Profiles is the bottom three drop-down boxes that let you set rendering by image *type*. Solid Color Intent defines the rendering intent for vector artwork, either natively drawn or imported somehow (place, paste, drop). Default Image Intent is the default raster or bitmap image rendering intent. Lastly, the confusingly named After-Blending Intent is the rendering intent to apply to objects that interact through transparency. For instance, if one image is overlaid on another and set to the Multiply blending mode, then the two objects will be mapped to in-gamut colors using the rendering intent specified here if different from the intent in Color Settings.

The handy Preview check box lets you see the results of your changes with the ability to hit cancel and revert to the pre–Assign Profiles state.

CONVERT TO PROFILE

Converting a profile is the opposite of *assigning* a profile. Instead of telling InDesign *the colors were off, they should have been this*, Convert to Profile (see Figure 10.7) says, *The color definitions were right—and they look fine onscreen—but now I need them mapped to this other gamut in* this *color profile*. As the dialog indicates, Convert to Profile fires up the UN translator to convert the document's speech from the Source Space color language into the Destination Space color language.

FIGURE 10.7
In Convert to Profile, document working spaces and rendering intent may be remapped.

When would you use Convert to Profile? A good example is when you have to begin a project ahead of knowing how it will output and on what substrate. In that case, you'd set the document working spaces to large gamut profiles like Adobe RGB (1998) and U.S. Web Coated (SWOP) v2. Later, once you've received the correct ICC profile for the printer and substrate, use Convert to Profile to remap the CMYK profile to that particular profile. Just be careful: Every time you convert the document profile, you're mapping colors between two separate gamuts, causing permanent, possibly destructive changes. *Once the document profile is converted, you can almost never go back.*

Proofing

Now that you've painstakingly configured your document's color management, it's time for that labor to bear fruit.

Proof Colors

There are three types of proofs in the print design and production business: *soft proofs* display onscreen simulating final output colors as close as RGB-based devices and a CMS can; prints to proof printers, those that are not the final output device, are called *hard proofs*; pudding proofs, the finished job, which we fervently hope matches the better of the other two. Because you were so punctilious in setting up your application, document, and individual image working spaces and rendering intents, you've unlocked the potential of InDesign's built-in soft proofing—Proof Colors.

Near the top of the View menu you'll find the Proof Colors command, which, if you choose it now, probably won't do much to your document. Above it is the Proof Setup menu, which lists the document CMYK profile, the working CMYK profile, and Custom. Choosing Custom opens the Customize Proof Condition dialog (see Figure 10.8).

FIGURE 10.8
Customize Proof Condition sets the conditions for the Proof Colors command.

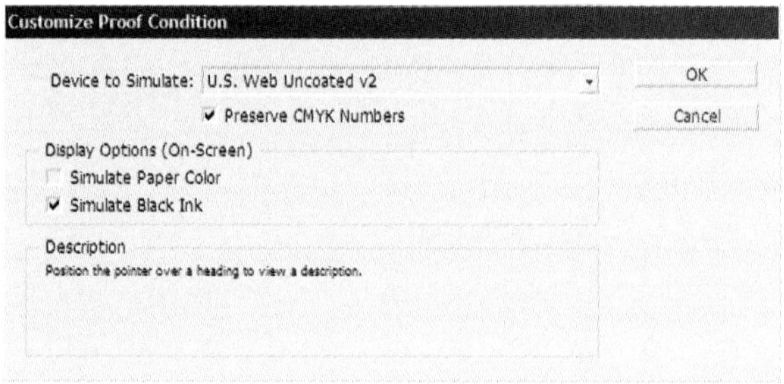

The purpose of soft proofing in InDesign is to approximate printing conditions live in the InDesign document window, which negates the old, time-consuming trick of printing to Post-Script using a specific PPD and then distilling the PostScript file into a PDF soft proof. Instead of using PPDs, the modern, color managed workflow relies on Rosetta stones—ICC profiles.

The Device to Simulate menu includes all the compatible ICC profiles installed on your system. Not just CMYK profiles, mind you; all the RGB profiles are there, too. In case you feel like broadcasting your InDesign document, you can also see what it would look like in video profiles like HDTV, PAL/SECAM, and NTSC. Actually, these are just available because InDesign is displaying every ICC/ICM profile on the system.

Selecting any profile other than the document's current working RGB or CMYK profile activates the Preserve (RGB/CMYK) Numbers check box. When Preserve Numbers is checked, InDesign will not alter the display colors of objects drawn natively in InDesign—including frames, strokes, text, and so on—nor will it alter the display color of images being managed by the document CMYK working space. Images would be so managed because either they don't have linked profiles of their own or you chose Preserve Numbers (Ignore Linked Profiles) as the CMYK (or RGB) policy in Color Settings. Unchecking the Preserve Numbers box adapts *all* colors to soft proof regardless of color management policies. If you'll be going to press with the Preserve Numbers (Ignore Linked Profiles) option, then you'll probably want to leave Preserve Numbers checked during soft proofing.

Simulate Paper Color and Simulate Black Ink read the characteristics for both as stored in the selected device profile. When Simulate Paper Color is checked, the CMS will try to ascertain the color of the paper and change the white point of the image display to match. For example, with parchment paper defined as the expected substrate for the job, all the white areas and highlights will turn yellowish tan, which will also shine through and tint areas of transparency and non-opaque inks—cyan, magenta, yellow, and many spot colors. Simulate Black Ink, which is automatically turned on if Simulate Paper Color is activated, uses the Black Ink Compensation I mentioned earlier to determine the actual value of black on the specific output device and adjusts the black point and gray values accordingly.

When you hit OK, the entire document will be thrown into soft proof or Proof Colors mode (see Figure 10.9). You can scroll around, change pages, zoom in or out, and even continue to work in Proof Colors mode, although screen redraws will be somewhat slower. To turn off soft proofing, select View ➤ Proof Colors.

FIGURE 10.9

The same document with different proof profiles selected. Left to right: Original (Proof Colors off), Europe ISO Coated FOGRA27 (simulating paper color and black ink), and U.S. Sheetfed Uncoated v2 (simulating paper color and black ink).

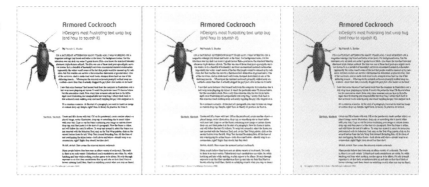

Note that InDesign will *try* to simulate spot color inks onscreen, but often that just isn't possible, particularly with special inks like PANTONE's pastel or metallic libraries. In those cases, ignore what you see onscreen and trust your swatch book. As long as you've specified the correct library and PMS color numbers, InDesign will accurately send the spot to press.

Proof Separations

Soft proofing doesn't end with simulating ink and paper colors. There's more yet to come, starting with viewing separations onscreen. If you're still printing seps to PDF, *stop*. There's a better way.

SEPARATIONS PREVIEW

I love the Proof Colors command, but Adobe's idea of putting onscreen separations into InDesign and then putting the controls for it on a panel instead of disuniting separations previews from the document in a dialog or a separate window is pure brilliance (see Figure 10.10). With these controls on a panel, the entire document can be proofed a page at a time or multiple pages at once by zooming out. Options can be changed on-the-fly—say, to get a deep look at just the black plate or to change the ink limit—and it can be turned off and on easily. Open the Separations Preview panel from Window ➤ Output ➤ Separations Preview.

FIGURE 10.10
The Separations Preview panel

From the View drop-down menu you have three choices: Off (the normal, working, nonpreviewed document state), Ink Limit, and Separations.

SEPARATIONS

Inks are managed on the Separations Preview panel the way layers are managed on their namesake panel. After you select Separations from the View drop-down, all inks in use anywhere within the current document will be presented as individual entries, including process and spot inks. To hide certain inks—for instance, to isolate a spot plate—click the eyeball icons beside the other inks. Activating the CMYK entry at the top of the list automatically turns on the individual Cyan, Magenta, Yellow, and Black plates. Any ink not visible will hide objects of that color in the document, which is very useful to guard against Black Ink Compensation turning black ink values into four-color rich black.

From the Separations Preview panel flyout menu you have the option to show single plates in black, meaning that, if only the yellow ink is shown, yellow objects will appear onscreen in black. Turning this off displays each plate in its ink color—Yellow shows yellow objects, Magenta magenta objects, and so forth.

Even better, with separations view active, hovering your mouse cursor over any object will display the ink densities for each individual color; hover the cursor beside CMYK for the combined total (see Figure 10.11).

FIGURE 10.11
Hovering the mouse cursor over a color shows the ink densities for each color.

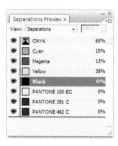

INK LIMIT

To check your design's ink densities more visually, choose Ink Limit from the View drop-down, and then set the ink coverage percentage limit in the field to the right. Any instances wherein the ink density exceeds the limit, InDesign will highlight in red while graying out any in-limit colors.

Proof Flattening

Transparency was one of the most difficult concepts to grasp for, well, a whole host of people and systems. RIPs were probably the most confused despite transparency being a core feature of Post-Script 3. Long-time QuarkXPress users saw no value in transparency because XPress didn't do it—the attitude was, to paraphrase *Saturday Night Live*'s Mike Myers (back when *SNL* was funny), if it's na' Quarkish, it's crap. Adobe itself was 20 years late to the party and, when they did build transparency into PostScript and their applications, had some trouble getting it just right. Despite propaganda, they *did* get it right quite a few years ago. A fair percentage of change-fearing print and prepress workers were frightened by transparency and so instinctively disparaged transparency with that most vile of epithets: *It shalt not print!*

Well, Adobe *did* get it right, even QuarkXPress uses transparency (as of version 7 in 2006), and, most important, *transparency does print*.

It prints natively in PostScript 3–compatible RIPs because PostScript 3, released in 1998, is built to print transparency (it's also built to handle color management internally). Nearly a decade later, many RIPs deserve walk-ons in VH1's *Stuck in the 90s* series; they still haven't updated to support PostScript 3.

If you happen to be stuck using one of these PostScript Level 2 has-been RIPs, don't fret: You can't send blended objects, drop shadows, or semitransparent strokes to RIP directly, but the ever courteous InDesign knows how to handle the RIPs of yesteryear. The secret is flattening.

FLATTENING

In any layout or graphics application, including InDesign, QuarkXPress, Illustrator, Photoshop, and so on, objects are not wholly two-dimensional. They have width and height (x and y) but also pseudo depth through stacking order or z-order (z for the third-dimensional z-axis). Objects in InDesign (or another program; layers in Photoshop) are stacked atop or below one another, allowing them to be independently manipulated as opposed to a single-layer raster image where artwork really is two-dimensional on the pixel grid. As we all know, printing is a two-dimensional process: Ink sits on drums, rollers, plates, or screens and then transfers onto a single two-dimensional substrate surface. Presses, printers, and imagesetters just don't do 3D—even object printers that print in revolution around a 3D package or other object are only applying 2D ink to a flat surface. A RIP—a raster image processor—converts everything into a raster image at the output device's resolution, creating halftone dots from solid areas of color. All that text, all those carefully drawn paths, get rasterized into the equivalent of a single-layer raster image. At some point, the stacking order of objects must be abandoned as well, incorporating or discarding areas of color blocked by objects higher in the stacking order. This is the process of *flattening*—squishing everything down to two dimensions and removing transparency.

During flattening, the notion of objects is secondary to the concept of colors. If you look at Figure 10.12, you'll see a few rectangles typical of InDesign objects on the left. They interact with one another through transparency—the green is 50% transparent, blending with the yellow; the red is opaque but has a drop shadow that forces it to blend with the yellow and green. Where areas of transparency overlap other objects, their colors mix to create new areas of color. On the right, flattening has carved each distinct area of color out to become its own flat, opaque, 2D object, which I've spread out so you can appreciate the effect of carving. Some—the drop shadow as well as the yellow and green rectangles it touched—are no longer vector paths; now they're raster images.

FIGURE 10.12
Top, three transparent objects interact. Flattened, three have become seven color-centric chunks (bottom).

Depending on the types of objects and how they interact with surrounding colors, some vector objects will be rasterized as a matter of necessity. Which objects retain their resolution independence as vectors (or remain separate raster objects) and which rasterize into solid imagery is the dominion of the InDesign Transparency Flattener, which, by and large, is under your control.

PREVIEWING AND CONTROLLING FLATTENING

The core of the Transparency Flattener controls is the Flattener Preview panel (see Figure 10.13). You'll find it on Window ➢ Output ➢ Flattener Preview.

FIGURE 10.13
The Flattener Preview panel

The Flattener Preview panel highlights objects containing, or affected by, transparency in red while sapping color out of the rest of the document's onscreen view. In Figure 10.14 you can see the results of highlighting raster-fill text and strokes on a document with blended mode images above or below text. By previewing the flattening before going to press, you can find and fix common problems. As you change flattening controls, the onscreen preview can be set to update with the Auto Refresh Highlight check box or you can manually update it by clicking the Refresh button.

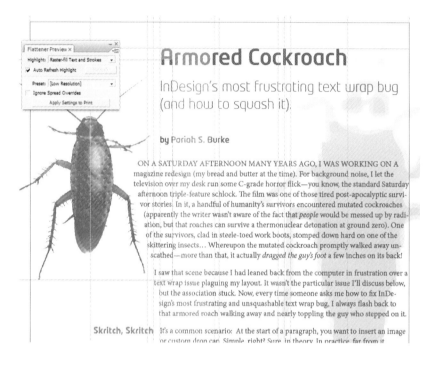

From the drop-down list at the top, choose what you'd like to see. All Affect Objects will high-light all *objects* affected by transparency; even if those objects are carved up into affected and non-affected regions, InDesign will highlight the entire object. All Rasterized Regions shows only those areas that have had to be rasterized. All the other options isolate specific types of flattening and specific types of objects.

If a region or objects require flattening, InDesign has three methods available to accomplish it:

Clip When it comes to the interaction of raster images and transparency, InDesign tries to accomplish flattening by making multiple, clipped copies of the images. For instance, in Figure 10.15, the logo on the left is a vector shape blended with the placed image background via 75% opacity and the Overlay blending mode. When flattened (on the right), the background becomes one raster image with the vector shape knocked out, but then two other copies of the background are included—one to fill the vector flame fill, the other to fill the vector flame out-line. Each image is whole and rectangular, but each has had a clipping path applied. Moreover, the copies of the image that were colored by the overlaid logo have been recolored at the pixel level to create the pre-flattened effect. (Note that I moved the pieces for clarity. Of course, once flattened, they would align as before.)

FIGURE 10.15
Pre-flattening (left),
and post-flattening
(right)

 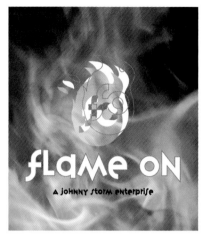

FIGURE 10.15
Pre-flattening (left),
and post-flattening
(right)

Divide Just like the Pathfinder Divide command, this primarily vector object method of flattening carves all the colors out into their separate objects. For a visual example, direct your peepers to Figure 10.16. Pre-flattening (left), three circles overlap one another and blend together using a Screen blending mode to create seven distinct areas of color. On the right, post-flattening, three objects have become seven, with no blending (I outlined them to make the differences easier to see).

FIGURE 10.16
Pre-flattening (left),
and post-flattening
(right)

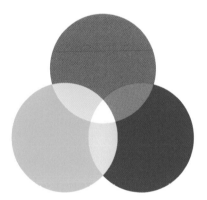 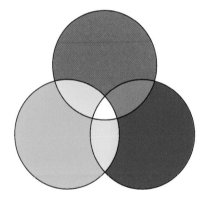

Rasterize The last and least desirable option available to the Transparency Flattener is to rasterize a region of transparency. When not rasterizing would make the flattened result too complicated, when it would create too many small chunks that might slow or even crash a RIP, InDesign will opt to rasterize an area. Rasterized areas become fixed resolution and can potentially output with lower quality than other areas. Spot colors forced to rasterize will convert to their nearest CMYK equivalents and may not match nonrasterized areas that use the actual spot.

Which flattening method InDesign employs depends on the specific artwork—whether it's raster or vector, how it blends with objects above and below, the colors used, and so on—and as determined by the chosen flattener preset. Presets are managed and customized via the Edit ➤ Transparency Flattener Presets menu command and the Transparency Flattener Presets command on the Flattener Preview panel's flyout menu. In any of these places, the Preset menu lists three default, bracketed (undeletable) presets. Each contains quality decision directives and has certain uses.

Low Resolution Best for low- to mid-grade desktop ink-jet and laser printers. Text and line art, if rasterized, is fixed at 288 ppi while gradients and meshes are rasterized to 144 ppi.

Medium Resolution Works with higher-grade or higher RAM desktop printers and provides a fairly fast print on proof printers. Uses 300 and 150 ppi.

High Resolution The highest quality, but the most complex output. Save this for imagesetters, platesetters, and high-end proof printers. Uses 1200 and 300 ppi.

The three default presets are general purpose and have large gaps between them. Ideally, you want to flatten all your for-press work with the High Resolution preset, which has everything cranked up. For most documents, that works. However, with lots of transparency on lots of pages, your RIP could error or timeout. So could a desktop printer with one of the other presets for that matter. You'll want to know how to make your own presets.

From the Transparency Flattener Presets dialog, choose New to open the Transparency Flattener Preset Options dialog (see Figure 10.17). At the top, give the preset a name you'll understand when you re-open this document six months down the road. Then, make your quality versus complexity decisions. It's all a trade-off.

FIGURE 10.17
Transparency Flattener Preset Options dialog

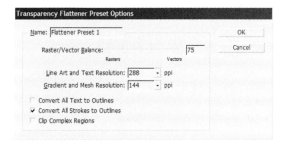

Raster/Vector Balance (Slider and measurement box) Although the other options are important, the Raster/Vector Balance slider is the most important part of determining flattening quality—and how long it takes to print a document. The slider adjusts the Transparency Flattener's priorities—how hard InDesign should try to maintain vectors before electing to rasterize transparent regions. On the right, identified as Vectors, is high quality. The closer to the right you take the slider, the more InDesign will try to use the divide (on vector objects) and clip (on raster) methodologies. Additionally, the closer to the right, the more complicated the document and longer to print. Conversely, moving the slider toward the left sets a lower threshold for rasterizing transparency and results in faster prints. Every document is different, so experiment with the slider on a few jobs to get a feel for how close to the right you can push the Raster/Vector Balance slider.

Resolution If these types of items must be rasterized, which resolution would you like? The drop-downs on these two fields offer common resolution settings, but you may also type custom values into the fields.

The values here are also used during the clipping flattening method because InDesign will downsample clipped images (that interact with transparency) to the higher resolution in the Line Art and Text Resolution field. Thus, a placed 600 ppi image with a semitransparent color box above it will be downsampled to 288 ppi resolution if the Low Resolution preset is used. If the resolution of an image is lower than the Gradient and Mesh Resolution value, InDesign may upsample images interacting with transparency to meet the Gradient and Mesh Resolution value. The upsamples are not very good, by the way, using the Nearest Neighbor interpolation method with which you may be familiar from Photoshop. In other words, *watch out*, particularly if you're working with a client's "high resolution logo from the home page."

Convert All Text to Outlines Don't gloss over this one. At first glance, most design and print pros tend to think, *Oh, I know all about converting type to outlines.* That may be true for converting type to outlines in general, but do you know the unique considerations inherent in doing it during flattening? When type interacts with transparency, one of two things must happen: It gets rasterized, or, preferably, it converts to outlines and becomes part of the divide or clip flattening methods; sometimes type even becomes a clipping path and contains a section of a raster image. Those things are going to happen regardless of whether this box is checked. What this box really does is decides how the rest of the type is treated.

When type is converted to outlines, it can get heavier—thicker, boldlike—onscreen and on some low- to mid-level printers (not on imagesetters). If type that doesn't interact with transparency isn't outlined, if it's left as live type, then suddenly a vertical half of a paragraph or even a few letters within a word can appear bolder than surrounding text just because they had strips of blended art close to them. Conversely, when type is rasterized, it rarely gets thicker. In fact, once in a blue moon, it appears *thinner*. So converting all text to outlines might not save you from type of visually disparate weights on your desktop and proof printers. Outline type is also slower to print.

So, which should you use—Convert All Text to Outlines on or off? I don't know. I can't see your document. Proof the flattening in the Flattener Preview panel before sending a document to print on your desktop or proof printer. You can use different flattener presets per spread (see below), so set an overall document preset, then spot-assign different presets to handle unique situations.

For final output, I recommend leaving this option off as I've yet to see the thickening or thinning issues appear with good-quality imagesetters or platesetters. Even though PDFs created either by printing or by exporting from InDesign do exhibit the same issues onscreen and in desktop or proof printers, just as they do when output directly from InDesign to desktop printers, I've never seen a PDF print thick (or thin) text to high-end devices.

Convert All Strokes to Outlines The description and potential problems with this choice are identical to Convert All Text to Outlines except that it deals with strokes instead of type.

Clip Complex Regions Raster images are rectangles; that's their nature. So when InDesign rasterizes a region of transparency, it creates rectangles. Sometimes, those rectangles bisect objects—it's not uncommon to observe a letter split in two, with one side remaining a vector path and the other rasterizing into a larger region. And sometimes, these are noticeable. In fact, they are *often* noticeable onscreen, on low- to mid-grade printers, and in PDFs, but in the majority of such cases they are *not* noticeable on final output to a high-end output device. Still, you may want to change the way InDesign relates objects and paths to areas that must be rasterized.

Turning on Clip Complex Regions will direct InDesign to try to only rasterize up to an object's path. If it can't do that—maybe half the letter *is* affected by transparency—it will incorporate the entire path. It does this by creating more and more complicated clipping paths, which, of course, slows down the flattening process and printing.

I apologize if I left you with more questions and answers in defining the purposes, pros, and cons of the Transparency Flattener Preset Options dialog. If you've read through the rest of this book, you know there are usually rules or at least guidelines or rules of thumb. Flattening, however, is like curves or levels in Photoshop—there are no hard rules because every document is different. Flattening is a process of trade-offs, quality versus complexity. Where the tipping points occur between acceptable and unacceptable quality and acceptable and unacceptable print speeds are subjective, only *you* can determine the location of those tipping points with *your* particular documents. If you care about quality and print speed, use the Flattener Preview panel to scrutinize your document.

A Few More Words about Flattening

Flattening can be accomplished in RIP with PostScript 3–compatible RIPs. When using older-technology RIPS, it has to be done at output time, either via printing or exporting to PDF in InDesign. You'll find the familiar list of Transparency Flattener presets on the Advanced pane of the Print dialog and the Advanced pane of the Export Adobe PDF dialog.

Acrobat version 5 and later (PDF 1.4 and later), being based on PostScript 3, natively supports transparency. There's no need to flatten prior to, or during, export to PDF when sending to PDF version 1.4 or later. However, when exporting to PDF 1.3 (Acrobat 4), flattening *will* occur, a fact many forget and wonder why they got output looking a lot like the default High Resolution flattening preset instead of their custom preset. Exporting to PDF/X-1a or PDF/X-3 requires flattened, PDF 1.3–compatible PDFs; PDF/X-4 uses PDF version 1.4.

When working in an Open Prepress Interface (OPI) workflow, it's important to remember that InDesign only flattens what it can see. If you have the high-resolution final images available, tell InDesign where to find them so it can properly flatten at output (InDesign will then handle the OPI replacement, too). Do this in two steps: First, check the box Read Embedded OPI Image Links in Import Options of placed EPS files. You'll need to have done that while initially placing the graphics, or relink them from the Links panel and do it then. Second, at output time, check OPI Image Replacement on the Advanced pane of the Print or Export EPS dialog. With both of those checked, InDesign will handle the OPI substitution and flatten using the high-resolution images instead of the low-resolution proxies. If your workflow requires that InDesign only have access to the proxy image and that replacements cannot be made until further down the line, *do not flatten the document*—do not print, export to PDF 1.3, or export to EPS.

Blend Spaces

On the Edit menu is the Transparency Blend Space submenu. Blend spaces override swatches to maintain consistent color across a spread in the event of transparency interaction. In other words, if you choose Document CMYK as the spread blend space (Edit ➢ Transparency Blend Space ➢ Document CMYK), all colors on the spread will be shown onscreen and be sent to press as CMYK— even if you draw an RGB object, even if you use an RGB swatch. Transparency output is a spread-level consideration, and InDesign doesn't want your flattened blues to be different from one side of the spread to the next. This is a definite gotcha for those who publish to PDF distributables because an otherwise RGB document can suddenly have two CMYK pages smack in the middle. If that's you, change the Transparency Blend Space to Document RGB.

Individual spreads (but not individual pages) can be assigned their own flattening presets. On the Pages panel, select one or more spreads and then, on the Pages panel flyout menu, you'll find the Spread Flattening submenu with these options:

◆ Default: Use the document preset, even if it has yet to be defined.

◆ None: Ignores transparency entirely and outputs opaque objects that do not blend (a bad idea unless troubleshooting).

◆ Custom: This option will let you customize flattener options for that particular spread.

The only way to gauge spot color transparency interaction onscreen is with Overprint Preview on (View ➢ Overprint Preview). The same is true in PDFs. When creating PDF proofs, check the Simulate Overprint box on the Output pane of the Export to Adobe PDF dialog to better render spot color interaction with transparency.

Color, Difference, Exclusion, Hue, Luminosity, and Saturation blending modes are generally not recommended for use on or in connection with spot colors.

Printing

Ultimately, the destiny of 99.9% of InDesign documents is to be printed to a substrate. Now that you know how to softproof those documents, it's time to prepare them for final output.

Ink Manager

The Ink Manager (see Figure 10.18), accessible from the panel flyout menus on the Separations Preview and Swatches panels and from within the Output pane of the Print and Export to PDF dialogs, enables direct management of individual inks. Each in-use ink is listed along with its type, neutral density, and trapping sequence. Icons matching the Swatches panel communicate the type of ink—such as process, with a CMYK icon ▨ , or spot, with a gray circle icon ◉ , or an aliased ink ▨ .

FIGURE 10.18
Ink Manager

INK TYPE

This field sets the trapping type for the selected ink, which can be one of four:

◆ Normal: Use this for process and most spot inks.

◆ Transparent: Set varnishes and die line inks with this option, which will take the selected ink out of trapping calculations, ensuring that ink beneath traps properly.

◆ Opaque: Heavy inks like metallics need special treatment. The Opaque setting traps along the edges of the selected ink but does not trap underlying inks.

◆ OpaqueIgnore: Similar to Opaque, OpaqueIgnore is used for heavy inks and does not trap underlying colors but *prevents* trapping along the edges of the selected ink.

NEUTRAL DENSITY

When trapping is enabled, Neutral Density fine-tunes trap placement. By default, the U.S. English and Canadian versions of InDesign use standardized SWOP ink density values, but it can be adjusted here for specific press needs.

TRAPPING SEQUENCE

Trapping Sequence changes the order in which inks are factored into trapping calculations.

INK ALIAS

Although decreasing in frequency thanks to the efforts of, and improved communications between, Pantone and software makers like Adobe, a common problem faced by print professionals is multiple instances of the same spot color in one document. The problem is usually caused by selecting a PMS color in one application, which lists it one way (for example, Pantone 346 U), and then choosing the same color in another application whose PMS library writes color names differently (for example, PMS 346 UC). They're both the same Pantone 346 solid uncoated, but because they're named differently, InDesign, and later PDF and RIP, will output them to separate plates. As I said, this problem is improving because creative pro applications are standardizing their color library naming schemes such that applications like Photoshop and Illustrator use the exact same name. Thus, placing a PSD and an AI, both containing the same spot color defined in their native applications, into InDesign results in a single ink. When using older imagery, however, particularly yesteryear's EPS files, you might still get two separate plates for the same color. Of course, because the colors are embedded in external assets, you can't simply delete one swatch on the Swatches panel and tell InDesign to replace it with the other as you can with objects created within InDesign. This is where the Ink Manager comes in.

Within Ink Manager, highlight one of the repetitive spots and then, from the Ink Alias field below, choose the other instance of the spot. Aliasing is the process of saying, *Don't print this color, use that ink instead.* At output time, InDesign will then replace all instances of one with the other, resulting in a single plate for both inks.

Real World Scenario

USING THE INK MANAGER TO CORRECT PHOTOSHOP CHANNEL DISASTERS

Every few months I see in person or read about in online forums someone who, through some weird accident, wound up creating a two- or three-color image in Photoshop using a dozen or more channels. In the document's Channels panel, he has multiple channels (plates) for each of the two or three spot colors. Why is this a disaster? Because each of those channels will be treated as a separate plate, turning a 2- or 3-color job into a 10- or 12-color job; the price of printing goes through the roof, as does the poor pressman who has to run the thing.

The worst I ever saw personally was a two-color PSD with 14 channels for a single spot and 11 more for the second color. As near as I could figure, the designer, whom we'll call Jane, had mistakenly used channels like layers, creating a new channel for every new object or section of color while she painted.

When these types of Photoshop images pop up, there isn't a great deal that can be done to fix them within Photoshop. Sometimes cutting all image data off the extraneous channels one at a time and pasting onto a single target channel works, sometimes it doesn't. Splitting the image into two, one to hold each color, merging the channels down into a single channel each, and then reconsolidating the images also works once in a while. Converting the image to grayscale and then back to duotone in Photoshop consolidates the channels easily but destroys the original color separations and usually requires copious recoloring work.

I spent two solid days working on Jane's PSD, trying these methods and others, to no avail. At the time, I had at my disposal the unlimited knowledge and resources of Adobe—including the direct assistance of several members from the Photoshop development team; none of us could come up with a solution that didn't require Jane to completely repaint her artwork, which she eventually did.

Since then, InDesign's Ink Manager has provided the solution to Jane's problem via ink aliases. If you find yourself dealing with such a Photoshop document, place it into InDesign and output from there. Select one instance of each doppelganger ink as the primary, and, using the Ink Manager, alias all the others to their primary. Upon output, you'll have just one plate for each color.

Often images such as those previously described are set in multichannel color mode, and InDesign does not support placing PSD images in multichannel. InDesign only handles images in the CMYK, RGB, and Lab color spaces. To get around the limitation:

1. Re-open the image in Photoshop.

2. On the Channels panel, create four empty new channels, and drag them to the top of the channels list.

3. Convert the document color mode to CMYK via Image ➤ Mode ➤ CMYK Color. The conversion will automatically turn the four empty channels into empty Cyan, Magenta, Yellow, and Black channels. Spot channels—the ones containing all the image data in this case—will be preserved, and upon save from Photoshop, InDesign will now be able to import the image.

Note: If the image will be the only content of the InDesign document, you'll wind up outputting blank C, M, Y, and K plates. When it's time to output, disable printing of the cyan, magenta, yellow, and black inks in the Print dialog Output pane.

Often when channel disaster images are made, they contain several identically named channels (e.g., PANTONE 462 C). Photoshop doesn't care that these are the names of spot colors, only that they're the name of channels, which is what leads to this problem in the first place. InDesign, however, *does* care about taking in two or more spots with the same name, and it will complain, preventing you from importing the image. If you get this, just go back to Photoshop's Channels panel and rename the duplicate channels to something like PANTONE 462 C copy 1, PANTONE 462 C copy 2, and so on. This will also make it easier to identify the target and aliased colors in InDesign.

Once correctly aliased, the extra inks will disappear off the Separations Preview panel, leaving only one of each ink.

I wish I'd had this method available years ago to fix Jane's image. At least now, if *you* encounter it, you'll have a solution that doesn't involve repainting the Photoshop document.

CONVERTING SPOTS TO PROCESS

To convert all spot colors in the document to their nearest process (CMYK) mix equivalents, check the All Spots to Process box at the bottom of the Ink Manager. Regardless of whether spots are embedded in external assets (e.g., a linked PDF), InDesign will, upon output, convert them to process.

To selectively convert just a single spot to process, click on its icon in the ink list. When the spot icon changes to a CMYK icon, the spot is defined to convert to process.

USE STANDARD LAB VALUES FOR SPOTS

As you saw earlier in this chapter, CMYK is a very small color gamut, particularly when compared with the absolutely mass Lab gamut. Although spot color swatchbooks have always contained CMYK values for spots, enabling conversion from spot to process, this has limited the display of spot inks to their process formulas. Newer swatchbooks, such as InDesign CS2's and CS3's DIC, HKS, PANTONE, and TOYO libraries, also contain Lab values for their swatches. The Lab values enable more accurate color throughout the process via better color management and higher-fidelity spot conversions—within workflows capable of handling conversion from Lab. The Use Standard Lab Values for Spots option is off by default for backward compatibility, but if your workflow can use Lab values, turn it on.

When Overprint Preview is enabled, InDesign will automatically *display* spot colors using the Lab color model onscreen without altering output spot color values. However, Lab values *will be used* for printing and exporting if Simulate Overprint is active in the Output pane of the Print or Export to Adobe PDF dialog.

Trapping and Overprinting

On a printing press, every ink is run separately. All sheets run through on one color, sit on a drying rack for a while, and are then reloaded into the press to receive the next color. With all that moving of paper, by human hands and machine grippers or rollers, you might expect that the paper could shift slightly and that ink colors might not perfectly align. And you would often be right. Paper shifts, and inks don't align—they *misregister*—which can leave ugly white gaps between areas of color such as those in Figure 10.19.

FIGURE 10.19
Slight misregistration in the magenta plate causes a sliver of white between inks (assuming the image was printed in registration, that is).

Trapping is the process of extending colors beyond object borders so they overlap—just slightly—to compensate for misregistration, eliminating ugly white gaps in any competently run print job. By default, InDesign keeps trapping turned *off*. It does that because most print service providers prefer to set their own traps further down the line in a dedicated trapping application or system or in-RIP process. If that isn't the case, if you need to set traps in InDesign—maybe *you* are the print service provider reading this—InDesign has both automated and manual trapping options. The automated traps are very good, and unless you really know what you're doing, I advise leaving it to InDesign to trap.

The built-in InDesign trapping engine calculates traps on the ink level based on the neutral densities of adjacent colors and typically spreads the lighter color into the darker at any intersection. As we discussed above, the Ink Manager offers methods of influencing the trapping engine's calculations, including how it handles special types of spot colors like varnishes, dies, and heavy inks. These types of spots in particular require an experienced hand because, in the case of varnishes and dies, there isn't a color to trap, and with heavy inks, trapping can often cause undesirable results (for example, you really don't want to mix magenta process ink with a metallic gold ink that contains real bits of metal).

Manually setting traps involves two panels: Attributes and Trap Presets.

OVERPRINT ATTRIBUTES

Overprinting is exactly what it sounds like: making one ink print on top of another. Black, for instance, is the most opaque of the CMYK foursome and typically overprints cyan, magenta, and yellow in small areas like type, strokes, and so forth. Overprinting ensures that there are no misregistration gaps because there are no gaps to worry about. In Figure 10.20, for instance, you can see a comparison between *overprint* and *knockout*. In a knockout, the upper shape is punched out of the color(s) below at separation time—the area filled by black text is knocked out of the cyan and yellow—which creates potential for obvious misregistration. If the paper moves slightly on press, a white gap will appear around the edge of the text. However, with overprint, the cyan and yellow are both continuous, even where they will clearly be hidden by the black, so a slight misregistration will be impossible to detect (in this one area).

FIGURE 10.20
Text knockouts out
of background color
(left), and the same
text set to overprint
(right)

What are the drawbacks to overprinting? Why not just set everything to overprint?

Good questions. Printing ink is not completely opaque. Even black ink isn't, though it's the least transparent of the four process inks. Check out Figure 10.21. See how the colors mix in the "CMYK"? Now see how the black star on the right looks more black than the pure black one in the center? That's because I've set the box on the right to be percentages of cyan, magenta, yellow, *and* black all overlaid (rich black). Even though the black ink was printed last, putting it atop the other three, they still shine through the 100% pure black ink to tint it, er, blacker. If the colors behind the black weren't even, if they were, say, colored stripes, those stripes would show through the black by creating two-toned black. Now, if I had set a cyan-filled object to overprint its background instead of knocking out the background, who knows what we'd get. Put a 100% pure cyan object overprinting a 100% yellow background and the ink colors will mix to create green. The only way to maintain the cyan is to knock out the yellow, subtracting the area of cyan from the yellow except for enough overlap to hedge against misregistration.

FIGURE 10.21
At left, overprinting
all four colors creates
undesired mixes.
Center, a 100% black
ink star, and right, a
rich black star—a
mixture of all four
process inks.

InDesign will handle its own knockouts by default—or leave them to the RIP or trapper. Again, InDesign does a very good job of choosing when to overprint and when to knock out, but you can override the settings with the Attributes panel accessible from the Window menu. With an object selected, some or all of the Attributes panel's four check boxes will become available. Each of these options is very simple:

- Overprint Fill: Overprint the object's fill.

- Overprint Stroke: Overprint just the object's stroke.

- Overprint Gap: This option is only enabled when a gapped stroke style such as dashed, dotted, or hashed is chosen and when a gap color has been selected.

- Nonprinting: Why the option to not print an object was stuck in the same place as the overprint controls has always baffled me. The vast majority of designers will leave overprinting decisions to their print service providers, so they'll typically never touch the Attributes panel.

However, just about everyone needs to define an object as nonprinting from time to time. Putting that particular option here means most designers can't find it when they need it.

To create an object that doesn't print—for instance, template slugs and labels—select the object and check this box. To temporarily override this setting and force objects with the non-printing attribute to print, check Print Non-Printing Objects on the General pane of the Print dialog.

Overprinting controls are only relevant to natively drawn objects—paths and text—and have no effect on placed images, which are managed by InDesign's trapping controls.

A few words about overprinting strokes: Strokes straddle a path—half inside, half outside—by default. If you overprint a stroke, it will therefore overprint the colors around the path *and* over-print the fill, which most of the time creates the appearance of two separate strokes. To avoid this situation, set the object stroke entirely within or without the path via the Stroke panel. Also, when you have a choice between overprinting a fill or a stroke, you'll get better results in most cases by overprinting the stroke because InDesign defines the stroke as higher in the stacking order than the fill.

On the View menu is the Overprint Preview command, which simulates overprinting results onscreen. Additionally, previewing separations automatically activates overprint preview.

TRAPPING

At the risk of sounding academic, Ink Manager's job is to manage ink across the entire document (or book, if multiple documents are sent to PDF or print as one unified document). The ink Type, Neutral Density, and Trapping Sequence fields control trap on an entire ink wherever it may appear, and in whatever type of objects—natively drawn paths and type as well as native assets. Overprint attributes are object-level, controlling fundamental trapping per fill or stroke on indi-vidual natively drawn objects. Beyond and between Ink Manager and overprint attributes are InDesign's precision trapping controls, which, again, trap based on neutral densities of inks, not objects, which accounts for objects containing multiple colors.

InDesign Trapping vs. In-RIP Trapping

InDesign can do the trapping internally or leave it to PostScript 3–compatible RIPs carrying the Adobe In-RIP Trapping feature (consult your RIP's documentation to see if this functionality is included). The main differences between them are that Adobe In-RIP Trapping can trap just about everything, while InDesign's internal trapping ability has a few limitations:

♦ InDesign's built-in trapping is limited to a maximum trap width of 4 points;

♦ It will *not* trap EPS, DCS, or OPI linked assets, nor will it trap native objects to any of these types of images.

♦ It *will* trap Illustrator AI files and PDFs, but only if they weren't already trapped natively and only if they were created by Illustrator 9 or later (when AI became PDF based).

How can you tell if a PDF was created with Illustrator 9 or later? Simple. In Acrobat, access the PDF Document Properties from the File menu or by pressing Cmd+D/Ctrl+D. In the middle of the Description panel (see Figure 10.22), the creating application will be listed in the Application field. Determining if the PDF has been previously trapped is just as easy— look on the Advanced tab of the Document Properties (see Figure 10.23).

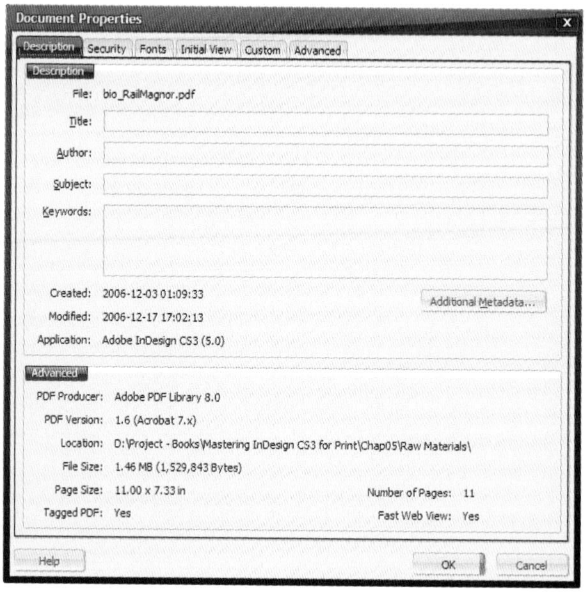

FIGURE 10.22
Acrobat's Document Properties dialog reveals the application that created the PDF.

FIGURE 10.23
Whether a PDF has been trapped is also contained in Acrobat's Document Properties dialog.

None of the above limitations apply to Adobe In-RIP trapping.

Where the heck do I choose between built-in trapping and Adobe In-RIP Trapping? That is an excellent question, one I hear often because most books and even the InDesign help file don't tell you where to make this choice—at least, they don't tell you in the context of discussion about the two options. The choice is in the Print dialog (see Figure 10.24).

On the Output pane of the Print dialog, you'll find first the Color drop-down menu. Choosing any composite color output option disables the Trapping and Screening fields. However, selecting Separations or In-RIP Separations activates them, although Adobe In-RIP may yet be disabled in the Trapping field. This option only becomes available once you've chosen a printer and PPD that support PostScript 3 and Adobe In-RIP Trapping. Assuming you're printing seps and have chosen a compatible printer and PPD, there is where to make your choice between the built-in trapping engine and Adobe In-RIP.

Whichever choice you make, trapping is controlled via customizable trap presets, which can be applied per page or to a range of pages via reusable, shareable trap presets.

FIGURE 10.24
Choosing between
built-in and Adobe
In-RIP trapping is
done at print time,
in the Print dialog's
Output pane.

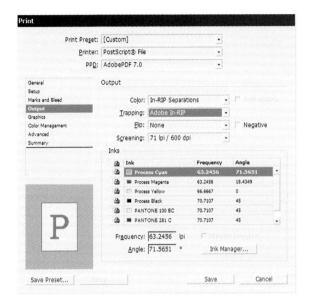

Setting Trap Options

Opened from the Window ➤ Output menu, you'll find the Trap Presets panel (see Figure 10.25). In this list-style panel you'll find the default and undeletable [No Trap Preset] and [Default] presets. Presets you create are saved as part of the document, which means every new document will be devoid of your previous presets. Fortunately, you can load them into any document from any other InDesign document with the Load Trap Presets panel menu command. Choosing said command will show a File Open dialog; just navigate to and choose the InDesign document containing the presets you need to load them into the current document. If you use the same trap settings more often than once in a blue moon, or if you need to share them across your shop, stick an otherwise empty template document on the file server from which anyone can load in the trap presets.

FIGURE 10.25
The Trap Presets
panel

Create new presets with the New button at the bottom of the panel or by duplicating an existing preset with the command on the flyout menu, and then modify its options with the menu's Preset Options command. The Modify Trap Preset Options dialog will then appear (see Figure 10.26). Clicking the New button while holding Opt/Alt will create the new preset and immediately open Modify Trap Preset Options for the new preset.

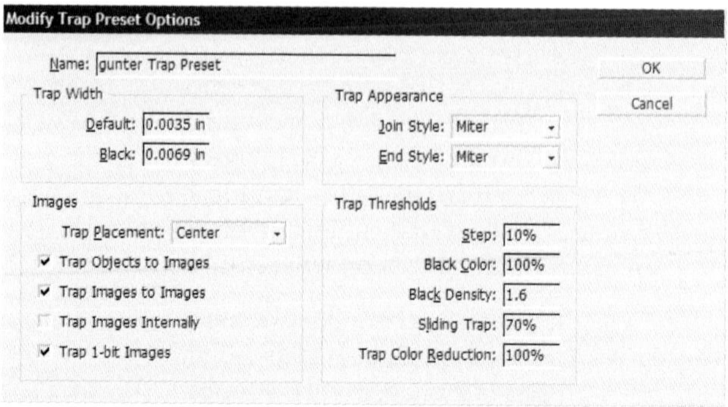

FIGURE 10.26
Modify Trap Preset
Options dialog

What are the controls?

Trap Width Default & Black The amount of ink overlap desired. InDesign's built-in trapping is limited to a maximum 4-point overlap, while Adobe In-RIP is capable of up to 8 points. Default controls the overlap for all ink colors except black, which has its own separate trap width.

Trap Appearance Join Style Identical to the way path segments are joined via the same option in the Stroke panel, this field offers miter, round, and bevel choices to shape corner points in two trap segments.

Trap Appearance End Style The End Style setting defines how trap lines behave at their end points. Selecting Miter keeps the lines tight and away from one another, while Overlap directs them to overlay one another.

Trap Placement When InDesign native objects abut placed images, Trap Placement determines the location of the traps.

> **Center** operates like a default stroke on a path, straddling the path edge to partially overlap the object and the image.
>
> **Choke** overlaps only the placed image, staying outside the vector path.
>
> **Spread** is the opposite of Choke, trapping based on the placed image colors, thus placing the trap inside the vector path and outside the image.
>
> **Neutral Density** restores the default trap engine priority of spreading lighter colors into the darker regions and thus can create traps with a ragged-edged appearance, jumping from one side of the object/image join to the other.

Trap Objects to Images (check box) Decides whether vector objects should use the above Trap Placement choice to trap to placed images they adjoin.

Trap Images to Images (check box) Specifies if images immediately adjacent to other images should trap to one another.

Trap Images Internally (check box) Off by default, Trap Images Internally asks if you would like to trap the colors appearing inside placed imagery to other colors inside the same imagery. Activating this option is only recommended for simple imagery with large areas of solid color and high contrast—business graphics, for instance—and should definitely not be used on continuous-tone photographic imagery. Trap Images Internally is subject to the limitations of the trapping engine—for example, this option will have no effect on DCS imagery, pre-separated images that contain layers for each plate as well as a composite preview layer. When enabled, this option will complicate and slow trapping calculations.

Trap 1-Bit Images (check box) 1-bit images are pure black and white. Even if tinted within InDesign, they are still treated as 1-bit images and thus need no internal trapping. If this option is activated, such images will be trapped with adjacent vector objects using neutral density and ignoring the Trap Placement setting.

Step Step defines what percentage of difference must exist between adjoining colors before trapping occurs. The lower the value of difference, the more traps result. Adobe recommends 8 to 20% for best trapping.

Black Color In this field, set the minimum percentage of black ink before Black Trap Width overrides Default Trap Width. The lower the value, the less black ink required in a color before Black Trap Width takes over.

Black Density When using dark spot colors, determine how dark the ink's neutral density must be to be considered black for the purposes of trapping and thus use Black Trap Width.

Sliding Trap When areas of variable tints such as gradients abut, trapping with a uniform color along the entire length of the gradient can cause noticeable contrast between the object and the trap. Therefore, a sliding trap adjusts the trap placement relevant to the neutral densities of colors throughout tint variances. A sliding trap begins by using a spread on the darker side. When the difference between two colors' neutral densities exceeds the percentage entered in the Sliding Trap field, the trap moves from a spread to a centerline, providing a smoother transition between colors. To force a constant spread trap that never switches, set Sliding Trap to 100%; use 0% to enforce a constant centerline trap.

Trap Color Reduction In the simplest terms, this field is the limit to how much is InDesign allowed to mix neutral densities from either side of a trap to create and lighten the trap itself. Setting Reduction to 0% prevents any reduction and sets the trap to the neutral density of the darker color, which is not necessarily the same color, just the same neutral density.

Assign Trap Presets

Once you've configured the needed trap presets, it's time to assign them to pages. From the Trap Presets panel flyout menu select Assign Trap Preset to open the simple dialog shown in Figure 10.27. At the top are all the presets available. Select one, then enter a range of page numbers—or All to assign the same trap preset to the entire document—and then click the Assign button. The assignments section at the bottom of the dialog lists all trap assignments for reference. Presets may be applied to any page or range of pages; different presets can even be assigned to left and right pages in the same spread.

FIGURE 10.27
Assign Trap Preset
dialog

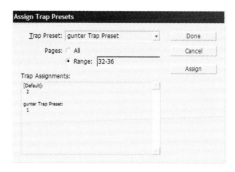

When you're synchronizing documents in books, all the trap presets from the master document will be added into the available trap presets of each document. Synchronizing will not, however, assign them. If you intend to assign the same trap preset to all pages of all documents, don't create a new one. Instead, assign the Default preset to all pages in all documents manually. Any changes, make to the Default preset in the master document. Then, when you're synchronizing, the master document version will overwrite all the other documents', applying the new settings.

Also important to note is that, when native InDesign objects are rasterized during flattening, they usually lose overprints and traps. This does not happen for placed AI and PDF documents that include their own overprints and traps, however; those survive flattening.

Preflight

For the uninitiated, *preflight* is the process of checking a document for potential printing issues before printing—flight. InDesign includes an introductory preflight function that I recommend all designers use. Press and pre-press shops will use a much more robust preflight system like FlightCheck, Preflight Pro, PitStop Pro, or PDF Checkup. Moreover, I advise print and pre-press shops to encourage their designer clients to run InDesign's basic preflight before submitting files to you. It does help stop many of the simple, common problems with InDesign documents.

With a document opened, go to File ➢ Preflight to initiate a check of the document. The Preflight report dialog should be easy to grasp, but let's quickly run through each of its panes anyway.

Summary (See Figure 10.28) As you might intuit from the title, this pane summarizes the more detailed data on the following panes. Of note here are two things: At the top it probably states Preflight: Entire Publication, alluding to the fact that you can also preflight multiple documents or an entire book at once. Refer back to the discussion about books and Book panels in Chapter 9, "Documents," for instructions on preflighting some or all of a book. The second thing to note is the check box at the bottom—Show Data for Hidden and Non-Printing Layers. Generally you want this checked to make sure there are no problems with documents that create multiple versions via layers (for example, a multilingual layout) and that fonts and assets used by non-printing labels and instructions won't cause problems.

Fonts (See Figure 10.29) All the fonts the document uses are listed here along with their names, types (TrueType, Type 1, OpenType, and so on), statuses (OK, missing, incomplete, etc.), and the fonts' protection statuses. The last is important. If the type foundry protected its font from embedding, it will not be embedded in an exported PDF; you'll need to coordinate with your service provider to make sure it has the same font.

FIGURE 10.28
The Preflight Summary pane

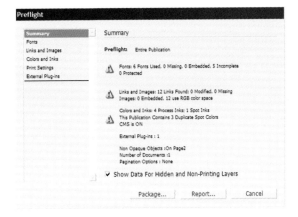

FIGURE 10.29
The Preflight Fonts pane

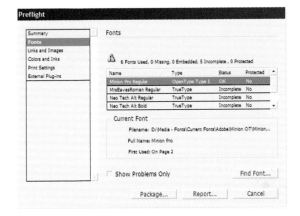

Click any font in the list to load more detailed information, including the location of its first use in the document, into the Current Font area below. If you need to replace a font, the Find Font button will open the standard Find Font dialog.

Links and Images (See Figure 10.30) The Links and Images pane does for, uh, links and images what Fonts does for fonts. You can see in the list each instance of a image, its file type and color space (RGB, CMYK, Lab), on which page it appears, its status (linked, embedded, modified, missing), and which, if any, ICC profile it's assigned or carries internally. If an image is listed as missing or modified, a Relink or Update button appears in the Current Link/Image area, which also displays other very useful information. Repair All updates all images listed as modified and helps relink all missing images more quickly than one at a time.

Colors and Inks (See Figure 10.31) What's missing here is a link to Ink Manager, but, oh well. All the document inks as well as their angles and *lpi*, or lines per inch, are listed. Any aliasing you've done via Ink Manager is reflected here by notations such as "this publication contains X duplicate spot colors" combined with the ink list only showing the actual, aliased to ink. Whether CMS is on is also noted at the top.

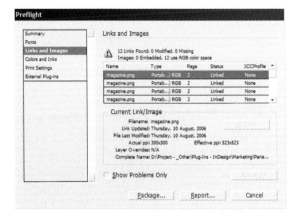

FIGURE 10.30
The Preflight Links
and Images pane

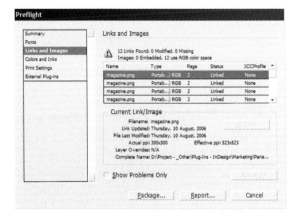

FIGURE 10.31
The Preflight Colors
and Inks pane

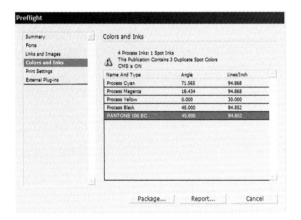

Print Settings (See Figure 10.32) A list of the settings from the Print dialog or assigned print style, which is useful for making sure things like PPD and OPI are correctly set.

FIGURE 10.32
The Preflight Print
Settings pane

External Plug-ins (See Figure 10.33) If, in creating your document, you use or even have installed a plug-in that didn't come out of the InDesign box and your print service provider doesn't have the same plug-in, there could be trouble. At the minimum, your providers or collaborators will be annoyed by a warning every time they open the document; at the worst, they won't be able to open or output your document. This pane exists so you can see what nonoriginal plug-ins are installed and communicate to your providers or collaborators, whereupon the two of you can work out how to handle the matter.

FIGURE 10.33

The Preflight External Plug-ins pane

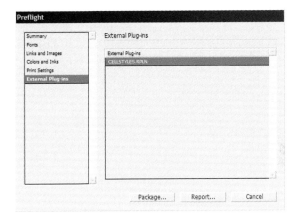

At the bottom of the Preflight dialog the Report button generates a plain-text report of everything in the graphical Preflight user interface ready for email to your provider. Package moves to the next logical step and, of course, the next logical section of this chapter.

Package for Output

In the olden days of the wild and wooly 1980s and 1990s, we had to spend hours rifling through our hard drives, other people's hard drives, file servers, and maybe even removable media manually collecting all the linked assets and fonts used in a single publication. Invariably, it seemed we always missed one, much to the consternation of our service bureaus. Nowadays, the software collects everything for us.

Choosing Package from the File menu or from the Preflight dialog initiates the packaging process, which will collect all the graphics and fonts, put copies of them in orderly folders, *and* create a new copy of the InDesign file (or files, if you're packaging a book) that links to the newly organized assets. Let's run through it, and then all will become clear, grasshopper.

When you tell InDesign to package an unsaved document, the first thing that will occur is that you'll be prompted to save. Next, InDesign will run a snappy preflight in the background. If it finds any problems, you'll be alerted with a message like the one in Figure 10.34. Choosing View Info opens the Preflight dialog. Fix the problems, take note of the warnings, and run Package again.

FIGURE 10.34

Before packaging, InDesign preflights and offers the opportunity to see the problem report.

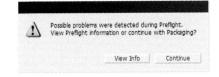

Next, a semi-useless Printing Instructions dialog appears. Every package operation generates an `Instructions.txt` file in the package folder. Most print service providers have their own job tickets for you to fill out—usually a PDF or HTML eform, or something you complete over the phone with your service rep. If you want to fill this out, go for it; you're not required to enter information, just to press the Continue button. The document generated does include the preflight report, which can be useful to your provider, though.

Finally, we're into the Package Publication dialog where everything happens. It looks a lot like a save dialog (Figure 10.35) because it is. Package will create a new folder into which it will place a new copy of the InDesign document(s) and subfolders for assets and fonts. In this step, pick the location and folder name for the package. It's important to remember that you can not choose the folder containing the current working version of the InDesign document(s) you're presently packaging. InDesign can't overwrite a file it's reading from. Create a new subfolder, or put it somewhere else. I often choose my Desktop so I can then just drag the packaged folder to a DVD-R or DVD-RW and then delete it after burning the disc.

FIGURE 10.35
The Package Publication dialog

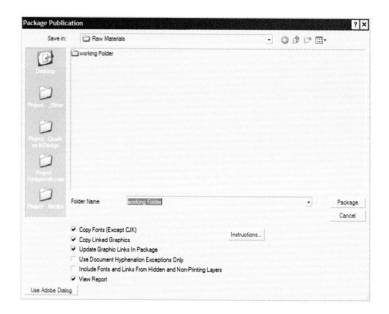

At the bottom of the Package Publication dialog are your options for the package.

Copy Fonts (Except CJK) Do you want it grab all the fonts used by your document so they can travel, or be archived, with the document? (Hint: *Yes*, yes you do.) CJK fonts (Asian fonts) will not be copied; if your document makes use them, you'll later have to manually grab them and copy them to the package's `Fonts` folder. The same is true of any fonts that restrict embedding; InDesign can't copy these, so you'll, um… have to find… your own solution for printing your document while respecting of the type foundry's intellectual property and font license.

Copy Linked Graphics Do you want it to copy all the linked images from all the hundreds of places they could have been and put them in the package's `Links` folder for easy travel and archival? (Same hint.)

Update Graphic Links in Package This option updates the InDesign document(s) to point to the linked assets in the package's Links folder rather than to the originals in their various locations. Because all the linked images will wind up in a folder beneath or inside the folder containing the INDD document, this option makes the document truly portable by using relative instead of absolute file paths. If you uncheck this, every time the document is opened off a CD or DVD, all images will need to be manually relinked before the document can be used. (Word of advice: This *will* make the recipient angry.)

Use Document Hyphenation Exceptions Only With this option *not* selected, the external user dictionary stored on your computer will merge with the document's embedded dictionary such that both will be used for determining hyphenation when InDesign composes text. When sending the job out to your service providers, they won't have access to your external user dictionary. Any relevant hyphenation exceptions stored therein won't be accessible, and text may reflow. If you've made use of a number of hyphenation exceptions, import your external user dictionary into the document's dictionary, and then check Use Document Hyphenation Exceptions only.

Include Fonts and Links from Hidden and Non-Printing Layers Do you also want to include the fonts and imagery used only in non-active or non-printing layers? If not, then the document will continue to generate image or font missing warnings.

View Report Launches your text editor with Instructions.txt loaded when packaging completes.

After clicking Package, you'll probably be given a friendly warning about the risk of copyright infringement when distributing fonts as part of a package. After that, sit back and let InDesign do its thing. It's a fast process, but, depending on the number of fonts, assets, and documents, you might have time to check email, pick a fight with the sales department, or have lunch. When it's done, you'll still be looking at your original document—the unpackaged one. You'll also have a new package folder—mine was Test Doc Folder—containing a complete copy of the InDesign document, the Instructions.txt report, and two other folders. Every linked image asset will be in the single Links folder and every font in the Fonts folder. To transport the whole document to someone else, or to archive it permanently, just zip or burn the Test Doc Folder folder. You'll never deal with a link missing warning again.

Print Dialog

We've talked about most of the Print dialog already, in context. Let's quickly run through what we haven't already covered.

GENERAL

In addition to printing all pages and sequential selections from the current document, InDesign allows printing of nonsequential pages. In the Range box (see Figure 10.36), enter a sequential range as *X-Y*. If you want to print nonsequentially, use commas, like this: *2, 4, 6, 8, 10*. Maybe, with a multiple-template magazine, for instance, you want to print about 10 pages, but they're spread out in 2- and 3-page chunks across the document's 36 pages. Simple: Combine range and nonsequential like so: *2-3,8-10,20-22*. If all you need is even or odd pages, for instance when doing manual duplexing, select the appropriate option from the Sequence drop-down.

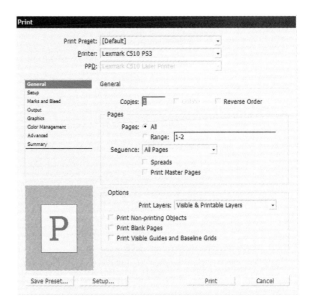

Printing master pages is useful for quite a few things, particularly when proofing or redesigning templates.

Under options, you can choose to print layers that are visible (on) and not tagged as non-printing, but you can also override layer visibility and non-printing status. I like this feature for variations and particularly document review markups. I can feel free to mark up a document with change notes right in InDesign as long as my collaborators or I do it on a layer set to non-printing. When I *want* to print those markups or other non-printing data, the Print Layers drop-down lets me print them. Thus, through *deliberate action* I can get a hardcopy of my document and markups, comments, and other non-printing data, but I don't have to worry that comments like "Were you high when you wrote this!?" will *unintentionally* go to press.

SETUP

If you need to scale pages to fit in a smaller space, make thumbnails, or tile large pages to span multiple sheets of smaller paper, do it here instead of in your printer's setup dialog (Setup button on the bottom left). Why? Because InDesign will scale or divide the pre-processed data; leaving it to your printer scales the post-RIP imagery. You'll get better quality letting InDesign take care of it. (See Figure 10.37)

The preview on the left will update with any changes here (or elsewhere in the Print dialog), which makes it easy to adjust thumbnails, scaling, page position, and tile overlap.

MARKS AND BLEED

This is cool (see Figure 10.38). Want color bars? You got 'em. Want crop marks with a custom offset? There they are. Need to print a proof with custom bleed widths without messing up the document? Well then, just uncheck Use Document Bleed Settings and set the new widths. You can even print information in the document slug area.

FIGURE 10.37
The Print dialog
Setup pane

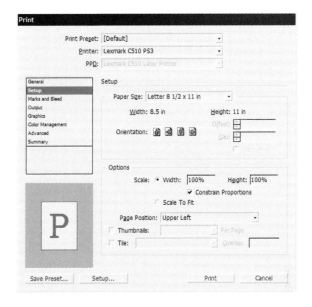

FIGURE 10.38
The Print dialog
Marks and Bleed
pane

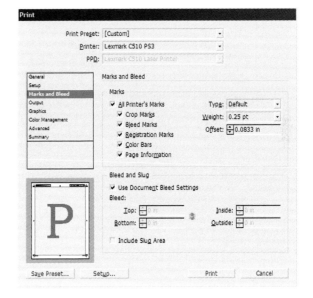

OUTPUT

We've already covered most of this pane (see Figure 10.39). The rest is as follows:

FIGURE 10.39
The Print dialog
Output pane

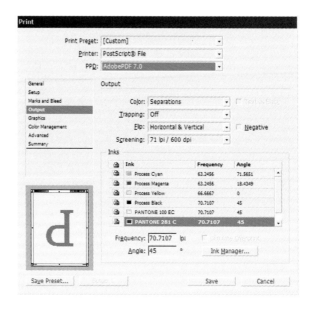

Text as Black Prints all text in black ink.

Flip This one tends to get some people who are used to other layout applications. Flip is how you set emulsion up or down (Flip Horizontal), but it also lets you rotate the image simultaneously.

Screening All the screen frequencies (in lines per inch and gots per inch) available for the selected PPD.

Inks Notice the little printer icon next to each ink? If you'd like to selectively print or omit from printing any inks, just click those icons just as you'd hide layers by clicking the eyeball. InDesign makes it really easy to create your own custom comps or seps or to print without including the colors taking the place of varnishes or dies.

GRAPHICS

See Figure 10.40. This should be called something else since there's really only one option for images, but…

Send Data If high-quality images aren't important to a particular proof, you can speed printing by sending subsampled, low-resolution proxy, or no images at all to the printer.

Fonts Should an entire font be sent to the printer, a subset comprising only the glyphs used in the document, or no fonts at all? The last option includes only a reference to the font in the PostScript file and is useful only when the printer has the needed fonts onboard. When you've used TrueType fonts or TrueType-flavored OpenTypes, it's generally best to download them.

FIGURE 10.40

The Print dialog Graphics pane

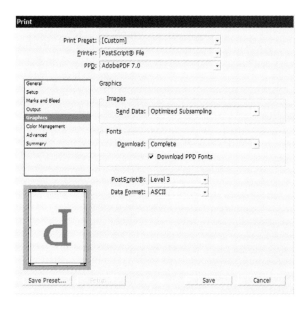

Download PPD Fonts Even if the fonts in use are printer resident, InDesign will download the fonts anyway. Typically, you want this on to guard against disparate versions of fonts causing glyph substitution or text reflow.

PostScript The version of PostScript encoding for the printed data. This option automatically sets itself according to the highest supported level of PostScript in the output device as reported by the PPD. Some desktop printers support emulated PostScript (a PS interpreter from someone other than Adobe), which often doesn't support the full set of features for a particular PostScript level. If you experience problems printing at PostScript 3 with a device that should support it, try changing PostScript to Level 2. Similarly, when printing to a Post-Script file with a generic PPD, you may need to knock the level down to PostScript Level 2 for compatibility.

Data Format Binary has better compression and is a little faster, but it can cause problems with EPS and DCS files and may not be compatible with many output devices. I've used Binary a couple of times, but only on direct request from a service provider. I've never had trouble sending ASCII-encoded PostScript code to a wide variety of devices.

COLOR MANAGEMENT

At the top (see Figure 10.41), choose whether to print using the document working space profile or the proof profile defined in the Customize Proof Conditions dialog.

Next, depending on the printer, PPD, and output options selected, Color Handling will offer options to let InDesign handle color management or to handle it in-RIP. Choose the latter only if you have a PostScript 3—compatible RIP with onboard color management.

Finally, choose the output device's specific ICC profile. The rest of the options you already know.

FIGURE 10.41
The Print
dialog Color
Management pane

ADVANCED

See Figure 10.42. In the OPI section, you can omit different types of proxy images from the print stream to leave just the OPI link comments in the PostScript code. Use this when OPI image insertion is to be handled further downstream.

FIGURE 10.42
The Print dialog
Advanced pane

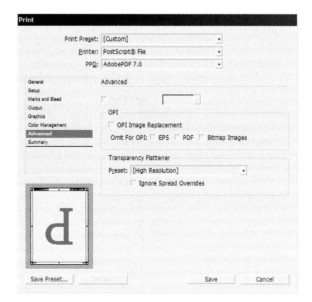

Above the omit options, OPI Image Replacement tells InDesign to handle OPI image replacement in the print stream. Leave it unchecked for an OPI server to do the replacement. In order for InDesign to take care of image replacement, the following conditions must be met:

♦ EPS images in the document must have OPI comments linking to high-resolution versions.

♦ When the EPS proxies were imported, the Read Embedded OPI Image Links check box must have been checked in Import Options.

♦ InDesign must be able to access the high-resolution images.

If conditions one and two are met but not three, InDesign will leave in place OPI comment links for images it can't access.

Last is Transparency Flattener presets and the ability to ignore or override spread overrides.

PRINT PRESETS

Once you've configured all your print settings the way you need them, do yourself a favor and save a preset with the button at the bottom. Next time you need the same configuration, you'll find all your arduously configured settings only two clicks away on the Presets menu.

Even better, from File ➤ Print Presets ➤ Define (see Figure 10.43), you can manage all your presets and even save them to external, shareable PRST files. Clicking New or Edit opens the Print dialog to create or modify a complete set of printing options in the familiar interface.

FIGURE 10.43
The Print Presets
dialog

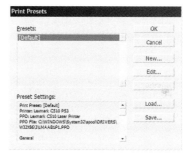

I frequently recommend to my print and pre-press shop clients that they generate PRST files for their common devices and workflows and then distribute those files to their customers as part of job preparation instructions. Save yourself—and your designer customers—some agony and delays. Just make sure to also include the appropriate PPD and ICC files.

The Bottom Line

Configure Color Management on Documents and Images   Consistent color throughout the workflow is critical—even in grayscale jobs. With each version of Creative Suite, Adobe makes color management smarter, easier, and more consistent across the Creative Suite applications. However, the nature of color management is such that it only works if you configure it for the devices specific to your workflow.

Master It   Configure Adobe Bridge to use the ICC profiles for your monitor and printer (or other output device) across all of Creative Suite. You can profile your devices yourself using

Mac's ColorSync or Windows's Image Color Management. If you're configuring a high-end output device such as an imagesetter or proofprinter, ask your print service provider for the most up-to-date ICC profile for the device. If you choose to configure color management for your desktop printer, either profile it yourself or visit the manufacturer's website; most OEMs included free, downloadable ICC profiles. These aren't specific to your printer's unique color rendering characteristics, but it will get you close.

Softproof Documents to Screen   When software makers say, *What You See Is What You Get (WYSIWYG)*, it's really not, not in the case of color, not from the typical working mode of applications. That's where soft proofing comes in. Its pixel-based preview still isn't a precise representation of what you can expect with ink on paper, but when configured correctly, InDesign gets it surprisingly close.

Master It   Using one of your own documents or a sample from another chapter on this book's download page, proof the approximate expected output colors on with your printer's ICC profile. Next, examine how the document will separate when sent to press and how transparency will flatten. Look for potential printing issues, and resolve them.

Preflight, Package, and Output to Print with Managed Inks and Trapping   Printing is about much more than just clicking the Print button. It requires planning and careful preparation. During design and certainly before output, a number of designs critical to your artwork's printed quality must be made. Then, when it is time to send away the job, you have options about how to do that.

Master It   While soft proofing the document, you may have noticed problems with inks, areas of overlapping color that might cause misregistration, and potential ink mixing problems. Using the Ink Manager, overprint attributes, and trapping, resolve these problems and reproof the results. When you're confident the document is ready for output, preflight it, print a hard copy proof on an available printer, and then package the document for delivery to a print service provider.

Chapter 11

Efficiency

Have you ever heard the term *prosumer*? Coined in 1980 by the futurist Alvin Toffler—in his book *The Third Wave*—as a blend of *producer* and *consumer*, the term was used to describe a possible future type of consumer who would become involved in the design and manufacture of products so they could be made to individual specification. These days, the term more often refers to amateurs or hobbyists who use professional-grade tools. A hobbyist's ideal page-layout application, used for birthday party invitations, band fliers, and custom Christmas cards, for instance, would be Serif PagePlus or Microsoft Publisher. A professional would choose a platform with more extensive features and finer control, something like InDesign or QuarkXPress. Prosumers are those who create invitations, fliers, and cards using gold standards such as InDesign or QuarkXPress.

For the prosumer, the key criteria in a page-layout application—and the most interesting parts of a book about the application—are those that unfetter creativity and ease usability. Print professionals have the same requirements, but equally important is the ability of the application to effect, and of the book to teach, the fastest, most efficient means of getting a job done.

This chapter is *not* about the prosumer.

In this chapter, you will learn to:

◆   Work efficiently with text

◆   Work efficiently with tables

◆   Work efficiently with objects

Working Efficiently with Text

Between InDesign's copious features and a little of the wisdom of experience, there are many ways to increase productivity when working with text and type objects, which is a good thing when you consider that setting and manipulating type is the biggest part of most professionals' work in InDesign.

Paragraph Styles

Paragraph styles are most definitely not a new concept. InDesign didn't invent them, and CS3 doesn't bring anything radically new to the concept. However, a remarkable number of professionals working under deadlines don't use them, thus wasting a tremendous amount of time and money. If you *do* use paragraph styles religiously *and* you're already adept at creating, modifying, and using them in InDesign, by all means, feel free to skim or even skip this short initial section—but do check out the following sections on style names, organization, and more, however.

What are paragraph styles? Why should I use them? A paragraph style is a record of all paragraph-level attributes of text—formatting options that apply to all text between the start of the paragraph and the end. It's a record that can be reused to instantly style additional text with all the same attributes—typeface, font size, indents, paragraph spacing, rules, justification, bullets or numbering, underline, color, and more. Moreover, once a paragraph style has been applied to text, every attribute of that text can be altered throughout the entire document (or book) just by changing the paragraph style. You can literally reformat the text of a thousand pages in seconds. If you do nothing else to improve your productivity, nothing else to save yourself time and frustration, use paragraph styles.

Paragraph styles are, predictably, managed from the Paragraph Styles panel, which can be opened from Window ➢ Type & Tables ➢ Paragraph Styles (see Figure 11.1). Styles are listed in the panel in the order of creation—a departure from prior versions of InDesign that enforced an alphabetic arrangement. If you want alphabetic arrangement, choose Sort by Name from the Paragraph Styles flyout menu.

FIGURE 11.1

The Paragraph Styles panel, with a few styles and groups already created

There are two ways to create a paragraph style: (1) define the style before formatting text, and (2) create a style *from* formatted text. The latter is the faster, more intuitive way because you set most, if not all, formatting on live text on the page and then simply create a style that records the formatting; you will work with familiar areas of InDesign such as the Paragraph and Character panels to *see* what the style will become.

So, set a line or paragraph of type on the page and format it however you like. Then, highlight all or part of the paragraph, or simply leave the I-beam cursor within the paragraph, and on the Paragraph Styles panel, click the new button at the bottom. A new style will appear in the list with a default name—Paragraph Style 1; additional styles will be numbered sequentially. Note that Paragraph Style 1 is *not* yet assigned to the text from which it was created. You'll still need to tag the text with the style by clicking once on Paragraph Style 1. The style assignment will last until the end of the paragraph, a hard carriage return, as indicated by the presence of a pilcrow (¶), which you'll see if viewing hidden characters. To apply the style to additional paragraphs, click within or highlight them (in whole or in part) and choose Paragraph Style 1 once more from the Paragraph Styles panel.

LOGICAL STYLE NAMES

Default style naming isn't very informative. *Was Paragraph Style 13 for figure captions or third-level numbered lists? Wait, wasn't it Paragraph Style 4 for figure captions and Paragraph Style 21 for third-level numbered lists?* You can see how confusing it can become quickly. Even if you know now exactly which default-named style is used for which text, will you remember six months from now? A year? If you need to bring in some help on the project or an update to, or derivation of, the project, will others know at a glance which style should be used for *this* text and which for *that*? In all cases, the correct answer is *very unlikely*. Give your styles descriptive names that make sense to you and to whomever else might have a reason to work with the document.

There are two ways to rename paragraph styles, and two ways to access each way. The fastest way is to first highlight the style in the list, then Option+click/Alt+click on the name itself. You'll be able to rename the style right on the panel. You can also double-click on the style name in the list to do the same. If you double-click right on the characters, you'll be able to rename in place. If your double-clicking is a bit off, you'll open the Paragraph Style Options, which is the second way to rename styles (see Figure 11.2).

FIGURE 11.2
Paragraph Style
Options

On the top of the General pane of the Paragraph Style Options dialog is the Style Name field. Rename it there. And, while you're here, why not get even more organized?

CASCADING STYLES

The Based On field presents a list of all other paragraph styles defined in the document. InDesign's styles are *cascading styles*, meaning that Style B can be based on Style A, C on B, D on C, and so on. This is an important concept to grasp because it means that by carefully basing styles on one another, you can effect broad changes across multiple styles by changing only one.

Let's say, for example, that you've chosen Adobe's Minion Pro type family for the majority of your document. Leaving out, for this example, styles not using Minion Pro, perhaps your paragraph styles would include the basic character formatting shown in Table 11.1.

TABLE 11.1: **Basic Character Formats in the Document's Initial Paragraph Styles**

PARAGRAPH STYLE	FONT FAMILY	STYLE	SIZE	LEADING	FIRST LINE INDENT
Body Copy	Minion Pro	Regular	10.5 pt	13.25 pt	0.25″
Body Copy First ¶	Minion Pro	Regular	10.5 pt	13.25 pt	0″
Kicker	Minion Pro	Bold Italic	12 pt	14 pt	1″
Caption	Minion Pro	Italic	8.5 pt	10 pt	0″
List - Num LVL 1	Minion Pro	Regular	10.5 pt	13 pt	0.5″
List - Num LVL 2	Minion Pro	Regular	10.5 pt	13 pt	1.0″
List - Unnum	Minion Pro	Regular	10.5 pt	13 pt	0.5″

Because more text will likely fall under the Body Copy paragraph style than any other, we'll designate that as the primary, or parent, style. Looking at the table, you should see many options among the other styles that are identical to those of Body Copy. Let's highlight them for clarity (see Table 11.2).

TABLE 11.2: **Common Character Formats in the Document's Initial Paragraph Styles**

PARAGRAPH STYLE	FONT FAMILY	STYLE	SIZE	LEADING	FIRST LINE INDENT
Body Copy	Minion Pro	Regular	10.5 pt	13.25 pt	0.25″
Body Copy First ¶	Minion Pro	Regular	10.5 pt	13.25 pt	0″
Kicker	Minion Pro	Bold Italic	12 pt	14 pt	1″
Caption	Minion Pro	Italic	8.5 pt	10 pt	0″
List - Num LVL 1	Minion Pro	Regular	10.5 pt	13 pt	0.25″
List - Num LVL 2	Minion Pro	Regular	10.5 pt	13 pt	0.5″
List - Unnum	Minion Pro	Regular	10.5 pt	13 pt	0.25″

Each of the styles shares at least one common characteristic—the Font Family Minion Pro. Except for the Kicker and Caption styles, the rest have four options matching those of Body Copy. Whenever two or more styles share formatting options, you're presented with the opportunity to save yourself some work. You see, each paragraph style isn't *required* to store all the formatting options for a passage of text; it can contain as many or as few settings as you like. By setting styles to be based on one another, you leave all the *common options to a single style*, storing *only the differences* in the dependent styles.

Considering the styles in our tables and the commonalities we identified, Body Copy is our primary style based on nothing (No Paragraph Style) and holding all the core formatting options.

Body Copy First ¶ will be based on Body Copy and therefore only itself contain the different first line indent; all other options it will inherit from its parent, Body Copy. The Kicker style will also be based on Body Copy, but it will only use its font family; the font style, size, leading, and first line indents are all different, and those unique settings will be part of the Kicker style. Each of the other styles will also be based on Body Copy, cascading from the parent Body Copy style for shared attributes and holding onto only their unique values. The result would produce styles that look like Table 11.3. With all styles based on the Body Copy paragraph style, common values are left out of dependent styles (indicated by empty fields).

TABLE 11.3: **Redundant Attributes Are Removed in Styles Based on One Another**

PARAGRAPH STYLE	FONT FAMILY	STYLE	SIZE	LEADING	FIRST LINE INDENT
Body Copy	Minion Pro	Regular	10.5 pt	13.25 pt	0.25˝
Body Copy First ¶					0˝
Kicker		Bold Italic	12 pt	14 pt	1˝
Caption		Italic	8.5 pt	10 pt	0˝
List - Num LVL 1				13 pt	
List - Num LVL 2				13 pt	0.5˝
List - Unnum				13 pt	

Now that you've got the concept down, you should be asking three questions:

◆ *What is the point and value of cascading styles?*

◆ *How do I leave common traits out of a paragraph style definition?*

◆ *There are other formatting attributes shared between some of the other styles. Should they cascade off one another as well?*

Let's start with the first question: *What is the point and value of cascading styles?* The point of cascading styles off one another is to eliminate redundancy in their definitions, and the value is that doing so increases efficiency. Looking once again at our cascading styles, they all share a font family, Minion Pro. What if you or the client decides that Officina Serif ITC Pro would be a better choice? Well, that's a single change—change the font family setting in the Body Copy style and the alteration will ripple down through all styles dependent upon Body Copy. Suddenly, and with no further action on your part, Body Copy First ¶, Kicker, Caption, and your lists will also all use Officina Serif ITC Pro. Text assigned to the Kicker style will be Officina Serif ITC Pro Bold Italic, and text in the Caption style will be Officina Serif ITC Pro Italic. Not happy with Officina Serif ITC Pro? Change Body Copy's font family to Palatino Linotype or Times New Roman or Garamond Premiere Pro—whatever—and all dependent styles will inherit the change from their parent. Change the font size in Body Copy and all styles except those with unique values will change as well. Basing styles on one another eliminates redundant settings that become impediments when a common trait must change. The formatting of some or all the text in an entire document can be modified in seconds, with a single, facile task.

As for your second question—*how do I leave common traits out of a paragraph style definition?*—the answer is simple. In the Paragraph Style Options dialog, on the General pane, the Style Settings area lists the Based On style and only those additional settings that differ from it (see Figure 11.3). Before you base the style on another, the Style Settings area will display all formatting options defined in the style. As soon as you make a selection in the Based On field above it, all common attributes disappear from the Style Settings area. InDesign assumes you want the shared attributes inherited from—and changed along with—the parent style and so removes them from the child style itself.

FIGURE 11.3
Style settings for the current paragraph style

If any unique settings remain in the Style Settings area that you don't want to be unique, that you want to instead inherit from the parent style, delete them. Go to the appropriate pane in the Paragraph Style Options dialog, and clear the contents of the text field for the specific attribute. For example, if you want to remove a 0.25-inch right indent, go to the Indents and Spacing pane, highlight the value in the Right Indent field, and press Delete or Backspace on your keyboard. The 0.25-inch setting will immediately be replaced by the inherited value of the parent style, whatever is its right indent. Check boxes, radio buttons, and drop-down lists are similar—just clear their values.

Finally, you observed that the styles we've been working with in our tables shared other common attributes and asked, *Should they cascade off one another as well?* Yes, they should if you want true style efficiency. Styles may be cascaded numerous levels deep—Style B can be based on A, C on B, D on C. Inheritance will follow through all the levels. For example, if we based List - Num LVL 1 on Body Copy and List - Num LVL 2 on List - Num LVL 1, List - Num LVL 2 would inherit the options from *both* List - Num LVL 1 and Body Copy.

Carefully setting styles to be dependent on one another may sound complicated, but it really isn't—no more so than a child's game of matching like characteristics—*which of these is like the others?* And, it yields tremendous productivity benefits.

AUTOMATIC SEQUENTIAL STYLES

Another area that helps greatly is the Next Style field on the General pane of Paragraph Style Options. The Next Style field poses a simple question: *When you hit Return/Enter, what style do you want to use for the next paragraph?* Paragraph styles apply to an entire paragraph, from the character after a carriage return through, and including, the next carriage return. After that, in the following paragraph, you can keep the same paragraph style or automatically switch to another. For example, rarely does a subhead precede another subhead without intervening text. Therefore, I would open the Paragraph Style Options for the Subhead style and set its Next Style field to Body Copy; thereafter, every time I type a document subhead and hit return, I automatically begin typing the next paragraph in the Body Copy style.

Next Styles can be strung together as well, thus creating, under some circumstances, fully automatic, cascading paragraph styles with no need to even reach for the Paragraph Styles panel after the first line of the document. Consider a directory-style listing (see Figure 11.4). Each line is its own paragraph, each line has—or can easily have—its own paragraph style, and most importantly, the paragraph formatting is cyclical. Each listing or dataset begins and ends with the same styles that begin and end lines in other listings.

FIGURE 11.4
Typical directory listings with styles called out

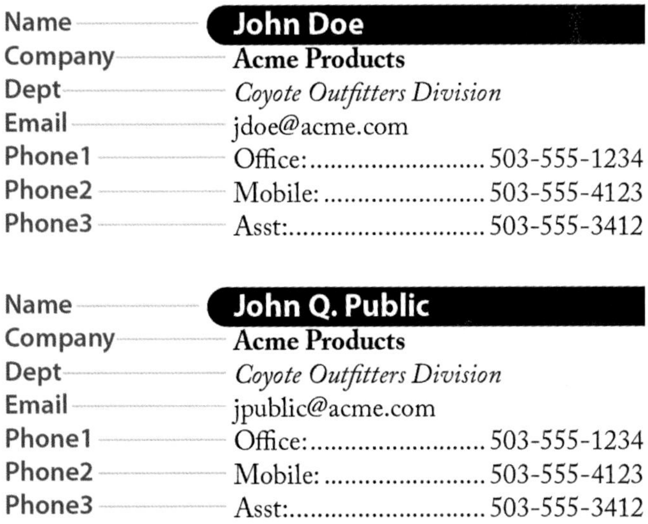

You can type a thousand of those listings, only touching the Paragraph Styles panel *once* thanks to Next Style. In the options for the Name style, set the Next Style field to the Company style; in Company, make Dept the next style; in Dept, set Email as the next style; and then Phone1 and Phone2 successively. With the Phone3 style, set its Next Style field back to the beginning (i.e., back to Name). Now, type the name, pick the correct paragraph style for the entry's name, and hit Return/Enter. Type the company name, which will automatically be in the Company style, hit Return/Enter. Type the contact's department in the Dept style, and so on. When you finish typing the assistant's phone number on the listing's last line and hit Return/Enter, the Next Style cascade will loop back to the beginning, setting the line after your carriage return in the Name style, ready for you to type the next contact's name.

Next Style saves a great many distracting trips to the Paragraph Styles and Character Styles panels in many, many types of documents. We'll get into the efficient use of characters styles later in this chapter. For now, let's keep the focus on paragraph styles.

STYLE GROUPS

In InDesign CS3, styles can be reordered and rearranged in the Paragraph Styles panel list simply by dragging and dropping. Even better—courtesy of RogueSheep, a group of InDesign programmers who left Adobe and were brought back into the flock temporarily to assist in the production of CS3—the styles can also be arranged in nested folder groups much like Illustrator's or Photoshop's layers (see Figure 11.5).

FIGURE 11.5
New style groups make organization even easier.

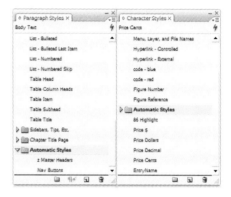

By clicking the New Folder button at the bottom of the panel, you can add expandable groups to the Paragraph Styles list (as well as to other styles panel's lists, which we'll discuss later in this chapter). Place styles in the groups by dragging them or by highlighting the styles and choosing from the panel flyout menu Copy to Group, which opens a destination group selection dialog, or New Group from Styles, which simultaneously creates a new group and moves the styles into it. You can even put one group inside another, nesting them.

Groups can be renamed like styles and can be opened or closed by clicking on the arrow to the left of the group name. Helpful Open All and Close All Style Groups commands are on the flyout menu.

CLEAN UP STYLES

Paragraph styles are major productivity aids, but only when in use. (So, uh, use 'em.) As you work, changing this passage of text, trying this visual effect or that, you'll undoubtedly end up with extraneous paragraph styles unused anywhere in the document. Leaving those alone makes for an unnecessarily bloated style list. Dump the styles you don't need. On the Paragraph Styles panel flyout menu is the Select All Unused command. When executed, it selects (highlights) all the styles that aren't assigned to any text, anywhere. Once they're selected, simply click the trashcan Delete icon at the bottom of the panel to delete those useless bits of clutter.

STYLE OVERRIDES

An *override* is any formatting that doesn't jibe with the style definition. For instance, if you set a paragraph in a roman (non-italic) typeface and then italicize a word or phrase within the paragraph, the italic text is overriding the paragraph style. Overrides are revealed as a plus sign (+)

beside the style name on the Paragraph Style panel, but only when the overridden text is selected. If you select or place the cursor within the italic text in the example, a plus sign will appear next to the paragraph style's name in the panel. Move the cursor to another word that does adhere to the style definition, however, and the plus sign will disappear despite the presence of overrides in the same paragraph. Selecting the entire paragraph also selects the overridden word and thus supplies the telltale plus sign. *Anything* done to a paragraph or a part of a paragraph that isn't specifically defined in the paragraph style is an override—text color, font, leading, paragraph indents, tabs, and so on.

In and of themselves, overrides are no big deal—they're just formatting options that aren't in the style definition. Heck, if all they are is an italic word or two, who cares, really? Many times, though, that plus sign signals something bigger than an emphasis here and there. For instance, an override in a collaborative layout could hint at a radical departure from the style guide by one of the layout artists.. One accidental press of Option+/Alt+ on the keyboard would increase the leading of a selected paragraph, potentially changing the text fitting for dozens of subsequent pages. Maybe someone inadvertently clicked on the Registration color swatch instead of the Black swatch on the Swatches panel. Registration, as you know, is 100% of cyan, magenta, yellow, and black; a paragraph colored with Registration will look just as black as pure black on screen, but it will print to all four CMYK plates and come off the press looking more like scorched mud than black. The plus sign is your only warning of these or other mishaps.

Restoring text formatting to the strict definition of the paragraph style is called clearing overrides. After selecting the word, words, paragraph, or story containing overrides, there are several ways to clear overrides:

◆ Choose the Clear Overrides command from the Paragraph Styles panel flyout menu.

◆ Force reapply the paragraph style by holding Option/Alt and clicking on the style name on the panel.

◆ Use the new Clear Overrides button at the bottom of the Paragraph Styles panel. Cmd+click/Ctrl+click to clear character-level overrides only (e.g., italics or kerning), or Cmd+Shift+click/Ctrl+Shift+click to clear only overriding paragraph-level attributes such as indents, spacing, and drop caps.

Be careful clearing overrides by any method: The process is indiscriminate, and all overrides will be wiped out, wanted or not.

If you like the override and want to make the style incorporate it, thus updating all other text assigned to the same paragraph style to match the overridden text, highlight or place your cursor within only the differently styled word and choose Redefine Style on the Paragraph Styles panel flyout menu. Redefine Style incorporates the formatting options of the selected text into the style definition. For most people (your humble host included), Redefine Style is a lifesaver because it saves them from having to go into the Paragraph Style Options to make changes. Instead, formatting options can be changed on the page and then the style quickly updated to incorporate the new aesthetic.

In an ideal world, your document would never have a plus sign beside any style. Practically speaking, however, it's far too much darn work to never have overrides. I mean, changing a kerning pair in a headline is an override and produces that plus sign. What are you going to do, create a character style for *every* little tweak and pluck? Certainly not. Just be careful, and, when it makes sense, use character styles. And, with that…

Character Styles

Paragraph styles are paragraph level and include in their definitions many character-level formatting options such as font family, font style, size, leading, scaling, color, OpenType options, and much more; paragraph styles apply to the entire paragraph, including the final paragraph mark (¶). If an entire paragraph will be formatted the same, a paragraph style will do the trick all by itself. However, if you expect words or phrases *within* paragraphs to differ in some respect from their surrounding text, regularly or occasionally, you'll want character styles defined to store, apply, and preserve those differences.

Predictably, character styles are managed on the Character Styles panel (Window ➤ Type & Tables ➤ Character Styles). I won't dwell on the panel itself because it's almost identical to big brother Paragraph Styles. You have a list of styles, style groups, and many of the same commands on the flyout menu. Even their respective new style and style options dialogs are identical, but the Character version contains a subset of the panes found in the corresponding Paragraph Style New and Options dialogs (compare Figure 11.6 with Figure 11.2 that we looked at earlier). Character styles can also be based on one another, although, because they don't have anything to do with carriage returns, there is no Next Style field.

FIGURE 11.6
The Character Style
Options dialog

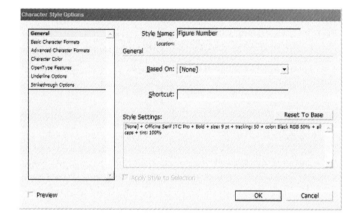

Think of character styles as sanctioned overrides. They change text formatting by the character or by the word, but they don't cause a plus sign and thus aren't wiped away by clearing overrides. Create character styles as you would paragraph styles—either by formatting text and then pressing the New button at the bottom of the Character Styles panel or by defining the style in the Character Style Options dialog ahead of placing text. To apply them, you must highlight text. Paragraph styles may be applied when the cursor is simply within a paragraph, even if no text is selected, but character styles require specific text selection.

Character styles are ideal for a variety of uses. Here are just a few examples (see Figure 11.7):

◆ Using *run-in* heads.

◆ Underlining URLs in a document destined for distribution as a PDF (and in which those URLs will be live, clickable links; don't underline them otherwise).

◆ Adding other nondefault underlines and strikethroughs without having to go through the Underline Options or Strikethrough Options dialogs every time.

◆ Highlighting text (see the sidebar "Underline Styles for Hyperlinks" in Chapter 3, "Characters").

◆ Setting italic or bold type that will survive a deliberate or accidental clearing of overrides.

◆ Changing the color of bits of text.

◆ Styling the first line of a story larger or in all caps.

◆ Differentiating the style of numbers or leaders in a directory- or TOC-style entry.

◆ Styling drop caps differently from the rest of the text in the paragraph. Note that drop caps themselves—whether to use them, how many lines tall they are, and how many characters wide they are—are paragraph-level attributes. Use character styles to alter typeface, color, and other options on drop caps already defined in paragraph styles.

FIGURE 11.7

Example uses for character styles

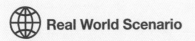

Chapter 1   My father's family name being Pirrip, and my Christian name Philip, my infant tongue could make of both names nothing longer or more explicit than Pip. So, I called myself Pip, and came to be called Pip.

MY FATHER'S FAMILY NAME BEING PIRRIP, AND my Christian name Philip, my infant tongue could make of both names nothing longer or more explicit than Pip. So, I called myself Pip, and came to be called Pip.

y father's family name being Pirrip, and my Christian name Philip, my infant tongue could make of both names nothing longer or more explicit than Pip. So, I called myself Pip, and came to be called Pip.

My father's family name being Pirrip, and my Christian name Philip, my infant tongue could make of both names nothing longer or more explicit than Pip (*see* www.Domain.com). So, I called myself Pip, and came to be called Pip.

My father's family name being Pirrip, and my Christian name Philip, my infant tongue could make of both names nothing longer or more explicit than Pip. So, I called myself Pip, and came to be called Pip.

1   My father's family name being Pirrip, and my Christian name Philip, my infant tongue could make of both names nothing longer or more explicit than Pip. So, I called myself Pip, and came to be called Pip.

⊕ Real World Scenario

FIND/CHANGE STYLES TO THE RESCUE

Joanna S. worked as the final stop in a publication workflow that involved nine layout artists, each working on different portions of a 320-page quarterly. Her job was to collect and proof everyone's work, stitch it all together into a single publication managed by an InDesign book, and fix any mistakes before imposing the issue and sending it to press. Of course, the publication had a style guide, templates, and preconfigured paragraph and character styles; invariably, however, the articles and sections Joanna received from the other creatives contained numerous style overrides in the form of local formatting—all of which Joanna had to fix before the publication went to press. Making matters worse, the publication also ran per issue anywhere between 1 and 10 articles and pieces of articles from outside agencies and filler libraries. The outside contributions were formatted in ways that rarely bore any resemblance to Joanna's templates.

Wrangling these wild styles should have been as easy as selecting paragraphs and applying or reapplying paragraph styles. Unfortunately, doing so cleared out *desired* overrides, most notably italic. Consequently, Joanna found herself spending days staring at side-by-side comparisons of original pages and pages with correct paragraph styles, locating italicized words in the former, and manually italicizing the same words in the latter. The process took so long that she had to push up the issue closing date—which, of course, some members of the team understood to mean more time between submission and press for making last-minute rewrites, leading to more formatting cleanup and often on the same story more than once.

The real solution to Joanna's problem lay with stricter enforcement of the publication's style guide, which was in the offing but still left her with a lot of extra work in the interim. Although style enforcement might improve the consistency of work from Joanna's coworkers, policy changes for content from external agencies wasn't likely to improve as quickly as internal policy changes. By way of retaining Joanna's direct control over fixing the publication, I enacted a two-step solution.

First, Joanna and I identified all the formatting options that fell under the heading of "desired override"— in other words, any appropriately used character-level formatting such as italic, a couple of different underline and coloring styles used for assorted kinds of URLs listed in stories, and small caps for acronyms and occasional other uses. We created character styles to hold each of the settings—one for small caps, one each for the types of URLs, one each for italic, bold-italic. We also created a Regular character style that specifically disallowed all the formatting options of all the other character styles; using the Regular style would instantly strip off the effects of, say, the bold-italic style, reverting the selected text to non-bold, non-italic. We added these styles to the main template.

Step two was building and enacting a procedure to replace wanted style overrides with character styles and then remove all unwanted overrides. No sweat. Using Find/Change (Edit ➤ Find/Change), we searched for any italic glyph and assigned it to the Italic character style. You see those settings in the screenshot of the Find/Change dialog. Similar searches were run for each of the other format overrides that had matching character styles. Each replacement criteria set was saved as a reusable query.

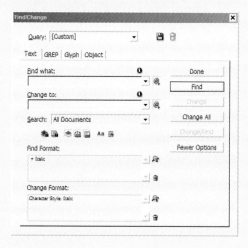

To revert undesirable overrides back to their correct paragraph styles, additional searches were performed, one for each paragraph style. In that case, it was even simpler: both Find Format and Change Format were set to the same paragraph style and no other options. When InDesign performs a Find/Change with such criteria, it automatically strips off any overrides—but not those properly assigned to character styles. So, to remove any unwanted overrides on the Body Copy style, Joanna set the Find Format to search for Paragraph Style: Body Copy; the Change Format was also set to only Paragraph Style: Body Copy. InDesign rolled through all the stories in the document, finding every instance of text in the Body Copy style, and force reapplying the paragraph style. Joanna's problem was solved.

To make things even faster, and with the help of a JavaScript programmer in Joanna's IT department, even all the Find/Change queries were automated. Now Joanna just executes the Style Cleanup script from the Scripts panel. Formatting cleanup that used to take her days is finished within a couple of minutes.

BREAKING STYLE LINKS

When you change a style definition, all text assigned to the style will update accordingly anywhere in the current document. Sometimes, you'd rather freeze a particular passage of text, leaving it unchanged regardless of what happens to the style definition. To do that, disassociate the text from the style with the Break Link to Style command on either or both the Paragraph Styles or Character Styles panels. The text will retain its formatting but will no longer update to reflect changes in the style.

Nested Styles

A nested style is a character style applied from Point A to Point B automatically. For example, you could specify that the first two words of any paragraph assigned to the First Graph paragraph style automatically adopt a different color, typeface, and an underline. If you're working on a product catalog, you could force every dollar sign ($) to one character style, the dollar amount to another character style, and the cents to a third style (perhaps one that makes the numerals superscript and underlined), all automatically.

Remember, when we discussed the Next Style choice on paragraph styles, how I said you can format an entire listing—and even multiple listings—by merely selecting the first paragraph style? Nested Styles is very similar, but operates *within* paragraphs instead of being triggered by carriage returns. In other words, you can format an entire paragraph of many different character styles by merely selecting the first paragraph style.

Open the Paragraph Style Options for any style, and go to the Drop Caps and Nested Styles pane (see Figure 11.8). In the upper portion, Drop Caps, is the introduction to nested styles. After defining the number of lines and characters to form the drop cap, you can choose a character style that applies only to the drop cap. After the drop cap, the character style will stop applying to text, leaving the rest of the paragraph untouched. Thus the beginning of the drop cap is Point A, the end Point B; it's a nested style.

FIGURE 11.8
The Drop Caps and
Nested Styles pane
of Paragraph Style
Options

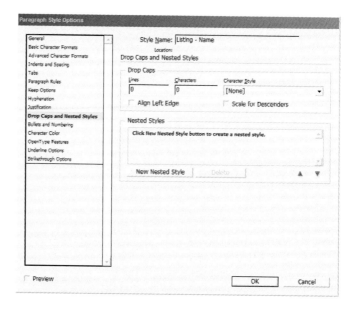

When you'd like to use something other than a drop cap as a nested style, move to the lower section and press the New Nested Style button, which will add a new row of four fields to the Nested Styles list. Before I describe the fields, though, I'd like to diagram the anatomy of a simple nested style so you can see what those fields do (see Figure 11.9). The character style (Heading 3 RunIn, it's called), begins with the paragraph and applies to text the *run-in head* up until it reaches the nested style end marker, which, in this case, is a tab.

FIGURE 11.9
A run-in head
nested style

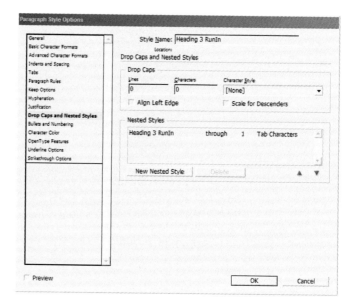

Back in the Nested Styles list, the row of fields is a statement—use *this* character style up to or through *X* instances of *that* stop character. In the first field, choose the character style to use. Next, decide whether to style the stop character itself as well as the text before it. For example, if you set a colon as the stop character, choosing Through will apply the character style to the colon as well as to the text that precedes it; setting this field to Up To will apply the style and stop before styling the colon. After that, choose how many instances of the stop character. You can, for instance, continue applying the character style through the third tab from the beginning of the paragraph, or the fifth tab, or the ninth… Finally, choose the stop character itself. You can use any single letter, number, punctuation, or symbol. The drop-down menu in this field presents several common options such as a tab character or forced line break, as well as sentences, words, and characters. Choosing Sentences, for example, you could style the entire first sentence of the paragraph whether that sentence is 2 or 40 words long. If the stop character you want isn't in the list, type it into the field, replacing whatever is there.

As you may surmise, you can add multiple nested styles that follow one another. In Figure 11.10 you can see a series of nested styles I might use for the prices in a catalog; on the right of the figure are the before and after of using the nested styles. (Note that the decimal point is still there, but it turned white by its character style.) The order of nested styles in the list is critical as each style picks up after the last has ended. I couldn't, for example, put my Price Cents style directive ahead of the Price $. If I did, none of the styles that need to be applied before Price Cents would be applied. The arrows beneath the Nested Styles list enable the rows to be reordered as needed.

FIGURE 11.10
At left, the chained nested styles create the effect at the lower right. In the upper right is the text before applying nested styles.

Your stop character can be just about any character you can type—and many invisible ones such as spaces, tabs, and returns. This is what makes nested styles so powerful. They apply automatically to text, adapting to the text itself. Still, this method assumes that an appropriate stop character can be found in the text where you want it. What if there isn't? What if you want to style only the first line of a paragraph regardless of how many words or characters that may be, regardless of whether the last word in the line is complete or hyphenated? Can you just set the nested style stop character to End of Line? Regrettably, no; it's a glaring omission in an otherwise extremely powerful feature. Fortunately, you *can* insert a special, invisible stop character marker in the text where you need it.

On the Type ➤ Insert Special Character ➤ Other menu is the End Nested Style Here marker, which corresponds to an option on the Stop Character field drop-down in the Paragraph Style Options's Drop Caps and Nested Styles pane. Placing the End Nested Style Here marker in text, and choosing that as the stop character, limits the effect of a nested style to precisely the point you decide.

Nested styles added to the paragraph style apply anywhere that paragraph style is applied. If you only want to use a nested style once, in a spot instance, choose Drop Caps and Nested Styles from the flyout menu on the Paragraph panel or the Control Panel in Paragraph mode.

Text Variables

As of the release of InDesign CS3—and for nine years before that—Adobe owns three page-layout applications: PageMaker, which reached an official end of life in 2003 yet continues to enjoy a large and loyal following; InDesign, which was conceived by PageMaker creator Aldus (acquired by Adobe in 1994) as the replacement for PageMaker; and FrameMaker, a robust technical-document-publishing application that is decidedly unfriendly to creative types. Although Page-Maker and InDesign differ in their approaches, there is nothing the former does that the latter doesn't. The same can't be said of FrameMaker. That application has always led the pack in its ability to create a unlimited assortment of adaptive text variables and automatically numbered items and lists. Maintaining three separate page layout applications is a strain for a company like Adobe because, to a large degree, its layout applications compete with one another. More impor-tantly, PageMaker and FrameMaker are both (by computer standards) ancient code bases that can-not be readied for the publishing demands of today much less tomorrow. In fact, FrameMaker for Mac hasn't even been updated to work with OS X; the Mac version was officially discontinued a few years ago because sluggish sales wouldn't justify the expense of rewriting the elderly code.

PageMaker's features were easily replaced by InDesign, but Adobe couldn't replace FrameMaker with InDesign without rendering InDesign as unintuitive and noncreative-friendly as the other. Slowly, however, Adobe is training InDesign users to expect more-advanced, more-powerful, more-complicated features. In expectation of the day when it can finally retire FrameMaker, in InDesign CS2 it introduced anchored objects. Now, CS3 continues the trend with better paragraph-numbering options, the restoration of a direct HTML export (absent since version CS in 2003), expanded script-ing and XML, and, most importantly, *text variables*.

When you insert a page number marker on a master page, you are really inserting a text vari-able. It isn't static data; rather, it updates itself with every page. In its simplest form, a page num-ber is a mere digit; activate section or chapter numbering and the page number will include the unique number of each section or chapter (and possibly text, too) as well as a numeric, alphabetic, or mixed-numbering page number. That's a text variable: text that changes automatically to meet current conditions.

The obvious benefit to productivity of using a text variable is that certain bits of text that would otherwise have to be written and edited by hand are inserted and changed automatically. Place the text variable once and forget about it; it will alter its information to match changing conditions in the document, computer, or what have you. Used wisely, the result can be a significant time sav-ings—particularly with repeating text such as a product name.

What would be a practical application of a custom text variable? Consider this scenario: You're the production manger at a direct-mail production house. As part of your company's services, you offer clients several predesigned, ready-to-fly templates. Your templates are built such that only the client's name, logo, and contact info (phone, fax, address, and URL) change; all other infor-mation and design is static from one client to the next. Instead of changing the client-specific information in its three or four locations manually—or even doing a Find/Change—insert text variables in the appropriate template locations. To change the client company name, simply change the single value in the text variable's definition and all instances of that variable in the layout copy will update to match. Setting up all the requisite custom data—company name, phone, address line 1, address line 2, and so on—would involve each being one text variable. If you hooked InDesign into your client or job database via scripting or XML, you could even automate the entire process of changing text variables and sending the document to print or PDF.

VARIABLE TEXT TYPES

InDesign CS3 ships with seven predefined, ready-to-insert text variables: Chapter Number, Creation Date, File Name, Last Page Number, Modification Date, Output Date, and Running Header. They can be inserted in a text frame by selecting Type ➤ Text Variables ➤ Insert Variable. Once inserted, a variable takes on the formatting of surrounding text and is thus ready to use upon installation of InDesign. Note that text variables *will not wrap* across multiple lines; instead they will overset. You may not want to use the defaults for everything, however, so you can define your own variables from Type ➤ Text Variables ➤ Define. In the Text Variables list are the defaults and any you've created or imported from other documents via the Load button.

As implied above, you can have numerous text variables of different or all the same types. You can, for instance, have several different running header type text variables all in use in the same document. Click the New button in the dialog to create a new text variable. In the New Text Variable dialog there are nine different types of variables available, and each has its own unique options to set:

Chapter Number This type of variable displays the current chapter number with optional text before and/or after and using the numbering style selected (see Figure 11.11). Flyout menus to the right of the Text Before and Text After fields enable easy input of special glyphs and markers. Although you may paste into the Before and After fields text that is copied from another field or the document text, special characters will not paste in correctly and must be inserted using the flyout menus.

FIGURE 11.11
Options for Chapter
Number text
variables

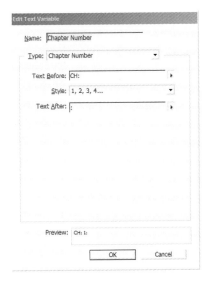

Creation Date Useful for inserting in the slug area or a note the date and/or time at which a document was created, this variable offers a highly customizable array of date/time formats from the flyout menu to the right of the Date Format field (see Figure 11.12). Naturally, the field also accepts text input, so you can separate date/time components with standard punctuation and marks.

FIGURE 11.12
Options for Creation
Date text variables

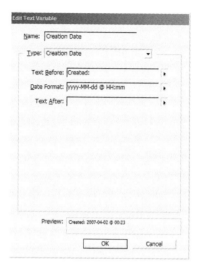

Custom Text This variable type offers but one text entry field that can accept pasted or typed content and special glyphs and symbols from the menu to the right of the field.

File Name Placing the name of the current document in the slug area is a common practice, one that this text variable makes a snap. Before and after text is complemented with two options, Include Entire Folder Path and Include File Extension, that, respectively, insert the complete path to the file on disk and the document file extension (see Figure 11.13).

FIGURE 11.13
Options for File
Name text variables

Last Page Number Undoubtedly among the most commonly used, the Last Page Number text variable can be used to create a folio in form of *Page X of Y* where X is the current page number inserted from the Type ➤ Insert Special Characters menu and Y is the number of the last page in the document. Standard optional before and after text is accepted, as is a numbering style (e.g., Arabic, Roman, alphabetic, etc.) and a scope—whether to use the last page number of the section or document (see Figure 11.14).

FIGURE 11.14

Options for Last Page Number text variables

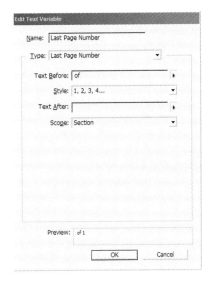

Modification Date With options identical to the Creation Date text variable type, Modification Date records the last, rather than the first, time the document was saved.

Output Date Again, like Creation Date and Modification Date text variable types, Output Date offers number options for formatting the date/time when the document was output—printed, packaged, or exported to PDF.

The last two text variable types, Running Headers (Paragraph Style) and Running Headers (Character Style) require a little more space to explain.

RUNNING HEADERS AND FOOTERS

When you insert text at the top or bottom of a page, you've created headers or footers. Adding the Current Page Number marker into master page headers and footers adds a relatively simple text variable with the page number and possibly section and chapter numbers or identifiers. In the same or a different text frame, you can also add the Section marker to enhance a folio with something to the effect of *Chapter 11* or *Section IV*. The dynamics at work with automatic page numbers and section numbering are excellent and very needed, but they only go so far. Page numbers, for example, are only cognizant of the current section and page numbers and any prefixes or suffixes added. Section markers don't even consider the page level. Wouldn't it be great if page headers noted not only the section or chapter number, but also the subsection? What if every instance of the Heading 1 paragraph style was reflected in the page header? In publications such as catalogs, directories, indexes, and glossaries, wouldn't it be cool to have the first product, person, entry, or definition on the left-read page noted at the top of that page and the last product, person, entry, or definition in the spread noted at the top of the right-read page for easy reference (as with the telephone book)?

All of that—and more—is now possible (without resorting to FrameMaker) with the new Running Header (and footer) text variable type. In Figure 11.15 you can see a single-page header from a fairly standard personnel or membership directory. The anatomy of this header, created entirely on the document master page, is very, very simple. First, on the left, is a standard Current Page Number marker. Beside it is the first running header text variable, with the second running header text variable anchored to the page's inside margin. Both variables listen for appearances of a particular character style (the EntryName character style in this case). The left variable uses the first instance of that character style on the page, echoing text set in that style, while the right variable repeats whatever it hears in the *last* instance of the character style. I would use identical variables—perhaps even the exact same master page—in a dictionary to include the first and last definitions of words on the page in the page header.

FIGURE 11.15
Text variables enable dynamic headers in this membership directory.

There are two variations of the Running Header text variable type: one that echoes text assigned to a specific paragraph style and one that watches for the use of a character style. It's simple to choose: do you want to echo an entire line of text or merely part of it? In the case of the personnel directory (see Figure 11.15), personal names were not set on lines by themselves; rather, they were set as the first part of a line with additional data—birthdates—tabbed off to the right. I didn't want the birthdates included in the header, so I used a nested style to automatically give each entry's personal name the EntryName character style and told the text variables to listen for that particular style.

A running header (footer, too, mind you) is entirely style dependent. If you want to take advantage of this new feature, you *must* use paragraph and/or character styles, as discussed earlier in this chapter. Moreover, you must be careful to use a particular style only to format the specific text you want to appear in the header (or footer; last time, honest). Once you have a document and text containing the appropriate styles, create a new text variable, choosing Running Header (Paragraph Style) or Running Header (Character Style) as appropriate. In Figure 11.16, you can see the settings I used in the Edit Text Variable dialog.

Style Choose the paragraph or character style the variable should echo.

Use Either the first or last instance of the selected style on the page.

Text Before/After As with other text variable types, these fields allow you to enter static text, punctuation, and symbols around the variable text.

Delete End Punctuation Use this option particularly when the variable is based on paragraph styles to strip off any punctuation appearing at the end of the echoed text.

Change Case A very nice little feature, the four options in this section allow you to change the case of echoed text without altering the original. For instance, if the trigger text on the page is mixed case (e.g., *Burke, Samuel D.*) and you'd rather it be all caps in the header (e.g., *BURKE,*

SAMUEL D.), choose the Upper Case radio button. To get fancy, setting just the last name in all caps and the rest in mixed case (e.g., *BURKE, Samuel D.*), use multiple variables and multiple character styles inserted via nested styles.

FIGURE 11.16
Options for
Chapter Number
text variables

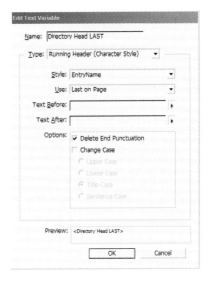

Once you've defined your text variables, simply insert them into text frames using the Type ➤ Text Variables ➤ Insert Variable menu. Any custom variables you've created will appear on that menu.

Note that text variables are document specific, like styles. Therefore, if you want to create a global text variable for use in several documents, or at least available for use in future documents, create the variable with no documents opened. Alternatively, if you've already created the variable in a document and want to make it globally available for future documents, close all documents and use the Load button in the (Define) Text Variables dialog.

Also in that dialog is the Convert to Text button, which, when clicked, will convert all instances of the highlighted variable throughout the document to static (nonvariable) text.

Data Merge

Digital printing is faster and, generally speaking, more efficient than traditional lithographic printing. There is little to no *run-up* or *run-down*, which saves paper, and even during the job, fewer raw materials are consumed. These, of course, are some of the major reasons digital printing is spreading so rapidly. Another significant reason is the fact that digital printing is *plateless*, meaning data flows directly from a computer to the ink impression system without film or plates. Consequently, it's not cost prohibitive to print in very small quantities as it is with offset printing. Each page printed on a digital press can be different without significantly increasing the production budget. That fact has caused the Variable Data Printing (*VDP*) mini-revolution in which everything from advertisements (Publix Supermarkets) to the cover of a 40-thousand-subscriber magazine can be customized to each individual receiving the piece (the June 2004 issue of *Reason*).

How is it accomplished on the design side? you may ask. In essence and execution, it's very simple. Designers and compositors lay out all the static elements within the original digital document; then, wherever customizable data must appear, they insert markers or tokens. The variable data is contained within a database. At one of two points during document production and output, the markers or tokens in the layout are replaced one at a time by the records in the database, creating unique *one-off* documents.

I say there are two points during which the database records may be inserted and unique pages generated. The more powerful and flexible of the two methods is to do it concurrently with output. Numerous high-end systems exist to host potentially very large databases of text and imagery and—just before, during, or just after RIP—to create the one-offs from a layout template. That's the production option. The other option, which works better for simple text and image replacement and in short runs of fewer than 500 versioned one-offs, is to perform the variable data, multiple one-off creation *before* sending the document to RIP. Using this latter option, the designer creates all the variations as a single, continuous document and sends it press, asking that every page be printed only once.

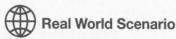 **Real World Scenario**

VDP OF 300 ONE-OFFS

Here is an example of creation-time variable data printing. It's a flyer distributed to attendees of the InDesign Conference Master Class in October 2006. Each of the 300 one-page flyers contained a unique software serial number (represented by the *X*s in the figure). Everything else about the flyers was static—same imagery, same ad copy, and so on. With only one line of text to change per copy, using a full-blown VDP system at press time would have been overkill. Instead, I used InDesign's built-in VDP function—data merge—to suck in the list of serial numbers and generate the 300 pages for me. After exporting the 300-page InDesign document to PDF, I had a single copy digitally printed for pennies per page.

Data merge can insert many different types of variable text into a layout. It can even insert images as variable data objects. In addition to using it for serial numbers and sales flyers, data merge can be used on numerous types of documents. Mailing labels and envelopes, of course, come immediately to mind. I've also used, or helped my consulting clients use, data merge for such things as the following:

◆ Rapidly producing new business cards for two hundred employees, pulling personnel names, titles, departments, e-mail addresses, phone extensions, and EPS images of special, employee-specific logos from a list generated out of the human resources database.

◆ On-demand printing of children's books in which each customer's child's name, age, sex, birth date, and description appear within the content of the book.

◆ Producing regionalized versions of association newsletters wherein local chapter information, events, contacts, photos, and maps are inserted among global material sent to all members nationally.

◆ Pulling requisite data from a FileMaker Pro database into visually interesting InDesign layouts for one-at-a-time estimates, invoices, contracts, and proposals.

◆ Laying out one hundred 500-page membership directories, including name, title, company, profession, legal specialties, certifications, honors, phone number, and photograph from Excel spreadsheets.

◆ Creating point-of-sale signage and shelf tags for the entire inventory of a national department-store chain by designing only a single layout (signage and shelf tags were printed on the same page and then separated in finishing) and then importing product name, price, SKU, and other information from the stock database the retailer maintains anyway.

These are but a few of the variable data projects I've worked on within InDesign (and Page-Maker before it). There are others, and there are many, many possible uses for which I've not had the chance to employ data merge. If you need content customization in three or more copies of the same layout, use data merge. It's very simple.

Let's get the basic terminology out of the way first. There are a few terms you need to know to work through a data merge in InDesign. It's a process of merging a list of data (*data source file*) into a layout document (*target document*) to produce a third, commingled set of data and layout, the *merged document*. The merged document is what you then send to press or a desktop printer.

THE DATA SOURCE FILE

The data source file is where all the unique data is stored. InDesign cannot *directly* use a database such as FileMaker Pro, Microsoft Access, or MySQL as a data source file; Adobe left such direct integration to third-party plug-in makers and system integrators. What InDesign *does* link to are *flat-file databases*—in other words, comma- or tab-separated text files. Every database and spreadsheet application built since the 1980s has the ability to export its data to comma- and tab-separated text files. Don't be deterred by the fact that you can't hook straight into InDesign from Excel or FileMaker; all you have to do is find the data you want in the source application and export it to comma-separated text as a CSV file or to tab-delimited text as a TXT file. In most cases, the export process can be automated in the database or spreadsheet application. If you aren't the database person in your organization, talk to the person who is; she'll know exactly how to get the data out into CSV or TXT files.

Within the data source file, as in any database, data is separated into fields—one piece of data (e.g., a person's name is one field, his address another field, his phone number a third)—and records. All the fields that make up a single entry is one record; the next person's name, address, telephone, and so on is another record. Records are separated in the data source file by paragraph returns. Every record will generate a new InDesign page when the merge is effected.

The very first record in your data source file should be a header row or list of field names (e.g., Name, Address, Phone). This helps you and InDesign identify what goes where. It's very important that each record have the same number of fields—even if the field is blank. For instance, if you're working with addresses, some entries may have a country listed while others do not. *All* such records *must* have a country field. When the record has no data in the field, leave it blank, ensuring that there is still a tab or comma position for that record's country field. The below lines, an example of an address-based, comma-delimited data source file, illustrate my point; note the second record.

```
CITY, STATE/PROVINCE, COUNTRY, ZIP/POSTAL
Beaverton, OR, USA, 97007
South Boston, MA, , 02127
Alberta Beach, AB, Canada, T0E 0A0
```

Because data source files may only be comma or tab separated, and because every instance of a comma or tab, respectively, communicates to InDesign that a new field has begun, you cannot use commas or tabs as actual text. For example, *red, white, and blue* is construed as three separate fields instead of a single field value. If you want to use commas in your text, either use tab delimitation for the data source file or enclose the text containing the comma in quotation marks—*"red, white, and blue."* For tabs in text, leave them out of the data source file entirely; instead, insert two separate field placeholders in the InDesign target document with a tab between.

THE TARGET DOCUMENT

The target document is an InDesign layout unremarkable save for the fact that placeholders stand in for the actual data to be printed. You may design the merged document and insert placeholders on either (but not both) the document or the master pages. If your variable data layout is more than one page, design it on document rather than on master pages. If, however, it's a single page or several pages that are each assigned their own master pages, there is a distinct advantage to putting the placeholders on a master page: the merged document may be updated to reflect changes in the data source file, something not available when the placeholders are on the document pages. A master page containing placeholder fields should be applied to the first page in the document.

After creating a data source file with the header row, lay out the target document exactly as it will ultimately print. Add all imagery and static text, but leave blank the variable data markers; you'll insert those in short order. First, you have to connect the data source file to the target document via the Data Merge panel.

INITIATING DATA MERGE

Open the Data Merge panel from Window ➤ Automation ➤ Data Merge. From the panel flyout menu, choose Select Data Source and navigate to the CSV or TXT data source file you created. Before clicking Open, check Show Import Options at the bottom of the dialog. You'll then be presented with the Data Source Import Options dialog box (see Figure 11.17). If InDesign does not correctly identify the delimiter in the file, you can change to Tab or Comma, adjust the file encoding and platform, and choose between keeping or stripping off leading and trailing spaces (spaces between words are preserved regardless). Click OK in Data Source Import Options, and the Data Merge panel will populate with the fields in the header row of your data source file (see Figure 11.18).

FIGURE 11.17
The Data Source Import Options dialog

FIGURE 11.18
After import, the Data Merge panel displays the header row fields in the first record.

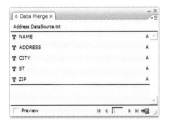

Return to the places in your layout where variable data should be inserted, and, positioning the cursor in the text at the correct point or points, click once on a field name in the Data Merge panel. Doing so will insert the placeholder for that field wrapped in double braces—for example, <<*Address*>>. Insert the remaining placeholders the same way. Figure 11.19 shows how a simple address label might look with field placeholders inserted.

FIGURE 11.19
Placeholders in place on a mail label

<<NAME>>

<<ADDRESS>>

<<CITY>>, <<ST>> <<ZIP>>

If you make changes to the data source file after import, choose Update Data Source from the Data Merge panel flyout menu. To replace one data source with another, choose Select Data Source again, or choose Remove Data Source, and then begin again.

Placeholders may be added anywhere text can go—alone in a text frame, amid lines of other text, in the middle of a paragraph, inside a table, within a text on a path object—and they are in all respects treated like normal, nondynamic text. Style placeholders using the same character, paragraph, and other formatting options; you can even use paragraph, character, table, and cell styles on them. In other words, variable data should be formatted to appear like any other text in your document, not like direct mail advertisements of old where one's name was inserted in the middle of a sentence in a different typeface with two inches of white space on either side. Take note that InDesign inserts only the variable text exactly as contained in the data source document. InDesign will neither add nor remove spaces, tabs, or anything else before or after the variable text. Therefore, be careful to insert any wanted spaces, tabs, and so on around the placeholder in the destination document. Similarly, make sure the data in the source is cleaned up and devoid of extraneous spaces, punctuation, tabs, and anything else you don't want in the final, merged document.

MERGING DATA

With your field placeholders in place, it's time to see what's going to happen in the merge. Switch to the target document page containing the placeholders. If you inserted them on a master page, go to a document page based on that master; note that you may need to create a document page or two or reapply the master. At the bottom of the Merge Data panel, check the Preview option, which will substitute one of the actual records of your data source file for the placeholders. It's always a good idea to preview the merge before actually merging data. Beside the Preview option, in the bottom right of the panel, navigation buttons enable you to proof how each record will look before finalizing the data merge operation.

If you notice blank lines in your merged data, go to the Merge Data panel flyout menu and choose Content Placement Options (see Figure 11.20). Check the option at the bottom, Remove Blank Lines for Empty Fields, to, well, remove blank lines created by empty fields. If a record contains a blank field, the space will be hidden. For example, when using two lines for addresses, those records wherein only one line is filled will leave the second address field blank, causing an ugly gap in the text. Remove Blank Lines for Empty Fields removes the line as if it was never there. To mitigate problems inherent in working with longer documents, you may also limit how many records are merged into one document file. If, working with one hundred records, you set a limit of 50, InDesign will create two merged documents. The remaining options should be familiar to you from working with placed images. Shortly I'll explain how use images in a data merge.

FIGURE 11.20
Content Placement
Options

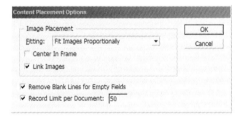

Once you're satisfied with the preview, choose Create Merged Document from the panel flyout menu, or click the button at the bottom of the panel. Up will pop the Create Merged Document dialog (see Figure 11.21). Here, you can specify exactly which records to merge. This is especially useful if a printer malfunction eats one or two pages; you don't have to run the entire merge again.

FIGURE 11.21
Create Merged Document dialog

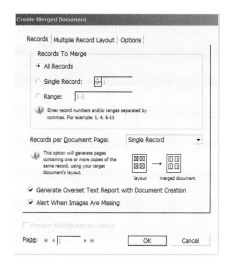

Records per Document Page determines how many copies of the merged data will appear on each page. For form letters, flyers, and other one-page-per-reader variable data documents, use Single Record per page. Choose Multiple Records per page for mailing labels and other *ganged* layouts where multiple, variable data content needs to appear on the same page. If the Records per Document Page drop-down is grayed out, there's a reason—two, possibly. InDesign will only allow one record per page merging if either of the following conditions is in effect in the target document:

◆ If the field placeholders are used on document pages in a multiple-page document (instead of on a master page).

◆ If placeholders appear on more than one master page (even both pages in a spread count as more than one master page).

For best results with placing multiple records per page, use nonfacing pages in the document.

Do check the Generate Overset Text Report with Document Creation and Alert When Images are Missing options because they provide important feedback about two common problems: (1) merged text doesn't completely fit within the area assigned to it (or merged text causes static text to not fit), and (2) images can't be found.

If you *are* setting multiple records per page, make sure to check out the Multiple Record Layout tab (see Figure 11.22). Here you can define the page margins, the gutters between columns and rows, and whether labels build left to right and then top to bottom (Rows First option) or top to bottom first (Columns First option).

The Options tab contains the same controls as the Content Placement Options dialog discussed a moment ago.

When you're ready, click OK to merge records into a new document. If you've elected to use a single record per page, you'll have one InDesign document with a page count equal to the record count. The merged document is what you'll save and send to print.

FIGURE 11.22
Create Merged
Document dialog
Multiple Record
Layout tab

If you put field placeholders on the master page, data can be updated later without regenerating the entire merged document. After making changes in the data source file or in the layout of fields on the master page, choose Update Data Fields on the Data Merge panel's (see Figure 11.18 for this panel) flyout menu. If your changes are more extensive than adding records or rearranging elements on the page—for instance, if you added a new field to every record—you will need to re-create the merged document from the target document.

MERGED IMAGES

Variable data isn't always textual data. Sometimes, you want to exchange images. That's easy. First, in the data source file, differentiate the field containing image paths with an "at symbol" (@), and then reference images by path in the fields. For instance, the following examples from a comma-delimited data source file reference full image pages on Windows:

```
NAME, @PHOTO
John Doe, D:\headshots\johndoe.jpg
Bob Roberts, D:\headshots\bobroberts.tiff
```

...And on Mac...

```
NAME, @PHOTO
John Doe, HD:headshots:johndoe.jpg
Bob Roberts, HD:headshots:bobroberts.tiff
```

Note: In Microsoft Excel and other applications, the @ symbol is used for special functions. Therefore, it could be problematic to make the @ the first character of a cell when organizing data sources in Excel. If this becomes an issue for your work, precede the @ with a straight single quote or foot mark (') such as: '@PHOTO.

Insert the image field placeholders just as you would text field placeholders. Instead of putting them in text frames, however, drag the placeholder from the Data Merge panel (see Figure 11.18) into a graphic frame—if you want a stand-alone image, that is; if you want an image inline among text, add it to a text frame. You can also put the image field placeholder inside table cells, which hold either text or imagery. Regardless of where you put it, until the merge is actually effected, an image placeholder will only display as the textual field name.

Working Efficiently with Tables

Tables and tabular data are common in printed matter and are becoming more common as InDesign gradually replaces Adobe FrameMaker as the long- and technical-document publishing tool of choice. With each new version of InDesign, tables become easier to work with and more feature rich. Table-related features aren't as cool or widely publicized as, say, attribute-level transparency or multiple-asset placing, so fewer people realize how InDesign can raise productivity when working with tables.

Live Linking to Excel Spreadsheets

Although tables are used for more than simply laying out spreadsheets, the fact remains that a great deal of the tabular data laid out on the InDesign page comes directly from Microsoft Excel. InDesign will place an Excel spreadsheet via File ➤ Place, which you probably already knew. And that's where a common problem begins.

Spreadsheets and other tabular data change *often*, frequently more often than editorial copy. Typically, designers place the Excel data and style the table, its cells, and their data with the Table panel (Window ➤ Type & Tables ➤ Table) and all the various options on the Table menu. It seems that, no matter what the data you're styling, someone always needs to revise it at the last moment. You'll no sooner finish styling the table, getting it just right, when a new version of the Excel spreadsheet arrives by email. At that point, many InDesign users find themselves faced with a choice: replace the old data with the new and then manually style the table all over again, or try to find the differences between the two versions and manually update the table one cell at a time. Either way, updating tabular data from an external source is a pain in the neck—but it doesn't have to be.

Squirreled away at the bottom of the Type pane of InDesign's Preferences is an important check box for anyone who places Excel spreadsheets. It's the option to Create Links When Placing Text and Spreadsheet Files. That option is disabled by default, which means that, when you place textual documents and spreadsheets, they instantly become embedded in InDesign; there is no link to the original, and, if the original document is changed, you have to place a whole new copy into InDesign. However, if you check Create Links When Placing Text and Spreadsheet Files, every time you place an Excel document into InDesign, it will be linked instead of embedded. If the original document is later changed or replaced, it can be updated in InDesign from the Links panel just like an image. Most of the formatting is retained, too!

What doesn't survive when a linked Excel document is updated are changes you've made to the data itself within the table on the InDesign layout page, the addition of running header or footer rows, and other structural attributes of or changes to the table. Styling *does* survive—particularly if you use the new table and/or cell styles (we're getting to those). Still, the time saved not having to reposition and restyle the entire table will usually outweigh the time required to rebuild the few elements that are lost when updating from the linked file. You'd have to rebuild and reconfigure them with or without linking the rest of the data anyway.

The downside to Create Links When Placing Text and Spreadsheet Files is that *all* textual assets placed into InDesign become linked. That includes Word, RTF, TXT, and other textual documents as well as Excel XLS files. For some, that's a benefit; for others, it's a liability. After all, most of the time you'll want to place copy into the layout and then not have to ship the original Word or RTF document to press as part of the package. Working around this consequence is no problem really. With such documents—and with Excel documents, if you like, right before going to press—highlight the appropriate file link in the Links panel and select Unlink from the panel flyout menu. The link to the original document will be broken, embedding the content in the InDesign layout. You can even select multiple assets in the Link panel list and unlink them en masse.

Table Styles

Yes, Virginia, there is a Santa Claus. And, yes, InDesign now has table styles.

For the last two versions, since tables were added to InDesign, table styles has been among the top feature requests from InDesign users. With CS3, we finally get them. In fact, there are two parts—table styles and cell styles. Tables styles record and apply table-level formatting attributes such as borders, row and column spacing, strokes, and fills—including alternating fills. No longer must you manually set the options for each table in the document!

Table styles and cell styles work just like paragraph and character styles. They have their own panels on the Window ➢ Type & Tables menu, the Table Styles and Cell Styles panels (see Figure 11.23). Styles are added the same way—with the New button at the bottom of the panel—and may be reordered or grouped into folders. To apply them, merely highlight the appropriate content—a table or some of its cells—and click the appropriate style in the Table Styles or Cell Styles panel. You can even load styles from other documents with the Load Table and Cell Styles commands on the flyout menu of either panel or the Load Table Styles or Load Cell Styles on the respective panel's flyout menu.

FIGURE 11.23

The Table Styles and Cell Styles panels

Editing a table style presents the Table Style Options dialog (see Figure 11.24), which looks very much like the Paragraph Style Options. On the General pane, one style can be based on another to take advantage of ultra-convenient cascading of styles. At the bottom, five drop-down fields enable choosing cell styles for different parts of a typical table: header and footer rows, left and right columns, and body rows (i.e., the rest of the table). Of course, the cell styles must be created on the Cell Styles panel before you can choose them in this dialog. The rest of Table Style Options is all the options you'll find in the Table Options dialog and Table panel.

Cell styles are to tables styles what character styles are to paragraph styles. In a cell style, you define individual cell attributes such as diagonal lines, strokes and fills, cell insets, vertical justification, baseline offset, clipping, and text rotation. Moreover, among the text formatting options is the ability to choose a paragraph style to apply to type within table cells.

You can also choose a table style at the time you *create* a table. With the Type tool inside a text frame, choose Table ➢ Insert Table to open the familiar Insert Table dialog. At the bottom of the dialog is a list of all existing table styles; choose one and your new table will insert with full formatting. Similar options appear when you place an Excel document and select Show Options during the place operation. Figure 11.25 shows both dialogs side by side. Selecting the table style at the time of insertion or creation of multipage tables spares the minor chore of having to select across pages and then choose appropriate table and cell styles.

FIGURE 11.24
Table Style Options
dialog

FIGURE 11.24
Table Style Options
dialog

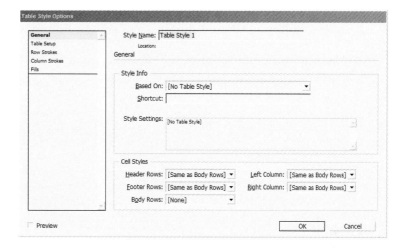

FIGURE 11.25
Insert Table dialog
(left) and Microsoft
Excel Import
Options (right)

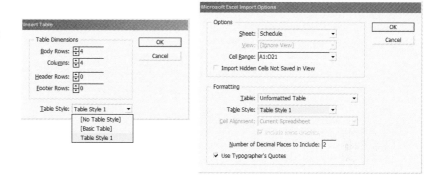

Working Efficiently with Objects

Working efficiently with objects also entails employing reusable styles but goes beyond to reusable *objects* as well.

Object Styles

Let's review: InDesign operates on a container-to-content model where everything in the document is either content—text, images, paths—or a container to hold content. Text, for instance, must be contained in either a text frame or a path text object. In addition to container and content, InDesign also cares about attributes. Thus, InDesign deals with containers and content and with the attributes of each. Paragraph and character styles govern text content formatting attributes but not the attributes of the frame containing the text. Paragraph styles, for instance, have no bearing on the number of columns in the text frame or the transparency of text. That and much more is left to the dominion of object styles, which record and apply the attributes of containers.

If you open the Object Styles panel from the Window menu, you'll find three preloaded entries—None, Basic Graphics Frame, and Basic Text Frame (see Figure 11.26). Each style is listed in brackets denoting that it is undeletable; you can edit these styles and change their definitions, but you can't get rid of them. The None style you want because it wipes out pretty much every attribute—fill, stroke, effects, everything. Basic Graphics Frame and Basic Text Frame reduce a selected object to default options; for a graphics frame, for example, that means 1 pt black stroke, no fill, nothing else.

FIGURE 11.26

Object Styles panel

One extremely useful option is the ability to set a user-created object style as the default for newly created graphics or text frames. Remember, a graphic frame is not only one into which you'll place imagery; it's also any unfilled decorative path such as a block of color, an ellipse, and so on. On the Object Styles panel flyout menu, choose any existing object style from the Default Graphic Frame Style submenu to format every new graphic frame *as you draw it*, which is an even faster and more efficient method of styling multiple objects than drawing and then applying the style. The Default Text Frame Style offers the same choice for text frames.

The rest of the panel is remarkably similar to the other four Styles panels, with a reorderable style list, the ability to group styles in nested folders, and buttons for New, Delete, Clear Overrides, and Clear Attributes Not Defined by Style. *What's the difference between the latter two?* Object styles can be defined to include every possible attribute but are rarely so defined. Instead, many attributes are simply not enabled. For instance, you may have an object style that doesn't include a drop shadow. Now, if you applied the style to an object and then selectively gave the object a drop shadow, that effect is an attribute not defined by the style. Clear Overrides, on the other hand, is relevant if the style *does* define a drop shadow but you later change the shadow angle on the individual object.

Double-clicking a style or choosing Style Options from the panel flyout menu will open the robust Object Style Options dialog (see Figure 11.27). *Every* attribute that may be given to a container—and many for content—is organized within this dialog. On the General pane, in the Style Settings area, is an expandable tree detailing the attributes defined in the style. The list of attributes on the left matches the summary of Style Settings and offers in one place access to just about every option you can set on the Swatches, Stroke, Effects, Story, Text Wrap, and other frames and in the Corner Options, Text Frame Options, Anchored Object Options, Effects Options, and other dialogs. Beneath the deceptively named Basic Attributes list is a replicated Effects Options section. Using the Effects For drop-down menu to select the element affected, you can apply the various Photoshop-esque transparency effects to containers and contents and individually to fills, strokes, text, and images.

Although most creatives prefer to design a live object on the page or pasteboard, applying needed attributes, *and then* produce an object style from the object, others know precisely what they want and can build the style in Object Style Options from scratch, by setting options without an object ready. Which way you choose depends on your particular work style. The Preview box at the bottom of the dialog will show changes in a selected object as you make them either during initial style creation or later tweaking.

FIGURE 11.27
The Object Style
Options dialog

Libraries

The utility of proprietary application object libraries has been greatly diminished with modern innovations such as placing native format graphic files (e.g., PSD, AI, PDF) into the layout; the ability to place one InDesign file as an asset inside another; *snippets*; accessible visual digital asset managers (DAMs); and the ability to drag and drop pictures from a DAM, the file system (e.g., OS X Finder and Windows Explorer), and other applications. Once upon a time, a library palette was the pinnacle of convenience and productivity. Now, libraries are no longer essential, but they're still very handy for improving efficiency in many solo and group workflows. Besides, they're kind of fun.

Libraries are floating, mini DAMs inside InDesign (see Figure 11.28). They allow objects created or placed in InDesign to be duplicated and placed elsewhere in the same or other documents without copying and pasting. Objects added to a library may be linked images that are, in reality, scattered about one or more hard drives or network resources. Library assets can be text frames (with or without text), native InDesign paths, objects with effects, groups of objects, even an entire page. These objects can be arranged and sorted in various ways within the library and then added to a document simply by dragging them out of the library and dropping on the page or pasteboard.

FIGURE 11.28
A library panel

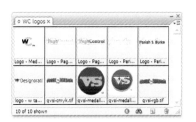

If you're a freelancer with no repeat clients or the print shop's in-house document fixer, you probably won't have much use for libraries these days. I recommend everyone *else* at least try using a library—or two, three, or more—because having at your fingertips all your frequently used objects can save massive amounts of time and effort over other methods of inserting objects. Consider some of the following uses:

◆ All your company's or client's logos can be stored—versions in RGB, CMYK process, CMYK plus spot colors, grayscale, black and white; logos with and without the tagline; full logos; iconic logos.

◆ Advertising-supported publications can store all their variously sized ad space placeholders and ready-for-content frames in a library ready for drag-and-drop placement (instead of keeping a list of ad sizes taped to the side of the monitor).

◆ Periodicals, catalogs, and other longer documents that use several layout templates for different types of pages can insert each page layout—inclusive of its text frames, graphic frames, and all other elements—as a single library entry and place all the pieces onto a blank page by dragging just one entry from the library.

◆ Photos and illustrations slated as potential use in a document can be collected from various sources and locations and organized together into a library for side-by-side evaluation.

◆ Any object or bit of text used once in a while in documents created for the same client or project can be collected into a library, keeping them always available for the next new document for the client or in the project.

Now that you're beginning to see the value of libraries, let's make one:

1. Open or create a document with several objects on a given page. These can be any type of object—text, placed imagery, paths drawn in InDesign, and so on.

2. Choose File ➢ New ➢ Library. InDesign will prompt you to save the library, which creates an INDL file.

   InDesign suggests the default name of *Library.INDL*. Don't use the default. Give the library a *meaningful* name. If this will be a library of logos for your client Acme Corp., name the file *Acme Logos.INDL* and save it in the folder where you save Acme Corp. assets or documents. If you use libraries well, you'll probably find yourself creating them for several clients, projects, and other purposes. Naming them all *Library.INDL* and saving them to a default location like My Documents or your Home folder won't seem like a very smart decision when you need to archive all documents related to one client or project to DVD-ROM.

3. After you save the library, a new panel will appear bearing as its title the filename you chose (e.g., *Acme Logos*). The library itself will be blank. One at a time, select objects on the document page and drag them into your library panel. Notice how each becomes a new library entry with a thumbnail and *Untitled* as its legend. We'll set aside the legend for now.

4. Move to another page in the document, and then drag an object *out* of the library panel onto the page. An exact duplicate of the original object appears on the page.

5. Create a new document (File ➢ New ➢ Document), and then do the same, dragging an object from the library panel onto the page. Now think about doing that for an identity package, quickly adding the client's logo and textual information—in the correct colors and typefaces—across the business card, letterhead, envelope, and other layouts.

Adding items to a library, as you saw, is as easy as drag and drop. If you need to add several items from the same page, however, there's an easier way. On the library panel's flyout menu, choose Add Items on Page or Add Items on Page as Separate Objects. The former adds all items on the page as a single library entry. Thus, if your page contains five objects, all five will be added as a single library entry. Dragging that entry from the panel to the page places all five objects back into the document simultaneously and as five separate objects. The latter menu command, Add Items on Page as Separate Objects, adds all items on the page as separate entries, one per object. A trick to quickly and easily populate a library is to place assets onto a page by dragging and dropping from their various locations in Bridge, Finder/Explorer, or elsewhere and then, once all objects are on the page, use the As Separate Objects command.

To delete items in the library, drag the items to the trashcan icon at the bottom, select them in the palette and click the trashcan icon, or select items and use the Delete Item(s) command on the flyout.

Each item may have a title, a type, and a description. Double-click the item or choose Item Information from the panel menu to open the Item Information dialog (see Figure 11.29). In a library with only a handful of items, names, description, and object type—collectively meta information—aren't very important because organization will be done visually. However, with larger libraries, or when the thumbnail detail in the panel isn't sufficient to differentiate items, adding meta information can be very helpful. Give the item a name and, optionally, a description. And then choose the type of object—image, EPS, PDF, Text, InDesign File (INDD), Structure (e.g., XML code chunk), Page (an entire page of objects as a single item), or Geometry (a vector path). None of the meta information is required; its only purpose is to help you or someone else find and identify items.

FIGURE 11.29

The Item Information dialog

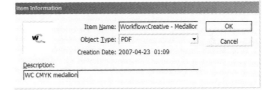

Large libraries may be sorted by, filtered to, and searched for specific items. All of these features depend on the meta information attached to each item. To search or filter the list, click the binoculars icon at the bottom of the panel (refer back to Figure 11.28), or choose Show Subset from the panel flyout menu. Up will pop the Show Subset dialog (Figure 11.30), which allows you to search across potentially thousands of library items (in the same library) for data that does or does not appear as Item Name, Creation Date, Object Type, or Description meta information. In fact, if you click the More Choices button, additional parameter rows may be added for highly focused searching and filtering. When you click OK, the library panel will filter to show only those results matching the query. To clear the query and see all items in the library, choose Show All from the menu.

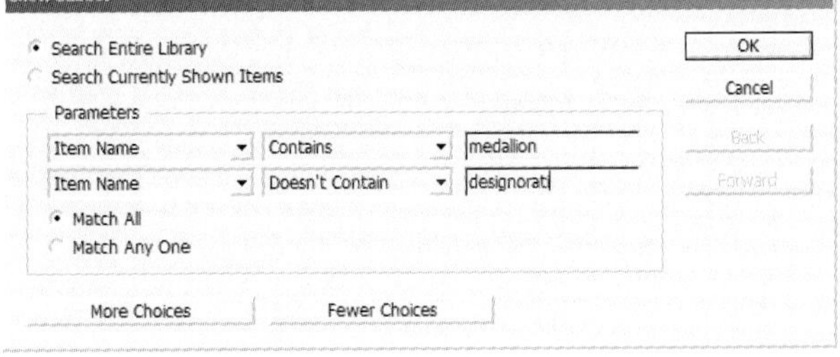

FIGURE 11.30

Show Subset enables searching and filtering based on meta information.

If, when adding content from a library to a new document, you choose an entry that includes a linked placed asset, the Links panel in the new document will show a link to the original asset just like the entry that appears on the Links panel in the document from which you dragged the object into the library. It's important to recognize that linked assets are *not* stored within the library any more than they are stored within documents; in both documents and libraries, *only the link*—the actual location on disk—is recorded. Don't make the common mistake of adding a linked image to a library and then deleting the original from your hard drive.

If the object included any custom swatches, strokes, or paragraph, character, table, cell, or object styles, they will be added to their respective panels as well.

Items in a library are independent of their original instances, the ones from which they were created. Similarly, items placed on the page *from* a library are *not* tied to the library instances. Changing one does not update the other. Think of a library as a sort of copy and paste operation; when copying and pasting, neither the original nor duplicate will update to reflect changes in the other. The same is true of library items. On the flyout menu, the Update Library Item command lights up when an object is selected on the page. Executing that command will replace the selected library item with the object selected on the page. That will not, however, alter any instances of the original library item added to the document. It only changes the copy stored in the library.

Confused? Let's try an example. Say you've created a black square as a library object and then dragged that black square from the library onto a document page. You now have two distinct, unrelated black squares—one on the page, one in the library. On the page, you can recolor the square to green, but the version in the library will remain black. Similarly, if you change the color of the black square in the library to blue, the copy on the page remains black (or green). Deleting one instance also doesn't affect the other.

You may have more than a single library open at any given time, and libraries are *not* dependent on a particular document. I, for instance, often work with several libraries at once, and with numerous documents, depending on the client or project. Except for the fact that library panels are tied to specific external files, they behave like any other panel—they can be docked, tabbed, stacked, rolled up, rearranged, and resized. Their inventory can be sorted by name, by newest or oldest addition, or by the type of asset, all from the Sort Items menu on the panel flyout menu. Closing a library is as simple as clicking the close button in its title bar or choosing Close library from the flyout menu; open libraries with InDesign's File ➢ Open command.

InDesign saves libraries automatically every few minutes, so changes you make to the panel's inventory are saved almost as you make them.

Libraries can be shared from one user to the next, which is among the most productive features of libraries for workgroups. If the library contains linked images, they will work as long as everyone using the library has access to the same images in the same path. Otherwise, InDesign will prompt them to locate missing links as it would with any document.

Snippets

Snippets are reusable content similar to libraries but with two key differences. First, whereas libraries collect multiple objects into a single list, snippets are new external assets not gathered together into a panel. Second, library objects do not remember positioning data, but snippets do.

A snippet is an encapsulated segment of XML code, but don't let that put you off—after finishing this sentence, you need never again consider the words *snippet* and *XML* together. What is important, and the reason I mention it, is that XML can contain text, path data, imagery, attributes—all the structural data and everything InDesign needs to re-create a container, its content, and their attributes. Snippets even remember their relative location on the page and the layer(s) on which they originated. In the simplest terms, a snippet is a piece of an InDesign page external-ized. Snippets may be passed around and traded like baseball cards.

Create a snippet by selecting one or more objects with the Selection tool, and then drag the object(s) out of InDesign to drop on your desktop. An INDS file will be created, which is like any other file and can be managed through the file system, Bridge, or what have you. If the idea of drag-ging something out of an application onto the desktop gives you the heebie-jeebies, use File ➤ Export; in the Export dialog, set Save As Type to InDesign Snippet.

Placing snippets in documents is just as easy—through File ➤ Place or by dragging from the desktop into InDesign. Upon dropping (or placing), the object(s) dragged to the desktop will instantly appear with all formatting and appearance intact and on the layer(s) from which they originated. By default in InDesign CS3, snippets will drop at the cursor location rather than at the position on the page from which they originated. Changing that behavior is a toggle. In Prefer-ences, on the File Handling pane, change the Snippet Import option. Position at Original Location will place the snippet in exactly the same place on the page as the original set of objects from which the snippet was created. Position at Cursor Location will place the snippet content wher-ever a loaded place cursor is clicked or where a snippet dragged from the desktop is dropped.

Style Shortcuts

All styles—paragraph, character, table, cell, and object—may be assigned to keyboard shortcuts on the General pane of their options dialogs. To set a keyboard shortcut, click in the Shortcut field and press the keyboard keys that will serve the particular style—for instance, Cmd+5/Ctrl+5. Assign-ing keyboard shortcuts to styles is not a new feature; neither is the fact that it's so limited as to be almost useless.

The primary limitation to style shortcuts, you see, is that they *require* use of the numeric keypad—the set of number keys out to the right of full-sized keyboards. Every shortcut must be one or more modifier keys—Cmd, Opt, Ctrl, Shift on Mac or Ctrl, Alt, Shift on Windows—plus a numeric keypad number. Thus, the first limitation is that usually alphabetically named styles must be bound to arbitrary numbers. *(Did I put the RunIn Head paragraph style on Ctrl+Shift+Num 5, Ctrl+Num 5, or was it something plus the 6?)* Next, you have to recognize that, on most keyboards, any of these options are two-handed keyboard shortcuts, which are only—and not always—slightly more con-venient than reaching for the mouse and clicking an entry on a panel. The choice of shortcuts is also limited by the fact that many key combinations are reserved for use by the operating system. On Windows, for example, you cannot use Alt and a number without also choosing Shift or Ctrl because Alt plus the numeric keypad numbers is reserved for systemwide insertion of special characters—for example, to insert a copyright symbol, press Alt+0169. Finally, the biggest limita-tion to keyboard shortcuts for styles is again the numeric keypad. Laptops don't have them, nor do many slim desktop keyboards. Most laptop keyboards have a pseudo-numeric keypad created by depressing the Function key (often labeled as *Fn* and unique to laptops) and then pressing other keys (such as U, I, and O for 4, 5, and 6 or another mapping of numeric keypad functions to existing keys). So, in addition to pressing one, two, or three modifier keys and a number key, those using laptops or slim keyboards must press Function. Worse, pressing Function often changes the function of a modifier key. Option on a Mac PowerBook, for instance, becomes Alt when the Func-tion key is depressed. Therefore, it is impossible to press Opt+Shift+Num 6 on a PowerBook's built-in keyboard.

Until Adobe adds styles to the customize Keyboard Shortcuts dialog and opens up the rest of the keyboard to style shortcuts, the feature is more of a hindrance than a help. The only exception I would proffer is default styles. Leave your custom styles unassigned to shortcuts, but binding the Basic Paragraph paragraph style, the None character style, and similar defaults for table, cell, and object styles to shortcuts can be very useful and universal because every document you create has these defaults (though you may not use them). For instance, some people find it very helpful to put Basic Paragraph on the numeric keypad's 1 key, the None character style on 2, and so on. For the rest of their styles they use something far more efficient: Quick Apply.

Quick Apply

Quick Apply was introduced in InDesign CS2, although most users have no idea it's there or what it does. Even if you *do* know Quick Apply, don't skip over this section—CS3 is the Col. Steve Austin version Quick Apply. Adobe sat down with InDesign, with Quick Apply, and Kevin Van Weil said, "Gentlemen, we can rebuild it. We have the technology. We have the capability to make the world's first bionic application menu. Quick Apply will be that application menu. Better than it was before. Better… stronger… faster."

In the last version, Quick Apply was a menu that consolidated all paragraph, character, and object styles into a single list for rapid access to any of them. Now, in InDesign CS3, its bionics enhance Quick Apply to include all those styles, table and cell styles, and menu commands and scripts all together in a single, rapid-action list. In other words, you might be able to hide the Paragraph Styles, Character Styles, Object Styles, Table Styles, Cell Styles, and Scripts panels and reclaim screen real estate they consume. You really have to see Quick Apply to understand it. Press Cmd+Return/Ctrl+Enter and the Quick Apply menu will appear (see Figure 11.31).

FIGURE 11.31

The Quick
Apply menu

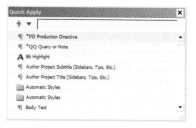

The basic operation of Quick Apply is simple: In the search field above the list, begin typing the name of a style in the current document. As you type, the list of available options will shrink, filtered to those styles, commands, scripts, and variables that begin with what you typed. The first option matching your input will be highlighted. To choose it, applying the style or whatever to a selected object or text, simply press Return/Enter. If the highlighted item isn't what you want, type more of the name or use the up and down arrows on your keyboard to navigate the list. *Can I select something with the mouse?* Of course; it's a scrollable list, after all. But the main point of Quick Apply, with its simple Cmd+Return/Ctrl+Enter activation shortcut—the ability to type a part of a name and use Return/Enter to apply it—is to *spare* you the need to take your hands off the keyboard. Its secondary point, which does just as much for productivity, saves you from searching through various panels and menus hunting for something whose name—but not exact location—you already know. When you press Return/Enter to apply a selected style, Quick Apply will retreat out of your way.

At the top of Quick Apply you have two buttons (see Figure 11.31). The lightning bolt hides the Quick Apply menu itself. You may recognize it as appearing on all the individual styles panels where the same button will hide or show Quick Apply. Next, the down-facing arrow lets you choose what to show in the Quick Apply menu (see Figure 11.32). That's right, Quick Apply includes not only all the styles, but also text variables, scripts, and every menu command in InDesign: those on the menu bar at the top of the application, those on panel flyout menus, and even many that don't appear anywhere else in the user interface. You can quite literally *run InDesign exclusively from Quick Apply.* (Note that scripts are, by default, not included in Quick Apply. To include them, activate that option from the Show/Hide menu.) You can even include in Quick Apply menu commands hidden by customizing menus.

FIGURE 11.32
The Show/Hide menu in Quick Apply toggles the inclusion of list contents as well as providing filter codes.

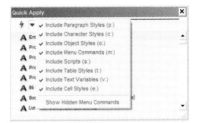

Beside each type of entry in the Show/Hide menu is a parenthetic special code—for instance *(p:)* beside Include Paragraph Styles. With so much now added to the Six Million Dollar Menu, typing just a few letters into the search field will undoubtedly return numerous commands, styles, and so on. The expanded focus of Quick Apply therefore becomes a hindrance to its own utility. Rather, it *would*, but for the filter codes. If you want a table style, for example, preface your search with *t:*, which filters the Quick Apply list to show only table styles. Use *m:* for menu commands, *v:* for text variables, *p:* for paragraph styles, and so on. The Show/Hide menu is a complete key to filter codes.

Quick Apply even makes it easy to *edit* a style. Pressing Cmd+Return/Ctrl+Enter opens Quick Apply, but pressing the shortcut again while Quick Apply is open will open the editing options for the selected style, command, script, or variable. With an object style selected, for instance, Cmd+Return/Ctrl+Enter will open the Object Style Options dialog editing that particular style. With a *text variable* selected, Cmd+Return/Ctrl+Enter opens the Text Variables dialog.

Scripting

To one degree or another, anything you can do manually in InDesign can be automated via a script. Such scripts can be written in Mac-only AppleScript, Windows-only Visual Basic Script, or cross-platform JavaScript. They can do something as simple as preload the Swatches panel with your corporate colors and they can perform highly complex, multistaged operations such as turning a blank page into a press-ready layout. Using scripts, InDesign can also be connected to other applications—for example, data from a spreadsheet or database can be sucked into InDesign and laid out automatically. The possibilities are limited only by your imagination and coding skill.

Covering what can be done and how to do it is far beyond the space available in this tome. Entire books have been written on the subject, and Adobe wrote one of the best—the *InDesign CS3 Scripting Guide*. There are three variations of the *InDesign CS3 Scripting Guide*: one each for Apple-Script, Visual Basic Script, and JavaScript. You'll find them as PDFs in the Adobe InDesign Documentation\Scripting folder on the InDesign or Creative Suite DVD. If you don't have your DVDs on hand, you can also grab copies free of charge from www.adobe.com/go/scripting_id. You'll want to begin with the *Adobe Intro to Scripting*, progress through *InDesign CS3 Scripting Tutorial*, and use the *JavaScript Tools Guide CS3* and the three script-language-specific versions of the *InDesign CS3 Scripting Guide* for reference.

Accompanying the scripting tutorial and reference documents are hundreds of sample scripts that do everything from creating printer presets to unlinking text frames, placing text files to laying out events calendars. In addition to those, there are hundreds of other scripts floating around the Internet, most created by other InDesign users to address specific workflow needs. A great place to look for them is the Adobe Exchange at www.adobe.com/cfusion/exchange/. There you can find many scripts (and more!) for InDesign and every other Adobe product. I would hope you'll find ones that function on your platform.

MAKE SCRIPTS PEER FRIENDLY

At this point, I would like to strongly ask that, should you create scripts for InDesign or InCopy, you do so in *JavaScript*. Only Mac-based InDesign and InCopy users can use AppleScript, and only Windows-based users Visual Basic Script (aka VBScript). Both, however, can use JavaScript scripts in InDesign. Few things are more frustrating than scouring the Adobe Exchange and the rest of the Internet in search of a script to solve a problem, finding the perfect script, and then realizing that you can't use it because it was written for the other platform.

While all three languages (JavaScript, AppleScript, and VBScript) offer unique advantages—and the latter two enable file system integration that, because of security concerns at the level of the operating system, JavaScript can't—most platform-specific scripts written by InDesign users *don't* use those advantages or integrate with the file system. In other words, they *could* have been written in cross-platform JavaScript but weren't. From what I've seen, many script writers have a tendency to write specifically for their own platform as a first choice, not even considering that their scripts might be of use to someone on the other platform. With the split between Mac- and Windows-based professional creatives rapidly approaching 50/50 (yes, I *am* certain of that), it's naïve to think that only Mac users will need or want to do *this* or *that* in InDesign. I'm not just talking about Mac-based script writers, either; there are plenty of highly useful VBScript InDesign scripts out there that confound Mac users with a need.

For the foreseeable future, Windows will never do AppleScript and Mac will never do VBScript. If you write a custom script, *please* write it in JavaScript if at all possible. Don't punish your fellow creatives and production people, a great many of whom have no say in which Operating System they get to use at work.

When you've written or obtained scripts you'd like to use, you have to give them to InDesign. Do that by closing InDesign and copying the scripts to the correct location for your platform:

Mac OS X: `Users/[username]/Library/Preferences/Adobe InDesign/Version 5.0/Scripts`

Windows XP: `Documents and Settings\[username]\Application Data\Adobe\InDesign\Version 5.0\Scripts`

Windows Vista: `Users\[username]\AppData\Roaming\Adobe\InDesign\Version 5.0\Scripts`

When you relaunch InDesign, the scripts will be available in the User group on the Scripts panel, which can be opened by choosing Window ➢ Automation ➢ Scripts. Under Application in the panel, you'll also see numerous sample scripts that are not in the locations noted above. If you want to delete these, you'll find them in the InDesign application installation location:

Mac OS X: `Applications/InDesign CS3/Scripts/Scripts Panel/Samples`

Windows: `Program Files\Adobe InDesign CS3\Scripts\Scripts Panel\Samples`

To execute a script on the Scripts panel, double-click it.

Note that many scripts function only when a specific condition has been met—such as preselecting certain types of objects or highlighting text. Indeed, many scripts that manipulate or work from objects require that objects be *named*. This is where the Script Label panel comes into play. The Script Label panel (Window ➢ Automation ➢ Scripts) has no buttons, no flyout menu, and, apparently, nothing else. Actually, the entire panel is a single text field. Select an object on the page or pasteboard, click once inside the Script Label panel, and begin typing a name or label for the object. That's it. That's all it does. But, once named with the label a script expects, the object can then be manipulated by the script.

Script writers can attach scripts and scripted functions to InDesign documents and to menu commands; doing so, while incredibly powerful, represents a security risk. Consequently, Adobe shipped InDesign with the ability to run such scripts turned off. In InDesign's preferences, on the General pane, the Enable Attached Scripts option is that control. To allow the execution of scripts attached to documents, check Enable Attached Scripts.

The Bottom Line

The bottom line is this: InDesign is a software application anyone with a little money can buy and use. What separates the professional from the prosumer is how efficiently it's used.

Work Efficiently with Text   Text comprises the most space in the average InDesign document. Unfortunately, editing and *re*styling text occupies the majority of a creative's time in the document. Used wisely, paragraph and character styles, nested styles, text variables, and data merge eliminate repetitive actions and hours of work.

Master It   Use Excel, a database, or Notepad/TextEdit to create a new flat-file database of information. The data may be anything you like—a mailing list, product listings for a catalog, directory listings, etc.—but should include at least three fields and three rows. Save the file as either comma or tab delimited; this will be your data source file.

Beginning with a blank InDesign document, build a variable data target document to hold the records from the data source file. Include static information as well as field placeholders. Format all text—static and placeholders—and create paragraph and character styles to make the initial and follow-up formatting easier. If you have appropriate places to employ nested styling, do so.

When the target document is ready, effect a data merge to generate a press-ready variable data project.

Work Efficiently with Tables   Barring additional investments in third-party plug-ins, each table created in prior versions of InDesign had to be individually and manually formatted. The more creative the formatting, the more arduous the task of styling multiple subsequent tables to match. New table and cell styles make it a one-click operation to format tabular data and to instantly update all tables to match future formatting changes.

Master It   Begin with a table of data. If you have tables in preexisting InDesign documents, use those (save the document under a different name, just in case). If you don't have such documents already, create a new layout and add at least two tables; the sports or financial sections of today's newspaper are excellent places to find tabular data you can use for FPO. Style one table with alternating fills, custom strokes of your choosing, and with appropriate text formatting using paragraph styles. When the first table is styled to your liking, build table and cell styles, and then use them to format the second table.

Work Efficiently with Objects   Working efficiently doesn't end with text and tables. Graphics, paths, and containers are part of any InDesign document, and creating and editing them productively is also important to the efficient InDesign-based workflow.

Master It   Using either your own or a client's various media logos (RGB, CMYK, grayscale; with and without taglines; iconic and full logos; and so on), build a shareable, reusable logo library. Now create a second library of text frames and other objects you use at least occasionally. Make sure to give each an object style before adding them to the library so that other objects can quickly be styled to match and so that formatting changes don't take too much time. Don't forget to label objects in both libraries for rapid identification and filtering by you or your coworkers.

Chapter 12

Collaboration

No man is an island, entire of itself; every man is a piece of the continent, a part of the main.

—*John Donne* Meditation XVII (1572–1631)

Few InDesign users operate in a vacuum, creating documents start to finish all on their own. The majority of modern workflows, even among freelancers, entails some form of collaborative content creation. Perhaps it's a group of designers cooperating on the packaging for a large product line; maybe it's designers and copywriters crafting the perfect advertising creative.

In the past, much like print and web, West Berlin and East Germany, the personnel, activities, and especially software tools employed by design and production have always been separate from, and often mutually unfriendly toward, copywriting and editorial. All of that is changing. More and more print workflows are embracing digital content delivery; Germany has been unified. Most importantly, the software, which has always been, at best, reluctantly compatible and, at worst, openly hostile toward one another is actually beginning to cooperate, coordinate, and collaborate. Creatives keep on designing while writers keep on writing, but the barriers that separated them from each other and their peers are being torn down as fast as the Berlin Wall.

However—and with whomever—you collaborate, InDesign can speed and improve the process.

In this chapter, you will learn to:

- ◆ Collaborate with other designers
- ◆ Collaborate with writers and editors
- ◆ Share reusable settings

Collaborating with Other Designers

Whether you need to collaborate with the person over the cube wall from you or across the planet, InDesign CS3 has several powerful ways to coordinate join efforts among creatives.

Saving to Older Versions of InDesign

Not all of us upgrade as quickly or regularly as others. For some, InDesign CS2 is ideal, with all the features needed for their particular work; they don't need or want CS3 and will not upgrade to it for a while if ever. (I doubt *you* are included in this group; after all, you obviously bought a book titled *Mastering InDesign CS3 for Print Design and Production*.) Others may lust after a new version but simply can't justify its price tag. Whatever the reason, it becomes necessary on occasion to move documents between the latest and earlier versions of InDesign.

The fact that InDesign CS (CS1, version 3.0) did *not* save backward for compatibility with 2.0 (the first commercially successful edition of InDesign) brought forth a public outcry so vociferous that it still echoes throughout the halls of Adobe and many press and pre-press shops around the world. Allow me to dispel another common misconception: Despite what you may have heard, InDesign *does* save backward. It has done so since CS2, which saved documents compatible with CS1.

To save a document such that it can be opened in CS2, choose File ➢ Export. In the Export dialog, change the Save as Type drop-down to InDesign Interchange format. When you save the document, it will be with the .inx file extension. InDesign Interchange documents are XML based, and may be opened in InDesign CS2 or CS3 with the File ➢ Open command. Both versions can also export them, although CS2 users sending documents to CS3 users can simply send documents in the standard INDD format. CS3 will open documents created by any prior version of the program. It will only save INDD files as CS3 version, however.

Maintaining a round-trip editing workflow between InDesign CS2 and CS3 is tedious, but doable. The CS2 user can send his work as either INDD or INX formats, but the CS3 user must send her work back as INX files, which the CS2 user can open and edit.

Note: An update to InDesign CS2 was released shortly prior to the release of CS3. Contained in the update was a new version of the INX filter that enables CS2 to open CS3-authored INX documents. If you or a CS2-based associate experiences any problems opening such documents, ensure that InDesign CS2 has been updated to the latest version. You can do that by opening InDesign and choosing Updates from the Help menu. The Adobe Updater utility will then check for recent updates to InDesign and all installed Adobe applications and present you with a list of available downloads. Install any available InDesign updates. While you're at it, it's a good idea to install available updates and patches for all your Adobe applications.

One Document, Many Designers

Dividing a multipage document into multiple documents of one or more pages each and then collecting the pieces under a book file is a common collaboration workflow. So common is it that I've given it a name—the Book File Collaboration Workflow (I hope no one has already coined this). Under this method, members of the design team work on pieces of the whole, and each piece is at least one full page. If the team members work from a single network file repository, each piece of the publication stays in synch with all other pieces with regard to section and page numbering, style consistency, and other shared document attributes. If they *don't* work off the network, shared attributes are updated when their pages are delivered to the person in charge of assembling and managing the parts into a whole publication (the paginator).

SETTING UP THE BOOK FILE COLLABORATION WORKFLOW

To set up book file collaboration, begin by analyzing the document to be created or edited. How many creatives will work on it? Does it have inherent break points for apportionment? For instance, if the publication is a magazine, could the "Letter from the Editor" column page be broken out into its own document for one designer to work on while the "New Bites" spread and subsequent department and features pages are given their own documents and handed to other designers? If logical content separators aren't as obvious, look for more subtle separations where the document could be divided.

Once you've identified where the publication can be separated, make the pieces.

1. Begin with the complete publication in a single document. Set on the master page(s) folios, page headers and footers, and any other common elements that will appear on all or at least the majority of the document's pages. Although you're unlikely to need the full publication document again, save it for safety anyway.

On the Pages panel (Window ➢ Pages), select all the pages that will *not* be in the first constituent part and delete them. You should then have a document containing only the page(s) that will be assigned to the first designer. The pages *must* be contiguous; if you want to give pages 2–5 and 10–15 to the same team member, make one document for pages 2–5 and another for 10–15.

If the document contains the Current Page Number special character, the document pages will renumber after the other pages are deleted. Ignore the page numbers. They'll be fixed automatically in a few steps.

If you manually insert page numbers, *stop doing that!* InDesign has robust section and page numbering options that can handle nearly any page enumeration scenario with far less work than the unnecessarily masochistic practice of manually inserting and changing page numbers. Read about *page numbers*, *section numbering*, and *text variables* in this book before you say, *Oh, InDesign won't do automatically what I need for page numbering and identification.*

3. Because you're still working in the one and only full publication document and you've probably just deleted the majority of the publication, *don't save*. Instead, choose File ➢ Save a Copy. When prompted, name the document something both you and the designer who will work on it will understand. If the section you're creating is the first of 10 parts of the May issue, a name like `May-p2-5.indd` would be ideal. Click OK when ready. Save a Copy saves a copy of the document without saving or closing the original document.

4. Press Cmd+Z/Ctrl+Z to undo the deletion of pages and return to the full document.

5. Repeat steps 1 through 4 for each subsequent section of the document, saving a copy of each part, until all the pieces are saved out to their own documents.

6. Go to File ➢ New ➢ Book and create a new InDesign book INBK file with the same name as your publication. After you save, a blank Book panel will appear; its name will be that of your publication.

7. On the Book panel's flyout menu, choose Add Documents. In the Add Documents dialog, choose all the publication part files you just created. Click on the first file in the list to select it, and then, holding the Shift key (on both Mac and Windows), click on the last file in the list. All interceding documents will also be selected. Click the Open button and the documents will populate the Book panel.

8. If the documents are not in their correct order, drag them within the list until they are correct. Automatic page numbers will update across all the files, putting them back into place in the scheme of the overall document.

9. Send the section documents to the designers who will be responsible for them.

Using the Book panel, you, as the publication manager, will be in control of the overall publication cohesion. If your team is working from a network file server, place all the component documents, the INBK book file, and documents' linked assets in a folder on the server, and have team members open from, and save to, the same documents and folder. Your view of the publication through the Book panel will then always be in synch with the most recently saved changes to any pages of the publication. If your team works remotely from one another or for another reason cannot open and save files in a central repository, ensure that, as each piece comes back to you, you overwrite originals with new versions, which will also keep your Book panel updated.

Rearranging the individual documents in the publication is as easy as dragging them within the Book panel. If section *A*, for instance, must now come after *C* instead of before section *B*, simply drag *A* down to the correct place in the Book panel. Pages throughout the rest of the publication will instantly renumber to reflect the change. You don't even need to involve the designer working on section *A*!

If you later need to make changes to the segments, to move pages between publication sections for instance, that's easy:

1. Open both the source and destination documents by double-clicking each in the Book panel.

2. In the source document, the one from which pages will be moved, choose Layout ➢ Pages ➢ Move Pages, which will open the Move Pages dialog (see Figure 12.1).

FIGURE 12.1

The Move Pages dialog

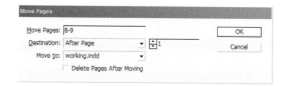

3. In the Move Pages dialog and the Move Pages field, enter the page number(s) of the page(s) to move from the source document to the target document. Use hyphen-separated numbers to specify a range (e.g., 1-3) and comma-separated numbers for nonsequential pages (e.g., 1,3). Change the Move To field from Current Document to the name of the destination document, and then, using the two Destination fields, tell InDesign precisely where to drop the page(s). Check Delete Pages After Moving so they will be removed from the source document.

    When you click OK, the pages will immediately move from the source to the target document. Save both, and you're done; the Book panel will update itself.

If you only want to *copy* pages between documents, leaving the originals in the source document but also adding them to the target, don't check Delete Pages After Moving. This is a handy trick for those situations wherein someone comes along and says, "Hey! Wouldn't it be cool if every chapter suddenly began with a splash page?" Folks who work on magazines, telephone directories, and other such advertising-supported periodicals love that particular trick because it makes it easy to insert newly sold full-page or full-spread ads into the middle of a feature article or other publication section that can't—or shouldn't—be broken into still more documents.

Speaking of periodicals...

WHEN BOOK FILE COLLABORATION WON'T WORK

The Book File Collaboration Workflow has one hard rule—in order for automatic page numbering and unified output to work, each component document must comprise strictly contiguous pages with no blank or extraneous pages. For magazines, newspapers, newsletters, magalogs, and other documents where stories jump, pausing on a particular page, skipping other content pages, and then picking up again farther into the publication, the one rule of book file collaboration could be a problem. (If your publication doesn't jump stories, it's not a problem.) InDesign can't thread a single, continuous story across multiple documents; threaded frames may only be in the same document. Therefore, if a feature article jumps from page 19 to page 32, you're left with a dilemma. You have a choice between four possible solutions for that dilemma:

A. Make pages 19–32 one document, inclusive off all content pages between, thus making it impossible for more than one designer to work at any given time on any page between 19 and 32.

B. Make pages 19–32 one document, but leave blank any pages not directly part of the single feature story. Any intervening pages and sections are still their own separate documents, enabling other designers to work independently and concurrently on their respective pieces. This method isn't new—it's what magazines and other periodicals typically employ. There are two downsides to this method: automatic page numbering goes haywire because of the extraneous pages, and it forces extra pagination work and a greater potential for mistakes immediately before going to press.

Many component documents using this method include numerous pages that serve no function other than as placeholders for content on which someone else is working. When the pages are locked down, just before the issue is put to bed, someone has to sit down and either combine all the components into a single document via drag and drop or go through each document, printing or exporting content pages manually while ignoring placeholder pages. When pages are exported to PDF, EPS, or another format, the numerous resulting files are then either combined into a single document (for instance, one large PDF), imposed in-house into a single document, or named after their page numbers and sent out for imposition (whereupon someone hopes very, very hard that the imposer doesn't make a mistake).

C. Continue with the Book File Collaboration Workflow, making page 19 one file, page 32 another, and dividing the intervening pages as needed and independently of the jumped story. In that case, the story is manually broken on page 19, with its last line tweaked and a jumpline inserted, and then the overflow copy is added manually and independently to page 32, again, with a manually inserted and maintained *Continued From* jumpline. Last-minute edits to the story or to the layout that affect story composition require editing two documents instead of one.

D. Augment or replace the Book File Collaboration Workflow with a different methodology. See if your workflow can employ the InCopy LiveEdit Workflow (Adobe's term, not mine) or the Placed Page Collaboration Workflow (I *am* pretty sure I'm the first to coin this one, so please send me a nickel every time you use it) or both. I'll discuss both of these methodologies below—the latter in the very next section, "One Page, Many Designers," and the former a few pages hence in the section "Collaborating with Editorial."

Just to be clear: If your publication *doesn't* jump stories outside the pages assigned to each creative, you *can* use the Book File Collaboration Workflow without the aforementioned problem. *Do* still read the rest of this chapter, though, as none of these methodologies is necessarily exclusive of the others.

One Page, Many Designers

Yesterday there was a one-to-one, one-designer-to-one-page, relationship so inflexible it may as well have been cast in iron. Today, the paradigm has shifted. Now, with InDesign CS3, a many-to-one relationship is possible. Many designers may work simultaneously on one page—or, more accurately, on *portions* of the same page. In Figure 12.2 you'll see a flowchart diagramming an example of what I've dubbed the Placed Page Collaboration Workflow.

FIGURE 12.2
Diagram of a Placed Page Collaboration Workflow in use on a single page

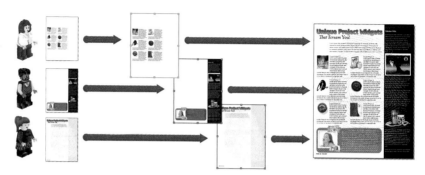

In the diagram, a single-page magalog layout is divided into three separate areas. Three separate designers will work concurrently, one on each area, all never leaving InDesign. Rachael (the redhead), is responsible for copyfitting and setting the six product listings in the middle of the page, while Carlos (in the middle) takes care of designing the sidebar and feature box. Kim (at the bottom with the ponytail) is the lead designer on the page, so she's designing the background imagery and setting the headline, deck, page introductory paragraph, and static elements like the folio. Previously, trying to split the work on one page among three designers meant each would have to take a turn, each one waiting to begin work until the last has finished. All three designers under this scenario *are* working concurrently, on the same page, in InDesign.

The principle is simple, one with which you're already intimately familiar. Let's look at the basics of your current workflow.

If you work on advertising-supported publications, for instance, you almost certainly accept PDF or EPS press-ready ads from agencies, right? Someone far away designs an ad, FTPs it to you, and you drop it as is into the appropriate slot in your layout. If you don't accept outside creative into your layouts, you *do* create elements and sections of at least some pages in Photoshop or Illustrator. That artwork (or agency art) is placed into InDesign as a linked asset. Should the asset need to be altered, it's edited in its native application and the link merely updated in InDesign. Thus, while you're working on the composed page in InDesign, someone else could be working at the same moment and independently in Illustrator on the pie chart for page 6. Neither of you will hinder the other's work because, as a linked asset, that AI or PDF pie chart is a wholly separate document from your INDD layout. You do this day in and day out with placed assets, so you know how it works.

Now, substitute another INDD file for the AI or PDF. Instead of a pie chart, page 6 contains a table or other elements better done in InDesign than outside it. InDesign CS3 now accepts *other InDesign files as placed and linked assets*. That's what Rachael, Carlos, and Kim are doing. Each is working in InDesign on a separate INDD or INX document. The final, composited page in the Figure 12.2 flowchart is a fourth document (or not; maybe Carlos is working in the master while Rachael's and Kim's pieces will be placed into his document). For the sake of argument, let's assume a fourth document collects the three designers' separate documents. The compositor uses File ➤ Place or drag and drop from Bridge, Finder, or Explorer to import the designers' three separate INDD files exactly as he would a trio of TIFFs, PSDs, PDFs, or whatever. The placed assets are then arranged to form the composite page—just like pages you lay out every day with images and artwork created outside InDesign. That's the Placed Page Collaboration Workflow.

Another cool aspect of compositing a page by placing INDD files is that the compositor's tasks of manual asset positioning and transforming can be completely eliminated. Glance again at Figure 12.2, paying particular attention to the component pieces. Notice that they're all the same size and, except for Kim's background, contain copious white space. Each piece is the exact size of the final page. If your composited INDD document is 8.5×11 inches, make each page asset 8.5×11 inches. The bounding box of each placed page will then also be 8.5×11 inches. Not only does that enable each designer to work with a sense of how his work fits into the page as a whole, it also means the asset can be placed with minimal positioning work. Rachael's, Carlos's, and Kim's art can all be placed at the same time, aligned to each other's top and left edges with two quick clicks of buttons on the Control panel or Align panel, and then easily positioned to the 0,0 origin. No one has to zoom in and precisely position the pieces to one another because they are all the same size, ready to align perfectly with one another. Cropping is unnecessary, too, because empty space on the InDesign document page is transparent; each asset will show through the negative space in the one above it. They'll even blend with each other if transparency or blending modes are used. In my flowchart, the black background of Carlos's sidebar is set to a Multiply blending mode at 85%. When it overlays the fingerprint image in Kim's section of the page, the sidebar will enable the white fingerprint ridges to show through as 85% black ridges. The red feature box also blends with the other part of the fingerprint via another blending mode.

How do I know what everyone else is doing? You can't lay out a page in a vacuum. Again, InDesign CS3 can place other InDesign files as assets. So, to keep abreast of what everyone else is doing in his portion of the page, place each page component document on the pasteboard. Assuming everyone is working from files stored on a network server accessible by all, Rachael can place on her pasteboard Carlos's and Kim's INDD documents, Carlos can place Rachael's and Kim's, and so on. When any one of them saves the document, InDesign will notify the others that the linked asset has been changed and ask if the link should be updated. If you've got a good group of people fastidious enough to clean up after themselves, they can even place the other designers' documents on the page instead of the pasteboard. The effect then is that three people are all working simultaneously on the composite layout. (Fair warning: It can be a little creepy at first to watch parts of your page change as if by supernatural means.)

SOLVING THE PROBLEM WITH BOOK FILE COLLABORATION

C'mon. Do you really *expect me to assign* three *designers to* one *page?* No, of course not, at least not in most workflows. Don't take me too literally. The one-page example and diagram can be interpreted literally or as an allegory for a much larger document. Collaborating via placed pages works just as well with multiple pages. Remember above when I listed the types of documents and circumstances under which a Book File Collaboration Workflow won't work? Well, the Placed Page Collaboration Workflow *does* work on those documents and under those circumstances.

Periodicals often follow a common workflow based on division and duplication—Divide and Copy and Conquer, I call it. Initially, a template is created containing all the pages in the book. Department and regular features pages are laid out, ad pages are assigned, and FPOs are inserted for feature article spreads and other content. Then you, the creative director, sit down and plan the page parceling. You may divide it equally among your designers and production artists. You would then save one additional copy of the template for each designer. Alternatively, you might apportion the template by logical structure. In that case, regardless of the number of people working on the next issue, you would divide the document into its spaces. For instance, the three pages blocked out for the first feature article would be a single space and one complete copy of the template, the two pages for the "Letters to the Editor" department another copy, and so on until all sections of the publication have been accounted for in copies of the initial template.

Figure 12.3 diagrams the common Divide and Copy and Conquer method of designing and laying out periodicals. In this case, the publication has been apportioned to the three production artists plus pages for yourself (you're at the bottom of the flowchart; I wouldn't be so presumptuous as to make a LEGO person of you). Earlier we talked about jumping a story from page 19 to page 32, which is where the flowchart picks up. Pages 1 through 18 we'll assume have been assigned to other production artists. Rachael, Carlos, and Kim are your best people, anyway. They're busy folks, but then they're LEGO designers; they have no lives and don't need coffee breaks. The green pages are Rachael's to design, the blue belong to Carlos, the red to Kim, and the goldenrod are yours. Ad pages are blocked out entirely, awaiting PDF and EPS ads that will be dropped in during pagination.

FIGURE 12.3
Flowchart of a common periodical publication workflow

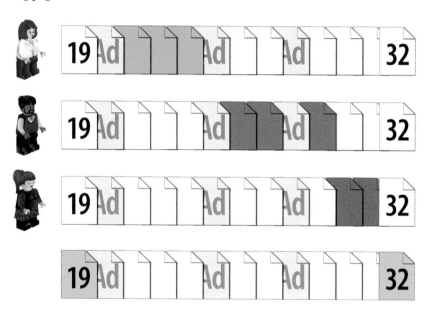

Examine the flowchart. This type of collaboration is common because it offers the benefit of maintaining automatic page numbering. The feature story jumps from pages 19 to 32, and, by leaving all intervening pages in place, page 32 is numbered as such without the need to manually type 32 into a text frame and change it should pages be added, deleted, or re-ordered. Because all four copies of the template are complete copies, Rachael knows she's working on pages 21–23 while Carlos has pages 25, 26, and 28, Kim has pages 30–31, and you have the feature story on pages 19 and 32. Everyone knows where her or his work falls within the book, and the publication TOC can then be built by hand with reasonable assurance of its accuracy (automatic TOC generation is impossible at this stage because there are four of every page, so the various versions cannot be tied together via a book file).

Regardless of its benefits, this type of collaboration has significant inherent problems. Can you spot them? I found several.

1. Let's start with the fact that there are no arrows. Flowcharts are supposed to have arrows, right? I mean, that's the *flow* part of *flowchart*. There are no arrows because nothing moves, nothing and no one interacts. Rachael does her thing, Carlos his, Kim hers, you yours. None of you has the slightest idea what the others are up to. That's a problem in itself, but it also leads to other problems. Such as…

2. You, the creative director, have no insight into, or oversight of, what your people are doing short of walking up behind them or asking them to stop productive work to print or email proofs. If you don't get proofs (or peer over shoulders), odds are good you'll be surprised by the pages at the eleventh hour and find yourself asking for changes. Even if you do get proofs, how often is it practical to check up on and coordinate with your designers? If Kim does something that doesn't work with Carlos's design, one of them has to change, but after how many work hours have been invested? How much does each change cost you?

3. Everyone is working from a separate and complete copy of the entire publication template. Magazine structures don't often change without rebuilding the entire template, but they do change from time to time. Pages in other types of multipage, team-effort publications are often shuffled around with pages added or removed here and there. In a workflow of the sort shown in the diagram, such a change is a nightmare. To add a page in the middle of the publication or shift one section behind another entails coordinating with each of the designers to make the identical change in every copy of the template. Done infrequently by very organized, detail-oriented creatives, such structural alterations can be accomplished smoothly. The difficulty and likelihood of mistakes increases in direct proportion to the frequency and number of such changes and with the level of stress on the creatives. One slipup and you could be spending quite a bit of time trying to puzzle your publication back together.

4. Pagination with this type of publication is a royal pain in the… neck. At the end of the publication cycle, someone must sit down with all the pieces of the publication and pull out only the original pages from each version and then combine all those pieces into a single publication. Typically this is done by saving each page individually to EPS or PDF and then placing those one at a time into yet another template duplicate.

The workflow presented in Figure 12.3 is extremely common. It's also a huge waste of time and money because, for many such workflows, there's a better way.

Let's review the key production problem that forces a Divide and Copy and Conquer workflow. If you have a magazine, newspaper, newsletter, magalog, or other document with jumped stories, you can't divide the publication into multiple Book panel–managed files without severing the threading between frames of jumped stories. You also can't break out the pages in between the story jumps and expect automatic page numbering to work across the book. You *can*, however, use placed pages in addition to a book file to give you everything—automatic page numbering, threaded jumped stories, and concurrent productivity—*without* risky structural alterations or grueling pagination work at the end.

The chart in Figure 12.4, which continues with the example of a story that jumps from page 19 to page 32, demonstrates placing pages in a multipage document. In this case, the creative director is using both a book file and placed pages. To handle the jumped story, one booked document includes pages 19 through 32 inclusive. Intervening pages are assigned out to Rachael, Carlos, and Kim. The designers work in separate INDD documents that are placed as linked assets in the main document; there are no redundant, unused pages in the documents the designers receive. Each component document is either single pages or multiple pages, whichever is needed. Multipage INDD document assets can be placed just as easily as can multipage PDFs—one page at a time. Therefore, even though Carlos's three pages are nonconsecutive, broken by the full-page ad on page 27, he can still carry a threaded story through all three pages. When his pages are placed into the main publication document, they're placed as pages 25–26 and 28; he *works on* consecutive pages even though they won't be *printed as* consecutive pages. He doesn't have to break the text flow; he can work in a single three-page document, enjoying threading and all the other benefits of working in only one document, without causing problems for the main document. In fact,

Carlos's pages can be moved around in the main document (and renumbered automatically) without the need to even involve Carlos.

FIGURE 12.4
Diagram of a Placed
Page Collaboration
Workflow in a multi-
page document

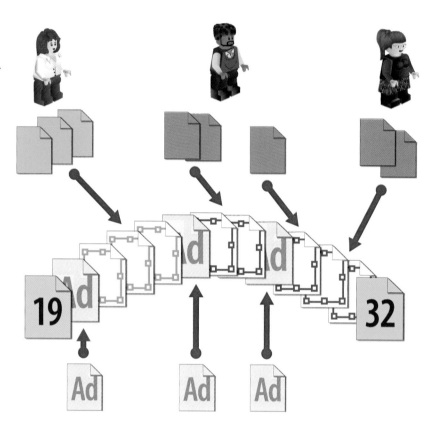

There is legitimate use for Placed Page Collaboration in the occasional one-page document. But, it's with multipage documents that it really shines—particularly if, for one reason or another, you can't use Book File Collaboration or using it alone doesn't solve your workflow problems. By freeing creatives from the need to sit on their hands or perform busywork while waiting to get access to documents, your organization saves money and time. You'll also save time and money by eliminating the need for a paginator to impose in a scramble at the last minute, going through all the full-document templates, selecting and imposing all the needed pages sitting here and there among dozens of empty or FPO pages.

GOING TO PRESS WITH PLACED PAGES

Point made, but there's no way it will print. Why not? Why is it that, every time someone presents a new way of doing things in InDesign, the first response is always, *I bet it won't print.* QuarkXPress doesn't suffer this kind of cynicism. Placing INDD files inside other INDD files is *exactly* like placing Illustrator AI files or even EPS images. It's another linked asset, albeit one that can have its own linked assets, but it prints, packages, and exports to PDF just fine. Again, I can personally attest to it.

So, how *do I output?* Same as any InDesign document you did yesterday or last week—print it, package it, or export it to PDF. You can also do all of those through a Book panel the same way you did it before you placed pages.

One thing you'll be glad to know is that InDesign's Package feature is placed-page aware. When you place INDD pages into another INDD document, you've created a layer of nesting. The *placed* INDD can have its own fonts and linked assets—and even contain other placed INDD files. Potentially you could build from placed pages an infinite Russian matryoshka doll where every placed INDD has inside it another placed INDD, and inside that is another INDD, and so on. How far into that nest of linking will the package command go? As far as I can tell, all the way. Just for kicks I tried six levels deep. Package found and collected unique images and fonts used at each level. So, if you have DocA.indd placed inside DocB.indd, File ➢ Package will find all the fonts and linked assets used by DocB.indd. One of those linked assets is DocA.indd, so InDesign will collect that and put it into the packaged project's Links folder, too. At the same time, InDesign recognizes that DocA.indd itself has font and asset dependencies, so it grabs all those as well. And, it updates the links in *all* collected INDD files to point to images and other assets in the Links folder.

Placed Page Collaboration Workflow. It just works. Remember where you heard it first.

Collaborating with Writers and Editors

Design—graphic designers, production artists, compositors, and typesetters—and editorial—copywriters, journalists, editors, and authors—have, since time immemorial, often been pitted against one another by the secular and incompatible tools and technologies on which they each depend. Editorial passes its text to design for copyfitting and layout, taking the copy out of the sight and control of its creators. Editorial must then wait for proofs to be returned from design. Changes—and there are often changes—have to be passed incrementally to designers to effect; after the first handoff, editorial must rely completely on design to update and correct what is editorial's own work. That could be frustrating for anyone. Equally frustrating is the other side of the process where design personnel frequently must interrupt work on current pages to go back and edit text on previously completed pages. Frustration could lead to resentment and to conflict between the two departments. At the heart of all of it is the software.

The sky is blue, water is wet, editorial uses Microsoft Word. This undisputable fact of life is not because Microsoft Word is perfectly suited for copywriting and editing. Far from it. It has numerous flaws and quirks that increase the difficulty of day-in, day-out writing and editing. It's the only choice for editorial for one simple reason: nothing better has come along. Or, maybe that should read, "nothing better has been presented to editorial." There *is* competition to Microsoft Word, but writers aren't using it for one of three reasons: they don't know what other options are out there; the other word processors don't integrate better than, or even as well as, Word with other applications in the workflow; or their employers, who suffer under one or both of the first two reasons, don't give editorial a choice.

When it comes to Word competitors like Corel WordPerfect, WordStar, OpenOffice.org Writer, the Mac-only Pages, and others, switching from Word offers no advantage to the design-editorial collaboration. None of these applications integrates into InDesign (or its competitors) any better or worse than Word. Not one of them addresses the potential frustrations and slowdowns in the design-editorial collaboration.

Solving the Design-Editorial Collaboration Problems

In Chapter 8, "Stories," you were introduced to InDesign's editorial companion, InCopy, and given an explanation of the basics for using it as a stand-alone word processor. I won't rehash that introduction here. This section is about how the designer or production person handles the InDesign side of the InDesign-InCopy collaboration. It's not about *you* writing and editing stories in InDesign this time. It's about you enabling *editorial staff* to write and edit stories in your InDesign documents. Before we get into the mechanics of that, however, I want to briefly explain why your design and editorial collaboration workflow needs InCopy.

InCopy addresses the largest and most common problems on both sides of the design-editorial collaboration.

Editorial's Biggest Problem Editorial must hand off its work to design and loses control of the copy at that point. Editors will not have direct interaction with the copy again before it goes to press, and changes must be sent to design to effect. Seeing the results of those changes means waiting on design to make them and then return a new proof. If multiple editors are involved in a story, proofs make the rounds before going back to design, meaning even more time is spent waiting to see the results of the copy edits.

Design's Biggest Problem Once designers receive original Word document copy, they place it into the layout, advise editorial of any overset or underset text, and often generate a printed or PDF proof for editorial. After the proof has been sent, designers move on to other tasks. From that point forward and until the document goes to press, designers typically can expect to be yanked out of whatever else they're doing to make changes to the copy as directed by editorial. Such changes are communicated through various mediums: new versions of the Word documents that must be placed and styled again; emailed editorial directives and fragments of new or updated copy; marked-up paper proofs that must be painstakingly re-created in the document; or over-the-shoulder edits made during a personal visit from the editor. If multiple editors are involved a story, the designer may receive redundant or conflicting change orders. Moreover, change requests from multiple well-meaning editors can create a constant stream of copy changes that prevent the designer from doing anything but editing one or a few stories for significant periods of time.

The InCopy Solution InCopy stories maintain live links to the InDesign layout. Editors using InCopy do *not* hand off their copy; it never leaves their hands. Instead, the InDesign user places it into the INDD document as a linked asset, applies the initial styling (if it wasn't done already within InCopy), and saves the InCopy story from within InDesign. Designers can work with the text as needed, but it actually lives in an InCopy document that may be modified by the editor at any time without waiting for proofs, without sending change orders to design. Through InCopy, editors no longer have to blindly imagine how changes will affect the layout of the story; they will *see* the changes live, as they write. In fact, they can write and edit directly in the layout page! For editors, InCopy is control—control over their copy, control they should never be made to give up—wrapped up in a purpose-built word processor that isn't littered with buttons and menu commands for envelope printing, electronic forms creation, Web design, and dozens of other features that have no relevance to writing and editing.

For designers, InCopy represents freedom. It frees them from having to be both designer and editor. By putting total control over the content of stories back into its rightful hands—the editors'—designers can focus entirely on *designing*. There will be no more complete replacement and restyling of text stories after the initial import, no more red-marked paper proofs, a dramatic reduction in email, and fewer instances of looking up to see editors' faces reflected in your monitor.

Assignments

The basis for this remarkable collaboration is *assignments*. Assignments are another type of container. Rather than images or text, however, assignments contain frames (other containers) that themselves contain text or graphics. More accurately, assignments are like book files. They're effectively an index of other files. Whereas INBK book files index INDD InDesign documents, assignments index INCX InCopy documents, which you, the designer, generate from the frames in your InDesign layout. Assignments and their indexed INCX documents are delivered to editorial and opened in InCopy. As opening a book file in InDesign gives you access to the individual layouts connected by the book file, opening an assignment in InCopy puts all the stories and frames *it* connects in front of the editor.

Before we get too much further, allow me to introduce the *dramatis personae* in Table 12.1.

TABLE 12.1: **File Types Involved in the InDesign-InCopy LiveEdit Workflow**

FILE EXTENSION	DESCRIPTION
.indd	An InDesign document.
.incx	A single story file created as part of an assignment. Users do not open these files directly.
.inca	An assignment file that connects one or more INCX documents. When opened in InCopy, the assignment will array all stories assigned to the user in a list for easy editing.
.incp	A packaged assignment generated by InDesign and destined for InCopy. The package contains the assignment, content, and linked assets in a single file and is easily emailed.
.indp	A packaged assignment generated by InCopy and sent back to InDesign. The package contains the assignment, content, and linked assets in a single file and is easily emailed.

Adobe calls assignments and the InCopy documents *managed files*. At least, that's the term in CS3; it changes with each version. "Managing files," in my experience, is something all together different and more comprehensive than exporting a story from one application and editing it in another. Therefore, I don't—and won't in this chapter—refer to them as "managed files," but I wanted you to know Adobe's term.

Let's go hands-on, and I'll explain creating and using assignments to set up a collaborative workflow as we actually build an assignment.

1. Open or create a suitable InDesign document. Choose one containing a page with one or more graphic frames and two or more unthreaded text frames. The text frames may be threaded or stand-alone, but you want at least two frames that are not connected to each other.

   In setting up assignments in a real project, you can use any page containing any number and type of frames. However, to complete this particular exercise and learn what you should, we'll need to work with a page containing specific elements.

   Figure 12.5 shows a page suitable for this exercise. It has several independent text frames, including the three-part title, the byline, the pullquote in the outside rail, and then the main story, which threads through the horizontal frame, the two-column frame beneath, and on to later pages. There are also two image frames in case we want to let editors fill in their own photos in InCopy. (*Maybe* the interview subject's headshot, but I would probably leave the ghosted background art for the designers to handle.)

FIGURE 12.5
A page containing multiple frames ready for assignment to editorial personnel

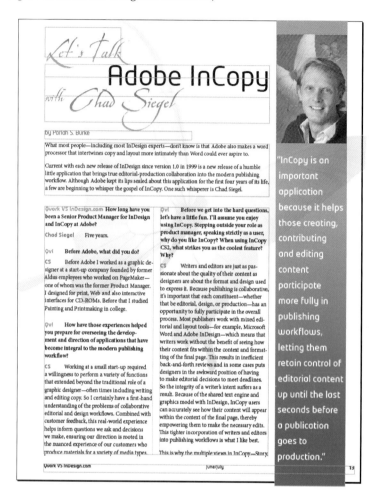

2. Choose File ➤ User to open the User dialog (see Figure 12.6). Here, you'll set options that identify you within the collaborative workflow. When you check out stories and frames for editing, anyone else who tries to check them out will be alerted that you, whatever user name you enter, already have the content checked out. Any notes you add to the stories will also bear your user name and be bracketed by rectangles in the color you select from the drop-down menu. By entering a unique user name and choosing a unique color, you let your collaborators know who to come to with questions or comments. Everyone in the workflow—in InDesign and InCopy—must fill in a name before the InCopy LiveEdit workflow will function, and they should coordinate to choose unique colors for ease of reference.

My user name field says *Pariah Burke (InD)* because InCopy has an identical User dialog, and I differentiate between work done in InDesign and InCopy with the parenthetic suffix.

FIGURE 12.6
The User dialog
identifies you in
the collaborative
workflow.

When you've entered your user name and chosen a color, click OK.

3. Open the Assignments panel from Window ➤ Assignments (see Figure 12.7). Here's where all the magic happens. As I said before, it's a lot like a Book panel. Instead of external documents, however, the Assignments panel manages stories and image frames within a document. At the top of the panel is your document. Beneath it, you'll see an empty entry for unassigned InCopy content. As long as the document contains any frame not part of an InCopy assignment, the Unassigned InCopy Content entry will be there. In other words, get used to it.

FIGURE 12.7
The Assignments
panel

Let's get a real assignment onto the list and begin the process of handing some of editorial's content back to them.

4. In the bottom of the Assignments panel, click the New button. Up will pop the New Assignment dialog (see Figure 12.8).

First, give your assignment a name. Both you and the editor will see the assignment name, and it will be used as the basis for exported filenames, which you can see reflected as you type the assignment name in the INCA file path in the Location for Assignment File section. So, give the assignment a meaningful name like *Let's Talk Page*. As you type, you'll see the proposed path to the file in the Location for Assignment File section update to include the assignment name. You can change the location if needed (see two paragraphs hence).

The Assigned To field is optional but lets you specify who will take on the assignment. If you name the assignee, set that person's particular user color as well. Note that InDesign and InCopy do not communicate about assignee names and colors, so it's a good idea to let the InCopy user choose his color first. Then he'll need to inform you of his color choice by phone, e-mail, or carrier pigeon so that you may set the same color within the assignment—or not. The Color field is entirely optional and exists solely to give you, the InDesign user, a visual cue in the Assignments panel of who owns what content. Assignments in the panel will be tinted to the assignee's color, but that's where the utility of this field ends.

FIGURE 12.8
The New Assign-
ment dialog

When you create an assignment file, an INCA document will be written to disk. Each story added to the assignment will be exported as an INCX. The Location for Assignment File section tells you where on your computer (or the network) these files will be saved. Clicking the Change button enables you to browse your system for a new place to save the documents. If your editorial department collaborators are on the same network, set the Location for Assignment Files to a shared folder on the network, one to which you, your fellow designers, and the editors have both read and write access. If your editors work remotely from other locations, you'll need to make use of packaged assignments, which we'll discuss later in this chapter; for now, choose a convenient location on the network or your computer.

The Include section is extremely important. Here is where you determine how much of the layout InCopy users see when they open the assignment and work with it in InCopy's InDesign-like Layout view. Story and Galley view, which do not show the layout, are unaffected by the Include options. Your choices are as follows:

◆ **Placeholder Frames:** If chosen, this option makes solid gray boxes of all frames not directly a part of the assignment. Any content within those frames will be hidden from InCopy users' view. Any frames that *are* in the assignment—including graphic frames— *will* be visible and editable in InCopy's Layout view.

   Recommendation: Choosing Placeholder Frames is very much like setting InDesign's display performance to Fast Display, with the same benefits: less distraction, and pages draw to the screen very quickly. If editors find themselves distracted by page elements that are not theirs, or if they report that InCopy moves sluggishly while they edit, consider using the Placeholder Frames option.

◆ **Assigned Spreads:** Assignments may consist of multipage threaded stories as well as multiple disconnected stories spread across several pages. Therefore, with the Assigned Spreads option, an InCopy user has the ability to see in InCopy's Layout view all the assigned *and* unassigned content from those pages (in spreads). Any pages or spreads that are *not* part of the assignment will be excluded. Of course, although visible, unassigned content will not be editable in InCopy. Like InDesign's Typical Display display performance mode, images included in the assignment to InCopy users are low-resolution proxies ideal for onscreen viewing and suitable for output on a desktop printer. The images and graphical elements are not, however, of a high enough quality that editors should rely on them for fine detail.

Recommendation: Assigned Spreads is already the default option, and I recommend that you consider using it most often. One of the key benefits to the tight integration between InDesign and InCopy is the ability for editors to see and write in the real WYSIWYG layout page within InCopy. Sending full views of assigned spreads gives editorial a window on the layout that, in most cases, helps them better visualize the impact of, and limitations on, their copy. Usually it benefits the publication overall; however, in some cases it can be a hindrance. Some editorial staffers find that looking at an in-progress or finished page is confusing (even though they don't *have* to look at it; InCopy has two other views that hide the layout).

◆ **All Spreads:** With this option, the entire document, not only the spreads containing assigned frames, will be sent and viewable in InCopy's Layout view. The InCopy user will only be able to edit the content assigned to him, however. Choosing this option generates larger files and may cause sluggish InCopy performance on computers with less RAM and hard drive space.

Recommendation: I only recommend using the All Spreads option in assignments for those who absolutely must see the entire document—namely, top of the chain editors. For most lower-level editors, it's overkill and can slow down InCopy running on low-spec computers.

Let's leave discussion of the Linked Image Files when Packaging check box option to the section "Collaborating with Remote Editors" coming up.

When you have all the options for your first assignment set, click the OK button.

5. Although you now have a new assignment in the Assignments panel, it's still empty, devoid of assigned content. On the document page, select one frame and go to Edit ➢ InCopy ➢ Add Selection to Assignment. You'll see the assignment you just created on that list; choose it as the destination for the selected content. If you haven't recently saved the document, InDesign will kindly prompt you to do so, and then it will export the content to an INCX file, which is indexed by the INCA assignment file. The INCX InCopy document will be created in a Content folder beneath the location you chose for the INCA. For instance, if you chose to save the assignment to your desktop in a folder titled MyDocument Assignments, the INCX will be saved to `MyDocument Assignments\Content`.

6. In the Assignments panel, your assignment will now list the assigned frame. It will also show a yellow, out-of-date caution sign beside the assignment name. InDesign does not automatically update assignments as it does INBK book files. Select the assignment in the panel's list and choose Update Selected Assignments from the panel flyout menu, which will write the change (the new INCX to index) to the INCA file.

If you and your editors are on the same network, call up an editor and tell her where to find the assignment. When she opens the assignment file (the INCA, not the INCX story file) in InCopy, she can edit the frame content all she wants. She can be editing in InCopy while you work on the layout in InDesign—even while you make changes to the frame size and positioning! When one of you saves your respective documents, the other will be notified and given the opportunity to update the view onto the other's content.

Congratulations! You've just assigned content to an editor. You were a good foster parent for the story, but it was time. You just returned the copy to the custody of its rightful parent. Now the *editor* will take care of raising the story to maturity while *you* focus on *your* baby, the layout.

 **Real World Scenario**

PUBLISH TO PRINT, PDF, AND WEB, WITH INCOPY AS THE PIVOT POINT

Pilsen Dynamics produces a bimonthly, magazine-style newsletter for its employees, shareholders, customers, and vendors. The newsletter, the *PD Report*, is a marketing tool featuring articles about the company's accomplishments, products, and research and development efforts, but it also takes a broader view of industry trends and concerns. The four-color and saddle-stitched printed edition is distributed to various points in North America via direct mail; it is sent to overseas customers and vendors as an RGB PDF. Although the print edition is the pride of the *PD Report*, various content from each issue—such as the feature articles, calendar of events, and letter from the CEO column—are simultaneously published to the Pilsen Dynamics's intranet, which is accessible by employees, contractors, and certain vendors. One of the chief benefits to the online version is the ability to spark discussion through bloglike comments appended to each article.

The workflow is the epitome of team-based collaboration.

Work on an issue begins with in-house writers submitting their INCX articles and accompanying photographs (often a selection of possible photos) directly to the production department. Production, working from an InDesign INDT template file, places the first-draft INCX files and photos and then generates InCopy assignments for the publication's editors. Because all work is done in-house, all files are written to a shared server, accessible by production and editorial personnel (and later by the intranet team).

Often a writer submits several possible photos for an article, or production itself offers stock photo or stock illustration candidates. All possible images are placed into a folder named to mirror the INCA filename, and the final selection is left to the article editor. Adobe Bridge is now included with all of Adobe's stand-alone, CS3 version applications, so even the InCopy-based editors can visually browse the folder, rate and label images, and, if they aren't happy with any candidate image, use the Adobe Bridge interface to Adobe Stock Photos to select and license a new photograph or illustration. Once an image is selected, editors place it into an assigned image frame directly within InCopy.

Editors and writers go back and forth perfecting the copy while production personnel continue designing the rest of the publication.

When a story has reached its final form, the editor executes a JavaScript script from the InCopy Scripting panel. The script performs a number of small but important tasks:

◆ Accepts and commits to all revisions and changes in the document

◆ Inserts a nonprinting "FROZEN COPY" note at the top of the story to prevent other editors from later modifying the story

◆ Exports the document dictionary to be later merged with other editors' dictionaries by a server-side script, thus creating a central repository of all new words and spelling or hyphenation exceptions (the single dictionary will be imported into every editor's copy of InCopy to ensure that everyone on the team has the most current list of words)

◆ Exports the story to an XML file

◆ Checks in the assignment

When all editors have completed their work and checked in their assignments, the production department updates and reviews content and generates a single RGB PDF version of *PD Report*. The PDF is made available to the personnel who will send it to overseas recipients. It is also sent to the printer, who will convert from RGB to CMYK in preflight and print the hard copy edition. But, the collaboration doesn't end there.

If a story were only going to press and PDF, there would be no reason to mark the story "FROZEN COPY," accept all revisions, or export an XML version. Editors could simply tell production when editing had been completed; no special mark inside the story would be necessary. Similarly, changes made to the article with InCopy's change-tracking enabled wouldn't mar the finished output; notes and markups are nonprinting. And, InDesign has no use for the XML version when content is linked via the Assignments panel. All of these functions are required to output the story to the company intranet.

While the print edition is in production at the outsourced print shop, the internal intranet team goes to work on the exported XML stories. Using a custom script as a bridge, they suck the XML stories into an MSSQL database running on their .NET server. The script maps InCopy's XML structure to required database fields and converts formatting tags to HTML, including CLASS and ID attributes so that the content can be styled by the site's existing CSS stylesheet. With the article now available via the intranet's content management system and, ostensibly, ready for publication, the intranet team turns to the story images. With the final publication PDF as a guide, they select the story images in Adobe Bridge and execute, from within Adobe Bridge, a Photoshop batch action to size and downsample images and to save Web-compatible PNG copies of the images in the same folder. Finally, they manually add references to the images to the online stories.

Using InCopy as the pivot point, all the departments can use the same content to publish to print, PDF, or the intranet with little wasted or duplicated effort. Each department maintains control over the content in its area of expertise while using technology to streamline the hand-off of content to the next department. Ahh, creative efficiency.

Assigned Content in InDesign

When you added the frame to the assignment above, the INCX file was created on disk and the assignment on the Assignments panel was updated. Something else happened, too.

As I worked through the steps above in *my* document, I created an assignment for Samuel John Klein, my frequent collaborator (and technical editor of this very book). Sam's first assignment is the pullquote frame in the interview layout's right rail (see Figure 12.9). Incidentally, in that figure, although the photo is in a separate graphic frame atop the assigned frame, the pullquote frame and blue gradient background is one object, not a text frame laid over an empty, colored graphic frame (this is the *efficient* way to do it). Insets in the text frame push text in from the four sides, and the Color blending mode applied only to the fill blends it with the butterfly in the background. Being that the frame is one object, you might fear that someone working in InCopy could change the insets, background color, or other attributes of the frame. (Nothing personal, Sam.) No need to fear, however; InCopy doesn't have any frame modification functions. They just aren't in there. InCopy users can edit the *content* and its attributes, but they can't touch the attributes of the *container*, the frame. No matter what he tries in InCopy, Sam won't be able to move, resize, or change any attribute of the frame itself. That just isn't what InCopy does; that's what InDesign alone does.

FIGURE 12.9

An assigned frame

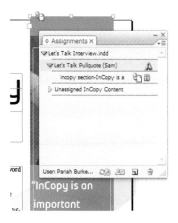

You should notice something different about the assigned frame. It's subtle, but you should see it. Yes, the icon. The little icon (it looks like a blue-green ball with a page in front of it) at the top-left corner of the frame indicates that it's assigned material. It also denotes that the content—text in this case—no longer lives within InDesign. It's been exported to the InCopy INCX story file and converted from content that lives only in the layout to content that lives in the linked asset INCX. The content of that frame is now a wholly separate document, and working with it now entails a rather significant change.

InDesign and InCopy communicate with one another via the LiveEdit Workflow plug-ins installed in both applications. Those plug-ins, the heart of assignments, prevent double-modification when both InDesign and InCopy users are working from files saved to a shared location. If Sam opens the INCA and begins editing the INCX story it contains, I won't be able to edit the sidebar copy until Sam is done. The reverse is also true—if I begin editing the text, Sam will have to wait for me to finish. I can still edit the frame and its attributes, however, even if the content is in use by someone else. I can change the frame insets, number of columns, blending mode, background color. I can move the frame on the page or to another page in the same document. I can even rearrange or resize the pages of the document, all while Sam is actively editing the content of that frame because I'll be working with the frame itself, not its content directly. It works with a simple checkout/check-in system. Whoever wishes to edit assigned content must check out the story (or graphic frame), which thereby prevents others from checking out and editing the same content.

There are several ways to check out an assigned frame (or series of threaded frames). After selecting the frame, there are several ways to check out an assigned frame (or series of threaded frames):

◆ Go to Edit ➢ InCopy ➢ Check Out;

◆ Right-click (Ctrl-click on a single-button Mac mouse) on the frame and choose InCopy ➢ Check Out from the context sensitive menu;

◆ Highlight the story in the Assignments panel; and choose Check Out from the panel flyout menu, or;

◆ Highlight the story in the Assignments panel and click the Check Out button at the bottom.

Yeah, Adobe *really* wanted you to be able to work with InCopy assignments easily.

I don't use any of those methods myself, not unless I want to check out several stories at once. Instead, when checking out only a single story or frame, I just begin editing. For instance, if I wanted to fix a typo in the pullquote, I'd switch to the Type tool and click inside the assigned frame. As soon as I type or delete something, InDesign will inform me that I "must check out the contents of this frame in order to make changes." It will present me with Yes and No buttons, asking if I'd like to go ahead and check out the story. When I click Yes, the story checks out to me, locks to everyone else, and my change occurs. The icon at the top of the frame will also change to a pencil indicating that I've checked out and am able to edit the content of the frame (see Figure 12.10).

FIGURE 12.10
The Pencil icon identifies the frame as being checked out to you.

If Sam had checked out the frame, I would see a different icon denoting that the content is checked out to someone else (see Figure 12.11; the Pencil icon now has a diagonal line through it). At the same time, none of those Check Out commands would be available. The change is instantaneous when InDesign and InCopy are used in a network environment, with users opening files from the same location. Within seconds of Sam checking out the story for editing in InCopy, I'll see the unavailable, checked-out-by-someone-else icon appear on the frame as well as on the Assignments panel. If I want to know who has the story checked out, hovering my mouse cursor over the icon will tell me by whom and in which application, InDesign or InCopy, the story is being edited.

FIGURE 12.11
When content is checked out to someone else, this icon appears on the frame.

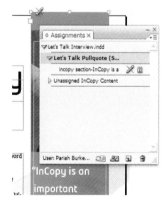

When you're finished editing content, be sure to check it back in so that others may access it. Few things steam collaborators more than needing to edit a story someone else has left checked out behind a password-protected screensaver when he went to lunch or home for the weekend. Checking in content is done through all the same means as checking it out—from the Check In menu command on the Assignments panel flyout menu, the context sensitive right-click menu, and Edit ➢ InCopy. There isn't a button for Check In on the Assignments panel, which would have been nice to have. Adobe made up for this inconvenience by also giving you the Check In All command, which at once returns *all* the document's checked-out content to an available state.

As you work, you'll probably also notice a Cancel Check Out command. The difference between Check In or Check In All and Cancel Check Out is whether changes you've wrought are written back to the INCX and INCA files or discarded, respectively.

When one person in the workflow changes content and checks it back in, the Assignments panel will inform everyone else with connected documents opened. The assigned content status icon will update to display two icons stacked (side by side in the Assignments panel; see Figure 12.12). First will be the available-for-checkout ball and page; beside it is a yellow caution sign indicating that the content has been updated outside the current application and is out-of-date as you see it. Select the assignment or assigned story entry in the Assignments panel, and then click the Update Content button at the bottom of the panel or choose Update Selected Assignments, Update All Assignments, or Update Content from the panel flyout menu.

FIGURE 12.12
Two icons indicate that content has been updated by someone else and the assigned frame is now available for check out.

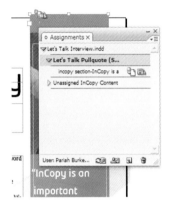

Managing Assignments

Assignments would be pointless if you could only give one frame to a single collaborator.

ADDING CONTENT TO ASSIGNMENTS

A document can contain numerous assignments, one for every person in your workgroup or organization. The Assignments panel will manage them all. I recommend that, when it is feasible and you know which InCopy users will work on a particular document, you create all your assignments at once and as early as possible in the document construction phase. Begin by creating a new assignment for each person. For instance, if I wanted this book's team to assist with the interview feature layout with which I've been working, I'd leave the previously built assignment for Sam and create a new one so Karen could check facts, readability, style usage, grammar, and spelling. If I was waiting for the production department to finish color correction of the interview subject's headshot, I might assign the photo frame to them as an InCopy story, too. The other editors—copyeditor Judy, production editor Deb, and managing editor Pete—would also need a pass at the copy, but they'll need to see the same copy that goes to Sam or Karen. Therefore, I wouldn't create assignments for them. Instead, Sam and Karen would send *their* assignments on to the next person in the chain from within InCopy. As the InDesign layout artist, my concern with the copy ends with the assignment and delivery to the first step in the chain and doesn't pick up again until just before going to press, when I perform my final proof of all pages.

Once you have all your empty assignments created, they'll appear on the InCopy ➢ Add to Assignment menu available from the Edit menu and all those other places. You can add each story or graphic frame one at a time to the correct assignment. That's a lot of clicking, though. Why not just drag? You can drag any frame from the layout and drop it onto an assignment in the Assignments panel to add the content to that assignment. When all content that must be assigned has been added to the correct assignment, choose Update All Assignments from the panel flyout menu to write changes into the INCA documents.

ASSIGNING PHOTOS

InCopy users can, if you let them, place and replace images in graphic frames. Reporters, for example, can supply their own story photos. Many designers use this ability to get the photo from the InCopy user but later tweak the cropping, scaling, and other attributes of images in InDesign. In other words, assigning a graphic frame to an InCopy user can lighten your workload a little bit more without sacrificing any control.

Graphic frames are assigned just like story frames—through the same menus and methods. Then, in InCopy, editors can use the File ➤ Place command and a Place dialog and options identical to InDesign's to insert imagery into the checked-out frame. Once the image is inserted, they can perform basic manipulation tasks like scaling and repositioning the image, but, again, they cannot edit the frame size, shape, position, or visual attributes.

REARRANGE ASSIGNED CONTENT

If you inadvertently add a story to the wrong assignment, or priorities change and you need to move content from one person's assignment to another's, just drag the content entry in the Assignment panel's list from one assignment to another and update all assignments. The INCX won't change or be overwritten. Only the INCA assignment files will change, removing the reference to the INCX from one and adding it to another.

From the Edit ➤ InCopy menu, you can quickly add all story frames, all graphics, or all story and graphic frames on the current layer to a particular assignment in one step. This is a handy way to get all content onto the Assignments panel quickly. Once they are there, you can drag and drop individual frames to other assignments.

UNASSIGNING CONTENT

To pull content out of an assignment altogether, highlight its entry in the Assignments panel and click the trashcan icon at the bottom and update the assignment. The content will then re-embed in the InDesign document. Note that this action does not delete the INCX file; it only breaks the link between the content in the layout and the external INCX document.

RENAMING ASSIGNED FILES

INCX files are named by combining the filename of the originating InDesign document with the first few words of the content in the INCX and exported frame. The INCX files *can* be renamed, but there's very little point in doing so because their names on the Assignments panel can *not* be altered from the first name InDesign gives them. Yeah, I know: *Whose brilliant idea was that?* If you'd still like to change the name of the INCX file, follow this procedure:

1. Open the InDesign file containing the assigned INCX file in question.

2. Rename the INCX file on disk.

3. In the InDesign Links panel, the linked INCX file will suddenly go missing because it was renamed (indicated by the red circle beside its name). Select the missing link in the list and click the Relink button.

4. In the Relink dialog, choose the newly renamed INCX and click Open. The missing link status will disappear, and the Links panel entry will change to reflect the new filename.

5. Switch to the Assignments panel, where the assignment containing the INCX story will show the yellow caution sign to indicate that the assignment is out-of-date. Select the assignment and choose Update Selected Assignments from the panel flyout menu.

Overriding Checkouts

In any team effort, someone must be in charge of the overall project. This is a matter of practicality, operational security, and workflow integrity. Indeed, if the LiveEdit Workflow afforded everyone equal power, if no one could override anyone else, one forgotten check-in the night before deadline could bring the entire project to a grinding halt. Fortunately, power is *not* shared equally between InDesign and InCopy. Although most publications are captained by someone who uses InCopy— a managing editor, editor in chief, or publisher—in the LiveEdit Workflow, it's the InDesign side of the collaboration that holds final technological authority.

It happens. Someone goes home sick or leaves for the night forgetting to check in stories on which they'd been working. In the InDesign document, you'll see content checked out, and you can't fix that typo on line seven. Do you call the missing editor at home? Should you call IT to come hack into the editor's computer? Nah. Start editing the story in InDesign. It will prompt you to check out the story, which will then generate a warning that someone else already has it checked out. At that point you'll be offered the option to re-embed the story, overriding the checkout and any unsaved changes the editor may have made. Once embedded back into the InDesign document, it's native, editable text (or a picture) again. Exercise caution in overriding a checkout because what gets embedded is the version already on the InDesign page—the version from the last read of the assigned INCX. If the absent writer made any changes to the checked-out content, those will be lost.

To give the assignment to another InCopy user, add the frame to an assignment again just as you did the first time.

Recovering from Broken Assignment Files

When you create assignments and generate story files, INCX documents are added to the Links panel (Window ➢ Links) as linked assets. Thus, even though a story is part of an assignment managed via the Assignments panel, it is also a linked external asset and is therefore under the dominion of the Links panel. I would say that better than 99% of the time, you won't need to even think about the fact that assigned stories are also managed through the Links panel. The only time you will care is if something goes wrong with the assignment.

If the INCA assignment file was lost, accidentally deleted, or somehow became corrupted, you could ostensibly be in a serious pickle. On a couple of occasions I've had clients call me in a panic because something happened to the INCA and they could no longer update stories in InDesign or even work on them in InCopy. Of course, as is the order of the universe, such catastrophes never happen earlier than mere hours before a deadline. There's no need to panic, though, because the Links panel rides to the rescue.

Remember, an assignment INCA is like a book file INBK. The assignment file contains nothing more than its own name, the name and color of the assignee, and a list of INCX documents; the actual content of stories is within INCX files. As long as they survive, your assignment file can be re-created.

Collaborating with Remote Editors

Up until now we've been talking mostly about collaborating with network peers who have read/ write access to the same shared folders as you. What about remote or mobile workers on either the InDesign or InCopy side of the assignment? Are you out of luck? If you were using InDesign CS2 and InCopy CS2, then, yeah, you'd be out of luck. You could generate and send assignment and story files, but there would be no check-in/checkout control and double-modification would always be a risk. This was a huge complaint from those who discovered Adobe's best-kept secret (InCopy).

In my experience migrating *many* workflows, *many* writers and editors, to collaborative InCopy-InDesign workflows, those that include at least one remote or mobile worker outnumber those that have all design and editorial personnel in-house. The fact that Adobe's LiveEdit Workflow was built entirely around the belief that everyone would have read/write access to the same central file location handicapped workflows that wanted collaborative efficiency, control, and freedom with InCopy and InDesign. Worse, because InCopy shows all stories in the assignment in a continuous interface, many editorial department recipients of INCA and INCX documents had difficulty with the idea that they needed to return multiple email attachments to the designer (see Figure 12.13). *It looks like one document, so why do I have to send several documents?* That confusion often led to only INCA assignment files being sent back to layout artists; of course, INCA files alone are useless to anyone. Additionally, using File ➢ Open in InCopy showed both the INCA and INCX files to the InCopy user. Given the fact that Mac and Windows applications may hide many document filename extensions by default, the editors' confusion was further compounded by having several similarly named files and no clear indicator of which they needed to select in the File Open dialog.

FIGURE 12.13
Opening an assignment file in InCopy presents a Story Editor view of all assigned stories inline for easy editing.

While building CS3, Adobe got hip to the fact that what it had wasn't working for a great many people. Its response was assignment packages, single files that, like a ZIP or StuffIt archive, include multiple files compressed into one. In this case, the contents of the package are assignment files, INCX stories, and, optionally, linked image assets used by the layout in the assignment. As I alluded to above, assignment packages are ideal for remote workers, but they aren't *solely* for remote workers. They also address the very real, very large problem of too many files confusing users and paralyzing the InCopy side of the workflow. Both InCopy and InDesign can open and work with assignment packages and send them to each other. InCopy users only have to deal with a single package file—InCopy will extract the INCA and INCX on-the-fly as part of the file-opening process and will recompress the files again after closing the INCP package. *And*, the act of sending a package to InDesign or InCopy users automatically checks out content to the recipient, preventing accidental double-modification by the sender or anyone else.

To create a package from within InDesign, begin by creating an assignment as usual and adding content. In the Assignment Options dialog, decide whether to check that option we skipped earlier, include Linked Image Files when Packaging. Including them allows InCopy users to see high-resolution images but increases the size of the package. Excluding them causes InDesign to generate and include low-resolution proxies that are fine for onscreen viewing and printing to desktop laser and ink-jet printers. I recommend the latter, especially if you intend to email the package. With the assignment and content created, choose Package for InCopy from the Assignments panel flyout menu. You'll be prompted to name the new package. After you save the package, a cute gift box in InCopy-purple will appear beside the assignment name in the Assignments panel (see Figure 12.14). At the same time, the content in the packaged assignment will be checked out.

FIGURE 12.14
Packaged assign-
ments are denoted
by special icons.

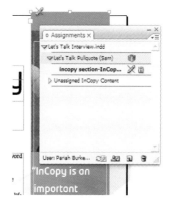

You can send the package to your editorial colleague by FTP, email, or even pocket flash drive. If your plan is to email the package, save a couple of steps. Instead of choosing Package for InCopy from the Assignments panel flyout menu, choose Package for InCopy and Email. In one fell swoop InDesign will package up the assignment, pop open an email, and attach the package to the email. Fill in the recipient's email address and maybe a friendlier message than "your assignment is attached," and click Send. Now get to work on the next project while editorial takes care of writing, editing, and polishing the copy without burdening you.

On the other side, your editorial collaborator will receive the package by email. She should then save it to disk and open it InCopy. When she's finished editing and it's time to send the content back to the layout, she should choose File ➤ Package ➤ Return for InDesign and Email to generate and send an IN*D*P package back to you (see Figure 12.15). Her InCopy package will lock down the content as checked out to someone else (you).

FIGURE 12.15

InCopy's Package menu

When it arrives, you can either double-click the INDP or choose Open Package from the flyout menu on the Assignments panel. The package will marry up with the INDD layout, updating and checking in the assigned frames in that publication.

Instead of sending the package back to you, the InCopy user can send it to other InCopy users. That's what the Forward for InCopy and Forward for InCopy and Email commands in the Package menu do. Either will create a new INCP InCopy package, lock and check out the content, and send it on to the next editor who needs to review the same content. That next editor will either send it back to you or on to the next editor in the chain for review and markup

Copy Before Layout

Up to this point, the way we've been talking, it may seem that everything, including the copy, begins in InDesign. That's not necessarily true. Often that's the case exactly—you design a frame-first layout or template and then build InCopy assignments from empty frames or frames filled with placeholder text. Just as common, however, are workflows that begin with editorial personnel writing first drafts and then you laying out those first drafts to build a document. How does collaboration and the LiveEdit Workflow fit into a workflow wherein copy is written before layout begins? Not too dissimilarly, as it turns out.

Here's one common scenario:

1. A freelance writer writes his first draft in Microsoft Word and submits the DOC file to his editor.

2. The editor imports the DOC file into InCopy for initial editing and saves the document as a native INCX InCopy document.

3. Even as the InCopy document is exported back to a Word-compatible RTF document and sent to the writer for revision, the editor passes the first-draft INCX to the design department so that page allocation, illustration, and layout may begin.

4. The designer places the INCX document and begins page composition.

From this point, the workflow can progress along two possible routes:

A. You can place the INCX document as a linked asset and forgo assignments altogether. INCX documents are native InCopy documents. Functionally, they are identical to the INCX story files generated when content is added to an assignment—except they are not wrapped in assignments. There will be no check-in/checkout control via the Assignments panel in either application. Double-modification is prevented by the fact that, in a network environment, only one person at a time may open the file from the shared location. If all parties are not working from the same shared folder, there is no protection against double-modification of the copy. Additionally, unassigned INCX files do not include layout information or a layout preview. Switching to InCopy's Layout view while editing such a story presents a blank page rather than the copyfit page. More importantly, because unassigned INCX files do not include bidirectional communication with InDesign, editors will not know if copy over- or undersets. The INCX remains in the custody of editorial personnel. When they change and save the file to a shared network folder, it is updated within InDesign like any external asset managed by the Links panel.

I don't recommend this option because it is functionally no different than placing native Word DOCs. Editorial isn't allowed the insight into how text fits into and looks on the page, and it will be up to you to verify their work after every revision, ensuring that copy hasn't overset, cutting off the end, or underset, leaving large empty spaces. This negates several of the most important benefits of using InCopy in the publication workflow. You're back to babysitting the page copy, and editorial is back to requesting proofs after every revision.

B. Instead of leaving the INCX document as a stand-alone linked asset, you place it the first time and then build an assignment around it. The assignment is then saved to a shared folder or sent as an assignment package back to the editor. The INCA then enables check-in/checkout, prevents double-modification, and gives the editor a window onto, and the ability to edit within, the laid-out page.

The downside to creating an assignment after beginning with an INCX is not a technological one but an habitual challenge. For everything to work, the editor must stop using his INCX file directly and switch to opening the INCA assignment or INCP assignment package. In fact, if the assigned version was saved to a different location than the original INCX, he must delete the original INCX. For some editors, these simple alterations to the familiar process of using the same story file from start to finish can be quite confusing, which leads to mistakes and frustration.

Keep in mind that the computer experience of some editorial people is limited solely to default, uncustomized installations of Web browsers, the corporate email client, and Microsoft Word. I'm not speaking derogatorily about writers and editors here (remember, I'm both as well as a designer). Rather, I'm pointing out the reality that editorial's work demands much less interaction with, and knowledge of, technology than does production's work. Technologically challenged personnel may save all their documents to a single location on their hard drives, leading to massively overcrowded Home (Mac) or My Documents (Windows) folders. They will therefore likely save the INCA or INCP to the same folder containing the original INCX, which, if they don't delete the original INCX, will probably result in the wrong file being edited at some point.

If you opt to generate assignments after receiving first-draft INCX documents for initial placement—and I heartily advise that you do—be prepared to assist members of the editorial team who are not comfortable with technology. I recommend you create a numbered list of steps to take after the assignment has been delivered to them. Include in the list how and where to save email attachments (if you email assignment packages); how to locate and delete the original INCX; how to open the INCA or INCP, paying special attention to the fact that some editorial computers will not show the .inca or .incp filename extension; and, if using assignment packages, how to send the package back to you or on to the next editor. Print out these instructions for each editor, and suggest that each affix it to the side of his monitor until he's gone through the new procedures a few times.

Collaborating with a Big Cheese

If the editor in chief, quality control, or other nondesign personnel needs access to edit the majority of stories in your publication, don't bother sending assignments. Instead, send the InDesign document (or documents) itself. InCopy can directly open and save (but not create) INDD files. Then, the InCopy-using Big Cheese can check out and edit the contents of *any* frame in the document. The Big Cheese can also use the track changes feature in InCopy to record his or her changes, as well as to approve or reject copy changes made by other editors. Of course, the frames themselves cannot be altered.

Sharing Reusable Settings

Collaboration doesn't just mean sharing a page or a document. Often designers work together on separate documents within the project, on different projects of a larger campaign, or, especially within in-house creative and production departments, with a variety of different projects and campaigns that share common attributes. Whenever a designer re-creates something that would more easily be obtained another way, time and money are wasted. I don't know about you, but I *hate* blowing time or money on anything that doesn't bring a smile to somebody's face.

Although everything that follows has been covered, in depth, in other chapters, a review is warranted. Besides, here it's all in one place, in succinct how-tos. The following settings may be saved out of InDesign as reusable settings and then shared to other InDesign or InCopy users.

Dictionaries

User dictionaries, including added, removed, ignored, and excepted spellings and hyphenations. (More on dictionaries in Chapter 8, "Stories.")

Export Go to Edit ➤ Spelling ➤ Dictionary and click the Export button. You'll be prompted to save a Word List.txt file. Change the filename to something unique and meaningful in case the recipient receives multiple exported dictionaries.

Import Go to Edit ➤ Spelling ➤ Dictionary and click the Import button. When prompted, locate the TXT file you received from a collaborator. Importing a dictionary adds it to the current document's document-level dictionary. If you import a dictionary with all documents closed, the word list will become part of the default InDesign dictionary and thus applicable to all new documents you create.

Paragraph, Character, Table, Cell, and Object Styles

The various styles aren't saved to external files but rather become part of the INDD documents in which they're used. Thus, there is no export instruction. (More on all of these in Chapter 11, "Efficiency"; paragraph and character styles are also discussed in Chapter 2 and object styles in Chapter 6.)

Import On each of the styles panels there is an Import command—for example, Import Character Styles on the Character Styles panel. Execute that command, and then, in the resulting Open dialog, navigate to and choose the INDD InDesign document or INCX InCopy document containing the styles you'd like to load into the current document. Loading styles with all documents closed make those permanent parts of InDesign, and the styles will therefore be available in every new document you create.

Both the Character Styles and Paragraph Styles panels offer the Load All Text Styles command, which will load both character and paragraph styles in one step. Similarly, the Table Styles and Cell Styles panels have a command to load both of those in a single step as well.

Swatches

As are styles, color swatches are saved as part of the documents in which they're used. Unlike styles, however, they can also be saved to external files that can then be shared among other InDesign documents as well as saved to Photoshop and Illustrator. (More on swatches in Chapter 6, "Objects.")

Export On the Swatches panel flyout menu, choose Save Swatches. This command is disabled until you select a nondefault swatch in the panel itself. When prompted, save the Adobe Swatch Exchange ASE file to disk.

Import Choose the Load Swatches command from the Swatches panel flyout menu in InDesign, Illustrator, or Photoshop and load the ASE file.

Stroke Styles

Custom-designed striped, dotted, or dashed stroke styles. (More on stroke styles in Chapter 6, "Objects.")

Export On the Strokes panel flyout menu, choose Custom Stroke Styles. If you have created any custom stroke styles, the Save button will be available. Click it and choose a destination for your stroke styles.

Import To import, return to the Custom Stroke Styles dialog and choose the Load button.

Autocorrect Word Pairs

The moment you create or alter an autocorrect word pair via the Autocorrect pane in InDesign's preferences, a new file is created on disk to store it. There is no export. (More on Autocorrect in Chapter 8, "Stories.")

Import Copy the language-specific XML file (e.g., `English USA.xml`) from the source system to the same location on the destination system. That location is as follows:

Mac: `Applications/Adobe InDesign CS3/Presets/Autocorrrect/`

Windows: `C:\Documents and Settings\[username]\Application Data\Adobe\InDesign\Version 5.0\Autocorrect\`

Find/Change Queries

The InDesign CS3 Find/Change dialog is much more powerful than previous iterations; it allows for extremely complex search and replace queries, which, fortunately, may be saved, reused, and shared. (More on Find/Change in Chapter 8, "Stories" and Chapter 11, "Efficiency.")

Export Open the Find/Change dialog from the Edit menu. There, set the criteria for the search and/or replace, and click the Save Query button at the top of the dialog. Doing so automatically writes an XML file to disk in the following location:

Mac: `Applications/Adobe InDesign CS3/Presets/Find-Change Queries/`

Windows: `C:\Documents and Settings\[username]\Application Data\Adobe\InDesign\Version 5.0\Find-Change Queries\`

Import The Find-Change Queries folder contains four subfolders, one each for the types of queries performed by Find/Change—Text, GREP, Glyph, and Object. Copy the XML query file from the source computer to the same location on the destination computer to make the query available to Find/Change on the latter.

Glyph Sets

Creating and sharing custom glyph sets makes it easy for workgroups to have instantaneous access to their most commonly used symbols, marks, and glyphs. After you create and populate a glyph set by choosing New Glyph set from the Glyphs panel's flyout menu, InDesign automatically saves the glyph set to disk as an XML-based file without a filename extension. (More about glyphs, the Glyphs panel, and glyph sets in Chapter 3, "Characters.")

Import Copy the desired glyph set from the source system to the destination. You will find the set as a file in the following location:

Mac: `Applications/Adobe InDesign CS3/Presets/Glyph Sets/`

Windows: `C:\Documents and Settings\[username]\Application Data\Adobe\InDesign\Version 5.0\Glyph Sets\`

PDF Export Presets

Ensuring that PDFs are exported identically across a workgroup is critical for sending PDFs to press, the Web, or just about anywhere else. PDF options created in InDesign can be shared to other InDesign or Creative Suite 3 users. (More on exporting to PDF in Chapter 10, "Output.")

Export Define PDF presets either in the Export to PDF dialog during an actual PDF export or ahead of time by choosing File ➤ Adobe PDF Presets ➤ Define. In the Adobe PDF Presets dialog, create a new preset and click the Save As button to save an Adobe PDF Creation Settings File (`.joboptions`) to a location on disk.

Import Click the Load button in the Adobe PDF Presets dialog and navigate to a `.joboptions` file. The preset will be available on the Presets drop-down list in the Export Adobe PDF dialog the next time it's used.

Print Presets

Setting all the necessary options for several final and proof print devices across a workgroup can be tedious but quite valuable for maintaining creative efficiency. (More on printing and print presets in Chapter 10, "Output.")

Export Choose File ➤ Print Presets ➤ Define; in the Print Presets dialog, click the New button. Define the options for a particular device, name the preset at the top of the dialog, and click OK. Back in the Print Presets dialog, click the Save button to save a shareable PRST file to disk.

Import Return to the Print Presets dialog and click the Load button to search for and load a PRST file. The preset will appear in the dialog and in the Print Preset drop-down menu in the Print dialog the next time you go to print.

Document Size Presets

Although not particularly complicated or arduous, defining the dimensions, margins, bleeds, slug, and other options of documents that differ from InDesign's defaults can become tedious. If you regularly—or even occasionally—create documents that *aren't* strictly using the default options, create a reusable preset to turn new document creation into a two-click operation. (More on about margins, bleeds, slugs, and other document setup options in Chapter 7, "Pages.")

Export In the Document Presets dialog (File ➢ Document Presets ➢ Define), create a new document setup preset. Save it to disk as a DCST file by clicking the Save button.

Import In the Document Presets dialog, click the Load button and navigate to the DCST file. The next time you create a new document by pressing Cmd+N/Ctrl+N or choosing File ➢ New ➢ Document, the preset will be in the drop-down list at the top of the dialog. Selecting it will populate all the settings in the rest of the dialog.

Transparency Flattener Presets

Choosing transparency flattening options is a critical part of ensuring quality printed output. Such options are directly related to the capabilities and characteristics of the output device, and everyone within your organization who sends similar work to the same device should use transparency flattener settings that begin with the identical options and then customize for the particular document. (Transparency flattening is discussed in depth in Chapter 10, "Output.")

Export Choose Edit ➢ Transparency Flattener Presets, create and name a new preset, and click the Save button to save a FLST file to disk.

Import Load the FLST file in the Transparency Flattener Presets dialog. Once loaded, the preset will appear in the Transparency Flattener Preview panel and the Print dialog on the Advanced pane.

InDesign Templates

InDesign INDT template files enable saving document size, margins, bleeds, slug, swatches, styles, and more all in one easily shared document. (More on template files in Chapter 7, "Pages.")

Export Choose File ➢ Save As. In the Save As dialog box, set the Save as Type field to InDesign CS3 Template, and click the Save button to save an INDT file to disk.

Import Choose File ➢ Open and open the INDT. InDesign will, by default, open a new document based on the template rather than the INDT itself. To open the INDT document itself for editing, change the Open dialog's Open As field selection to Original instead of Normal or Copy.

Workspaces

Sharing saved workspaces—panel arrangements and menu customizations—is not often done among coworkers. Typically one designer will create a workspace on her office machine and then carry the same workspace to her laptop and home computers so that the interface matches her work habits wherever she works. Some organizations, however, *do* standardize the InDesign user interface for its workstations to leverage productivity—any designer may sit down at any workstation and immediately work in a familiar environment. (More on workspaces and panel organization in Chapter 1, "Customizing.")

Export After setting panel arrangements and options and any menu customizations, save the workspace by choosing Window ➢ Workspace ➢ Save Workspace. In the Save Workspace dialog, check the appropriate choices to capture either or both panel locations or menu customization and name your new workspace. A workspace XML file will be saved to disk and the workspace will immediately appear on the Window ➢ Workspace menu.

Import Copy the workspace file from the source system to the destination system. You will find the workspace saved as an XML file in the following locations:

Mac: `Applications/Adobe InDesign CS3/Presets/Workspaces/`

Windows: `C:\Documents and Settings\[username]\Application Data\Adobe\InDesign\Version 5.0\Workspaces\`

Keyboard Shortcuts

Customizing keyboard shortcuts is among the most significant ways you can improve your productivity in InDesign CS3. Although only a few organizations standardize on a custom set of shortcuts, just as you would with workspaces, you'll definitely want to use the same shortcuts on all of your own workstations. (More on keyboard shortcuts in Chapter 1, "Customizing.")

Export Open the Keyboard Shortcuts dialog (Edit ➢ Keyboard Shortcuts) and click the New Set button, which will prompt you to name the set. Make your customizations and then click the Save button to update your set. Close the Keyboard Shortcuts dialog by clicking OK; InDesign will automatically write your set to disk as an INDK file.

Import Copy the INDK shortcut set from the source system at the below locations and drop it into the destination computer at the corresponding location.

Mac: `Applications/Adobe InDesign CS3/Presets/InDesign Shortcut Sets/`

Windows: `C:\Documents and Settings\[username]\Application Data\Adobe\InDesign\Version 5.0\InDesign Shortcut Sets\`

The Bottom Line

Collaborate with Other Designers   Teamwork and workgroup-based creativity is common among larger publications. Collaborating efficiently is crucial but rare—until now.

Master It   Working alone or together with colleagues, create or convert a preexisting, multipage document into a candidate for the Placed Page Collaboration Workflow. Assign content to coworkers, and have them design or alter the existing design of their portions of the publication and deliver their respective INDD documents back to you so that you may update and finalize the overall publication.

Collaborate with Writers and Editors   It's a control thing, man. Laying out the page is the domain of the designer; editing the copy is the realm ruled by editors. Neither group wants governorship of either material forced upon (or even really given to) the other group. Thankfully, with InCopy, Adobe's best-kept secret, there's no longer a need for either editorial or design to give up its control, freedom, or field of view.

> **Master It**   Open or create a layout containing at least two separate stories. Create assignments for two collaborators, assigning at least one story to each, and then generate and email an InCopy package for each assignment to its assignee.
>
> If your collaborators have InCopy CS3 on hand, have them edit the stories and return them to you as InDesign packages. Finally, update the content in the layout from those packages.

Share Reusable Settings   They say the definition of the word *insane* is doing something over and over while expecting different results. I agree with that definition, but I would like to propose my own addendum: doing the same thing over and over when there's no reason to do it more than once is also insane. In this thing we do, there is more than enough insanity thrust upon us by deadlines, clients, limited budgets, malfunctioning software, temperamental RIPs, and so many other sources; we must do what we can to salvage our own peace of mind and maintain productivity. Save a brain cell; share a setting.

> **Master It**   Examine your work, the typical documents you create and contribute to, the styles, swatches, and other reusable settings you use at least once a month. Save them all. Put them on a USB flash memory stick or email them home to yourself. Then, send them to your coworkers or lab partners, and ask for their reusable settings in return. Each of you should then load pieces you've exchanged into your respective versions of InDesign. It's time to collaborate efficiently

The Bottom Line

Each of The Bottom Line sections in the chapters suggest exercises to deepen skills and understanding. Sometimes there is only one possible solution, but often you are encouraged to use your skills and creativity to create something that builds on what you know and lets you explore one of many possible solutions.

Chapter 1: Customizing

Organize Panels and Use the New Panel Docks   New docks and other options make organizing panels in the workspace easier than ever before.

Master It   Beginning with the default workspace, open all the panels you expect to use in most projects and close those you won't. Now, using grouping, stacking, docking, or just free floating panels, arrange the panels to fit your work style and leave you as much room to work on documents as possible.

Solution   Which panels are visible and how they're arranged will vary with each learner. The important part of the exercise is that learners learn to arrange the panels and customize the workspace to maximize efficiency and the document working area.

Customize Keyboard Shortcuts   Adobe couldn't assign a keyboard shortcut to everything—there just aren't enough keys—so it did its best. Many of your favorite commands may not have shortcuts or may have shortcuts you dislike. You can add or change keyboard shortcuts for any command in InDesign.

Master It   Just for fun, create keyboard shortcuts for each of the object effects—Basic Feather, Bevel and Emboss, and so on.

Solution   Using the procedure described in "Keyboard Shortcuts" in this chapter, learners should use the Keyboard Shortcuts dialog to first create a new shortcut set and then to add shortcuts to the nine object effects in the Object Menu product area.

Remove Parts of InDesign to Create Lean, Workflow-Specific Installations   By customizing menus and disabling plug-ins, you can now easily remove features and functions of InDesign not required by your workflow. Doing so streamlines the interface, reduces errors, and ultimately increases productivity among workflows that do not require the entirety of InDesign.

Master It   To test your hand at removing features from InDesign, find all the features that are new or improved in CS3 and hide their menu commands. Then, color green the first 10 still enabled menu commands about which you'd like to learn more. Finally, disable the plug-ins that show panels you or your team aren't likely to need.

Solution   If learners need help finding which menu commands are new or improved in InDesign CS3, remind them that the Window ➢ Workspace menu contains the New and Improved in CS3 workspace, which, when active, will highlight such commands in blue. In the Edit ➢ Menus dialog then, all the menu commands and submenus that must be disabled will note *Blue* in the right column. The directive to color additional menu commands green is another hint about how to accomplish the first part of the exercise. In the last part, disabling plug-ins, the results will vary. However, the only plug-ins disabled under Help ➢ Configure Plug-ins should be nonrequired APLN files with *Panel* in the name.

Change the Default Font, Colors, and More   Out of the box, InDesign uses Times New Roman 12/14.4 pt as the default text style and includes swatches for process magenta, cyan, and yellow and RGB red, green, and blue. These defaults are fine if your average document uses 12/14.4 Times New Roman and only solid process or RGB colors. But, if the average document you create requires another typeface, size, or leading or other colors, or virtually any other option different from the defaults, change the defaults and save yourself some time.

Master It   Think about the documents you create most often. What is the type style—font family, font style, size, leading, and other formatting attributes—you use more than any other? Make those your new defaults. Do the same with your swatches, eliminating any colors you rarely use while adding those you use frequently.

Solution   All changes should be made with no documents opened. The end result will vary widely from learner to learner, but at least something should be different about the Character and Swatches panels from the out-of-the-box configuration.

Carry Your Personalized InDesign Work Environment in Your Pocket or on Your iPod   From freelancers brought into agency offices to assist with crunch time to students working in school labs, from round-the-clock production teams where different shifts use the same equipment to those dedicated enough to bring work home, seldom do creatives work solely on a single machine anymore. Creative and production personnel who switch computers waste a significant portion of their time customizing the InDesign environment of each computer on which they work even for a few minutes. To save time, nearly everything customizable about the InDesign CS3 working environment is portable. Customize one copy of InDesign, and carry your unique environment with you, making you instantly productive at any workstation.

Master It   After arranging your panels and customizing your keyboard shortcuts and menus, it's time to take your InDesign workspace with you. If you have a USB flash drive, an iPod, a PDA, or even just a floppy disk handy, copy the files containing your customized environment to the storage device. Now, if a second computer is available with InDesign CS3 installed, install those files to that computer and set up InDesign CS3 your way.

Solution   The first step learners should undertake is to save a workspace as discussed in the section "Workspaces" in this chapter. While customizing keyboards and menu commands, they would have already created new sets of each but may need to save those sets again to reflect later changes. Once everything has been saved, they should follow the instruction in the section "InDesign in Your Pocket" to back up on the one system, and restore and activate on the second, their own workspaces, menus, and shortcuts.

Chapter 2: Text

Create and fill text frames   Setting type is InDesign's primary function, and it performs that function better than any other application. The fundamental building block of type in InDesign is the text frame container and the text content.

Master It   Create a new text frame, and then place the flawed text file, bad-lorem.txt, into it. Clean up the resulting text to make it readable. When finished with that, place the document REVstory.doc into the same text frame after the first imported document.

Solution   As described in the how-to exercises under the "Getting Text into Text Frames" heading, students should import bad-lorem.txt and then the REVstory.doc document, making use of Show Import Options in both cases.

Format text frames   Correctly formatting and configuring text frames will save effort and time not only now, but also every time a frame or its content changes.

Master It   Using the text frame created above, convert it from a single column into three, with a 0.25-inch gutter. At the same time, give the text some breathing room by setting top and bottom insets of 0.1667 inches and no inset on the sides.

Solution   Using the Text Frame Options dialog, students should set the number of columns to three, change the gutter width, and uncheck Fixed Column Width. To effect the inset spacing, they will need to disable the Make All Settings the Same chain-link and individually set the top and bottom insets.

Format paragraphs   Paragraphs must be separated and styled to enable legibility and facilitate readability. That can be accomplished through alignment, indents, paragraph spacing, and drop caps.

Master It   Continuing with the multicolumn frame of placed stories, let's make them readable. In the first full paragraph of each story, add a drop cap of 2 to 3 lines. Separate the same paragraphs from anything that may come before with a comfortably large paragraph space before. Give the rest of the paragraphs a correct first line indent and, to control runts, a last line right indent. Because we've got three probably narrow columns, let's make clean, rag-less paragraphs.

Solution   The end result should have two drop caps, first and last line indentation on all paragraphs except those with drop caps, and vertical spacing on the two lead paragraphs (those containing the drop caps). All should be set to force justify (no ragged edge).

Compose paragraphs   Paragraph composition is essential to good typography. A poorly composed paragraph is one of those things that both trained and untrained eyes immediately notice—even if unconsciously—and that marks the document as the product of an amateur. From this book you should learn first that efficiency and economy of motion equate to more creative time, second that coffee is your friend, and third that practicing good paragraph composition is very, very important to the quality of your documents, your clients and employers, and the future marketability of you as represented by your portfolio.

Master It   Undoubtedly by this point we have three columns of unsavory composition. You may have widows and orphans, paragraphs may be split all over the place, hyphenation may be off or run amok, and word and letter spacing could be just horrendous. Even if it isn't that bad, you've got some areas in your document that need work.

First, duplicate the text frame and work on the copy, keeping the original above or beside it as a reference.

Begin the cleanup by asking InDesign to highlight problem areas and violations. Then, working through the highlighted text and keeping an eye out for problems InDesign didn't notice, employ the skills you learned about paragraph composition to eliminate all runts, widows, and orphans; then optically align hanging punctuation and tweak hyphenation and word and letter spacing.

Solution   Results will vary due largely to the discrepancy between frame sizes and type styling employed by the learners. Comparing the original and (hopefully) properly composed frames, the latter should display marked improvement in composition.

Chapter 3: Characters

Format Characters   Formatting characters is more than just choosing a size and font.

Master It   Build a single-page magazine article, using FPO copy if needed, and include typical features of an article: headline, kicker, byline, subheads, body copy, and writer bio block.

Solution   Results will vary, but each item has its own degree of importance in the article, and it should be styled to reflect its order of importance relative to other text. Headlines should be large type, often sans-serif or thicker in stroke than other bits of text and usually tightened by reducing tracking, kerning, or both. Subheads should be similarly styled. Writer bio blocks and kickers are often italicized, and bylines should be offset by some other styling means—color, weight, alignment, position, baseline shift, or another aesthetic choice.

Transform Characters   InDesign includes much more control over character attributes than the basic styling options on the face of the Character panel, but they're scattered about.

Master It   Creating a highlight (including reversed) effect on type is common enough that designers have cobbled two means of doing it. The first and more common method, within InDesign, is to place a colored rectangle behind text as a separate object. While it gets the job done, it creates yet another object that must be moved and resized to reflect changes to copy, text style, and reflow—and arduously at that because the text frame sits in front of the colored box, making the latter difficult to select. Less common and infinitely more risky is the Acrobat highlighting method. Within Acrobat is a commenting tool called the Highlighter. Choose the tool and highlight color (from common colors such as yellow, pink, and blue), and drag-select type. The highlight appears on screen and looks great. Unfortunately, it doesn't print unless the user deliberately changes a setting in the Acrobat Print dialog, the existence of which most Acrobat users are totally unaware.

Using the same article, and using the skills learned in this chapter, highlight or reverse a few words in the correct, printable, and flexible way. Then, insert at least two URLs in the article and style them appropriately but distinctly from each other.

Solution   The user should employ a custom underline with a weight at least equal to the size of the type and a negative offset that forces the underline to completely underlap the highlighted text. Colors and tints will likely vary but should always contrast with the highlighted text to afford legibility. The underline stroke type should be Solid. URL styles should employ techniques taught in the sidebar "Underline Styles for Hyperlinks."

Insert Special Characters   Not everything can be typed without phalangeal acrobatics worthy of an Olympic gold medal.

Master It   Continuing your work with the mockup article, find at least three places where trademark and registered trademark symbols belong (use your imagination if you're using gibberish FPO copy). Declare your work with a properly formatted copyright notice beneath the article. Find a few proper name phrases that shouldn't break across lines, and ensure that they don't. And, finally, insert em and en dashes where they belong, with slight padding around the em dashes.

Solution   Most symbols and punctuation should be inserted from the Insert Special Characters menu and nonbreaking spaces and the padding around em dashes (hair spaces) from the Insert White Space menu.

Work with OpenType Font Features   OpenType fonts fix most of the woes of digital typography—and open entire worlds of typographic freedom and control.

Master It   Create pullquotes in separate frames, complete with quotation marks, unique styling, and—because pullquotes garner much more attention than body copy and draw the reader into a story—pull out all the stops by using OpenType features to style them perfectly.

Solution   Results will vary wildly here, but all should have correct, so-called typographer's quotes as well as at least one or two OpenType style features such as swashes, contextual alternates, discretionary ligatures, titling alternates, and genuine small caps.

Use the Glyphs Panel   Every glyph in every font can be accessed by this one, elegant panel and then inserted into the text.

Master It   Concluding the work on the mockup article, cap the story with a custom endmark chosen from a symbol font and inserted into the last line of the article (ahead of the writer bio block). Once done, build a new custom glyph set to make reuse of the endmark easy for the next issue. Send the glyph set to a co-worker or friend so she may try inserting the same endmark.

Solution   Any symbol glyph will do, but it must be chosen and inserted from the Glyphs panel.

A new glyph set containing a single glyph should be created and made ready for sharing. In a classroom or other multi-student environment, have the students title their custom glyph sets with their own names, pair up, and then exchange their sets with partners for installation and trial.

Chapter 4: Drawing

Draw Precise Paths with the Pen Tool   Precision drawing, the ability to create any shape, requires mastery of the Pen tool.

Master It   Re-open `pathtrace01.indd` from the files that you downloaded from the Web. Instead of tracing it with merely straight path segments, use what you've learned about corner anchor points and smooth anchor points to trace it faithfully—straight where needed, curved where needed. Set the fill for your traced letters to contrast with the original orange ones, and when you've finished tracing, zoom in to examine how closely you were able to come to the original shapes.

Solution Each letter should be traced over, with straight path segments where appropriate. Nonstraight areas should also match the originals' curvature and be broken with anchor points where needed to affect the curves. When the "Trace This" source layer is unlocked and the anchor points in a given letterform counted, the count should match those in the student's resulting tracing.

Freehand Draw Paths with the Pencil Tool The Pen tool is synonymous with precision, and the Pencil tool with freedom. Sometimes, quickly drawing something with a natural feel is more important than precision.

Master It Open a new document and, using the Pencil tool, draw your own cartoonish self-portrait. Get it all sketched out before worrying about the paths themselves. Once it's done, go back with the Smooth tool and, if needed, the Erase tool to clean it up.

Solution Results will vary depending upon learners' freehand drawing skills and their dexterity with the input device (mouse, trackball, or tablet and stylus). The end result should be several overlapping open and closed paths smooth where appropriate, sharp where not.

Combine and Subtract Shapes, and Convert from One Shape to Another Many complex paths begin with simple geometric shapes. Indeed, most objects you create in InDesign will *be* simple geometric shapes, alone or compounded with other shapes.

Master It

1. Draw three shapes—a circle, triangle, and a square—each exactly 2 inches in diameter.

2. Convert the triangle and square to circles.

3. Manually position the circles into a rough triangular formation. Each circle should overlap its neighbors, with all three overlapping in the center. Select all three.

4. Exclude the overlaps.

5. Release the compound path, and fill each resulting shape with color individually.

Solution Except for color differences, the result should look like this:

Modify Any Vector Artwork Precision drawing mastery requires precision path editing.

Master It Beginning with a pentagon, employ the Convert Direction Point tool and Direct Selection tool to convert the straight segment shape into a five-pointed star with concave sides like this:

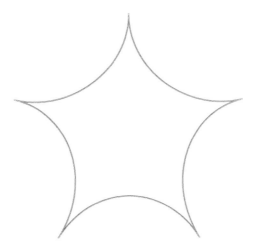

Solution The result should look like the figure and still contain only five points.

Turn Type into a Container to Hold Images or Text Strictly speaking, the technique of converting readable type into frames should be used infrequently. When used on symbol font glyphs, though, it's a great way to make short work of creating complicated shapes for use as frames or merely decorative elements.

Master It Using a font installed on your computer—preferably a symbol font—locate a suitable glyph using the Glyphs panel. Set and style it on the page and convert it to frame. Fill the frame with text—your own or InDesign's placeholder text.

Solution Results will vary with learners' choice of glyph, applied style, and the text and style of text used to fill it. If a suitable symbol font is not available, a letter may be used.

Chapter 5: Images

Place Image Assets Focusing on efficiency with this version of InDesign, Adobe seeded numerous tiny improvements in the task of placing image assets and three big overhauls—increased support for Photoshop PSD layers, frame-fitting options, and simultaneous multiple asset import.

Master It Create a frame-first layout containing 6 to 10 image frames. Preset the blank frame fitting options to Fit Content Proportionately, and then, using any folder of images available, import and place, in one operation, all the images needed to fill the frames.

Solution After creating the frames, learners should access the Frame Fitting Options and set fitting as indicated. Once the frames are ready, multiple images should be selected in the Place dialog, resulting in a loaded cursor with all images on deck. Image assets should be placed in waiting frames one after the other by clicking once in each frame in rapid succession.

Import Images without Place   Drag and drop enables visual selection and import of image assets while copy and paste, under the right conditions, offers a more natural way of moving assets from one place to another in the same document or between InDesign and other applications.

Master It   Create another empty frame layout similar to the previous one, and then, using Adobe Bridge and ensuring that both Bridge and the InDesign layout are visible onscreen, visually choose and place image assets from within Bridge to fill the empty frames.

Solution   Learners should launch Bridge from within InDesign and, following the directions in the section "Drag and Drop" earlier in this chapter, drag image assets from the Bridge window and drop them atop the empty frames in succession.

Manage Placed Assets   Getting image assets into the layout is only half the job; you must also know how to manage—and even replace—assets once they're on the page.

Master It   Use one of the two documents created in the preceding Master It exercises, and, without using File ➤ Place, drag and drop, or even copy and paste, replace three of the images (in the same frames) with other assets. If you have Photoshop and/or Illustrator installed, choose another image already placed on the page and edit the image itself in Photoshop or Illustrator *without* opening the application from the Dock or Start menu.

Solution   This exercise revolves around the Links panel, discussed in the section "Links Panel." In the first part of the exercise, learners should select an asset on the page (which will also highlight its entry on the Links panel) and use the Relink command or button to select a replacement asset. If they have access to Photoshop or Illustrator—for raster or vector assets, respectively—learners should select one asset and use the Links panel's Edit Original command or button to launch the image editor with the asset loaded. Once inside Photoshop or Illustrator, they should make some change to the image data, save and close the document in the image editor, and then exit that application. InDesign will automatically update the linked asset on its page.

Chapter 6: Objects

Use Attribute-Level Transparency and Object Effects   InDesign CS3's new attribute-level transparency and transparency-based object effects allow more to be done inside InDesign with live object effects than ever before.

Master It   Place an image onto the page. Above that image, create a text frame and fill it with placeholder type. Fill and stroke the frame. Using the new attribute-level transparency and effects…

◆ Give the frame an inner glow and blend it back with the photo such that the frame tints the photo.

◆ Make the type gradually disappear into its background as it moves from the top down.

◆ Give the stroke a drop shadow and blending mode that alters the background image just in the area of the stroke.

Solution Results will vary widely with the images, colors, and blending modes chosen, but learners should all do each of the following:

♦ Select in the Effects dialog Settings for Fill, add an inner glow, and either alter overall transparency of the fill or change its blending mode.

♦ Select in the Effects dialog Settings for Text and apply the default gradient feather with either a –90° angle or 90° and reversed.

♦ Select in the Effects dialog Settings for Stroke, change its blending mode, and apply a drop shadow.

Design Custom Stroke Styles Although the stroke styles that come with InDesign are perfect for many occasions, they fall short of perfect in others. That's why InDesign lets you create your own.

Master It Create a new Dash type stroke style that looks like the graphic below—dot-dot-dash-dot-dot—which is Morse code for *ID*, InDesign's identifier among the Creative Suite 3 icons.

Solution Learners should create a new stroke style that looks like the one depicted below. Some variance in pattern length and individual dash length and spacing is to be expected.

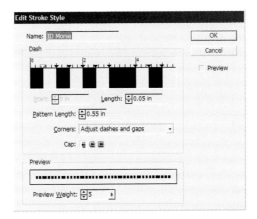

Mixed Ink Swatches and Sharing Swatches Between creating mixed inks swatches and mixed ink swatch groups and sharing swatches across applications and documents, InDesign CS3 makes color fidelity and productivity easy.

Master It Pick a new spot color and create shades of that spot by mixing black into a mixed ink group. Generate 10% tint swatches in the group. Save the document and exchange it with a partner. Both you and the partner should then add the mixed ink group swatches you both created into InDesign's default Swatches panel. If you're working alone, you can still do this portion of the exercise with the single document you created.

Solution   Following the instructions in the section "Mixed Inks" in this chapter, learners should first create a spot color swatch and then generate a mixed ink group with nine swatches, beginning with 10% black mixed with 100% spot color and progressing upward to 100% black. After saving and closing the document containing the mixed ink group, ensuring that no other document is opened in InDesign, learners should use the Load Swatches command on the Swatches panel to import swatches from that document into the panel to become part of InDesign's new default swatch list.

Work with Anchored Objects   Anchored objects replace the old-style inline graphics that had limited options. They also completely eliminate the need to manually reposition text-supported figures, illustrations, charts, pullquotes, tip boxes, sidebars, and other objects when document text reflows.

Master It   Beginning with several pages of text linked into a single story (again, use this chapter's sample file if you like), insert at least one above line graphic and at least two objects (images, nonthreaded text frames, natively drawn objects, or a group of objects) as anchored objects that float outside the text. Make the above line image appear on a line by itself, with at least 0.25 inches of vertical padding above it, and make the floating objects align to the outside margin of whichever page they fall on. Check your work by inserting text above the marker points to push the marker points and anchored images to subsequent pages.

Solution   The details of anchored object positions and alignments in this exercise are left up to the learner, as is the size and type of object anchored, though the Anchored Object Options dialogs for the above line and floating objects should look *similar* to the below graphics (inline on this page, floating on the next page).

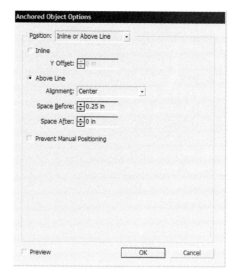

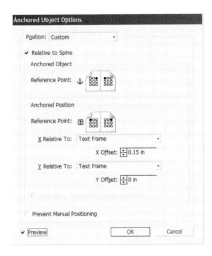

Set Type on a Path   Type on a Path allows text to go anywhere paths can go, in any shape a path may take, which is anywhere, any shape.

Master It   Let's combine a few of the things we've learned in this chapter to create a cool type on a path creative technique. Begin by drawing a broad arc open path. Add type to the path—whatever you'd like to say, perhaps a line from a favorite poem—and give it faux depth. Make the stroke disappear such that the text floats free. Then, using object effects, make the text gradually fade out from opaque at one end of the arc to completely transparent at the other end.

Solution   Using the Pen tool, learners should draw an arc of preferably two anchor points. After clicking on it with the Type on a Path tool and typing their line of text, they should remove the path stroke color on the Swatches panel. In the Effects dialog, they should choose Settings for Text and apply a gradient feather rotated to achieve the desired effect.

Chapter 7: Pages

Create Pages with Bleed, Slug, and Live Areas   Properly setting up a for-press document involves more than choosing paper stock and ink colors. To ease the burden of setting up pages, InDesign includes ways to automate creation of similar documents after the first.

Master It   Examine this book's cover. Don't redesign it, but set up a new, blank InDesign document as if you were designing the cover for this or another Mastering series book. Include the appropriate features—bleed, slug, and live areas—and create reusable cover presets and a template.

Solution   If possible, provide measuring rulers to learners. If not, expect variance in the document dimensions. Dimensions aside, all documents should have a 0.125-inch bleed area all around, a 0.125-inch live area constructed from manually positioned and colored ruler guides within the trim, and at least some type of slug area, which will likely vary per document. Once the document is created, learners should save it as an InDesign INDT template file and create a Document Preset based on it.

Manage Pages in and between InDesign Documents   Any multipage document requires familiarity with the Pages panel and related features. Working *well* with multipage documents requires practiced proficiency.

Master It   Create two new InDesign documents of one page each. Now, using the skills learned in "Managing Pages," insert four additional pages in each document for a total of five pages each. In very large type (at least 200 pts), label each page with a text frame containing the page number. In the first document, preface page numbers with the Roman numeral I and the second with II such that pages are numbered I1, I2, I3, I4, I5 and II1, II2, II3, II4, II5. Save both documents. Copy all five pages from the II document into the I, and then arrange pages in order such that page II1 follow I1, II2 follows II2, and so on.

Solution   Because there are various methods for inserting pages—the Create New Page button on the Pages panel, the Insert Pages command, duplicating pages, and dragging and dropping master pages into the pages list—how learners accomplish this part of the exercise will vary. Once both documents are created, the merge should be accomplished by using the Move Pages command in the II document to add its pages to the I document (without deleting them in the original). Following the merge, learners will either manually drag page icons in the Pages panel or use the Move Pages command to rearrange pages into the correct order.

Master Master Pages   Master pages are the key to efficient initial layout and especially document revisions. Mastering their use is essential for design that uses common elements across multiple document pages.

Master It   Refer back to the hands-on instruction in the section on nested master pages. Follow the instruction in that section to build all the master pages required for the proposal project. Check your results against mine. Once you have the master pages built correctly, use the other skills learned in this chapter to add document pages (a few for each proposal section or chapter) and to assign to them the appropriate master pages.

Solution   All the steps required to perform this exercise are detailed in the section "Nested Master Pages." Learners should follow the step-by-step instructions to produce nested master pages conforming to the master page plan in Figure 7.27 and then produce several pages for each with the appropriate master pages assigned.

Chapter 8: Stories

Thread and Unthread Text Frames and Flow Text   Threaded text frames are the foundation of multipage documents, and, whether manual, auto, or semi-auto, flowing text is the way to pour that foundation.

Master It   Create a new document with a two-column master page text frame and employ the skills learned in this chapter to lay out a multipage Word or other text document. There should be no overset text when you've finished.

Solution   Learners will create a new document with two columns and the Master Text Frame option checked in the New Document dialog. They must then override the master text frame on the first page of the document, and pursue the technique described in "Autoflow in Master Page Frames" to lay out a multipage textual document in threaded frames.

Create Bulleted and Numbered Lists   InDesign CS3 offers more creative and structural control in updated bullets and numbering features and the new Lists property.

Master It   In a new document, use Lists and Bullets and Numbering to re-create the headings from this chapter's section "Threading and Unthreading Text Frames" as a hierarchical list.

Solution   Learners should create three levels of lists in the Lists dialog, and then in Bullets and Numbering, set options to create the following hierarchical list, although the numbering systems may vary.

1. Threading and Unthreading Text Frames
    A. QuarkXPress vs. InDesign
    B. Threading Frames
        i. Threading Pre-Created Frames
        ii. Threading without Pre-Created Frames
        iii. Threading Upon Import
        iv. Threading without Text
    C. Threading Tips
    D. Viewing Threads
    E. Managing Threads
        i. Unthread Text Frames
        ii. Removing Frames from a Thread
        iii. Adding Frames into a Thread
        iv. Duplicating Frames in a Thread
    F. Autoflowing Text
    G. Autoflow in Master Page Frames
        i. Autoflowing Immediately
        ii. Use the Master Text Frame
    H. Jumplines

Write and Word Process in InDesign   The world is changing, and writing and editing in the layout application is no longer such a crazy idea.

Master It   In Story Editor, write a paragraph or two discussing how something you've learned in this chapter will benefit your work. Include at least one footnote, and set its options for a pleasing appearance on the page.

Solution   After creating a new text frame, learners should open Story Editor with the menu command or keyboard shortcut and write the essay. They should also insert and, through the Type ➤ Document Footnote Options, style the footnote.

Fixing, Finding, and Changing Text and More   In addition to beefing up its already solid text support systems of spell checking, hyphenation, and Autocorrect, InDesign CS3 completely revamps Find/Change with incredible new capabilities.

Master It   Using the two-column, multipage document created just a few moments ago, use the new Find/Change features to convert the text frame to three-columns with a 0.25-inch column gutter. At the same time, give the text frames a semitransparent background color (while keeping the text fully opaque) and a frame inset.

Solution   Learners should use the Object tab in Find/Change, searching for all text frames, and setting the described graphical attributes in the Change Object Format Options dialog.

Chapter 9: Documents

Interact with Documents Visually, Change Zoom Level, View Modes, and Display Perfor-mance   InDesign provides numerous means of changing the way you interact with documents, how fast they move, how you see them, and what you see.

Master It   Open any InDesign document containing text and images on the same page. Open three different views of the same document, arranged simultaneously onscreen, zooming all to fit the page within the document window, and compare the views according to the following options:

- View 1: Preview mode with High-Quality Display display performance.

- View 2: Layout mode with Fast Display display performance.

- View 3: Bleed mode with Typical Display display performance.

Solution   Learners should open a document and then, using the Window ➢ Arrange ➢ New Window command, create two other views on the same document. They should then manually arrange the trio comfortably onscreen, and by changing the View ➢ Display Per-formance setting and the different modes at the bottom of the Tools panel, establish the comparison described above.

Build and Manage Grids and Guides   The foundation of any well-laid-out document is a well-thought-out grid.

Master It   Create a new document and build a grid on the master page consisting of six equal columns and three equal rows within the page margins. Once that's done, apportion the top row into three equal sections.

Solution   Learners should use the Layout ➢ Create Guides utility to create the initial grid with six and three, no gutters, and Fit Guides to Margins. Next, to divide the top row, they will have to manually drag down two horizontal ruler guides. After unlocking guides, they will precisely position the new manually created guides with the Transform or Control panel's Y field.

Create and Manage Book Files   Often one person finds it easier to work on longer documents by breaking them up into chapters or sections and connecting them via a Book file. For work-groups wherein different people are responsible for different sections of the document, a Book file is essential to productivity.

Master It   Working alone or in a group, create at least three InDesign documents of several pages of text each. Save each document, and then create a Book file to connect the documents. Finally, create a single PDF from the entire book.

Solution   Learners should preferably team up to create InDesign documents and then designate one individual to create the Book file. Once the book is set, the Export Book to PDF command should be chosen from the Book panel flyout menu.

Index Terms and Create an Index   An index helps readers find content. From simple keyword lists to complex, multilevel, topic-driven indices, InDesign handles them all, marrying index entries to referenced text through index markers.

Master It   Open or create an InDesign document containing a story of at least three pages in length. Working through the document, create index entries and cross-references for at least 10 words, one of which should be a word that repeats numerous times throughout the story (use a common word such as *the* if needed). Once the terms are indexed, generate and place the index story on a new page.

Solution   Learners may take several routes to accomplishing the indexing depending on the story and words chosen, although their methods should conform to those described in the sections "Creating Index Entries," "Cross-References," and "Power Indexing" under "Indexing" in this chapter. With all the options available to them in the Generate Index dialog, the final output will likely vary as well from learner to learner.

Create Tables of Contents   Tables of contents direct readers in logical or virtually any order to content, and InDesign's TOC options are varied and powerful for myriad uses.

Master It   Open or quickly create a rudimentary book-style document containing body text and several heading paragraphs utilizing at least two levels of headings. Create and assign paragraph styles for the body text and headings. Using what you've learned in this chapter, generate and place a hierarchal TOC.

Solution   Before beginning with the Layout ➢ Table of Contents command and the corresponding dialog, learners should create a document that has text and styles in the format of Heading 1, Heading 2, and Body Text, with several paragraphs of each style. Then, in the Table of Contents dialog, the Heading 1 and Heading 2 styles should be moved into the Include Paragraph Styles list, assigned Levels 1 and 2 respectively, and then the TOC placed into the document. The other options available for formatting the TOC will vary by learner.

Chapter 10: Output

Configure Color Management on Documents and Images   Consistent color throughout the workflow is critical—even in grayscale jobs. With each version of Creative Suite, Adobe makes color management smarter, easier, and more consistent across the Creative Suite applications. However, the nature of color management is such that it only works if you configure it for the devices specific to your workflow.

Master It   Configure Adobe Bridge to use the ICC profiles for your monitor and printer (or other output device) across all of Creative Suite. You can profile your devices yourself using Mac's ColorSync or Windows's Image Color Management. If you're configuring a high-end output device such as an imagesetter or proofprinter, ask your print service provider for the most up-to-date ICC profile for the device. If you choose to configure color management for your desktop printer, either profile it yourself or visit the manufacturer's website; most OEMs included free, downloadable ICC profiles. These aren't specific to your printer's unique color rendering characteristics, but it will get you close.

Solution   Learners should profile their monitors using the basic above method described immediately above and obtain an ICC profile for an output device. Both should be installed through Adobe Bridge's Creative Suite Color Settings or even InDesign's individual Color Settings dialog.

Softproof Documents to Screen   When software makers say, *What You See Is What You Get (WYSIWYG)*, it's really not, not in the case of color, not from the typical working mode of applications. That's where soft proofing comes in. Its pixel-based preview still isn't a precise representation of what you can expect with ink on paper, but when configured correctly, InDesign gets it surprisingly close.

Master It   Using one of your own documents or a sample from another chapter on this book's download page, proof the approximate expected output colors on with your printer's ICC profile. Next, examine how the document will separate when sent to press and how transparency will flatten. Look for potential printing issues, and resolve them.

Solution   Using the Customize Proof Conditions dialog and the Proof Colors command, learners will first observe their document colors shift into the chosen output device's gamut. Next, employing the Separations Preview and Flattener Preview panel, they'll look for problem areas.

Preflight, Package, and Output to Print with Managed Inks and Trapping   Printing is about much more than just clicking the Print button. It requires planning and careful preparation. During design and certainly before output, a number of designs critical to your artwork's printed quality must be made. Then, when it is time to send away the job, you have options about how to do that.

Master It   While soft proofing the document, you may have noticed problems with inks, areas of overlapping color that might cause misregistration, and potential ink mixing problems. Using the Ink Manager, overprint attributes, and trapping, resolve these problems and reproof the results. When you're confident the document is ready for output, preflight it, print a hard copy proof on an available printer, and then package the document for delivery to a print service provider.

Solution   Results in the first part of this exercise will vary with the learners' documents. Look for improper traps, missing overprints, ink mixing issues, and extra or incorrectly defined spot inks. In the second half of the exercise, learners will need to preflight the document, looking for broken image links, other typical image and font problems, and any other issue that may affect printability. Following the preflight, learners will configure the Print dialog with the options specific to the output device—including the correct ICC profile on the Color Management pane of the Print dialog—and then print a hard copy proof of at least a page or two. Assuming the proof is of suitable quality, they will finally use the Package command to prepare a portable version of the InDesign document, its linked assets, and fonts.

Chapter 11: Efficiency

Work Efficiently with Text   Text comprises the most space in the average InDesign document. Unfortunately, editing and *re*styling text occupies the majority of a creative's time in the document. Used wisely, paragraph and character styles, nested styles, text variables, and data merge eliminate repetitive actions and hours of work.

Master It   Use Excel, a database, or Notepad/TextEdit to create a new flat-file database of information. The data may be anything you like—a mailing list, product listings for a catalog, directory listings, etc.—but should include at least three fields and three rows. Save the file as either comma or tab delimited; this will be your data source file.

Beginning with a blank InDesign document, build a variable data target document to hold the records from the data source file. Include static information as well as field placeholders. Format all text—static and placeholders—and create paragraph and character styles to make the initial and follow-up formatting easier. If you have appropriate places to employ nested styling, do so.

When the target document is ready, effect a data merge to generate a press-ready variable data project.

Solution   Owing to the multiple steps and complexity of this exercise, a great deal of variance in learners' results is to be expected. Upon completion, the learner should have a merge document with all data correctly imported. Additionally, all text in the document should be assigned to paragraph and/or character styles.

Work Efficiently with Tables   Barring additional investments in third-party plug-ins, each table created in prior versions of InDesign had to be individually and manually formatted. The more creative the formatting, the more arduous the task of styling multiple subsequent tables to match. New table and cell styles make it a one-click operation to format tabular data and to instantly update all tables to match future formatting changes.

Master It   Begin with a table of data. If you have tables in preexisting InDesign documents, use those (save the document under a different name, just in case). If you don't have such documents already, create a new layout and add at least two tables; the sports or financial sections of today's newspaper are excellent places to find tabular data you can use for FPO. Style one table with alternating fills, custom strokes of your choosing, and with appropriate text formatting using paragraph styles. When the first table is styled to your liking, build table and cell styles, and then use them to format the second table.

Solution   Results will vary, but learners should end up with two (or more) identically formatted tables. Additionally, all text within the tables should be assigned to paragraph styles and cell styles.

Work Efficiently with Objects   Working efficiently doesn't end with text and tables. Graphics, paths, and containers are part of any InDesign document, and creating and editing them productively is also important to the efficient InDesign-based workflow.

Master It   Using either your own or a client's various media logos (RGB, CMYK, grayscale; with and without taglines; iconic and full logos; and so on), build a shareable, reusable logo library. Now create a second library of text frames and other objects you use at least occasionally. Make sure to give each an object style before adding them to the library so that other objects can quickly be styled to match and so that formatting changes don't take too much time. Don't forget to label objects in both libraries for rapid identification and filtering by you or your coworkers.

Solution   When finished, learners should have two INDL libraries. Every object in each library should be labeled. The majority of objects in the second library should have object styles assigned to them.

Chapter 12: Collaboration

Collaborate with Other Designers   Teamwork and workgroup-based creativity is common among larger publications. Collaborating efficiently is crucial but rare—until now.

Master It   Working alone or together with colleagues, create or convert a preexisting, multipage document into a candidate for the Placed Page Collaboration Workflow. Assign content to coworkers, and have them design or alter the existing design of their portions of the publication and deliver their respective INDD documents back to you so that you may update and finalize the overall publication.

Solution   Learners should apportion a multipage document such that one or more separate pages are assigned to each member of the learner's workgroup. Content on those pages should be removed to separate InDesign documents and then placed back into the original locations as placed and linked INDD documents. The other members of the workgroup should edit their assignments and return the art to the team leader working with the core document. The leader will then update linked assets to bring the document current. Watch out for pages with duplicated content, which indicates that the learner forgot to delete the original objects from the core document subsequent to generating the assigned component documents.

Collaborate with Writers and Editors   It's a control thing, man. Laying out the page is the domain of the designer; editing the copy is the realm ruled by editors. Neither group wants governorship of either material forced upon (or even really given to) the other group. Thankfully, with InCopy, Adobe's best-kept secret, there's no longer a need for either editorial or design to give up its control, freedom, or field of view.

Master It   Open or create a layout containing at least two separate stories. Create assignments for two collaborators, assigning at least one story to each, and then generate and email an InCopy package for each assignment to its assignee.

If your collaborators have InCopy CS3 on hand, have them edit the stories and return them to you as InDesign packages. Finally, update the content in the layout from those packages.

Solution   If learners do not have access to InCopy or coworkers with InCopy, forgo the second part of the exercise. In the first part, the result should be an Assignments panel that lists two assignments with at least one content item each. Both assignments should display the purple gift box icon denoting that they've successfully been packaged. Also check File ➤ User to ensure that the learner correctly identified himself to InDesign, per the instructions in this chapter.

Share Reusable Settings   They say the definition of the word *insane* is doing something over and over while expecting different results. I agree with that definition, but I would like to propose my own addendum: doing the same thing over and over when there's no reason to do it more than once is also insane. In this thing we do, there is more than enough insanity thrust upon us by deadlines, clients, limited budgets, malfunctioning software, temperamental RIPs, and so many other sources; we must do what we can to salvage our own peace of mind and maintain productivity. Save a brain cell; share a setting.

Master It   Examine your work, the typical documents you create and contribute to, the styles, swatches, and other reusable settings you use at least once a month. Save them all. Put them on a USB flash memory stick or email them home to yourself. Then, send them to your coworkers or lab partners, and ask for their reusable settings in return. Each of you should then load pieces you've exchanged into your respective versions of InDesign. It's time to collaborate efficiently.

Solution   Given that each learner will likely opt to save and share different types of reusable settings, there is no check against their progress other than that *something* was transferred between the InDesign users and successfully loaded into their copies of InDesign.

Glossary

A

alpha channel
An alpha channel is a special color channel within pixel-based images containing transparency. Opacity is measured in 256 levels and generally represented in the onscreen alpha channel as 256 levels of gray. Although applications such as InDesign will read, interpret, and display the transparency of an alpha channel, there is no way to specifically view or directly manipulate the alpha channel without an interface such as Photoshop's Channels panel. Image formats that support alpha channel transparency include Photoshop documents (PSD, PSB), PDFs, and PNGs.

alpha transparency
See *alpha channel*.

anchor point
Vector drawings are made up of paths—more specifically, coordinates on a two-dimensional grid. An anchor point is the path-defining point plotted on the grid. It contains an x-axis horizontal location coordinate and a vertical coordinate on the y-axis; it may also contain angle and curvature data, which control the angle and curve of path segments emanating from either side of the anchor point. When a second anchor point is plotted on the grid, a path segment may be drawn between the two points to create a path. Repositioning the anchor point alters the shape, angle, and length of the path, and manipulating the anchor points' curve handles changes the curvature or angle of attached path segments.

anchored object
An anchored object is any object—graphic frame, text frame, or other object—that is tethered to a specific point in another frame or story. The anchored object is actually tied to a special, invisible marker placed inside the other frame or story, and the anchored object will follow the marker to maintain a specific relative distance. If page recomposition causes an anchored object's marker to flow from page 2 to page 6, for instance, the anchored object itself will also jump from page 2 to page 6 automatically. Inline images, those pasted into text, are also anchored objects. The relative position, alignment, and numerous other options regarding the placement of anchored objects relative to their markers, columns of text, the page, and document spine are available in the Anchored Object Options dialog.

ascender
The portion of a glyph that extends above the x-height (the height of a typeface's lowercase *x*). Glyphs with ascenders include *f, h, l,* and *t*.

ASCII
(Acronym for American Standard Code for Information Interchange) This is the computer language that represents human-readable text. The English-based ASCII contains 95 characters, including the Latin alphabet and standard punctuation. TXT files are ASCII-encoded and thus are often referred to as ASCII files. More robust text-based file formats such as RTF and DOC are based on, but extend beyond, ASCII.

assignments
Within InDesign and its sister application InCopy, an assignment is a collection of one or more text or graphic frames separated from an InDesign publication and made available for work by an InCopy user or another InDesign user. Only one user may have any one InDesign INDD document opened for editing at a time. When assignments are used to apportion the document into linked and semi-autonomous sections of content, however, that single document may be edited by several people concurrently. A bidirectional check-in/check-out system further assists by maintaining version control and preventing double-modification of assigned content.

B

baseline
The invisible line on which type stands. Glyphs such as *j*, *g*, and *y* have lower portions—called descenders—that descend below the baseline.

Bézier
In vector drawing, paths are created by placing *anchor points* on a virtual grid and then connecting those anchor points with *path segments*. In the Bézier drawing system of vector illustration, path segment angle and curvature are controlled by the anchor points rather than by the path segments. Bézier curves are parametric, meaning that the curvature in one end of a path segment affects and interacts with the curvature in the other end.

The vector drawing tools in all of Adobe's applications—InDesign, Illustrator, Photoshop, and others—use Bézier curves.

blow out
When a device such as a printer or camera cannot render low percentages of color (in subtractive color models) or high percentages (in additive color models) and the result is a jump to 0% color, or pure white, the color is said to "blow out." For example, many offset presses cannot render less than 4% of a given ink, thus an area painted in 3% of a color will blow out and become no color at all. *Plugged* is the opposite of blow out; when very dark the values become 100% color, or black.

C

calibrate
To calibrate a device is to bring its color rendering or capturing ability as close as possible into alignment with the actual colors presented to the device.

cap height
The height of a given typeface's capital letter X.

CJK
Shorthand for Chinese, Japanese, and Korean; most often used to describe a group of fonts containing glyphs for one or all three languages.

clipping path
A vector path embedded into, or attached to, an image or object that causes parts of the object to appear transparent. Unlike alpha transparency, clipping-path transparency does not offer levels of opacity; areas of color are either completely transparent (clipped) or fully opaque. Clipping paths may be added to images in Photoshop or Illustrator and are understood by InDesign and other page-layout applications. If an image does not contain a clipping path, one may be created inside InDesign to mask out (render transparent) parts of the image.

CMS
(Abbreviation for Color Management System; also for Content Management System and for the *Chicago Manual of Style*, which factored heavily into the editing of this book) A color management system connects calibrated color capture or render devices and their respective profiles, translating color data from one device to the next in an attempt to ensure consistently accurate portrayal of colors at each step.

CMYK
(Abbreviation for Cyan Magenta Yellow blacK) CMYK is a subtractive color model wherein the more color added, the further the mix moves from white. CMYK, or process ink, is the standard for printing in North America and most of the world. Although CMYK has an extremely limited color *gamut*, it may be augmented through the use of spot color inks.

color profile
When a color rendering or capture device such as a computer monitor or scanner is profiled, its unique color interpretation characteristics are examined and recorded into a color profile and saved as an ICC or ICM file to be read by a color management system that translates and maintains consistent color between several devices' color profiles.

compound path
Two or more vector paths behaving as one.

compound shape
Two or more complete shapes (closed paths) behaving as one shape.

contextual orphan

An orphan is the first line of a paragraph left behind at the bottom of a column or page while the rest of the paragraph flows to the next column or page. A *contextual* orphan is what the author calls a short or single-line paragraph that, in context, should remain in the same column and on the same page as the paragraph it precedes but is instead left behind at the bottom of the previous column or page. For example, a single-line heading is its own paragraph but should always appear in the same column and page as the first paragraph it describes. (See also *orphan*.)

contextual widow

Similar to a contextual orphan, a contextual widow is a term coined by the author to describe a single-line or short paragraph pushed to the next column or page even though logic dictates that it should remain directly beneath the preceding paragraph. For example, a contextual widow would be the final, single-line paragraph of a bulleted or numbered list. (See also *widow*.)

counter

The holes or large open spaces within letter forms—for example, the holes in the letters *o* and *g*.

curve handles

In vector drawing, anchor points contain angle and curvature data to affect path segments. Curve handles are always present but only visible when the anchor point has more than 0° of curvature and/or more than a 0° angle. Dragging curve handles alters the angle and depth of curvature of path segments emanating from an anchor point.

D

data source file

When creating variable data printing (VDP) documents using InDesign's mail merge features, the set of comma- or tab-delimited variable data is stored in a data source file (a CSV or TXT file).

descender

The portion of a glyph that extends below the text baseline, such as with the lowercase letters *g*, *q*, and *j*.

drop rule

A vertical rule or line separating columns or rails.

duplexing

Printing on both sides of a piece of paper.

E

em

A relative measurement equal, in theory, to the width of a typeface's capital *M* and to the cap height of the typeface. For example, type set in 12 pt should theoretically have a 12 pt em measurement; 10 pt type should have a 10 pt em. In practice, with digital fonts, the capital *M* is rarely the width of a full em, although an em is still usually same in width as the cap height of the font.

em dash

A horizontal dash one em wide.

en

A relative measurement equal, in theory, to the width of a typeface's capital *N* and slightly more than half width of an em.

en dash

A horizontal dash one en wide.

endpoint

An anchor point at the beginning or end of an open path.

F

flat-file database

A collection of data stored in an ASCII-based format such as a comma- or tab-delimited TXT file rather than in a traditional database.

flattening

The process of removing transparency and generating opaque objects from the areas of color created by overlapping one or more transparent objects with nontransparent objects.

flush
The clean edge of type. For example, this page is printed with type flush left, meaning that the type aligns along the left to create a clean edge.

flush left
Text aligned uniformly to the left margin.

flush left and right
See *force justified*.

flush right
Text aligned uniformly to the right margin.

folio
A page number. Also refers to the page itself and to large sheets of paper that are folded once and bound.

force justified
Text aligned to flush, clean edges on both the left and right sides of the column is justified. In most justified paragraphs, last lines that are too short to fill the width of the column remain left, right, or center aligned. However, when even short last lines are made to justify, creating a uniform rectangle but with large gaps possibly introduced between words or letters, the paragraph is called force justified. Some newspapers, for example, force justify text.

FPO
(Abbreviation for For Position Only) Temporary content—text or imagery—placed to estimate size, position, or usage of other content to be inserted later.

G

gamma
The frequency of radiation that turned Dr. Bruce Banner into the Incredible Hulk. Also the luminescence value of color as measured in tones of gray.

gamut
The range of color values possible in a particular color space, device, or color-production process.

gang
Printing multiple pages from one or more jobs on a single, large sheet of paper to save production time and costs.

ganged
See *gang*.

glyph
A single character, pictogram, mark, or entity within a font or language.

greeking
Content—usually text—that is used in place of final copy (aka FPO text). In InDesign, when text appears onscreen below a size limit set in the preferences, the text is replaced by black-and-white patterning, which is also greeking. The term derives from the expression "it's all Greek to me," indicating that something cannot be read or is gibberish.

gutter
Traditionally either the space between pages in a spread or the space between columns or both. In InDesign, the gutter is only the space between columns.

H

hanging punctuation
Punctuation and parts of glyphs allowed to shift in part or wholly beyond the flush edge of text to create a more optically balanced flush edge instead of a physically clean flush edge.

hard proof
Any printed version of a document short of the final output.

HSL
(Abbreviation for Hue, Saturation, and Luminosity [or Lightness]) A color model that describes a color in terms of its hue, saturation, and luminosity values; interchangeable with HSB (Hue, Saturation, and Brightness).

ICC profile
See *color profile*.

in port

The place on a threaded text frame through which text flows into the frame. The in port is located near the upper-left corner of a text frame and on the left end of a type on a path object. Opposite the in port is the out port.

inset

A margin on the interior of a text frame that pushes type inward from one or more edges of the frame.

J

jumpline

A directive to readers that a threaded story resumes at a later point. For example, "continues on page 83."

K

kerning

The relative distance between a pair of letters. Kerning values are adjusted on the Character panel or the Control panel's character mode to reduce or increase space between two characters whose shapes create awkward gapping or collision.

knockout

When two or more colors overlap, the foreground color can either *overprint*, which often causes mixing of colors from the background into the foreground color, or knockout such that the lower or background ink is removed, punching a hole through it in the shape of the foreground color area, thus preserving the appearance of the foreground color.

L

layer comp

In Photoshop, a layer comp is a recording of the state of an image's layers at a given moment in time. Layer comps register the visibility, opacity, blending mode, and position of individual layers and may be used to switch between design variations without the need for creating multiple documents. InDesign honors and employs layer comps stored in Photoshop PSD documents such that design variations

created in Photoshop may be placed and changed on the InDesign page without a return trip to Photoshop.

leader

Marks, glyphs, or symbols representing or preceding a tab. For instance, in many tables of contents, entries are connected to their page numbers by a series of dots/periods or a continuous rule (really underscores). Those dots or underscores are the leader.

left-read

In a bound publication or facing-pages document, the page to the left of the spine. In English- and other Latin-based-language publications, the left-read pages are even numbered. In Japanese, Hebrew, and sinistral publications reading from right to left, left-read pages are odd numbered.

ligatures

Two or more letters tied into a single character. Generally, when certain pairs, triplets, or quartets of individual letters or glyphs are combined, their shapes cause awkward collisions—for example, *f-i* and *f-t*. In old metal and block type as well as older TrueType and Type 1 fonts, ligatures were extra, single characters added to fonts that combined the shapes of individual colliding letters in a way that voided collision. In modern OpenType fonts, ligatures are created by combining special variants of each individual character drawn to accommodate such combinations and avoid collision while maintaining the individuality of each letter.

live area

Approximately ⅛ inch inside the trim, the "safe" area of a page inside of which content should be safe from harm in the event of a slight paper shift on the cutting machine.

LPI

(Abbreviation for lines per inch) A measurement of the resolution of printed output that is the number of halftone dots per linear inch. The greater the number of dots, the higher the resolution. Also known as screen ruling or screen frequency.

M

marker
In InDesign, markers are invisible but important characters that act as placeholders or tethers for different types of content. For example, anchored objects are tied to their descriptive text via markers, as are footnotes.

merged document
When variable data documents are created via InDesign's mail merge feature, the merged document is the ready-to-print result of combining the source document containing variable data markers with the data source document that holds the variable data.

metadata
Information stored within a special layer of a document to identify, categorize, or define the file. Metadata do not print with a document but are accessible to numerous XML-aware applications and databases for file management, asset management, and other purposes.

misregister
Inadvertently registering for Early European Economics 301 instead of for Early European Arts & Culture 301 because you woke up on the dormitory roof with a hangover. Also, when plates fail to align perfectly on a printer, colors fall out of register or alignment and are said to misregister.

mixed ink
In InDesign, a mixed ink is one that is a combination of two or more spot color inks or one spot color ink and one or more process color inks.

mixed ink group
Multiple swatches generated as incremental tint variants resulting from mixing spot and process inks.

more often than not
A mantra by which efficient designers live. If you do something in InDesign—use a particular document setup, need certain colors, and so on—more often than you don't do it, whatever it is should be automated or made the default value.

O

onomatopoeia
A special kind of word named to closely approximate the sound described by, or associated with, the subject of the word. For example: bang, pow, smash, and numerous other examples from the 1960s *Batman* television show.

OpenType
The latest, er, *first* generation, in my not so humble opinion, of intelligent font software. Based on Unicode, OpenType fonts (or simply OpenTypes) have predefined spaces for more than 65,000 glyphs from more than a dozen languages. These fonts often contain variant designs such as true small caps, swashes, contextual alternates, ordinals, and several versions of numerals in a single file, replacing several separate fonts required to achieve the same functionality in Type1 or TrueType fonts. OpenType fonts are identified on a computer by the extension .otf, although in many cases they bear the old TrueType .ttf file extension revealing the fact that, at their cores, OpenType fonts are structured as either Type1 or TrueType. OpenType fonts are 100% cross-platform; the same font functions and renders identically on Windows, Mac OS 9, Mac OS X, and several flavors of Unix.

OPI
(Abbreviation for Open Prepress Interface) The process of inserting a low-resolution or FPO image to be exchanged automatically further on in the production process for a high-resolution or final image. Using InDesign, OPI image substitution can be performed at output time or left to be done in-RIP.

orphan
In a paragraph, a line left behind at the bottom of a column or page while the rest of the paragraph flows to the next column or page. Bringhurst limits the definition of *orphan* to the paragraph's first line ending a page, although common usage has expanded the definition to also include the paragraph's first line ending a column. (See also *contextual orphan*.)

out port
The place on a threaded text frame through which text exits the frame to connect with and enter another text frame. The out port is located near the

lower-right corner of a text frame and on the right side of a type on a path object. Opposite the out port is the *in port*.

overprint
When two or more colors overlap, they can be printed over one another, each color layed down successively, which usually results in the colors mixing to form a new, combined color. This is over-printing. Conversely, the uppermost ink can be set to *knockout* lower inks to preserve the appearance of the foreground color.

override
In terms of styles, an override is a formatting option not specifically defined in the style assigned to the text, object, table, or cell. For instance, using the Cmd+Shift+I/Ctrl+Shift+I keyboard shortcut to apply italic to text is an override of a paragraph style in which the text is defined to be roman, or not italic. Overrides are indicated by a plus sign (+) beside the style name in Paragraph Style, Character Style, Object Style, Table Style, and Cell Style panels.

overscore
A rule above text, as opposed to an underscore.

overset
When a text frame (or type on a path object) is not large enough to hold all of the text placed into it, any overage is said to be overset. A frame containing overset text displays a red plus sign (+) in its out port.

P

palette
The pre-CS3 name for the floating utility boxes that contain the majority of InDesign's functionality.

panel
CS3 name for the floating utility boxes that contain the majority of InDesign's functionality; formerly called palettes.

path
A vector drawing consisting of anchor points and path segments.

path segment
Segment of a path connecting one anchor to another.

plugged
When a device such as a printer or camera cannot render high percentages of color (in subtractive color models) or low percentages (in additive color models) and the result is a jump to pure black, the resulting color is said to plug. For example, many offset presses cannot render ink tints greater than 95%; thus, an area shaded in 97% black will plug and become solid black. *Blow out* is the opposite, when very light color values become 0% color.

polyglot
A person or computer application fluent in more than one language, or a book or other long publica-tion that prints the same information in more than one language.

PostScript
The printer language that translates computer-drawn graphics and text into high-quality printed output on a PostScript-enabled printer or other device. PostScript was created by Adobe Systems, Inc., founders John Warnock and Chuck Geschke and was the foundation technology for that com-pany. Coupled with a computer—the Apple Macin-tosh—and printer—the Apple LaserWriter—both with onboard PostScript interpreters, Adobe's Post-Script launched the Desktop Publishing Revolution in 1985.

preflight
Preparing a document for print output.

prosumer
Coined in 1980 by the futurist Alvin Toffler—in his book *The Third Wave*—as a blend of producer and consumer, the term *prosumer* was used to describe a possible future type of consumer who would become involved in the design and manufacture of products so they could be made to individual specification. The term also refers to amateurs or hobbyists who use professional-grade tools such as InDesign CS3.

Q

quad

Spacing added to align text to the left, right, or center. Also often used to describe simply the flush edge of text. See *flush*.

quad left

See *flush left*.

quad right

See *flush right*.

R

rag

The uneven side of flush left or flush right type, as in "the rag edge."

ragged

The uneven side of flush left or flush right type.

rail

A column. The term is most often used in newspaper publishing.

rebate

On photographic film, the margin surrounding the image area. In desktop, object, and certain other printers, the area of the substrate required to be gripped by the printer's rollers or grips; no image may be printed in the rebate.

rendering intent

When a color management system must convert colors from one *gamut* to another, and when some of the colors in the source *gamut* do not fit into the destination, the rendering intent determines *how* out-of-*gamut* colors are brought into *gamut*. For instance, are out-of-*gamut* colors clipped to the nearest values in the same range, are they converted based on their relative distances from the color space's white point, or is another method used? The four rendering intents available in Adobe's CMS are described in detail in Chapter 10, "Output."

RGB

(Abbreviation for Red, Green, and Blue) An additive color model encompassing the visual portion of the radiation spectrum. The more color added, the closer the combination moves toward pure white. RGB has a vastly wider *gamut* than CMYK but is smaller than the Lab color *gamut*.

rich black

Black created by mixing a percentage of cyan, magenta, yellow, and/or black process inks. Rich black is so named because it is a richer, deeper black than pure black process ink; however, because it requires the use of at least three different inks, its use increases the risk of misregistration. Nearly every press, pre-press, and graphics professional has a different opinion of the ideal formula to produce rich black, and the formula often varies depending on the print image and the substrate in use.

rich text

Based on but an extension to ASCII text, rich text incorporates basic word processor–level formatting such as bold and italic, color, underlines, wrapping lines, tabs, indents, and an expanded character set. (See also *RTF*.)

right-read

In a bound publication or facing-pages document, the page to the right of the spine. In English- and other Latin-based-language publications, right-read pages are odd numbered. Right-read pages are even numbered in Japanese, Hebrew, and southpaw publications.

RIP

(Acronym for Raster Image Processor) When digital artwork is sent to press, it often includes pixel-based raster images, resolution-independent vector type and paths, transparency, and Z-order stacking of objects. Printers—including imagesetters, platesetters, digital printers, and desktop laser and inkjet printers—can only render two-dimensional, flat images and in screened raster form. The job of the RIP is to convert all data in the document to screened rasters at the resolution of the output device.

river

An unsightly optical effect created by white space gaps between words or letters aligning, or nearly aligning, vertically. Rivers are prevalent especially among justified type and narrow columns such as one finds in newspapers. InDesign's composition engine, particularly effective when using the paragraph composition option, eliminates most rivers.

RTF

(Abbreviation for Rich Text Format) A universal format based on rich text content. RTF files can be read and created by all modern word-processors, page-layouts, and many other applications. RTF files are cross-platform.

run-on

Extra copies run at the end of a print job to provide a buffer in case some earlier pages turn out to be unsuitable for delivery to the client. Also known as run-out and run-down. Also, what the ersatz informant Huggy Bear always gave Starsky and Hutch.

run-in head

A subhead with text immediately following it on the same line.

runt

A term coined by David Blatner, a runt is a single word residing on a line by itself within, or at the end of, a paragraph. In the case of forced justified text, runts space out their constituent glyphs horribly to fill the entire column width.

run-up

Extra sheets printed at the beginning of a job to prepare a press to print the actual job and to test ink and press accuracy and readiness. Run-up is typically done with cheap, low-quality paper such as newsprint or paper left over from a previous job rather than the paper actually ordered for the job, thus not risking the stock required to complete the job.

S

separations

Digital, film, paper, or other material wherein each ink used in a job is created as its own image distinct and separate from other inks.

seps

Slang for *separations*. (See *separations*.)

slug

Any piece or set of information placed in a document outside the trim and bleed area of the page. Slugs will appear on film and, generally, even on the printed substrate but will be trimmed off during finishing. Common information inserted as a slug includes the job name and number, client information, name and contact information for the designer, color scales, and special instructions to the pre-press or press operators.

slug area

The area of the InDesign document in which slugs may be placed. The dimensions of the four sides of the slug area are defined together or individually in the New Document and Document Setup dialogs in CS 3.

snippet

InDesign objects—text frames, paths, placed assets, or other objects—or portions or whole pages saved as external files. Snippets are XML-based chunks of layout data that may be reused, restoring InDesign objects into any document, and shared with other InDesign users.

soft proofs

A digital version of a document used to check the document on screen.

solidus

The unique slash appearing between the numerator and denominator in a fraction; often called simply the fraction slash (for example, 9/10). The slope of the solidus is not as steep as the virgule—the so-called "forward slash" found on keyboards and used as a substitute for the words *or, and or,* and *per* in English grammar. The solidus is not found on computer or typewriter keyboards.

OpenType fonts have separate virgule and solidus glyphs. Through InDesign's Glyphs panel, or by activating the Fractions OpenType option, InDesign will convert a virgule between two numbers into a solidus (and make the numbers properly sized and positioned numerator and denominator).

spot colors
(Also known as spot inks, spots, or PMS colors after the PANTONE Matching System, the most widely used set of spot color inks in North America) Pre-mixed ink colors that expand upon the limited *gamut* of CMYK process inks. Spot colors come in a rainbow of colors, including some—such as neons and metallics—that cannot be rendered onscreen.

spread
What Mom lays out for Thanksgiving dinner. Also, any set of two consecutive pages in a bound book or facing-pages document.

Stacking order
See *Z-order*.

sticky
When options and settings entered into an application or one of its dialog boxes remain as set between sessions, the settings are said to be sticky settings. An example is InDesign's Print dialog, where basic options set once will be retained for the next print operation.

substrate
Any material on which an image may be printed. Paper is, of course, the most common example of a substrate, but others include plastic, metal, and wood.

T

thread
A thread is a story that flows freely between several text frames. The frames themselves are said to be threaded.

transparency flattening
See *flattening*.

trapping
Because offset printing applies only one ink color to the page per run, slight misalignment of the substrate on any subsequent pass may cause misregistration and gaps between adjacent colors. Trapping, also called choking and spreading, is the process of overlapping inks slightly to hide minor misregistration and to eliminate gaps.

U

Unicode
An international standard in which glyphs from all the world's written languages are encompassed and included in a form understandable by computers. In Unicode, every glyph from each language has its own predefined and inviolable position in the table of glyphs. OpenType fonts are built on Unicode.

V

variable data printing
The process of customizing each copy of printed output to include unique text, imagery, or both.

VDP
See *variable data printing*.

Version Cue
A rudimentary server-based workgroup collaboration system included with Adobe Creative Suite and several stand-alone Adobe applications. Version Cue includes check-in/check-out controls and file versioning.

W

widow
A paragraph's last line appearing as the first line in a new column or page. Bringhurst limits the definition of widow to only the paragraph's last line beginning a page, but the definition has expanded through common usage to also include the last line beginning a new column. (See also *contextual widow*.)

wireframe
A skeletal representation of the shape of a three-dimensional object.

workspaces

In InDesign and other Adobe applications, the workspace is the entire environment of the application interface, including menu configurations and panel arrangements. Most such applications enable the user to save, recall, and often even share his environment settings as a "workspace" file. InDesign comes with several predefined workspaces on the Window ➤ Workspace menu.

WYSIWYG

(Acronym for What You See Is What You Get) Basically, what you see onscreen is what will print. InDesign is the first page-layout application to offer true WYSIWYG, particularly with regard to transparency, vector graphics, and object interactions on the page.

X

XMP

(Abbreviation for eXtensible Metadata Platform) A technology coauthored by Adobe that allows metadata to be embedded in file formats based on XML or containing an XML layer. Common XMP *metadata* include author and copyright holder information, camera settings (for photographs), licensing restrictions, and archival data such as categories, description, and keywords. The extensible part of XMP is its ability to go beyond predefined metadata fields and include any information a file author sees fit to store in the XMP layer.

Z

Z-order

Three-dimensional (3D) space is plotted on three axes: X (the horizontal plane), Y (the vertical plane), and Z (the depth plane). Within two-dimensional or pseudo-three-dimensional applications such as InDesign, full understanding of, and support for, the z-axis and 3D objects is not available. Out of necessity, however, objects can be stacked above or below, in front or behind, one another. This stacking is done along the z-axis and is referred to as the Z-order of objects.

Index

Note to the reader: Throughout this index **boldfaced** page numbers indicate primary discussions of a topic. *Italicized* page numbers indicate illustrations.

Symbols & Numbers

@ (at) symbol, **396**
© (copyright), 70, 81
€ (euro), 70
¶ (pilcrow), 24, 70, 81
   character-level attributes for, 61
® (registered trademark), 70, 75, 81
§ (section symbol), 81
~ (tilde), for discretionary hyphen, 274
• (waisted bullet), 70, 81
¥ (yen symbol), as anchored object
   marker, *195*, 195–196
1-bit images, trapping, 355
3D objects, InDesign vs. Illustrator, 155
3D Ribbon effect, for type on path, 206

A

A-Master, 237
Absolute Colorimetric rendering
   intent, 332
acronyms, case changes and, 73
Actual Size icon (Command Bar), *10*
Add Anchor Point tool, *6*, 112
Add Bullets dialog, *255*, 255
Add Documents dialog, 413
Add Unnamed Swatches
   command, 186
Adobe applications, user interface, 2
Adobe Bridge, 8, *153*, **153–154**, 428
   color management with, **324–327**
   templates in, 225
   for viewing document colors,
      191, *192*
Adobe Caslon Pro font, *89*, 89
   figures, 94
Adobe Digital Editions reader
   software, 302
Adobe Exchange, 408
Adobe Graphics Engine, 287
Adobe Illustrator (AI) file format, 141
Adobe Illustrator Clip Board
   (AICB), 156
Adobe In-RIP Trapping, 351–352
Adobe Jenson Pro typeface, 254
Adobe Myriad Pro font, *89*, 92
Adobe Stock Photos, 161
Adobe Swatch Exchange (ASE) file, 191
AdobeRGB (1998) color profile, *329*,
   329, 330
AI (Adobe Illustrator) file format, 141
AICB (Adobe Illustrator Clip
   Board), 156

Align panel icon, *3*
align stroke, 179, *179*
alignment
   of anchored objects, 199
   of bullets, 256
   optical margin, 49–50
   of paragraphs, **37–39**
All Spreads option for InCopy Layout
   view, 427
Allow Document Pages to Shuffle
   command, 234
alpha channels, 142, 465
alpha transparency, 107
alphanumeric headings, in indexes, 313
AM/PM (time notations), 75
American Standard Code for
   Information Interchange (ASCII), 465
Americana typeface, 65
anchor points in vector shapes, 104,
   105, 465
   adding and removing, **112**
   for curves, *108*
   editing, with Direct Selection tool,
      128–132
   fill and/or stroke color, 187
   moving, 131
   selecting, 131
Anchored Object Options dialog, *194*,
   196, 196–198
   Custom mode, *198*, **198–202**
   for object
      close to page bottom, *202*
      column-wide or less, *203*
      outside frame, *200*
      at top of frame and
         centered, *202*
      at top of page, *201*
anchored objects, **192–202**, 465
   anatomy, *195*–196
   benefits, 192–193
   creating, **193–195**
   custom options, **198–202**
   inline options, **196–198**
   preventing manual positioning, 198
AppleScript, 407
application defaults, customizing,
   19–20
Application menus, 13
Apply Color tool, *6*
Apply Gradient tool, *6*
Apply None tool, *6*
Arial font, 265
art box, cropping PDF to, 149
artwork. *See* images

ascender, 465
ascender line, 69
ASCII (American Standard Code for
   Information Interchange), 465
ASE (Adobe Swatch Exchange) file, 191
Asian language fonts, 59
assets. *See also* images; text
Assign Profiles dialog, *334*, 334
Assign Trap Preset dialog, 355–356, *356*
Assigned Spreads view, 426–427
Assignment Options dialog, 436
assignment packages, 436
assignments, **423–428**, 465
   adding content to, 432–433
   changing, 433
   changing names, 433–434
   checking in, 431
   checking out, 430
      overriding, 434
   content in InDesign, **429–432**
   of photographs, 433
   recovery from broken files, 434
   unassigned content, 433
   updating, 427
   user name and color for, 424
Assignments panel, 425, *425*
   checking in/out, *431*
   drag and drop frame into, 433
   icon, *3*
   Package for InCopy, *436*, 436
attribute-level transparency, 170,
   170–171
attributes, Object Style Options dialog
   for accessing, *400*, *401*
Attributes panel icon, *3*
Auto-Collapse Icon Panels, 4
auto leading, 47, 60
Autocorrect, **275–276**, *276*
   sharing word pairs, **440**
autoflowing text
   into frames, **251**
   in Master page frames, **252–253**

B

Balance Ragged Lines command, **50**
Based On field, for styles, 371
baseline, 69, 466
   offset for footnotes, 270
   and underline offset, 77
baseline grid, *293*, **293–295**
baseline shift, **69–70**, *70*
basic feather effect, 174–175
bevel and emboss effect, *174*, 174

Bézier, 466
Bickham Script Pro font, *90*
bid generation, book file for portfolio, **301–302**
binary data format, printing, 365
black point compensation, 333
black, showing single plates in, 337
blank lines, in data merge, 394
Blatner, David, 473
bleed area, cropping PDF to, 149
bleed guides, color of, 222
bleed marks, in slug area, 218
Bleed mode for view, 288
Bleed tool, *6*
bleeds, 216, *217, 220*, **220–221**
blend spaces, 344–345
blowout, 333, 466
bold type
    character styles for, 379
    preserving in imported Word
        text, 29
book design workflow. *See also*
    workflow
        redefining and optimizing, 228–229
Book File Collaboration Workflow,
    412–414
Book Page Numbering Options dialog,
    298, 298
Book panel, *297, 298*
    for multiple page sizes, **227**
Bookmarks panel icon, *3*
books, **297–302**. *See also* indexes
    beginning file, **297**
    for collaboration, 412
    generating index for all
        documents, 312
    outputting, **301–302**
    page, chapter and section
        numbering, **298–300**, *299*
    portfolio for proposal and bid
        generation, **301–302**
    synchronizing styles, **300–301**
    table of contents, **314–318**, *317*
bound documents, facing pages for, *215*
bounding box, cropping PDF to, 149
broken link, fixing, 160
buffer space of live area, 221
Bulleted List icon (Command Bar), *10*
bullets, 81, **254–257**
    converting in Word text, 29
    fonts for, 256
    overriding, **262**
Bullets and Numbering dialog, *255, 258*
Button tool, *6*

C

Caflisch Script Pro font, *91*
calibrating, 466
    monitor, 323

Calibri font, 265
canceling assignment checkout, 432
cap height, 466
cap of stroke, 178
capital letters, and attention, 95
Capitalize dialog, 306, *307*
caret code metacharacters, 278
carriage returns, 24
    removing, 26
cascading styles, **371–374**
    benefits, 373
case sensitivity
    for adding words to dictionary, 274
    in search and replace, 278
catalog, design, 139–140, *140*
cell styles, 398
    sharing, 439–440
Cell Styles panel, 398, *398*
    icon, *3*
Center Content command, 163
chain link icon, and margins, 214
change requests, for designers, 422
change tracking, in InCopy, 265
Channels panel (Photoshop CS3), 142,
    347–348
Chapter Number text variable, 300
    options, 385, *385, 389*
chapter numbering in books,
    298–300, *299*
Character mode, for Control Panel, 8, **80**
Character panel, *57–72, 58*
    All Caps, 74
    Font Size, 60–61
    icon, *3, 10*
    Language attribute, 271
    Leading, 60–61
    No Break option, 75–76
    OpenType menu, 86, *87*
    Small Caps, 74
    strikethrough, **77–78**
    underline, 76–77
character sets, for text import, 26
Character Style Options dialog, *378*
character styles
    breaking links, 381
    for bullets, 256
    clearing paragraph style overrides
        and, 378
    efficiency from, **378–379**
    for headers and footers, 388
    kerning in, 64
    sharing, 439–440
Character Styles panel, 378
    icon, *3*
characters. *See also* special characters
    drop caps for multiple, 43, *43*
    formatting, **57–80**
        baseline shift, **69–70**, *70*
        font families and type style,
            57–60

font size and leading, **60–61**
kerning, *62*, **62–64**
language, **71–72**
skew, **70–71**, *71*
tracking, 64, **64–67**
vertical and horizontal scaling,
    68, **68–69**
horizontal spacing, 47
InDesign vs. Word style
    conflicts, 30
transformations, **72–80**
    changing case, **72–73**
    strikethrough, **77–78**
    superscript and subscript, *74*,
        74–75
    underline, 76–77
Check Spelling dialog, 272
Check Spelling icon (Command Bar), *10*
chemical formulas, subscript for, 75
Chinese language font, 59
circle
    for frames, 117
    path of, 110, *110*
CJK fonts, 59, 466
clearing
    paragraph style overrides, 377
        and character styles, 378
clipboard, 207
clipped copies, flattening and, 340
clipping path, 142
close path, 127
CMYK color, converting RGB to, 330
collaboration
    copy before layout, **437–438**
    example, 428–429
    with other designers, **411–421**
        one document with many
            designers, **412–415**
        one page with many
            designers, **415–421**
        saving to older InDesign
            versions, **411–412**
    sharing reusable settings, **439–443**
        Autocorrect word pairs, **440**
        dictionaries, **439**
        document size presets, **442**
        Find/Change queries, **440–441**
        glyph sets, **441**
        keyboard shortcuts, **443**
        PDF Export Presets, **441**
        print presets, **441–442**
        stroke styles, **440**
        styles, **439–440**
        swatches, **440**
        templates, **442**
        transparency flattener
            presets, **442**
        workspaces, **442–443**
    with upper level nondesign
        personnel, **439**

with writers and editors, **421–439**
  assignments, **423–434**
  design-editorial problem
    solving, 421–422
  remote editors, **435–437**
color
  Adobe Bridge for viewing, 191, *192*
  for anchor points, 187
  for assignments, 424, 425
  disabling menu for, 15
  of drop shadow, 173
  of grid lines, 292
  of paragraph rules, 54
  proofing, **335–337**
  of ruler guides, 290
  for stroke gap, 180
  for text frames, 36
  of underline, 77
color blindness, 323
color-coding menus, 14
color gamut, *329*, 329, 330
  process for bringing color
    inside, 332
color library colors, in QuarkXPress
  swatch, 190
color management, **321–335**. *See also*
  ICC color profiles
  color profile changes, **333–335**
  configuring, **324–333**
    black point compensation, 333
    Bridge color management sets,
      324–327
    engine, 332
    policies, 331–332
    rendering intent, 332
    working spaces, 329–331
  per-image, **333**
  purpose, 321–322
Color Management Off set, 327
color models, 156
Color panel icon, *3*
Color Settings dialog, *328*
  Expanded List of files, 327
colorimeter, 323
column guides
  color of, 222
  and text frame creation, 248
columns
  edge for anchored object
    alignment, 200
  QuarkXPress vs. InDesign, 246
  setup, 213
  specifying number, **34–35**
comma-separated text file, for data
  merge, 391
Command Bar, **10**, *10*
commands, hiding, 13
composer, 44
compound paths, *123*, **123–126**, *124*, *125*

computers, custom environment when
  switching, 19
condensed type, vs. scaling down
  horizontally, 69
Configure Plug-ins dialog, *17*
content-first workflow, **158**
Content Placement Options dialog, for
  merge, *394*, 394
Context & Panel menus, 13
Context, for keyboard shortcuts, 12
contextual orphan, 467
contextual widow, 467
Control panel, *8*, **8–9**
  Character mode, **80**
  customizing, *9*
  Fitting command buttons, *163*
  Paragraph mode, *37*, 254
    Apply Bullets, 257
    Apply Numbering, *257*
    number of columns, 37
Convert Bullets to Text/Convert
  Numbering to Text command, 262
Convert Direction Point tool, *6*, 111, 130
Convert to Profile command,
  334–335, *335*
copy and paste
  effects, 176
  graphics, **155–157**
  objects, layer impact, 296
  pages, **236**
  text, 31
copy before layout process, **437–438**
Copy Link(s) To command (Links
  panel), 161
copyright (©), 70, 81
corner anchor points, 109
  converting anchor points between
    smooth and, **111**
Corner Options dialog, 120–121, *121*
corrupted documents, 162
  and undeletable swatches, 190
counter, 467
counting words in text frames, **33**
Create Guides dialog, *291*
Create Merged Document dialog
  Multiple Record Layout tab,
    395, *396*
  Records tab, 395
Creation Date text variable, options,
  386, 386
Creative Suite, 1
  color synchronization between
    applications, 333
Creative Suite Color Settings dialog
  (Adobe Bridge), *325*
crop marks
  printing, 362
  in slug area, 218

cropping
  in Frame Fitting Options, 164–165,
    165
  PDF (Portable Document Format),
    options, 149
cross-platform fonts, 85–86
cross-references in indexes, 305,
  308–310
Current Page Number special character
  marker, 298
cursor, loaded, *31*, 31, 150
curve flattening, 107
curve handles, 108, *109*, 467
curves, Pen tool for, *108*, **108–111**
custom cross-reference, 310
Custom Text text variable, *386*
Customize Proof Condition dialog, 335,
  335, 365, *366*
customizing InDesign
  application defaults, **19–20**
  Command Bar, **10**, *10*
  to create workflow-focused
    workstations, 14–15
  InDesign settings on portable
    drive, **19**
  keyboard shortcuts, **10–13**
  menus, **13–15**, *14*
  panels, **1–10**
    arranging, **4–5**
    Control panel, *8*, **8–9**
    dock, *2*, *3*, **4**
    multi-state, **5–6**, *6*
    stacked, **5**
    Tools panel, *6*, **6–7**
    unneeded, **9–10**
  plug-ins, **16–17**
  workspaces, **18**
cutting and pasting images, 193

D

Dante MT Std font, 90, *91*
dashed stroke, defining custom,
  180–181, *181*
data merge, **389–396**
  data source file, **391–392**
  with images, **396**
  initiating, **392–393**
  merge process, **394–396**
  target document, **392**
Data Merge panel, 392
  header row fields display, *393*
  icon, *3*
data source file, **391–392**, 467
Data Source Import Options dialog, *393*
database records, inserting and
  printing, 390
Decrease Font Size icon (Command
  Bar), *10*

Decrease Left Indent icon (Command Bar), *10*

Default Fill and Stroke tool, *6*

default styles, 405

default swatches, **191**

Default Workspace, 18

defaults, customizing application settings, 19–20

Define Lists dialog, *259*

Delete Anchor Point tool, *6*, 112

deleting
  footnotes, 268
  guides, 290
  index marker, 308
  items in library, 403
  pages, **236**
  unused swatches, 186

dependent styles, in cascading styles, 372

descenders, 69, 467

design elements, proximity to trim edge, 221

Device to Simulate menu, 336

dialog boxes, vs. panels, 2

dictionaries, 72
  adding word to, 273
  editing, **273–275**
  sharing, **274–275**, **439**
  for spell check, language attribute and, 271

Dictionary dialog, *273*, 273
  Import and Export buttons, 274

digital asset manager (DAM), 153

digital editions, exporting book to, 302

digital printing, 389

Direct Selection tool, *6*, 124, 171
  for editing anchor points, **128–132**
  for selecting anchor points, 131

direction of paths, 115

directional feather effect, 175

discretionary hyphens, 80–81, 274

discretionary ligatures, **86–88**, *88*

display font, in Story Editor, 265

Divide and Copy and Conquer workflow, 417
  potential problems, 418–419

Divide method, of flattening, 341

dividing shapes, 122–123

.doc file extension, 27, 32

dock, 2, *3*, *4*
  adding panel to, 4
  expanding or contracting, 4

Document Numbering Options dialog, 298–299, *299*

Document Properties dialog (Acrobat), for application creating PDF, *352*

documents. *See also* books
  creating master pages from pages in, **243**

displaying, **285–288**
  display performance, **287–288**
  multiple windows, **287**, *287*
  Navigator panel, **286**, *286*
  view modes, **288**
  zoom, **285–286**
grid, *292*, **292–293**
  baseline grid, *293*, **293–295**
guides, **289**, **289–291**
  Guides Manager, **291**
  options, **290–291**
layers, **295–296**
loading master pages from other, 243
moving pages between, **235**
placing snippets in, 405
preflight check, **356–359**
reusable setups, **222–225**
setup, **213–222**
sharing size presets, **442**
templates, **224–225**

dotted stroke styles, 182

drag and drop
  to add items to library, 403
  master page, 232
  pages, 233
  to place assets, **153–154**
  in Story Editor, 265

drawing. *See also* paths in vector shapes
  editing paths and shapes, **126–135**
  with shape tools, **117–135**
    Ellipse Frame tool, **117**
    Polygon Frame tool, **118**
    reshaping shapes, **120–126**

drop caps, **42–44**, *43*
  character styles for, 379
  hanging, 44

drop rule, 467

drop shadow effect, *172*, **172–173**

DTP Tools, 229

dual monitors, 2

duplex printing, 215, 467

duplicating
  effects, 176
  pages, **236**

E

Edit Glyph Set dialog, *98*
Edit menu
  ➤ Color Settings, 328
    ➤ Assign Profiles, 333
    ➤ Convert to Profile, 333
  ➤ Duplicate, 207
  ➤ Edit in Story Editor, 263
  ➤ Find/Change, 380, 440–441
  ➤ InCopy
    ➤ Add Selection to Assignments, 427

  ➤ Add to Assignment, 432
  ➤ Check Out, 430
  ➤ Keyboard Shortcuts, 11, 443
  ➤ Paste in Place, 157
  ➤ Paste Into, 157
  ➤ Paste without Formatting, 157
  ➤ Preferences, *7*. *See also* Preferences dialog
  ➤ Spelling
    ➤ Autocorrect, 275
    ➤ Dictionary, 273, 439
    ➤ Dynamic Spelling, 275
  ➤ Step and Repeat, 207
  ➤ Transparency Blend Space, 344
  ➤ Transparency Flattener Presets, 342, 442
Edit menu (Bridge), ➤ Creative Suite Color Settings, 324
Edit Original command
  and Illustrator, 189
  and other applications, 189
  and Photoshop, 188
Edit Original command (Links panel), 160
Edit Text Variable dialog, 388
editorial team, instructions for assignment management, 438
effects, **171–175**
  basic feather, 174–175
  bevel and emboss, *174*, 174
  dialog box, *171*
  directional feather, 175
  drop shadow, *172*, **172–173**
  global light, **176–178**, *177*
  gradient feather, *175*, *175*
  inner glow, 173–174, *174*
  inner shadow, 173
  moving and replicating, **176**
  outer glow, 173
  satin, 174
Effects panel, 170
  fx icon, 175, *176*
  icon, *3*
  for placing image, *171*
efficiency
  lists maintenance, 275
  numbering, 260–262
  with Quick Apply, **406–407**
  vs. realism in lighting, 178
  reusable documents setups for, **222–225**
  with scripting, **407–409**
  snippets for, **404–405**
  style shortcuts for, **405–406**
  working with objects, **399–409**
    libraries, **401–404**
    object styles, **399–400**
  working with tables, **397–398**
  working with text, **369–396**
    with character styles, **378–379**

with data merge, **389–396**
with nested styles, **381–384**
with paragraph styles, **369–377**
with text variables, **384–389**
Ellipse Frame tool, *6*
Ellipse tool, *6*
ellipsis (...), 81
em, 64, 467
em dash, 80, 467
em space, *83*, 83
email, attaching package to, 436
Embed File command (Links panel), 161
embedded assets
vs. linked, 162
spreadsheet, 397
EMF (Enhanced Windows Meta File) format, 141
empty fields, in data merge, 394
empty frames, pre-threading, 248–249
empty layers, deleting, 296
en, 467
en dash, 80, 467
en space, *83*, 83
Encapsulated PostScript (EPS), 141
exporting layout page as, and placing inside other layout, 151
placing with EPS Import Options dialog, *143*, **143–144**
End Nested Style Here character, 82, 384
end of stroke, 180
end style, for trap segments, 354
endmark, 97
endnotes, **271**
in imported Word text, 28
endpoint, 467
engine, for color management, 332
Enhanced Windows Meta File (EMF) format, 141
EPS (Encapsulated PostScript), 141
exporting layout page as, and placing inside other layout, 151
placing with EPS Import Options dialog, *143*, **143–144**
.epub file extension, 302
Erase tool, *6*, 116
euro (€), 70
Excel spreadsheets, live links to, **397–398**
Export Adobe PDF dialog, *219*
Export Adobe PDF icon (Command Bar), *10*
Export Book to Digital Editions command, 302
Export dialog, 412
exporting book to PDF, 302
Eyedropper tool, *6*
plug-in for, 16

F

facing pages display
master text frames in, 253
vs. nonfacing, **214–215**
Fast Display, *288*, 288
feathering, for drop shadow, 173
fields in data source file, 392
inserting placeholder in target document, 393
figure space, *83*, 83
file formats, InDesign support for, 32
File menu
➢ Adobe PDF Presets ➢ Define, 441
➢ Document Presets ➢ Define, 442
➢ Export, 151, 190, 405, 412
➢ New
  ➢ Book, 297, 413
  ➢ Document, 223
  ➢ Document from Template, 225
  ➢ Library, 402
➢ Open in InCopy, 435
➢ Package, 359
  ➢ Return for InDesign, 436
➢ Place, 24, 141, 158, 252, 397, 405
➢ Preflight, 356
➢ Print Presets ➢ Define, 367, 441
➢ Save a Copy, 413
➢ Save As, 224
  for templates, 442
➢ User, 424
File Name text variable, *386*, 386
files, selecting sequential in list, 152
fill color, for shapes in compound path, 124
Fill Frame Proportionally command, 163
Fill tool, *6*
Find/Change utility, **276–281**
Glyph tab, *280*, 280
GREP tab, *279*, 279–280
icon, *10*
Object tab, 280–281, *281*
saving searches, 276, *277*
sharing queries, **440–441**
for styles, 379–381, *380*
Text tab, **276–279**, *277*
Find Object Format Options dialog, *281*
first line indents, for paragraphs, 40
First Line Left Indent field, 41
Fit Content Proportionally command, 163
Fit Content to Frame command, 163
Fit Frame to Content command, 163
Fit Spread in Window icon (Command Bar), *10*
fitting images, **162–166**

fixed-page autoflow, 251
flash drive, InDesign on, 19
flat-file database, 467
for data merge, 391
Flattener Preview panel, 339, *339*
icon, *3*
Transparency Flattener Presets, 342
flattening, 467
proofs, **338–344**
FlightCheck, 356
floating panel, 4
flush, 71, 468
flush left, 468
flush right, 468
flush space, 83, *83*
flyout menu, for Control Panel, 8
folders
for assignment files, 426
for packaging publication, 360
for personal, per-user settings, 19
for plug-ins, 16
for scripts, 408
folio, 218, 468
font families, **57–60**
listing, *58*
fonts. *See also* OpenType fonts
for bullets, 256
connection with glyph, 98
copying with Package Publication, 360
default, 20
errors from missing versions, 133
preflight checking, 356
replacing, *282*, **282**, 283
shortcut for changing, 61
size of, 60–61
fractional points, 66–67
and symbol use, 80
footers, **387–389**
Footnote Options dialog
Layout tab, *270*, 270–271
Numbering and Formatting tab, 268–269, *269*
footnotes, *267*, **267–271**, *268*
formatting, **268–271**
in imported Word text, 28
search and replace, 278
force justified, 468
formatting
characters, **57–80**
baseline shift, **69–70**, *70*
font families and type style, **57–60**
font size and leading, **60–61**
kerning, 62, **62–64**
language, **71–72**
skew, **70–71**, *71*
tracking, 64, **64–67**
vertical and horizontal scaling, *68*, **68–69**

finding, 279
footnotes, **268–271**
in imported Word text,
removing, 28
paragraphs, **37–44**
alignment, **37–39**
drop caps, **42–44**, *43*
Last Line Right Indent field,
42, *42*
left and right indent, 39
separating paragraphs, **39–41**
in Story Editor, 263
when dragging and dropping text,
265
Formatting Affects Container tool, *6*
Formatting Affects Text tool, *6*
FPO (For Position Only), 468
fractions, in OpenType fonts, *88*, **88–89**
frame break, 249
Frame Fitting Options, *164*, **164–166**
FrameMaker, 384
frames. *See also* text frames
converting text to image, **132–135**
Ellipse Frame tool for, **117**
removing existing content
from, 119
vs. shapes, 118–119
Free Transform tool, *6*
fully justified text, 38

G

galley view, in InCopy, 266, *267*
gamma, 468
Gamma Correction, for PNG file, 143
gamut, 468. *See also* color gamut
gang, 468
gap color, for stroke, 180
gap in underline, options for, 77
Garamond Premier Pro font, 92
Generate Index dialog, *311*, 311–313
GIF (Graphical Interchange
Format), 141
global baseline grid, 294
global light effect, **176–178**, *177*
glyph tables, 84
glyphs, 26, 468
Glyphs panel, **95–99**, *96*
Font Family menus, 96
glyph sets, **97–99**, *98*
sharing, **441**
icon, *3*
sorting on, 97
Go to Selected Marker command, 307
gradient feather effect, 175, *175*
tool, *6*
Gradient panel icon, *3*
Gradient tool, *6*

gradients, applying to multiple
paths, 125
graphic file formats, InDesign support
for, 141
Graphical Interchange Format
(GIF), 141
graphics. *See* images
Gravity effect, for type on path, 206
gray boxes, for images, 288, *288*
greeking, 468
grid, *292*, **292–293**
baseline grid, *293*, **293–295**
Grotesque MT Std font family, 68
grouped panels, *4*, 4
grouping objects, 296
guides, *289*, **289–291**
color of, 222
for drawing, 106
Guides Manager, **291**
options, **290–291**
unlocking, *222*
gutter, 34, 35, 468
setup, 213

H

hair space, *83*, 83
Hand tool, *6*, 286
hanging drop caps, 44
hanging indents, 40–41
hanging punctuation, 49, 468
hard line breaks, in imported text,
24, *25*
hard proofs, 335, 468
header row, in data source file, 392
headers and footers, **387–389**
heart shape, creating, 128–132, *129–131*
Hebrew font, 59
Help icon (Command Bar), *10*
Help menu (Windows) ➢ Configure
Plug-Ins, 16
Helvetica font, 265
hidden layers
including table of contents text
on, 318
for index entries, 306
search and replace, 278
High Quality Display, 288, *288*
high school newspaper, workflow for,
14–15
horizontal scaling, 66
of characters, *68*, **68–69**
horizontal spacing of characters, 47
hot-lead typesetting fonts, 82
HSL (Hue, Saturation, Luminosity)
color model, 157, 468
hyperlinks
table of contents entries as, 316
underline for, **78–79**

Hyperlinks panel icon, *3*
hyphenation, 47–48
exceptions, **274**
and document package, 361
preventing, 75–76
Hyphenation Settings dialog, *48*
Hyphenation Zone, 48

I

ICC color profiles, 322, **323–324**
changing, **333–335**
removing or assigning to
document, **334**
and soft proofing, 336
specifying, 142
v2 versus v1, 327
.icc file extension, 324
.icm file extension, 324
icon-only mode, for dock, 2
icons, for InDesign panels, *3*
identifier, for master page, 237
Illustrator, 103
for custom brush stroke, 182
drag and drop from, 154
for drawing, 155
Edit Original command and, 189
performance, vs. InDesign, 121
troubleshooting pasting from, 156
Image Color Settings dialog, *333*
Image Import Options dialog, 142
images
assignments of, 433
cutting and pasting, 193
fitting, **162–166**
identifying source of undeletable
color swatch, 187–188
importing, **141–152**
EPS (Encapsulated PostScript),
143–144
InDesign INDD, **151–152**
multipage PDFs, **150**
PDF (Portable Document
Format), **148–150**
PNG (Portable Network
Graphics), **143**
PSD (Photoshop) file format,
145–147
raster graphics, **142**
merging, **396**
placing, **139–158**
content-first workflow, **158**
with copy and paste, **155–157**
with drag and drop, **153–154**
frame-first workflow, **139–140**
planning for bleed, 221
profiles, vs. working space
profiles, 331
resizing, 226

as variable data, data merge
for, 391
vectors, **103–105**
Import Options dialog (Excel), *399*
Import Topics command (Index
panel), 310
importing. *See also* sharing reusable
settings
dictionaries, 439
graphics, **141–152**
EPS (Encapsulated PostScript),
143–144
InDesign INDD, **151–152**
multipage PDFs, **150**
PDF (Portable Document
Format), **148–150**
PNG (Portable Network
Graphics), **143**
PSD (Photoshop) file format,
145–147
raster graphics, **142**
text into text frame, **24–31**
threading when, 248
in port, 246, 247, *247*, 469
.inca file extension, 423, 426
troubleshooting problems with,
434
.incd file extension, 32, 266
InCopy, 30, **265–267**
assignment view options, 426–427
Layout view, *266*
problem solving with, 422
Story Editor view, *435*
story view, *266*
Track Changes option, 29
InCopy LiveEdit Workflow, 415, 424
.incp file extension, 423
Increase Font Size icon (Command
Bar), *10*
Increase Left Indent icon (Command
Bar), *10*
.incx file extension, 32, 266, 423, 426,
427, 437
.indd file extension, 422, 423
Indent to Here character, 82
indents, 35, *35*, **39**
for bullets, 257
hanging, 40–41
for paragraph rules, 54
of type on path, 205
InDesign
installation folder, 16, 19
OpenType fonts use, 86
regionalized version of, 72
Track Changes option, 29
InDesign CS3 Scripting Guide, 407
InDesign-InCopy LiveEdit Workflow,
file types for, 423
InDesign INDD, **151–152**
InDesign Interchange INX file, 190, 412

InDesign menu (Mac)
➢ Configure Plug-Ins, 16
➢ Keyboard Shortcuts, 11
➢ Preferences, 7
➢ Units & Increments, 214
index marker, *308*, 308
Index panel, 303
Generate Index, 311
icon, *3*
menu, 306–307
Reference mode, *303*, 303, 306
Topic mode, 303, *303*, 310
index text, in imported Word text, 28
indexes, **302–313**
adding new reference to existing
topic, 310
alphanumeric headings in, 313
creating entries, **303–306**
cross-references, 305, **308–310**
generating, **311–313**
managing entries, **306–308**
nested or run-in, *312*, 312
power indexing, **310–311**
searching entry list, 307
setting end of page range, 304–305
.indl file extension, 402
.indp file extension, 423
.inds file extension, 405
.indt file extension, 224
Info panel
for content counts, 33
icon, *3*
information, on plug-ins, 16
ink alias, **346**
Ink Manager, *345*, **345–348**
for Photoshop channel corrections,
347–348
inline anchored objects, options,
196–198
inline graphics, 193
in imported Word text, 29
inner bevel, 174, *174*
inner glow effect, 173–174, *174*
inner shadow effect, 173
inport, on path object, 204
Insert Number Placeholder
submenu, 259
Insert Pages command, 232
Insert Pages dialog, 235, *235*
Insert Pages icon (Command Bar), *10*
Insert Table dialog, 398, *399*
inset, 469
inside margin, 215
Interface pane, 7
invisibles (QuarkXPress), displaying, 24
.inx file extension, 412
iPhoto, 154
Isolate Blending setting, 171
italics
character styles for, 379

negative skew for, 71
preserving in imported Word
text, 29
Item Information dialog, for library
items, *403*

J

Japanese dots, *182*
Japanese language font, 59
JavaScript, 407
benefits, 408
for style cleanup, 381
join, for stroke, 179
join style, for trap segments, 354
JPEG (Joint Photographic Experts
Group), 141
jumplines, **253–254**, *254*, 469
justification
options, **47**
for text frames, vertical, *36*, **36**
Justification dialog, *47*

K

Keep Options dialog, **50–52**, *51*
for footnotes, 271
Keeper of the List, 275
kerning, 62, **62–64**, 469
in character styles, 64
vs. tracking, 64
keyboard shortcuts, **10–13**
for hidden Tools panel features, 7
multiple sets, 12
sharing, **443**
for styles, **405–406**
zoom in and zoom out, 286
Keyboard Shortcuts dialog, 11
knockout, 349, 350, *350*, 469
Knockout Group setting, 171
Korean language font, 59

L

lab values for spot color, 348
languages, Photoshop layers for
multiple, 146
Last Document State option, 147
Last Line Right Indent field, **42**, *42*,
42, 42
Last Page Number text variable, *387*,
387
layer comps (Photoshop), **146–147**, 469
Layer Options dialog, 296
layers, **295–296**
on master pages, 238
in Photoshop, for language
versions, 146
printing, 362

Layers panel
    icon, *3*
    Merge Layers command, 296
Layout Adjustment dialog, *225*, **225–226**
Layout menu
    ➤ Create Guides, 291
    ➤ Margins and Columns, 225
    ➤ Numbering & Section
        Options, 298
    ➤ Pages
        ➤ Add Page, 232
        ➤ Move Pages, 233–234, 414
    ➤ Ruler Guides, 222, 290
    ➤ Table of Contents, 314
    ➤ Table of Contents Styles, 314
    ➤ Update Table of Contents, 318
Layout view in InCopy, *266*
leader, 256, 469
leading, 60–61, 66–67
left indent, for paragraphs, **39**
left-read, 469
levels, in hierarchical table of
    contents, 316
libraries, **401–404**
    creating, 402
    deleting items, 403
    panel, *401*
        Add Items on Page, 403
        Add Items on Page as
            Separate Objects, 403
    saving, 404
    sharing, 404
ligatures, 84, 469
    discretionary, **86–88**, *88*
lighting effects, global light,
    176–178, *177*
Lightroom, 154
Line tool, *6*, 112
line wraps, manual control over, 46
lines. *See also* rules (lines)
lines per inch (LPI), 469
lining numerals, 94–95, *95*
Link File Info command (Links
    panel), 161
Link Information dialog, 159–160, *160*
linked assets, 159
    vs. embedded, 162
    updating for package, 361
linked graphics, copying with Package
    Publication, 360
Links panel
    assigned stories and, 434
    icon, *3*
    for managed content, *159*, **159–161**
    menu, 160–161
        Unlink, 397–398
lists, **259–260**
live area of document, 217, **221–222**, 469

live links, to Excel spreadsheets,
    397–398
Live Workflow
    with copy before layout, 437
    plug-ins for InDesign/InCopy
        communication, 430
loaded cursor, *31*, 31, 150
    for threading frames, 246, *247*
local overrides, preserving in imported
    Word text, 29
locked guides, 290
locked layers, search and replace, 278
locked stories, search and replace, 278
logo, creating, 132
lowercase, 73
LPI (lines per inch), 469

M

Macintosh, ColorSync, 323
Macromedia applications, user
    interface, 2
magnification level, and gridline
    display, 294
mail merge. *See* data merge
managed files, 423
manual control over line wraps, 46
manual kerning, 63
manual page breaks, in imported Word
    text, 29
manual text flow, 251
margin guides, *217*
margins, 221
    color of, 222
    and Master Text Frame, 222
    measurement system for, 214
marker, 470
Marker menu, 240
Marlett typeface, 256
master dictionary list, 275
Master Options dialog, *238*
master pages, **237–243**
    autoflowing text in frames,
        252–253
    creating from document pages, **243**
    creating text frame on, 214
    drag and drop, 232
    index entries on, 306
    layers on, 295
    layout adjustment, **225–226**
    linked assets on, 159
    nested, **240–242**
    overriding items, **238–239**
    page number marker on, 384
    with placeholder fields for data
        merge, 392
    printing, 362
    in QuarkXPress, 246
    restoring items, **239**

    search and replace, 278
    setup, **237–238**
    text frames on, **239–240**
Master Text Frame option, 213, 214, 222
    in facing pages display, 253
    text input and, 246
MDF (multiple document format), 226
Measure tool, *6*
measurement system, 214
menu command, hiding, 13
Menu Customization dialog, 15
menus, customizing, **13–15**, *14*
Merge Swatches command, 186–187
merged document, 391, 470
merging. *See also* data merge
    paths with Pencil tool, 117
    shapes, 122–123
metadata, 470
    for library items, 403
metric kerning, 63, *63*
Microsoft Word, 27
    editorial use of, 421
    endnotes, 271
    Import Options dialog, 27–31, *28*
    indents, 41
minimize/maximize button, for
    stacked panel, 5
misregister, 348, *349*, 470
miter limit, for stroke, *179*, 179
mixed ink group, 470
Mixed Ink Group Options dialog, 185
mixed inks, 470
    for swatches, **183–186**
Modification Date text variable, 387
Modify Trap Preset Options dialog,
    353, *354*
Monitor Color, for color management
    settings, 325
monitors, color variations, 323
Moonglow Bold Extended font, *93*
MOV (QuickTime Movie), 141
Move Pages dialog, 233–234, *234*,
    414, *414*
Move tool, *6*
moving
    anchor points in vector shapes, 131
    effects, 176
    pages, 232
        between documents, **235**
    selected object between layers, 295
moving and replicating effect, **176**
multi-ink colors, in QuarkXPress
    swatch, 190
multi-state panels, **5–6**, *6*
multipage PDFs, placing, **150**
multiple concurrent asset placement
    option, **152–153**
multiple document format (MDF), 226
Myriad Web font, 265

N

names
    for assigned files, changing, 433–434
    for assignments, 425
    for colors, 346
    indexing, 310
    for master pages, 237
    for paragraph styles, **370–371**
Navigator panel, *286*, **286**
    icon, *3*
nested index format, *312*, 312
nested master pages, **240–242**
nested styles, efficiency from, **381–384**
New Assignment dialog, 425–427, *426*
New Doc Sizes.txt file, 223–224
New Document dialog, 34, 213, *214*, 223, *223*
    icon, *10*
    Master Text Frame option, 252
New Document Setup dialog, Bleed and Slug area, *219*
New List dialog, *260*
New Mixed Ink Group dialog, *185*
New Mixed Ink Swatch dialog, *183*, 183
New Page Reference dialog, 303, *303*, 305
    for cross-references, 309, *309*
New Stroke Style dialog, *181*, 181–182
New Text Variable dialog, 385
noise, for shadow, 173
Non-Joiner character, 82
non-Latin fonts, removing unused, 59
non-printing layers, 296
    for notes, 362
Nonbreaking Hyphen, 80–81
nonbreaking space, *83*, 83
    and index sort, 311
nonfacing pages, vs. facing, **214–215**
nonprinting characters, displaying, 24
nonprinting object, 351
Normal mode for view, 288
Normal tool, *6*
North America General Purpose 2, for color management settings, 325
North America Prepress 2, for color management settings, 326
North America Web/Internet, for color management settings, 326
Note tool, *6*
notes
    assigning to layer comps, 147
    non-printing layers for, 362
Notes panel icon, *3*
Numbered List icon (Command Bar), *10*
numbering
    for footnotes, 268
    for lists, **258–259**
        overriding, **262**
    pages, chapters and sections, in books, **298–300**, *299*

numbers, converting in Word text, 29
numerals, tabular vs. proportional, 94, *94*
numeric keyboard, limitations as shortcuts, 405

O

Object Knocks Out Shadow setting, 172
Object Layer Options dialog, *148*
object-level transparency, 170
Object menu
    ➢ Anchored Object
        ➢ Insert, 202
        ➢ Release, 196
    ➢ Content, 119
    ➢ Convert Shape, 120
    ➢ Corner Options, 120–121
    ➢ Fitting, 162–164, *163*
    ➢ Image Color Settings or Graphics, ➢ Image Color Settings, 333
    ➢ Pathfinder
        ➢ Add, 122
        ➢ Exclude Overlap, *124*, 124
        ➢ Intersect, 122
        ➢ Subtract, 122
    ➢ Paths, 127
        ➢ Release Compound Path, 124, 134
        ➢ Reverse Path, 127, 180
    ➢ Text Frame Options, 213
    ➢ Transform, *208*
    ➢ Transform Again, *208*, 208–209
Object Style Options dialog, 400, *401*
object styles, **399–400**
    sharing, **439–440**
Object Styles panel, *400*
    icon, *3*
objects
    anchored, **192–202**
        anatomy, **195–196**
        creating, **193–195**
        custom options, **198–202**
        inline options, **196–198**
    attribute-level transparency, *170*, **170–171**
    effects, **171–175**
        applying to multiple paths, 125
        basic feather, 174–175
        bevel and emboss, *174*, 174
        directional feather, 175
        drop shadow, *172*, **172–173**
        global light, **176–178**, *177*
        gradient feather, *175*, 175
        inner glow, 173–174, *174*
        inner shadow, 173
        moving and replicating, **176**
        outer glow, 173
        satin, 174

efficiency working with, **399–409**
    libraries, **401–404**
    object styles, **399–400**
moving between layers, 295
and rearranged pages, **236–237**
Step and Repeat, **207–208**
strokes, **178–183**
    custom styles, **180–183**
styles, **399–400**
swatches, **183–192**
    finding unfindable, 187–189
    managing, **186–190**
    mixed inks, **183–186**
    sharing, **190–192**
transformations, **208–209**
type on path, *203*, **203–207**
    editing, **204–205**
    options, *206*, **206–207**
oblique style, negative skew for, 71
offset
    for paragraph rules, 54
    for underline, 77
oldstyle numerals, 94–95, *95*
onomatopoeia, 470
opacity, changing settings, 171
Open a File dialog, 224, *225*
Open Document icon (Command Bar), *10*
Open Illustrator icon (Command Bar), *10*
open paths, Scissors tool and, 127
Open Photoshop icon (Command Bar), *10*
Open Prepress Interface (OPI) workflow, and flattening, 344
Open Style Add Documents dialog, 297
OpenType fonts, **84–95**, 470
    features, **86–95**
        contextual alternates, 90–91, *91*
        discretionary ligatures, **86–88**, *88*
        figure styles, *94*, 94–95
        fractions, *88*, **88–89**
        ordinals, *90*, 90
        positional forms, 93
        positional numerals, 93–94
        slashed zero, *92*, 92
        small caps, 91, *92*
        stylistic sets, 92, *93*
        swashes, 90, *90*
        titling alternates, 90
    with small caps, 74
    upgrading to, 86
OPI (Open Prepress Interface) link, 143–144, 470
    image replacement, 367
optical kerning, *63*, 63
optical margin alignment, 49–50
ordinal numbers, 70, 75, 90, *90*
Origin field, for horizontal ruler, 216
orphaned anchor point, 187

orphans, 50, 470
    tracking to eliminate, 65
orthogonal line, 120
out-of-gamut colors, mapping to in-
    gamut, 332
out port, 246, 247, *247*, 470–471
outer bevel, 174, *174*
outer glow effect, 173
outline
    converting text to, 343
    converting to, 133
outport, on path object, 204
output. *See also* color management;
    printing
    package for output, **359–361**
    proofing, **335–345**
        colors, **335–337**
        flattening, **338–344**
        separations, **337–338**
Output Date text variable, 387
outputting books, **301–302**
outside margin, 215
overprinting, **348–356**, 471
    stroke, 351
    for underline, 77
overriding, 471
    assignment checkout, 434
    bullets, **262**
    master page items, **238–239**
    paragraph styles, **376–377**
        clearing, 477
overscore, 471
overset, 471
overset marker, 264

P

Package Book for Print command, 302
package for output, **359–361**
Package menu (InCopy), *437*
    ➢ Forward for InCopy, 437
Package Publication dialog, 360, *360*
padlock, 16
page breaks, manual, in imported Word
    text, 29
Page Control plug-in, **229–230**
Page Edge, for anchored object
    alignment, 200
Page Margin, for anchored object
    alignment, 200
page numbers, 218, **240**
    in collaboration documents, 413
    in jumplines, 253
    on table of contents, 315
Page Reference Options dialog, *304*
PageMaker, 384
    migrating from, keyboard shortcut
        sets for help with, 12
PageMaker Plug-in Pack, 254

pages
    assigning trap presets to, 355–356
    creating, **213–230**
        in document setup, **213–222**
    duplicating and deleting, **236**
    facing vs. nonfacing, **214–215**
    inserting, **232**
    layout, **216–217**
    managing, **230–237**
    moving between documents, **235**
    multiple sizes, **226–230**
        Book panel for, **227**
    numbering in books, **298–300**, *299*
    object placements with paste, 157
    printing nonsequential, 361
    rearranging, **232–234**
        and objects, **236–237**
Pages panel, *230*, **230**
    Allow Master Item Overrides on
        Selection, 243
    Apply Master to Pages, 243
    Create New Page button, 232
    customizing, *231*, **231**
    Duplicate Master Spread, 241
    facing pages display, 215, *216*
    Hide Master Items, 243
    icon, *3*
    Load Master Pages, 243
    Remove All Local Overrides, 239
    Remove Selected Local
        Overrides, 239
    Save as Master from, 243
palettes, 471. *See also* panels
Panel Options dialog, for Pages panel,
    231, 231
panels, **1–10**, 471
    arranging, **4–5**
    changing defaults, 19–20
    Control panel, *8*, **8–9**
    dock, **2**, *3*, **4**
    expanding from dock, 4
    flyout menu, Show Options
        command, 6
    multi-state, **5–6**, *6*
    saving arrangements as
        workspaces, 18
    stacked, **5**
    Tools panel, *6*, **6–7**
    unneeded, **9–10**
Paper Size menu, customizing, 223–224
paper stock color, 324
    simulating in soft proof, 336
Paragraph Composer, 39, **44–46**
Paragraph dialog, 40
    Indents and Spacing tab, 41
paragraph keeps, 50
paragraph mark (pilcrow; ¶), 24, 70, 81
    character-level attributes for, 61
Paragraph mode, for Control Panel, 8

Paragraph panel, 37, *37*
    Balance Ragged Lines
        command, **50**
    Bullets and Numbering, 254
    hyphenation, 47–48
    icon, *3*, *10*
    Justification, 47
    Keep Options, **50–52**
Paragraph Rules dialog, 53, *53*
Paragraph Style Options dialog
    for bullets and numbering, *257*
    Drop Caps and Nested Styles pane,
        381–384, *382*
    General pane, *371*, 374
        Next Style field, 375
paragraph styles
    adding bullet and numbering, 257
    automatic sequential, **375–376**
    creating, 370
    efficiency from, **369–377**
    groups, **376**
    for headers and footers, 388
    names for, **370–371**
    overriding, **376–377**
    removing unused, 376
    sharing, **439–440**
    in Story Editor, 263
    and table of contents generation,
        314, 315
Paragraph Styles panel, *370*, 370
    Clear Overrides, 477
    icon, *3*
paragraphs
    applying leading to entire, 61
    composition, **44–46**
        highlighting violations, **52**, *53*
    formatting, **37–44**
        alignment, **37–39**
        drop caps, **42–44**, *43*
        Last Line Right Indent field,
            42, *42*
        left and right indent, **39**
        separating paragraphs, **39–41**
    InDesign vs. Word style conflicts, 30
    rules (lines) for, **53–54**, *55*
pasting. *See* copy and paste
path segments, 471
    in vector shapes, 104
Pathfinder panel, 128
    icon, *3*
paths for type, *203*, **203–207**
    editing, **204–205**
    options, **206**, **206–207**
paths in vector shapes, 104, **105–117**, 471
    compound, **123**, **123–126**, *124*, *125*
    direction of, 115
    Pen tool
        adding and removing anchor
            points, 112

converting anchor points between corner and smooth, 111
for curves, *108*, **108–111**
straight path segments with, 112
for straight paths, **105–107**
Pencil tool, **113–117**
cleaning up paths, **116**
for merging paths, **117**
for modifying paths, **114–116**
Scissors tool for editing, **126–127**
pattern matching, for search and replace, 276
PDF (Portable Document Format), 141
Adobe Illustrator (AI) file format as, 148
blend spaces and distributables, 345
cropping, options, 149
Document Properties dialog (Acrobat) for application creating, *352*
exporting book to, 302
exporting, including slug area, 219
high resolution, 150
live hyperlinks, underline styles, 78
PDF bookmarks, 316
PDF Checkup, 356
PDF Export Presets, sharing, **441**
Pen tool, *6*
adding and removing anchor points, 112
converting anchor points between corner and smooth, 111
for curves, *108*, **108–111**
for drawing open path, 203
straight path segments with, **105–107**, 112
Pencil tool, *6*, **113–117**
cleaning up paths, **116**
for merging paths, **117**
for modifying paths, **114–116**
per-image color management, **333**
per text frame baseline grid, 294–295
Perceptual rendering intent, 332
performance, resolution of display and, 287
periodicals
Divide and Copy and Conquer workflow for, 417–418, *418*
potential problems, 418–419
photographs, assignments of, 433
Photoshop
copy and paste from, 156
drag and drop from, 154
Edit Original command and, 188
Quick Mask in, 142
Photoshop Album, 154
Photoshop (PSD) file format, 141
import options dialog, *145*
placing, **145–147**

PICT file format, 141
pilcrow (paragraph mark; ¶), 24, 70, 81
character-level attributes for, 61
pillow emboss, *174*, 174
PitStop Pro, 356
Place dialog, 141
Replace Selected Item, 158
Place icon (Command Bar), *10*
Place PDF dialog, 148
General tab, *149*
Placed Page Collaboration Workflow, 415–417, *416*, *420*
output from, 420–421
Placeholder Frames view, 426
placeholders, 32
for data merge image field, 396
for data merge text, 392
pages as, in collaboration documents, 415
platform, for text import, 26
Plug-in Information dialog, *17*
plug-ins, **16–17**
plugged color values, 333, 471
PNG (Portable Network Graphics), 141
placing with Import Options dialog, **143**
policies, for color management, **331–332**
polyglot, 471
Polygon Frame tool, *6*, **118**, 120
options dialog, *118*
Polygon Settings dialog, 120
Polygon tool, *6*
Portable Document Format (PDF). *See* PDF (Portable Document Format)
portable drive, InDesign settings on, **19**
Portable Network Graphics (PNG), 141
placing with Import Options dialog, **143**
portfolio for proposal and bid generation, book file for, **301–302**
positional forms, in OpenType fonts, 93
positional numerals, in OpenType fonts, 93–94
PostScript, 471
EPS files as, 144
exporting layout page as, and placing inside other layout, 151
placing with EPS Import Options dialog, *143*, **143–144**
printing, 365
PostScript fonts, limit to number of glyphs, 84
Preferences dialog
Advanced Type pane, 74
Composition pane, 52, *52*
Display options, for Story Editor, *264*
Grids pane, 292, *293*
baseline grid options, *294*
Guides & Pasteboard pane, *290*

Type pane, 59
Create Links When Placing Text and Spreadsheet Files, 397
Units & Increments, 214, 216, *217*
preflight, **356–359**, 471
Preflight pane
Colors and Inks, 357, *358*
External Plug-ins, 359, *359*
Fonts, 356, *357*
Links and Images, 357, *358*
Print Settings, *358*
Summary, 356, *357*
Preflight Pro, 356
Preserve Embedded Profiles policy, 331
presets for trapping, loading from other InDesign documents, 353
Preview mode for view, 288
and guides, 290
Preview tool, *6*
previews
of data merge, 394
of EPS file, 144
of type, size of, 59
Print Book command, 302
Print dialog, **361–367**
Advanced pane, *366*, 366–367
for built-in trapping vs. Adobe In-RIP Trapping, 352, *353*
Color Management pane, 365, *366*
General pane, **361–362**, *362*
Graphics pane, 364–365, *365*
Marks and Bleeds pane, 219, *220*, 362, *363*, 364
Output pane, *364*, 364
plug-in for, 16
Setup pane, 362, *363*
Print icon (Command Bar), *10*
Print Instructions dialog, 360
Print Presets dialog, 367, 441
printers, color characteristics, 323–324
printing, 321, **345–367**
Ink Manager, 345, **345–348**
master pages, 362
preflight, **356–359**
sharing presets, **441–442**
trapping and overprinting, 348–356
overprint attributes, **349–351**
Private Use area, for OpenType fonts, 99
Pro OpenType fonts, 86
process colors
converting mixed ink swatches to, 185
converting spot color to, 348
productivity. *See* efficiency
proofing, **335–345**
colors, **335–337**
flattening, **338–344**
separations, **337–338**
proper names, indexing, 303

ProPhoto RGB color profile, *329*, 329, 330
proportional numerals, 94, *94*
proposals, book file for portfolio, **301–302**
prosumer, 369, 471
PRST files, 367
PSD (Photoshop) file format, 141
punctuation, hanging, 49, 468
punctuation space, 83, *83*
Purchase This Image command (Links panel), 161

Q

quad, 472
quad left, 38
quad right, 38
QuarkXPress, 119
   master pages, 238
   migrating from, keyboard shortcut sets for help with, 12
   swatches from, 190
   threaded vs. stand-alone frames, 245–246
quarter space, *83*, 83
Quick Apply, **406–407**
   menu, *406*
Quick Mask, in Photoshop, 142
QuickTime Movie (MOV) format, 141
quotation marks, 82

R

rag, 472
ragged edge, 38, 472
   balancing, **50**
rail, 472
Rainbow effect, for type on path, 206
raster graphics, 103, **142**
   InDesign preview generation of placed PDF pages, 150
   resizing, 103
Raster/Vector Balance slider, 342
rasterize to flatten, 341
rastor image processor (RIP), 107, 338–339, 472
   flattening in, 344–345
realism, vs. efficiency in lighting, 178
rebate, 472
Recently Used Set, of glyphs, 97
records, in data source file, 392
Records per Document Page option, for merge, 395
Rectangle Frame tool, *6*
Rectangle tool, *6*
rectangular path, creating, 106
red squiggly line, for misspelled words, 275
Reference mode, for Index panel, *303*, 303, 306

reference point, for anchored object, 198
regionalized version, of InDesign, 72
registered trademark (®), 70, 75, 81
registration marks, in slug area, 218
Relative Colorimetric rendering intent, 332
Relative to Spine option, for anchored object, 194
Relink dialog, 434
remote editors, collaboration with, **435–437**
Remove Pages icon (Command Bar), *10*
rendering intent, 142, 330, **332**, 472
   changing, 333
rendering machine, 287
repeating elements, master pages for, 237
replacing fonts, **282**, *282*, *283*
replicating effects, 176
resizable panels, 5
resizing vector graphics, 105
resolution
   of display, and performance, 287
   when flattening, 343
Restart Numbering command, 262
Reveal in Bridge command (Links panel), 161
Reveal in Finder/Explorer command (Links panel), 161
reverse path, 127
RGB color, 472
   converting to CMYK, 330
rich black, 331, 350, 472
rich text, 472
Rich Text Format (RTF), 27, 32, 473
rich text word processors, importing text from, 27
right indent for paragraphs, **39**
Right Indent Tab character, 82
right-read, 472
RIP (rastor image processor), 107, 338–339, 472
   flattening in, 344–345
rivers, 45, 473
Rotate tool, *6*
.rpln file extension, 16
.rtf file extension, 27, 32, 473
ruler
   changing units, 214
   origin for, 216, *217*
Ruler Guide dialog, *291*
Ruler Guide Options dialog, *222*
ruler guides
   creating, *289*, 289
   layout adjustment and, 226
rules (lines)
   for footnotes, 271
   for paragraphs, **53–54**, *55*
run-in head, 382, 473
   character styles for, 378
run-in index format, 312, *312*

run-in table of contents, 316, *317*
run-on, 473
run-up, 473
runts, 45, 50, 473
Russian Cyrillic font, 59

S

sans-serif typefaces, for screen display, 265
satin effect, 174
Saturation rendering intent, 332
Save As EPS Options dialog (Illustrator CS3), 144, *145*
Save icon (Command Bar), *10*
Save Link Verson command (Links panel), 161
saving
   book files, 297
   libraries, 404
   to older versions of InDesign, **411–412**
   printing presets, 367
   templates, 224
Scale tool, *6*
scaling, 68, 68–69
   of characters, *68*, **68–69**
   horizontal, 66
   pages when printing, 362
Scissors tool, *6*, **126–127**
screening, 364
Script Label panel, 409
   icon, *3*
scripting, **407–409**
   folder for, 408
   peer friendly, 408
Scripts panel icon, *3*
Section Indicator, 295
section marker, 299
section symbol (§), 81
sections, numbering, in books, **298–300**, *299*
See Also reference, 309
See reference, 309
Select All Unused command, 186
selected object
   moving between layers, 295
   Transform Again for group, 209
selecting, sequential files in list, 152
Selection tool, *6*, 24
   for threading frames, 246
semi-autoflow mode, 247, *248*, 251
Sentence Case, 73
separating paragraphs, **39–41**
separations, 473
   checking, 331
   proof, **337–338**
Separations Preview panel
   icon, *3*
   for ink management, 337, *337*
separators, in indexes, 313

seps, 473
sequential styles, automatic, **375–376**
serif typefaces, for print, 265
service mark, 75
Shadow Honors Other Effects, 173
shapes
    compound paths, *123*, **123–126**, *124, 125*
    vs. frames, 118–119
    Scissors tool for editing, **126–127**
    tools for, **117–135**
        merging, dividing, *122*, **122–123**, *123*
        reshaping, **120–126**
sharing reusable settings
    Autocorrect word pairs, **440**
    dictionaries, **439**
    document size presets, **442**
    Find/Change queries, **440–441**
    glyph sets, 99, **441**
    keyboard shortcuts, **443**
    libraries, 404
    PDF Export Presets, **441**
    print presets, **441–442**
    stroke styles, **440**
    styles, **439–440**
    swatches, **190–192**, **440**
    templates, **442**
    transparency flattener presets, **442**
    workspaces, **442–443**
Shear tool, *6*
shuffling, 234
Single-Line Composer, 39, **44–46**
sixth space, 83, *83*
Skew effect, for type on path, 206
skewed text, **70–71**, *71*
slashed zero, in OpenType fonts, 92, *92*
sliding trap, 355
slug, 473
slug area, 217, *217*, 473
    color of guides, 222
    contents, **218–219**
Slug mode for view, 288
Slug tool, *6*
small caps, 69
    from Character panel, 74
    in OpenType fonts, 91, *92*
smooth anchor points, 109
    converting anchor points between corner and, **111**
Smooth tool, *6*, 116
snap zone, 106, 226
    changing distance, 290
snapping, 290
snippets, **404–405**, 473
soft proofs, 335, 473
    purpose, 336
solidus, 473–474
Sort By fields, for index entries, 304
Sort Options dialog, *307*, 307

sorting
    on Glyphs panel, 97
    libraries, 403
    table of contents entries, 316
spacing
    after paragraphs, *40*
    of characters, horizontal, 47
special character marker, Current Page Number, 298
special characters, **80–99**. *See also* OpenType fonts
    in Find/Change utility, 276, 277, 278
    Glyphs panel, **95–99**, *96*
    white space characters, **82–84**
spectrophotometer, 323
spell check, **271–273**
    dictionary editing, **273–275**
    dynamic spelling, **275**
    ligatures and, 87
spine
    alignment relative to, 39
    anchored object position relative to, 197
    and facing pages, 215
    as ruler origin, 216
splitting footnotes, 270
spot colors, 474
    converting to process color mix, 188, 348
    in mixed colors, 183
spreads, 474
    multipage, **234**, *235*
sRGB color profile, *329*, 330
stacked panels, *5*
stacking order, 103, 338
Stair Step effect, for type on path, 206
star, for frames, 118
start of stroke, 180
Start Paragraph option, 52
State panel icon, *3*
Std (standard) OpenType fonts, 86
Step and Repeat dialog, *207*
step for trapping, 355
sticky, 474
stop character, for nested styles, 383
Story Editor, *263*, **263–265**, *264*
    customizing, **264–265**
    drag and drop, 265
    for editing footnotes, 267, *268*
    Preferences dialog, Display options, *264*
Story panel
    icon, *3*
    Optical Margin Alignment, 49
Story view, in InCopy, 265, *266*
strikethrough, **77–78**
Strikethrough Options dialog, *78*
stripes, for custom stroke, 182
Stroke panel, 178, *179*
    icon, *3*

Stroke tool, *6*
strokes, **178–183**
    color, for Pen tool, 106
    custom styles, **180–183**
    default assigned to frames, 164
    overprinting, 351
    sharing styles, **440**
styles. *See also* character styles; paragraph styles
    editing, Quick Apply for, 407
    enforcing, 380
    for footnotes, 268
    for hyperlink underline, 79
    in imported Word text
        name conflicts, 29
        removing, 28
        unused, 29, 30
    for index levels, 313
    for index title, 312
    nested, **381–384**
    for objects, **399–400**
    redefining when changing font, 282
    for section numbers, 299
    sharing, **439–440**
    shortcuts for, **405–406**
    synchronizing for book, **300–301**
    for tables, 398
stylistic sets, in OpenType fonts, 92, *93*
subscript, *74*, **74–75**
substrate, 474
    color of, 324
superscript, *74*, **74–75**
Swap Fill and Stroke tool, *6*
swashes, *90*, 90
swatches, **183–192**
    default, **191**
    deleting unused, 186
    finding unfindable, 187–189
    managing, **186–190**
    mixed inks, **183–186**
    sharing, **190–192**, **440**
    undeletable, 187, 190
    viewing without opening or importing, **191–192**, *192*
Swatches panel, 183
    customizing, 20
    icon, *3*
    in Illustrator, 189
    ink type, 345
    New Mixed Ink Group, 184
Swatches Panel icon (Command Bar), *10*
Synchronize Options dialog, 300, *300*

T

tab character, 82
tab position, for bullets, 257
tab-separated text file, for data merge, 391

Table menu ➤ Insert Table, 398
table of contents, **314–318**, *317*
Table of Contents dialog, 314, *314*
Table of Contents text, in imported
  Word text, 27
Table panel icon, *3*
Table Styles Options dialog, *399*
Table Styles panel, 398, *398*
  icon, *3*
tables
  efficiency working with, **397–398**
  in imported Word text, 29
  styles, **398**
  sharing, 439–440
Tabs icon (Command Bar), *10*
tabs, to replace spaces in imported
  text, 27
tabular numerals, 94, *94*
Tagged Image Format (TIF), 141
Tags panel icon, *3*
target document for data merge, 391, **392**
templates, **224–225**
  saving, 224
  sharing, **442**
  for trap presets, 353
tethered objects, 192. *See also* anchored
  objects
text
  converting to outline, 133, 343
  cutting to fit space, 66
  efficiency working with, **369–396**
    with character styles, **378–379**
    with data merge, **389–396**
    with nested styles, **381–384**
    with paragraph styles,
      369–377
    with text variables, **384–389**
  pasting without formatting, 157
  placing without frame, **31–32**
text files, in Bridge, 154
Text Frame Options dialog, **33–37**, *34*
  Baseline Options tab, *295*
Text Frame Options icon (Command
  Bar), *10*
text frames
  converting to image-filled frame,
    132–135
  counting words in, **33**
  creating, **23–24**
  filling with placeholder text, **32**
  importing text file, **24–31**
  inset spacing, **35–36**, *36*
  on master pages, **239–240**
  matching columns and gutters
    in, 213
  resizing, 24
  threading, **245–254**
    adding frame, 250–251
    autoflowing text, **251**

and multiple documents,
    414–415
  pre-created frames,
    246–248, *247*
  removing frame, 250
  when importing, 248
  without pre-created
    frames, 248
  without text, 248–249
  vertical justification, **36**, *36*
Text Import Options dialog, 26, *26*
text macros, in InCopy, 265
Text tool, 78
text variables, **384–389**
  Chapter Number, 300
  page number, 384
  types, **385–387**
text wrap, and hidden layers, 296
Text Wrap panel, 193
  icon, *3*, *10*
thesaurus, in InCopy, 265
thin space, *83*, 83
third space, *83*, 83
threading, 474
  text frames, **245–254**
    adding frame, 250–251
    autoflowing text, **251**
    and multiple documents,
      414–415
    pre-created frames,
      246–248, *247*
    removing frame, 250
    when importing, 248
    without pre-created
      frames, 248
    without text, 248–249
  tips, 249
  unthreading, 249
  viewing, 249, *250*
threshold for gridline display, 294
thumbnail drive, InDesign on, 19
thumbnails
  of pages, in Page panel, 230, *230*
  viewing in Bridge, 154
ThumbsPlus, 154
TIF (Tagged Image Format), 141
tilde (~), for discretionary hyphen, 274
tiling pages when printing, 362
time notations (AM/PM), 75
tint build, 183
tint, for underline, 77
title
  of index, 312
  of table of contents, 314
Title Case, 73
titling alternates, in OpenType fonts, 90
™ (trademark), 70, 75, 81
Toffler, Alvin, 369
Tools panel, *6*, **6–7**
  arrangement options, *7*

Polygon Frame tool, 120
  view modes, 288, *289*
Topic mode, for Index panel, 303,
  303, 310
Topic Options dialog, 306, *307*
topics in index, creating before
  references, 310
tracking, *64*, **64–67**, *67*
  tightening, 66
trademark (™), 70, 75, 81
Transform panel icon, *3*
transparency
  alpha channels for, 142
  attribute-level, *170*, **170–171**
  copy and paste impact, 156
  for PDF background in
    Acrobat, 149
  in PNG file, 143
Transparency Flattener Preset
  dialog, 342
Transparency Flattener Preset Options
  dialog, 342, *342*
  sharing settings, **442**
Transparency palette, 170
Trap Presets panel, 353, *353*
  Assign Trap Preset, 355–356
  icon, *3*
trapping, **348–356**, 474
  assigning presets to page, 355–356
  data in PDF document, 148
  InDesign vs. In-RIP, 351–352
  loading presets from other
    InDesign documents, 353
trim area, 217, *217*
  cropping PDF to, 149
trim edge, proximity of design elements
  to, 221
troubleshooting, pasting from
  Illustrator, 156
TrueType fonts, 86
  limit to number of glyphs, 84
.txt file extension, 32
Type 1 fonts, 86
Type menu
  ➤ Bulleted & Numbered Lists ➤
    Define Lists, 259
  ➤ Change Case, 73–74
  ➤ Create Outlines, 133
  ➤ Document Footnote
    Options, 268
  ➤ Find Font, 282
  ➤ Font, *60*, 60
  ➤ Insert Footnote, 267
  ➤ Insert Special Character, 387
    ➤ Frame Break, 249
    ➤ Hyphens and Dashes, 80
    ➤ Marker ➤ Current Page
      Number, 240, 299
    ➤ Marker ➤ Footnote
      Number, 268

➢ Marker ➢ Next Page Number, 253
➢ Marker ➢ Section Marker, 299
➢ Other, 384
➢ Symbols, 80
➢ Insert White Space ➢ Nonbreaking Space, 311
➢ Show Hidden Characters, 24, 308
➢ Text Variables
➢ Define, 385
➢ Insert Variable, 385, 389
➢ Type on a Path
➢ Delete Type from Path, 205
➢ Options, 206–207
Type on a Path tool, *6*
type on path, *203*, **203**, **207**
editing, **204–205**
options, *206*, **206–207**
type style, **57–60**
Type tool, 6, 23, 80
Type on a Path tool, 204
typeface design, 62
typesetting
to fit text, 66–67
vertical scale increase for emphasis, 68
Typical Display display performance setting, 287, *288*
typographer's quotes, in imported text, 27, 28

U

undeletable swatches, 187, 190
underline, 76–77
for hyperlinks, **78–79**
Underline Options dialog, 76, 76–77
undoing page move, 234
Unicode, 474
Unicode font table, 85
for Glyphs panel sort, 97
uniformity, of global light effect, 177, *177*
unlocking guides, *222*
unthreading text frames, 249
Update Link icon (Command Bar), *10*
uppercase, 73
U.S. Web Coated (SWOP) v2 color profile, 329, *329*, 330
USB stick, InDesign on, 19
User dialog, *424*, 424
user names, for assignments, 424

V

Variable Data Printing (VDP), 389, 474
vector graphics, **103–105**. *See also* paths
in vector shapes
resizing, 105

Verdana font, 265
Version Cue, 474
Versions command (Links panel), 161
vertex, 104
vertical justification, for text frames, **36**, *36*
vertical scaling of characters, *68*, **68–69**
View menu
➢ Display Performance, *288*
➢ Clear Object-Level Display Settings, 288
➢ Grids & Guides
➢ Lock Guides, 222, 290
➢ Snap to Guides, 290
➢ Proof Colors, 335, 336
➢ Screen Mode, 288
➢ Show Text Threads, 249
➢ Story Editor
➢ Collapse All Footnotes, 268
➢ Expand All Footnotes, 268
➢ Hide Style Name Column, 265
➢ Show Depth Ruler, 265
virgule, 473–474
visibility of layer, 295
Visual Basic Script, 407

W

waisted bullet (•), 70, 81
WebDings font, 97, 99
weight
of paragraph rules, 54
of strikethrough, 78
of stroke, 178
of underline, 76
white, in QuarkXPress swatch, 190
white space
characters, **82–84**
need for, 222
between story column and footnotes, 270
whole word search and replace, 278
widows, 50, 474
width
of columns, 34–35
of paragraph rules, 54
Window menu
➢ Arrange ➢ New Window, 287
➢ Assignments, 425
➢ Automation
➢ Data Merge, 392
➢ Scripts, 408, 409
➢ Effects, 170
➢ Object & Layout
➢ Command Bar, 10
➢ Navigator, 286
➢ Pathfinder, 128
➢ Output, 353
➢ Flattener Preview, 339
➢ Separations Preview, 337

➢ Text Wrap, 193
➢ Type & Tables, 398
➢ Character, 57
➢ Character Styles, 378
➢ Glyphs, 95
➢ Index, 303
➢ Paragraph, 37
➢ Paragraph Styles, 370
➢ Story, 49
➢ Table, 397
➢ Workspace
➢ New and Improved in CS3, 13
➢ Printing and Proofing, 13
➢ Save Workspace, 18, 443
Window menu (Photoshop), ➢ Layer Comps, 146
Windows, Image Color Management (ICM) user interface, 323
Windows Meta File (WMF) format, 141
wireframe, 474
wireframe cube, 104
WMF (Windows Meta File) format, 141
Word. *See* Microsoft Word
word processing, **262–271**
Autocorrect, **275–276**, *276*
endnotes, **271**
Find/Change, **276–281**
fonts, replacing, **282**, *282*, *283*
footnotes, 267, **267–271**, *268*
InCopy, **265–267**
story view, *266*
spell check, **271–273**
dictionary editing, **273–275**
dynamic spelling, **275**
Story Editor, *263*, **263–265**
customizing, **264–265**
drag and drop, 265
WordPerfect, RTF for, 32
words
adding references to index for all instances, 305
preventing hyphenation, 274
in text frames, counting, **33**
workflow
for book design, redefining and optimizing, 228–229
Book File Collaboration Workflow, **412–414**
content-first workflow, image placement in, **158**
Divide and Copy and Conquer workflow, 417–418, *418*
potential problems, 418–419
frame-first workflow, image placement in, **139–140**
InCopy LiveEdit Workflow, 415, 424
InDesign-InCopy LiveEdit Workflow, file types for, 423

Live Workflow
with copy before layout, 437
plug-ins for InDesign/InCopy
communication, 430
Open Prepress Interface (OPI)
workflow, and flattening, 344
Placed Page Collaboration
Workflow, 415–417, *416, 420*
output from, 420–421
workstations with focus on, 14–15
workflow-focused workstations,
creating, 14–15
working spaces (color), **329–331**
changing, 333
converting to, 331
workspaces, 475
customizing, **18**
sharing, **442–443**

workstations, creating workflow-
focused, 14–15
Wrap Around Bounding Box, 193
WYSIWYG onscreen preview, 287, 475

X

x-heights, of typeface, 65
X Offset field, for anchored
object, 200
XHTML-based Digital Editions
format, 302
.xls file extension, 32
XML code, snippet as, 404
XMP (eXtensible Metadata
Platform), 475
XMP metadata dialog, 161

Y

Y Relative To field, 199, 201
yen symbol (¥), as anchored object
marker, *195,* 195–196

Z

Zapf Dingbats typeface, 97
Zapfino Extra LT Four font, *70*
zero-point of ruler, 216
zero, slashed, in OpenType fonts, *92, 92*
zoom, for Glyphs panel, 97
Zoom In icon (Command Bar), *10*
Zoom Out icon (Command Bar), *10*
zoom percentage field, *286*
Zoom tool, *6, 285,* 285
zooming, **285–286**
z-order, 338, 475